Shaping Rule of Law Through Dialogue

Europa Law Publishing, Groningen 2010

Shaping Rule of Law Through Dialogue

International and Supranational Experiences

Edited by Filippo Fontanelli, Giuseppe Martinico & Paolo Carrozza

Europa Law Publishing is a publishing company specializing in European Union law, international trade law, public international law, environmental law and comparative national law.
For further information please contact Europa Law Publishing via email: info@europalawpublishing.com or visit our website at: www.europalawpublishing.com.

Typeset in Scala and Scala Sans, Graphic design by G2K Designers, Groningen/Amsterdam

NUR 828; ISBN 978-90-8952-057-9

'Constitutional Justice' Requires Judicial Cooperation and 'Comity' in the Protection of 'Rule of Law'

Ernst-Ulrich Petersmann*

1 Introduction

All contributions to this book on *Shaping Rule of Law through Dialogue: International and Supranational Experiences* explore diverse dimensions of national and international adjudication and of interactions among national and international courts of justice in their protection of 'rule of law'. This Foreword introduces some of the common constitutional principles and constitutional problems underlying these 'judicial dialogues', notably the idea of 'constitutional justice' justifying and limiting courts of justice, constitutional democracies and multilevel 'judicial governance' for the collective supply of 'public goods', like 'rule of law', protection of human rights and peaceful settlement of disputes in conformity with 'principles of justice'.

2 Conservative and Reformative Conceptions of Justice

Law as an instrument of governance needs justification. Since antiquity, justice has been recognized as the main guiding principle and objective of law and of judicial settlement of disputes. The independent, impartial judge applying rules of law in fair procedures in order to settle disputes peacefully belongs to the oldest paradigms of justice, as illustrated by instructions in the Old Testament to set up courts of law ('Justice, and justice alone, you shall pursue') as well as by judicial settlement of disputes in Greek city republics (*e.g.* in the court of Areopagus in ancient Athens), inspired by much older ideals of judicial dispute settlement as discussed in ancient Athenian tragic drama.[1] The judicial acquittal of *Orest* in the third part of Aeschylos' *Oresteia* offers an early example for the task of impartial judges to apply not only existing rules of law (like the ancient 'golden rule' of retaliation: 'what you do shall be done to you', *e.g.* a killer like Orest deserves to be killed himself); in addition to this 'conservative function' of judges to uphold 'legality' by applying existing rules of law, judges also have to review whether the particular circumstances of a dispute may require 'equitable' dispute settlements, for instance by judicial 'gap-filling' in the existing rules of law based on judicial justification and clarification of new interpretations of customary rules and principles of law (*e.g.* justifying rectification of past injustices so as to avoid a 'miscarriage of justice', or identifying particular merits or needs of the parties to the dispute calling for 'equitable' interpretations of general or too rigid rules of law by judgments based on meritorian or needs-based conceptions of justice). By 'giving reasons',[2] courts

* Professor of International and European Law and Head of the Law Department, European University Institute, Florence. Previously professor at the University of Geneva and its Graduate Institute of International Studies (1993-2001) and legal advisor in GATT and the World Trade Organization.

1 On justice in the Bible and in Greek tragedies and Greek philosophy see: Raphael (2001).

2 Schauer (1995), 633 ff.

of justice contribute to the clarification of 'public reason' and to its continuous adaptation to changing public conceptions of justice.

3 Universal and Particular Conceptions of Justice

Plato's *Republic* (*Politeia*) and Aristotle's *Nicomachean Ethics* offer early efforts at systematizing different dimensions of justice. Plato's citation of the Greek poet Simonides' conception of justice as 'rendering to every man his due' became the standard definition of justice in the Roman law tradition (*justitia est suum cuique tribuere*), referring to justice not only as a personal virtue but as being dependent on the whole system of law aimed at – as defined in the Justinian Code – *honeste vivere, neminem laedere, suum cuique tribuere* (to live uprightly, to harm no one, to render to each person what is his). Yet, as explained by Perelman, what exactly is 'due' to each person beyond the principle of 'formal justice' (*e.g.* in the sense of 'beings of the same essential category must be treated in the same way'), has always remained contested.[3] Aristotle's distinctions between moral and legal justice, universal justice (*e.g.* in terms of the 'lawful') and particular justice (*e.g.* in terms of distributive justice based on conceptions of 'proportionate equality' and fairness, commutative exchange justice, corrective justice, equity as a 'rectification of legal justice') introduced distinctions among different branches of justice that remain important to date, notwithstanding the emergence of additional conceptions of justice like 'social justice' and 'egalitarian justice' as defined by human rights.

4 Constitutional Conceptions of Justice

Limitation and separation of powers (*e.g.* between *gubernaculum* and *jurisdictio*), like 'mixed constitutions' with mutual 'checks and balances' among monocratic, oligocratic and democratic governance structures, have been used since antiquity in order to prevent monopolization and abuses of power and constrain 'rule by men' through 'rule of law'.[4] The designation – in many

3 Perelman (1963), who distinguishes (at 7) the following six 'most current conceptions of justice': (1) to each the same thing; (2) to each according to his merits; (3) to each according to his works; (4) to each according to his needs; (5) to each according to his rank; (6) to each according to his legal entitlement. Perelman defines 'formal justice' as 'a principle of action in accordance with which beings of one and the same essential category must be treated in the same way' (at 16). Yet, there is no agreement on how to define the 'essential characteristic' justifying equal or different treatment in the administration of justice.

4 On the ancient legal ideal of 'rule of law', and its dialectic development on the basis of constitutional rights and principles of justice restraining the instrumental 'governance by law', see already Aristotle (1996), book III, para. 16, at 1287 a-b. On the history of separation and constitutional limitation of powers see: McIlwain (1947); Riklin (2006).

languages – of judges as 'Mr. Justice', and of tribunals as 'courts of justice', reflects these ancient interrelationships between law (*jus*), judges (*judex*) and justice (*justitia*). Many national constitutions emphasize that their objectives include, *inter alia*, to 'establish Justice' (Preamble of the US Constitution); and that 'the judicial power shall extend to all cases, in law and equity' (Article III.2 US Constitution).

Since the beginning of modern political philosophy with T. Hobbes – whose *Leviathan* (1651) identified justice with *pacta sunt servanda* ('That men perform their Covenants made'),[5] applying the term 'justice' to the system of law as a whole -, constitutional conceptions of justice and of 'courts of justice' continue to differ enormously, even among constitutional democracies. The 'human rights revolutions' since the 18th century, inspired by J. Locke's claims of natural rights to 'life, liberty and estate', led to constitutional recognition of egalitarian conceptions of justice in terms of 'inalienable' human rights to be free and equal, thereby challenging positivist conceptions of justice (*e.g.* in terms of conformity to legislation). The delimitation of constitutional, legislative, executive and judicial powers often differs among countries; yet, the case law of many supreme courts and 'constitutional courts' includes cases where 'new' judicial interpretations of constitutional rules – like the US Supreme Court judgment of 1954 in *Brown v. Board of Education* that segregated schools for children of different colour denied 'equal protection of the laws' in violation of the Fourteenth Amendment in 1868 – were accepted by citizens and governments even if the judicial interpretations of the rules ran counter to the historical intentions of the law-makers. Hence, in constitutional democracies with judicial review at national and international levels, protection by legislation is no guarantee that a legal right is in conformity with constitutional principles of justice of a higher legal rank.

Adam Smith's *Inquiry into the Nature and Causes of the Wealth of Nations* (1776) 'was centrally concerned with the issue of justice, with finding a market mechanism capable of reconciling inequality of property with adequate provision for the excluded'.[6] In the field of economic law, this tension between unequally distributed property rights and social claims of the poor (as formulated by L. Blanc in 1839: 'from each according to his ability, to each according to his needs') continues to be often decided by the courts in favour of acquired property rights recognized by legislation,[7] or by judicial deference to parliamen-

5 Hobbes (1968), p. 202.

6 Hont-Ignatieff, (1983), 2, 42.

7 Nozick (1974), conceives rights of justice as historical entitlements resulting from either just, direct acquisition by the rights holder or just transfer from some other person through voluntary exchanges or gift. He recognizes rectification of holdings arising from past injustice as a third principle of justice (in addition to the two principles of just acquisition and just transfer). But Nozick opposes a welfare state in view of the individual responsibility to better one's condition and the need for protecting innocent individuals against the inevitable, continuous interferences by welfare state governments with people's lives.

tary economic regulation aimed at maximizing utilitarian happiness of domestic citizens (notwithstanding the frequent arbitrariness of governmental distribution of economic benefits and 'protection rents' in favour of powerful interest groups to the detriment of general consumer welfare). Yet, in other fields of law (like human rights, labour and social law), different conceptions of social structures led to the emergence of different conceptions of rights-based justice (*e.g.* as defined by human rights, social and labour rights).

John Rawls' *Theory of Justice* emphasizes that – in view of the 'fact of reasonable pluralism' and 'the fact that in a democratic regime political power is regarded as the power of free and equal citizens as a collective body' – the democratic exercise of coercive power over one another is democratically legitimate only when 'political power [...] is exercised in accordance with a constitution (written or unwritten) the essentials of which all citizens, as reasonable and rational, can endorse in the light of their common human reason.'[8] According to Rawls and other philosophers (like B. Barry), impartiality (*e.g.* in the reasoning about a 'social contract' behind a 'veil of uncertainty' promoting a 'desire for reasonable agreement') is of crucial importance not only for settlement of disputes, but also for inducing rational participants in a 'social contract' to agree on constitutional 'principles of justice' that respect and protect the legitimate diversity of moral, religious and political conceptions of citizens; according to Rawls, recognition of equal liberties as 'first principle of justice', and of a 'difference principle' as 'second principle' of justice favouring the least advantaged in society, is essential for an 'overlapping consensus' among citizens in a constitutional democracy that respects the enduring reality of often diverse conceptions of citizens for a good life and for the 'just' regulation and constitutional and legislative limitation of governance powers.[9] Yet, Rawls' later acknowledgment that 'the first principle covering the equal basic rights and liberties may easily be preceded by a lexically prior principle requiring that citizens' basic needs be met, at least insofar as their being met is necessary for citizens to understand and to be able fruitfully to exercise those rights and liberties',[10] leaves open under what conditions the lexical priority of liberty rights (as justified by I. Kant's doctrine of respect for human dignity, autonomy, freedom of choice and responsibility as vital constituents of a person) should be limited by 'needs claims' as preconditions for exercising equal rights and liberties. Even if it may be true that 'lexical priority for maximum equal liberty implies that unequal liberty may never be considered at all',[11] respect for human dignity, autonomy

8 Rawls (2001), 41.

9 On the Rawlsian 'idea of a well-ordered society' respecting the 'fact of reasonable pluralism' and pursuing only a limited conception of 'political justice', see: Rawls (1993), 35 ff. For a different 'contractual impartiality theory', defining justice in terms of 'reasonable agreement' among all citizens affected by the rules and of 'mediating between conflicting conceptions of the good', see: Barry (1995), 7-8 and 11-12.

10 Rawls (note 9), 7.

11 Raphael (note 1), 209.

and responsibility also requires conceiving citizens as free, equal and responsible persons that must be presumed to be capable to increase their individual welfare through mutually beneficial, voluntary cooperation.

5 Constitutional Justice as Institutionalized 'Public Reason'

The reasoning and justifications of independent, impartial judges, concluding transparent judicial procedures after all parties have been heard, tend to be more 'principle-oriented' than political compromises in majoritarian legislation and instrumental reasoning of periodically elected politicians and administrations. Hence, John Rawls' theory of justice argues that 'in a constitutional regime with judicial review, public reason is the reason of its supreme court'; it is of constitutional importance for the 'overlapping, constitutional consensus' necessary for a stable and just society among free, equal and rational citizens who tend to be deeply divided by conflicting moral, religious and philosophical doctrines.[12] The separation of legislative, executive and judicial powers, like the hierarchies between 'courts of justice' and judges at different levels of national and international governance (*e.g.* 'chief justices' in Supreme Courts, WTO appellate review of WTO panel reports), reflect not only the historical experience that 'rule by men' and their 'rule by law', like judgments of first-instance courts, may be contested as unjust; institutionalized dialogues inside and among legislative, executive and judicial powers at national and international levels also promote 'public reason', 'deliberative democracy' and regular review of past interpretations and progressive development of 'rule of law.' In common law systems, for example, judges and 'courts of equity' could temper the rigor of the law by recourse to principles of 'equity', thereby reconciling 'general justice' with requests by citizens for 'particular justice', or with requests to adapt the interpretation of past legislation to new conceptions of democratic governance.

Rule-following, equal application of existing rules of law ('*idem cuique*') and preservation of 'public order' (*e.g.* by punishing infringements of criminal law) are widely seen as primary functions of judges. Yet, rendering to each person what is his right, may also require the judge to review whether rule-following would 'do justice' to the particular circumstances of the dispute, for example if judicial enforcement of a contract would run counter to dynamically evolving conceptions of 'public morals', 'public policy' and democratic governance. Hence, legal systems and courts of justice have not only 'conservative functions' to preserve the existing legal rules; they also have 'reformative functions' to do justice to the citizens governed by the legal system (*e.g.* by rectifying majoritarian abuses of legislative and executive powers, removing discrimination, taking

12 Rawls (note 9), 231 ff.

into account new democratic legislation, or 'making the whole community responsible for the basic needs of those who cannot help themselves').[13]

6 Justice Requires Multilevel Constitutionalism Limiting Multilevel Governance

The 'globalization' of international economic, environmental, political and legal relations, and its ever larger impact on the legal regulation and social stability of societies, have transformed national constitutions into 'partial constitutions' that can no longer effectively protect general citizen interests in ever more areas of social life without international law and international organizations as essential instruments for 'multilevel governance' for the collective supply of 'international public goods' (like international rule of law, a mutually beneficial division of labour, transnational protection of human rights and 'sustainable development'). Yet, conceptions of 'international justice' in transnational relations among individuals as well as among states tend to be even more controversial than inside countries.

The changing functions of law and justice (*e.g.* compared with the Westphalian system of 'international law among states' from 1648 to 1945) are explicitly recognized in modern international law, for example in the Vienna Convention on the Law of Treaties' codification of the customary law requirement of settling 'disputes concerning treaties, like other international disputes, [...] in conformity with the principles of justice and international law', including 'universal respect for, and observance of, human rights and fundamental freedoms for all' (Preamble VCLT). The universal recognition of human rights by all 192 UN member states, notwithstanding their often diverse conceptions of the legal protection of civil, political, economic, social and cultural rights (*e.g.* by liberty rights and social 'claim rights') and of the underlying normative premises of 'inalienable' human rights (*e.g.* their derivation from respect for 'human dignity'), calls for citizen-oriented conceptions of international law focusing on protection of human rights and democratic governance in the collective supply of national and 'international public goods'.[14] In European and worldwide international economic law, national and international courts (like the EC Court, the EFTA Court, WTO dispute settlement bodies, investor-state arbitration) have taken the lead in interpreting intergovernmental guarantees of freedom, equality, human rights and 'rule of law' for the benefit of citizens and their individual rights.[15]

Immanuel Kant was the first legal philosopher who extended his constitutional conceptions of law (as 'the sum total of those conditions within which the will of one person can be reconciled with the will of another in accordance

[13] Raphael (note 1), 2-3.

[14] Petersmann (2010).

[15] Petersmann (2008/2009), 101-152.

with a universal law of freedom')[16] and of 'rule of law' to international law. In his proposals for *Perpetual Peace: A Philosophical Sketch* (1795), Kant explained why – in order to institute lasting peace among rational, antagonistic egoists with limited reasonableness and 'unsocial sociability' (I. Kant) – 'all men who can at all influence one another must adhere to some kind of civil constitution' of the three following types:

1) a constitution based on the civil rights of individuals within a nation (*ius civitatis*);
2) a constitution based on the international rights of states in their relationships with one another (*ius gentium*);
3) a constitution based on cosmopolitan right, in so far as individuals and states, coexisting in an external relationship of mutual influence, may be regarded as citizens of a universal state of mankind (*ius cosmopoliticum*). This classification, with respect to the idea of a perpetual peace, is not arbitrary, but necessary. For if even one of the parties were able to influence the others physically and yet itself remained in a state of nature, there would be a risk of war, which it is precisely the aim of the above articles to avoid.'[17]

The Kantian conception of multilevel constitutionalism as a morally necessary 'categorical imperative' for protecting human dignity and equal freedoms of individuals in all their social interactions at national, transnational and international relations reflects not only moral self-limitation by rules of a higher rank. Kantian multilevel constitutionalism also rests on Kant's insight that – since rules cannot specify all the conditions of their own application – the application of every rule requires interposition of an authority determining what the rule should mean in a particular situation, and whether applying the rule might be better than resorting to an exception.[18] Hence,

> '(a) constitution allowing the greatest possible human freedom in accordance with laws which ensure that the freedom of each can coexist with the freedom of all the others (not one designed to provide the greatest possible happiness, as this will in any case follow automatically), is at all events a necessary idea which must be made the basis not only of the first outline of a political constitution but of all laws as well.'[19]

Kant was also the first legal philosopher emphasizing that the 'problem of establishing a perfect civil constitution is subordinate to the problem of a law-

---

16 Kant (1977), 133. Kant follows from his moral 'categorical imperative' that 'every action which by itself or by its maxim enables the freedom of each individual's will to co-exist with the freedom of everyone else in accordance with a universal law is *right*' (at 133).

17 Kant (1977), 98.

18 Kant (1991), 140 f.

19 Kant (1977), 191.

governed external relationship with other states, and cannot be solved unless the latter is also solved.'[20] Kant's proposals for separating and limiting representative legislative, executive and judicial powers by multilevel constitutional restraints were aimed at institutionalizing and promoting 'public reason' (*e.g.* in the sense of political support for the moral judgments of law-appliers in determining what equal freedoms and other 'principles of justice' might require in real word conflicts and contestation); for, according to Kant, it was only through antagonistic, historical learning processes that individuals and states could be expected to progressively transform the lawless state of nature into law-governed national, transnational and international relations protecting 'conditions under which the choice of one can be united with the choice of another in accordance with a universal law of freedom.'[21] Like human rights, such multilevel constitutional restraints not only provide for 'principles of justice' as constitutional restraints on 'rule by law'; they also promote 'rule of law' by empowering and protecting individuals and law-appliers to interpret and apply indeterminate rules in reasonable ways respecting equal freedoms and universal 'principles of justice'. The progressive extension of rule of law thus depends not only on the 'justice' of national and international rules and on 'reasonable judgments' in applying them, but also on 'struggles for rights' and multilevel constitutional and judicial guarantees enabling 'public reason' to prevail in the inevitably antagonistic rivalries among rational individuals and states and their instrumental conceptions of law and intergovernmental 'legal regimes.'[22]

In European Community law, in the European Economic Area (EEA) among the 27 EC countries and three EFTA countries as well as in the context of the European Convention on Human Rights (ECHR), the EC Court, the EFTA Court and the European Court of Human Rights have interpreted the international EC and EEA agreements, as well as the ECHR, as 'constitutional instruments' that were progressively transformed – in close cooperation with national courts and with subsequent approval by national parliaments and civil society – into effective, multilevel legal and judicial guarantees of equal freedoms, human rights and rule of law for the benefit of some 500 Million EU citizens and other citizens in the 47 ECHR member states.[23] According to a widely shared view, the 'coherence of the judicial system of the European Union does not rest solely on the Community courts, but rather on the interlocking system of jurisdiction of the Community courts and the national courts which is cemented together by the principle of upholding the 'rule of law' in the Union legal order.'[24] In conformity

[20] Kant /1977), 47.

[21] Kant (1996), 230.

[22] On 'constitutional approaches' as ways for reducing 'fragmentation' of international legal regimes and limiting instrumental, managerial conceptions of 'rule by law' see also: Koskenniemi (2007); van Aaken (2009).

[23] Petersmann (2008).

[24] Lenaerts (2007), 1659.

with the Kantian conception of multilevel constitutional protection of human rights as the most effective safeguard of 'democratic peace' inside and among republican states, the European integration agreements have become the most effective 'peace treaties' ever concluded among European states, offering European citizens more economic and social welfare, rule of law and transnational, individual rights than citizens ever enjoyed before.

In the UN Charter, all 192 UN member states reaffirmed – on behalf of 'We the peoples of the United Nations' – their 'faith in fundamental human rights, in the dignity and worth of the human person, in the equal rights of men and women and of nations large and small' so as 'to establish conditions under which justice and respect for the obligations arising from treaties and other sources of international law can be maintained' (Preamble). Yet, as long as UN human rights conventions do not provide for effective judicial remedies and only about one third of UN member states submit to the compulsory jurisdiction of the International Court of Justice (ICJ) and other worldwide courts (such as the International Tribunal for the Law of the Sea), the UN objective 'to bring about by peaceful means, and in conformity with the principles of justice and international law, adjustment or settlement of international disputes' (Article 1 UN Charter) is not effectively secured. Most constitutional democracies (including the USA) distrust 'rule of international law' and prefer the 'realistic' view that governments should pursue 'international rule of law',[25] submitting to 'rule of international law' only 'as long as' international law rules remain consistent with the constitutional guarantees of human rights, democracy and justice in domestic jurisdictions.[26] Due to the diversity of domestic constitutional traditions, of democratic preferences and of international 'bargaining power' among states, national conceptions of 'international rule of law' often differ among the 192 UN member states and fail to protect 'rule of international law' and human rights in many UN member states.

7 Need for Multilevel Constitutional Theories of Transnational Adjudication and 'Rule of Law'

According to the European Court of Human Rights (ECtHR), 'the Court's obligation is to have regard to the special character of the Convention as a constitutional instrument of European public order for the protection of individual human beings and its role, as set out in Article 19 of the Convention, is to ensure the observance of the engagements undertaken by the Contracting Parties.'[27] Similarly, the EC Court, the European Free Trade Area (EFTA) Court and investor-state tribunals emphasize their judicial function of protecting rule

25 Ikenberry-A.M.Slaugther (2006).

26 Petersmann (note 23), 780 ff.

27 ECtHR, Grand Chamber, *Bankovic and Others against Belgium and Others*, inadmissibility decision of 12 December 2001.

of international law with due regard to the rights of producers, investors, traders, consumers and other citizens against arbitrary interferences by governments and other abuses of public and private power. Just as the idea of 'rule of law' has always been related to justice,[28] so do human rights instruments emphasize 'that human rights should be protected by the rule of law'[29]; 'international rule of law' cannot become effective unless national and international courts respect and apply more effectively the customary law requirement of settling 'disputes concerning treaties, like other international disputes, [...] in conformity with the principles of justice and international law', including 'universal respect for, and observance of, human rights and fundamental freedoms for all' (VCLT, Preamble).

The ever more comprehensive, national and international regulation of human rights, economic law, environmental law and international organizations with legislative, executive and judicial functions requires adapting national constitutional theories to the new realities of 'globalization' and international law. The abuses of foreign policy powers under the Westphalian system of 'international law among states' suggest that, as inside states, 'courts of justice' – through their judicial protection of citizen rights (*e.g.* of EU citizen rights, investor rights, trading rights, social, labour and other human rights) and of transnational 'rule of law' against abuses of discretionary governance powers – must take the lead in protecting constitutional democracy and rule of law also in the ever more important, transnational cooperation among citizens. International human rights law tends to prescribe only *minimum standards* that respect the freedom of states to protect higher standards of civil, political, economic, social and cultural rights and to interpret their international legal obligations in conformity with their domestic constitutional guarantees of human rights. Many international trade and economic agreements, by contrast, commit countries to *higher standards* of freedom, non-discrimination and rule of law than are provided for in their autonomous economic laws.[30] As governments often conclude international treaties that leave the meaning of human rights and of other international law rules and their underlying 'principles of justice' indeterminate and contested, 'international rule of law' depends on judicial dialogues, 'judicial comity', judicial clarification of contested rules and on conditional, judicial cooperation among national and international courts in the protection of 'rule of law', based on 'judicial comity' and reciprocal respect for their respective jurisdictions and constitutional foundations.

28 On the ancient Greek concept of 'law as participation in the idea of justice', and the need to relate justice not only to the value of equality, see: Friedrich (1963), chapters II and XX.

29 Universal Declaration of Human Rights (1948), Preamble.

30 On these often neglected, diverse functions of multilevel human rights law and multilevel market integration law see: Petersmann (2008).

8 Multilevel Judicial Protection of 'Rule of Law' in International Economic Law

The emergence of 'rule of law' in international trade, investments and transnational economic integration is due to such multilevel constitutional restraints of abuses of power and multilevel judicial protection of 'constitutional justice', for example in the judicial review and recognition of foreign arbitral awards and court judgments, in international annulment proceedings challenging arbitration awards (*e.g.* pursuant to the procedures of the International Centre for the Settlement of Investment Disputes), in the ever more comprehensive appellate review of dispute settlement rulings in the World Trade Organization (WTO) and their enforcement through arbitral awards on the 'reasonable period of implementation' and alternative sanctions, or in the review of first-instance judgments by the EC Court as well as in the close cooperation among the EFTA Court and national courts in EFTA countries. As discussed in various chapters to this book, also other areas of international law – like human rights law, international criminal law and the international law of the sea – are increasingly shaped by cooperation among national and international courts in their settlement of disputes and judicial clarification and progressive development of international law rules. Public review and discussion of this 'multilevel judicial governance' and cooperation among national and international courts are preconditions for strengthening rule of law beyond state borders.

The need for more comprehensive 'constitutional theories' of transnational adjudication[31] and of 'rule of law'[32] is illustrated by the variety of alternative dispute settlement *fora* for international investment disputes – like private commercial arbitration, national courts, investor-state arbitration based on bilateral investment treaties (BITs) or regional agreements (like Chapter 11 of NAFTA), regional economic or human rights courts, worldwide courts (like the International Court of Justice) and alternative dispute settlement bodies (*e.g.* in the WTO), whose 'administration of justice' and occasionally incoherent jurisprudence continues to remain controversial.[33] In order to reduce the risks of legal and jurisdictional fragmentation in international law, national and international courts should review their textual, contextual and teleological interpretations of international treaties more thoroughly from the constitutional perspective of the judicial task of settling disputes 'in conformity with principles of justice' and the universal human rights obligations of governments. As in European integration law, international 'rule of law' may be advanced most effectively beyond Europe by means of such multilevel judicial cooperation and

---

31 Petersmann (2009).

32 See notably the contribution by G. Palombella to this book.

33 Petersmann (note 31).

comprehensive 'judicial balancing' in international economic adjudication of individual rights and legal obligations of governments.[34]

9 International 'Rule of Law' and 'Judicial Comity' Depend on Respect for the Legitimacy of Multilevel 'Constitutional Pluralism'

Public international law has historically evolved as a decentralized coercive order respecting state sovereignty over domestic affairs and the power-oriented realities of national legal systems'.[35] While rulers have invoked, applied and enforced rules of 'international law' since legal antiquity (*e.g.* international trade agreements in the Mediterranean), the changing structures and 'legal system' of international law (*e.g.* in the sense of H. Hart's 'concept of law' as consisting of 'primary rules' of conduct and 'secondary rules' about the recognition, amendment and enforcement of rules[36]) are shaped no longer only by (inter)governmental decisions: as explained by the 'Yale School' (founded by M. McDougal and M. Reisman), the authoritative decision-making processes constituting international norms are increasingly influenced also by domestic constitutional systems, parliaments, courts, non-governmental organizations and civil society committed to protection of human rights. Even though 'the need for universal adherence to and implementation of the rule of law at both the national and international levels' is recognized in a few UN resolutions,[37] neither the UN Charter nor other UN treaties constitute an effective, 'multilevel rule of law' system as a constitutional restraint on 'the rule of men' and their 'rule by law' in transnational relations.[38] As national law and international law rely on each other for the collective supply of international 'public goods' (like international rule of law), the effectiveness of international rules depends on their consistency with, and respect for, the legitimate diversity of domestic constitutional laws. Just as international law cannot be effective without its good faith implementation inside domestic legal systems, so are domestic legal systems risking to become ineffective in a globally interdependent world without international legal

---

[34] On 'rationality tests' and 'reasonableness tests' in the 'proportionality balancing' of European and other international courts see: Petersmann (note 14), Sections 22-25.

[35] On Kelsen's unified conception of national and international law as deriving from the same basic 'Grundnorm' see: Kelsen (1945 and 1952), where Kelsen formulated the basic customary norm of the national and international legal order as follows: 'The states ought to behave as they have customarily behaved' (at 417-418), allowing revolution and the principle of effectiveness to be law-creating facts.

[36] Hart (1994).

[37] The quotation is from paragraph 134 of UN General Assembly Resolution A/60/L.1, adopted during the 2005 World Summit meeting on 25 October 2005 (in the same paragraph, UN member states also 'reaffirm our commitment [...] to an international order based on the rule of law and international law, which is essential for peaceful coexistence and cooperation among States').

[38] Cf. note 4 above and Brownlie (1998).

coordination of their often adverse 'external effects' on other polities and legal systems.[39] While European integration law reflects the recognition that national constitutions have become 'partial constitutions' that can no longer unilaterally ensure many 'public goods' demanded by citizens, most countries outside Europe continue to focus on 'constitutional nationalism' without attempting to 'constitutionalize' intergovernmental power politics.

The effective supply of international public goods (like the EC's common market based on rule of law) through European integration law, like the increasing 'globalization' of human rights, market integration, market regulation and of judicial protection of 'international rule of law' since the fall of the Berlin wall (1989), offer empirical evidence that multilevel constitutionalism can succeed in transforming power politics into rule of law systems also beyond state borders. European law and courts increasingly focus on common constitutional principles and on multilevel parliamentary, governmental and judicial cooperation for limiting 'governance failures' at national levels, with due respect for the reality of 'constitutional pluralism' in diverse national and international legal regimes. Several contributions to this book discuss how – in its *Kadi* judgment of 3 September 2008 – the European Court of Justice rightly concluded that UN Security Council sanctions against alleged terrorists can be implemented inside the EC only in conformity with European constitutional guarantees of fundamental rights (*e.g.* rights to be heard, rights to effective judicial protection, rights to respect for private property) and with due respect for judicial remedies.

10 Multilevel Judicial Extension of 'Rule of Law' Beyond the State and Beyond International Economic Law Depends on 'Constitutional Justice'

Many contributors to this book argue that – rather than relying on formal 'monist claims' of supremacy of international law (*e.g.* based on Articles 103 UN Charter, Article 27 VCLT) or 'dualist claims' of the legal autonomy of domestic legal systems – national and international courts should clarify, and reconcile, the complex legal interdependencies among national and

39 American international lawyers focusing on 'state interests' (as defined by the state's political leadership) openly admit that their power-oriented international law approaches are 'not necessarily, or even usually, the policy that would maximize the public good within the state' or 'collective international public goods' among states, Goldsmith-Posner (2005), 17; in view of the 'democratic process pathologies such as interest group capture' and 'collective action problems in performing cosmopolitan duties', the 'absence of democratic support' for the collective supply of international public goods is viewed as 'an inherent feature of democratic process' and insurmountable 'hurdle to cosmopolitan action': 'Information and power asymmetries, as well as the absence of a centralized enforcement mechanism, make international collective action problems difficult to overcome even when there is a plausible argument that the international regime, if successful, would enhance the welfare of every participating state' (at 206-217).

international legal systems in more differentiated ways. Just as the EC Court's judgment in the *Kadi* case aimed at reconciling EC constitutional law (*e.g.* its requirement that 'the European Community must respect international law in the exercise of its powers') with the EC's international obligations under UN law by requiring to bring the EC's implementation of UN sanctions into conformity with the EC's human rights obligations,[40] so can national and international courts reconcile also other national and international legal obligations through mutually coherent interpretations. UN human rights law justifies that, in the absence of adequate guarantees of human rights and judicial review at the UN level, UN member states and European courts must remain entitled to comply with their human rights obligations, and to protect judicial remedies, at national and European levels. Hence, 'rule of law' may legitimately differ in domestic and international jurisdictions depending on their often diverse constitutional and international legal obligations and democratic and judicial conceptions of the 'rule of law prevailing in this jurisdiction', as illustrated also by the 2006 US Supreme Court judgment in *Hamdan v. Rumsfeld*.[41]

It is so far only in the field of international trade and investment law that most UN member states have been willing to submit to multilevel judicial protection of international rule of law based on more than 2,500 Bilateral Investment Treaties (BITs), regional trade and investment agreements (like NAFTA), WTO law and its compulsory dispute settlement system, and other agreements on international judicial cooperation (*e.g.* under the 1958 UN Convention on Recognition and Enforcement of Foreign Arbitral Awards) and international judicial remedies (*e.g.* under the 1965 ICSID Convention on the Settlement of Investment Disputes between States and Nationals of other States). In European economic law, the treaties establishing the EC, the EU, the EEA and the ever larger number of EC free trade agreements with third countries are based on common constitutional 'principles of freedom, democracy, respect for human rights, fundamental freedoms and rule of law' (Article 6 EU), justifying their provision for effective legal and judicial safeguards not only of sovereign rights of states but also of the individual rights of their citizens. Just as UN human rights conventions explicitly recognize 'that these rights derive from the inherent dignity of the human person', so does the EU Charter of Fundamental Rights base the human rights approach to European economic law, and the rights-based conception of the EC's international 'market freedoms' as fundamental freedoms of individuals to be protected by national and European courts,

---

40 Cf. Joined Cases C-402/05P & C-415/05P, *Kadi v. Council of the EU*, in: [2008] Common Market Law Reports 41, 1207, 1240 ff. On the EC as a 'community of law' based on 'rule of law', the conceptual independence of rule of law from democracy and its content-dependent, constitutional assessment see also Palombella-N. Walker (2008).

41 *Hamdan v. Rumsfeld*, 548 U.S. 557 (2006), where the Supreme Court defined the 'rule of law in this jurisdiction' in conformity with the 'judicially enforceable' Geneva Conventions on the law of war and Article 21 of the US Uniform Code of Military Justice (Opinion of the Court at p. 635). Cf. also the contribution by Palombella to this book.

on 'the indivisible, universal values of human dignity, freedom, equality and solidarity' as well as 'on the principles of democracy and the rule of law.'[42]

This successful, constitutional as well as judicial protection of 'international rule of law' and of democratic citizen rights in EC law, EEA law and in the ECHR refutes the prevailing North American view that rule of law and democracy can be effective only inside nation states. 'Constitutional nationalism' and power-oriented foreign policies neglect that collective supply of international public goods depends on multilevel judicial protection of international rule of law, as universally recognized in the customary law requirement of settling 'disputes concerning treaties, like other international disputes, [...] in conformity with the principles of justice and international law', including 'universal respect for, and observance of, human rights and fundamental freedoms for all' (VCLT, Preamble). The editors of this book are to be congratulated for their promotion of academic and judicial discussions on the needed changes in 'public reason' necessary for 'international rule of law' beyond 'constitutional nationalism'.[43] As the 'fragmentation' and 'systemic crisis' of modern international law have been caused by intergovernmental power politics and 'national parochialism' disregarding the international law obligations of states and their 'constitutional functions' for protecting human rights and rule of law for the benefit of citizens, the 'systemic unity' of national and international legal systems can be re-asserted only by stronger legal and judicial protection of human rights and rule of law in mutually beneficial international cooperation beyond states. Yet, rather than relying on UN law as 'the gentle civilizer of nations',[44] citizens, parliaments and courts may rightly insist on legal and judicial respect for domestic constitutional guarantees of human rights and rule of law, including compliance with international law 'as long as' the international legal obligations of states remain consistent with domestic constitutional guarantees of human rights and democratic self-governance as legitimate constitutional restraints on international 'rules of recognition'.[45]

---

42 The quotation is from the Preamble to the Charter of Fundamental Rights of the European Union, as adopted first in December 2000 and subsequently incorporated into the 2004 Treaty establishing a Constitution for Europe (Official Journal of the EU C 310 of 16 December 2004) and into EU law by the 2007 Lisbon Treaty.

43 Petersmann(2008).

44 M. Koskenniemi (2004).

45 On the '*solange* case-law' of European courts 'as long as' (which is the English translation of the German term 'solange') as an appropriate paradigm for protecting 'constitutional justice' in multilevel judicial governance see: Petersmann (note 23).

References

A. van Aaken, Defragmentation of Public International Law through Interpretation: A Methodological Proposal, in: *Indiana Journal of Global Legal Studies* 16 [2009], 483-512.

Aristotle, *The Politics and the Constitution of Athens* (ed. by S.Everson), Cambridge: Cambridge University Press, 1996.

B. Barry, *Justice as Impartiality*, Oxford University Press, 1995.

I. Brownlie, *The Rule of Law in International Affairs*, Kluwer Law International, 1998.

C. McIlwain, Constitutionalism: Ancient and Modern, New York: Cornell University Press, 1947.

C.J. Friedrich, *The Philosophy of Law in Historical Perspective*, Chicago, University of Chicago Press. 1963.

J.L. Goldsmith-E.A. Posner, *The Limits of International Law*, Oxford University Press, 2005.

H.L.A. Hart, *The Concept of Law* (2nd ed), Clareondon University Press, 1994.

T. Hobbes, *Leviathan* (ed. by C.B.Macpherson), Penguin, 1968.

I. Hont-M. Ignatieff, Needs and Justice in the Wealth of Nations, in: Hont-Ignatieff (eds), *Wealth and Virtue* (1983), 2, 42.

G.J. Ikenberry-A.M. Slaugther, *Forging a World of Liberty under Law: U.S. National Security in the 21st Century* (Princeton Project Paper September 2006).

I. Kant, The Metaphysics of Morals, in: I. Kant, *Political Writings* (ed. by H.Reiss), Cambridge University Press,, 1977.

I. Kant, Perpetual Peace: A Philosophical Sketch in I. Kant, *Political Writings* (ed. by H.Reiss), Cambridge University Press, 1977.

I. Kant, Appendix from 'The Critique of Pure Reason', in I. Kant, *Political Writings* (ed. by H.Reiss), Cambridge University Press, 1977.

I. Kant, Idea for a Universal History with a Cosmopolitan Purpose, in in: I.Kant, *Political Writings* (ed. by H. Reiss), Cambridge University Press, 1977.

I. Kant, *Critique of Pure Reason* (ed. by V.Politis, 1991).

I. Kant, The Metaphysics of Morals (ed. by M.Gregor), Cambridge University Press, 1996.

H. Kelsen, *The General Theory of Law and State*, Harvard University Press, Cambridge Ms, 1945.

H. Kelsen, *Principles of International Law* New York, Rinehart & Co., (1952).

M. Koskenniemi, Constitutionalism as Mindset: Reflections on Kantian Themes about International Law and Globalization, in: *Theoretical Inquiries in Law* 8 [2007], 9-36.

M. Koskenniemi, *The Gentle Civilizer of Nations. The Rise and Fall of International Law 1870-1960*, Cambridge University Press 2004.

K. Lenaerts, The Rule of Law and the Coherence of the Judicial System of the European Union, in: *Common Market Law Review* 44 [2007], 1625 ff.

R. Nozick, *Anarchy, State and Utopia*, Basic Books, 1974.

G. Palombella-N. Walker (eds), *Relocating the Rule of Law*, Hart: Oxford, 2008.

C. Perelman, *The Idea of Justice and the Problem of Argument* (ed. by J. Petrie), Routledge & Kegan Paul, London, 1963.

E.U. Petersmann, State Sovereignty, Popular Sovereignty and Individual Sovereignty: From Constitutional Nationalism to Multilevel Constitutionalism in International Economic Law? in: W. Shan/P. Simons/D. Singh (eds), *Redefining Sovereignty in International Economic Law* (2008), 27-60.

E.U. Petersmann, *Human Rights, Multilevel Constitutionalism and International Economic Law in the 21st Century*, forthcoming, 2010.

E.U. Petersmann, Multilevel Judicial Governance as Guardian of the Constitutional Unity of International Economic Law, in: *Loyola International and Comparative Law Review* 30 (2008/2009), 101-152.

E.U. Petersmann, Human Rights, International Economic Law and 'Constitutional Justice', in: *European Journal of International Law* 19[2008], 769-798.

E.U. Petersmann, Multilevel Constitutionalism and Judicial Protection of Freedom and Justice in the International Economic Law of the EC, in: A. Arnull (ed), *Continuity and Change in EU Law. Liber amicorum Francis Jacobs* 2008, 338-353.

E.U. Petersmann, Constitutional Theories of International Economic Adjudication and Investor-State Arbitration, in P.M. Dupuy-F. Francioni-E.U. Petersmann (eds), *Human Rights in International Investment Law and Arbitration* 2009, 137-194.

E.U. Petersmann, Introduction and Summary: 'Administration of Justice' in International Investment Law and Adjudication, in: P.M. Dupuy-F. Francioni-E.U. Petersmann (eds), *Human Rights in International Investment Law and Arbitration* 2009, 137-194.

D.D. Raphael, *Concepts of Justice* Oxford University Press, 200) 1.

J. Rawls, *Justice as Fairness: A Restatement*, (ed. by E.Kelly), Cambridge, MA., Harvard University Press, 2001.

J. Rawls, *Political Liberalism*, New York, Columbia University Press, 1993.

A. Riklin, Machtteilung. *Geschichte der Mischverfassung*, Wissenschaftliche Buchgesellschaft, 2006.

F. Schauer, Giving Reasons, in: *Stanford Law Review* 47 [1995], 633 ff.

Introduction

Filippo Fontanelli, Giuseppe Martinico & Paolo Carrozza

We are very delighted to spend a few words to introduce this volume devoted to the judicial interaction between national and supranational/ international judges. This book is the final outcome of two seminars series organized in Pisa, at the Scuola Superiore Sant'Anna (Sant'Anna School of Advanced Studies) in 2008 and 2009, and implemented within the STALS (Sant'Anna Legal Studies) project (www.stals.sssup.it).

STALS is neither a journal nor a mere paper archive; it is in fact something different. STALS is – first and foremost – a 'space' where both young and experienced scholars can debate by publishing short papers. These papers are collected and classified by topic (European politics and policies; local law and devolution; new constitutional experiences; judicial dialogue; welfare and markets; global legal pluralism; human rights), the editors committed to choose and publish contributions by authoritative scholars and young researchers, whilst the authors, as well as the readers, are invited to comment or discuss the legal issues treated in the written essays. This parallelism between discussion and research is the main feature of the STALS project, and we think that it will foster the interplay between Italian and foreign scholars.

The STALS project started as an initiative of a group of Sant'Anna School students, who are interested and active in the field of constitutional legal studies. It is designed to provide young scholars from all around the world with a concrete opportunity of having their ideas published along with contributions by long-time professors: our strict policy is to favour the discussion between students and lecturers, rather than stressing their formal role, and to accept papers written not only in English but also in French or Spanish; our purpose is to enlarge as much as possible both the pool of contributors and the reach of the audience: everyone is invited to submit a paper, and everyone is welcome to read and discuss STALS on-line materials.

This project represented a splendid opportunity to invite in Pisa prominent scholars or young colleagues who are interested in European Constitutional and EU Law: along these lines, we were enthusiast to plan and take part in these seminars. Our firm belief is that the judicial dialogue is a privileged point of view to read the relationship between legal orders: that is why the core subject of this book is the struggle for the interpretation among the courts.

The process of fragmentation of the international legal order and the absence of constitutional devices governing the connections between the various legal regimes can be reduced to a rational picture only through the activity of the judges. Against this background, the judges play a crucial role in creating connections between legal regimes and proceedings, as Shany recently pointed out in his fundamental studies on judicial relations between international and national judges.

The metaphor of dialogue has been vastly used by the literature and this concept was variously understood in different meanings: vehicle for transplants, informal way of communication between judicial and political bodies, new paradigm of judicial relations between actors not belonging to the same legal order.[1] Starting from this assumption we attempted to put together scholars belonging to different fields of research (Constitutional Law, EU Law, WTO Law, Public International Law, Jurisprudence) in order to carry out a comprehensive appraisal of this phenomenon.

After the first essays, whose purpose is to provide the 'grammar' of judicial dialogue, we attempted to classify several relevant experiences of such a phenomenon by focusing first on the role of the ECJ (by analysing on the one hand the relations between the ECJ and – respectively – national ordinary, administrative and constitutional courts, on the other hand the ECJ's approach towards the ECHR, WTO judiciary bodies) and then on certain particular experiences of the international panorama.

Ideally, the structure of this book draws inspiration from the schematization proposed by Allan Rosas,[2] who recently distinguished between vertical (*e.g.*, ECJ and CFI), semi-vertical (*e.g.*, ECJ and ECHR, or ECJ and WTO Appellate Body), horizontal (ECJ and EFTA Court, at least formally) relationships, cases of overlapping or competing jurisdictions (*e.g.* ICJ and the Law of the Sea Tribunal in Hamburg) and – last but not least – cases where there is a '*special relationship which exists between the ECJ and national courts of the EU Member States faced with problems of interpretation or validity of EU law, notably Community 'First Pillar' law*'.[3]

Later, we realized that this list did non exhaust the variety of judicial relations and that these cases of dialogue between judges only could not provide a complete portrait of the phenomenon as such, since there can be cases of dialogue between judges and political or technical bodies that are as important as these already mentioned.

One instance is the case of the *Kadi* saga, where the ideal interlocutor of the ECJ is not a judge but an entire legal order (the UN one) that probably lacks the basic procedural rights. One example of the second category, instead, is the case of the relation between judges and experts: to what extent the expertise of the scientist represents a limit to the judicial discretion?

In order to deal with these issues outstanding scholars and young promising colleagues have been asked to give their contribution to this work: we hope this mix of expertise and fresh energies might provide an interesting contribution to the debate in this field.

Finally, we would like to thank all those people who made this volume possible, in particular Prof. Emanuele Rossi, whose efforts were precious in collect-

1 Recently Luc Tremblay proposed an interesting distinction between dialogue as a conversation and dialogue as a deliberation. The former implies a conversation not aiming at reaching a specific purpose in mind, this is the case of a casual meeting between friends talking about trivialities while the latter is aimed at a specific purpose and attempting to achieve a common agreement, at solving problems collectively; Tremblay (2005).

2 Rosas (2007).

3 *Ibidem.*

ing the funds for the launch of the STALS project two years ago, and all the other invited speakers of this two years whose contributions are not included in this volume: Leonard Besselink, Monica Claes, Marco Francesco Dal Canto, Sir Robert Carnwath, Antonio D'Aloia, Marco Dani, Bruno de Witte, András Jakab, Andrea Lollini, Petros Mavroidis, Francesco Palermo, Oreste Pollicino, Jens Woelk and Lorenzo Zucca.

Bibliography

A. Rosas, 'The European Court of Justice in Context: Forms and Patterns of Judicial Dialogue', in EJLS, 2007, http://ejls.eu/index.php?mode=htmlarticle&filename=./issues/2007-12/RosasUK.htm.

L.B. Tremblay, 'The legitimacy of judicial review: The limits of dialogue between courts and legislatures', International Journal of Constitutional Law, Number 4, 2005, pp. 617-648.

CHAPTER I

Dédoublement fonctionnel and the Mixed Loyalties of National and International Judges

Yuval Shany*

Introduction

What makes international courts *international?* We are used to think of international courts as permanent judicial institutions that were created by international instruments in order to apply international law to disputes presented before them.[1] Domestic courts clearly do not meet these characteristics: They are created by a national legislative process, not an international one, and primarily apply national law, not international law. Hence, the study of international courts and tribunals – a branch of international law research that has grown exponentially in recent years – has focused almost exclusively on judicial institutions operating at the international level – i.e., about 25 existing international courts, and a somewhat larger number of ad hoc and quasi-judicial bodies.[2]

But the sharp dichotomies between internationally-created and non-internationally-created courts, and between international law-applying and non-international law-applying courts, appear no longer to offer an exhaustive description of adjudicatory venues. Arguably, the emergence of hybrid institutions, such as investment arbitration panels and mixed criminal tribunals, established by procedures which are not uniquely international or non-international, and that apply norms deriving from a plurality of sources, renders irrelevant the old dichotomies and casts doubt on the propriety of some of the legal implications that ensue from such distinctions.[3] At the same time, the movement by some national courts towards assuming a more robust international law-applying role

---

* Hersch Lauterpacht Chair in Public International Law, Faculty of Law, Hebrew University of Jerusalem. The research for this contribution was supported by a European Research Council Starting Grant for Frontier Research. I am grateful for participants in the Sant'Anna School of Advanced Studies, Pisa seminar on the relationship between courts in the multilevel legal system and in particular to Giuseppe Martinico, Filippo Fontanelli and Nikolaos Lavranos.

1 For example, Cesare Romano defines an international judicial body as a body entrusted with five features: a) permanence; b) established by an international instrument; c) decides cases on the basis of international law; d) decided cases according to pre-existing rules of procedures; and e) a process leading to a binding decision. Romano (2009) 389 (International Courts are created 'by definition' by multiple governments); Alvarez (2006) 458; Shany (2003) 12, at note 44 (international tribunals are bodies manned by independent decision-makers and created by international legislative processes that operate and decide cases according to law by issuing binding decisions). Interestingly enough, Christian Tomuschat's definition of international courts omits reference to the body's method of creation. Tomuschat (2008) (defining international courts and tribunals as 'permanent judicial bodies made up of independent judges which are entrusted with adjudicating international disputes on the basis of international law according to a pre-determined set of rules of procedure and rendering decisions which are binding on the parties').

2 See *e.g.*, Alter (2008) 56-62; Avarez, *supra* note 1, 521 *et seq*; Shany, *supra* note 1, 5-7; Romano, *supra* note 1, 723-728.

3 For example, the immunity of serving heads of state may depend on the characterization of the relevant as national or international. See *Prosecutor v. Taylor* (SCSL -2003-01-I-059), AC decision of 31 May 2004.

suggests a growing functional assimilation between such national courts and their international counterparts.

The upshot of this narrative of judicial diversification may therefore be that the dichotomous approach to the study of international courts and tribunals, focusing on a small number of institutions with clear international attributes, should give way to a more open-ended or elastic understanding of international adjudication. Such a 'spectrum approach' would emphasize the international law functions of some judicial institutions, at certain points in time, and downplay the significance of more rigid institutional characteristics.

The current article surveys in Part One a few examples illustrating the blurring of distinctions between national and international adjudicatory bodies. In Part Two, I discuss the continued relevance of Georges Scelle's *dédoublement fonctionnel* theory to national courts applying international law and respond to some of the criticism directed against regarding national judges as potentially fulfilling an international judicial function. In Part Three, the concluding part of this article, I present some thoughts on the remaining differences between national and international courts and on the implications for the field of international law adjudication of expanding our definition of what constitutes an international judicial function.

1 The Blurring of Traditional Distinctions

According to the theory of legal dualism,[4] national and international judicial institutions operate on different normative planes: They are established by different law-makers, apply different laws and serve different political constituencies, who, in turn, confer upon them different types of legitimacy. Hence, the contact points between national and international courts under dualism are minimal and insignificant.

There is little question that the sharp dichotomies between national and international judicial bodies are being gradually eroded. First, more and more internationally-created courts are authorized to apply norms deriving from bodies of law other than international law. For example, arbitration tribunals operating under the auspices of the International Center for the Settlement of Investment Disputes (ICSID) and its constitutive treaty[5] may arbitrate disputes on the basis of any body of norms selected by the parties –their contractual obligations, national law, international law or a combination thereof. Significantly, the default rule prescribed by Article 42 of the ICSID Convention is that arbitra-

4 For a discussion, see *e.g.*, Gaja (2007) 52; Slyz (1996); Jennings and Watts (1992) 53; Klami (1992) 139-48; Starke (1936) 66.

5 Convention on the Settlement of Investment Disputes between States and Nationals of Other States, 18 March 1965, 575 U.N.T.S. 159 (hereinafter 'ICSID Convention').

tion be governed by the domestic law of the host state (and the applicable rules of international law).[6]

The invocation of 'umbrella clauses' found in many bilateral investment treaties (BITs) and the private-public method of creation of investment tribunals further accentuates the blurring of the national and international, and the futility of drawing clear normative lines between them. 'Umbrella clauses' are treaty provisions that authorize investment tribunals to monitor the host state's compliance with all of the obligations it has assumed.[7] One possible understanding of 'umbrella clause' type of provisions is that such clauses serve as conduits that transfer obligations created under national law, including contractual obligations, onto the international level.[8] In fact, the very characterization of 'umbrella clauses' as entailing the application of national law or international law requires an elaborate act of analytical hair-splitting, which does not adequately reflect the actual inter-dependence of obligations in the world of investment relations.[9] At the same time, the fact that investment arbitral tribunals are created by a combination of a framework inter-governmental agreement (a BIT or a general investment treaty) and a private contract between a foreign investor and the host government, further complicates the process of ascertaining the 'true nature' of such tribunals.

Moreover, some judicial institutions have recently been created pursuant to legal processes involving both national and international legislatures. Hybrid criminal tribunals, such as Special Court for Sierra Leone and the Extraordinary Chambers in the Courts of Cambodia, established through an international

---

6 ICSID Convention, Article 42 ('The Tribunal shall decide a dispute in accordance with such rules of law as may be agreed by the parties. In the absence of such agreement, the Tribunal shall apply the law of the Contracting State party to the dispute (including its rules on the conflict of laws) and such rules of international law as may be applicable'). For an authoritative interpretation of this provision, see Schreuer (2009) 545-639.

7 See *e.g.*, Agreement between The Kingdom of Saudi Arabia and The Republic of Austria concerning the Encouragement and Reciprocal Protection of Investments, 30 June 2001, Article 8(2), http://www.unctad.org/sections/dite/iia/docs/bits/saudi_austria.pdf ('Each Contracting Party shall observe any other obligation it has assumed with regard to investments in its territory by investors of the other Contracting Party'); Agreement between the Government of the Republic of Singapore and the Government of the Republic of Peru on the Promotion and Protection of Investment, 27 Feb. 2003, Article 15, http://www.unctad.org/sections/dite/iia/docs/bits/Singapore-Peru.pdf ('Each Contracting Party shall observe any commitment in accordance with its laws additional to those specified in this Agreement entered into by the Contracting parties, its investors with investors of the other Contracting Party as regards their investment').

8 See *e.g.*, *SGS v. Philippines*, Decision of the Tribunal on Objections to Jurisdiction of Jan. 29, 2004, para. 128, http://icsid.worldbank.org/ICSID/FrontServlet?requestType=CasesRH&actionVal=showDoc&docId=DC657_En&caseId=C6; Schreuer, *supra* note 6, at p. 279.

9 See Douglas (2009) 239.

agreement backed up by domestic legislation,[10] present classical examples of such dual-source institutions. Such institutions may also typically apply a combination of national and international law.[11] As a result, it is difficult, if not impossible, to neatly categorize them as either national or international in nature.[12]

Parallel to the growing influence of national law-making processes on international adjudication, one may identify a movement in the opposite direction. Indeed, certain national courts have been applying in recent years international norms in a way which appears to represent an advancement on past practices. Of course, the phenomenon of national courts applying international law is not new. Still, what may be innovative about some of the more recent international law cases decided by national courts, is their high profile, on the one hand, and the level of seriousness and credibility which attaches to the application of international law to these high profile issues, on the other hand. Recent cases such as the UK House of Lords 'war on terror' cases,[13] the Israeli Supreme Court 'Second

---

10 Agreement between the United Nations and the Government of Sierra Leone on the Establishment of the Special Court for Sierra Leone, 16 January 2002 (hereinafter' SCSL Agreement'), http://www.sc-sl.org/LinkClick.aspx?fileticket=CLk1rMQtCHg%3d&tabid=176; The Special Court Agreement Ratification Act (2002), http://www.sc-sl.org/LinkClick.aspx?fileticket=BcKTbFltxZk%3d&tabid=176; Agreement between the United Nations and the Royal Government of Cambodia concerning the Prosecution under Cambodian Law of Crimes Committed during the Period of Democratic Kampuchea, 6 June 2003, http://www.eccc.gov.kh/english/cabinet/agreement/5/Agreement_between_UN_and_RGC.pdf; Law on the Establishment of Extraordinary Chambers in the Courts of Cambodia for the Prosecution of Crimes Committed during the Period of Democratic Kampuchea 2001 (as amended in 2004)(hereinafter 'ECCC Law), http://www.eccc.gov.kh/english/cabinet/law/4/KR_Law_as_amended_27_Oct_2004_Eng.pdf.

11 See Statute of the Special Court for Sierra Leone, Annexed to SCSL Agreement, Articles 2-5; ECCC Law, Art. 2-3. One may also cite the examples of the Special Tribunal for Lebanon – an internationally created court that is authorized to apply only national law (See Statute of the Special Tribunal for Lebanon, annexed to S.C. Res S/RES/1757 (2007), Art. 2) and the Iraqi Special Tribunal (also referred to as the Supreme Iraqi Criminal Tribunal) – a nationally created court authorized to apply primarily international norms. Law of the Supreme Iraqi Criminal Tribunal No. 10/2005, Art. 1, 14, http://www.ictj.org/static/MENA/Iraq/iraq.statute.engtrans.pdf.

12 The case law on the matter also appears not to be fully consistent: The SCSL has regarded itself as an international court for the purpose of depriving a head of state from legal immunity. *Taylor, supra* note 3. However, the International Criminal Tribunal for Yugoslavia (ICTY) has held that the internationalized panels in Bosnia should be viewed as national courts for the purpose of 11bis transfer of cases procedures. *Prosecutor v. Stankovic*, TC Decision on 11bis Referral of 17 May 2005, at para. 26.

13 See *e.g.*, *A v. Secretary of State for the Home Dept.*, [2005] 2 AC 68 (ordering the release of detained foreign terrorists); *A v. Secretary of State for the Home Dept.*, [2006] A.C. 221 (proclaiming the inadmissibility of evidence procured through torture); *Secretary of State for the Home Department v. AF* [2009] UKHL 28 (suspected terrorists must have access to secret evidence in proceedings against them).

Intifada' cases[14] and the Italian Cour de cassation's 'Second World War reparations' cases[15] seem to share the following four characteristics:

a) the decisions rely exclusively or almost exclusively on international law;
b) the decisions do not differ much in style and methodology from decisions of national courts exercising judicial review on the basis of national constitutional or legislative texts;
c) the decisions do not appear to be parochial or tendentious in nature, and it is not clear that international courts would have analyzed the same cases much differently, or would have reached significantly different outcomes. It is particularly instructive that in many of the cases the courts ruled against the positions of the executive branch of government; and
d) the application of international law appears to have been based on a belief that courts are obliged to apply international law (either by way of *renvoi* from domestic legislation,[16] because of domestic law doctrines that require courts to use international law in the interpretation of local laws,[17] or by way of extrapolation from general 'rule of law' notions).[18]

Arguably, if some national and international courts apply international law in a similar fashion, they engage in a qualitatively comparable international law-application project or perform an analogous judicial function. As a result, a definition of the international judicial function that is based on one factor only – the formal legislative method in which a court has been historically created, appears to be too broad and too narrow, at the same: It is too broad because it will encompass internationally created courts such as the Lebanon Special Tribunal that exclusively apply Lebanese law or courts operating in internationally-administered territories and applying local law; and it is too narrow, because it excludes the contribution of national courts to the creation and implementation of international law. As noted above, there would also be difficult border-line cases such

---

14 See *e.g.*, H.C.J. 3799/02 *Adalah v. IDF Chief of Central Command*, 45 ILM 491 (2006)(IDF cannot solicit assistance in arrest operations from local Palestinians); C.J. 3239/02 *Mar'ab v. IDF Commander in Judea and Samaria*, 57(2) P.D. 349 (in Hebrew); English version available at http://elyon1.court.gov.il/files_eng/02/390/032/A04/02032390.a04.htm (a military order permitting detention of security suspects for 18 days without judicial review is unlawful); H.C.J. 2056/04 *Beit Sourik Village Council v. Gov't of Israel*, 43 ILM 1099 (2004) (route of separation barrier creates disproportional harm to Palestinian interests and is therefore unlawful).

15 *Ferrini v. Germany*, Appeal decision, no. 5044/4; ILDC 19 (IT 2004); *Germany v. Mantelli*, Preliminary order on jurisdiction, No 14201/2008; ILDC 1037 (IT 2008).

16 See *e.g.*, *Hamdan v. Rumsfeld*, 548 U.S. 557 (2006) (referring through Authorization for Use of Military Force and the Uniform Code of Military Justice to the Geneva Conventions); *A v. Secretary of State* (2004), *supra* note 13 (referring through the Human Rights Act 1998 to the European Convention on Human Rights).

17 See *e.g.*, *Murray v. The Schooner Charming Betsy*, 6 U.S. 64 (1804); South African Constitution, Sec. 39(1). For a discussion, see Shany (2006) 360-366.

18 See Shany (2009) 9-13.

as ICSID or the Special Courts for Sierra Leone, which a definition exclusively based on formal attributes, may fail to adequately capture.

Hence, the traditional dichotomy between national and international courts – a distinction which for many years has shaped our theoretical and practical understanding of international law (and domestic law) and its enforcement mechanisms, ought to be revisited. We should consider substituting our existing definition of the international judicial function that is based on the formal identity of the institution creating the law-applying institution with a more functional definition, which views the application of international law in a judicial process as the key attribute of the international judicial function. Arguably, national courts whose work meets the four aforementioned characteristics could be deemed as part of this function-based international judiciary.

True, a functionality-based definition of what constitutes international adjudicatory bodies also raises problems and encounters difficult borderline cases (*e.g.*, individual judge opinions, or decisions only partly based on international law). Personally, I would support the position that, in some cases, we should regard national courts as assuming a limited international judicial function or a judicial function with some international attributes. In other words, there could be a spectrum of international judicial functions ranging from the exclusive application of international lay by internationally created courts, such as the International Court of Justice (ICJ) to application of international law to some specific issues by some members of a non-internationally created court. Still, discussing borderline cases before addressing the strong objections to treating even paradigmatic international law decisions issued by national courts as international decisions, or as a manifestation of an international judicial function appears to me to be premature at this point in time.

2 The Conceptual Problems of Multiple Constituencies and Mixed Loyalties

One possible set of counter-arguments to the 'national judges as part of the international judiciary' approach presented above, is that national and international courts serve different normative purposes and cater for the needs of different constituencies. Arguably, the differences in goals and 'clients' affect the judicial motivations or loyalties of the two sets of judges and, as a result, change the essence of their function. Another set of possible counter-arguments points at the distorting effect of national law on the application of international law by national courts, and questions the quality of international law-application by domestic judges.

Dédoublement fonctionnel

It can hardly be disputed that national and international courts serve, most of the time, different policy goals and distinct constituencies. The critical question, however, is whether national courts have the capability of transforming themselves, at times, into international law-applying bodies. Even if national courts were mainly created to serve national policies and constituencies, cannot one argue that the very application of international norms – norms created, *inter alia*, to advance international policy goals and to cater for the need of an international constituency – entails an international judicial function? In other words, should we necessarily regard the goals of the legal norms to be undermined by the identity of the judicial institution that (mis)applies them?

The very insight that national courts may, at times, assume an international function underlies Georges Scelle's famous *dédoublement fonctionnel* theory.[19] According to Scelle, as long as there exists an institutional vacuum at the international level, national actors should be regarded as fulfilling, at times, the role of international actors. Consequently, national courts that apply international law should be viewed according to Scelle as acting – when they engage in such law-application exercises – as international courts.

Of course, the Scelle's theory has been discredited by many commentators particularly because of the theory's ambitious attempt to detach social functions from actual sources of authority.[20] Arguably, national courts remain national institutions even when they engage with international law materials. Although I accept the difficulties associated with detaching institutions from their core constituencies, as Scelle has tried to do, I do not subscribe to the equally sweeping rejection of overlaps between national and international goals, constituencies and sources of legitimacy, which some of Scelle's critics seem to have embraced.

First, one may note that national courts often apply international law pursuant to a legal authority vested upon them by international law. Even if one does not adopt Kelsenian positions on the actual links between national and international law,[21] international law sometimes clearly permits, at times, actively encourages and, at other times, directly requires states to apply international law. For example, legal remedies before domestic courts ought to be exhausted before certain proceedings are initiated before international courts;[22] and the principle of complementarity in international criminal law channels, as a default rule, international crimes to prosecution by local authorities.[23] Moreo-

[19] See *e.g.*, Scelle (1934) 10-12; Scelle (1956) 324.

[20] See *e.g.*, Truyol y Serra (1981) 276-277; Beaulac (2007) 7.

[21] See Kelsen (1952) 435-438; Kelsen (1945) 403-404.

[22] See *e.g.*, Convention for the Protection of Human Rights and Fundamental Freedoms, 4 Nov.1950, Art. 35(1), 213 U.N.T.S. 222; American Convention on Human Rights, 22 November 1969, Art. 46(a), 9 ILM (1970) 673.

[23] Rome Statute of the International Criminal Court, 17 July 1998, Art. 1, 2187 U.N.T.S. 90.

ver, a number of human rights treaties require local courts to offer 'an effective remedy'[24] or to prosecute (or extradite) international criminals.[25]

These legal provisions suggest that international law-makers regard national courts as useful, at times, indispensible legal tools for meeting certain international policy goals. Consequently, it is not implausible to assert that given the institutional deficiencies that exist at the international level of global governance, there may a functional necessity to authorize national court to promote international policy goals through their operation as international law-appliers. In other words, it is not impossible to view national courts as operating, at times, also on behalf of an international constituency.

Second, as I already noted, some national courts have been acting in recent years as if they were international courts, issuing decisions that resemble in style, direction and outcome international court decisions. This empirical fact suggests that national courts may be capable of transforming themselves into *de facto* international courts. Hence, although Scelle's *dédoublement fonctionnel* theory may have been divorced from social reality at the time of its promulgation, subsequent developments in some national jurisdictions may have conferred upon the theory some retroactive explanatory power.

Mixed loyalties

One of the most serious challenges to Scelle's theory emerges not from legal formalism, but rather from legal realism. Eyal Benvenisti has argued recently that even when national courts apply international law their motivation is strategic in nature – i.e., driven by particular domestic agendas, which may conflict in the long run with the project of international governance.[26] According to Benvenisti, national courts are apprehensive about the increased dominance of international institutions and are using international law in order to reclaim national sovereignty – that is, to generate alternative positions which could challenge sooner or later international institutions.

Antonio Cassese has also suggested in his writings that the 'litmus test' of the international judiciary is found in the realm of motivations:

> '[W]hat matters is to enquire into when and why they promote *metanational* values or long-term, communal objectives (peace, human rights, self-determination of peoples, etc.) or instead take action for the exclusive purpose of safeguarding *national* (or short-term, self-centered) interests. The distinction between the two classes can in effect become the litmus test for assessing to what extent the

[24] See *e.g.*, International Covenant on Civil and Political Rights, 16 Dec. 1966, Art. 2(3), 999 U.N.T.S. 171; Convention on the Elimination of All Forms of Discrimination against Women, 18 Dec. 1979, Art. 2(c), U.N. Doc. A/34/46 (1979).

[25] See *e.g.*, Convention against Torture and Other Cruel, Inhuman or Degrading Treatment or Punishment, 10 Dec. 1984, Art. 7, U.N. Doc. A/39/51 (1984); International Convention for the Suppression of Terrorist Bombing, 15 Dec. 1997, Art. 7, U.N. Doc. A/52/49 (1998).

[26] Benvenisti (2008) 241.

> international community is still anarchical and individualistic or is instead moving towards solidarity and common welfare'.[27]

The subtext of Benvenisti and Cassese's argument appears to be that a functional approach focusing too much on the incidence of international law-application may be misleading, as there may be a qualitative difference between international law-application intended to promote international policy goals and one designed to accommodate domestic policy concerns. Since the motivations of national judges may be very different from those of international judges, the two groups of judges should continue to belong to different legal universes.

I concede that at 'moments of truth', when national judges have to choose between the interests of their core constituency (i.e., the national community in which they live and operate) and the interests of an amorphous international community, we have every reason to believe that judges will prefer the former over the latter. Although far from certain, it is possible that for international judges the outcome of this conflict of interests may be different – hence, that they would prefer the interests of the international community over the immediate interests of the state whose nationally they carry.[28] Still, it is important to evaluate how frequent and significant are these 'moments of truth' in which national and international interests and values clash – i.e., point in diametrically opposed direction. To my mind, such conflicts are few in number, and their impact on the international judicial role of national judges is, at best, marginal.

First, there appears to be no inherent contradiction between the interests of the national and international constituencies: International law is after all created by states in order to accommodate their cumulative interests and common values. The fact that the creation of international norms is subject, as a rule, to the explicit or implicit consent of states, reduces the probabilities for chronic conflicts of interest between national and international constituencies.[29] Moreover, violating international law always entails certain costs – i.e., adversely affect the national interest.[30]

Hence, when national courts rely on international law and rule against their own government, one should not jump to the conclusion that the court has accorded preference to the international interest (reflected in the international norm) over the national interest (reflected in the government's position). More probably, this state of affairs is indicative of a difference of opinion between the court and some of the other branches of government as to where does the true

27 Cassese (1990) 213.

28 Some research work suggests that judges sitting on the ICJ tend to side with the litigation position of the state which appointed them and with other countries belonging to the same political bloc as their state of nationality. See *e.g.*, Smith (2005) 197; Posner and Figueiredo (2005) 599.

29 One could argue, in fact, that the majoritarian law-making process existing at the national level is equally amenable to produce inconsistencies between law and the national interest as perceived by large parts of the population.

30 See *e.g.*, Henkin (1995) 49.

national interest lie. For example, the court and government may disagree as to whether the benefits accruing to the national security interest from locking up terrorists without trial for an indefinite period of time outweigh the reputational harm that this inflicts on the nation, the ensuing erosion of domestic human rights protections that such practices facilitate, etc. It is not surprising that judges, who are trained to think of problems from a principled and long-term perspective, and are more sensitive to abuse of power concerns,[31] tend to assimilate the international interest to restrict certain potentially abusive governmental practices with the national interest.

Second, in cases where there is a clear divergence between the national and international interest, it is more likely than not that international law will not be incorporated into domestic law or overridden by the local legislature. Put differently, the very availability of international law to national judges may, in itself, signify the absence of strong political opposition to the judicial application of international law, and a good measure of approximation between the two sets of interests. Moreover, national judges that identify a strong conflict between national and international interests may look for a variety ways to dis-apply international law (i.e., 'avoidance techniques').[32] Their willingness to apply international law may therefore be in itself an 'act of faith', suggestive of a perceived compatibility between the relevant national and international interests.

If judges nowadays increasingly regard the national and international interests and value systems to be compatible with one another (a perception that may be influenced by the process of globalization that emphasizes the commonality of interests and values and increases the costs of non-compliance with common norms),[33] then the choice between these interests – Cassese's 'litmus test' of the international rule of law – becomes largely irrelevant. In short, the problem of mixed loyalties constitutes a serious problem only if national judges are actually confronted with a stark choice between incompatible set of interests and world views which the cannot avoid (*e.g.*, by way of dis-applying international law); it is a much less pronounced predicament when the two sets of interests and values are viewed as largely compatible with one another.

At a deeper level, however, Benvenisti and Cassese's emphasis on judicial motivations in understanding judicial functions appears to me to be exaggerated. To be sure, the question of judicial motivations is important from a

---

[31] See *e.g.*, McGinnis and Rappaport (2005) 286-287 ('Justices' preferences are often, albeit not always, based on more principled, long-term considerations than elected politicians-considerations that may over the long run lead to greater stability and prosperity for the republic'); Petersmann (2000) 256 (comparing the attributes of judicial and political settlement decisions). See also Petersmann's Foreword to this Volume.

[32] See Benvenisti (1993) 159.

[33] See *e.g.*, Joyner (2003) 448 ('some attempt can be made to equate national interests with international interests, and these arguments will likely be persuasive to a good many in foreign policymaking circles, particularly as the process of globalization and international institutional enmeshment makes the interdependency of nations in an array of issue areas increasingly manifest').

sociological perspective, and has some interesting predictive value (for example, it may enable us to make more educated guesses about future court decisions). Still, it should not control the definition of what constitutes a judicial function – i.e., what should attain a normative status as a judicial decision under the relevant legal system. Presumably, judges that decide legal cases (under national or international law) are motivated by a variety of factors (ideological leanings, professional conviction, personal empathy, peer pressure, self-interest, etc.) and qualifying only some of their judicial decisions as the proper exercise of a judicial function could destabilize our legal systems. It will also require legal theorists and practitioners to undertake an impossible mission– i.e., to enter the 'black box' of judicial mindsets.

Unless proven otherwise, we have no reason to believe that national judges who apply international law behave in a way that is qualitatively different from the way in which international judges apply international law (or from the way in which the same domestic judges apply national law). Moreover, the more national judges will grow accustomed to regard the application of international law norms as part of the 'rule of law', the more difficult it will be to distinguish between the motivations that control the application of national law and international law.

My proposal is therefore simple and straight forward: If we can ascertain that some national courts render decisions which apply international law *qua* law in a serious and credible manner, then we should regard these courts, when they are adopting such decisions, as fulfilling an international judicial function. The motivations we attribute to the judges in question may affect, over time, the persuasive weight of the legal opinions in question; it may also influence our normative assessment of the desirability of assigning national courts with an international judicial function. It should not, however, change the conclusion that rendering international law-based judicial decision constitutes an international judicial function.

But what about the distorting effect of national laws on the application of international law by international judges? Is this not an important distinguishing factor between national and international judicial bodies? Here, an important analogy can to be drawn between national courts and specialized international courts.[34] Like national courts that accommodate the needs of a domestic and international constituency, regional courts such as the European Court of Justice (ECJ) and the European Court of Human Rights (ECHR) also serve more than one constituency when they apply general international law. In exceptional cases, they may also encounter conflicts between norms deriving from different legal sources and should decide if and how to apply general international

34 In fact, one could conceptualize national courts as specialized courts: Like the ECJ or the ECHR they operate in the context of a specific legal regime (domestic law), which is almost self-contained, but invoke at times the provisions of general international law, which the regime tolerates. For some support, see International Law Commission (2006), 15.

law (especially, if it runs contrary to intra-regime norms).[35] Still, the existence of such normative tensions does not, and should not lead us to exclude such courts from the purview of the international judiciary or to deny the important international judicial function they fulfill.

In fact, most courts we regard as international courts – regional and specialized courts – constantly contend with the problem of the interplay between specific and general international law and the legal fragmentation that may ensue there from. The challenge of normative distortion faced by national courts is a real challenge, which threatens the prospects of applying international law in a uniform, or at least, similar manner; but this predicament is hardly unique to national courts. It is, in fact, a central challenge of the modern international judicial function. Again, a 'spectrum approach' can assist us in distinguishing acts of 'pure' international law-application from other international law-application acts 'tainted' with non-international norms, and in attributing different normative weights to the different judicial decisions.

3 Concluding Observations

If national judges apply international law in a serious and credible manner to settle cases before them, then they fulfill an international judicial function – engage in the same project of international law-application like international courts. Still, it is important to emphasize that there remain some crucial differences between national and international courts: national courts do not become international courts and remain, even when they apply international law, a relatively 'junior partner' in the international law-application project.

First, whereas 'real' international courts employ international norms (specific or general international law) all of the time, national judiciaries' involvement with international law norms and methods is bound to be much more limited in scope. This means that national judges serve as part of the international judiciary, at best, only on a part time or ad hoc basis – a fact affecting the way national judges perceive their international role. It also means that the national judges' level of international law professionalism, and their consequent ability to impact the development of international law, is expected to be considerably lower than that of international judges *par excellence*.

Second, not all national courts will fulfill an international judicial function, as their national legal system may restrict their ability to apply international law in the first place. Paradoxically perhaps, states that have fully integrated international law standards into their law books, and are applying those standards now as national laws, will not be an integral part of the international adjudicative process. In order to engage in a dialogue among international judicial

35 See *e.g.*, Joined Cases C-402/05 P and C-415/05 P *Kadi v. Council*, judgment of 3 Sept. 2008; *Al-Adsani v. UK*, judgment of 21 Nov. 2001 [2001] E.C.H.R. *35763/97* (dissenting opinion of Judges Rozakis and Caflisch).

institutions on the meaning of international law one has to use the 'common language'.[36] Arguably, the interest of national legal systems in participating in global governance through influencing the contents of international norms may create incentives for enabling national judges to invoke international law in their case law (and may create disincentives against the adoption of 'water-tight' incorporating legislation that prevent s national judges from invoking international norms).

Third, even when they apply international law, national judges fulfill dual functions under international law: they act simultaneously as international law adjudicators, but also as national organs. Under this latter capacity, if they misconstrue international law they may generate international responsibility for their own state. Here, Scelle's *dédoublement fonctionnel* theory operates in a reversed manner (an international actor fulfilling a role under national law), and other international courts who are reviewing international law decisions of national courts should view the latter as their judicial counter-parts, but also as the subjects of international judicial review. While such vertical/horizontal duality also takes place when international courts review the decisions of one another,[37] the introduction of state responsibility through the exercise of judicial functions might lead to more confusing, even disorienting results.

What is the upshot of the analysis offered above? In other words, what are the implications of regarding national courts as part of the international judiciary? To my mind, the most important consequences are methodological: if national courts, when they apply international law, are part of the international adjudicative machinery then their work should be treated as procedurally and normatively meaningful and attract deference from other actors involved in the same process – i.e. international courts, other national courts and other international law-applying agencies. More broadly, the work of national courts should be acknowledged by academics and decision makers as part of the building blocks of international law and should be studied with appropriate levels of care and attention.

At the same time, if national courts were to increasingly view themselves as taking part in the international legal system whenever they apply the system's norms, they should arguably be expected to adopt some methodological constraints vis-à-vis international law-application and employ to their work certain interpretive considerations. Like other law-applying bodies, national courts applying legal norms are arguably required to strive for a proper application of the law. In the case of international law, this implies the application of specific norms in light of overarching second-order principles, which are reflective of the systemic preferences of the international legal system: harmony, order, substantive justice, etc. In short, perceiving national courts as international adjudicators may impose on them a professional, if not a legal obligation, to apply specific legal norms in light of the overarching principles that govern

36 See Francioni (2001) 587.

37 See *e.g.*, Arbitral Award of 31 July 1989 (*Guinea-Bissau v. Senegal*), 1991 I.C.J. 53.

the application of international norms. It also requires national courts to monitor relevant international law decisions issued by other national and international courts in the same way that they monitor the application of domestic law by their domestic counterparts. In short, operating within a legal system (the international legal system) entails systemic consequences.

Ultimately, the weight that national and international courts will accord to the decisions of their judicial counterparts depends on the degree of confidence in their work. The more credible national courts the work will be regarded, the more deference they will attract from other national and international courts; in the same vein, the more appropriate and legitimate international proceedings appear in the eyes of domestic courts, the greater will be their willingness of the latter to defer to international courts decisions. The wish to influence the decisions of other institutions may serve as the ultimate 'quality check' on the records of national and international courts operating within the new loosely defined international legal system.

Bibliography

K. J. Alter, 'The Law And Politics Of International Delegation: Delegating To International Courts: Self-Binding Vs. Other-Binding Delegation' [2008] *Law & Contemp. Prob.* 37-76.

J. Alvarez, *International Organizations as Law-makers* (OUP, Oxford, 2006).

S. Beaulac, 'Westphalia, Dualism and Contextual Interpretation: How to Better Engage International Law in Domestic Courts' [2007] EUI Working Paper, MWP 2007/03, available at http://cadmus.eui.eu/dspace/bitstream/1814/6923/1/MWP_2007_03.pdf.

E. Benvenisti, 'Judicial Misgivings Regarding the Application of International Law: an Analysis of the Attitudes of National Courts' [1993] *Eur.J.I.L.* 159-183.

E. Benvenisti, 'Reclaiming Democracy: The Strategic Uses Of Foreign and International Law by National Courts' [2008] *Am.J.I.L.* 241-274.

A. Cassese, 'Remarks on Scelle's Theory of "Role Splitting" (*dédoublement fonctionnel*) in International Law' [1990] *E.J.I.L.* 210-231.

Z. Douglas, *The International Law of Investment Claims* (CUP, 2009).

F. Francioni, 'International Law as a Common Language for National Courts [2001] *Tex. Int'l L.J.* 587-598.

G. Gaja, *Dualism - A Review*, in A. Nollkaemper, J.E. Nijman (eds.), *New Perspectives on the Divide Between National and International Law* (OUP, 2007) 52-63.

H. Kelsen, *Principles of International Law* (Rinehart & Company, New York, 1952).

H. Kelsen, *General Theory of Law and State* (Harvard University Press, Cambridge, 1945).

L. Henkin, *International Law: Politics and Values* (M. Nijhoff, Dordrecht / Boston, 1995).

R. Jennings, A. Watts (eds.), *Oppenheim's International Law* (Longman, London, 1992).

D.H. Joyner, 'Bridging the Gap between International Law and Foreign Policymaking' [2003] *Denv. J. Int'l L. & Pol'y* 437-459.

H.T. Klami, *Monism and Dualism in Law: National Versus International or Supranational Law* in B. Brouwer et al., *Coherence and Conflict in Law* (Kluwer Law and Taxation, Deventer / Boston, 1992) 139-150.

J.O. McGinnis, M.B. Rappaport, 'The Judicial Filibuster, the Median Senator, and the Countermajoritarian Difficulty' [2005] *Sup. Ct. Rev.* 257-306.

E.U. Petersmann, 'Prevention and Settlement of International Trade Disputes Between the European Union and the United States' [2000] *Tul. J. Int'l & Comp. L.* 233-260.

E.A. Posner, M.F.P. de Figueiredo, 'Is the International Court of Justice Biased?' [2005] *J. Legal Stud.* 599-630.

C. Romano, 'The Proliferation of International Judicial Bodies: The Pieces of the Puzzle' [1999] *N.Y.U. J. Int'l L. & Pol.* 709-751.

G. Scelle, *Précis de droit des gens: principiés et systématique* (Sirey, Paris, 1934).

G. Scelle, *La phénomène juridique de déboulement fonctionnelle*, in W. Schätzel, H.J. Schlochauer (eds.), *Rechtsfragen der internationalen Organisation* (1956), 324-342.

C.H. Schreuer, *The ICSID Convention: a Commentary* (CUP, 2009).

A.M. Smith, '"Judicial Nationalism" in International Law: National Identity and Judicial Autonomy at the ICJo' [2005] *Tex. Int'l L.J.* 197-232.

Y. Shany, 'How Supreme is the Supreme Law of the Land? Comparative Analysis of the Influence of International Human Rights Treaties Upon the Interpretation of Constitutional Texts by Domestic Courts' [2006] *Brooklyn J. Int'l L.* 341-404.

Y. Shany, 'National Courts as International Actors: Jurisdictional Implication' [2009] *federalismi.it*, available at www.federalismi.it.

G. Slyz, 'International Law in National Courts' [1996] *N.Y.U. J. Int'l L. & Pol.* 65–113.

J.G. Starke, 'Monism and Dualism in the Theory of International Law' [1936] *Brit. Yearbook Int'l L.* 66-81.

C. Tomuschat, *International Courts and Tribunals*, in *Max Planck Encyclopaedia of Public International Law* (Rudiger Wolfrum ed., 2008)(on-line edition)

A. Truyol y Serra, 'Théorie du droit international public: cours général' [1981] *Recueil des cours* 9-444.

E. Voeten, 'The Politics of International Judicial Appointments' [2009] *Chi. J. Int'l L.* 387-406.

CHAPTER 2

Forum Shopping before International Tribunals

(Real) Concerns, (Im)Possible Solutions

Joost Pauwelyn, Luiz Eduardo Salles*

Introduction

This article pursues Professor Yasuhei Taniguchi's inclination for procedural questions and applies it to the central problem in one of Taniguchi's most celebrated rulings – *Mexico – Soft Drinks*, a case he chaired on appeal – namely: forum shopping before international tribunals. The *Soft Drinks* dispute between Mexico and the United States originated because of contested sugar quotas allocated to Mexico under the North American Free Trade Agreement (NAFTA).[1] When Mexico attempted to enforce those alleged quota rights under NAFTA, the procedure was stranded in the panel selection stage where, according to Mexico, the United States simply refused to appoint panelists in violation of NAFTA. To retaliate against this state of affairs, and instead of gaining larger quota shares on the U.S. sugar market, Mexico imposed a discriminatory tax on imports of U.S. soft drinks. The United States then decided to challenge the Mexican tax, not under NAFTA, but at the World Trade Organization (WTO). In the WTO proceedings, Mexico insisted that the larger U.S.-Mexico 'sugar war' be decided under NAFTA, where Mexico had already requested a panel. The United States, in contrast, insisted that it had the right to a WTO ruling on the consistency of the Mexican tax. Both the panel and the Appellate Body sided with the United States and found that the tax violated the General Agreement on Tariffs and Trade (GATT). Mexico's claim before NAFTA remains undecided.

The goal of this article is not to critically examine the *Soft Drinks* ruling.[2] Rather, the article examines the nature and potential concerns of the relatively new phenomenon of forum shopping among international tribunals. Further, it asks the question whether domestic law principles such as *res judicata, lis pendens* and *forum non conveniens* could be used to alleviate such concerns. The article finds that, to the extent these principles apply before international tribunals, they fail to address the problem. Instead, states should regulate forum shopping explicitly in their treaty regimes, and international tribunals should defer to such explicit treaty clauses. The article indentifies the distinction between questions of a tribunal's jurisdiction and questions of admissibility of claims as key to the implementation of jurisdictional coordination – be it through general principles of law or treaty rules on forum-selection. This distinction is generally applicable before international tribunals but has been overlooked in the WTO context. The article also argues that to deal with the rise of forum shopping in international adjudication, more thought should be given to the question of whether tribunals have or should have some margin of judicial discretion not to exercise jurisdiction in cases in which forum shop-

* Respectively, Graduate Institute of International and Development Studies (HEID), Geneva, and Barretto Ferreira, Kujawski, Brancher e Gonçalves (BKBG), São Paulo. Paper originally printed in 42 *Cornell Int'l L.J.* 77-118 2009. We thank the Editors of *CILJ* for giving us the permission to reprint the article.

1 Panel Report, *Mexico–Tax Measures on Soft Drinks and Other Beverages*, WT/DS308/R (Oct. 7, 2005) [hereinafter Panel Report, *Mexico–Soft Drinks*].

2 In the interest of full disclosure, one of the authors of this paper drafted the *amicus curiae* brief submitted by the Mexican sugar industry to the Appellate Body in *Soft Drinks*.

ping is at stake. To put these proposals in dynamic context, the article uses four variables, or scales, that will impact the assessment of both concerns and solutions for forum shopping among international tribunals, namely (1) a regime vs. system approach to international tribunals, (2) a partyfocus vs. legality-focus, (3) consensual vs. compulsory jurisdiction, and (4) specific vs. general jurisdiction.

The article proceeds in the following manner. Part I assesses the main concerns with forum shopping in domestic law, compares these concerns to international law, and identifies a number of variables that condition the emergence of this phenomenon internationally. Part II discusses where one could look for solutions to these concerns, briefly surveys domestic law solutions, and suggests that, to avoid the risk of inconsistent rulings, states should explicitly regulate forum selection when creating new tribunals or new treaties. In Part III, we explain the procedural technique through which general principles of law and treaty clauses on forum-choice can play a role in jurisdictional coordination between WTO adjudicative bodies and other international tribunals by introducing a distinction between jurisdiction and admissibility. Part IV discusses why 'general principles' such as *res judicata, lis pendens*, and *forum non conveniens* do not appropriately address the problem of forum shopping at the international level. This finding reinforces the argument that states should address the problem explicitly when negotiating their dispute settlement obligations. Part V argues that, given the move along the four scales identified earlier, some room for judicial discretion is needed to provide the necessary flexibility for jurisdictional coordination and advocates the emergence of the notion of *le juge naturel* or the 'natural forum' as a possible solution.

I Forum Shopping in International Law: Identifying the Real Concern

The problem of overlapping jurisdictions and forum shopping across domestic courts has assumed increasing relevance, but is in essence an old one.[3] In international law, however, this problem is relatively new. For a long time, and in most cases, there was simply no international court to turn to, let alone *two* tribunals whose jurisdiction overlapped.[4] With the recent boom in international tribunals, it is well-documented that international law now also faces the 'luxury problem' of multiple, overlapping courts.[5] This development is, first and foremost, a welcome one. Multiple courts are better than no courts at

3 See, *e.g.*, Bell (2003); Von Mehren (2002) 179.

4 In his 1986 collection, Gerald Fitzmaurice wrote: 'Just as in the domestic field it is rare for no court at all to have jurisdiction, and the issue is usually which of two or more possible forums is the correct one [...] conversely, is it a rarity in the international field for there to be any possibility of more than one forum.' Fitzmaurice (1986) 437. Writing as recently as 2006, Shabtai Rosenne had this to say: 'Questions of the conflicting jurisdictions, or conflicting competences, of international tribunals are rarely encountered.' Rosenne (2006) 518.

5 See Shany (2003). See also Alford (2000) 160; Pauwelyn (2001) 197; Romano (1999) 797.

all.[6] Clearly, to have several fora available is a boon for complainants. It may also guarantee that all elements of a multi-faceted dispute are actually resolved, such as a dispute over territorial delimitation at the International Court of Justice (ICJ) and a related trade restriction at the WTO.[7] A healthy level of competition among tribunals may also improve the quality of rulings and the expediency of proceedings. One tribunal keeping a critical eye over another can, finally, offer a welcome level of control over international tribunals and indirectly enhance their legitimacy.[8]

That said, there is no doubt that sequential or overlapping proceedings before international tribunals can and do raise concerns. Those concerns can be divided in two broad types: party-related concerns and society – or system-related – concerns. The tables below summarize these concerns and compare them as they arise under domestic law and international law.

Table 1: PARTY Concerns With Forum Shopping

Domestic law	*International law*
Cost of multiple proceedings	*Often less of a concern* Given that most parties in international disputes are states, litigation cost is less of an issue.[9] The cost of multiple proceedings can be a serious concern, however, for poor countries and for certain private parties (*e.g.* individuals or small or medium-sized corporations).
Finality of rulings; avoidance of oppressive litigation tactics	*Same concern* Note, however, that finality of rulings only applies to *sequential* proceedings, not to *parallel* proceedings where no ruling has been issued yet.
Inconsistent rulings may leave the dispute unresolved	*Of greater concern* The absence of a 'supreme court' in international law that can settle inconsistent rulings amplifies the party-concern of inconsistent rulings which, as a result, may leave the dispute unresolved or even create new disputes.
Avoidance of double jeopardy or double compensation	*Same concern*
Party equality	*Same concern* Because choice of forum may alter the substantive outcome of a dispute, there is an abstract interest that the 'right' forum be used.

6 See Higgins (2006) 791; Karagiannis (2003) 7; Rao (2004) 929, 958-959.

7 See, for example, the Minutes of the DSB Meeting of 7 April 2000, WT/DSB/M/78, referring to Nicaragua's taxes on imports from Honduras and Colombia (see WT/DS188 and WT/DS201), allegedly imposed as a response to an agreement on maritime delimitation between Honduras and Colombia which would have violated Nicaragua's rights. Honduras highlighted that 'the subject of maritime delimitation did not fall within the WTO mandate, and should be dealt with by the competent forum such as the International Court of Justice.' The ICJ eventually drew the maritime boundary between Nicaragua and Honduras. See *Territorial and Maritime Dispute in the Caribbean Sea (Nicar. v. Hond.)*, 2007 I.C.J. 1, 93 (Oct. 8).

8 See Cogan (2007) 411.

9 See Lowe (1999) 191, 201.

Table 2: SOCIETY or SYSTEM concerns with forum shopping:

Domestic law	*International law*
Waste of resources for society as a whole	*Often less of a concern* The amount and total cost of international law litigation remains relatively small.[10]
Stability and security of the 'system' (similar to finality argument as party-concern)	*Depends* on whether the different tribunals consider themselves as operating within the same 'system.' If not, inconsistent rulings amongst them cannot threaten the 'system' since there is none in the first place.[11] To give examples: do investor-state tribunals operating under different Bilateral Investment Treaties (BITs) belong to the same investment 'system';[12] do MERCOSUR tribunals and WTO panels operate in the same 'system';[13] do WTO panels disagreeing with an earlier WTO Appellate Body report operate in the same 'system' or do they decide distinct disputes?[14]
Inconsistent rulings can undermine the legitimacy and credibility of the 'system'	

10 See generally Romano (2005) 281, 303. The cost to society is arguably more of a concern where the cost of the tribunal is covered by all parties to it through the institution's general budget (not just the disputing parties), as in the WTO or the ICJ (but unlike in investor-state arbitration where the disputing parties alone pay all costs).

11 See Kingsbury (1999) 678, 692.

12 Compare *Lauder v. Czech Republic* (UNCITRAL Arb. 2001) *with CME Czech Republic B.V. (The Netherlands) v. Czech Republic* (UNCITRAL Arb. 2003) (reaching different conclusions on the merits of disputes dealing with the same measures).

13 See Appellate Body Report, *Brazil–Retreaded Tyres*, WT/DS332/AB/R (Dec. 3, 2007) (considering that exempting Uruguayan imports pursuant to a MERCOSUR ruling led to 'arbitrary or unjustifiable' discrimination in the application of Brazil's import ban under the chapeau of GATT Article XX); Panel Report, *Argentina–Poultry*, WT/DS241/R (Apr. 22, 2003) (accepting that the same measure be challenged sequentially before a MERCOSUR arbitral tribunal under the Protocol of Brasilia, and WTO dispute settlement) [hereinafter Panel Report *Argenina–Poultry*].

14 Compare Panel Report, *United States–Anti-Dumping Measures on Stainless Steel from Mexico*, WT/DS344/R (Dec. 20, 2007) (deciding it had 'no option but to respectfully disagree with the line of reasoning developed by the Appellate Body regarding the WTO-consistency of simple zeroing in periodic reviews') *with* Panel Report, *United States–Measures Relating to Zeroing and Sunset Reviews* WT/DS322/R (Sept. 20, 2006) *and* Appellate Body Report, *United States–Measures Relating to Zeroing and Sunset Reviews*, WT/DS322/AB/R (Jan. 9, 2007) (the Panel considering that 'simple zeroing' is permissible, the Appellate Body considering it is not). In a recent report, the Appellate Body reversed the Panel's findings in *United States–Anti-Dumping Measures on Stainless Steel from Mexico*, noting: 'We are deeply concerned about the Panel's decision to depart from well-established Appellate Body jurisprudence clarifying the interpretation of the same legal issues. The Panel's approach has serious implications for the proper functioning of the WTO dispute settlement system' and emphasized that 'the legal interpretation embodied in adopted panel and Appellate Body reports becomes part and parcel of the *acquis* of the WTO dispute settlement system.' Appellate Body Report, *United States–Final Anti-Dumping Measures on Stainless Steel from Mexico*, ¶ 162, WT/DS344/AB/R (Apr. 30, 2008). 'Ensuring 'security and predictability' in the dispute settlement system, as contemplated in Article 3.2 of the DSU, implies that, absent cogent reasons, an adjudicatory body will resolve the same legal question in the same way in a subsequent case.' *Id.* at ¶ 160.

Based on the summary analysis above, the biggest concern with forum shopping among international tribunals seems to be, therefore, the *concern of inconsistent rulings* because:

1) inconsistent rulings may leave the dispute unresolved (a party-related concern amplified in international law because of the absence of a hierarchy of courts); and
2) inconsistent rulings can threaten the stability and legitimacy of the broader 'system' within which the tribunals operate (of course, only if such a 'system' exists in the first place).

Note, however, that even if no 'system' exists, and the concern of system stability or legitimacy does not arise, the party-concern of inconsistent rulings and of not seeing the dispute settled, remains.[15] The party-concern of inconsistent rulings (point 1) may, therefore, dominate the system-concern of inconsistent rulings (point 2).[16]

Two further elements specific to international law may limit the problem of sequential or overlapping proceedings before international tribunals. These elements often lead international tribunals to decide cases that other fora have already decided, or might decide, in the future.

First, international tribunals traditionally operate under the principle of *party consent*. In domestic law, by contrast, courts operate on constitutional or statutory authority. As a result, if parties give an international tribunal explicit jurisdiction to decide a dispute, the tribunal often feels hard-pressed to fulfill its mandate and to decide the case, even where a second tribunal is also competent, or a parallel or sequential proceeding is, or can be, initiated. The tribunal may then be inclined to decide the case because 'that is what the parties asked it to do'.[17]

Second, there is no top-down division of labor among international tribunals. The 'international judiciary' is such that the authority of each body is limited by its own governing instruments, and there is no statute defining the authority of tribunals in relation to each other. Further, in practice, the jurisdiction of international tribunals is specific and depends not on geographical factors (as is often the case in domestic law[18]), but rather on the treaty it is enforcing (*e.g.*, WTO panels enforce WTO agreements; NAFTA panels enforce NAFTA). The

---

15 As Giles Cuniberti puts it: '[T]he existence of conflicting decisions in different legal orders can cause harm [...] [T]he situation of the parties will be intolerable, with each of them in danger of being deprived in one place of what it has been awarded in another.' Cuniberti (2006) 381, 421.

16 *Id.* at 395-6 (arguing that substantive inconsistencies and the absence of settlement can be more fundamental a problem than the concern with intra-systemic coherence and therefore submitting that mechanisms should be available to avoid inconsistent decisions even across different systems).

17 See, for instance, the painstaking efforts by the Arbitral Tribunal in *Iron Rhine Railway (Belgium v. The Netherlands)*, Award of 24 May 2005, to decide the case on the basis of international law, including European law, while respecting the exclusive jurisdiction of the European Court of Justice. *Contra* Lavranos (2006) 223.

18 See, *e.g.*, Michaels (2004) 105.

treaty-based jurisdiction of international tribunals often means that even where there is overlapping jurisdiction, each tribunal decides a different aspect of the dispute (say, the ICJ decides issues of territorial delimitation and the WTO decides issues of trade).[19] Even if different tribunals decide the same issue, they often do so from a distinct legal angle (for example, national treatment under the GATT, versus national treatment under NAFTA Chapter 11). In many cases, therefore, overlapping jurisdictions among international tribunals are less of a concern as compared to overlapping jurisdictions of domestic courts.

In sum, whether or not forum shopping before international tribunals is of genuine concern depends on at least three variables. First, the more a tribunal considers itself as operating within a broader 'system' of inter-connected tribunals (rather than a self-contained 'regime' limited to, say, the WTO) the more problematic forum shopping becomes (the regime v. system variable referred to earlier). In particular, the system-based concerns of inconsistent rulings (between, for example, a WTO panel and a MERCOSUR tribunal) and the threat to stability and legitimacy that such inconsistent rulings may bring about could necessitate better coordination. Second, the more international tribunals shift from *ad hoc* consent-based jurisdiction (as in a *compromis* before the ICJ) to compulsory jurisdiction (as in the WTO or BITs), the more forum shopping will raise concerns and the more tribunals will be forced to look beyond the increasingly weak argument that they must decide the case because 'this is what the parties asked us to do.' This is illustrated in the consensual vs. compulsory jurisdiction variable that Cesare Roman recently highlighted,[20] which is a variable that also dovetails with the move from party-focused to legality-focused international dispute settlement. Third, the more that international courts move away from specific jurisdiction towards broader bases of jurisdiction,[21] the more forum shopping will become a genuine problem (similar to overlaps between domestic courts).

Put differently, whereas forum shopping before international tribunals traditionally raised less concerns than its domestic counterpart (mainly because there are few international courts to begin with; costs in inter-state disputes are not a big issue; the jurisdiction of international tribunals is consent-based; no 'system' of international tribunals exists; and the division between tribunals is precarious), over time the problem has grown. It is destined to continue to rise in prominence given the shift in the four variables outlined earlier, namely the moves: (1) from a regime to a system approach; (2) from a party-focus to a legal-

[19] See *infra* note 7 and related text.

[20] Romano (2007) 791.

[21] A good example of this shift, or difference, is BITs conferring jurisdiction to arbitrate legal claims under the BIT only, versus BITs conferring jurisdiction more generally in regard to disputes 'relating to investments made' under the BIT, without limitation as to the legal cause of action of such disputes (be it the BIT or an investment contract). Compare *SGS Société Générale de Surveillance S.A. v. Republic of the Philippines*, Decision on Objections to Jurisdiction, ICSID Case No. ARB/02/06 131-35 (2004) with *SGS v. Pakistan*, Decision on Objections to Jurisdiction, ICSID Case No. ARB/01/13 161 (2003).

ity-focus; (3) from strictly consensual to compulsory jurisdiction; (4) and from specific to general jurisdiction.

II Where to Look for Solutions

A. Domestic Law Solutions

In domestic law, one can discern three common scenarios of forum shopping, and reactions thereto.

First, there are sequential proceedings in which one court is seized of a dispute that another court already decided earlier. In that scenario, both common and civil law systems may apply the principle of *res judicata* (*l'autorité de la chose jugée*). Second, there are parallel proceedings in which one court is asked to decide a dispute while another court is also looking at it. In that scenario, civil law systems may apply the principle of *lis pendens* or rules on 'related actions.'[22] Common law systems, in contrast, may apply the principle of *forum non conveniens* or other abstention doctrines. There, *lis pendens* may sometimes play a role as one of several factors to be looked at, but is not normally an independent principle to decide jurisdictional overlaps. Third, there are alternative proceedings in which one court is asked to decide a dispute over which another court also has jurisdiction, but this second court has not yet been or will never be seized. In that scenario, common law systems may also apply the *forum non conveniens* doctrine. Most civil law systems, in contrast, do not have a *forum non conveniens* doctrine;[23] and where they find jurisdiction, the civil law courts would not normally have the discretion to decline from exercising it – notwithstanding the presence of an alternative forum.

Another way to describe domestic law reactions to forum shopping is to distinguish broadly between three types of doctrines the seized court may eventually apply. (There are no watertight dividing lines between the doctrines, yet the distinction is, in our view, useful.)

Firstly, there are preclusion doctrines: Preclusion doctrines bar either the jurisdiction of a court or else the plaintiff's right to have her substantive claims examined.[24] Under preclusion doctrines (at least the way we define them), the second court does not have any discretion and *must* decide that it does not have jurisdiction or that the action (or claim) is precluded. The immediate consequence is similar in both cases: the dismissal of the case before a judgment on the merits. For instance, if another court already decided the dispute, *res judicata* can preclude the examination of the substantive claims before a second court. *Lis pendens* operates similarly if the dispute is pending elsewhere.

Secondly, there are abstention doctrines: These are doctrines or principles that do not preclude or take away the jurisdiction of the seized court. Instead,

---

[22] See *infra* notes 140-143.

[23] See *infra* note 113 and accompanying text.

[24] See *infra* Section III, on the distinction between jurisdiction and admissibility.

they lead that court, following a discretionary judicial evaluation, not to *exercise* its powers to pronounce on claims based on some factor extrinsic to the merits of the claims (for instance, the jurisdiction of another court). In other words, both courts can have jurisdiction over the specific case, but one of them may decide not to rule on one or more aspects of the claim because of the jurisdiction (pending or potential) of the other. Some measure of discretion *not to exercise established substantive or field-jurisdiction* (as we define this notion below) is inherent in abstention doctrines. Such judicial discretion is generally alien to civil law systems.[25] In many common law systems, however, that is exactly what happens under the *forum non conveniens* doctrine, which is a discretionary abstention doctrine. In the United States, more specific types of abstention doctrines also cover certain interactions between state and federal courts.[26]

Finally, there are the doctrines of consolidation or joinder: Rather than simply declining jurisdiction or not exercising it, domestic courts can also consolidate several related actions and rule on them in one proceeding.[27] A similar concept is joinder, which allows or mandates the coupling of several parties, claims or remedies in a single action.[28] Both consolidation and joinder

---

[25] Note, however, that rules on 'related actions,' discussed below, grant judicial discretion to exercise or not to exercise jurisdiction in civil law systems. Moreover, note that civil law systems may grant a wide margin of discretion within the appreciation of the law by courts through open-textured jurisdictional rules. Thus, Section 11 of Article 429c of the Code of Procedure of the Netherlands provides that 'a court has no jurisdiction if the petition is insufficiently connected with the legal sphere of The Netherlands.' See Freudenthal – Van Der Velden (1995) 67. In Greece, a discretionary power within the application of the law exists by virtue of the prohibition on abuse of rights and the obligation to act in good faith. See Kargados – Moustaira (1995) 235, 242. See also Hironaka (2004) 1317; Hayes (1992) 42, 56 (envisaging that the objectives of *forum non conveniens* could also be achieved in Japan through the prohibition on abuse of rights or of dual suits).

[26] See *Colorado River Water Conservation District et al. v. United States*, 424 U.S. 800, 813 (1976); see also Staver (1998) 1102.

[27] See North American Free Trade Agreement Art. 1126 [hereinafter NAFTA] (allowing the consolidation of proceedings with 'a question of law or fact in common,' 'in the interests of fair and efficient resolution of the claims'); see generally Alvarez (2000) 414. So far, two tribunals have decided consolidation claims. The *Corn Products* tribunal, on the one hand, focused on the unfairness to investors of a consolidation they did not agree to, and which would negatively affect their procedural interests. The *Softwood* tribunal, on the other hand, focused on efficiency to the resolution of the claims in terms of procedural economy. Compare *Corn Products International, Inc. v. Mexico*, ICSID Case No. ABR(AF)/04/1 and *Acher Daniel Midlands Company and Tate & Lyle Ingredients Americas, Inc. v. Mexico*, ICSID Case No. ARB(AF)/04/5, Order of the Consolidation Tribunal (May 20, 2005) with *Canfor Co. v. United States and Tembec et al. v. United States*, and *Terminal Forest Products, Ltd. v. United States*, Order of the Consolidation Tribunal (Sept. 7, 2005).

[28] See the WTO intra-systemic rules on multiple complaints in Article 9 of the DSU, which states that a single panel should examine complaints related to the 'same matter' whenever feasible (Article 9.1), and, when more than one panel is established, the same persons shall serve as panelists and the timetables should be harmonized.

presume that the court deciding the case has jurisdiction to do so in respect to all aspects and parties to the dispute. The consolidation or joinder of different but related actions before a common adjudicator, and possibly in one single proceeding, is a major tool for fostering coherence and saving judicial resources both in common law and in civil law systems.[29] In both systems, consolidation and joinder normally occur based on explicit statutory provisions, not based on general principles or unwritten doctrines.[30]

B. Alternatives for the International Judge

When a situation of forum shopping presents itself, several options – which are not necessarily mutually exclusive – are open to the international judge. First, the international judge could limit herself to the rules explicitly agreed on by the parties within the forum she is operating (for example, a WTO panel looking only at Dispute Settlement Understanding (DSU) rules).[31] In many cases, this will mean that the international judge will simply proceed and decide the case. In *Soft Drinks* the United States advocated this position, arguing that '[I]f a panel were to decline to exercise jurisdiction over a particular dispute, it would diminish the rights of the complaining Member under the DSU and other covered agreements [contrary to Articles 3.2 and 19.2 of the DSU].'[32] Similarly, China, a third party in *Soft Drinks*, submitted that:

> [A] WTO panel does not have an implied power to refrain from performing its 'statutory function' [...] [I]f a panel that is 'empowered and obligated' to assist the DSB in the settlement of a dispute declines to exercise jurisdiction, such a decision would create legal uncertainty and be contrary to the aim of providing security and predictability to the multilateral trading system as well as the prompt settlement of disputes as provided for in Article 3.3 of the DSU.[33]

Second, a slightly more adventurous judge could wander outside the four walls of the *lex fori* and ask whether there are general principles of law or domestic law analogies, on which she could rely to resolve the problem. Mexico advocated this position in *Soft Drinks*, relying on, among other things, an old Permanent Court

[29] See 'related actions' in civil law systems discussed *infra* notes 137-139 and accompanying text.137

[30] See, *e.g.*, Fed. R. Civ. P. 42; see also Council Regulation 44/2001, Art. 29, 2000 O.J. (L 12/8).

[31] Some authors argue this to be the only option for a WTO adjudicator. See, *e.g.*, Kwak – Marceau, *Overlaps and Conflicts of Jurisdiction between the World Trade Organization and Regional Trade Agreements*, *in* Regional Trade Agreements and the WTO Legal System (2006) 465, 483 ('If an RTA contains an exclusive forum clause, nothing appears to prevent a WTO panel from proceeding to examine a claim of WTO violation even if, in doing so, one of the parties to the WTO dispute would be in violation of its RTA obligation'); see also *id.* at 481 ('It is difficult to see how WTO panels could decline jurisdiction for reasons of *res judicata, lis pendens,* or *forum non conveniens.*').

[32] Appellate Body Report, *Mexico–Tax Measures on Soft Drinks and Other Beverages*, 23, WT/DS308/AB/R (Mar. 6, 2006). [hereinafter Appellate Body Report, *Mexico–Soft Drinks*].

[33] *Id.* at p. 34.

of International Justice (PCIJ) ruling expressing a variant of the so-called clean hands theory.[34] The panel showed some willingness to rely on general principles (in particular, *res judicata*), but quickly found that these principles would not undermine its obligation to decide the dispute.[35] Defendants in other WTO disputes in which forum shopping was an issue have similarly relied on general principles such as good faith, abuse of process, and estoppel in an attempt to convince the WTO not to rule on the dispute. For instance, in *Argentina–Poultry*, Argentina (unsuccessfully) argued that Brazil's double-challenge of the same measures, first before MERCOSUR and subsequently before the WTO, violated the principle of good faith and warranted application of the principle of estoppel.[36]

Third, the judge could insist upon relying only on party-agreed solutions (as in option 1), but be willing to look for those solutions outside of the forum within which she is operating (as in option 2). More specifically, the judge could then examine whether the parties in, for example, a WTO dispute, have agreed on forum selection or conflict clauses in the outside treaty which created the forum shopping problem in the first place (for example, in a WTO dispute, a fork-in-the-road clause in NAFTA or another free trade agreement ('FTA')).[37] This article argues that deferring to explicit treaty clauses on forum-election is the best solution for the problem of forum shopping in the current context. In the next section, we propose a conceptual framework for applying this solution before the WTO by distinguishing between the jurisdiction of tribunals and the admissibility of claims made before them.

Returning to *Soft Drinks*, it is worth noting that Mexico explicitly refused to rely on NAFTA's fork-in-the road provision[38] before the WTO panel, even though Mexico could have made a plausible argument, given its earlier submission of the broader sugar dispute to NAFTA, that this fork-in-the-road clause precluded the United States from bringing its claims before the WTO. In its *amicus curiae* brief submitted on appeal by the Mexican sugar industry did, however, rely

---

34 '[O]ne party cannot avail himself of the fact that the other has not fulfilled some obligation, or has not had recourse to some means of redress, if the former party has, by some illegal act, prevented the latter from fulfilling the obligation in question, or from having recourse to the tribunal which would have been open to him.' *Factory at Chorzów*, 1927 P.C.I.J. (ser A) No. 9, at 31 (July 26). See also Gabcikovo-Nagymaros Project (*Hungary v. Slovakia*), Judgment, 1997 I.C.J. Reports 7, at ¶ 133.

35 Panel Report, *Mexico–Soft Drinks, supra* note 1, at ¶ 7.14 (stating that neither the subject matter, nor the respective positions of the parties, would be equivalent in the disputes under the NAFTA and the WTO).

36 Panel Report, *Argentina–Poultry, supra* note 13, at ¶¶ 7.18-7.20.

37 For a fuller explanation of why also WTO panels can apply such treaty clauses outside WTO covered agreements, see (a) Pauwelyn (2003) 997.

38 NAFTA Article 2005.6 reads, in relevant part: 'Once dispute settlement procedures have been initiated under Article 2007 or dispute settlement proceedings have been initiated under the GATT, the forum selected shall be used to the exclusion of the other.' NAFTA, Dec. 17, 1992, *U.S.-Can.-Mex.*, 32 I.L.M. 289 (chs. 1-9); 32 I.L.M. 605 (chs. 10-22).

heavily on this NAFTA clause.[39] To its credit, the Appellate Body also considered the clause and left the possibility open that similar clauses could in the future constitute a 'legal impediment' for the WTO to rule on the merits of a case in the future.[40]

---

[39] Brief for Camara Nacional de las Industrias Azucarera y Alcoholera – Mexico as Amici Curiae at ¶ 19, Appellate Body Report, *Mexico–Tax Measures on Soft Drinks and Other* Beverages, WT/DS308/AB/R (Jan. 12, 2006), on file with the authors:

10 NAFTA Article 2005.1 states that 'disputes regarding any matter arising under both [NAFTA] and [GATT/WTO], may be settled in either forum at the discretion of the complaining party.' The US does not contest that Mexico's tax at issue here is just one part of a broader US-Mexico sweetener dispute. Nor does the US contest that this sweetener 'dispute' regards a 'matter' arising under both NAFTA and the GATT/WTO.

11 Now, in 2000, Mexico, exercising the discretion offered to NAFTA parties in Article 2005.1, decided to bring this 'dispute' to NAFTA. As of that point in time, though, Article 2005.6 reserves *exclusive* jurisdiction to NAFTA and *precludes* any WTO jurisdiction over the dispute. Article 2005.6 provides, indeed, that

[o]nce dispute settlement procedures have been initiated under [NAFTA] Article 2007 [...][...] the forum selected shall be used to the exclusion of the other [*in casu* the WTO] [...]

[...]

12 Unlike the principle of *res judicata* (implicitly referred to by the Panel in paragraph 7.13), Article 2005 of NAFTA is *not* conditioned on the fact that the same specific 'measure' is before both NAFTA and the WTO. Rather, Article 2005 relates to 'disputes' regarding a 'matter'. As the US concedes, the 'matter' in the US-Mexico sweetener 'dispute' is not limited to the US quota, nor to the Mexican tax. It covers both. Hence, the fact that the specific 'measure' before the NAFTA (a US quota) is not the same as the specific 'measure' before the WTO (a Mexican tax), is irrelevant under Article 2005 *for as long as these specific measures are part of one and the same 'dispute' or 'matter'.*

13 Similarly, Article 2005 is *not* conditioned on the fact that 'the respective positions of the parties' are 'identical' in both NAFTA and the WTO (Panel report, paragraph 7.15). Rather, once a dispute is before either forum (here, NAFTA), 'the forum selected shall be used to the exclusion of the other'. Article 2005.6 does not limit this restriction to the original complainant (in this case, Mexico). In other words, once Mexico brought the sweetener dispute to NAFTA, both Mexico *and* the United States were precluded from bringing it also to the WTO. Yet, this is what the US is trying to do here.

14 Finally, there can be no doubt that in this case 'dispute settlement procedures have been initiated under Article 2007' of NAFTA, *even if no NAFTA Panel has actually been established.* What counts is the initiation of procedures under NAFTA Article 2007, that is, the second step of NAFTA Chapter 20 procedures, namely consideration by the Free Trade Commission. Panel proceedings are the third step and covered by Article 2008. The US itself has explicitly acknowledged that Mexico thus 'initiated' NAFTA proceedings and that such proceedings remain pending to this day (and, therefore, continue to preclude WTO proceedings on the same dispute) [...].

[40] Appellate Body Report, *Mexico–Soft Drinks, supra* note 32, at ¶ 54. Mindful of the precise scope of Mexico's appeal, *we express no view as to whether there may be other circumstances in which legal impediments could exist that would preclude a panel from ruling on the merits of the claims that are before it.* In the present case, Mexico argues that the United States' claims under Article III of the GATT 1994 are inextricably linked to a broader dispute, and that only a NAFTA panel could resolve the dispute as a

A choice between the three options set out above – forum rules only, general principles, and treaty clauses outside the forum – largely depends on two variables.[41]

First, to what extent does the tribunal regard itself as a self-contained 'regime' operating in isolation, versus a dispute settlement mechanism operating as a part of a broader 'system' of international law and tribunals (the regime v. system variable)?[42] Second, and related to the first, does the tribunal construe its task as simply resolving a dispute between two parties, or is it rather also responsible for expanding the legality or rule of law within the forum it operates (the party-focus vs. legality-focus variable)?[43]

Where a tribunal shifts from a 'regime' to a 'system' approach, it will be more open to rules and solutions outside the *lex fori*, be it general principles or domestic law analogies (option 2) or clauses in other treaties (option 3). Where a tribunal shifts from a party-focus to a legality or rule of law focus, it is likely to consider not only rules or solutions explicitly agreed to by the disputing parties themselves (as in options 1 and 3), but also general principles or domestic law analogies (as in option 2) which often require a degree of gap-filling or law-making by the tribunal itself.

In our view, the best way to develop rules to address the novel problem of overlaps between international tribunals is through the inclusion of explicit

whole. Nevertheless, Mexico does not take issue with the Panel's finding that 'neither the subject matter nor the respective positions of the parties are identical in the dispute under the NAFTA [...] and the dispute before us.' Mexico also stated that it could not identify a legal basis that would allow it to raise, in a WTO dispute settlement proceeding, the market access claims it is pursuing under the NAFTA. It is furthermore undisputed that no NAFTA panel as yet has decided the 'broader dispute' to which Mexico has alluded. Finally, we note that Mexico has expressly stated that the so-called 'exclusion clause' of Article 2005.6 of the NAFTA had not been 'exercised'. *We do not express any view on whether a legal impediment to the exercise of a panel's jurisdiction would exist in the event that features such as those mentioned above were present. In any event, we* see *no legal impediments applicable in this case*' (emphasis added).

41 Recall that the three stylized options laid out are not mutually exclusive. A tribunal could, for example, be willing to look at all three sets of rules (forum rules, general principles and treaty clauses outside the forum) to eventually apply the forum or outside treaty rule based on the principle of *lex specialis*.

42 Compare Dispute Concerning Access to Information under Article 9 of the OSPAR Convention (*Ireland v. United Kingdom*), 42 I.L.M. 1118, at ¶ 143 (Perm. Ct. Arb. 2003) ('the OSPAR Convention contains a particular and self-contained dispute resolution mechanism in Article 32, in accordance with which this Tribunal acts') *with* The MOX Plant Case (*Ir. v. U.K.*), Order No. 3, 42 I.L.M. 1187 (Perm. Ct. Arb. 2003) (considering the possibility of the existence of exclusive jurisdiction of the European Court of Justice (ECJ) and opting for a stay in the proceedings until further clarification of the issue); see generally, Shany (2007) (contrasting the two underlying judicial policies under the labels of 'integrationism' and 'disintegrationism').

43 Georges Abi-Saab recently underlined the importance of this variable: '*la question fondamentale de la politique judiciaire à suivre se pose, ici comme ailleurs: est-ce que le but est simplement de régler un différend particulier dont on est saisi, ou doit-on se situer dans un contexte plus large, celui de contrôler et même d'affermir la légalité ?*' Abi-Saab (2007) 97.

conflict and overlap clauses in the relevant treaties, that is, rules to which the parties themselves have explicitly agreed (option 1 and option 3). The alternative of relying on general principles and domestic law analogies (option 2) is at first blush convincing. Because domestic legal systems had to deal with similar problems, why not copy their rules, instead of reinventing the wheel through specific treaty clauses that are often difficult and time-consuming to negotiate? Whereas domestic law analogies are appropriate in some respects (*e.g. res judicata*), this article argues that in other respects (such as *lis pendens* and *forum non conveniens*), they are not necessarily appropriate. More importantly, even where the incorporation of domestic law principles into international law makes sense (as with *res judicata*), in most cases, these principles do not address the problem as most of the time the conditions for these principles to be triggered (especially the requirement that the other forum addresses the 'same cause of action') will usually not be met anyway.

Therefore, until international law develops its own general principles to deal with forum shopping (a first attempt to do so is made at the end of this article), reference to domestic law analogies in the current state of international law operates at best as a fig leaf for the tribunal in question to exercise jurisdiction anyway. Instead, in the current context, both defendants (who are concerned with forum shopping) and tribunals (who see themselves as part of a broader, though heavily decentralized, system of international tribunals), are better off applying forum clauses set out in other treaties (*e.g.* WTO panels applying a NAFTA fork-in-the-road clause). Complainants also stand to gain from this solution as they will at least have explicitly agreed to these clauses, a safeguard that is not always met in cases in which tribunals start to 'discover' general principles of law based on domestic law analogies. One of the beauties of international law is that, given its decentralized nature, solutions to new problems can be creatively developed in new treaties (as long as the state-parties agree to them) or case-by-case in specific disputes. If they work, those solutions can then be generalized to other fields and disputes. This piecemeal process, in which treaties such as bilateral FTAs operate as test laboratories, can be particularly receptive to new ideas.

III Jurisdiction vs. Admissibility: Implementing Jurisdictional Coordination Between Autonomous International Tribunals

Before we turn to the applicability in international adjudication of the domestic law principles identified above, it is essential to identify the procedural technique to be used in applying these principles. We suggest employing preliminary objections to the *admissibility* of the request. This technique is based on the distinction between questions of *jurisdiction* and questions of *admissibility* (a distinction that has been well-developed before other international tribunals but has so far been overlooked in the WTO context).

In international law, including WTO law, it is well-accepted that certain questions of a preliminary character which are independent from the merits may nonetheless stop the proceedings before findings on the merits are made.[44] This eventuality need not be expressly stated in the governing instruments of the judicial body concerned.[45] Questions of jurisdiction and admissibility are both part of the universe of preliminary questions that, while leaving the merits of the case untouched, have the potential to prevent or postpone a final judgment on the merits.

The difference between jurisdiction and admissibility is a feature of the general international law of adjudication. Besides the ICJ, the European Court of

---

44 In international law, this notion is generally uncontested. See, *e.g.*, Abi-Saab (1967); Bos (1957); Witenberg (1932) 5. At the WTO, preliminary objections have the potential to stop proceedings. In *Mexico–Anti-Dumping Investigation of High Fructose Corn Syrup*, WT/DS132/AB/RW (Oct. 22, 2001), Mexico asked the Appellate Body to reverse the substantive findings of the Panel based on procedural deficiencies identified in the panel process that were allegedly ignored by the Panel. The Appellate Body recognized the potential of Mexico's claim, but denied it on substance due to Mexico's failure to raise those deficiencies as 'objections'. Note also that preliminary defences that fall outside the terms of reference have the effect, if accepted, of precluding findings of merit in the same panel proceedings concerning such claims. See, *e.g.*, Panel Report, *European Communities–Customs Classification of Frozen Boneless Chicken Cuts*, WT/DS269/R (Sept. 12, 2005).

45 The Panel in *Soft Drinks* stated, in relation to Mexico's request for a preliminary ruling on the question of the propriety of exercising jurisdiction:

Nothing in the DSU, or in the Panel's working procedures, required the Panel to address Mexico's request in a preliminary ruling. Instead, the Panel could have waited to rule on the request until its final report. It was the Panel's opinion, however, that both parties and the panel proceeding were better served by an early ruling on the request. Had it been appropriate for the Panel to decline to exercise its jurisdiction, *an early decision to this effect would have saved time and resources.* On the other hand, if the Panel – as in the event it did – rejected Mexico's request, an early decision would allow the parties to concentrate on the other aspects of the dispute.

Panel Report, *Mexico–Soft Drinks, supra* note 1, at ¶ 7.2 (emphasis added). The PCIJ Statute and original Rules of Court also did not foresee preliminary objections at all. Notwithstanding the lack of explicit regulation, the Court dealt with those objections ever since the first cases. For example, in Mavrommatis Palestine Concessions, the Court noted:

Neither the Statute nor the Rules of Court contain any rule regarding the procedure to be followed in the event of an objection being taken *in limine litis* to the Court's jurisdiction. The Court therefore is at liberty to adopt the principle which it considers best calculated to ensure the administration of justice, most suited to procedure before an international tribunal and most in conformity with the fundamental principles of international law.

Mavrommatis Palestine Concessions (*Greece v. England*), 1924 P.C.I.J. (ser. A) No. 2, at 16 (Aug. 30); see also *Certain German Interests in Polish Upper Silesia*, 1925 P.C.I.J. (ser. A) No. 6, at 19 (Aug. 25).

Human Rights (ECHR)[46] and arbitral tribunals have also made this distinction. For example, in *SGS v. Philippines*,[47] the tribunal found that it did have *jurisdiction* to consider a contractual claim under the so-called 'umbrella clause' of the bilateral investment treaty at issue. The tribunal, however, declined to exercise this jurisdiction, concluding that the claim was not *admissible* because of a forum clause in the contract stating that contractual claims must be brought to domestic courts.[48] Importantly, neither the ICJ Statute,[49] nor the Convention on the Settlement of Investment Disputes Between States and Nationals of Other State (ICSID Convention) (under which *SGS v. Philippines* was decided) explicitly includes the distinction between jurisdiction and admissibility. The DSU does not contain this distinction either, but that alone is not a reason to disregard the distinction out of hand. In fact, the dichotomy between jurisdiction and admissibility is embedded in the separation between the authority of the tribunal (determined by its own constitutive instruments; jurisdiction) and the more general procedural relationship between the parties (determined by the set of legal norms binding on them; admissibility). The development of this distinction before the ICJ, and its spill-over to the ECHR and arbitral tribunals, indicates that there is a more general role for it in international dispute settlement. Analogously, in our view, the distinction between jurisdiction and admissibility should also be applied in WTO dispute settlement.

The distinction between matters of jurisdiction and admissibility stems from the distinction between the *scope* of *a tribunal*'s decisional authority and the conditions governing the exercise of the *specific action or process* before the tribunal. As is well-known, one's right of action does not depend on the fact that a tribunal would uphold the claims made. In other words, action and process are independent from the ultimate merits of the claim.[50] Moreover, action and

[46] Article 35 of the European Convention of Human Rights and Fundamental Freedoms, entitled 'Admissibility criteria', lists, *inter alia*, the exhaustion of domestic remedies, anonymity of application, previous related actions and applications that are manifestly ill-founded or an abuse of the right of application. European Convention for the Protection of Human Rights and Fundamental Freedoms Art. 35, Nov. 4, 1950, 213 U.N.T.S. 222, as amended by Protocol No. 11, E.T.S. No. 155, 33 I.L.M. 960 (1944) [hereinafter ECHR Art. 35].

[47] *SGS Société Générale de Surveillance S.A. v. Republic of the Phillipines*, ICSID Case No. ARB/02/6, Decision of the Tribunal on Objections to Jurisdiction, ¶¶ 113-19 (2004).

[48] In other words, the tribunal regarded forum clauses (analogous to NAFTA Article 2005 at issue in *Soft Drinks*) not as an obstacle or legal impediment to jurisdiction, but as an obstacle or legal impediment to admissibility.

[49] The Court recognized objections to admissibility as such in the exercise of its *compétence de la compétence*, when it has felt it necessary. See, *e.g.*, Panevezys-Saldutiskis Railway (*Est. v. Lith.*), 1939 P.C.I.J. (ser A/B) No. 76, at 16 (Feb. 28). It is on the basis of this practice that the current ICJ Rules of Court, drawn by the judges themselves, do make the distinction. See I.C.J. Rules of Court, Art. 79.1 (1978, amended 2005).

[50] See also Morelli (1937) 253, 363: '*L'action doit être conçue, dans l'ordre international, comme un pouvoir juridique non seulement autonome, mais même abstrait. Elle ne se confond pas avec l'éventuel droit subjectif en contestation et elle n'est pas subordonné à l'existence du droit subjectif.*'

process have their own conditions independent not only from the question of merit of the substantial claims, but also from the question of jurisdiction of the tribunal. Consequently, notwithstanding a tribunal's jurisdiction to decide a case, and despite the possible merit of the claims made, there may be circumstances that represent 'legal impediments' – to use the words of the Appellate Body in *Soft Drinks* – to proceed to a ruling on the merits. Carefully monitoring these circumstances and legal impediments is all the more important if jurisdiction is compulsory, as it is in the case of WTO adjudicative bodies. Indeed, the problem of a defective action is minimized in cases in which parties jointly and explicitly agreed to resort to adjudication in a specific dispute. By contrast, in a situation of compulsory jurisdiction, the floodgates for complaints are open and the impartial adjudicator is the only gatekeeper ultimately responsible for guaranteeing respect for the integrity of the action and the process.[51]

The analysis of conditions or legal impediments for a specific action – that is, the question of *admissibility* of a request – is particularly well developed before the ICJ.[52] Thus, the ICJ may have jurisdiction to decide on the substance of a claim, and yet be unable to decide it because the action or complaint is inadmissible.[53] The ICJ in the *Oil Platforms* case explained the notion as follows:

> Objections to admissibility (*recevabilité*) normally take the form of an assertion that, even if the Court has jurisdiction and the facts stated by the applicant State are assumed to be correct, nonetheless there are reasons why the Court should not proceed to an examination of the merits.[54]

Objections to jurisdiction and objections to admissibility are similar in that they are both preliminary. They are analyzed before the merits and their intended effect is to avoid findings on the merits. However, they are different on at least four accounts. First, as explained above, objections to jurisdiction are primarily directed to the authority of the court to rule on the claims (i.e. the court's competence or *field-jurisdiction* as defined below). Objections to admissibility, in contrast, are targeted at the conditions for the specific action or complaint.[55] As

---

51 See Cuniberti (2006) 1715 (discussing the role of consent in minimizing the problem of forum-shopping.) Conversely, the problem is amplified where consent is given *ex ante*.

52 See generally *supra* note 44. See also Amerasinghe (2003) 245-308; Fitzmaurice 438-40.

53 Examples of legal impediments that make a complaint inadmissible before the ICJ are the nationality of the claimant, non-exhaustion of local remedies and undue delay. See, *e.g.*, Ahmadou Sadio Diallo (*Rep. Guinea v. D.R.C.*), 2007 I.C.J. 27 (May 24); Interhandel (*Switz. v. U.S.*), 1959 I.C.J. 5, 25-26 (Mar. 21); Nottebohm (*Liech. v. Guat.*), 1953 I.C.J. 111, 123 (Nov. 18); Ambatielos (*Greece v. U.K.*), 1952 I.C.J. 28, 43-44 (July 1).

54 Oil Platforms (*Iran v. United States*), 2003 I.C.J. 161, 177, ¶ 29 (Nov. 6).

55 Article 79.1 of the I.C.J. Rules of Court highlights that jurisdiction relates to the Court, and admissibility relates to the application: 'Any objection by the respondent to the jurisdiction *of the Court* or to the admissibility *of the application* [...] ' I.C.J. Rules of Court, *supra* note 49 (emphasis added).

a result, objections to admissibility often come into play only after a finding of jurisdiction.[56]

Second, whereas the governing law of jurisdictional objections refers to the tribunal's jurisdictional field (*ratione materiae* or *ratione personae*, in the case of WTO disputes set out in the DSU and the panel's terms of reference), objections to admissibility are governed by principles and rules binding on the parties to the dispute and not necessarily incorporated in the clause or instrument granting the tribunal jurisdiction.[57] As such, an objection to admissibility leaves untouched the jurisdiction of the court to decide the case. In fact, if a tribunal refuses to examine substantive claims based on their inadmissibility, the court is, by definition, *exercising jurisdiction*, albeit to decline to rule on the merits of the case. Hence, the question of a panel being *deprived of* jurisdiction based on an outside treaty or principle does not arise. Rather, what a panel does in these cases is to *exercise* its jurisdiction (albeit *incidental-jurisdiction* as defined later) so as to recognize the *inadmissibility* of the action and stop the proceeding without findings on the merits.

Third, qualifying an objection as a matter of jurisdiction or admissibility is important for the purpose of establishing the burden to raise such an objection. Lack of jurisdiction is an issue that a tribunal must examine at its own initiative.[58] In contrast, the question of admissibility of claims normally has

---

56 Theoretically, they should come into play only after jurisdiction is established. See, *e.g.*, Armed Activities on the Territory of Congo (*D.R.C v. Rwanda*) (new application), 2006 ICJ ¶¶ 18 and 126. Note, however, that there have been cases in which a claim has been found to be inadmissible while the objections to jurisdiction had not been thoroughly disposed of. See, *e.g.,, Interhandel, supra* note 53, at 8-9.

57 [T]he real distinction and test seem to be based on, or arises from, the jurisdictional clause or clauses under which the Tribunal is said to exist. If so, the objection is basically one of jurisdiction. If it is founded on the considerations outside the ambit of any jurisdictional clause, and not involving the interpretation or application of such a provision, then it will normally be an objection to the receivability of the claim.

Northern Cameroons (*Cameroon v. U.K.*), I.C.J. Rep. 1963, Separate Opinion of Judge Sir Gerald Fitzmaurice, at 102-3 (Dec. 2).

58 A WTO panel 'is entitled to consider the issue of its own jurisdiction *on its own initiative*, and to satisfy itself that it has jurisdiction in any case that comes before it.' Appellate Body Report, *United States–Anti-Dumping Act of 1916*, WT/DS136/AB/R, WT/DS162/AB/R, note 30 (Aug. 28, 2000) (emphasis added); see also *Prosecutor v. Tadić*, Case No. IT-94-1-AR72, Decision on the Defence Motion for Interlocutory Appeal on Jurisdiction, ¶¶ 15 and 18 (Oct. 2 1995). What is more, '[P]anels cannot simply ignore issues which go to the root of their jurisdiction [...] Rather, panels *must* deal with such issues – if necessary, on their own motion – in order to satisfy themselves that they have authority to proceed.' *Mexico–Corn Syrup, supra* note 44, ¶ 36 (emphasis added); see also Fisheries Jurisdiction (*Spain v. Can.*), 1998 I.C.J. ¶ 38 ('there is no burden of proof to be discharged in the matter of jurisdiction'); Border and Transborder Armed Actions (*Nic. v. Honduras*); I.C.J. Rep. 1988, at 76.

to be raised by the parties.[59] This distinction relates to the very nature of the lack of jurisdiction versus the inadmissibility of a claim. As lack of jurisdiction concerns the scope of the tribunal's authority to decide the issue, the tribunal must sort this out for itself, even if neither party raises the question.[60] Inadmissibility, however, relates to the specific application and centers on the legal relationship between the parties; for example, must the complainant first exhaust domestic remedies or, conversely, has the complainant previously waived or exhausted its right to bring a case?. In this sense, the analysis of admissibility is subject to implied waiver and acquiescence by the other party.[61] Thus, depending on whether one qualifies *res judicata, lis pendens, forum non conveniens* or forum-election clauses in outside treaties as relating to the admissibility of a claim, or to the jurisdiction of a tribunal, parties must raise the objection (admissibility) or the tribunal must consider them at its own initiative (jurisdiction). This difference may explain the Appellate Body's attitude in *Soft Drinks* in which it did not examine NAFTA's fork-in-the-road clause in any detail arguably on the ground that Mexico explicitly refused to rely on this NAFTA clause.[62] Had the Appellate Body considered this clause to be a matter of its own jurisdiction, it could have examined the clause even if Mexico did not invoke it. Because the clause relates, in our view, to admissibility, and Mexico therefore should have invoked it, we believe that the Appellate Body correctly decided not to further examine the NAFTA clause.

Fourth, and related to the question of waiver and acquiescence, a decision on inadmissibility does not acquire the full force of *res judicata* when the problem underlying the admissibility of the application may be cured. In contrast, a decision on jurisdiction cannot be cured unilaterally, and to this extent does carry the force of *res judicata*. A decision of inadmissibility based on the non-exhaustion of local remedies, for instance, does not influence further proceedings after local remedies have been exhausted. A decision proclaiming the inadmissibility of a WTO-complaint based on the inadequacy of consultations, likewise,

---

59 See *Mexico–Corn Syrup, supra* note 44, ¶ 53. Where the Appellate Body drew a distinction between issues that could deprive the panel of its 'authority' and held that '[i]f so, then the Panel was bound to address them in its own motion' and issues that the parties should raise. See also Amerasinghe, *supra* note 52, at 286. Notice, however, that the authority to examine issues of admissibility *ex officio* may also be expressly granted by the governing instruments of the tribunal. See, *e.g.*, *ECHR Article 35*, *supra* note 46, at Article 35.4.

60 Note, however, that in the context of the ICJ's ad hoc consent-based jurisdiction, a party who wishes to contest jurisdiction should raise the issue, given the potential operation of the doctrine of *forum prorogatum*. See generally, Yee (1999) 147.

61 See *Mexico –Corn Syrup, supra* note 44 (stating, at ¶ 50, that '[a] Member that fails to raise its objection in a timely manner, notwithstanding one or more opportunities to do so, may be deemed to have waived its right to have a panel consider such objections'; and at ¶ 64, that '[a] lack of prior consultations is not a defect that, by its very nature, deprives a panel of its authority [...] and that, accordingly, such a defect is not one which a panel must examine even if both parties remain silent thereon').

62 See Brief for Camara Nacional de las Industrias Azucarera y Alcoholera – Mexico, *supra* note 39, at 19.

should not preclude the complainant from making the same request under the same cause of action in new proceedings after proper consultations have taken place. In this sense, a decision on inadmissibility would not have the force of *res judicata*.

The notion of admissibility also sheds new light on the broader debate of jurisdictional overlap among international tribunals. Recognizing that principles such as *res judicata* and forum selection clauses are questions of admissibility of the request (not questions of jurisdiction of the respective tribunals) shifts the discussion away from a 'clash of legal regimes'[63] or 'conflicts of law/conflicts of jurisdiction' perspective. Instead, it frames the question in terms of an assessment of the legal conditions linked to the specific action or complaint before a particular tribunal. Previous works have centred on the role of non-WTO law in the jurisdictional stages of WTO disputes through the lens of conflicts of laws[64] and conflicts of jurisdiction.[65] As a result, the question of jurisdictional coordination has revolved around the possibility of bilateral derogation from WTO rules and rules of conflict such as *lex specialis* and *lex posterior* (for example, is the NAFTA fork-in-the-road clause more specific or later in time than the DSU's jurisdictional clause in Article 23?). In contrast, under the framework sketched above, forum-election clauses in outside treaties or general principles of coordination apply procedurally to preclude a *party* from resorting to WTO dispute settlement on the grounds that the *claims* become inadmissible, not on the grounds that there is a conflict of norms or jurisdiction *between tribunals* or *treaty-regimes* which plays out in favour of the non-WTO treaty and undermines the panel's jurisdiction. Indirectly, through the notion of inadmissibility, those rules and principles provide a panel with the basis to refrain from deciding a case irrespective of whether bilateral modifications affect the jurisdiction of panels. Indeed, under the analysis of admissibility, both the jurisdiction of the panel (*field-jurisdiction*) and the substantive rights of the complainant remain untouched. As a result, the thorny problem of conflict of laws or jurisdiction, at least the way it has been framed so far, simply does not come into play. Faced with inadmissible claims, a panel *exercises jurisdiction* (albeit *incidental jurisdiction*) if only not to rule on the substantive claims before it.

The concept of jurisdiction, as applied to international tribunals, has at least three different meanings. First, in its broadest sense, jurisdiction (from the Latin *jurisdictio* or *jus dicere*, literally 'speak the law') describes the *power* of a tribunal to state the law on a particular issue (hereinafter *power-jurisdiction*). This power is defined by two *spheres* of jurisdiction. The narrower sphere determines the *class of cases* a tribunal has the power to decide. It can be referred

63 See Fischer-Lescano – Gunther Teubner (2004) 999; see also Koskenniemi – Päivi Leino, (2002) 553, 574.

64 See, *e.g.*, (b) Pauwelyn (2003).

65 See Kwak & Marceau 465 (2006).

to as a tribunal's 'jurisdictional field,'[66] 'jurisdiction in a field sense,'[67], or also 'substantive,' 'original,' or 'primary' jurisdiction[68] (hereinafter *field-jurisdiction*). 'Competence' is another term that describes this field-jurisdiction of a tribunal, particularly in the French language and is referred to there as *compétence*.[69] The scope of field-jurisdiction is crucial in international law, as it is generally recognized that an international tribunal only has field-jurisdiction where such jurisdiction was explicitly granted to it by the parties (i.e., international tribunals are tribunals of specific jurisdiction). Thus, in the WTO context, the field-jurisdiction of adjudicative bodies is limited, first, to disputes under WTO covered agreements (DSU Article 1:1) and, second, to the terms of reference of the specific panel (DSU Article 7). Consequently, a panel's ultimate 'recommendations' on compliance or violation in a given dispute between WTO members must fall under the WTO-covered agreements and within the specific panel's terms of reference. These are the limits to be applied in an objection to field-jurisdiction as defined above.

There is, however, another sphere of jurisdiction which is often referred to as the 'incidental'[70] or 'inherent'[71] jurisdiction of international tribunals (hereinafter *incidental-jurisdiction*). This type of jurisdiction can also be called interlocutory jurisdiction, because it refers to questions intervening before the end of proceedings that are decisive to some point or matter, but are not a final decision of the whole controversy.[72] Incidental-jurisdiction is asserted when an international tribunal faces a question that affects its ability to exercise the judicial function assigned to it. This sphere of jurisdiction guarantees that a tribunal maintains the integrity of its judicial function[73] in exercising the limited field-jurisdiction granted to it.[74] To decide, for example, on preliminary objections to

---

66 Fitzmaurice (1986) 434.

67 *Id.*

68 See, *e.g.*, *Prosecutor v. Tadić*, Case No. IT-94-1-I, Decision on Defense Motion for Interlocutory Appeal on Jurisdiction, ¶ 17 (Oct. 2, 1995).

69 See Abi-Saab (1967) 60.

70 See, *e.g.*, *Tadic*, Case No. IT-94-1-I at ¶17; see also Briggs (1960) 87.

71 *Tadic*, Case No. IT-94-1-I at ¶ 14.

72 See Black's Law Dictionary 815 (6th ed,, 1990).

73 As Kenneth Carlston observed: 'A State, in submitting its dispute with another to the decision of an international tribunal, has certain fundamental rights which it may expect in full confidence will be respected [...] The tribunal must respect the law governing its creation and defining its powers as laid down in the *compromis*, and it must likewise *observe certain other established rules of a fundamental character which inherently, under the* generally *accepted rules of law and justice, regulate the conduct of any judicial body*.' Carlston (1946) 36 (emphasis added).

74 Notice, for example, the ICJ's limited field-jurisdiction in the *Namibia* opinion and in the *Lockerbie* case. In both cases, although the ICJ had undoubtedly no power to judicially review resolutions of United Nations organs, it assessed those resolutions as a matter of course, in the exercise of its judicial function, in order to decide on the merits of the cases, which were under its field-jurisdiction. See Legal Consequences for States of Continued Presence of South Africa in Namibia (South West Africa)

either jurisdiction or admissibility, a tribunal must exercise incidental-jurisdiction. Since, with regard to objections to jurisdiction, the very question is whether the tribunal has field-jurisdiction in the first place, a preliminary decision on jurisdiction cannot possibly be an exercise of field-jurisdiction (hence the notion of *kompetenz-kompetenz* or *la compétence de la compétence*).

The distinction between field-jurisdiction and incidental-jurisdiction is graphically represented here. Based on this distinction, the field-jurisdiction of WTO panels (circumscribed by WTO covered agreements and a panel's terms of reference) must be distinguished from the incidental-jurisdiction of WTO panels (inherently held by all judicial decision-makers). Notice the Appellate Body's agreement with Mexico in *Soft Drinks* that 'WTO panels have certain *powers that are inherent in their adjudicative function*.'[75] These powers are not set out in the WTO covered agreements, nor are they normally within a panel's explicit terms of reference. They are inherent in the judicial function,[76] and their existence reveals that the power-jurisdiction of panels (as defined earlier) expands beyond their field-jurisdiction, i.e., it includes both field and incidental-jurisdiction.

Figure 1. Distinction between Field-Jurisdiction and Incidental Jurisdiction

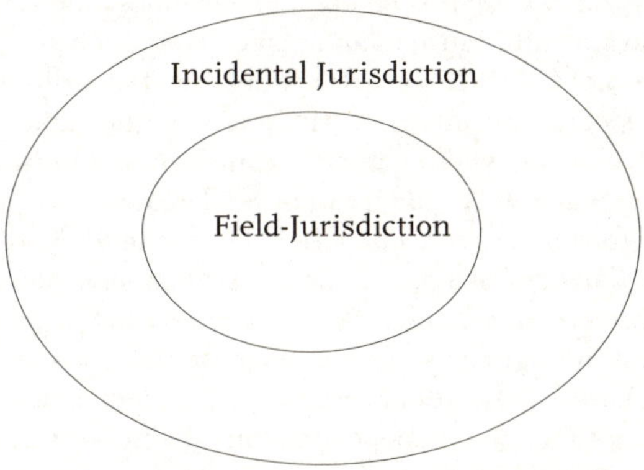

One notable example of power-jurisdiction exercised incidentally is the doctrine of *la compétence de la compétence*, which is well-recognized in the WTO.[77] But the

Notwithstanding Security Council Resolution 276, 1970 I.C.J. 16 at ¶ 89 (July 29); see also Questions of Interpretation and Application of 1971 Montreal Convention Arising from Aerial Incident at Lockerbie (*Libya v. U.S.*), 1992 I.C.J. 114 at ¶ 42 (Mar. 3).

75 Appellate Body Report, *Mexico–Soft Drinks*, *supra* note 32, at ¶ 45.

76 See also Van-Damme (2008).

77 'Notably, panels have the right to determine whether they have jurisdiction in a given case, as well as to determine the scope of their jurisdiction.' See Appellate Body Report, *Mexico–Soft Drinks*, *supra* note 32, at ¶ 45; see also Appellate Body Report, *United States–Anti-Dumping Act of 1916*, ¶ 30 (Aug. 28, 2000); Nottebohm (*Liech. v. Guat.*), Preliminary Objections, 1953 I.C.J. Rep. 119 (1953); Rio Grande Irrigation and Land Co.(*U.K. v. U.S.*), 6 R. Int'l Arb. Awards 131, 135-36 (1923).

incidental-jurisdiction of panels is broader than *la compétence de la compétence.* For instance, as the Appellate Body has confirmed, 'as a matter of due process, and the *proper exercise of the judicial function,* panels are *required to address* issues that are put before them by parties to a dispute.'[78] This dictum fits squarely with incidental-jurisdiction as defined above. More recently, the panel ruling on *US–Hormones Suspension* provided yet another example of incidental-jurisdiction as broader than field-jurisdiction, this time not focused as much on preliminary or procedural questions (for example, under objections to jurisdiction or admissibility) but on questions related to substance. In that ruling, the panel determined that in order to decide the EC's claim that the United States violated DSU Article 22.8 (in other words, whether the U.S. suspension should continue after the inconsistent measure was removed), it was necessary to examine issues under the SPS Agreement, namely whether the new EC measure complied with it).[79] These issues were flagrantly outside the panel's terms of reference or field-jurisdiction, but, in our view, perfectly within the panel's incidental-jurisdiction.[80] Hence, incidental or interlocutory questions trigger the tribunal's power-jurisdiction to consider law (in that case, the SPS Agreement) which may not strictly fall within the panel's field-jurisdiction (here, the WTO covered agreements or a panel's terms of reference). The same would be true when a panel decides on the admissibility of claims before it and is, in this incidental exercise, called upon to refer to a forum clause in an outside treaty such as NAFTA. Even if NAFTA clearly does not fall within a WTO panel's field-jurisdiction, a WTO panel may be called upon to consider it in the exercise of the panel's incidental-jurisdiction (in its decision on whether a WTO complaint is admissible).

In sum, the notion that a WTO panel can never decline to exercise its jurisdiction rests on a confusion between a panel's field-jurisdiction and its incidental jurisdiction. The yardsticks of a panel's field-jurisdiction are, as the United States and China argued in *Soft Drinks,* DSU Article 1:1 and the panel's terms of reference. These are the signposts of a panel's authority to make substantive findings of compliance or violation. Conversely, incidental jurisdiction is inherent in the judicial function and dependent on the opposing arguments raised by both parties. It includes those preliminary and incidental issues that a panel must assess before definitively deciding the merits of the case. Hence,

78 Appellate Body Report, *Mexico–Soft Drinks, supra* note 32, at ¶ 36 (emphasis added).

79 See Panel Report, *United States–Continued Suspension of Obligations in the EC–Hormones Dispute,* ¶ 6.54, WT/DS320/R (Mar. 31, 2008); upheld by the Appellate Body in Appellate Body Report, *United States–Continued Suspension of Obligations in the EC–Hormones Dispute,* ¶¶ 322-332, 736, WT/DS320/AB/R (Oct. 16, 2008).

80 *Id.* at ¶ 7.276.

[W]e want to stress that in reviewing the EC claims of violation of Article 23.1 read together with Article 22.8 and Article 3.7 of the DSU, our intention is not to substitute ourselves for a compliance panel under Article 21.5 of the DSU. We will make findings with respect to the second series of main claims of the European Communities with the only purpose to reach a conclusion on the violation of the provisions referred to in those claims.'

unlike what the United States and China were implying in *Soft Drinks*, the fact that a panel or the Appellate Body has field-jurisdiction in a specific case does not mean that it must necessarily make a ruling on the merits. Notwithstanding this field-jurisdiction, legal impediments, such as a forum selection clause in NAFTA, can make the specific claim inadmissible and thereby can prevent the panel or Appellate Body from making a ruling on the merits. However, the fact that the field-jurisdiction of a WTO panel is limited (i.e. only provisions in WTO covered agreements are included in the panel's terms of reference), does not speak to a panel's incidental jurisdiction or the possibility that a WTO panel may have to consider treaty provisions outside its field-jurisdiction when exercising incidental jurisdiction (be it a NAFTA clause or, in *US–Hormones Suspension*, SPS provisions).

IV Why Domestic Analogies Do Not Work in the International Context

A. Res Judicata

With the difference between jurisdiction of a tribunal and admissibility of a claim explained, let us now revert to the relevance and possible impact of domestic law principles to deal with forum shopping on an international scale. First, *res judicata* – a preclusion doctrine dealing with sequential proceedings – is generally considered a principle that is also applicable before international tribunals.[81] Under the framework outlined above, *res judicata* is a legal impediment precluding sequential claims; in other words, it relates to admissibility (not field-jurisdiction). Most importantly, if the criteria for *res judicata* are met, the tribunal does not have any discretion to decide the case, making the principle a preclusion rather than an abstention doctrine, as were defined earlier).

The reluctance of WTO panels and the Appellate Body to apply the principle of *res judicata* is difficult to understand.[82] If the Appellate Body decides to apply judicial principles on burden of proof, good faith and due process – on which nothing is explicitly said in the DSU – there is no reason for it to reject

---

81 See Application of Convention on the Prevention and Punishment of Crime of Genocide (*Bosn. & Herz. v. Serb. & Mont.*), 2007 I.C.J. 91, at ¶ 115-20 (Feb. 26); see also *Waste Management, Inc. v. United Mexican States*, ICSID Case No. ARB (AF)/00/03, Preliminary Objection, ¶ 39 (Apr. 30, 2004); *Petrobart Ltd. v. The Kyrgyz Republic*, Arb. No. 126/2003 at 55, SCC Arb. Awards (Mar. 29, 2005); see generally Leonardo Brant, L'autorité de la Chose Jugée en Droit International Public (2003); Vaughan Lowe, *Res Judicata and the Rule of Law in International Arbitration*, 8 *African Y.B. Int'l L.* (1996); *The Pious Fund (U.S. v. Mexico)* (Oct. 14, 1902) 2 *Am. J. Int'l L* 900 (1908).

82 See Panel Report, *India–Measures Affecting the Automotives Sector*, ¶¶ 7.57-7.59, WT/DS146/R, WT/DS175/R (Dec. 21, 2001) [hereinafter *India–Autos*] (considering that there is neither textual nor case-based clear guidance on the applicability of the doctrine, since 'many important interpretative issues would thus need to be considered in determining whether the doctrine of *res judicata* applies in WTO dispute settlement […] ' (at ¶ 7.59)).

the principle of *res judicata*.[83] The WTO reluctance to apply the principle of *res judicata* is all the more surprising because *res judicata* is only rarely triggered in international litigation. Put differently, if it is only rarely triggered what is the WTO afraid of?

It is, indeed, commonly acknowledged that *res judicata* only applies if (1) the parties are the same; (2) the object or subject matter (*petitum*) is the same; and (3) the cause of action (*causa petendi*) is the same.[84] The third condition most often means that an earlier ruling by one international tribunal will not constitute *res judicata* for another. This is so because of the treaty-based, category-specific nature of the jurisdiction of most international tribunals, referred to earlier For example, if the International Tribunal for the Law of the Sea (ITLOS) previously decided a dispute, the admissibility of the claims in a subsequent WTO panel between the same parties and on the same factual background, will most likely not be precluded by the earlier ITLOS decision. The *causa petendi* before ITLOS will be a claim under the United Nations Convention on the Law of the Sea (UNCLOS), and before the WTO a claim under a WTO agreement. Similarly, even if a NAFTA panel decided earlier that a given tax violated national treatment, this decision might not, strictly speaking, trigger the preclusive effects of *res judicata* for a subsequent WTO panel even between the same parties, on the same tax, because the *causa petendi* before the WTO is the WTO obligation to provide national treatment. Before the NAFTA panel, however, the *causa petendi* was the NAFTA obligation of national treatment.[85]

---

83 *But* see Appellate Body Report, *European Communities–Anti-Dumping Duties on Imports of Cotton-Type Bed Linen from India*, ¶ 93, WT/DS141/AB/R (Apr. 3. 2003) [hereinafter *EC–Linen*] (confirming at least implicitly the *res judicata* effect of unappealed Panel reports adopted by the DSB). '[...] [I]n our view, an unappealed finding included in a Panel report that is adopted by the DSB must be treated as a final resolution to a dispute between the parties in respect of the particular claim and the specific component of a measure that is the subject of that claim.' See *EC–Bed Linen, supra*, at ¶ 93. The Appellate Body thereby also confirmed the three pre-conditions for *res judicata* effect to be triggered: (1) same parties; (2) same object matter ('specific component of a measure'); and (3) same cause of action or claim. The Appellate Body equally confirmed the binding effect as between the parties of its own reports, once adopted by the DSB. Appellate Body Report, *United States–Import Prohibition on Certain Shrimp and Shrimp Products*, ¶¶ 92-96, WT/DS58/AB/R (Oct. 12, 1998).

84 *Factory at Chorzów*, Interpretation of Judgments Numbers 7 and 8, 1927 I.C.J. (ser. A) No. 11 (Dec. 16). (dissenting opinion of Judge Anzilotti); *India–Autos, supra* note 80, at ¶ 7.65. See also Shany (2003) 22-23.

85 The MOX Plant Case (*Ir. V. U.K.*), Request for Provisional Measures, 2001 I.T.L.O.S. No. 10, ¶ 53 ('[T]he application of international rules on interpretation of treaties to identical or similar provisions of different treaties may not yield the same results, having regard to, *inter alia*, difference in the respective contexts, objects and purposes, subsequent practices of parties and *travaux préparatoires*.' See also *Panel Report Argentina–Poultry, supra* note 13; see also *Petrobart*, Arb. No. 126/2003 (refusing to apply *res judicata* in an Arbitral Tribunal operating under the Stockholm Arbitration Institute to neither domestic proceedings in a Kyrgyz Court nor an UNCITRAL arbitration). On the difference between national treatment in trade and investment agreements, see Nicolas DiMascio & Joost Pauwelyn, *Nondiscrimina-*

In the *Soft Drinks* dispute, the Appellate Body saw no problem exercising jurisdiction to decide the merits of the claims by the United States, even though Mexico had earlier brought a claim to NAFTA, because, *inter alia*, 'neither the subject matter nor the respective positions of the parties are identical in the dispute under the NAFTA [...] and the dispute before us.' Before NAFTA, Mexico was complaining about U.S. quotas, while before the WTO, it was the United States that was complaining about a Mexican tax.[86]

In the current context of international law, where jurisdiction and cause of action are intimately linked, applying *res judicata* to deal with overlaps between *different* international tribunals will, therefore, mostly be a waste of time. The cause of action will be different and the doctrine thus will not be triggered. In those cases, *res judicata* is at best a fig leaf allowing the tribunal to go ahead and decide the case anyway; at worst, it is false judicial deference or comity. The tribunal gives the impression that it has an open mind and is ready to apply general principles, yet it knows beforehand that these general principles will not apply and will not stop it from deciding the case.

This situation could, however, change if tribunals were willing to soften the three criteria for *res judicata* to apply. To do so they could borrow from common law notions such as 'issue estoppel' or civil law notions such as 'related actions.'[87] Tribunals could also define the 'same parties' broadly as some investor-state awards have done, albeit to expand, rather than to decline to exercise, their jurisdiction.[88] In the current context of international law it may, however,

tion in Trade and Investment Treaties: Worlds Apart or Two Sides of the Same Coin?, 102 Am. J. Int'l L. 48 (2008).

86 *Appellate Body Report, Mexico–Soft Drinks, supra* note 32, at ¶ 54 (citing *Panel Report, Mexico–Soft Drinks, supra* note 1, at ¶ 7.14. Granted, since there was no previous decision by a NAFTA panel, one of the conditions for the application of *res judicata* would not have been met anyway. At any rate, the discussion remains relevant for the question of *lis pendens*. See also *Panel Report Argentina–Poultry, supra* note 13, (refusing to consider *res judicata* even though the same measure at issue had been previously found legal under Mercosur).

87 *Carl Zeiss Stiftung v. Rayner & Keeler Ltd.* [1967] A.C. 853, at 935 (emphasizing that the doctrine of 'issue estoppel' in common law systems is neighbour to the notion of *res judicata* but does not require the 'same cause of action'). See also *Allen v. McCurry*, 449 U.S. 90, 94 (1980) (citing *Montana v. United States*, 440 U.S. 147, 153 (1979)). For the doctrine of 'related actions,' see *infra* notes 140-143.

88 Some investment tribunals have applied the 'same parties' requirement broadly to assert jurisdiction over claims. See, *e.g.*, *Dow Chemical France v. Isover Saint Gobain*, 9 *Y.B. Comm. Arb.* 131, 136 (1984) ('[I]rrespective of the distinct juridical identity of each of its members, a group of companies constitutes one and the same economic reality (*une realité economique unique*) of which the tribunal should take account'); *Amco v. Indonesia*, Decision on Jurisdiction, 1 ICSID Rep, 389, 400 (1983) ('PT Amco was but an instrumentality through which Amco Asia was to realize the investment. Now, the goal of the arbitration clause was to protect the investor [...]: would it not be fully illogical to grant this protection to the controlled entity, but not to the controlling one?'); *Klöckner v. Cameroon* 2 ICSID Rep, 9, 17 (1983) ('This Agreement, although formally signed by the Government and SOCAME, was in fact negotiated between the Government and Klöckner [...] [I]t is undeniable that it was manifestly concluded in the interest of

be difficult, and risky, to apply more lax to *res judicata* for two reasons. First, it is difficult to distil true 'general principles' to this effect. Rules on 'related actions' are, for example, only applied when explicitly provided for, they are not a self-standing doctrine or principle. Second, even where actions are 'related,' for example, national treatment in NAFTA and the WTO, the origin, objectives and institutional contexts of these related actions may still be different, and, therefore, it may be unwise for one decision to legally preclude another.[89] This should not, however, prevent softer means of judicial deference). That said, in exceptional cases, doctrines such as good faith, estoppel or abuse of process could be applied to curb genuinely abusive sequential litigation.[90]

Finally, if one qualifies *res judicata* as undermining the tribunal's very jurisdiction to decide the case, the tribunal must consider the principle at its own initiative. If, in contrast, *res judicata* relates to admissibility (or the application or complainant and not the tribunal as such), a position that conforms to the framework offered above and that we find more convincing at least in the current context of international law,[91] the tribunal must only consider *res judicata* if either party invokes it.[92] Put differently, in our view, *res judicata* relates to the admissibility of the claim, not the jurisdiction of the tribunal.

B. Lis Pendens

Whereas *res judicata* no doubt applies to international tribunals, it is more controversial whether the same is true for *lis pendens*, a preclusion doctrine dealing with parallel, rather than sequential proceedings. August Reinisch argues that *lis pendens* applies in the international context;[93] Gilles Cuniberti submits that it does not;[94] Yuval Shany says that the answer is unclear.[95]

Klöckner. Reinisch argues that this argument should work both ways; tribunals should also interpret the 'same parties' criterion broadly so as to *decline* jurisdiction); Reinisch (2004) 37, 57-77.

89 See *supra* note 83.

90 See Lowe, *supra* note 9, at 191.

91 Indeed, if an issue is to be examined by the tribunal at its own initiative, it should logically be something that the court can examine relatively easily by looking at the constituent documents that confer the court jurisdiction. In contrast, in the current context of widely diverse and loosely integrated international courts and tribunals, the fact that another tribunal has already decided the dispute is not normally something that a second tribunal can find out for itself without the parties bringing the issue to the tribunal's attention. Hence, if only for purely practical reasons, *res judicata*, in the current international law context, would seem to relate more to the application /or earlier conduct by the complainant, than to the very jurisdiction of the tribunal itself.

92 Consider Article 35 of the Convention for the Protection of Human Rights and Fundamental Freedoms, which lists the situation of where an application 'is substantially the same as a matter that has already been examined by the Court', that is, an extended version of *res judicata*, as a question of admissibility, not jurisdiction.

93 See Reinisch (2004) 48.

94 Giles Cuniberti (2006) 406.

95 See Shany (2003) 241.

Cuniberti supports the view that *lis pendens* is not, nor should be, a principle of international law on two grounds. First, in his view, *lis pendens* is not a 'general principle of law' because it is essentially a civil law doctrine.[96] Other legal traditions approach the same problem with very different jurisdictional tools (*e.g.* the common law principle of *forum non conveniens* or the U.S. courts' abstention doctrines). Incorporating *lis pendens* as a general principle of law into international law without the ancillary doctrines that come with it, such as the civil law rules on 'related actions,'[97] would, in Cuniberti's opinion, offer an 'incomplete picture'.[98] Second, and more importantly, the time factor of *lis pendens* – the court first seized decides the case – makes sense between hierarchically equal and similarly expert and legitimate domestic courts. It does not make sense among international courts that are not necessarily comparable, be it for reasons of hierarchy, procedural efficiency, legitimacy or expertise. To apply, in those circumstances, the guillotine approach of 'the first court seized decides' is, according to Cuniberti, not appropriate:

> [T]he fundamental goal of the institution [of *lis pendens*] has been to discriminate between adjudicators who were comparable in most respects. As it would not have been acceptable to find that one given first instance court was superior to or more legitimate than another first instance court of the same country, it was only natural that the institution would ultimately rely on a test that would be as neutral as possible [i.e. a simple time factor] to distinguish between them and designate the one that should retain jurisdiction. In an international setting, however, neither the equality nor the legitimacy of all adjudicators should be assumed. The issue of parallel litigation can therefore be addressed by discriminating between the competing adjudicators on very substantive grounds [...] the policy decisions behind the *lis pendens* doctrine have no legitimacy to regulate parallel litigation in an international setting.[99]

Although Cuniberti overlooks the fact that, much like between two courts of first instance within the same country, no inherent legal hierarchy exists between international tribunals, on the merits, his arguments are convincing.[100]

96 See Cuniberti (2006) 383.

97 See *infra* notes 144-146.

98 See Cuniberti (2006) 412.

99 *Id.* at 383-4.

100 Moreover, even when it comes to formal, legal hierarchies between tribunals, Cuniberti has a point as his prime example there is the hierarchical superiority of an *international* tribunal over a *domestic* court. Cuniberti refers, with support, to an early P.C.I.J. case which decided that overlapping proceedings before, on the one hand, a mixed arbitral tribunal and a Polish domestic court and, on the other hand, the P.C.I.J. cannot trigger *lis pendens* as these are 'not courts of the same character.' Certain German Interests in Polish Upper Silesia (*F.R.G. v. Pol.*), 1925 P.C.I.J. (ser. A) No. 6, at 20. Yet, Cuniberti then discovers with dismay that I.C.S.I.D. tribunals started to disregard this hierarchy and now commonly apply *lis pendens* also to overlap between international (I.C.S.I.D.) proceedings and domestic court or

In the current context of international law – particularly given the treaty-based jurisdiction of most international tribunals as well as their diverse institutional and historical context, proceedings, applicable law, remedies, expertise, and legitimacy – it is hard to start from the presumption that *ceteris paribus* – other than the time factor – two international proceedings are 'the same' or even 'comparable.' On the contrary, to apply the guillotine of time in the brave new world of diverse international tribunals of all colours and stripes could then be rather artificial. Indeed, even Reinisch, who supports application of *lis pendens* by international tribunals, agrees that one of the prerequisites for *lis pendens* is that the two tribunals operate in the same legal order.[101]

Consider, for example, whether the WTO panel should have applied *lis pendens* in *Soft Drinks*. Assuming that NAFTA's choice-of-forum provision did not apply, should the WTO panel have dismissed the case in favour of the earlier-initiated NAFTA proceeding? Given the United States' refusal to appoint a panelist, *lis pendens* would have left the case in limbo. Although it may not be politically correct to posit the superiority of the WTO panel system, it could be argued that, at least in procedural terms, WTO and NAFTA (Chapter 20) panels are not 'comparable.' If so, the purely time-based logic of *lis pendens* should not apply. From this perspective, it may, therefore, not be appropriate to apply *lis pendens* before both international tribunals in question have matured procedurally.

So much for Cuniberti's arguments against applying *lis pendens* in the international context. What convinced Reinisch to advocate the opposite position?[102] First, Reinisch argues that *lis pendens* is a general principle of law in the sense of Article 38 of the ICJ Statute. In support of his arguments, he points to '[t]he

arbitration proceedings, thereby implicitly accepting that the jurisdiction of an IC.S.I.D. tribunal is comparable to, or of the same hierarchy, as that of a domestic court or tribunal. In *SGS v. Pakistan*, for example, the I.C.S.I.D. tribunal explicitly considered – but ultimately did not apply – the *lis pendens* doctrine even though the parallel proceeding was one brought before a single *ad hoc* arbitrator pursuant to the arbitration clause of an investment contract. *SGS v. Pakistan*, Decision on Objections to Jurisdiction, ICSID Case No. ARB/01/13 (2003); *S.A.R.L. Benvenuti & Bonfant v. People's Republic of the Congo*, ICSID Case No. ARB/77/2; *Compañía de Aguas del Aconquija SA and Vivendi Universal v. Argentine Republic*, ICSID Case No. ARB/97/3; *Empresas Lucchetti SA and Lucchetti Peru SA v. Peru*, ICSID Case No. ARB/03/4 (2005); and *Noble Ventures Inc. v. Romania*, ICSID Case No. ARB/01/11 (2005). In *Noble Ventures*, the tribunal recognised a difference of order between international and domestic law, but reasoned that the umbrella clause led to an exception to this separation. But, in contrast to *SGS v. Pakistan*, note, however, *SPP v. Egypt*, ICSID Case No. ARB/84/3 (1992), (where the tribunal refused to apply *lis pendens* when faced with parallel proceedings before 'two unrelated and independent tribunals').

101 See Reinisch (2003) 52.

102 Reinisch has written that he was asked to write a legal opinion in the Czech Republic's case before Swedish courts to set aside the ruling in *CME Czech Republic B.V.*, see *supra* note 12, which found the Czech Republic liable for $ 269,814,000. See Reinisch, *supra* note 86, at 37. Reinisch wrote in favor of the earlier Lauder case, which denied all claims against the Czech Republic on the same facts. *Id.* From that perspective, he may have had an incentive to write in favour of a broad application of *lis pendens* and *res judicata* in the international context.

widespread use and similarity of the concept of *lis pendens* in the national procedural laws of States of all legal traditions, [...] its inclusion in a number of bi- and multiparty agreements'; and its appearance in a number of international court cases.[103] Second, and more interestingly, Reinisch argues that if international courts and tribunals were to accept the principle of *res judicata*, they would be logically compelled to also accept the principle of *lis pendens*:

> As a matter of legal logic it would be inconsistent to permit parallel proceedings between the same parties in the same dispute [i.e. not to apply *lis pendens*] before different dispute settlement organs up to the point where one of them has decided the case and then prevent the other ('slower') one from proceeding as a result of *res judicata*.[104]

Is this necessarily the case? Are there no reasons to let parallel proceedings continue until one proceeding ends, and only then demand that the other stop? Of course, such an approach imposes the 'extra' cost of letting parallel proceedings continue, but as we saw earlier, cost is not that important an issue (except perhaps for very poor countries and some individuals or small and medium sized corporations).[105]

Cost aside, there may be two additional reasons to apply *res judicata* but not *lis pendens*. First, *res judicata* directly preserves the finality of rulings (*l'autorité de la chose jugée*) and the stability and security of the legal system. Allowing parallel proceedings to continue, in contrast, does not upset any past ruling by another court.[106] Second, as the *Soft Drinks* example illustrates, declining jurisdiction on the ground that another proceeding is pending does not necessarily guarantee that the other proceeding will ultimately resolve the dispute. In the *res judicata* context, by definition, the other proceeding has already been completed.[107]

Further, because some international courts and tribunals may take years to resolve a single dispute, it may not be a bad idea to pressure them to expedite their proceedings. Encouraging a race to a ruling (that is, applying *res judicata* only, not *lis pendens*) will be more effective than encouraging a race to court (that is, applying *lis pendens* as well as *res judicata*). A tribunal's decision will prevail

---

103 *Id.* at 48-50.

104 *Id.* at 50; see also Salvioli (1957) 533, 609 (deriving the notion of *lis pendens* from the applicability of a rule of *res judicata*).

105 See *supra* text accompanying notes 9-14.

106 Note that the Appellate Body in *Mexico–Soft Drinks* highlighted that it was 'undisputed that no NAFTA panel as yet has decided the 'broader dispute' to which Mexico has alluded.' Appellate Body Report, *Mexico–Soft Drinks*, *supra* note 32, at ¶ 54.

107 The Permanent Council of International Justice faced an analogous problem in *Factory at Chorzów* and considered that 'the Court, when it has to define its jurisdiction in relation to that of another tribunal, cannot allow its own competency to give way unless confronted with a clause which it considers sufficiently clear to prevent the possibility of a negative conflict of jurisdiction involving the danger of a denial of justice.' Factory at Chorzów, (*F.R.G. v. Pol.*), 1927 P.C.I.J. (ser. A.) No. 9, at 30 (July 26).

– even though the tribunal was seized last – so long as the tribunal's decision comes first.

Taken together, Cuniberti's arguments against *lis pendens* and the previously mentioned reasons in support of applying *res judicata* but not *lis pendens* lead to the conclusion that, in the context of contemporary international law, courts should not automatically apply the principle of *lis pendens* as a preclusion doctrine to resolve overlaps between international proceedings.[108] Put differently, *lis pendens* and its underlying time-based rationale should, at best, be applicable only on a case-by-case basis, on condition that the competing fora are the same or comparable, and other conditions are satisfied. Indeed, other than as a strict preclusion doctrine, the rationale behind *lis pendens* remains useful in at least three ways. First, *lis pendens* considerations may sometimes justify a temporary stay in the proceedings of the second seized court. Second, *lis pendens'* underlying rationale must be stressed as a starting point for the drafting of treaty clauses on forum selection to avoid the multiplication of proceedings. An ongoing procedure should then stop a later one in the event explicit treaty clauses exist to this effect (such as a fork-in-the-road provision that, after all, has *lis pendens* features).[109] Third, *lis pendens* can be one of several factors to be looked at under abstention doctrines or emerging principles of coordination in international law (such as the notion of 'natural forum' discussed here).[110]

In addition, and perhaps most importantly, even if international courts and tribunals were to apply *lis pendens,* the conditions for its application are so strict that, in effect, the principle would rarely ever apply.[111] Specifically, the traditional requirement of full competence – that the earlier court be able to resolve the legal cause of action (*causa petendi*) brought in the later court – would hardly

[108] The *SPP v. Egypt* tribunal put it more bluntly: 'When the jurisdiction of two unrelated and independent tribunals extends to the same dispute, there is no rule of international law which prevents either tribunal from exercising its jurisdiction.' *SPP v. Egypt*, Jurisdiction I, 3 ICSID Reps. 112, 129 (1995) (Nov. 27, 1985). Similarly, the Inter-American Court of Human Rights refused to decline jurisdiction because similar proceedings were pending before the ICJ. The Right to Information on Consular Assistance in the Framework of the Guarantees of the Due Process of Law, 99 Inter-Am. Ct. H.R. (ser. A) No. 16, at 43-45). Further, the Court held that it was an autonomous adjudicator and that conflicting interpretations of one same body of law was the sad consequence of a non-integrated legal system. *Id.*; see also Camouco (*Pan. v. Fr.*), 39 I.L.M. 666, 678 (Int'l. Trib. L. of the Sea 2000), where the ITLOS refused to decline jurisdiction on the ground of *lis pendens* because similar proceedings were pending before French domestic courts. Courts ruled similarly in *Upper Silesia, Holiday Inns* and *SPP v. Egypt*; *but* see *SGS v. Pakistan*, ICSID Case no. ARB/01/03, Decision on Objectiosn to Jurisdiction, and other cases at note 98, *supra.* Although those cases reference differences between international and domestic courts, respectively, the fact remains that, to date, tribunals within the international system are generally less comparable than courts in many domestic systems.

[109] Of course, in this case, the effect of the first proceeding would flow from the treaty clause, and not from the principle of *lis pendens.*

[110] See *infra* Section V.

[111] See *supra* notes 82-90 and accompanying text.

ever apply across international tribunals. To wit: a *causa petendi* before a WTO panel is a claim of violation of a WTO rule, whereas a *causa petendi* before a NAFTA panel it is a claim of violation of a NAFTA rule. Traditional *lis pendens* doctrine would allow parallel proceedings in this case. Applying *lis pendens* then is at best a fig leaf designed to cover cracks in the international system; at worst, it is false judicial deference or comity. Courts or tribunals applying *lis pendens* give the impression of an open mind and readiness to apply general principles but know that they do not apply or do not solve the problem.

Finally, as with *res judicata*, to the extent that *lis pendens* applies as a general principle of law, it would, pursuant to the distinction set out earlier between jurisdiction and admissibility, relate to admissibility, not to jurisdiction.[112] If so, tribunals should not normally consider *lis pendens* unless either party raises it.

C. Forum Non Conveniens

If *lis pendens's* chronological rule fails because it presumes too much similarity between different international fora, *forum non conveniens* – a doctrine that stays or dismisses a proceeding when another forum is more 'convenient'[113] – initially seems to offer a way out. *Forum non conveniens,* however, is not the answer, however. First, because it is almost exclusively known in common law systems and it could be difficult to sell it as a 'general principle of law.'[114]

Second, and more importantly, the original and often decisive criterion for a court to declare itself a *forum non conveniens* are arguments of 'convenience to the parties' such as practical claims of hardship to the defendant, not arguments as to the appropriateness of the court or its proceedings as such. The standard case is an individual or corporation being sued before a foreign court and that court declaring that forcing a foreign defendant to defend itself before it is 'unduly burdensome' (evidence must be moved, witnesses transported, experts in foreign law hired etc.), thereby making the forum 'inappropriate.' Put differently, one of the main reasons to apply *forum non conveniens* is territorial and relates to the physical distance or lack of connection between the defendant and the forum. In inter-state disputes before an international tribunal, this geographical factor is almost irrelevant. As Vaughan Lowe points out

Unlike municipal litigation a move in the location of an inter-state action before an international tribunal does not entail the need to employ experts to

---

[112] Article 35 of the European Convention on Human Rights classifies at least one instance of *lis pendens* – where the application 'has already been submitted to another procedure of international investigation or settlement and contains no relevant new information' – as an issue of admissibility, not jurisdiction. ECHR Art. *35*, *supra* note 46.

[113] See Kwak – Marceau (2006) 480.

[114] But note that civil law traditions often have rules regarding so-called 'related actions,' discussed *infra* notes 144-146. Although these laws share core features of the common law principle of *forum non conveniens,* they derive from statutory provisions may therefore be difficult to reconcile with common law approaches. See Brand – Jablonski (2007) 2 (noting that common law rules presume greater judicial discretion than analogous civil law rules).

handle questions of foreign law, or the need to maintain separate legal teams [...] In inter-state disputes, the lawyers prepare the case; they get on the plane; they get off and they litigate. Where they do it is a matter of little legal significance.[115]

Third, and equally crucial in the domestic context, a court will generally declare itself an 'inconvenient' forum if the alternative, foreign court would have jurisdiction to decide the whole dispute before it.[116] Now, as pointed out earlier, the division of labour among international tribunals is not territorial but functional and/or treaty-based. Hence, even though in, for example, the *Soft Drinks* case one could have argued that NAFTA was a more appropriate forum than the WTO, the WTO could (strictly speaking) only apply *forum non conveniens* if it was sure that the dispute before it could also be decided before NAFTA. Yet, a NAFTA tribunal cannot decide claims of violations of WTO law (and vice versa[117]); and, as pointed out earlier, NAFTA Chapter 20 proceedings are procedurally deficient. In overlaps between a trade tribunal and other specialized international tribunals the problem is even more acute. ITLOS may consider that a dispute is better settled at the WTO; yet, at present, the WTO could never deal with the dispute's claims of violation of UNCLOS; therefore, to refer the case from ITLOS to the WTO based on the principle of *forum non conveniens* as it is known in domestic law, would be impossible. As Cuniberti pointed out: '[i]t would not be permissible, for any adjudicator, to decline jurisdiction without ensuring that the competing adjudicator would have jurisdiction over the whole dispute. Any decision to the contrary would amount to a denial of justice'.[118]

Finally, the principle of *forum non conveniens* in common law systems is a discretionary abstention doctrine, that is, the court has field-jurisdiction over the dispute but decides not to rule on the claims based on propriety considerations. *Forum non conveniens* involves, by definition, a weighing and balancing between the interests of the plaintiff and those of the defendant and the administration of justice more generally. As noted earlier, civil law systems are wary about

---

115 Lowe (1999) 201.

116 This would be the case in most common-law jurisdictions, one exception being Australia. See generally Brand – Jablonski (2007); *Spiliada Maritime Court v. Consulex Ltd* [1987] AC 460; *Gulf Oil Corp. v. Gilbert*, 330 US 501 [1947], and contrast to *Oceanic Sun Line Special Shipping Co. v. Fay* [1988], 165 CLR 197 (Austl) (Deane J), 243.

117 The Appellate Body explicitly pointed this out, noting that 'Mexico also stated that it could not identify a legal basis that would allow it to raise, in a WTO dispute settlement proceeding, the market access claims it is pursuing under the NAFTA' (at para. 54). Indeed, Mexico's alleged right to higher sugar quotas in the U.S. market was only enshrined in NAFTA, not in the WTO. Thus, even where a NAFTA panel would somehow find itself an 'inconvenient' forum, it could not refer the dispute to the alternative tribunal, here the WTO, since the WTO cannot decide on Mexico's sugar quota claims. In such event, the principle of *forum non conveniens* as it is known in domestic law cannot apply.

118 Cuniberti, *supra* note 15, at 421; see also the PCIJ reasoning as in note 107 above, and the *Recommendations on Lis Pendens and Arbitration*, Resolution 1/2006 of the International Law Association, at para. 5.1.

giving this kind of discretion to courts.[119] The same is true for international tribunals where the fear of judges as 'law-makers' is even greater.

For this reason, it was bad strategy for Mexico in the *Soft Drinks* dispute to concede up front that the WTO *had* jurisdiction over the case, and to argue only that the WTO should decline to *exercise* this jurisdiction based on its inherent discretionary powers as a judicial body (not based on admissibility as argued above). In civil law systems, as well as before international tribunals, once a judge *has* jurisdiction, it will be difficult to convince her not to *exercise* it without identifying a legal impediment to such exercise.[120] Not surprisingly, therefore, based on Mexico's defence strategy, the panel in *Soft Drinks* found that 'under the DSU, it had no discretion to decide whether or not to exercise its jurisdiction in a case properly before it.'[121] Mexico should instead have argued that the WTO did not have (or had lost) jurisdiction in the first place, or more precisely and based on the distinction between jurisdiction and admissibility, that the United States was precluded from having a WTO remedy by the operation of NAFTA's fork-in-the-road clause. Put differently, Mexico could have made the case that even though the panel had jurisdiction over the dispute, in these specific circumstances the United States' request was simply not admissible.

The Appellate Body was, fortunately, more careful, finding that, although in this case it saw no reason to decline jurisdiction, it expressed 'no view as to whether there may be other circumstances in which legal impediments could exist that would preclude a panel from ruling on the merits of the claims that are before it.'[122] When concluding, the Appellate Body upheld the panel's ruling that 'under the DSU, it ha[d] no discretion to decline to exercise its jurisdiction in the case that ha[d] been brought before it.'[123] The Appellate Body did leave the door open for future panels to decline jurisdiction or to find jurisdiction and to decide not to exercise it on the ground that the claim is inadmissible by adding that it finds it 'unnecessary to rule in the circumstances of this appeal on the propriety of exercising such discretion.'[124]

There can be no doubt that the U.S. claim of a violation of GATT Article III as it related to the Mexican sweetener tax falls within the field jurisdiction of WTO panels as well as within the terms of reference of the specific *Soft Drinks* panel that decided the case (as defined by the U.S. panel request and DSU Article 7). There is, however, another question, namely, whether there are legal

---

119 *But* see the rules on 'related actions' which do grant judicial discretion, discussed *supra* notes 137-140.

120 Put differently, both before civil law courts as well as international tribunals, it is better to make preclusion arguments ('you do not have jurisdiction' or 'the claim is inadmissible') rather than abstention arguments ('you have jurisdiction but should not exercise it').

121 *Mexico – Soft Drinks* (Panel), ¶¶ 7.1 and 7.18.

122 *Mexico – Soft Drinks* (AB), ¶ 54 (highlighting a *caveat* repeated later in this paragraph as: '[w]e do not express any view on whether a legal impediment to the *exercise* of a panel's jurisdiction would exist in the event that features such as those mentioned above were present') (emphasis added).

123 *Id.* at ¶ 57.

124 *Id.*

impediments which may take away this jurisdiction or preclude the United States from obtaining a ruling on the merits because of the inadmissibility of the claim. It remains to be seen what these legal impediments may be, as well as whether these impediments take away or preclude a panel's jurisdiction as such or whether they only render the claim inadmissible. As discussed earlier, the distinction between jurisdiction and admissibility is commonly upheld by international tribunals and should also find a place in WTO jurisprudence. If so, one of the consequences of classifying, for example, *res judicata* or a forum clause in, say, NAFTA or another FTA, as a claim of inadmissibility (not jurisdiction), is that this claim must be raised by either party and could then not be decided by a WTO panel at its own initiative.

V A Reformulated Forum Non Conveniens Principle: *Le Juge Naturel* or Natural Forum

Notwithstanding the above four arguments[125] that make it difficult to apply *forum non conveniens* to overlaps among international tribunals, *forum non conveniens* does have features that make it attractive in an international context, especially as compared to *lis pendens*.

First, whereas *lis pendens* assumes that the competing tribunals are the 'same' or at least 'comparable' (and, therefore, applies a mechanical time factor), the very reason to apply *forum non conveniens* is that the alternative tribunals are 'different'.[126] More specifically, when *forum non conveniens* is applied, there is substantial evidence that the seized court is not 'convenient' or 'appropriate' as compared to another forum which, by definition, is more convenient and, therefore, quite different.[127] English case law, for example, requires that the foreign forum be clearly and distinctively more appropriate.[128] As discussed earlier, in the newly emerging field of overlapping international tribunals, tribunals are divided on treaty lines and are both substantively and procedurally quite different. The fact that the *forum non conveniens* principle is a rule on overlap between tribunals that are inherently different makes it attractive for application in the current international context (or, at least, more attractive than the mechanical time factor of *lis pendens*). Nonetheless, *lis pendens* would remain relevant to some extent as one of possibly several elements in a *forum non conveniens* analysis. Thus, in cases where multiple forums are considered to be similarly appropriate, an adjudicator could factor the evolution of parallel proceedings elsewhere in the *forum non conveniens* analysis.

125 The four arguments are difficulties stemming from: the common law roots of *forum non conveniens*; that convenience is largely geographical; an alternative forum must be able to decide the whole dispute; and that the principle of *forum non conveniens* implies judicial discretion.

126 Cuniberti (2006) 383.

127 *Id.* at 406.

128 *Spiliada Mar. Corp. v. Cansulex Ltd.*, [1987] 1 A.C. 460, 476-78 (UKHL 1986) (appeal taken from B.C.).

Second, whereas *forum non conveniens* focuses on geographic 'convenience to the parties,' it also considers broader demands of the efficiency in the administration of justice.[129] Such broader elements include, for example, references to connections of the competing adjudicators to the dispute, focusing on which of two international tribunals is 'more appropriate.' Even though *forum non conveniens* traditionally (with the exception of U.S. law) excludes a comparison of the merits of the procedural laws of each adjudicator, the skills of the judges, or the substantive quality of the justice provided (including remedies and enforceability) for overlaps between international tribunals these factors may be worth looking at, especially given the diverse stages of development, institutional contexts, expertise, and levels of legitimacy or support that surround today's panoply of international courts and tribunals.[130]

Finally, the fact that the jurisdiction of most international tribunals is treaty-based – with the result that few overlaps will address the same legal cause of action and, therefore, trigger *res judicata* or *lis pendens* – would not stop the operation of a *forum non conveniens*-type principle, adapted to international law. Indeed, when an English court declares itself as 'inconvenient' to decide a dispute, it need not first assure itself that there is a foreign court which can or is currently examining the dispute under the exact same cause of action.[131] Although the dispute must fall within the jurisdiction of the alternative court, there is no requirement that this court examine the dispute under the same cause of action (unlike for *res judicata* or *lis pendens*). On the contrary, in many cases, before the English court, the cause of action would be English law, and the foreign court would use its own law (unless, of course, either forum applies foreign law). As Cuniberti points out, 'the emphasis is not put on actions or disputes, but on courts and processes.'[132] Once more, this type of overlap between tribunals examining a cause of action that is different makes *forum non conveniens* a principle particularly attractive in an international context.

In sum, if a general principle to regulate overlaps among international tribunals would need to be developed in the medium to long term, the best candidate to use as a starting point would be *forum non conveniens* adapted to the specificities of international law. For those who fear the common law roots of this notion, a different term could be utilized, such as the principle of searching for *le juge naturel* or the 'natural forum' to decide a particular dispute. There is a common quest across legal systems for the *forum conveniens* or the natural forum to decide specific disputes,[133] often defined as the adjudicator 'with which the action ha[s] the most real and substantial connection.'[134] Common law systems

[129] Cuniberti (2006) 383.

[130] *Id.* at 424; see also Ernest A. Young, *Institutional Settlement in a Globalizing Judicial System*, 54 *Duke L.J.* 1143, 1236-43 (2005).

[131] See Cuniberti (2006) 406-07.

[132] *Id.* at 407.

[133] See generally Bell (2003).

[134] *Spiliada Mar. Corp. v. Cansulex Ltd.*, [1987] 1 A.C. 460, 478 (UKHL 1986) (appeal taken from B.C.).

focus on judicial discretion to manage unfair assertions of jurisdiction whereas civil law countries endeavour to establish the natural forum through general jurisdictional organization and protect that forum through the individual guarantee of the independence and impartiality of the court consecrated in the principle of *le juge naturel*.[135] However, one must recognize that establishing *a priori* natural fora in domestic systems is hard, but it may be even harder in international law, as the latter generally lacks traditional connecting factors of a territorial character. Because the struggle for the international *juge naturel* or natural forum is likely to operate on the basis of the subject matter of the dispute, rather than the geographic origin of the relevant facts or the nationality of the parties – and will, therefore, vary case by case – some room for judicial definition of the natural forum in international law seems to be unavoidable. Moreover, because international law is decentralized and jurisdiction is defined by focusing on one tribunal's constitutive instruments, granting some measure of judicial discretion could ease judicial calibration of unfair assertions of jurisdiction.[136]

To further comfort possible critics who may feel that *forum non conveniens*-type rules are wedded to common law systems, it is important to note that many civil law countries have statutory provisions that operate much like *forum non conveniens*, namely rules on so-called 'related actions.'[137] Unlike *forum non conveniens*, rules on 'related actions' can only be triggered when parallel proceedings are pending; yet, like *forum non conveniens*, rules on 'related actions' are triggered even if the cause of action is not the same (it is enough that they are 'related').[138] Similarly, the decision whether or not to stay or relinquish jurisdiction is within the discretion of the judge who can evaluate, *inter alia*, which of the two fora is more convenient or appropriate.[139] Explicit forum selection

135 Dictionnaire de l'Académie Française Dedié au Roi (Jean Baptiste Coignard ed., 1694): '*à qui naturellement, ordinairement et de droit appartient la connaissance d'une affaire.*' See, e.g., International Commission of Jurists, International Principles on the Independence and Accountability of Judges, Lawyers and Prosecutors, A Practitioner's Guide 7-11 (2004); Shetreet (1985).

136 See Michaels (2006) 1003 (contrasting the United States' 'in or out' approach to jurisdiction and the European 'us or them' approach, and arguing that judicial discretion, in the American context, tempers excessive assertions of jurisdiction). According to Michaels, it is this 'externalization' which allows the U.S. to maintain its 'unilateral' posture (at 1037). Analogously, the international law's approach to jurisdiction, which is based on the constitutive instrument of each individual tribunal, might gain, in a context of expanded judicial settlement, from some form of judicial calibration such as *forum non conveniens*.

137 See The French Code of Civil Procedure in English 20, Art. 101 (Nicolas Brooke, trans., 2007) ('If there is a link between matters which are before two different courts, which in the interest of justice requires that they should be determine together, one of the courts may be asked to decline jurisdiction and to refer the whole matter to the other').

138 Cuniberti (2006) 406-07.

139 See Council Regulation 44/2001, Art. 28, 2000 O.J. (L 12) 1.

[W]here related actions are pending in the courts of different Member States, any court other than the court first seized *may* stay its proceedings [...] [f]or the purposes of this Article, actions are deemed to be

clauses[140] and so-called fork-in-the-road clauses[141] similarly regulate 'related' – though not exactly the same – 'actions'.

In sum, further development of any regulating principle such as the natural forum will most likely come hand in hand with a further move on all four of the scales or variables hinted at earlier, especially: (1) from a party-focus to a legality-focus in international dispute settlement; (2) from a regime to a system approach; (3) from consensual to compulsory jurisdiction; and (4) from specific to general jurisdiction. On the basis of such a nascent principle of the 'natural forum,' the history, prior procedures, substantive content and/or core issue in dispute could then make, for example, the WTO or ITLOS the natural forum to decide a specific dispute.[142] Doctrines asserting inherent powers of international tribunals already provide some leeway for declining or asserting jurisdiction (or deciding on the admissibility of a claim)[143] on the basis of *forum non conveniens*-like considerations directed at the subject matter of the dispute. In particular, international tribunals possess the jurisdiction to 'interpret the submissions of the parties' so as to 'isolate the real issue in the case and to identify the object of the claim,'[144] as part of their well-established power to determine their own competence.

related where they are *so closely connected that it is expedient to hear and determine them together to avoid the risk of irreconcilable judgments* resulting from separate proceedings. (emphasis added).

This provision has been described as 'a robust doctrine of *forum non conveniens*' except in that only the second-court seised can apply it. See Von Mehren (2002) 370.

140 ECHR Art. 35, *supra* note 46 ('The [European] Court [of Human Rights] shall not deal with any application submitted under Article 34 that is *substantially the same* as a matter that has already been examined by the Court or has already been submitted to another procedure of international investigation or settlement and contains no relevant new information') (emphasis added).

141 NAFTA, *supra* note 38, at Art. 2005.

[D]isputes regarding *any matter arising under both this Agreement and the [GATT]*, any agreement negotiated thereunder, or any successor agreement (GATT), may be settled in either forum at the discretion of the complaining Party [...] Once dispute settlement procedures have been initiated under Article 2007 or dispute settlement proceedings have been initiated under the GATT, the forum selected shall be used to the exclusion of the other [...] (emphasis added).

142 See Rosenne (2006) 519 ('[T]he true nature of the dispute at hand is the real factor to determine to which court or tribunal a particular dispute should be submitted').

143 For the reasons discussed under *res judicata* and *lis pendens* (*supra* notes 89 and 111), it may, indeed, be more appropriate to classify the principle of *le juge naturel* or the natural forum as one that relates to admissibility rather than jurisdiction.

144 Nuclear Tests (*Austl. v. Fr.*), 1974 I.C.J. 253, 262 at ¶ 29; see also Nuclear Tests (*N.Z. v. Fr.*), 1974 I.C.J. 457, 466, at ¶ 30; Fisheries Jurisdiction (*Spain v. Can.*), 1998 I.C.J. 432, 437.

VI Conclusion

The main purpose of this article is to demonstrate that domestic law principles addressing forum shopping between domestic courts – *res judicata, lis pendens* and *forum non conveniens* – do not resolve potential concerns of forum shopping among international tribunals. Even where these principles apply as 'general principles of law,' the conditions for their application are so strict – especially the requirement that the 'cause of action' be the same – that they will hardly ever be triggered. Indeed, where international tribunals do consider, in particular, *res judicata* or *lis pendens*, one cannot help but think that these principles are merely used as a fig leaf to go ahead and decide the case anyhow. In the short to medium term, the best way to address forum shopping among international tribunals is to regulate overlaps explicitly in the relevant treaties.[145] General principles of law will simply not do. Yet, for these explicit treaty clauses to have effect, international tribunals, including the WTO Appellate Body, must be ready to refer to those clauses even if they were included in a treaty other than the forum treaty.[146] Procedurally, reference to such clauses is possible under objections to admissibility, which are distinct from the question of jurisdiction. Fortunately, the Appellate Body in *Soft Drinks* has left this possibility open.[147] As a result, if a WTO panel is, for example, asked to decide a dispute which was previously brought to NAFTA or MERCOSUR, and the fork-in-the road clause in NAFTA Article 2005:6 or Article 1.2 of the Olivos Protocol applies, the WTO panel should simply apply the fork-in-the road clause agreed to by both parties instead of going through general principles such as *res judicata* or *lis pendens*. Based on such a forum-selection clause, the panel should then decline to rule on the substance of the claims made before it based on the *inadmissibility* of the specific WTO complaint (to be distinguished from the field-*jurisdiction* of the panel over the facts, which remains intact). In addition, even if as a result of the strict conditions for *res judicata* to apply, the decisions of one international tribunal will only rarely preclude proceedings before another, the tribunals should at least exercise mutual deference and comity by staying their

---

[145] See The Olivos Protocol for the Settlement of Disputes in MERCOSUR Art. 1(2), Feb. 18, 2002, 2251 U.N.T.S. A-37341, *NAFTA, supra* note 38, at Art. 2005. See also Consolidated Version of the Treaty Establishing the European Union, Art. 292, 2002 O.J. (C 325) 148; Foreign Investment Protection and Promotion Agreement Art. 13(3), Can.–Thail., Jan. 17, 1997, C.T.S. 1998/29 ('An investor may submit a dispute [...] ' to arbitration 'only if the investor has consented in writing thereto; and the investor has waived its right to initiate or continue any other proceedings [...] '); United Nations Convention on the Law of the Sea Art. 282, Dec. 10, 1982, 1833 U.N.T.S. 397 (underlying the stay in the proceedings in *MOX Plant*); *Waste Management Inc. v. Mex.*, I.C.S.I.D. ARB(AF)/98/2, 15 *Foreign Inv. L.J.* 214, § 27 (2000) (citing *NAFTA, supra* note 38, at Art. 1121).

[146] See generally Pauwelyn, *supra* note 37, at 997-1030.

[147] See Appellate Body Report, *Mexico–Soft Drinks* (2003) ¶ 7.4

proceedings in some cases[148] and avoiding double counting the remedies they award.[149] In the medium- to long-term, if general principles would develop to address forum shopping among international tribunals, the best starting point is a reformulated *forum non conveniens* clause adapted to the requirements of international law. Any notion of the *juge naturel* or natural forum should focus not on mechanical criteria, such as time, but on material criteria, such as connections of the case with a tribunal's jurisdiction, the history, prior procedures, substantive content or core issues in dispute as well as the institutional context, expertise and legitimacy of the respective tribunals.

[148] See *Mox Plant Case* (*Ir. v. U.K.*), Order 3, ¶¶ 14-28 (Perm. Ct. Arb. 2003) (where the Permanent Court of Arbitration opted for a stay in the proceedings pending the resolution of issues of E.C. law, including the possibility that Article 292 of the E.C. Treaty precluded the Permanent Court of Arbitration's jurisdiction in its entirety); see also *Commission of the Eur. Communities. v. Ir.*, Judgment, Court of Justice of the European Communities (Grand Chamber) May 30, 2006, 2006 O.J. (C-459/03); *Southern Pacific Properties Ltd. v. Egypt*, ICSID (W. Bank) ARB/84/3 (1992) (where the ICSID tribunal stayed its proceedings pending a decision of the French *Couer de cassation* based on comity considerations).

[149] See Decision of the Arbitrator, *United States–Tax Treatment for 'Foreign Sales Corporations,'* ¶¶ 6.27-6.30, WT/DS/108/ARB (Aug. 30, 2002) (holding that compensation corresponding to the full amount of the subsidy were 'appropriate countermeasures,' but stating that the determination of 'appropriate countermeasures' should take into account the existence of multiple complainants, whenever this is the case).

Bibliography

G. Abi-Saab, *Les Exceptions Préliminaires dans la Procédure de la Cour Internationale* (1967).

G. Abi-Saab, *Commentaire*, in H. Ruiz Fabri – J.M. Sorel (eds.) *La Preuve devant les Juridictions Internationales* (2007).

R. Alford, 'The Proliferation of International Courts and Tribunals: International Adjudication in Ascendance', [2000/94] *Am. Soc'y Int'l L. Proc.*

H. Alvarez, 'Arbitration Under the North American Free Trade Agreement', [2000/16] *Arb. Int'l.*

C.F. Amerasinghe, *Jurisdiction of International Tribunals* (2003).

A. Bell, *Forum Shopping and Venue in Transnational Litigation* (Oxford, 2003).

M. Bos, *Les conditions du procès en droit international public* (1957).

R.A. Brand – S.R. Jablonski, *Forum non Conveniens: History, Global Practice, and Future under the Hague Convention of Choice of Court Agreements* (OUP, 2007).

H. Briggs, *The Incidental Jurisdiction of the International Court of Justice as Compulsory Jurisdiction*, in K. Zemanek (ed.) *VöLkerrecht und Rechtliches Weltbild Festschrift für Alfred Verdross* (1960).

K. Carlston, *The Process of International Arbitration* (1946).

J. Cogan, *Competition and Control in International Adjudication*, [2007/48] *Vand. J. Int'l L.*

G. Cuniberti, *Parallel Litigation and Foreign Investment Dispute Settlement*, [2006/21] *ICSID Rev.*

A. Fischer-Lescano – G. Teubner, 'Regime-Collissions: The Vain Search for Legal Unity in the Fragmentation of Global Law', [2004/25] *Mich. J. Int'l L.*

G. Fitzmaurice, *The Law and Procedure of the International Court*, vol. 2 (1986).

M. Freudenthal – F. Van Der Velden, *The Netherlands*, in J.J. Fawcett (ed.) *Declining Jurisdiction in Private International Law* (1995).

E.L. Hayes, 'Forum Non Conveniens in England, Australia, and Japan: The Allocation of Jurisdiction in Transnational Litigation' [1992/26] *U. Brit. Col. L. Rev.*

R. Higgins, 'A Babel of Judicial Voices? Ruminations from the Bench' [2006/55] *Int'l & Comp. L.Q.*

A. Hironaka, 'Jurisdictional Theory 'Made in Japan': Convergence of U.S. and Continental European Approaches' [2004/37] *Vand. J. Transnat'l L.*

S. Karagiannis, *La Multiplication des Juridictions Internationales: Un Système Anarchique?*, in *SFDI*, *La juridictionnalisation du droit international* (Lille, 2003).

B. Kingsbury, 'Is the Proliferation of International Tribunals a Systemic Problem?' [1999/31] *N.Y.U. J. Int'l L. & Pol.*

M. Koskenniemi – P. Leino, 'Fragmentation of International Law? Postmodern Anxieties' [2002/15] *Leiden J. Int'l L.*

K. Kwak – G. Marceau, *Overlaps and Conflicts of Jurisdiction between the World Trade Organization and Regional Trade Agreements*, in L. Bartels – F. Ortino (eds.) *Regional Trade Agreements and the WTO Legal System* (2006).

P. Kargados – E. Moustaira, *Greece*, in J. J. Fawcett (ed.) *Declining Jurisdiction in Private International Law* (1995).

N. Lavranos, 'The MOX Plant and the Ijzeren Rijn Disputes: Which Court is the Supreme Arbiter?' [2006/19] *Leid J. Int'l L.*

V. Lowe, 'Res Judicata and the Rule of Law in International Arbitration', [1996/8] *African Y.B. Int'l L.*

V. Lowe, 'Overlapping Jurisdiction in International Tribunals', [1999/20] *Austl. Y.B. Int'l L.*

R. Michaels, *Territorial Jurisdiction after Territoriality*, in P.J. Slot – M. Bulterman (eds.) *Globalisation and Jurisdiction* (2004).

R. Michaels, 'Two Paradigms of Jurisdiction' [2006/27] *Mich. J. Int'l L.*

G. Morelli, 'La Théorie Générale du Procès International' [1937/ 61] *Recueil des Cours III.*

J. Pauwelyn, 'Adding Sweeteners to Softwood Lumber: The WTO-NAFTA 'Spaghetti Bowl' is Cooking' [2001/9] *J. Int'l Econ.* L.

(a) J. Pauwelyn, 'How to Win a World Trade Organization Dispute Based on Non-World Trade Organization Law: Questions of Jurisdiction and Merits' [2003/ 37] *J. Of World Trade.*

(b) J. Pauwelyn, *Conflict of Norms in Public International Law: How WTO-Law Relates to Other Rules of International Law* (2003).

P. Rao, 'Multiple International Judicial Forums: A Reflection of the Growing Strength of International Law or its Fragmentation?' [2004/25] *Mich. J. Int'l L.*

A. Reinisch, 'The Use and Limits of Res Judicata and Lis Pendens as Procedural Tools to Avoid Conflicting Dispute Settlement Outcomes' [2004/3] *L. & Prac. Int'l Cts & Tribunals.*

C. Romano, 'The Proliferation of International Judicial Bodies: The Pieces of the Puzzle' [1999] 31 N.Y.U. *J. Int'l L. & Pol.*

C. Romano, 'The Price of International Justice' [2005/3] *L. & Prac. Int'l Cts. & Tribunals.*

C. Romano, 'The Shift from the Consensual to the Compulsory Paradigm in International Adjudication: Elements for a Theory of Consent' [2007/39] *N.Y.U J. Int'l L. Pol*, 791.

S. Rosenne, *The Law and Practice of the International Court 1920-2004*, vol. 2 (Oxford University Press, USA, 2006).

G. Salvioli, 'Problèmes de Procédure Dans la Jurisprudence Internationale' [1957] 91 *Recueil des Cours.*

Y. Shany, *The Competing Jurisdictions of International Courts and Tribunals* (Oxford University Press, Oxford 2003).

Y. Shany, *Regulating Jurisdictional Relations Between National and International Courts* (2007).

S. Shetreet, *Judicial Independence: New Conceptual Dimensions and Contemporary Challenges*, in S. Shetreet – J. Deschenes (eds.) *Judicial Independence: the Contemporary Debate* (1985).

S. Yee, 'Forum Prorogatum in the International Court' [1999/42] *German Y.B. Int'l L.*

M. Staver, 'The Abstention Doctrines: Balancing Comity with Federal Court Intervention' [1998/28] *Seton Hall L. R.*

I. Van-Damme, *Inherent Powers Of and For the WTO Appellate Body*, Centre for Trade and Economic Integration Working Paper (2008), available at http://www.graduateinstitute.ch/webdav/site/ctei/shared/CTEI/publications/CTEI%20Working%20Papers/WPCTEI-InherentPowersAB29Aug.doc.

A. Von Mehren, 'Theory and Practice of Adjudicatory Authority in Private International Law: A Comparative Study of the Doctrine, Policies and Practices in Common Law and Civil Law Systems' [2002] 295 *Recueil des Cours* (2002).

J.C. Witenberg, 'La Recevabilité des Réclamations devant les Juridictions Internationales' [1932] 41 *Recueil des Cours III.*

CHAPTER 3

In the Court(s) We Trust?

On the Need for Hierarchy and Differentiation in the Preliminary Ruling Procedure*

Jan Komárek**

I Introduction

There is certainly no shortage of articles devoted to the judicial system of the European Union and proposals for its reform, particularly with respect to the preliminary ruling procedure. Although the backlog of cases pending before the Court of Justice has been reduced in the last two years, the present shape of the preliminary ruling procedure cannot be considered satisfactory. This is particularly so with regard to the time it requires. Most of the proposals, made either by academics or various institutions, have rejected one option, which would reduce the Court of Justice's caseload significantly: limiting the procedure to national courts of last instance only. Arguments put forward against this option are many and have considerable weight. Very often, however, they are based on an implicit distrust of national courts and their competence or even willingness to make EU law effective in their respective legal orders.

Contrary to these voices, this article suggests the following:

1) limiting preliminary ruling procedure to courts of last instance as a rule;
2) as a *necessary* exception to 1, when a lower court considers that one or more arguments for invalidity, put forward by the parties or as the case may be raised by it of its own motion, are well founded, it must stay proceedings and make a reference to the Court for a preliminary ruling on the act's validity;
3) as a *possible* exception to 1, the Council can decide which EU law measures may be subject to preliminary references from lower courts.

The article therefore opposes a recent Commission's Communication,[1] which illustrates well the prevailing attitude to the preliminary ruling procedure.

* This article was first published by Sweet & Maxwell in *European Law Review*, (2007), 32 , 4 , 467-491 and is reproduced by agreement with the Publishers.

** Somerville College, The University of Oxford. Many people have helped with their stimulating comments in the course of the writing and I would like to thank Michal Bobek, Tomáš Boček, Petr Bříza, Paul Craig, Gareth Davies, Xavier Groussot, Zdeněk Kühn, Koen Lenaerts, Zuzana Maršálková, Martin Mörk, Sean O'Toghda, Jan Passer, Daniel Sarmiento, Imola Streho, Jana Šamánková, Stephen Weatherill and Adrian Zuckerman, as well as the participants in a discussion circle at the University of Oxford, a seminar at the University of Lund and a conference entitled 'The Treaty of Rome – 50 Years On!' organised by the British Centre for English Legal Studies, Warsaw University, where I presented various drafts of the article. Finally, I would like to thank to this Review's editors for their helpful suggestions when finalizing the article. Some of the people mentioned here would disagree with quite a few of the ideas presented in the article and all errors and opinions, of course, remain my own. Comments are welcome at jankomarek@centrum.cz.

1 'Adaptation of the provisions of Title IV of the Treaty establishing the European Community relating to the jurisdiction of the Court of Justice with a view to ensuring more effective judicial protection', COM(2006) 346 final, hereafter 'the Communication.' The Court of Justice issued two discussion papers related to the Communication, both available at <http://www.curia.europa.eu/en/instit/txtdocfr/index.htm>, hereafter 'the Discussion Paper' and 'the Discussion Paper Supplement'.

The Communication proposes to make the ordinary Article 234 EC preliminary reference procedure fully applicable to the provisions of Title IV of the EC Treaty. Title IV encompasses provisions dealing with visas, and asylum and immigration policies, together with judicial cooperation in civil matters. Today, the jurisdiction of the Court of Justice in this field is limited and only courts of last instance may refer preliminary questions.[2] The Communication resulted in a proposal for a Council decision, which should make Article 234 EC fully applicable in Title IV. The main argument on which the Commission bases its proposal is a need for uniformity of EC law, effective judicial protection of individuals' rights, and trust in the proper functioning of the Court of Justice, which according to the Commission is now prepared to cope with its inevitably increased caseload.

The Commission's proposal is based on a prevailing, but certainly not the only possible conception of the Union judicial system; a conception, which sees the Court of Justice as the superior and exclusive judicial institution for making the EU legal system functional. This understanding distrusts national courts, when it turns the preliminary ruling procedure from a tool for achieving unity and coherence of EU law to a mechanism for the judicial protection of individuals. At the same time, the goal of uniformity is pushed to absurdity and serves as a justification of the Court of Justice's excessive intervention into the national judicial process. As will be shown, due to its structural characteristics the preliminary ruling procedure can never serve these aims properly, although the Court of Justice itself contributes to this expectation, largely supported by the legal doctrine.[3]

This article offers an alternative conception of the EU judicial system: a conception which sees national courts as *true* parts of the EU judicial system. Too often national judges are only reminded of their Union mission when obligations in the name of effective application of EU law are imposed upon them. But this mission must also entail more trust in them, as well as a consideration of problems which these obligations may cause to national judicial processes. National and Union judicial processes are connected vessels and problems at one level inevitably cause problems at another.

This article sees hierarchy as an important element of any judicial process, which makes the process rational and effective. The current preliminary ruling procedure undermines national judicial hierarchies when it allows any court to enter into a dialogue with the Court of Justice. While this openness certainly played an important role in the formative years of the EU legal order, maintaining it today seems less justified. The alternative conception of the preliminary ruling procedure would thus suggest limiting the possibility to refer prelimi-

[2] Article 68 EC.

[3] For a thoughtful critique of the Court of Justice's distrust of national courts' independent application of EU law see Gareth Davies, 'Abstractness and concreteness in the preliminary ruling procedure: implications for the division of powers and effective market regulation', in: Shuibhne (2006). Davies calls this 'infantilising and marginalising the role of national courts in interpreting Community law' (p. 212).

nary rulings to last instance courts only, as is now the case in Title IV matters. Hence 'the need for hierarchy'.

In addition, the preliminary ruling procedure covers too divergent types of judicial procedures concerning various fields of substantive law. It does not distinguish whether it arises in a criminal procedure, where the rights of individuals must be particularly carefully treated, a dispute between two undertakings, which concern a considerable amount of money, or a matter of constitutional importance. This calls for a 'differentiation', which in certain cases makes desirable the allowing of references from lower courts as well and in some cases inserting a truly expedited procedure, not a procedure which takes almost the same time as an ordinary one.[4] The article asks whether we trust courts and is intentionally formulated ambiguously. It also asks whether we should trust the Court of Justice's ability to fulfil the role ascribed to it by the EU founding treaties. At the same time, the article examines whether we sufficiently trust national courts as European courts.

The article will proceed as follows: Firstly it will take issue with arguments presented against limitation of the preliminary ruling procedure to last instance courts only (part II). It will be seen that these arguments often contain much deeper normative claims, which are not discernible on the surface. Identifying them will help clarify the debate about the Union judiciary, and focus it on the real issues instead of slogans. After this, the Court of Justice's improved efficiency will be critically assessed (part III). Finally, after providing an account of the Court of Justice's role and showing why hierarchy is important in securing efficiency of the judicial system, a more detailed proposal on how the preliminary reference should look will be provided (part IV).

II Arguments against Limitation of the Preliminary Ruling Procedure to Last Instance Courts

This part will discuss the main arguments put forward against limitation of the preliminary ruling procedure to the last instance courts only. As will be seen, too often are some concepts used in the debate without their being critically examined. The following hopes to clarify these concepts in order to steer the debate to the real issues posed by the limitation of the Court of Justice's jurisdiction in the preliminary ruling procedure.

a) Uniformity and authority of EU law

Uniformity is like a magic formula, preventing many proposals on decentralization of the preliminary ruling procedure. Consider the following words used by the Court of Justice:

---

4 See part III. a) *infra*.

> Any weakening, even if only potential, of the uniform application and interpretation of Community law throughout the Union would be liable to give rise to distortions of competition and discrimination between economic operators, thus jeopardizing equality of opportunity as between those operators and consequently the proper functioning of the internal market. One of the Court's essential tasks is to ensure just such a uniform interpretation, and it discharges that duty by answering the questions put to it by the national courts and tribunals. The possibility of referring a question to the Court of Justice must therefore remain open to all those courts and tribunals.[5]

The first problem arising here is what the Court of Justice means by uniformity. Is it an *absolute* 'sameness', suggested by the warning that even potential weakening of uniformity could have disastrous consequences for the internal market? If so, it would make EU law indeed unique, since no legal system can achieve such a degree of uniformity as the Court of Justice suggests. Practices of the highest national courts show that this cannot be the case. As Chalmers puts it:

> Unity of interpretation does not mean that the highest court should provide rulings on every provision. Within most national legal systems, higher national courts, with far more wide-ranging jurisdictions, guarantee the unity and ordered development of their legal systems through setting out a number of steering judgments each year, which define the hallmarks of that legal order and guide other actors in how to apply the law.[6]

One important note must be made here. There are some supreme courts,[7] whose caseload is not controlled by any means. The most extreme example is the Italian Supreme Court, *Corte di Cassazione*, which must decide every case arising before it as a matter of constitutional right, guaranteed to all citizens.[8] Consequently, this court decides about 12 000 civil cases and 35 000 criminal cases a year. For such a task it is composed of 400 judges. However, it would be erroneous to think that the *Corte di Cassazione*'s massive intervention in the judicial system's operation achieves greater uniformity of law. To the contrary: '[an] essay concerning conflicts [judgments] in civil matters, which consider[ed] only five years and judgments published by 12 legal journals, show[ed] that the court ha[d] fallen into contradiction no less than 864 times.'[9] More 'precedents' simply does not mean more uniformity.

---

5 Report of the Court of Justice on certain aspects of the application of the Treaty on European Union, 1995, point 11.

6 Chalmers (2004) 22.

7 *E.g.* Italy, Spain or Poland. However, civilian systems also have adopted some measures to limit access to its supreme courts. See Taruffo (1997) 445-446.

8 See Taruffo – Torre (1997) 144.

9 *Ibid* at p. 165.

The example of the U.S. Supreme Court also shows that striving for uniformity through case law does not mean that the Supreme Court decides every case brought forth. The Supreme Court sometimes leaves the lower or State (!) courts to work out a new rule and intervenes only after some decisions have significantly differed among these courts. As (now former) Justice O'Connor says:

> While uniformity is a necessary and desirable goal, its immediate achievement is not always possible. Nor is immediate action necessarily desirable. Part of the beauty of our federalism is the diversity of viewpoint it brings to bear on legal problems. State court judges may have a different approach to a problem than might a federal judge; the lessons that can be learned from being a judge in one part of our country will not be immediately obvious to those who have always lived, practiced, and judged in another part. [...] When those courts encounter an unresolved question of federal law, their differing perspectives may lead them to different conclusions. The resulting divergence provides a valuable moment in the law -- a moment of dialogue among different jurists in which they may share their views on a common issue. There can be no doubt that the dialogue is a profitable one or that the Court on which I sit listens to the voices in the debate.[10]

Problems stem from an unclear meaning of uniformity in general. Whereas uniformity is used as a part of law's rhetoric, the examples above show that virtually no legal system may ever achieve it. Recently, the very dogma of uniformity in Community law application has started to be questioned, most prominently by Dougan, who advocates a differentiated approach to the system of national remedies, which would reflect regulatory differentiation that is real in certain sectors of Community policy.[11] What may be added to Dougan's arguments is that no legal system, even unitary, achieves or even aims at uniformity in such absolute terms as Community law claims (but necessarily fails to provide) for itself.[12] All mechanisms of case filtration existing in various jurisdictions confirm this regardless of the criteria these mechanisms adopt – it means that some questions are not important enough to be decided by the supreme interpretative authority of the system. Why should the Community legal system be different?

The argument of uniformity in fact contains far more than the need for coherent legal order. Dyberg's words explain it a little: 'Uniform application is rather a sort of existential problem to which the Community legal order has to relate.'[13] To see the importance of this 'existential problem,' we must understand what uniformity may actually mean for a legal system: '[I]n the national legal

---

[10] O'Connor (1994) 181-82.

[11] See Dougan, (2004) 113-226.

[12] See Chalmers (2004) 22-23.

[13] Dyberg (2001) 295.

systems, uniform application is mostly taken for granted.'[14] As we know, it is not necessarily always true, but the core of this assertion lies in the fact that there is a *presumption of uniformity* in the national law. The fact that we do not even think what uniformity really means only confirms how deeply we connect it with a functional legal order in which we are used to live. On the other hand, EU law must fight for these *presumptions* being attached to it in the national legal orders. Only then may it claim its authoritative status of the law of the land.

The control over national courts' practices regarding EU law is another element underlying the Court of Justice's desire for uniformity. The Court of Justice is not greatly troubled about EU law being applied with some discrepancies before various national courts. After all, the Court of Justice itself contributes to non-uniform application of EU law in certain areas. Chalmers gives an example of the state regulation of gambling and its relationship to the internal market freedoms, where the Court has been giving inconsistent answers in almost every judgment it delivered,[15] but other examples could certainly be found as well. In some cases the Court of Justice even denied creating a uniform rule, although this was badly needed and asked for.[16] Thus uniformity cannot be the main concern. The Court rather fears that EU law would not be applied at all. The strong (and unrealistic) strive for uniformity serves as a justification for the Court of Justice's involvement in cases of minor importance for EU legal order as a whole, where an ordinary supreme court in a mature system of law would never intervene. This intervention does not aim at uniformity, but supremacy of Union law.[17]

For a better understanding of this aspect of the Court of Justice's construction of the notion of uniformity, which in fact serves as a justification for its broad involvement in national courts' decision-making activity, the U.S. concept of 'federal question jurisdiction' may provide some insights. The federal jurisdiction clause in the U.S. Constitution determines what kinds of cases may be heard before federal instead of state courts.[18] Justification for federal jurisdiction is based on three considerations: more experience of federal judges to deal with federal law, hope of uniformity in application of federal law, and finally, more solicitude for its proper application than could be expected from state courts

---

14 *Ibid.*

15 Chalmers (2004) 23.

16 Consider *e.g.* a distinction between discriminatory and non-discriminatory obstacles to the free movement, important for their possible justification (whether it is possible on express grounds enlisted in the Treaties only or on the case-law based justifications as well). Advocate General F. Jacobs in his opinion in Case C-136/00 *Danner* [2002] ECR I-8147 expressly pointed out the two lines of cases, each of them leading to different results, and invited the Court to clarify the correct application. The Court, however, did not respond to his call.

17 This point is nicely proven in a recent contribution of Lenaerts – Corthaut (2006) 289-291, where they argue for the supremacy of the second and third pillar EU law from uniformity.

18 U.S. Const. Art. III, § 2, cl. 1.

judges.[19] So it is not only the need for correct application of federal law (hence 'experience'), nor uniformity which justifies jurisdiction of federal courts in certain cases. One limb of the justification for federal jurisdiction lies in the protection of federal law from unfaithful treatment by state courts. A similar point can be made in a historical perspective: 'Historically, Congress' regulation of the Supreme Court's jurisdiction in relation to the state courts demonstrates a congressional perception that the Supreme Court's main role is to ensure the supremacy rather than the uniformity of federal law.'[20] The Court of Justice, by its broadly construed construction of uniformity, does the same.

However, this is rooted in the Court of Justice's distrust in national higher courts. Of course, there are examples where some supreme courts failed to refer important questions to the Court of Justice or even ignored its rulings. The most famous would probably be the French *Conseil d'Etat*, which did not recognize the direct effect of directives for a considerable period of time.[21] This may be true, but the remedy for this situation was certainly not the possibility of the lower courts sending preliminary references to the Court of Justice. It was the *Conseil d'Etat* itself which eventually changed its attitude and confirmed that directives may have a direct effect in its celebrated *Nicolo* decision.[22] Even if lower courts could send references to the Court of Justice, asking whether directives were or were not directly effective, it was ultimately the *Conseil d'Etat* which determined whether this would be true in France (or before French administrative courts at least, as the *Cour de Cassation* took a different approach).[23] Similarly, in the case of the German *Bundesfinanzhof*, it was the Federal Constitutional Court *(Bundesverfassungsgericht)* which made this court accept the same doctrine,[24] regardless of the Court of Justice's unequivocal response to a reference coming from a lower court,[25] since the *Bundesfinanzhof* quashed its decisions.[26] The highest courts hold a veto power over the Court of Justice's rulings within their legal orders[27] and lower courts have only limited means to change it.

Another response, which could satisfy those who share this sceptical approach to national supreme courts, is the fact that the Court of Justice now has a greater control over supreme courts than ever before.[28] A national judge is no more immune from causing liability of the state – either in relation to individuals or the Community in infringement proceedings. This stems from the

---

19 See *Grable & Sons Metal Products Inc. v. Darue Engineering & Manufacturing Co.*, 125 U.S. 2363 (2005) at p. 2368.

20 Wallace (1983) 917.

21 Judgment of 22.12. 1978, *Minister of the Interior v. Daniel Cohn-Bendit* [1980] 1 C.M.L.R. 543.

22 Judgment of 20.10. 1989, *Raoul Georges Nicolo and Another* [1990] 1 C.M.L.R. 173.

23 See Claes (2006) 224-231.

24 Judgment of 8.4. 1987 *Kloppenburg* [1988] 3 C.M.L.R. 1.

25 Case 70/83 *Kloppenburg* [1984] ECR 1075.

26 Judgment of 16.6. 1981 [1982] 1 C.M.L.R. 527. See on the story Claes (2006) 429-431.

27 Chalmers (1997) 180.

28 See generally Komárek (2005).

recent case law of the court in *Köbler*[29] and *Commission v. Italy*.[30] Although viability of the principles set in these judgments may be seriously questioned, their power lies outside actual cases where they could be successfully invoked – it lies in their dissuasive effects. Parties may use them to warn national judges not to disregard EU law[31] and it seems that Court of Justice judges themselves never let slip an opportunity to remind their national counterparts of these judgments, of course, in an atmosphere of sincere cooperation and mutual understanding.[32] Equally, although the Commission will scarcely (if ever) pursue a case of infringement based on judicial breaches ultimately to the Court of Justice, it may use *Commission v. Italy* as a precedent to dissuade the Member States. Actually, Sweden has recently had to change its rules of civil procedure and, whenever a court dismisses an appeal without referring to the Court of Justice although parties have sought this, it must give reasons.[33]

Having hopefully satisfied sceptics, this article is nevertheless based on a different approach: on the real trust in national courts. The instances of national highest courts' open rebellions against the Court of Justice have been few, although they (regrettably) serve as perfect evidence for anyone wishing to point them out as proofs of the danger of our trusting in these courts. It is submitted, however, that in most instances when these courts did not send references to the Court of Justice, they acted thus for good reasons. As Chalmers suggests:

> Even a brief perusal of the cases suggests this was not some systematic rejection of the Court of Justice's authority. The overwhelming majority of cases involved significant commercial interests where speedy resolution and legal certainty were considered to be particularly important. If a matter was not general and important, national courts of last resort do not refer.[34]

Reports from the Conference of the national Supreme Administrative Courts seem to confirm this.[35] These courts know that their main objective is to solve the disputes brought to them by the parties rather than create a new legal order in sincere cooperation with the Court of Justice, which means that some questions remain without their reference.

One may object that such confidence is no longer possible in times where in 2004 ten Member States acceded to the Union. It is accurate to say that these

[29] Case C-224/01 *Köbler* [2003] ECR I-10239.

[30] Case C-129/00 *Commission v. Italy* [2003] ECR I-14637.

[31] See *e.g.* Drijber (2004) 35.

[32] See *e.g.* contribution of Jann (2005) or contribution of Skouris (2004).

[33] See Bernitz (2006).

[34] Chalmers (2004) 34.

[35] This was discussed by the Association of the Councils of State and Supreme Administrative Jurisdictions of the European Union at its 19th Colloquium. See the General Report from the Colloquium, <http://193.191.217.21/colloquia/2004/gen_report_en.pdf> at pp. 71-73.

Member States' judiciaries still meet serious problems.[36] However (although it involves some measure of an informed guess rather than empirically based evidence), these courts do not contest the authority of EU law or the Court of Justice. One should not be misled by some constitutional courts' rhetoric used in the judgments in which they define the relationship of their constitutions to EU law. The rhetoric is intended for internal discourse. What these courts *actually* show is their respect for obligations arising from EU law.[37]

In sum, whether or not we take an optimistic approach towards the highest national courts, there are no longer any good reasons for allowing the lower courts to circumvent their authority, either because the EU has the mechanisms for making disobedient courts toe the line or because there is no reason to believe that these courts' intention be to compromise the Court of Justice's authority in a systematic manner.

b) Judicial protection of individuals and economy of the judicial process

Effective judicial protection of individuals together with procedural economy is a second powerful argument against reserving preliminary reference procedure to last instance courts. The time and effort of private litigants is said to justify the direct link of even the lowest courts to the Court of Justice. However, the very same argument may be used the other way round: preliminary ruling procedure considerably delays the final judgment and causes additional costs. So where to strike the balance?

One thing should be made clear: while the preliminary ruling procedure may serve individual justice in a *wider* perspective, by guiding national courts in their application of EU law, and thus making the whole system deciding more correctly and just, it can never systematically provide justice in every single case. Chalmers suggests that the problem of the Court of Justice's caseload would be particularly acute in the Area of Freedom, Security and Justice, as it 'will no longer cover narrow fields of law, which rarely generate matters of headline-generating sensitivity. It will now dominate the heartlands of domestic judicial activity and intrude regularly into areas of acute national sensitivity.'[38] This would mean even more references sent to the Court of Justice. To propose widening the scope of Article 234 EC to Title IV of the EC Treaty, as the current Commission's proposal does, is to ignore this. To the contrary, limitation of the Court of Justice's jurisdiction should be seriously considered.

A potentially powerful argument against limiting lower courts' competence to ask the Court of Justice lies in the possible threat to the economy of national procedure. The argument goes that a party would have to climb the judicial hierarchy to the point where there was no appeal for its being allowed to raise its EU

---

[36] See *e.g.* Kühn, '*Worlds Apart. Western and Central European Judicial Culture at the Onset of the European Enlargement*' [2004/52] *Am.J.Comp.L.* 531.

[37] See Sadurski, (2006). For an excellent overview of the ordinary courts' practice in the Member States, which acceded in 2004, see Bobek (2006) 3.

[38] Chalmers (2004) 16.

law arguments before a court with the ultimate authority to hear them and make a decision. However, this presumes that every question of EU must be dealt with by the Court of Justice, and disregards the fact of the same painful exercise the parties must undertake if they whish to get the national supreme court to clarify some important point of purely national law. Why should the litigants, playing the 'EU law card', be treated differently?

It must be stressed that such an exercise in the appellate procedure may significantly reduce the number of instances where the top of the system is eventually reached. And this is exactly the point. Only if the litigants are sure of their claim and the lower courts have not persuaded them of the correctness of their judgment, have they sufficient incentives to undertake the whole appellate exercise. The effect of this is fewer cases of greater importance arising before the supreme court. It is painful, no doubt, but it is a necessary price for the judicial system's effective functioning. The only possible exceptions to the hierarchical organization of the judicial procedure are perhaps referrals to constitutional courts existing in some legal systems. But these concern the most fundamental questions of constitutionality and not *e.g.* the tariff classification of pyjamas.[39] The attempt to attach fundamental status to every provision of EU law is contradicting the premise that EU law has become part of national law. If it has, then EU law can no longer be treated as 'supranational' law having some special force in each instance, rather must the weight of its rules reflect their actual nature.

Preliminary ruling procedure must be seen as a deviation from normal organization of the judicial process, not as its natural component. This is because it allows obviating the existing hierarchy amongst the courts, which plays an important role in the rationalization of the judicial process,[40] and delays final resolution of the dispute, thus potentially bringing an element of injustice. Again, it is a question of how we want to see the EU judicial system: whether it really comprises national courts *as* European courts, or whether we use this label only for highlighting their obligations resulting from EU law. If we see it in the former sense, than we must accept that it means to see the EU judiciary as a judicial system without qualifications. Nice labels may only hide some (of course hard) choices we must inevitably make when we perceive national courts as 'Community courts of general jurisdiction'[41] – thus fully competent to decide questions concerning interpretation of EU law. Insisting on all courts' possibility to refer to the Court of Justice questions their competence to give effective protection to individuals without the Court of Justice's assistance. At the same time, it implies that the Court should be involved in an everyday dispute settlement whenever a question of Community law arises, regardless of its importance for the EU legal system as a whole. The result is an unreasonable distri-

39 The 'Pyjama Case' (Case C-338/95 *Wiener* [1997] ECR I-6495) is the famous one, where Advocate General Jacobs proposed that the Court of Justice change its criteria for obligatory references.

40 On the role of hierarchies in national judicial systems see part IV b) *infra*.

41 Case T-51/89 *Tetra Pak* [1990] ECR II-309, para. 42, cited in Claes (2006) 3.

bution of the Court of Justice's judicial capacity throughout the Union judicial system.

Moreover, one may doubt whether the preliminary ruling procedure can truly be considered to serve individual justice, if the Court of Justice itself holds that 'Article 234 EC establishes direct cooperation between the Court and the courts and tribunals of the Member States by way of a non-contentious procedure excluding any initiative of the parties, who are merely invited to be heard in the course of that procedure'.[42] So, individual rights are said to be at stake before the Court of Justice, but those to whom these rights pertain are 'merely invited to be heard', not to defend their case, with all the consequences which would follow from this (such as the right to defence, the right to be heard or, more broadly, the right to a fair trial). Such a dismissive attitude to the parties is particularly striking if we realize that, in references concerning alleged invalidity of a Community measure, it is solely the Court of Justice which may decide. So far the European Court of Human Rights has taken a very benevolent attitude, *e.g.* when it did not take into account the time necessary for the preliminary procedure on assessing whether the final judgment of a Greek court which referred to the Court of Justice was excessively delayed.[43] It is an open question whether this did not change after the ECHR confirmed the importance of the preliminary ruling procedure in the system of judicial protection of the EU in *Bosphorus v. Ireland*.[44] The Human Rights Court, however, clearly misrepresented the standing of individuals in the preliminary ruling procedure, when it said that '[t]he parties to the domestic proceedings have the right to put their case to the Court of Justice during the Art. [234] process. It is further recalled that national courts operate in legal systems into which the Convention has been incorporated, albeit to differing degrees.' No such right exists, at least as a matter of Community law, and the Court of Justice has confirmed this on several occasions.

There should, however, be room for at least one exception allowing lower courts' preliminary references. Individuals who believe that their rights have been violated by a Community measure adopted under Title IV must now, according to *Foto-Frost*,[45] go through the national judicial hierarchy to the court of last instance to be able to plead invalidity before a court solely competent to review Community measures: the Court of Justice. Many rightly criticize this[46] and there are no compelling reasons to prevent lower courts from questioning validity of Community law in cooperation with the Court of Justice.

Allowing the lower courts to do so does not contradict the approach suggested here, an approach which promotes rational distribution of the Court of Justice's judicial capacity by limiting its jurisdiction to cases of importance for

[42] Case C-496/04 *Slob*, not yet reported, para. 34.

[43] Case *Pafitis v. Greece* [1999] 27 E.H.R.R. 566, para. 95.

[44] Case *Bosphorus v. Ireland* [2006] 42 E.H.R.R. 1, para. 164.

[45] Case 314/85 *Foto-Frost* [1987] ECR 4199.

[46] See Claes (2006) 578-583 with further references and Communication, p. 5.

the legal system. Questions of validity are without a doubt important. Moreover, *Foto-Frost* does not imply that the national court must refer every single case, which raises doubts about the validity of a Community measure. If the national court is not convinced by arguments claiming invalidity, it may decide without the Court of Justice's assistance.[47] The exclusion of lower courts from referring questions concerning validity of Community measures goes in the opposite direction to the Court of Justice's construction of the Community system of remedies reinforced in *Unión de Pequeños Agricultores v. Council*;[48] this restricts individuals' direct access to the Court of Justice and refers them to national courts, which are then obliged to ask the Court for a preliminary ruling. The system of individuals' effective judicial protection becomes even more illusory if there is no possibility for national courts to refer the question of validity to the Court of Justice. These courts may only invite the parties to appeal to a higher court (competent to turn to the Court of Justice) in order to obtain a judgment, which the deciding lower court itself believes to be right or just.

In addition to this exception, it may be considered that in some cases the exclusion of lower courts from the preliminary ruling procedure compromises economy of the judicial process as a whole. The Brussels regulation[49] is a perfect example since it is a basic principle to determine jurisdiction of a court at the earliest stage of the procedure possible so that judicial resources are not wasted in producing a decision, which would eventually be annulled because an incompetent court had delivered it.[50]

Judicial protection of individuals and procedural economy therefore may justify allowing in certain instances references from lower courts. This should however be the exception and not the rule, as it is today.

c) Broader considerations concerning the role of lower courts in the development of EU law

The last set of arguments concerns the overall role of lower courts in the development of EU law. It is asserted that almost three fourths of all references come from these courts and that without these references the Court of Justice would have no possibility of creating the doctrines now widely accepted as most fundamental for the Community legal order. It has been claimed that it is a kind of tradition to allow all courts to enter into a dialogue with the Court of Justice. From the point of view of national legal orders, it has been argued that 'the ability of any national court or tribunal to refer has been of importance in emphasizing the penetration of EC law to all points of the national legal system.'[51] These are strong arguments which touch the more fundamental questions concerning

47 See *e.g.* recently Case C-344/04 *International Air Transport Association*, not yet reported, paras. 27-32.

48 Case C-50/00 P *Unión de Pequeños Agricultores v. Council* [2002] ECR I-6677.

49 Council Regulation (EC) No 44/2001 of 22 December 2000 on jurisdiction and the recognition and enforcement of judgments in civil and commercial matters, OJ 2001, L 12, p. 1.

50 This principle can be derived by analogy from Case 34/82 Peters [1983] ECR 987, para. 17.

51 Craig (2001) 196.

the role of lower courts in the European legal integration project – similarly as with the 'hidden' core of the argument from uniformity, discussed above. But still, the arguments are not as incontestable as they may seem.

The argument regarding the number of references is easy to rebut – the very aim of our proposal is to make the Court of Justice's caseload more reasonable. Similarly, lower courts do not have to feel isolated from EU law by its being impossible for them to consult the Court of Justice. Today, it is almost impossible to find a field of national law untouched by EU law. Not only are judges much better educated, so are the parties who invoke EU law before these lower courts – which are often not competent enough and would rather send a reference to Luxembourg, pressed by the parties' advocates, than try to find for themselves the correct response to the problem posed by EU law. This need to find an answer without the possibility of easily avoiding the problem by referring it to the Court of Justice would be 'a most valuable training ground, and [would] be a development in conformity with the principle of subsidiarity'[52] and not a step isolating lower courts from all EU law. It would only highlight their responsibility as Community courts of general jurisdiction, by signalling that finding solutions based on EU law is not only work for the Luxembourg oracle, but also for them.

Whether the development of EU law would be threatened by limiting preliminary references to the highest courts is only questionable – first, because it cannot be excluded that an 'important' preliminary reference from a lower court would reach the Court of Justice as a reference from a higher court too. Second, all depends on how we define 'important' questions. It has been proposed elsewhere that preliminary references are 'another infant disease' of the Community legal order.[53] It may well be the time to reflect on whether we need the Court of Justice to give a ruling on the interpretation of every provision of EU law that we can think of or whether its role should be more that of a genuine Supreme and Constitutional Court of the Union, in a more mature legal system. The latter view is well characterised by Advocate General Jacobs:

> [T]he Court's primary task in preliminary rulings is not to decide specific cases on the basis of narrowly distinguished facts, or to solve a problem for the national court in the particular case, but to state clearly and coherently for the benefit of everyone in the Community what the correct understanding of the law is, and to give rulings of general significance. It is only that broader function which justifies the system of preliminary rulings and explains the unique procedure whereby Member States and the Commission are systematically invited to submit observations and indeed why the judgment of the Court and the Opinion of the Advocate General in every case are published in no fewer than 11 languages.[54]

---

52 Rasmussen (2000) 1107.

53 Allot (2000).

54 Opinion of Advocate General F. Jacobs in Case C-136/00 *Danner* [2002] ECR I-8147, para. 38.

This article reflects this appeal. Unfortunately, the Court of Justice seems to be heading in the opposite direction.

III Efficiency of the Court of Justice

a) 'Trust in the proper functioning of the Court of Justice' – through the looking glass

In its Communication, the Commission considers that 'the Court, the efficiency of the means of internal organization which it now enjoys and the new possibilities created by the Nice Treaty must be trusted.'[55] The President of the Court of Justice is similarly optimistic about the increasing effectiveness of the Court of Justice.[56] Should we therefore still care about the caseload in the preliminary ruling procedure?

The Communication highlights the fact that 'the Court has managed to significantly reduce the average duration of preliminary ruling proceedings.'[57] However, the Commission fails to add that, since 1 May 2004, the Court has had 10 more judges while the number of cases arising from the new Member States (taking into account all kinds of cases, not only preliminary references) has remained insignificant. Thus the celebrated 3.1-month reduction in the length of proceedings in preliminary references[58] may be easily explained by the fact that there were more judges to decide almost the same number of cases. It is doubtful whether this is a systemic change that will outlast the new Member States courts' shyness about making preliminary references and/or new litigants' lack of experience in using Community courts. Moreover, even 20.4 months of the preliminary ruling procedure is far too much time in some cases where a speedy solution is particularly needed.

The Commission refers to the special procedures, which in its opinion allow closing the case faster than usual. Alas, a closer look at the practice of the Court of Justice and the results of this practice suggest something *very* different. The expedited procedure pursuant to Article 104a of the Rules of Procedure cannot be used as a tool which the Court may use in urgent cases where individual justice or the need for a speedy procedure are at stake – for example criminal procedures where the person concerned awaits the court's judgment in custody, cases of asylum seekers who must often wait for a decision while their personal liberty is restricted or economic operators seeking speedy judgment in order to not be put out of business. Out of 26 cases where the referring court asked

55 Communication at p. 8.

56 See Skouris (2006) 21-22.

57 Communication at p. 8.

58 The Commission refers to the Court's press release No. 14/06 of 13 February 2006, 'Statistics concerning judicial activity in 2005 – consolidation and continuation of the progress recorded in 2004', available at <http://www.curia.europa.eu/en/actu/communiques/cp06/info/cp060014en.pdf>.

for an expedited procedure, the Court satisfied only one request,[59] which is the result of a particularly restrictive standard.[60] It is true that the Court could relax the standard, but Article 104a of the Rules of Procedure itself speaks about granting the expedited treatment only in matters of *exceptional* urgency. In other words, expedited treatment cannot be a rule – otherwise the provision would lose its meaning. Thus it cannot be considered as a systemic remedy for the length of proceedings before the Court of Justice.[61]

Another suggested solution, the simplified procedure, which in accordance with Article 104(3) of the Rules of Procedure allows the Court of Justice to decide by a reasoned order, does not seem to be a real solution either, although it is considered to be more promising than the expedited procedure.[62] Again, it is scarcely used. In 2005, 12 reasoned orders were issued, 22 in 2004, 11 in 2003 and 12 in 2002. Perhaps it is a matter of taste. Presidents of the Court of Justice have constantly described the procedure as being 'regular' or 'frequent.'[63] But even if we were ready to accept that 4.72% (i.e. 12 orders out of the total of 254 preliminary references completed in 2005) is a significant percentage, there would be other reasons to believe that the simplified procedure does not help in urgent cases. Statistics of judicial activity do not provide information on the average length of procedure dealt with by reasoned order. So, take a seat and a deep breath; in 2005 it was 18.6 months![64] Even if in our calculation we do not take into account the probably extraordinary case *Azienda Agricola Nardoni*,[65] which took almost 5.5 years to decide, the average length remains at 13.8 months. Would this improve judicial protection available to a person in custody or an asylum seeker?

However, the most compelling reason showing that the simplified procedure is not an instrument speeding up the proceedings in urgent cases lies (as in the case of the expedited procedure) in its very nature. It may be used only in cases where:

---

59 Court of Justice's Annual Report for 2005 at p. 204. Annual reports are available at <http://www.curia.europa.eu/en/instit/presentationfr/rapport.htm>.

60 See de la Serre (2006) 783.

61 After all, the Court of Justice admits this in its Discussion Paper at p. 2.

62 De la Serre (2006) 811.

63 'The Court made frequent use of the simplified procedure' said President G.C. Rodríguez Iglesias in 2002 (Court of Justice's Annual Report for 2002 at p. 8), while in 2004 President V. Skouris qualified the use as 'regular' (Court of Justice's Annual Report for 2004 at p. 13).

64 Inghelram (2005) 452, gives statistics on all years when the procedure was applied, in comparison to the ordinary procedure (number in parenthesis). Thus in 2004 it was 18.4 months (23.5), in 2003 20.2 months (25.5), in 2002 17.1 months (24.1), in 2001 16.2 months (22.7), in 2000 30.5 months (21.6), in 1999 8.3 months (21.2) and in 1998 20.2 months (21.4).

65 Joined Cases C-483/00, 485/00-488/00, C-492/00-C-494/00, C-496/00 and C-500/00 *Azienda Agricola Nardoni*, not yet reported.

> [a] question referred to the Court for a preliminary ruling is identical to a question on which the Court has already ruled, where the answer to such a question may be clearly deduced from existing case-law or where the answer to the question admits of no reasonable doubt.[66]

Recall that the Commission's proposal concerns the Area of Freedom, Security and Justice, one of the most dynamically developing areas of EU law. The questions arising before national courts will hardly be identical, clearly deducible from the Court of Justice's previous case-law or raising no reasonable doubts, and the simplified procedure will be excluded in most cases.[67]

In sum, due to a relatively small proportion of cases dealt with by reasoned orders and the still considerable length of the procedure, it is not true that the simplified procedure can significantly help the Court of Justice to reduce its backlog of pending cases, which could shorten the average length of proceeding before the Court of Justice. At the same time, the procedure cannot help in individual cases due to its very nature and purpose.

b) Judicial efficiency and the need for a real discourse in the EU judicial process

The Court of Justice may speed up the procedure by another measure. According to Article 20 of the Statute the Court may determine cases without an Opinion of the Advocate General where they do not raise any new point of law. According to the Court's Annual Report for 2005, about 35% of judgments in 2005 were delivered without an Opinion (compared with 30% in 2004).[68] Again, as in the case of the simplified procedure, the Report does not tell us how much time this saved. However, not only should this interest us here. Much more noticeable is the fact that the Court is willing to cut off an important component of its argumentation[69] for the sake of the expeditiousness of its work. It is a mark of a broader development, which indicates that the Court of Justice has decided to deal with its caseload by focusing on the *quantity* rather than on the *quality* of its judicial production. This, perhaps unconsciously, significantly undermines its role as a veritable Supreme or even Constitutional Court of the EU.[70] Critical evaluation of the argumentative practices of the Court of Justice would deserve detailed consideration, which cannot be made here; an often-quoted passage from J. Weiler's article is submitted instead:

> [T]he Court should abandon the cryptic, Cartesian style which still characterizes many of its decisions and move to the more discursive, analytic and conversational style associated more with the common law world – though practiced by others as well, notably the German Constitutional court. As noted above, espe-

66 Article 104(3) of the Rules of Procedure.

67 See also n. 38 *supra*.

68 Court of Justice's Annual Report for 2005 at p. 11.

69 See Lasser (2004).

70 Discussed in part IV. a) *infra*.

> cially in its Constitutional jurisprudence, it is crucial that the Court display in its judgments that national sensibilities were fully considered and taken into account. And it must amply explain and reason its decisions if they are to be not only authoritarian but also authoritative. The Cartesian style with its pretense of logical legal reasoning and inevitability of results is not conducive to a good conversation with national courts.[71]

The Court has remained deaf to this appeal. Moreover, it seems to prefer the exact opposite. This may be illustrated by a recent and quite unfortunate development in the structure of the Court of Justice's judgments. To make them shorter (and thus reduce translation costs), the Court now sometimes leaves out all arguments submitted to the Court by participants – including the Member States. A sublime example is a recent judgment in *Banca popolare di Cremona*.[72] The case concerned compatibility of an Italian tax with the Community VAT system. Advocate General Jacobs suggested declaring the Italian tax incompatible with EC law and at the same time proposed to the Court that it limits the temporal scope of its judgment. Retroactive effects of the judgment (which is a general rule) would have caused serious economic difficulties for Italy resulting from the duty of Italian authorities to reimburse the amounts collected contrary to EC law.[73] The Court re-opened the oral stage of the procedure, asking the parties and the Member States to present further observations concerning interpretation of the relevant provisions of the Sixth Directive and also the possibility of limiting the temporal effects of its decision.[74] At the second hearing, fourteen Member States submitted their views, and Advocate General Stix-Hackl[75] – who delivered the second opinion – again proposed declaring the Italian tax incompatible.[76] However, in its judgment the Court presented the case as a straightforward issue, without mentioning the dissenting opinions of both advocates general, the existence of the second hearing, or the arguments of the Member States.

Quite frustrating for the participating governments (but also for the Court of Justice's observers) must be the judgment in *i-21 Germany*,[77] where the Court in answering the second question reproduced only the arguments of the applicant in the main proceedings and the Commission, which conveyed its analysis while totally ignoring the arguments presented by governments arguing against its

71 Weiler (2001) 225, references omitted.

72 Case C-475/03 *Banca popolare di Cremona*, not yet reported.

73 Opinion of Advocate General Jacobs of 17 March 2005 in Case C-475/03 *Banca popolare di Cremona*, not yet reported.

74 Order of the Court of 21 October 2005 in Case C-475/03 *Banca popolare di Cremona*, not yet reported.

75 Advocate General Stick-Hackl was called to give the second opinion as in the meantime Advocate General Jacobs had resigned from office.

76 Opinion of Advocate General Stix-Hackl of 14 March 2006 in Case C-475/03 *Banca popolare di Cremona*, not yet reported.

77 Joined Cases C-392/04 and C-422/04 *i-21 Germany*, not yet reported.

conclusion. One cannot help but ask whether this respects the fundamental principle of equal treatment in judicial procedure.

Elimination of the Member States' arguments from the Court of Justice's judgments does not only mean that the judgment cannot be properly justified; how do we *e.g.* know that the Court of Justice did not simply overlook some compelling arguments, presented by a Member State or a party to the main proceedings in contradiction to the solution adopted by the Court?.[78] The Court is thus diminishing the importance of the Member States in the European legal discourse, ignoring implications of this for its own legitimacy.[79] When the President of the Court of Justice discusses potential criticisms of the 'quality of the Court of Justice's case law', he does not address the quality of the Court's reasoning at all. He instead 'confutes' attacks on the Court for its activism or faintheartedness in cases concerning controversial questions, an issue which relates far more to a substantive evaluation of the Court's decision-making activity than to something close to the 'quality' of its work.[80]

The little care for real discourse in the EU judicial process is also illustrated by the Court of Justice's proposal for an 'urgent preliminary ruling procedure', discussed further below. Efficiency is seen in cutting off some (perhaps disturbing?) voices, which stand in the way of the Court's expediency. It is the legitimizing potential of the real discourse, which should urge all concerned to a very careful use of this new procedure, although its adoption seems necessary.[81]

It may be argued that the Court of Justice only adjusts its way of reasoning for its audience – which consists predominantly of lower courts that are not interested in long justifications and are only keen to get an answer from the Luxembourg oracle. This may be true, but then the Court of Justice can hardly expect such improperly reasoned answers to seem authoritative before national supreme courts, which probably are much more critical. It again questions the suitability of the Court of Justice's talking to all courts in Europe. While perhaps all listen, some obey only with hesitation.

78 Although, until the submissions of the participants to the procedure are not publicly available (as is the case of *e.g.* the U.S. Supreme Court), we may never properly control the Court as it always depends on how it presents these arguments (and this is the case even of the Reports for the Hearing –these actually present the *answer* proposed by the party, not its supporting *argumentation*).

79 There is no space to analyse the concept of the Court of Justice's legitimacy. For a possible view see Lasser (2004) 69.

80 See Skouris (2006) 24-25. Would we *e.g.* discuss whether the principle of EC law primacy, stated by the Court of Justice in Case 6/64 *Costa v. ENEL* [1964] ECR 585, was of 'first-rate quality'? No, but we would perhaps ask whether the Court properly justified the judgment, in which the principle was inserted into EC law.

81 For the constitutional significance of a true discourse in the EU judicial process see *e.g.* Maduro (2005) 52.

IV A Model Proposed: Hierarchy and Differentiation Combined

a) The Court of Justice as part of national judiciaries – Supreme and Constitutional Court

The starting point of the following section is non-controversial. We must look at the EU judicial system as a whole – not as a mere conglomerate of the central courts in Luxembourg and the national courts in the Member States, each having a different *quality* – the former being 'supranational' courts having tasks similar to all international courts, and the latter 'wearing Community law hat' only when EU law enters their court-rooms. They *all* form part of the EU judiciary. While this has 'become a truism' in relation to national courts[82] (perhaps to remind them of obligations they have because of EU membership in the EU), the implications of this understanding for the Court of Justice itself seem to go unnoticed.

The Court of Justice is not merely a 'supranational' court. This label is often used to avoid difficult questions. The Court of Justice is a civil, criminal and administrative law court, and in these fields it has *become part of national* judicial structures. It is not like an international court acting *outside* national judicial systems, but rather a supreme court, whose task is to guide lower courts in their application of EU law ('supreme' and 'lower' are metaphors; this is not to propose that an actual hierarchy, at least as in national legal systems, exists[83]). Apart from this 'ordinary' law jurisdiction, it acts as the EU Constitutional Court – deciding disputes concerning the division of powers, systemic principles of EU law or fundamental rights of those who are bound by it. This mixed nature makes understanding the Court of Justice and its role within the EU judicial system very complicated.

One of the reasons for this confusion is that the Court of Justice may fulfil all these roles using a single means – the preliminary ruling procedure. This procedure was modelled according to procedures dealing with constitutional questions only, important because of their very nature, and not questions concerning the interpretation of ordinary civil, criminal, or administrative legislation. This has far-reaching implications for today's EU preliminary ruling procedure, as there is no mechanism ensuring that only important questions will arise before the Court of Justice or make the Court of Justice's workload through the preliminary references more reasonable. Every court may turn to the Court of Justice and the latter must respond regardless of the importance of the question referred.

In most national judicial systems, the highest courts deal with questions of greater importance. The higher the court, the more the system cares for maintaining its coherence, which at the same time means that individual interests

82 Claes (2006) 3.

83 Although there are tendencies in the Court of Justice to establish similar means of control to those existing in federal judicial systems – see Komárek (2005) 28.

give way to these broader considerations. The Court of Justice and the widely opened doors it has towards all national courts (and litigants before them) contradict this, in the name of the judicial protection of individuals. Why are individuals so important to the Court of Justice?

For the most part this is because the Court of Justice builds its legitimacy and authority (as well as the legitimacy and authority of the whole EU legal order) on its direct relationship to all EU citizens.[84] As Chalmers puts it: 'The operationability and authority of the EU legal order, time and again, became equated with the assertion of EC individual rights before a court and the precedence of judicial authority over other administrative actors.'[85] Equally, individuals have become an important vehicle for EU law enforcement within the Member States.[86]

Unlike the Court of Justice, *e.g.* the U.S. Supreme Court does not need to fight for its authority in such a way. That is (probably) why the balance of the EU judicial process is so much deflected in favour of individuals, whilst the Supreme Court justices dare to state publicly that their function is 'not to correct errors in the lowest courts, but to secure harmony of decision and the appropriate settlement of questions of general importance.'[87] As C. Shapiro observes, '[t]he Supreme Court, [...], has cast itself not as a source of justice for individual litigants or the forum to correct aberrations in the application of law, but rather as providing the structure and guidance necessary for the lower courts to correct or avoid errors.'[88]

Another question immediately arises: if the purpose of the preliminary ruling procedure is to ensure coherent interpretation and application of EU law, is it necessary for the Court of Justice to solve every single case when EU law is unclear? As we have already observed above, experience of other highest courts shows that this is not so.[89] For example the intensity of the U.S. Supreme Court's control over the application of federal law by lower courts is relatively low, as it believes that it 'can best serve the needs of the national law by laying down broad principles, leaving their application and elaboration largely to the federal courts of appeals and the state appellate courts.'[90] Thus the Supreme Court not only avoids mere 'error correction,' it leaves a great scope of independent action in developing federal law to lower courts. An issue which should be seriously examined is the intensity of the Court of Justice control over EU law application on a national level, and the means as to how to achieve it.[91]

---

84 See *e.g.* Halberstam (2005) 775.

85 Chalmers, (2004) 3.

86 See *e.g.* Timmermans (1994).

87 Hellman (1996) 403 quoting at p. 432 U.S. Supreme Court Justices.

88 Shapiro (2006) 279.

89 See the text accompanying n. 6-10.

90 Hellman (1996) 433.

91 For inspiring discussions concerning the U.S. Supreme Court's control over application of federal law by lower courts see Hellman (1996) or Shapiro (2006). See also discussion accompanying n. 5-10 *supra*.

One of the options would be some kind of a selection mechanism, a 'European certiorari.'[92] Much has been written about case-selection by the Court of Justice but, in the event, proposals to this effect have never been adopted. This article will not be a further attempt to change the mind of those who have previously rejected case selection. Nevertheless, contrary to the 'certiorari option,' limitation of preliminary references to the courts of last instance have always been dismissed too quickly, using the same or similar arguments.[93] In addition, this limitation may bring about other beneficial outcomes, resulting from the institutional structures of the national judiciaries, which the Court of Justice's open doors threaten. Let us consider these advantages.

b) Hierarchy as a means of bringing rationality to the judicial process

Problems that judicial systems must face today do not concern only the supreme courts. They reach far wider and concern all courts in the system, not only its apex. This is caused by the increasingly important role of law and its institutions in the life of society, which has brought about a 'litigation explosion,' resulting in an unmanageable caseload for courts. Paradoxically, this simultaneously undermined trust in the courts' work because the quality of their work diminished due to their workload.[94] Inevitably, the objective of providing 'ideal' justice must be balanced against other interests and constraints limiting the effectiveness of the judicial system. The following will show that establishing the hierarchy of courts is a means of finding a proper balance between various interests and an effective distribution of resources in the judicial system. In fact, the hierarchy of courts is one of the prerequisites for a functioning judicial system. The preliminary ruling procedure, in its current design, destabilizes that balance. This has detrimental effects, not only for the national judicial systems but for the EU judiciary as a whole. The Court of Justice's capacity is treated not as a scarce resource, but as an ordinary part of the judicial process. In the Commission's words (which reflect the view of the Court of Justice): '[a]n essential element of the procedure is the principle that *all* national courts can dialogue with the Court.'[95] The consequences will be seen below.

Judicial hierarchy guarantees a rational distribution of resources in several ways. Time and other resources of an economic nature are factors determining whether the judicial system is able to produce just results and whether it is sufficiently inclusive. Another, inherent limitation of the judiciary stems from the unequal competence of individual judges. Being a judge requires experience, education and skills not possessed by all judges to the same extent. 'Judicial wisdom' is distributed throughout the system unevenly – more experienced judges generally sit at higher courts, as these courts must solve more difficult

92 For a general evaluation see Heffernan (2003) 907.

93 For one of the (most probably few) exceptions see Rasmussen (2000).

94 See Fix-Fierro (2004) 1-33.

95 Communication at p. 4. The 1999 Report is on the same wave-length as the Commission. See particularly pp. 22-23.

questions.[96] We do not necessarily have to explain the smaller number of references from national supreme (or higher) courts by their unwillingness to submit themselves to the Court of Justice authority. An equally sound explanation may actually be that they are more competent to deal with complex legal questions.[97]

The varied distribution of 'judicial wisdom' does not only concern competence of a purely 'legal' nature possessed by an experienced judge. The judicial process involves different tasks and requires different skills which are allocated to different levels of the judicial decision-making process. Fact-finding requires, among other things, an ability to examine witnesses or assess their reliability and is usually done at a first instance (trial) level. On the contrary, higher courts do not generally determine facts –rather do they develop law in difficult, 'unsettled' cases.[98] This is particularly true of supreme courts. Their activity must be based not only on a considerable legal expertise, but also on their ability to see the wider societal consequences of their decisions, since in such situations they make law. Again, allowing references from the lower courts means that judges, who do not possess competence or experience to take decisions in a complex institutional and societal context, are involved in difficult cases involving hard choices surpassing the domain of ordinary law in which they are used to operate. A case in point is the Irish abortion litigation, which produced one of the most difficult cases for the Court of Justice, as it had to face a conflict between the constitutional prohibition of abortion and the principles of free movement. Although it may be frustrating for those who want the Court of Justice (or courts) to give definite answers in cases, even if they can reach beyond their institutional competence and scope of law in general, the Court of Justice at the end avoided judging the conflict and so did the Irish Supreme Court. The troubling reference came from a lower court.[99]

The separation of fact finding from law making on a higher level of the judicial process has more than this rationale. As Damaška puts it:

> Initial decisionmakers are closer to the messy details of life, including human drama, and therefore can less readily be immunized from individual aspects of cases. Meanwhile, higher officials face realities prepackaged or edited by their subordinates; individual destinies are less visible. Because of this mediation, higher-ups can more easily disregard the 'equities' of the cases they must decide. The advantage of their insensitivity to individual circumstances is that they are free

[96] See Damaška's examination of varied approaches to distribution of authority within his models of the judiciary (hierarchical and coordinate) depending on qualities valued by a particular system: Damaška (1986) 16-28.

[97] See Chalmers (2004) 34 who also rejects a priori distrustful stance towards higher courts.

[98] Lasser convincingly shows that this is the case also in France, known for its historically determined distrust in the judiciary (see Lasser (2004)). The question is not whether courts make law, but how openly they do so.

[99] See Claes (2006) 526-531. For a general argument showing limitations of courts when deciding constitutional conflicts between supranational and national law see Komárek (2007) 34-39.

> to concern themselves with correcting inconsistencies in low-level decisions and with cultivation of broad ordering schemes for decision-making.[100]

This advantage is lost when the first instance court makes a reference to the Court of Justice before the problem has been properly elaborated in the national judicial process. No wonder that the Court of Justice inclines to do justice in particular cases instead of searching for proper interpretation of law, which could be applied in a more general context. 'Early' references have another adverse consequence: they may actually eliminate the higher court's desire to clarify EU law in collaboration with the Court of Justice, as the higher court does not want to prolong the procedure for another two years; although it may consider that it would be desirable to ask different questions to those that had been asked by the lower court.[101]

More instances at a national level also mean more accuracy in identification of what is necessary to be decided by the Court of Justice. This is explained by the Condorcet theorem which, put briefly, presupposes that 'more heads know more':

> [U]nder certain conditions, [...] the cumulative vote of a group of independent decisionmakers, each of whom is more likely than not to get a decision right, will approach greater and greater accuracy as the number in the group increases. More heads are better than fewer, so long as each head is probably right. A related point is that consensus reduces the variance of opinions and thus dampens the effect of extreme views. The typical structure of hierarchical judicial systems illustrates these institutional principles: The number of judges hearing a given case usually increases as the case ascends through the judicial hierarchy, which emphasizes that the most controversial decisions will tend to be made by a larger group of judges.[102]

The need for increasing the quality of the questions referred to the Court of Justice and possible involvement of higher court judges in their formulation is sometimes mirrored in rather odd proposals: Chalmers *e.g.* suggests that a possible way to select meaningful references 'would be for a judge from the Court of Justice and a senior judge from the national jurisdiction to consider together whether a reference made by a national court is appropriate for a ruling by the Court of Justice.'[103] Instead of creating some kind of 'selection committee' composed of the Court of Justice and national supreme courts judges, alien to

[100] Damaška, (1986) 20.

[101] Such a shortcoming may be eliminated by the possibility of challenging decisions to refer before the higher courts. This seems to be allowed by the Court of Justice (Case 146/73 *Rheinmühlen-Düsseldorf* [1974] ECR 139, para. 3), and is now being reconsidered in Case C-210/06 *Cartesio*, OJ C 165, of 15.07.2006, p. 17.

[102] Vermuele (2000) 117, footnotes omitted. As to the last point, see the text accompanying n. 99 *supra*.

[103] Chalmers (2004) 33-34.

the judicial process, a national judicial hierarchy through which higher courts would control the activity of lower instances by ordinary procedural means may do the same job.

Thus the division of labour between lower and higher courts enables the latter to fulfil their task, which of course sometimes requires leaving a minor injustice without remedy. In other words, hierarchy ensures (more or less) a rational distribution of cases in the system.[104] The lowest courts decide all issues, and by way of appeals their superior courts check how they succeeded in particularly complicated cases and correct their failures. However, the superior courts' control is not endless and overwhelming. There is only a limited number of instances wherein one may pursue his case, and the higher one climbs in the hierarchy, the less the system cares for his particular case and rather turns its attention to the wider consequences of the judgment for the legal system as a whole. This is achieved by filtering mechanisms, which does not necessarily entail case selection but encounters a much wider means of control.[105] All these advantages are lost if the lowest court in the hierarchy is allowed to turn immediately to the 'supreme'[106] interpretative authority. This produces disturbances at national level, which the Court of Justice often ignores, and also burdens the proper functioning of the Union judiciary.

c) The proposal – hierarchy and differentiation

From the foregoing we can formulate a proposal for the preliminary reference procedure regime:

1) limiting preliminary ruling procedure to courts of last instance as a rule;
2) as a *necessary* exception to 1, when a lower court considers that one or more arguments for invalidity, put forward by the parties or as the case may be raised by it of its own motion, are well founded, it must stay proceedings and make a reference to the Court for a preliminary ruling on the act's validity;[107]
3) as a *possible* exception to 1, the Council can decide which EU law measures may be subject to preliminary references from lower courts.

There is not much to be added to points 1 and 2 of the proposal since arguments supporting them have been discussed at some length. As regards point 3, it has already been mentioned that in some instances it may serve the economy of the judicial process to allow references from first instance courts. A case in point was the Brussels regulation,[108] but there would certainly be other measures too.

[104] For an analysis using political science modelling, see Kornhauser (1994-1995) 1605.

[105] See *The Role and Future of the European Court of Justice*, (The British Institute of International and Comparative Law, 1996) at pp. 114-115, which gives examples of such selection mechanisms.

[106] See n. 83 for an explanation of the term 'supreme' here.

[107] Case C-344/04 *International Air Transport Association*, not yet reported, para. 30; see the text accompanying n. 47.

[108] See the text accompanying n. 50 *supra*.

In addition, some form of an urgent preliminary ruling procedure may be created, as the Court of Justice suggested in its Discussion Paper.[109] The Court was less optimistic than the Commission about the sufficient efficiency of its existing procedures. It proposed creating an 'urgent preliminary ruling procedure', since in some instances the ordinary procedure takes too long and limitation of the Court of Justice's caseload cannot help with it. The Court of Justice's Discussion Paper[110] mentions the regulation concerning jurisdiction and the recognition and enforcement of judgments in matrimonial and parental responsibility matters;[111] this lays down a number of time-limits applying to the national courts, including a time-limit of six weeks for giving a ruling (except where exceptional circumstances make this impossible) where proceedings are brought before a court seeking the return of a child who has been wrongfully removed. References in criminal cases involving persons in custody represent another example.

The Court of Justice's proposal cannot be examined in detail here; however, brief perusal of it shows that its simplification consists primarily in the limitation of a true discourse and exchange of opinions between the parties, Member States and EU institutions. This would be acceptable in cases of minor importance; but, such cases should never arise before the Court of Justice, if it ever wants to become a veritable supreme and constitutional court for the whole Union. Such cases should be dealt with primarily by national courts and only if important reach the ultimate authority of the Court of Justice.

This does not mean, that in matters of urgency, the protection of individuals would somehow suffer because of their need to climb the national judicial pyramid. National procedural law may provide itself for an expedited procedure, whereby such cases would reach the national supreme court more speedily. Moreover, expediency of the national procedures is often underestimated. In a recent case *Bot*,[112] a reference from the French *Conseil d'Etat*, it took only six weeks since a decree of deportation had been issued against the appellant in the main proceedings until the *Conseil d'Etat*'s referred to the Court of Justice, when a lower court had rejected an application for the decree's annulment. The urgent procedure should therefore be possible only after a last instance court's reference and not in every case concerning individual rights. It could easily become a standard procedure, and the legitimacy of the EU judicial process would be further undermined.

---

109 See n. 1.

110 Discussion Paper at p. 2.

111 Council Regulation (EC) No 2201/2003 of 27 November 2003 concerning jurisdiction and the recognition and enforcement of judgments in matrimonial matters and the matters of parental responsibility, repealing Regulation (EC) No 1347/2000, OJ 2003 L 338, p. 1.

112 Case 241/05 *Bot*, not yet reported.

V Conclusion

Narrowing down the possibility of lower courts to send preliminary references reflects the philosophy of the Court of Justice's role as a veritable Supreme Court for the Union and its courts. Supreme, not because of its hierarchically superior position over the national courts –this article does not advocate such a position. The article believes that the fundamental Court of Justice's task, when ensuring that in the interpretation and application of the Treaties the law is observed,[113] is to provide national courts with authoritative guidance. However, to be able to speak with authority, the Court must speak clearly and persuasively. This cannot be done if it pulverizes its authority into hundreds of (sometimes) contradictory and (often) insufficiently reasoned answers. The current system of preliminary reference, which undermines national judicial structures by allowing the lowest parts of the judicial pyramid to talk directly to the ultimate interpretative authority, has negative effects both for the national judicial process and for the Court of Justice's mission.

This article has considered an option which thus has received scant attention – limiting the power of lower courts to refer while at the same time adopting differentiated procedures in accordance with the nature of the instrument to be interpreted. The article showed that many arguments against such an approach are not sufficiently thought out and are used rather mechanically. Even if the proposal contained here does not persuade the reader, perhaps – and still importantly – the article will facilitate an open-minded discussion of the current structure of the EU judicial system.

---

[113] Article 220 EC.

Bibliography

P. Allot, 'Preliminary Rulings – Another Infant Desease' [2000/25] *E.L. Rev.* 538.

M. Bobek, 'A New or Non-Existent Legal Order? Some (Early) Experience in the Application of EU Law in Central Europe' [2006/3] *Croatian Yearbook of European Law and Policy* 265.

M. Claes, *The National Courts' Mandate in the European Constitution* (Hart Publishing, 2006).

P. Craig, *The Jurisdiction of the Community Courts Reconsidered* in: G. De Búrca, J.H.H. Weiler (eds.) *The European Court of Justice* (Oxford University Press, 2001).

E.B. de la Serre, 'Accelerated and Expedited Procedures before the EC Courts: A Review of the Practice' [2006/43] *C.M.L. Rev.* 796-801.

M. Damaška, *The Faces of Justice and State Authority. A Comparative Approach to the Legal Process* (Yale University Press, 1986).

M. Dougan, *National Remedies before the Court of Justice. Issues of Harmonisation and Differentiation* (Hart Publishing, 2004).

P. Dyberg, 'What Should the Court of Justice Be Doing?' [2001/26] *E.L.Rev.* 291-295.

D. Chalmers, 'Judicial Preferences and the Community Legal Order' [1997/60] *M.L.R.* 164-180.

D. Chalmers, 'The Dynamics of Judicial Authority and the Constitutional Treaty' in: J.H.H. Weiler, C.L. Eisgruber (eds), *Altneuland: The EU Constitution in a Contextual Perspective*, Jean Monnet Working Paper 5/04, <http://www.jeanmonnetprogram.org/papers/04/040501-18.html>.

J. Clifford Wallace, 'The Nature and Extent of Intercircuit Conflicts: A Solution Needed for a Mountain or a Molehill?' [1983/71] *Calif.L.Rev.* 913–.

H. Fix-Fierro, *Courts, Justice and Efficiency: A Socio-legal Study of Economic Rationality in Adjudication* (Hart Publishing, 2004).

D. Halberstam, 'The Bride of Messina: Constitutionalism and Democracy in Europe' [2005/30] *E.L.Rev.* 775.

L. Heffernan, 'The Community Courts Post-Nice: A European Certiorari Revisited' [2003/52] *I.C.L.Q.* 907.

A.D. Hellman, 'The Shrunken Docket of the Rehnquist Court' [1996/9] *Sup. Ct.Rev.* 403.

J.F.K. Inghelram, 'Enkele kanttekeningen bij de vereenvoudigde procedure voor de beantwoording van prejudiciële vragen door het HvJ EG' [2005] S.E.W. 452.

J. Komárek, 'Federal Elements in the Community Judicial System: Building Coherence in the Community Legal Order' [2005/42] *C.M.L.Rev.* 9.

J. Komárek, 'European Constitutionalism and the European Arrest Warrant – In Search of the Limits of 'Contrapunctual Principles'' [2007/44] *C.M.L.Rev.* 9 34-39.

L.A. Kornhauser 'Adjudication by a Resource-Constrained Team: Hierarchy and Precedent in a Judicial System' [1994-1995/68] *S.Cal.L.Rev.* 1605.

Z. Kühn, 'Worlds Apart. Western and Central European Judicial Culture at the Onset of the European Enlargement' [2004/52] *Am.J.Comp.L.* 531.

M. Lasser, *Judicial Deliberations. A Comparative Analysis of Judicial Transparency and Legitimacy* (Oxford University Press, 2004).

K. Lenaerts and T. Corthaut, 'Of Birds and Hedges: The Role of Primacy in Invoking Norms of EU Law' [2006/31] *E.L.Rev.* 289-291.

M.P. Maduro *Sovereignty in Europe: The European Court of Justice and the Creation of a European Political Community* in: M.L. Volcansek – J.F. Stack (eds), *Courts Crossing Borders* (Carolina Academic Press 2005).

S.D. O'Connor, 'Proceedings of the Middle Atlantic State-Federal Judicial Relationships Conference' [1994/162] *Fed.Rules Dec.* 181-82.

H. Rasmussen, 'Remedying the Crumbling EC Judicial System' [2000/37] *C.M.L.Rev.* 1071 – 1107.

W. Sadurski, *'Solange, chapter 3': Constitutional Courts in Central Europe – Democracy – European Union,* EUI Working Paper Law 2006/40, available at <http://hdl.handle.net/1814/6420>.

C. Shapiro, 'The Limits of the Olympian Court: Common Law Judging Versus Error Correction in the Supreme Court' [2006/63] *Wash. & Lee L. Rev.* 279.

N.N. Shuibhne (ed), *Regulating the Internal Market* (Edward Elgar, 2006).

V. Skouris *Self-Conception, Challenges and Perspectives of the EU Courts,* in: I. Pernice- J. Kokott – C. Saunders (eds): *The Future of the European Judicial System in a Comparative Perspective* (Nomos 2006).

M. Taruffo, *Institutional Factors Influencing Precedents* in: N. MacCormick and R.S. Summers (eds), *Interpreting Precedents: A Comparative Study* (Aldershot, 1997).

M. Taruffo – M. La Torre, *Precedent in Italy* in: N. MacCormick, and R.S. Summers (eds), *Interpreting Precedents: A Comparative Study* (Aldershot, 1997).

C.W.A. Timmermans, *Judicial Protection against the Member States: Articles 169 and 177 Revisited* in: D. Curtin – T. Heukels (eds.), *Institutional Dynamics of European Integration. Essays in Honour of Henry G. Schermers. Vol. II.* (Martinus Nijhoff Publishers, 1994).

A. Vermuele, 'Interpretive Choice' [2000/75] *N.Y.U.L.Rev.* 74.

J. Weiler, *Epilogue: The Judicial Après Nice* in: G. de Búrca – J.H.H. Weiler (eds) *The European Court of Justice* (Oxford University Press, 2001).

CHAPTER 4

Revisiting Article 307 EC

The Untouchable Core of Fundamental European Constitutional Law Values and Principles

Nikolaos Lavranos*

1 Introduction

This contribution seeks to analyze and clarify the relationship between international law and Community law in the light of the most recent jurisprudence of the ECJ regarding Article 307 EC.

The main argument that will be developed is that the ECJ has recently identified a new untouchable core of fundamental European constitutional law values and principles more explicitly and more forcefully than before by interpreting the obligations arising out of Article 307 (2) EC in an extremely extensive way. It is further argued that this new untouchable core of European constitutional values and principles is actually copied from national constitutional law, which in turn illustrates the fact that the ECJ is increasingly performing the function of a true constitutional court of Europe.

However, before embarking on a journey to the boundaries between international law and Community law, it will be appropriate to first disclose and explain the author's mindset regarding the relationship between international law and Community law, since this inevitably influences the subsequent analytical framework. Based on that, the ECJ's most recent jurisprudence on Article 307 EC, i.e. the *Kadi*[1] and *BITs* judgments,[2] will be discussed in more detail. The analysis will focus on two main aspects: (i) the new concept of the 'very foundations of the Community legal order' as established by the ECJ in its *Kadi* judgment, and (ii) the concept of 'hypothetical incompatibility' as elucidated by the ECJ in the *BITs* judgments. Finally, the contribution will be wrapped up with an outlook.

2 The Author's Mindset: The Asymmetric Relationship Between International Law and Community Law

The interplay between international law and EC law may be analyzed from different perspectives. This paper scrutinizes this linkage by adopting a Eurocentric perspective,[3] which partially but not entirely coincides

---

* LL.M., Max Weber Fellow, European University Institute, Florence, Italy. This contribution is based on presentations and discussions held at the EUI in Florence, the University of Siena, the University of Rome La Sapienza and the Sant'Anna School of Advanced studies. The author is indebted to Prof. Pieter Jan Kuijper, Prof. Riccardo Pavoni, Prof. Marise Cremona, Prof. Bruno de Witte, Prof. Panos Koutrakos, Dr. Sara Poli, Prof. Cannizzaro, Dr. Giuseppe Martinico, Filippo Fontanelli, Valentina Vadi, Stanislas Adam. The usual disclaimer applies. The author can be contacted at: nlavranos@yahoo.com.

1 ECJ: Case C-402/05 P *Kadi* [2008] ECR II-3649; ECJ: Case C-415/05 P *Yusuf and Al Barakaat* [2008] ECR II-3533.

2 ECJ: Case C-249/06 *Commission v. Sweden* [2009], not yet published; ECJ: Case C-205/06 *Commission v. Austria* [2009], not yet published.

3 This is also in answer to Klabbers, (2009) 140, who asks what explains the Eurocentric attitude of the ECJ and many Community law specialists. He provides two explanations: a sociological and a technical one. This is another one.

with the approach adopted by the ECJ.[4] According to this perspective, the following three pillars are determinant for the relationship between international law and Community law: (i) the autonomy of the Community legal order; (ii) the hierarchy of norms within the Community legal order and (iii) the scope of the exclusive jurisdiction of the ECJ.

The starting point is the seminal *Van Gend & Loos*[5] and *Costa v. ENEL*[6] judgments of the ECJ. Since these judgments, we know that the Community legal order is a separate – *sui generis* – legal order that must be distinguished from the international legal order. Therefore, it is submitted that their relationship can be best described as 'two different planets belonging to the same universe of law.' As a result, the ECJ has established the autonomy of the Community legal order, which, as will be discussed below, is of fundamental importance since it determines the internal understanding of international law.

Based on this professed autonomy of the Community legal order and based on the fact that the EC Treaty does not specify the legal status of international norms within the Community legal order, the ECJ has been able through its jurisprudence to determine a Community hierarchy of norms.[7] According to that jurisprudence, this hierarchy is as follows: (i) primary EC law (EC Treaty and the European Convention of Human Rights (ECHR)) is the 'supreme law' of the land, that is, at the top of the hierarchy; (ii) all international law sources (international treaties, decisions of International Organizations (IOs), international customary law) are situated below primary EC law, but supersede (conflicting) secondary EC law (Regulations, Directives); and (iii) at the bottom we find national (constitutional) law.

Thus, from the EC law point of view, international law and Community law are not on an equal footing, but rather are asymmetric in the sense that international law is subordinated to primary EC law.[8] Any attempts to change or reverse this hierarchy of norms – as the CFI tried with its *Kadi/Yusuf* judgments[9] – are forcefully rejected by the ECJ.[10]

---

4 For instance, the author has always strongly criticized and continues to criticize the ECJ's and CFI's refusal to take WTO law, including adopted DSB reports, into account and to set conflicting secondary EC law aside. See, *e.g.*, Lavranos (2005) 313-338; Jans/Lavranos, (2009) 356-362 (A).

5 ECJ: Case 26/62 *Van Gend & Loos* [1962] ECR 1.

6 ECJ: Case 6/64 *Costa v. ENEL* [1964] ECR 585.

7 See, *e.g.*, Opinion of AG Kokott in ECJ: Case C-308/06 *Intertanko* [2008] ECR I-4057, para. 48. See further: Lavranos (2004).

8 However, the ECJ has on occasion nuanced this point by explicitly stating that the EC and its institutions must in principle respect International law. See, *e.g.*, ECJ: Case C 162/96 *Racke* [1998] ECR I-3655, para. 45; ECJ: Case C-286/90 *Poulsen & Diva Nagivation* [1992] ECR I-6019, para. 9. Of course, this is self-evident and does not question the proposed asymmetric relationship between EC law and international law.

9 ECJ: Case T-315/01 *Kadi* [2005] ECR II-3649; ECJ: case T-306 *Yusuf and Al Barakaat* [2005] ECR II-3533. See further: Lavranos (2007) 1-17 (A).

10 See, *e.g.*, Lavranos (2009) 343-359 (B).

Regarding the scope of jurisdiction of the ECJ, its *MOX plant*[11] judgment is authoritative. In that judgment the ECJ clearly stated that it has a very wide exclusive jurisdiction which cannot be modified or affected by any other dispute settlement system that may have been established by another international treaty.[12] Consequently, no international or national court other than the ECJ has the authority to interpret and apply Community law *in fine*. Accordingly, EC Member States are obliged to bring any dispute between them that potentially involves Community law exclusively before the ECJ – as is also provided for in Article 292 EC.[13]

From the above, it becomes apparent that the ECJ plays a central role in determining the legal status and effect of international law within the Community legal order.[14] Essentially, the ECJ functions as a gatekeeper that decides on a case-by-case basis what the legal effect of an international law provision is within the Community legal order.[15] Obviously, this case-by-case approach enables the ECJ to exercise this gatekeeper function in a flexible way: it does not treat every international law norm in the same way. For example, while the ECHR[16] is fully integrated within the Community legal order, the WTO[17] and, more recently, the UNCLOS[18] are denied any direct effect within EC law. As a result, any search for consistency in the ECJ's jurisprudence towards international law is in vain – simply because it is not there.

3 Article 307 EC: The Awakening of a Sleeping Giant

Although, as mentioned above, the EC Treaty is basically silent on the relationship between international law and Community law, Article 307 EC (formerly Article 234 EEC Treaty) is an exception to this in that it provides a specific rule of conflict for solving incompatibilities between pre-accession treaties of the EC Member States and their Community law obligations.

---

11 ECJ: Case C-459/03 *MOX plant* [2006] ECR I-4635.

12 *Ibid.*, paras. 123, 132-135. Although the ECJ has accepted that EC Member States may conclude an international agreement that sets up a judicial system which would also be binding on the ECJ. But at the same time, the ECJ made clear that such an extra-EC law judicial system may not encroach upon the exclusive jurisdiction of the ECJ and may not affect the autonomy of the Community legal order, see in particular: ECJ: Opinion 1/91 EEA agreement [1991] ECR I-6079.

13 See further: Lavranos (2007) 83-94 (B).

14 As has also been explicitly pointed out by AG Maduro in his Opinion in Case C-402/05 P *Kadi*, 16 January 2008, para. 23.

15 On the gatekeeper function of the ECJ see: Snyder (2003) 313-367.

16 See, *e.g.*, ECJ: Case C-229/05 P *PKK* [2007] ECR I-439; ECJ: Case C-112/00 *Schmidberger* [2003] ECR I-5659.

17 See, *e.g.*, Joined Cases ECJ: Case C-120/06 P *FIAMM* [2008]; ECJ: Case C-121/06 P *Fedon* [2008].

18 See, *e.g.*, ECJ: Case C-308/06 *Intertanko* [2008] ECR I-4057.

Over the past 50 years Article 307 EC has been practically dormant, featuring only a few times in the jurisprudence of the ECJ.[19] Until very recently only very few Community law specialists and even fewer international law specialists were aware of its existence, not to mention its scope and effect.[20] Therefore, it seems appropriate to first have a closer look at this Article. Paragraph 1 of Article 307 EC proclaims that so-called pre-accession treaties[21] shall not be affected by the obligations of the EC Treaty.[22] Essentially, this is an expression of the principle of conformity of the European integration process with public international law (*Grundsatz der völkerrechtskonformen Integration*)[23]. Or to use the words of Prof. Koutrakos,

> '[...] instead of introducing an exception to the principle of supremacy of Community law, Article 307 EC acknowledges that the establishment of the Community legal order cannot possibly run counter to one of the foundations of public international law,' i.e. the *pacta sunt servanda* principle.[24]

Thus, Article 307 (1) EC acknowledges the existence of pre-accession international law obligations of the EC Member States, which should, in principle, also be honoured in light of existing Community law.[25] Indeed, it should be noted that the ECJ considers the principle to be generally applicable to *all* international treaties that fall within the scope of Article 307 EC.[26] As a result, Article 307

---

[19] See for instance: ECJ: Case 812/79 *Burgoa* [1980] ECR 2787; ECJ: Case C-84/98 *Commission v. Portugal* [2000] ECR I-5215; ECJ: Case C-62/98 *Commission v. Portugal* [2000] ECR I-5171; ECJ: Case C-307/99 *OFT Fruchthandelsgesellschaft* [2001] ECR I-3159; ECJ: Case T-2/99 *T. Port* [2001] ECR II-2093; ECJ: Case T-3/99 *Banatrading* [2001] II-2123; ECJ: Case C-203/03 *Commission v. Austria* [2005] ECR I-935; ECJ: Case C-216/01 *Budvar* [2003] ECR I-1361; ECJ: Cases C-466, 467, 468, 469, 471, 472, 475 and 476/98 *Commission v. UK, Denmark, Sweden, Finland, Belgium, Luxemburg, Austria and Germany* (open skies) [2002] ECR I-9519; see, *e.g.*, Lavranos (2003) 81-91.

[20] For the exceptions see: Schütze (2007) 387-440; Franklin (2005) 79-115; Manzini (2001) 781-792; Klabbers (2001) 187-197; Klabbers (2009).
See also generally: de Witte (2000) 31-58.

[21] Pre-accession treaties are international agreements signed and ratified by Member States before their accession to the EC. Due to the various enlargements of the EC/EU over time, the pre-accession treaties can date back various decades, i.e. ranging from before 1957 to before 2007.

[22] Article 307(1) EC reads as follows:
'The rights and obligations arising from agreements concluded before 1 January 1958 or, for acceding States, before the date of their accession, between one or more Member States on the one hand, and one or more third countries on the other, shall not be affected by the provisions of this Treaty.'

[23] See: Petersmann/Spennemann (2004).

[24] Koutrakos (2006) 301.

[25] Klabbers (2009) 148, writes in this context '[...] one can only reach the conclusion that Article 307 TEC is more about balancing Community law with international law than it affords outright protection to international commitments'.

[26] ECJ: Case 812/79 *Burgoa* [1980] ECR 2787.

EC has been misunderstood by some EC Member States as a *carte blanche* that allows them to continue to fulfil their international obligations arising out of their pre-accession treaties by disregarding conflicting EC law obligations. In particular, this misunderstanding seems to have been based on the fact that the ECJ had accepted in *Centro-Com*[27] that derogations – even from primary EC law – may be allowed on the basis of Article 307 (1) EC.[28] However, paragraph 2 of Article 307 EC clearly states that in the case of a conflict between the obligations arising out of pre-accession treaties and obligations arising out of the EC Treaty, the EC Member States are obliged to eliminate any incompatibilities in favour of their Community law obligations.[29] More specifically, the ECJ clarified that the obligation of eliminating any incompatibilities goes as far as denouncing the international agreement if an adjustment to it proves impossible or fails.[30]

In short, while the consequences of Article 307 (2) EC are potentially far reaching in obliging EC Member States – if necessary – to ultimately denounce pre-accession international treaties, in practice so far this seems not to have been a frequent issue. Therefore, until recently, little attention was paid to the jurisprudence of the ECJ on Article 307 EC. However, as will be discussed below in more detail, the dormant state of this Article has now most certainly changed.

---

27 ECJ: Case C-124/95 *Centro-Com* [1997] ECR I-81.

28 *Ibid.*, paras. 56-61. See also Eeckhout (2008) 111.

29 Article 307(2) EC reads as follows:

'To the extent that such agreements are not compatible with this Treaty, the Member State or States concerned shall take all appropriate steps to eliminate the incompatibilities established. Member States shall, where necessary, assist each other to this end and shall, where appropriate, adopt a common attitude.'

See, *e.g.*, ECJ: Case C-62/98 *Commission v. Portugal* [2000] ECR I-5215.

Klabbers (2009) 141, pointedly remarks '[...] there is no longer any point in trying to squeeze an anterior treaty in paragraph 1; the best a member state can hope for is that it will not be asked to immediately denounce the anterior treaty, so that a failure to denounce will not be regarded as a violation of Community law by the Court'.

30 See, *e.g.*, Opinion of Advocate General Kokott in ECJ: Case C-308/06 *Intertanko* [2008] ECR I-4057, in which she summed up the ECJ jurisprudence on Article 307 EC as follows:

'77. Accordingly, the Community can in principle require the Member States to take measures which run counter to their obligations under international law. This is already demonstrated by Article 307 EC, which governs inconsistencies between pre-existing international agreements and Community law. Even if the Member States' obligations under pre-existing agreements are initially unaffected by conflicts with Community law, the *Member States must nevertheless take all appropriate measures to put an end to such conflicts. This may even require the denunciation of international agreements.* Member States cannot in principle invoke agreements concluded after accession as against Community law.' [emphasis added].

See for detailed analysis regarding the various options for eliminating any incompatibilities: Koutrakos (2006) 304 ff; Eeckhout (2004) 338 ff.

3.1 The *Kadi* Judgment – The New Concept of the 'Very Foundations of the Community Legal Order'

The wake-up call for Article 307 EC came from a few paragraphs contained in the seminal *Kadi*[31] judgment of the ECJ. However, the court had already prepared the ground for this breakthrough almost two decades before with its *Opinion 1/91*[32] on the compatibility of the proposed agreement on the European Economic Area (EEA), in particular with regard to the provisions on the jurisdiction of the proposed EEA Court. In *Opinion 1/91* the ECJ argued that the EEA agreement's objective of ensuring homogeneity of the law throughout the EEA would determine not only the interpretation of the rules of the agreement itself but also the interpretation of the corresponding rules of Community law.[33] Consequently, according to the ECJ, in so far as the EEA agreement conditioned the future interpretation of the Community rules on the free movement of goods, persons, services and capital and on competition, the machinery of courts provided for in the EEA agreement would be in conflict with Article 220 EC [formerly Article 164 EEC Treaty] and, more generally, with the very foundations of the Community. As a result, the ECJ found the EEA agreement to be incompatible with Community law.[34]

The ECJ concluded its analysis by opining that Article 310 EC [formerly Article 238 EEC Treaty] does not provide any basis for setting up under an international agreement a system of courts which conflicts with Article 220 EC and, more generally, with the very foundations of the Community.[35]

To the knowledge of the author, this is the first time that the ECJ had used the term the 'very foundations of the Community.' This term indicates that there exists something more fundamental than primary EC law. The ECJ could have simply referred only to the EC Treaty, whereas it felt the need to add the expression 'more generally'. In other words, the ECJ emphasized that there is a 'core' of Community law that contains such fundamental values that even the EC Member States as *Herren der Verträge* [Masters of the Treaties] cannot simply abrogate or modify them.

As is well known, after some modifications the EEA agreement eventually entered into force.[36] Thus, it seems as if the impact of this newly-introduced concept of the 'very foundations of the Community,' which at the time did not include the term 'Community legal order,' remained dormant or was simply overlooked.[37] Moreover, it should be noted that, of course, *Opinion 1/91* did not

---

31 *Supra* note 1.

32 ECJ: Opinion 1/91 (EEA agreement) [1991] ECR I-6079.

33 *Ibid.*, para. 45.

34 *Ibid.*, para. 46.

35 *Ibid.*, para. 71.

36 For the text of the EEA agreement see: OJ [1994] L 1/3, 3.1.1994.

37 Although in Opinion 1/92 (*EEA agreement II*) [1992] ECR I-2821 on the revised EEA agreement the ECJ explicitly emphasized the autonomy of the Community legal order that must be respected by the EEA

touch on Article 307 EC because the EEA agreement was not a pre-accession agreement – at least as far as the EC Member States of the time were concerned.

Nonetheless, the notion that there is something higher 'out there' than primary EC law was born. As is well known, the *Kadi*[38] case concerned the issue of the implementation of UN sanctions through EC Regulations. This raised the general issue of the relationship between Community law and UN law, in particular the UN Charter, which dates back to 1945 and to which all EC Member States are parties, but not the EC/EU.[39] In the first instance ruling in *Kadi*[40] and *Yusuf*,[41] the CFI had ruled that UN Security Council Resolutions adopted on the basis of Chapter VII UN Charter supersede primary EC law. Therefore, according to the CFI, UN Security Council Resolutions must automatically be implemented by the EC and cannot be reviewed by the European courts – with the exception of *jus cogens* violations.[42]

However, in the *Kadi* appeal proceeding, the ECJ flatly rejected this approach by sticking to the normal hierarchy of norms described above, i.e. primary EC law is the 'supreme law of the land'. More specifically, with regard to Article 307 EC, which was raised by several EC Member States as a justification for derogating from primary EC law and fundamental rights in order to fulfil their UN obligations, the ECJ emphasised that Article 307 (and 297) EC

> 'do not authorize any derogation from principles of liberty, democracy and respect for human rights and fundamental freedoms enshrined in Article 6 (1) TEU as a foundation of the Union.'[43]

In addition, the ECJ stressed that Article 307 EC

> '*may in no circumstances permit any challenge to the principles that form part of the very foundations of the Community legal order*, one of which is the protection of fundamental rights, including the review by the Community courts of the lawfulness of Community measures as regards their consistency with those fundamental rights.'[44] [emphasis added]

This very sweeping and categorical line of reasoning by the ECJ regarding Article 307 EC reveals an important new aspect (although it echoes what the

---

agreement and the parties to it.

38 *Supra* note 1. For detailed analyses see: Harpa (2009) 65-88; Tridimas/ Guitierrez-Fons (2009) 660-730; Tridimas (2009) 103-126; Lavranos (2009) 157-183; Gattini (2009) 213-239; Heun-Rehn (2008) 322-338.

39 See further: Halberstam/Stein (2009) 13-72; Kunoy/Dawes (2009) 73-104.

40 CFI (*Kadi*) *supra* note 9.

41 CFI (*Yusuf*) *supra* note 9.

42 *Ibid.*

43 ECJ (*Kadi*), para. 303.

44 *Ibid.*, para. 304.

ECJ had stated in *Opinion 1/91*), namely the introduction of a new *supra*-constitutional law level termed the 'very foundations of the Community legal order,' which stands at the apex of the hierarchy of norms of the Community legal order. This new *supra*-constitutional law level apparently enjoys an even higher status than primary EC law. This follows from the fact that rather than reversing its remark made in *Centro-Com* allowing EC Member States to derogate from primary EC law, the ECJ introduced this new level of core fundamental European constitutional law values and principles from which in no circumstances any derogations are allowed – even if they are required by pre-accession treaties. In other words, while derogations from primary EC law within the context of Article 307 EC and in the light of *Centro-Com* apparently still remain possible, the ECJ signalled to the EC Member States that such derogations can never affect the 'very foundations of the Community legal order.'

After having identified the existence of the new concept of the 'very foundations of the Community legal order,' the next question to be addressed is: what elements does it consist of? As usual, the ECJ kept things vague and flexible for future refinement and development of the concept. However, a close reading of the relevant parts of the ECJ's *Kadi* judgment reveals the following non-exhaustive list of elements which make up the 'very foundations of the Community legal order':

- the allocation of powers fixed by the EC Treaties;
- the autonomy of the Community legal system;
- the exclusive jurisdiction of the ECJ conferred on it by Articles 220 and 292 EC;
- judicial review of EC acts in the light of fundamental freedoms;
- the protection of fundamental rights.

In addition to these, the ECJ also referred – apparently as a distinct group of elements – to the following principles that are common to the EC/EU Member States (Article 6 TEU):

- liberty;
- democracy;
- respect for human rights and fundamental freedoms;
- the rule of law.

This list is a mixed bag, aiming to protect the institutional architecture of the EC, some of the most fundamental political values and principles underpinning the European integration process and several basic fundamental rights. As such, these elements are not surprising, but rather reflect what is commonly understood as the essentials of European constitutional law.[45]

An interesting aspect of the new concept of the 'very foundations of the Community legal order,' besides the fact that it modifies the hierarchy of the Community legal order, is that it resembles very much the attitude of some of

45 See extensively: Von Bogdandy/Bast (2007).

the EC Member States' constitutional courts towards their own constitutions.[46] In particular, the resemblance to the German Constitutional Court's concept of the *Ewigkeitsklausel*, i.e. eternity clause, is striking. This concept was developed on the basis of Article 79 (3) German Constitution,[47] which prohibits modifications of the Constitution that would affect the federal structure of Germany, the federal states' rights of participation or the fundamental principles underpinning the main fundamental rights as listed in Articles 1-20 German Constitution. This does not mean that the fundamental rights or the structure of Germany cannot be changed, but rather that their core elements may never be modified or abrogated by the German legislator.[48] Obviously, what exactly belongs to the untouchable core within the meaning of Article 79 (3) German Constitution remains debatable.[49]

More specifically, in its jurisprudence regarding the Maastricht Treaty, the German Constitutional Court (*Bundesverfassungsgericht*) expanded and applied this *Ewigkeitsklausel* to the relationship between German constitutional law and Community law. The *Bundesverfassungsgericht* accepted the advancing integration of the EC/EU only under the condition that Article 79 (3) German Constitution is respected.[50]

---

46 Besides the German Constitutional Court, which is discussed in more detail below, reference can be made to similar approaches by the Italian and Spanish Constitutional courts. For instance, Article 139 of the Italian Constitution reads as follows: 'La forma repubblicana non può essere oggetto di revisione costituzionale' (the republican structure cannot be modified). In 1988, the Italian Constitutional Court added the idea of fundamental rights being part of the untouchable core, distinguishing between two different procedures of revision, judgment 1146 of 1988, available at: http://www.cortecostituzionale.it/giurisprudenza/pronunce/schedaDec.asp?Comando=RIC&bVar=true&TrmD=&TrmDF=&TrmDD=&TrmM=&iPagEl=1&iPag=1.
In Spain, while legal scholarship has been arguing for a similar approach to an untouchable core of the constitution, the Spanish Constitutional Court has denied such an approach, stressing that there are no limits to the revision of the constitution. See decision D-48/2003, http://www.tribunalconstitucional.es/en/jurisprudencia/Pages/Sentencia.aspx?cod=8016. For an overview see: Palermo 2005. I thank Valentina Vadi and Giuseppe Martinico for providing me with this information.

47 Article 79 (3) German Constitution reads as follows: Eine Änderung dieses Grundgesetzes, durch welche die Gliederung des Bundes in Länder, die grundsätzliche Mitwirkung der Länder bei der Gesetzgebung oder die in den Artikeln 1 und 20 niedergelegten Grundsätze berührt werden, ist unzulässig.

48 See, *e.g.*, Badura (1992) 23 ff.

49 See for a discussion: Sannwald (2004) 32 ff.

50 German Constitutional Court (Maastricht Treaty) BVerfGE 89, 155, judgment of 12 October 1993, available at: http://sorminiserv.unibe.ch:8080/tools/ainfo.exe?Command=ShowPrintVersion&Name=bv089155. More recently and in a different context, in the judgment BVerfGE 102, 370 at 392 (Zeugen Jehovas) of 19 December 2000 the *Bundesverfassungsgericht* summarized its jurisprudence on Article 79 (3) up as follows: 'Art. 79 Abs. 3 GG entzieht die in Art. 1 Abs. 1 und Art. 20 GG niedergelegten Grundsätze jeglicher Änderung. Das Grundgesetz erklärt damit neben dem in Art. 1 Abs. 1 GG verankerten Grundsatz der Menschenwürde und den von ihm umfassten Kerngehalt der nachfolgenden Grund-

In its very recent judgment concerning the constitutionality of the *Lisbon Treaty*, the *Bundesverfassungsgericht* has not only unequivocally repeated its position on the untouchable character of Article 79 (3) German Constitution adopted in its *Maastricht* judgment, but has gone one step further by reserving its right to generally review the conformity of any acts of the EU with Article 79 (3) German Constitution.[51] Consequently, the *Bundesverfassungsgericht* considers itself the ultimate guardian of the core of German constitutional law values and principles. In other words, the *Bundesverfassungsgericht* still does not accept the final authoritative exclusive jurisdiction of the ECJ, but operates as a gatekeeper by continuing to determine the impact Community law is allowed to have on the German constitutional legal order.

If one compares the 'very foundations of the Community legal order' concept of the ECJ with the 'Ewigkeitsklausel' approach of the *Bundesverfassungsgericht*, it becomes quite clear that the ECJ is acting as a true European Constitutional court by protecting the European Constitution or (because of the failure to adopt it) the European Constitutional legal order from any modifications of its fundamental structure originating from international law. In fact, it is interesting to note that the elements that make up the 'very foundations of the Community legal order' contain a very strong fundamental rights dimension, which proves that the ECJ is serious about its notion that the Community is based on the rule of law and will always continue to be so.

Of course, ever since the *ERT*[52] judgment we have known that the ECJ grants the ECHR and fundamental rights in general a very special status within the Community legal order.[53] The interesting new aspect, though, is that unlike in, for instance, *Schmidberger*[54] and *Omega Spielhallen*,[55] in which it struck a balance

rechte (vgl. BVerfGE 84, 90 [120 f.]; 94, 12 [34]) auch andere Garantien für unantastbar, die in Art. 20 GG festgehalten sind. Dazu gehören die Prinzipien von Rechtsstaat und Demokratie (vgl. BVerfGE 89, 155 [182]; 94, 49 [103]).'

51 BVerfG, 2 BvE 2/08, judgment of 30.6.2009, available at: http://www.bverfg.de/entscheidungen/es20090630_2bve000208.html.

52 ECJ: Case C-260/89 *ERT* [1991] ECR I-2925.

53 *Ibid.*: '41. With regard to Article 10 of the European Convention on Human Rights, referred to in the ninth and tenth questions, it must first be pointed out that, as the Court has consistently held, fundamental rights form an integral part of the general principles of law, the observance of which it ensures. For that purpose the Court draws inspiration from the constitutional traditions common to the Member States and from the guidelines supplied by international treaties for the protection of human rights on which the Member States have collaborated or of which they are signatories (see, in particular, the judgment in ECJ: Case C-4/73 *Nold v. Commission* [1974] ECR 491, paragraph 13). *The European Convention on Human Rights has special significance in that respect* (see in particular ECJ: Case C-222/84 *Johnston v. Chief Constable of the Royal Ulster Constabulary* [1986] ECR 1651, paragraph 18). *It follows that, as the Court held in its judgment in ECJ: Case C-5/88 Wachauf v. Federal Republic of Germany [1989] ECR 2609, paragraph 19, the Community cannot accept measures which are incompatible with observance of the human rights thus recognized and guaranteed.*' [emphasis added].

54 ECJ: Case C-112/00 *Schmidberger* [2003] ECR I-5659, paras. 76-81.

55 ECJ: Case C-36/02 *Omega Spielhallen* [2004] ECR I-9609, paras. 34-40.

between fundamental rights and the free movement rights of the EC Treaty,[56] with the introduction of the 'very foundations of the Community legal order' concept, the ECJ has taken fundamental rights out of the scope of this balance by proclaiming their core untouchable.

In fact, the concept and elements of the 'very foundations of the Community legal order' are comparable to the first part of the German Constitution, which contains the programmatic preamble, the basic institutional structure of Germany and an enumeration of the most important fundamental rights which may not be abrogated at all or only under certain very limited circumstances.

On a more general level, the explicit elucidation of the 'very foundations of the Community legal order' concept is a very significant development in that it further restricts the freedom of the EC Member States to modify the fundamental core of the EC/EU Treaties as they wish. The ECJ clearly established a red line called the 'very foundations of the Community legal order' that may not be crossed – not even for the purpose of fulfilling pre-existing international obligations. Clearly, this development also serves the ECJ because it further strengthens its exclusive final authoritative jurisdiction to determine the relationship between international law and Community law, which is another illustration of its gatekeeper function.

In short, this conclusion further underlines the point previously made by the ECJ in *Opinion 1/91* that the E(E)C Treaty is of constitutional character.[57] Nowadays, obviously, there is no doubt that the EC/EU Treaties are the Constitution of Europe – despite the fact that the European Constitution was not ratified by all Member States and despite the still undecided legal status of the Lisbon Treaty.[58]

3.2 From the 'Effect-Based' Test to the Concept of 'Hypothetical Incompatibilities'

The other concept that is important for our purposes is the concept of 'hypothetical incompatibilities,' which was recently applied by the ECJ in the context of Article 307 EC. Its origins – albeit under a different label and in the context of post-accession treaties – can be traced back to the early 1970s in the ECJ's *AETR* judgment.[59]

As is well known, the *AETR* case concerned – among other issues – the question of the extent to which EC Member States are still able to operate at the inter-

---

56 But see ECJ: Case C-341/05 *Laval* [2007] ECR I-11767, paras. 90 ff. in which the ECJ favoured Community law freedoms instead of fundamental rights.

57 ECJ: Opinion 1/91 (EEA agreement), *supra* note 12, para. 21:

'[...] the EEC Treaty, albeit concluded in the form of an international agreement, none the less constitutes the constitutional charter of a Community based on the rule of law'.

But already in ECJ: Case *Les Verts* 294/83 [1984] ECR 3325 para. 23, the ECJ called the EEC Treaty '[...] the basic constitutional charter'.

58 See, *e.g.*, Lenaerts (2007) 815-831.

59 ECJ: Case 22/70 *AETR* [1971] ECR 263.

national level when the competence of the EC is potentially affected by actions of the Member States. In its *AETR* judgment the ECJ ruled that:

> '17 In particular, each time the Community, with a view to implementing a common policy envisaged by the Treaty, adopts provisions laying down common rules, whatever form these may take, the Member States no longer have the right, acting individually or even collectively, to undertake obligations with third countries which *affect those rules*.'[60] [emphasis added]

The ECJ further clarified that:

> '22 If these two provisions are read in conjunction, it follows that to the extent to which Community rules are promulgated for the attainment of the objectives of the treaty, the Member States cannot, outside the framework of the Community institutions, assume obligations which might *affect those rules or alter their scope*.'[61] [emphasis added]
>
> Therefore, the Member States are essentially precluded or pre-empted from acting on the international plane by, for instance, concluding treaties with third states whenever Community legislation has been adopted in a certain area. This is referred to as the principle of implied external competence of the EC, which becomes exclusive once internal Community legislation is in force.[62]

However, the more important aspect for our purposes is the use of the verb 'affect,' which implies a high degree of flexibility and dynamism because it is usually debatable whether or not a certain action of a Member State affects Community rules and is therefore prohibited. Clearly, the introduction of this 'effect-based' approach favours Community competence by putting the protection of the Community legal order first. Indeed, the *AETR* ruling has been instrumental in vastly expanding the EC's external competence and activities in almost all areas of law.[63] As a result, the EC Member States' external activities have been progressively marginalized and conditioned by their Community law obligations as interpreted by the ECJ.

The scope of this 'effect-based' test became particularly apparent many years later. For example, in *Opinion 2/91*[64] the ECJ was asked to opine whether the EC Member States could still ratify ILO Convention 170 or whether this fell within the exclusive competence of the EC. Referring to its *AETR* judgment, the ECJ stressed that:

---

60 *Ibid.*

61 *Ibid.*

62 See further: P. Koutrakos (2006); Eeckhout (2004).

63 *Ibid.*

64 ECJ: Opinion 2/91 *ILO Convention* 170 [1993] ECR I-1061.

> '10. [...] the authority of the decision in that case [*AETR*] *cannot be restricted to instances where the Community has adopted Community rules* within the framework of a common policy. In *all the areas corresponding to the objectives of the Treaty*, Article 5 [now Article 10 EC] *requires Member States* to facilitate the achievement of the Community's tasks and *to abstain from any measure which could jeopardize the attainment of the objectives of the Treaty*.
>
> 11. The Community's tasks and the objectives of the Treaty would *also be compromised if Member States were able to enter into international commitments containing rules capable of affecting rules already adopted in areas falling outside common policies or of altering their scope*.'[65] [emphasis added]

In other words the 'effect-based' test is not only applicable to the provisions of an international agreement and the corresponding EC legislation adopted within common policies, but extends to all Community law in force. In this context, the ECJ pointed out that Community law is already 'affected' if the Community has regulated the policy area concerned to a 'large extent.'[66] Nevertheless, it should be noted that subsequently in its *Opinion 1/94*[67] regarding the WTO Agreement, the ECJ took a more restrictive approach by requiring that the EC has fully harmonized a policy area in question before it will accept the exclusive competence of the EC.

Despite this, a few years later the ECJ again started to expand the application of the 'effect-based' test in its *Opinion 1/03*[68] regarding the new Lugano Convention. In this Opinion, the principal question was whether or not Community law would be affected if the envisaged Convention were also to be ratified by the EC Member States rather than by the EC alone. In applying the 'effect-based' test the ECJ not only took into account the extent of existing Community legislation and the level of harmonization achieved (finding harmonization to a 'large extent' to be sufficient),[69] but also included the nature and content of the envisaged agreement and future developments in Community law.[70] In particular, this last criterion of taking future developments of Community law into account introduces even more flexibility and dynamism, by making it virtually impossible for EC Member States to forecast whether or not an envisaged international treaty with a third state could affect Community law that is not even in force.

Obviously, the application of the 'effect-based' test gives the ECJ a wide margin to determine whether or not an envisaged agreement 'affects' the uniform and coherent application of Community law. Consequently, it is not surprising that the ECJ tends to conclude quite easily that Community law is indeed 'affected'. In fact, in its *Opinion 1/03* the ECJ opined that the ratification

---

65 *Ibid.*

66 *Ibid.*, para. 25.

67 ECJ: Opinion 1/94 *WTO Agreement* [1994] ECR I-5267.

68 ECJ: Opinion 1/03 *Lugano Convention* [2006] ECR I-1145; Lavranos (2006) 1087-1100 (A).

69 ECJ: Opinion 1/03 *Lugano Convention* para. 126.

70 *Ibid.*

of the Lugano Convention by the EC Member States in addition to the EC would affect Community law. Consequently, the Lugano Convention had to be ratified exclusively by the EC.

The ECJ's continual expansion of the 'effect-based' test by including future developments of Community law, that is Community legislation that has not even been adopted, was most recently taken one step further. In the *IMO* case,[71] the issue was whether Greece was still competent to table a proposal to the International Maritime Organization (IMO) which may affect existing Community law. In this context, it should be noted that while the Community is not a member of the IMO, it has adopted Community legislation in the policy area concerned. Indeed, the Commission argued that the EC has obtained exclusive external competence in this area by virtue of existing internal Community legislation, which therefore would prevent Greece from acting in this field. Essentially following the Commission's argument, the ECJ stated that:

> '30 Similarly, the Hellenic Republic's argument that an obligation to abstain from active participation in the IMO will not ensure that the Community interest is protected, since the Community is not a member of that international organisation, cannot be accepted. The mere fact that the Community is not a member of an international organisation in *no way authorises a Member State*, acting individually in the context of its participation in an international organisation, *to assume obligations likely to affect Community rules* promulgated for the attainment of the objectives of the Treaty. [emphasis added]
>
> 31 Moreover, the fact that the Community is not a member of an international organisation does not prevent its external competence from being in fact exercised, in particular through the Member States acting jointly in the Community's interest (see, to that effect, Opinion 2/91 [1993] ECR I-1061, paragraph 5).
>
> 32 The Hellenic Republic also relies on Article 9(1) of the Regulation, which in its submission confers exclusive competence on the Member States for implementing the safety requirements laid down by that regulation, which are based on the amendments to the SOLAS Convention and the ISPS Code.
>
> 33 In that connection, it is sufficient to note that the *competence of the Member States, which stems from that provision, does not imply that they have an external competence to take initiatives likely to affect* the provisions of the regulation.' [emphasis added]

Thus, the ECJ ruled that by submitting a proposal for monitoring the compliance of ships and port facilities to the IMO, Greece had failed to fulfil its obligations under Articles 10 EC, 71 EC and 80(2) EC. In other words, the ECJ concluded that Greece had violated its Community obligations by the mere fact of initiating a procedure which could lead to the adoption by the IMO of new rules and that the adoption of such new rules would 'affect' Community law.

[71] ECJ: Case C-45/07 *Commission v. Greece* [2009], judgment of 12 February 2009, nyr.

Again, it is important to note the decisive role of future possible legislative developments and the hypothetical impact: Greece had only submitted a proposal to the IMO, and it was still far from certain that the IMO would actually adopt this proposal, and if that were the case it is still not certain that relevant Community law would actually be affected by it. Nonetheless, this totally hypothetical, possible, future effect on Community law was sufficient for the ECJ to find Greece in breach of its EC law obligations.

Clearly, the ECJ's extensive application of the 'effect-based' approach in this manner further conditions and restricts the external relations activities of the EC Member States, and it is respectfully submitted that the ECJ went too far by disproportionately limiting the external competence of the Member States, in particular since any potential 'affect' on or conflict with Community law provisions was still purely hypothetical.

On a more general level, it is interesting to note that a kind of 'effect-based' test has also been developed and applied by the ECJ in the context of Article 47 TEU,[72] which regulates the relationship between the first pillar (EC Treaty) on the one hand, and the second (Common Foreign and Security Policy within the EU Treaty) and third (Police and Judicial Cooperation in Criminal Matters within the EU Treaty) pillars on the other hand. Essentially, Article 47 TEU is intended to ensure that no second or third pillar measures 'affect' Community law. In recent cross-pillar cases, notably the *ECOWAS*[73] and *data retention*[74] judgments, the ECJ has clarified that using a second or third pillar legal basis rather than a first pillar legal basis would 'affect' the relevant EC competences within the first pillar.[75] The consequences that follow from this approach are comparable to the ones resulting from the 'effect-based' test discussed above. In the first place, the ECJ is able to extend and protect its exclusive jurisdiction by favouring a first pillar legal basis whenever it can be argued. In the second place, the room for manoeuvre of the Member States is further restricted as they need to prove that a certain measure can only be based on a second or third pillar legal basis if they want to avoid a first pillar legal basis. Obviously, with the expanding competences of the EC by virtue of past EC/EU Treaty revisions and the ECJ's jurisprudence, it becomes increasingly difficult to argue that a measure could not also have a first pillar legal basis.[76]

---

72 Article 47 TEU reads as follows:

Subject to the provisions amending the Treaty establishing the European Economic Community with a view to establishing the European Community, the Treaty establishing the European Coal and Steel Community and the Treaty establishing the European Atomic Energy Community, and to these final provisions, *nothing in this Treaty [TEU] shall affect the Treaties establishing the European Communities or the subsequent Treaties and Acts modifying or supplementing them.* [emphasis added]

73 ECJ: Case C-91/05 *ECOWAS* [2008].

74 ECJ: Case C-301/06 *Data retention* [2009].

75 See further: Lavranos (2008) 311-319; Lavranos (2009) 158-163 C.

76 See the cases mentioned in notes 74 and 75.

The key similarity to the 'effect-based' test discussed above lies in the common aim of protecting the Community legal order from 'external' interferences – be they in the form of international law or second or third pillar measures. However, it should be noted that Article 47 TEU would be affected by the Lisbon Treaty in that the third pillar would be integrated into the first pillar, thereby limiting the application of Article 47 TEU to protecting the first pillar from being affected by second pillar measures.

3.3 The *BITs* Judgments – The Concept of 'Hypothetical Incompatibilities'

Even though the 'effect-based' test was not elaborated within the context of Article 307 EC, the ECJ has developed and applied a similar and even more far-reaching test in regard to this Article. In the *BITs*[77] cases, the ECJ was explicitly asked to interpret Article 307 EC. This time the main question was whether or not a hypothetical, potential, as yet unmaterialised conflict between pre-accession bilateral investment treaties (BITs) and primary EC law provisions could be considered as an incompatibility within the meaning of Article 307 EC.[78]

The facts of the two quite similar cases can be summarised as follows. From the late 1980s on, Austria had concluded several BITs with third countries, such as China, Russia, Korea and Turkey, before its accession to the EC. Those agreements contain a so-called 'transfer clause,' which guarantees investors of either party the free transfer, without undue delay, of capital connected with their investment.

Sweden, before its accession to the EC, had also concluded a number of BITs with third countries, such as Vietnam, Argentina, Egypt, China and Pakistan, containing a 'transfer clause'. In Sweden's agreements, that clause authorises the transfer of several types of capital related to investment, namely profits, liquidation sums, the reimbursement of loans, and the payment of expenses. In certain agreements it is stated that the transfer will be made in accordance with the applicable national laws and regulations. Essentially, these 'transfer clauses' are comparable to the free movement of capital provisions contained in the EC Treaty. In particular, Article 56 EC prohibits any restrictions on the movement of capital as well as any restrictions on payments between Member States and to and from third countries.[79] However, the EC Treaty permits certain restrictions

---

77 ECJ: Case C-205/06 *Commission v. Austria* [2009]; ECJ: Case C-249/06 *Commission v. Sweden* [2009].

78 See, *e.g.*, Eilmansberger (2009) 383-429; Burgstaller (2009) 181-216.

79 Article 56 EC reads as follows:

'1. Within the framework of the provisions set out in this chapter, all restrictions on the movement of capital between Member States and between Member States and third countries shall be prohibited.

2. Within the framework of the provisions set out in this chapter, all restrictions on payments between Member States and between Member States and third countries shall be prohibited.'

See further: Hji Panayi (2007) 121-132; Stahl (2004) 47.

to be imposed by Member States (notably in Article 58 EC, which sets out several justifications) and, more importantly for the present cases, by the Community itself. For instance, Article 57(2) EC enables the Community to regulate the movement of capital to and from third countries, including the introduction of restrictions.[80] Moreover, the Community may also enact safeguard measures to address difficulties with economic and monetary union, as detailed in Article 59 EC.[81] Finally, under Article 60(1) EC the Community may restrict economic relations with third countries, including the movement of capital, on the basis of a joint action relating to the common foreign and security policy, in particular the freezing of funds in the fight against terrorism.[82]

Despite the above possibilities, the Community has yet to introduce any restrictions that would affect the free movement of capital to and from the third countries that are party to the BITs entered into by Austria and Sweden. In particular, the Community has still not made use of Article 57(2) EC to regulate the area; there has been no need to introduce the safeguard measures provided for in Article 59 EC against the third countries at issue; and while the Council has already made use of Article 60(1) EC against a number of third states, it has not yet targeted any of those third countries with which Sweden and Austria have concluded BITs.

---

80 Article 57(2) EC reads as follows:
'Whilst endeavouring to achieve the objective of free movement of capital between Member States and third countries to the greatest extent possible and without prejudice to the other Chapters of this Treaty, the Council may, acting by a qualified majority on a proposal from the Commission, adopt measures on the movement of capital to or from third countries involving direct investment – including investment in real estate – establishment, the provision of financial services or the admission of securities to capital markets. Unanimity shall be required for measures under this paragraph which constitute a step back in Community law as regards the liberalisation of the movement of capital to or from third countries.'

81 Article 59 EC reads as follows:
'Where, in exceptional circumstances, movements of capital to or from third countries cause, or threaten to cause, serious difficulties for the operation of economic and monetary union, the Council, acting by a qualified majority on a proposal from the Commission and after consulting the ECB, may take safeguard measures with regard to third countries for a period not exceeding six months if such measures are strictly necessary.'

82 Article 60 EC reads as follows:
'If, in the cases envisaged in Article 301, action by the Community is deemed necessary, the Council may, in accordance with the procedure provided for in Article 301, take the necessary urgent measures on the movement of capital and on payments as regards the third countries concerned.'
Article 301 EC, referred to in that provision, states:
'Where it is provided, in a common position or in a joint action adopted according to the provisions of the Treaty on European Union relating to the common foreign and security policy, for an action by the Community to interrupt or to reduce, in part or completely, economic relations with one or more third countries, the Council shall take the necessary urgent measures. The Council shall act by a qualified majority on a proposal from the Commission.'

Nonetheless, the Commission started infringement proceedings based on Article 226 EC against both EC Member States[83] arguing that the mere existence of the BITs containing such transfer clauses, which do not provide for the possibility of imposing restrictions, is in conflict with the potential introduction of restrictions by the Community, and therefore constitutes an infringement of Article 307 EC, which in turn obliges Austria and Sweden to eliminate the alleged conflict. Sweden and Austria denied the existence of such an incompatibility, arguing that an incompatibility between the BITs and the EC law provisions mentioned above could only exist after the Community has actually adopted restrictive measures. Moreover, both Member States stressed that in the case of an actual conflict between the BITs and adopted EC legislation, international law offers mechanisms to deal with the situation, such as suspension, re-negotiation or even denouncement of the agreements. Thus, both countries argued that they are still in a position to eliminate any incompatibility if and when it actually becomes necessary. Therefore, both Member States rejected the notion that a currently purely potential, hypothetical situation could be construed as an incompatibility within the meaning of Article 307 EC.

However, the ECJ sided fully with the Commission and with the conclusion of the Opinion of Advocate General Maduro,[84] although it must be noted that Advocate General Maduro based his conclusion on an incompatibility of the BITs with Article 10 EC in conjunction with Articles 57, 59, 60 (1) EC, which in turn triggered a violation of Article 307 EC.

While the ECJ acknowledged that the transfer clauses are, in principle, consistent with Community law,[85] it considered the lack of any provision in the BITs allowing the EC Member States concerned to impose restrictions on the free transfer of capital as unacceptable under EC law. The ECJ stressed that the EC law provisions mentioned above empower the Council to unilaterally take restrictive measures against third states, which may also include states with which the two EC Member States have concluded BITs.[86] In order to be effec-

---

83 According to Burgstaller, *supra* note 78, at 196-197, the Commission has also targeted other EC Member States. See Press Release 'Free movement of capital: infringement procedures against Denmark, Austria, Finland and Sweden concerning Bilateral Investment Treaties with non-EU countries' IP/04/618, 10/05/2004, available at: http://europa.eu/rapid/pressReleasesAction.do?reference=IP/04/618&format=HTML&aged=1&language=EN&guiLanguage=en.

For example, the Commission brought an action against Finland on 27 February 2007, OJ C 95/30, *28.4.2007. The case is still pending before the ECJ. Originally, the Commission had also targeted Denmark, in particular because of its BIT with Indonesia, which supposedly violated Article 307 EC. Meanwhile, Denmark has terminated the BIT and negotiated a new one that was signed on 22 January 2007, but has apparently not yet entered into force.*

84 Opinion of AG Maduro in ECJ: Case C-205/06 *Commission v. Austria* [2009]; ECJ: Case C-249/06 *Commission v. Sweden* [2009], 20 July 2008, nyr.

85 ECJ: Case C-205/06 *Commission v. Austria* [2009]; ECJ: Case C-249/06 *Commission v. Sweden* [2009], judgment of 3 March 2009, nyr, paras. 25-27.

86 *Ibid.*, paras. 36-37.

tive, such restrictive measures must be applied immediately by all EC Member States.[87] Accordingly, the ECJ concluded that the discrepancy between the BITs and EC law provisions regarding the possibility of imposing restrictions immediately constitutes an incompatibility within the meaning of Article 307 EC which must be eliminated by the EC Member States.[88] In particular, the ECJ was not convinced that the various international law mechanisms allow the Member States concerned to guarantee that restrictive measures adopted by the Community could be effectively applied.[89] In other words, the ECJ was not persuaded that Austria and Sweden would be able to take the appropriate steps of suspending, re-negotiating or denouncing the bilateral investment treaties quickly enough in order to ensure the full effectiveness of EC law.

However, it is respectfully submitted that the *BITs* judgments are misguided. The imposition of the obligation to denounce pre-accession treaties even in the case of possible hypothetical conflicts with Community law goes much too far. While it is understandable that the ECJ aims to protect the autonomy of the Community legal order, the burden it imposes on the EC Member States and third states is – in the view of the present author – disproportionate. This is the case in particular because the ECJ (and Advocate General Maduro) failed to provide convincing arguments why Austria and Sweden would not be able to effectively suspend their BITs by invoking, for instance, the *clausula rebus sic stantibus* principle as enshrined in Article 62 Vienna Convention on the Law of Treaties. This generally principle of public international law provides precisely the possibility of suspending a treaty because of unforeseen circumstances,[90] thereby enabling Austria and Sweden to fulfil their Community law obligations.

Moreover, while it is true that the imposition of restrictions on capital and payments once imposed should be implemented immediately in order to be effective, at the same time it cannot be denied that such decisions are normally prepared months before and need to pass many political and legislative hurdles. This gives EC Member States sufficient time to start to re-negotiate their BITs, or at least inform the third state concerned that the BIT will be affected by upcoming Community legislation. In this way, EC Member States would have sufficient time to find a practical solution by protecting the investments of their 'own' investors covered by the BITs concerned and respecting the legitimate interests of the third states and the investments of 'their' investors, while at the same time demonstrating their seriousness in implementing their EC law obligations.

However, in the present author's opinion, the true reason for the ECJ to develop and apply the 'hypothetical incompatibility' concept in such an extensive manner is the fact that BITs usually provide for the use of international arbitral tribunals to solve disputes between the BIT parties. As in the *MOX plant* and

87 *Ibid.*

88 *Ibid.*, para. 38.

89 *Ibid.*, paras. 39-41.

90 See further: Heintschel van Heinegg (2006); Schwarzenberger (1992) 611 ff.

IJzeren Rijn cases, this again raises the issue of the exclusive jurisdiction of the ECJ and its increasing anxiety that international arbitral tribunals may find themselves in a position to interpret and apply Community law, thereby potentially undermining its uniformity and consistency as well as endangering the exclusive jurisdiction of the ECJ itself.[91]

This issue is further exacerbated by the existence of many intra-EC Member State BITs. This has created the real possibility that arbitral tribunals established by, for instance, The Netherlands and Hungary to adjudicate a dispute on investments within the framework of their BIT may quite likely end up interpreting Community law. Besides the risk of endangering its exclusive jurisdiction, the ECJ (and the Commission) seems to be particularly concerned with the discriminatory element that is inherent in BITs. Since the main aim and purpose of BITs is to protect the investments of the parties more favourably than investments of non-parties, this could result in discrimination between German investments in Hungary not covered by a BIT compared to Dutch investments covered by a BIT. This would clearly constitute a violation of Article 56 EC, whereas an international arbitral tribunal established on the basis of a BIT may not deal with Article 56 EC at all, or may find an apparent violation of EC law fully consistent with the BIT it is asked to interpret. Since the ECJ is unable to seize a case *ex officio*, it has to rely on the Commission to bring such a dispute before it to enable it to condemn the EC law violation and request its termination. Understandably, the ECJ would not consider this situation to be a sufficient guarantee of the uniform and consistent application of Community law.

In fact, in view of the discriminatory effect of intra-EC Member State BITs, the Commission has been pushing for the denouncement of all these treaties, so far, however, without success.[92] In order to break the resistance of the Member States, the Commission decided to bring the *BITs* cases before the ECJ – apparently in the hope that the ECJ would support the Commission's quest to eliminate intra-EC Member State BITs and, more generally, make all other BITs compatible with Community law. Clearly, the ECJ *BITs* judgments contain more support than the Commission could have hoped for. Thus, it can be expected that the Commission will once again step up the pressure on the Member States to denounce all intra-EC Member State BITs and all other pre-accession BITs that constitute a hypothetical incompatibility with Article 307 EC.

In this context, it should be noted that if and when the Lisbon Treaty enters into force, Article 207 incorporates foreign investment treaties into the explicit exclusive common commercial policy (CCP) competence of the EC/Union. Accordingly, sooner rather than later, many problems currently associated with BITs will be taken care of by the EC institutions.[93]

---

91 See on this point: Lavranos (2006) 223-246 (B).

92 See further: Wehland (2009) 297-320; Söderlund (2007) 455-468.

93 Article 207 (ex Article 133 TEC) Lisbon Treaty reads as follows:

1. The common commercial policy shall be based on uniform principles, particularly with regard to changes in tariff rates, the conclusion of tariff and trade agreements relating to trade in goods and

In sum, the *Kadi* and *BITs* judgments are important further building blocks in the ECJ's jurisprudence on Article 307 EC. The ECJ has developed and applied in a very short time span (from September 2008 to March 2009) a two-pronged approach based on Article 307 EC that significantly reduces the possibility of EC Member States using international obligations as a justification for derogating from their EC law obligations. Both the 'hypothetical incompatibilities' concept and the 'very foundations of the Community legal order' concept mark a qualitative new jump. More specifically, the ECJ has made it clear to the EC Member States that they cannot use obligations arising out of pre-accession treaties, or post-accession treaties for that matter, in order to avoid the full and effective application of Community law – even if Community law were 'affected' only hypothetically. This obligation has been further expanded by the introduction of the 'very foundations of the Community legal order' concept, which prohibits EC Member States from derogating from the core of fundamental European constitutional law values under any circumstances.

4 Outlook

The analysis above has illustrated that, taken together, the two concepts of 'hypothetical incompatibilities' and the 'very foundations of the Community legal order' enable the ECJ to effectively insulate the Community legal order from significant influences of international law, thereby reinforcing its autonomy. Indeed, it has become apparent that Article 307 EC as interpreted by the ECJ has a constitutional impact that hitherto was invisible. In particular, the huge importance of this Article as a tool for regulating the relationship between international law and Community law, with the ECJ having the central gatekeeper function, has been demonstrated.

More specifically, it has become clear that the ECJ uses Article 307 EC as a tool for both internal and external purposes. Internally, Article 307 EC allows the ECJ to continue to shape the distribution of external competences between the EC and the Member States in favour of the former and at the expense of the latter. Essentially, it is able to further restrict and reduce the remaining external

services, and the commercial aspects of intellectual property, *foreign direct investment*, the achievement of uniformity in measures of liberalisation, export policy and measures to protect trade such as those to be taken in the event of dumping or subsidies. The common commercial policy shall be conducted in the context of the principles and objectives of the Union's external action. [emphasis added]

[...]

4. For the negotiation and conclusion of the agreements referred to in paragraph 3, the Council shall act by a qualified majority. For the *negotiation and conclusion of agreements* in the fields of trade in services and the commercial aspects of intellectual property, as well as *foreign direct investment*, the Council shall act unanimously where such agreements include provisions for which unanimity is required for the adoption of internal rules. [emphasis added]

[...]

competence of the EC Member States, to the extent that they basically cannot effectively exercise their external competence any more since this could very easily 'affect' any future developments of Community law or create 'hypothetical incompatibilities'. These extraordinarily vague and flexible concepts enable the ECJ to tilt the balance in favour of the EC practically every time that there is a dispute between the Member States and the EC on this point. Besides, the introduction of the concept of the 'very foundations of the Community legal order' enables the ECJ to further develop the constitutional foundations of the EC/EU. It seems that irrespective of the failure of the ratification of the European Constitution and the still unclear fate of the Lisbon Treaty, the ECJ is willing to strengthen the core of fundamental European constitutional law values and principles by declaring them untouchable. Indeed, the use of very sweeping terms such as 'in no circumstances,' 'any incompatibility' and 'likely to affect' gives the ECJ a powerful *carte blanche* in its quest for further constitutionalization of the European legal order. At the same time, this enables the ECJ to protect its leading role in exclusively determining the institutional balance of powers within the Community, which naturally continues to favour the EC.

Nevertheless, it must be pointed out that the leading role of the ECJ is still not accepted by all. In particular, the German *Bundesverfassungsgericht* has made it clear in its judgment on the *Lisbon Treaty*[94] that it continues to exercise a 'reserve jurisdiction' by reviewing EC/Union acts and the extent of the European integration process in general as to their compatibility with the German Constitution.

Externally, the application of both concepts enables the ECJ to further export Community law to the world. It can impose the supremacy of EC law and thus EC law itself on third states and on international agreements. In particular, the obligation to denounce pre-accession treaties even in the event of 'hypothetical incompatibilities' has strong implications not only for the EC Member States but also for the rights and legitimate interests of third states arising out of pre-accession treaties. Indeed, one may question whether this obligation to denounce pre-accession treaties is not going too far by disproportionately affecting the rights and legitimate interests of the third states concerned. After all, third states are hardly in a position to determine whether a treaty could 'affect' the (future) Community law obligations of the EC Member States concerned. Therefore, it is submitted that the obligation to denounce pre-accession treaties can only be imposed as far as it is in conformity with international law, which also entails the adequate protection of the rights and legitimate interests of the third states concerned.

Nevertheless, the ECJ has so far not appeared to be greatly concerned with the international law consequences of the obligation to denounce international agreements that it so easily imposes on EC Member States. Of course, while it has accepted that this obligation should be carried out in compliance with international law,[95] the question arises of who is to judge that. An international

94 See *supra* note 51.

95 See, *e.g.*, ECJ: Case C-216/01 *Budvar* [2003] ECR I-13617.

arbitral tribunal? The ICJ? And if these courts found that the obligation were not in conformity with international law, would the ECJ care about it? Would it 'affect' Community law? Most probably not.

To sum up, the ECJ found in Article 307 EC a tool that allows it to determine to a large extent the relationship between Community law and international law. To do this, as has been demonstrated, it uses a two-pronged approach, insulating Community law from the interference of international law and thereby creating an untouchable core of fundamental European constitutional law values and principles.

While the creation of this untouchable core must be wholeheartedly welcomed and supported, the consequences of using the two concepts, especially for the rights and legitimate interests of third states, should not be overlooked. The interest of protecting the autonomy of the Community legal order must be balanced against the fundamental principles of public international law, such as *pacta sunt servanda* and the legitimate interests of third states that enter into treaties with EC Member States. In the view of this author, the ECJ has so far not paid sufficient attention to this point. In particular, the application of the 'hypothetical incompatibilities' test favours Community law interests in a biased way.

Indeed, the inherent but increasingly open hegemonic tendency to export and impose Community law to and on the world may in the long run not be in the interest of the Community.[96] In fact, as a consequence of the ECJ's jurisprudence, long term investments by European investors under the thousands of existing BITs with third countries may be endangered because all these BITs may have to be denounced or re-negotiated – possibly with less advantageous conditions. Besides, third states and their investors may not like to see their claims adjudicated by the ECJ rather than by arbitral tribunals. In other words, there is no reason why third states and foreign investors should accept submission to Community law and the jurisdiction of the ECJ. A less pro-active attitude on the part of the ECJ in protecting the autonomy of the Community legal order may therefore – in the long term – not be such a bad idea.

---

96 It is interesting to note that Klabbers (2009), approaching this topic from an international law perspective comes to essentially the same conclusion. He concludes '[...] there is but a single rule, and according to that EU law shall prevail. That is to some extent understandable, and perhaps the inevitable result of being able to adopt only one prism at a time [...]. Yet, the evidence presented above suggests that the EC courts, and the Commission, have over the years become less interested in balancing than might legitimately have been expected. That may help protect European integration in the short run, but is bound to give rise to some resentment along the road on the part of the treaty partners of the EU's member states – and quite possibly on the part of those member states as well.' at 231.
So, eventually, whatever perspective or mindset one has, at the end of the day the same conclusion must be drawn, namely, that Article 307 EC as applied by the ECJ in its recent judgments may be detrimental to the EC. Thus, in a way, Article 307 EC unites international law and Community law specialists.

References

P. Badura, Verfassungsänderung, -wandel, -gewohnheitsrecht, in: J. Issensee / P. Kirchhof (eds.), Handbuch des Staatsrecht, Vol. VII, C.F. (Müller 1992).

M. Burgstaller, 'European Law and Investment Treaties' [2009] *Journal of International Arbitration*, 181-216.

B. de Witte, Old-Fashioned Flexibility: International Agreements between Member States of the European Union, in: G. de Búrca / J. Scott (eds.), *Constitutional Change in the EU. From Uniformity to Flexibility?*, (Oxford 2000) Hart Publishing, 31-58.

Th. Eilmansberger, 'Bilateral Investment Treaties and EU law' [2009] *Common Market Law Review*, 383-429.

P. Eeckhout, EC law and UN Security Council Resolutions – in search of the right fit, in: A. Dashwood / M. Maresceau (eds.), *Law and Practice of EU External Relations* (2008) CUP, 104-128.

P. Eeckhout, *EU External Relations* (2004) OUP.

P. Eeckhout, *EU External Relations* (2004) OUP.

Ch. Franklin, 'Flexibility v. Legal certainty: Article 307 EC and other issues in the aftermath of the Open skies cases' [2005] *European Foreign Affairs Review*, 79-115.

A. Gattini, 'Case-note on Kadi' [2009] *Common Market Law Review*, 213-239.

D. Halberstam / E. Stein, 'The UN, the EU and the King of Sweden: Economic sanctions and individual rights in a plural world order' [2009] *Common Market Law Review*, 13-72.

G. Harpaz, Judicial Review by the ECJ of UN 'smart sanctions' against terror [2009] *European Foreign Affairs Review*, 65-88.

W. Heintschel van Heinegg, Commentary on clausula rebus sic stantibus, in: Max Planck Encyclopedia of Public International Law, OUP electronic version, last update August (2006).

S. Heun-Rehn, Kadi und Al Barakaat, 'Der EuGH, die Gemeinschaft und das Völkerrecht' [2008] *European Law Reporter*, 322-338.

Ch. Hji Panayi, 'The effect of Community law on pre-accession tax treaties' [2007]*EC Tax Review*, 120-132.

J. Jans/N. Lavranos, Case note on FIAMM, *SEW* (2009) *Tijdschrift voor Europees en Economisch Recht*, 356-362.

J. Klabbers, Moribund on fourth of July? The Court of Justice on prior agreements of the Member States [2001] *European Law Review*, 26 ff.

J. Klabbers, *Treaty Conflict and the EU* (2009) CUP.

P. Koutrakos, *EU International Relations Law* (2006) Hart.

B. Kunoy/A. Dawes, 'Plate Tectonics in Luxembourg: The Ménage à Trois between EC law, International Law and the European Luxembourg: The Ménage à Trois between EC law, International Law and the European Convention on Human Rights following the UN sanctions cases' [2009] *Common Market Law Review*, 73-104.

N. Lavranos, Case-note on open skies agreements, *Legal Issues of Economic Integration* (2003), 81-91.

N. Lavranos, *Legal Interaction between Decisions of International Organizations and European law*, (Europa Law Publishing Groningen 2004).

N. Lavranos, 'The communitarization of WTO dispute settlement reports: An exception to the rule of law' [2005] *European Foreign Affairs Review*, 313-338.

N. Lavranos, 'The MOX plant and IJzeren Rijn disputes: Which court is the supreme arbiter?' [2006] *Leiden Journal of International Law* (B), 223-246.

N. Lavranos, 'Case-note on Opinion 1/03' [2006] *Common Market Law Review* (A), 1087-1100.

N. Lavranos, 'The scope of exclusive jurisdiction of the Court of Justice' [2007] *European Law Review* (B), 83-94.

N. Lavranos, 'Judicial Review of UN Sanctions by the CFI' [2007] *Nordic Journal of International Law* (A), 1-17.

N. Lavranos, 'In dubio pro first pillar: Recent developments in the delimitation of the competence of the EU and EC' [2008] *European Law Reporter*, 311-319.

N. Lavranos, 'Case-note on Kadi' [2009] *Legal Issues of Economic Integration*, 157-183.

N. Lavranos, 'Data retention: First or third pillar instrument for fighting terrorism?' [2009] *European Law Reporter*, 158 ff.

K. Lenaerts, La constitutionnalisation de l'ordre juridique de l'Union européenne, in: R. Andersen (ed.), *Mélanges en hommage à Francis Delpérée. Itinéraires d'un constitutionnaliste*, (Bruxelles/Paris 2007) Bruylant/L.G.D.J.

P. Manzini, The priority of pre-existing treaties of EC Member States within the framework of International law [2001] *European Journal of International Law*, 781-792.

F. Palermo, *La forma di stato dell'Unione europea* (Padova 2005) Cedam.

Petersmann/Spennemann, Commentary on Art. 307, in: von der Groeben/ Schwarze, *Kommentar zum EU/EG Vertrag*, Vol. 4, 6th ed., (Nomos 2004).

Sannwald, 'Commentary on Article 79', in: B. Schmidt-Bleibtreu / F. Klein, *Kommentar zum Grundgesetz*, 10th ed., (Luchterhand 2004).

R. Schütze, EC Law and International Agreements of the Member States – An Ambivalent Relationship? (2007) *Cambridge Yearbook of European Legal Studies*, 387-440.

G. Schwarzenberger, Commentary on clausala rebus sic stantibus, in: R. Berhardt (ed.), *Encyclopedia of Public International Law*, Vol. I, Elsevier (1992).

F. Snyder, 'The gatekeepers: The European courts and WTO law' [2003] *Common Market Law Review*, 313-367.

Ch. Söderlund, 'Intra-EU BIT investment protection and EC Treaty' [2007] *Journal of International Arbitration*, 455-468.

K. Stahl, 'Free movement of capital between Member States and third countries' [2004] *EC Tax Review*, 47 ff.

T. Tridimas/J. Guitierrez-Fons, 'EU law, International law and economic sanctions against terrorism: The Judiciary in distress?' [2009] *Fordham International Law Journal*, 660-730.

T. Tridimas, 'Terrorism and the ECJ: The Empowerment and democracy in the EC legal order' [2009] *European Law Review*, 103-126.

A. Von Bogdandy/J. Bast (eds.), *Principles of European Constitutional Law* (2007) Hart.

H. Wehland, 'Intra-EU Investment agreements and arbitration: Is EC law an obstacle?' [2009] *International Comparative Law Quarterly*, 297-320.

CHAPTER 5

Judicial Review of United Nations Counter-Terrorism Sanctions in the European Multilevel System of Human Rights Protection

A Case Study in Ineffectiveness

Federico Fabbrini*

I Introduction

The purpose of this chapter is to assess how effective the protection of fundamental rights is in the European multilevel system of human rights protection: the issue of judicial review of United Nations (UN) counter-terrorism sanctions in the European legal space is taken into account as a case study. My argument will be that the European human rights architecture still has gaps where the protection of fundamental rights is severely undermined. I will claim however that the substantive transformations produced by the jurisprudential dialogue among the highest European courts and the formal transformations that would be generated by the entry into force of the European Union (EU) Reform Treaty adopted in Lisbon show the potential for overcoming these *lacunae* of the European multilevel system, thus enhancing the protection of fundamental rights.

The chapter is structured as follows. In part II I will briefly outline the main traits of the European multilevel system of human rights protection and introduce the problem of ineffectiveness conceptualizing it as one of the major shortcomings of the European human rights architecture. In part III I will argue that the problem of ineffectiveness of human rights protection manifested in the European multilevel system because of the early impossibility for the individuals and the entities targeted by the UN counter-terrorism sanctions of having a court review the lawfulness of such measures. I will maintain, however, that a recent evolution in the jurisprudence of the European Court of Justice (ECJ), especially if coupled with the innovations that might be introduced by the Lisbon Treaty, has provided an answer to this situation. A brief conclusion will follow in part IV.

II Multilevel Protection of Fundamental Rights in Europe and the Problem of Ineffectiveness

The European human rights architecture is characterized by a three-layered structure.[1] Fundamental rights in Europe are protected by

* PhD student, Law Department, European University Institute. I would like to thank prof. Marise Cremona and prof. Martin Scheinin for their comments on an early draft of this paper. Many thanks also to Nicola Owtram for revising the language of the text and to Maria Diletta Damin for helping me in the editing process. E-mail: federico.fabbrini@eui.eu.

1 In this chapter, following Walker (2009) 1, I use the concept of multilevel constitutionalism in a broad sense. Whereas *stictu sensu* multilevel constitutionalism is linked to a particular school of thinking about contemporary constitutional developments centred around the work of Pernice (1999) 703; Pernice (2002), 511; Mayer (2003); *lato sensu*, the label refers to any scholarly position maintaining that constitutional ideas, institutions, norms and practices apply in settings beyond the State (*e.g.* the theory of compound constitutionalism). See: Barbera (2000) 59; S. Cassese (2002); Della Cananea (2003); Besselink (2007).

national, supranational (EU) and international (European Convention of Human Rights - ECHR) norms and institutions.[2] The protection of human rights is based on substantive rights backed up by institutional remedies through the method of judicial review.[3] The protection of human rights is thus the combination of rights on the books with remedies in action. Rights are proclaimed in national Constitutions and in the ECHR, and are recalled in the EU Treaty, that identifies the constitutional traditions common to the member states and the ECHR as general principles of community law.[4] National courts, the ECJ (which includes the Court of First Instance – CFI)[5] and the European Court of Human Rights (ECtHR), then, provide remedies against rights' infringements.[6]

Notwithstanding its apparent comprehensiveness the European system of human rights protection has manifested a number of problems. Several criticisms have been addressed by scholars to *particular* features of the protection of fundamental rights in the (various layers of the) European multilevel structure.[7] I propose here, however, to identify and define a clearly framed problem of the European human rights architecture *as a whole.* By resorting to the Hartian idea of the 'hard case'[8] I argue that it is possible to categorize theoretically (some among) the most serious empirical setbacks that have emerged in the European system of human rights protection by using the concept of 'ineffectiveness'.[9] I consider as falling under this category all the situations arising when the

---

2 The literature on multilevel protection of fundamental rights in Europe is vast, see among many: Zagrebelsky (2003); D'Atena (2004); Douglas-Scott (2006b) 629; Cartabia (2007) 13; Krisch (2008) 183.

3 Weiler (1991) 555, 559.

4 See De Witte (1999a) 859; Von Bogdandy (2000) 1307; De Burca (2001); Pizzorusso (2002).

5 It shall indeed be remembered that the CFI is part of the ECJ and that according to Article 220 EC Treaty (OJ 2006 C 321/E/46), they both 'shall ensure that in the interpretation and application of this Treaty the law is observed'. Note that the European judicial system is composed by 'the ECJ, with its ancillary body, the CFI, on top, and by national courts': Cartabia & Weiler (2000). See also Craig (2001) 177, 178.

6 See Harlow (1999); Lenaerts & De Smijter (2001) 90; Wildhaber (2002) 161; Schimmelfenning (2007) 100.

7 See, *e.g.*, A. Cassese, Clapham & Weiler (1991) 1; Besselink (1998) 629; Alston & Weiler (1999) 3, 9; Harlow (cf. *supra*: note 6) 190; Spielmann (1999) 757; De Witte (cf. *supra*: note 4) 883; Scheeck (2005); Gennusa (2007) 91; Harpaz, (2009) 105.

8 I borrow the concept of 'hard case' from Hart (1983) who employs it in his celebrated theory of interpretation to distinguish those cases where the meaning of a normative disposition is unclear from those cases where, on the contrary, the situation falls within the core of the normative disposition. For the purpose of this work the Hartian concept of 'hard case' will be utilized to identify those cases laying in the 'penumbra' of the application of the multilevel rules of human rights protection, raising the biggest concerns for the integrity of the European multilevel system. On Hart's legacy see Barberis (2005) 224.

9 The identification of the problem of ineffectiveness used in this paper is therefore essentially inductive: it is an attempt to organize (some among) the multiple and contingent criticisms that are addressed to the (various layers of) the European multilevel system of human rights protection (see *supra* note 7) by abstracting them in a more general theoretical category. For an argument that the role of scholars in the

European multilevel system does not provide protection against rights' infringements, given a lack of available rights and remedies at any layer of the structure.

If there are no rights and remedies, the system has a *lacuna*, a legal gap, where human rights are in peril. As such, the problem of ineffectiveness represents one of the major shortcomings of the European multilevel system of human rights protection.[10] When the system is ineffective, the protection of human rights is frustrated since there are cases in which no safeguards are available to protect individuals against the illegitimate activity of public authorities. What distinguish a constitutional system based on the 'rule of law' from other kind of polities or social compacts founded on other values, however, is exactly the possibility for the individuals illegitimately affected by the exercise of public authority to obtain justice.[11] In normative terms, a well-functioning system for the protection of human rights should hence be framed in order to provide the most effective protection against all sorts of violations.[12]

It is submitted that the view that underpins my research is largely rooted in the principles of John Locke's constitutionalism[13] and based on the idea that fundamental rights are natural and inalienable endowments of every individual that must be protected against the encroachment of the majoritarian political power.[14] In this liberal tradition, the institutions whose purpose is to ensure the protection of individual rights are essentially the courts of law.[15] From this point of view, therefore, the parameter on the basis of which to assess the effectiveness of human rights protection is the possibility for individuals adversely affected by the action of public authorities to obtain judicial redress.[16] I do not need to say, however, that there are other possible ways of looking at the effectiveness of a system of human rights protection, based on different conception of constitutionalism and rights.[17]

---

field of constitutional law is precisely to start from empirical evidences to elaborate doctrinal concepts that may help in explaining and rationalizing the complexities of reality see Morrone (2001) 7.

10 A. Cassese, Clapham & Weiler (cf. *supra*: note 7) 3.

11 See Shapiro (1981); Barak (2006) 51; Zagrebelsky (2008) 116.

12 A. Cassese, Clapham & Weiler (cf. *supra*: note 7) 7.

13 See Locke (1690, reprinted 1980).

14 See among many: Bobbio (1992); Zagrebelsky (1992); Barbera (1997); Saio (1999); Breyer (2005); Haberle (2006); Cheli (2006).

15 According to the renowned theory of McIlwain (1947) the development of an independent judiciary guarantor of the fundamental rights and liberties of the individuals historically originated from the distinction between the concepts of *gubernaculum* and *iurisdictio* in Middle-Age England.

16 For similar statements at the national level see Cheli (1996); Morrone (cf. *supra*: note 9); Bin (2004). With regard to the EU and the international (global) system see Weiler (cf. *supra*: note 3) 565; Poiares Maduro (2005) 332; Von Bogdandy, Dann & Goldmann (2008) 1375, 1376.

17 In the so called 'Jacobinian' constitutionalist tradition, for example, rights are not considered as pre-political endowment of the individual but rather as the product of activity of the political powers. In this vision the role of courts in ensuring the effectiveness of human rights protection is far more limited since it is believed that the main instrument to attribute rights to individuals is the exercise of legisla-

The constitutional systems of the European countries, nonetheless, confirm the importance of an effective judicial protection of fundamental rights.[18] In the civil law countries, which recognize the principle *ubi ius ibi remedium*, access to justice has progressively emerged as an autonomous individual rights whose purpose is to make all the other substantive rights effective.[19] In the common law countries, because of the tradition of the forms of action, the existence of an effective remedy precede the attribution of an individual rights as only *ibi ius ubi remedium*.[20] Both constitutional models acknowledge that human rights shall be effectively protected, be it through a general right of access to court or a specific remedy in front of an independent tribunal. In addition, with the constitutionalization of the European legal space, such principles have moved to the international and supranational systems, increasing the convergence between the two models.[21]

At the international level, Article 6 of the ECHR codifies a right to fair trial and Article 13 states that 'everyone whose rights and freedoms as set forth in this Convention are violated shall have an effective remedy before a national authority notwithstanding that the violation has been committed by persons acting in an official capacity.'[22] In *Golder*,[23] the ECtHR, drawing from the concept of the 'rule of law' in the preamble of the ECHR, interpreted Article 6 as not being 'limited to guaranteeing in substance the right to a fair trial in legal proceedings which are already pending, [but also as] secur[ing] a right of access to the courts for every person wishing to commence an action in order to have his civil rights and obligations determined.'[24] On the other hand, it is a fairly established statement of the ECtHR, that the ECHR 'is intended to guarantee

tive powers expressing the general will. See Barbera (cf. *supra*: note 14) 10; Troper (2007). It may be debated whether this idea of constitutionalism is compatible with the growing pluralism of values that characterize multicultural societies. See Habermas (2005) 63; Facchi (2006).

18 See Trocker (2007) 421, 435. As affirmed by De Vergottini (1998) 11, this testify the spreading of the principles of liberal constitutionalism Europe-wide in the second half of the XX century.

19 See, *e.g.*, Article 24(1) of the Italian Constitution recognizing that 'tutti possono agire in giudizio per la tutela dei propri diritti ed interessi legittimi' and the similar notion of 'one's natural judge' developed under German constitutional law. For a comparative overview of the concept Europe-wide see Storskrubb & Ziller (2007) 177.

20 See Mattei (1996), who recalls the celebrated statement of Maitland (1948) according to which 'the forms of action are a part of the structure upon which rests the whole common law of England and, though we may have buried them, they still rule us from their graves.'

21 Trocker (cf. *supra*: note 18) 435; Storskrubb & Ziller (cf. *supra*: note 19) 184.

22 According to Wildhaber (2004) 83, 'the principal and overriding aim of the system set up by the ECHR is to bring about a situation in which in every Contracting State the rights and freedoms are effectively protected.'

23 *Golder v. United Kingdom* ECHR [1975], Application No. 4451/70.

24 Id. at §25. See Harlow (cf. *supra*: note 6), 203.

not rights that are theoretical or illusory but rights that are practical and effective.'[25]

Also the ECJ has recognized in its landmark *Johnston* decision[26] that 'the requirement of judicial control [...] reflects a general principle of law which underlies the constitutional traditions common to the member states. That principle is also laid down in articles 6 and 13 of the ECHR [...] and as the Court has recognized in its decisions, the principles on which that convention is based must be taken into consideration in Community Law.'[27] By virtue of this judgment, therefore, 'all persons have the right to obtain an effective remedy in a competent court against measures which they consider to be contrary to' their fundamental rights. By enshrining in Article 6 of the EU Treaty[28] the principle that the EU 'is founded on the principles of liberty, democracy, respect for human rights and fundamental freedoms, and the rule of law' the Masters of the Treaty have furthermore reasserted the need for effective judicial review.[29]

In addition, Article 47 of the EU Charter of Fundamental Rights (CFR)[30] – which is entitled 'Right to an effective remedy', just as Article 13 of the ECHR – clearly recognizes that 'everyone whose rights and freedom guaranteed by the law of the Union are violated has the right to an effective remedy before a tribunal in compliance with the conditions laid down in this article.' Although the CFR does not have legal value yet and is not binding over the EU institutions and the Member States when concerned, its formal and solemn proclamation by the EU Parliament, Council and Commission in Nice in 2000 and its subsequent inclusion in the Treaty Establishing a Constitution for Europe[31] and in the Lisbon Treaty confirm that the Member States and the EU institutions 'have agreed to the wording of the Charter as being representative of the contents of the rights it endeavours to protect.'[32]

De iure, therefore, in every layer of the European multilevel system the availability of effective judicial remedies is considered as essential to guarantee respect and protection of fundamental rights. There is however 'a number of possible human rights violations [that] may, in fact, never reach'[33] a judge or another officer authorized by law to exercise judicial power. 'In every legal system there is a gap between the law in the books and the law in action.'[34] In

25 *Airey v. Ireland*, ECHR [1979], Application No. 6289/73, at § 24. See also *Artico v. Italy*, ECHR [1980], Application No. 6694/74 at §33; *Goodwin v. United Kingdom*, ECHR [2002], Application No. 28957/95, at §74.

26 Case 222/84, *Johnston v. Chief Constable of the Royal Ulster*, [1986] ECR 1651.

27 Id. at §18.

28 OJ 2006 C 321/E/1.

29 Gaja (1999) 780, 794; Shelton (2004) 349.

30 OJ 2000 C 364/1.

31 OJ 2004 C 310/1.

32 Strosrkrubb & Ziller (cf. *supra*: note 19) 184. See also Ward (2004) 123.

33 De Witte (cf. *supra*: note 4) 883.

34 Snyder (1993) 19, 26.

the field of human rights protection, nonetheless, the existence of a gap should be a cause for concern.[35] It is hence important 'to identify the gaps which exist; to explain why they exist; to identify and distinguish those gaps which are likely to be long-term features of the [...] system; and, if possible, to focus on those [...] gaps which pose real difficulties for the operation and the development of'[36] the European multilevel structure of human rights protection.

From this point of view, addressing the developments in the protection of fundamental rights in Europe may prove particularly useful. The European system of human rights protection, indeed, is currently at the heart of several transformations. A substantive transformation is produced by the constant jurisprudential activity of the highest European courts[37] dialoguing one with another in the joint effort to overcome the new human rights challenges.[38] A formal transformation might derive then by the entry into force (hopefully late in 2009 or at the beginning of 2010) of the Reform Treaty, which was signed in Lisbon in December 2007 – but has not been ratified yet by all 27 EU member states.[39] It is hence fruitful to take into account these transformations to evaluate whether they may reasonably solve the problem of ineffectiveness of the European multilevel system of human rights protection.

The issue of judicial review of UN counter-terrorism economic sanctions provides a good example of the problem of ineffectiveness, highlighting the pernicious effects that the lack of adequate human rights protection in any layer of the European multilevel structure may cause. On the other hand, this case

---

35 A. Cassese, Clapham & Weiler (cf. *supra*: note 7) 75 who argue that 'human rights protection is a question of constant vigilance.' See also Alston & Weiler (cf. *supra*: note 7) 24.

36 Snyder (cf. *supra*: note 34) 26.

37 I follow and generalize here the approach adopted by Shapiro (1999) 321 who argues that any analysis of the 'ECJ must be placed within two evolutionary contexts. One is the evolution of the Union itself. [...] The other is the evolution of the courts engaged in higher law judicial review.' On the dynamic character of human rights jurisprudence see McCrudden (2000) 499, 500. On the recent transformation in the case law of the highest European courts in the field of human rights see Canor (2000) 3; De Burca (2003); Shapiro (2005).

38 On judicial dialogue the literature is now vast. See Slaughter (1994), 99; Slaughter (2003) 191; Lavranos (2008); S. Cassese (2009). With specific reference to judicial dialogue in the European legal space see Jacobs, (2003) 547; Martinico & Fontanelli, (2008) 351; Cartabia (2009) 5.

39 OJ 2007 C 306/1. The Lisbon Treaty has already been ratified by 26 of the 27 EU Member States. However the Treaty has been approved by Parliament but still awaits presidential signature in the Czech Republic. In Germany the constitutionality of the ratification act has been acknowledged by the Constitutional Tribunal – BverfG judgment of 30 June 2009 – on the condition of the enactment of an additional statute strengthening the responsibility of Parliament in EU affairs. In Ireland a popular referendum held on 12 June 2008 rejected the ratification of the Treaty, but a new referendum held on 2 October 2009 as requested by the Presidency Conclusions of the European Council of 11 and 12 December 2008, Council of the European Union Doc. 17271/08 eventually approved it. For the data concerning the advancement of the ratification procedure in the various EU Member States see: http://www.euractiv.com/en/future-eu/ratifying-treaty-lisbon/article-170245 (last visited on 14 October 2009).

study has the advantage of illustrating how the current substantive and formal transformations may have a positive outcome in filling the gaps in the European multilevel system of human rights protection. To this end, in the next section, the issue of judicial review will be considered diachronically, from a European constitutional law perspective.[40] The chronological approach has the advantage of highlighting the gradual transformations in the protection of fundamental rights and the dynamics of the relationship between national, supranational and international courts in the European multilevel system.

III A Case Study: Judicial Review of UN Counter-Terrorism Sanctions

One of the major strategies adopted by the UN to fight against the phenomenon of international terrorism[41] has been, especially in the wake of 9/11/2001,[42] the adoption of economic sanctions targeting specific individuals or entities suspected of being involved in the financing of terrorism, and freezing their assets.[43] The highly political and confidential mechanisms through which such counter-terrorism measures are established, however, has raised concerns as to the respect of the fundamental rights of the natural and legal persons affected[44] and has raised the question of whether the judiciary should have the authority to step into the thorny field of national security to ensure an effective

40 For a thorough assessment of the topic from a public international law perspective see Scheinin (2009).

41 On the UN global counter-terrorism strategy see: A/RES/60/228 (2006); A/60/825 (2006); A/RES/62/272 (2008). For an overview of UN policies in the field of counter-terrorism see: Bianchi (2006) 881; Frowein (2006) 785. The literature on international terrorism is wide: Sterba (2003); Walter et al. (2004); Ramraj et al. (2005). For the problems raised by the normative definition of the phenomenon see instead A. Cassese (2001) 993 and Saul (2006).

42 See Condorelli (2001) 829; Fitzgerald (2002) 957. The employment of counter-terrorism sanctions at the UN level began prior to 9/11/2001 (see, *e.g.* S/RES/1267 (1999), S/RES/1333 (2000), S/RES/1363 (2001)) but steadily grew after the terrorist attacks in the US (see, *e.g.* S/RES/1373 (2001), S/RES/1452 (2002), S/RES/1455 (2003), S/RES/1526 (2004), S/RES/1535 (2004), S/RES/1566 (2004), S/RES/1617 (2005), S/RES/1730 (2006), S/RES/1735 (2006), S/RES/1822 (2008)). See Frowein (cf. *supra*: note 41) 787.

43 See Ciampi (2007); Halberstam & Stein (2009) 13. On the UN sanction regime more generally see Cortright & Lopez (2000); Farrall (2007).

44 See the report of the UN *Special Rapporteur* on the promotion and protection of human rights and fundamental freedoms while countering terrorism, Martin Scheinin, A/61/267 (2006), the conclusions of the UN High Commissioner for Human Rights on the protection of human rights and fundamental freedoms while countering terrorism, A/HRC/8/13 (2008) and Resolution 1597 (2008) and Resolution 1824 (2008) of the Parliamentary Assembly of the Council of Europe. The literature on the UN sanctioning system and respect of human rights is now vast, see among many: Mégret & Hoffman (2003) 314; Cannizzaro (2006) 195.

protection of human rights by reviewing the compatibility of the counter-terrorism measures established by the UN with human rights standards.[45]

I will argue that the problem of ineffectiveness of human rights protection manifested in the European multilevel system because of the early impossibility for the natural and legal persons targeted by the UN counter-terrorism sanctions of having a court review the lawfulness of such measures. I will claim, however, that a recent development in the jurisprudence of the ECJ, partly anticipating the reforms about to be introduced by the Lisbon Treaty, has provided an answer to this situation and has enhanced the protection of fundamental rights of the persons targeted by the counter-terrorism measures under suspicion of being involved in the financing of terrorism.

Indeed, although European courts had previously exercised judicial review over the legality of (the domestic implementation acts of) UN authorized sanctions addressing conditions of war or international crisis,[46] in the first decisions dealing with UN *counter-terrorism* sanctions all European courts either lacked or declined the power to exercise judicial review of the acts under scrutiny. This situation was perhaps generated by the attitude of judicial deference of the European judiciaries *vis à vis* the political branches of government acting under the auspices of the UN in the aftermath of a terrorist emergency.[47] Nonetheless, it severely jeopardized the effectiveness of the protection of fundamental rights in Europe. The *revirement* of the ECJ in the *Kadi* judgment[48] however, has filled this *lacuna* in the protection of fundamental rights, by acknowledging that all UN anti-terrorism sanctions transposed into the EU legal space are subject to judicial review.

The structure of the section is as follows. Part A introduces the context, briefly outlining the dynamics of the adoption of counter-terrorism sanctions

---

45 Dugard (2005) 83; Almqvist (2008) 303; Tridimas & Gutierrez-Fons (2008) 660.

46 The ECJ had already engaged in human rights review in several cases involving UN sanctions adopted by the Security Council under Chapter VII of the UN Charter in the context of the wars in Yugoslavia and Iraq. See for example: Case C-84/95 *Bosphorus v. Minister of Transports* [1996] ECR I-3953; Case C-177/95 *Ebony Maritime SA v. Prefetto della Provincia di Brindisi* [1997] ECR I-1111; Case C-237/98 P *Dorsch Consult mbH v. Council and Commission* [2000] ECR-4549. For an overview see Kapteyn (2003) 57. Review of national measures implementing UN law had also been customary in many domestic legal systems, especially those adopting a dualist position toward international law: see for example the decisions of the Italian and the German Constitutional Courts relating to the status of international law, C. Cost. s. 73/2001; BVerfG 111, 307 (2004) *Görgülü*. For an overview see Herdegen (2003) 77.

47 I have tried to argue elsewhere, Fabbrini (2009), that a common trend exists in the behaviour of the European and US judiciaries in times of terrorist emergencies: in the aftermath of a terrorist attack courts tend to be extremely deferent *vis à vis* the political branches of government sanctioning most restriction of individual liberties in the name of national security; only in the long run courts reassert their institutional position and exercise a strict scrutiny over the compatibility with human rights of the acts adopted by the executives and the legislatures.

48 Joined Cases C-402/05 P and C-415/05 P *Yassin A. Kadi & Al Barakaat International Foundation v. EU Council and Commission* [2008], nyr.

at the UN level and their implementation in the European legal space. Part B focuses on the specific problem generated by the original absence of effective judicial review of terrorism sanctions in either the law in the books or the law in action of any of the layers of the European multilevel system of human rights protection. Part C discusses several developments that have taken place in the case law of the European courts but that have proven to be unsatisfactory because of their inability to provide an effective protection of human rights. Part D analyzes how the recent change in the jurisprudence of the ECJ – acknowledging the power to exercise judicial review of counter-terrorism measures – has instead provided a solution to the problem of ineffectiveness of human rights protection, in line with the reforms that could be introduced with the Lisbon Treaty. Part E draws some *interim* conclusions.

A. Context

Counter-terrorism sanctions are *ab origine* established by a resolution of the UN Security Council (SC) adopted under Chapter VII of the UN Charter, which grants to the UNSC the power to take on all measures necessary for the maintenance of international peace and security.[49] In the simplest hypothesis, UNSC resolutions charge the UN Member States of the task of identifying the target of the sanctions.[50] If this is the case, the listing of suspected terrorist by the national authorities is subject to domestic standards of fundamental rights protection.[51] This chapter focuses however on another hypothesis, which raises bigger concerns for the protection of fundamental rights.[52] With resolution 1267 (1999),[53] in fact, the UNSC has started drawing up directly at the UN level a black list of the persons whose assets are to be frozen by all UN Member States:[54] Specifically, the UNSC established an auxiliary committee (on

49 For an introduction to the dispositions of Chapter VII of the UN Charter and a comment article by article see Frowein & Krish (2002) 701; See also De Wet (2004); Denis (2004). On the expansion of the powers of the UN Security Council in the last years, see Matheson (2006).

50 See, *e.g.*, S/RES/1373 (2001) §1c which decides that Member States shall 'freeze without delay funds and other financial assets or economic resources of persons who commit, or attempt to commit, terrorist acts or participate in or facilitate the commission of terrorist acts; of entities owned or controlled directly or indirectly by such person.'

51 See in general Kuijper (2003) 39. For the EU legal order this has been confirmed by the CFI in Case T-228/02 *Organisation des Modjahedines du peuple d'Iran (OMPI) v. Council of the EU* [2006] ECR II-4665. See also Della Cananea (2007) 896; Cappuccio (2007) 416; Defeis (2007) 1449; Guild (2008) 173.

52 See Miller (2003) 46; Flynn (2007) 371; Van Den Herik (2007) 729 and the literature cited *supra* in note 44.

53 S/RES/1267 (1999).

54 See Frowein (cf. *supra*: note 41) 787; Ciampi (cf. *supra*: note 43) 42; Halberstam & Stein (cf. *supra*: note 43) 28.

which all the members of the UNSC are represented) and endowed it with the power to list and delist the persons who are to be targeted by the sanctions.[55]

In this case, for the European countries that are part of the EU, the implementation at the domestic level of the UNSC resolutions follows a three-step procedure.[56] To begin with, a common position listing the individuals and entities identified by the UNSC is adopted in the framework of the II pillar of the EU, which establishes a cooperation among the EU Member States (EUMS) in the field of Common Foreign and Security Policy (CFSP).[57] Subsequently, a regulation is enacted under the I pillar of the EU, the European Community (EC), on the joint basis of Articles 60, 301 and 308 of the EC Treaty.[58] The regulation orders the freezing of the assets of all natural and legal persons reported in the Annex to the regulation, and empowers the Commission of the EC to update the Annex following the changes made at the UN level by the auxiliary committee of the SC.[59] Finally, EUMS give effect to the regulation at the national level, with administrative acts that materially freeze the financial assets of the blacklisted individuals and entities.[60]

55 The Committee was established by S/RES/1267 (1999). Its powers and rules of procedure were then modified by successive resolutions. See, e.g, S/RES/1333 (2000), S/RES/1363 (2001), S/RES/1390 (2002), S/RES/1452 (2002), S/RES/1455 (2003), S/RES/1526 (2004), S/RES/1566 (2004), S/RES/1617 (2005), S/RES/1730 (2006), S/RES/1735 (2006), S/RES/1822 (2008). See: Rosand (2004) 745. In the auxiliary committee, the diplomatic representatives of the members of UNSC directly identify the persons who are to be targeted by the sanctions (so called: smart sanctions). The listing procedure is essentially informal, governed by consensus and based on the (often) limited, confidential and non-shared information gathered by the security services of the member states of the UNSC. For an overview of the administrative procedure that governs the functioning of the Sanctions Committee see Feinaugle (2008) 1513.

56 See Nettesheim (2007) 567, 571. For a general overview of the constitutional foundations of the external relations of the EU see: Eeckhout (2004); Cremona (2007) 1173. For an assessment of the increase in importance of the EU as a global actor see: Cremona (2004) 553.

57 See, *e.g.*, Council Common Position 1999/727/CFSP OJ 1999 L 294/01; Council Common Position 2001/154/CFSP OJ 2001 L 57/01; Council Common Position 2002/402/CFSP OJ 2002 L 139/04. See also Koutrakos (2007) 257.

58 For a discussion concerning the existence of an EC competence to adopt and implement economic sanctions targeting individuals and entities, see Garde (2006) 284; Tzanou (2009) 123, 126. Articles 60, 301 and 308 have been considered as a sufficient legal basis for the adoption of target sanctions by the EC both by the CFI in Case T-351/01 *Yassin A. Kadi v. Council of the EU and Commission of the EC* [2005] ECR II-3649 and by the ECJ in Joined Cases C-402/05 P & C-415/05 P *Yassin A. Kadi & Al Barakaat International Foundation v. EU Council and Commission* [2008], nyr, albeit with different arguments.

59 See, *e.g.*, Council Regulation 337/2000/EC OJ 2000 L 43/01; Council Regulation 881/2002/EC OJ 2002 L 139/09; Council Regulation 561/2003/EC OJ 2003 L 082/01.

60 According to Article 249(2) EC Treaty 'a regulation shall be binding in its entirety and directly applicable' in all EUMS. The intervention of national administrative agency (*e.g.*, banking authorities, police forces etc.) is however necessary to give full effect to the regulation. See, as far as the Italian discipline of assets freezing is concerned, Savino (2008) 497.

B. Lack of Judicial Review

UN counter-terrorism sanctions have a significant impact over the fundamental rights of the targeted individuals and entities.[61] At the substantive level, both the right to property and the right to privacy are at stake. At the procedural level, the right of due process comes into play and requires, at the very least, that before the adoption of the sanctions or in their immediate aftermath interested persons be informed of the reasons justifying the approval of restrictive measure against them and have the right to defend themselves. Due process rights are well acknowledged in each level of the European system of human rights protection.[62] Wide consensus exists nonetheless among scholars about the deficiencies of the procedure by which the auxiliary committee of the UNSC identifies the targeted-persons: because of the political and diplomatic mechanism by which the listing takes place, significant violations of fundamental rights have been lamented.[63]

A posteriori judicial review is hence essential to ensure respect for these fundamental rights. Indeed, 'the key to the notion of rule of law is [...] reviewability of decisions of public authorities by independent courts.'[64] In the first challenges against the UN counter-terrorism measures, however, no court was available to review the compatibility of targeted sanctions with the fundamental rights of blacklisted persons. No judicial institution has ever been established at the UN level before which individuals can activate legal proceedings.[65] Even supposing that the International Court of Justice (ICJ) could have been competent to review the acts of the UNSC – a possibility, nonetheless, which is far from certain[66] – the individuals and entities targeted by the UNSC sanctions 'lacked *locus standi* before the ICJ, traditionally conceived as a judge between states.'[67]

---

61 See Fassbender (2006) 437; Ciampi (cf. *supra*: note 43) 123. See also De Wet (2003) 7.

62 Such principles historically originated and were codified in the *corpus* of administrative law of the EUMS and then circulated at the supranational and international level, see: S. Cassese (2006a) 1; Tridimas (2006) 370; S. Cassese (2006b); Harlow (2006) 206. Article 41 of the CFR now recognizes a right to 'good administration' defined as the 'right of every person to be heard, before any individual measure which could affect him or her adversely is taken'. Whereas the CFR is not yet binding, the CFI has acknowledged the importance of such principles in its decisions in Case T-228/02 *Organisation des Modjahedines du peuple d'Iran (OMPI) v. Council of the EU* [2006] ECR II-4665 and Case T-256/07 *People's Mojahedin Organization of Iran v. Council of the EU* [2008], nyr.

63 See Reisman & Stevick (1998) 226; Reinish (2001) 851 and literature quoted *supra* in note 44, 45 and 52.

64 Jacobs (2007) 35. See also the literature cited *supra* note 11, 14, 16 and accompanying text.

65 Nettesheim (cf. *supra*: note 56) 568. See also Akande (1997) 341.

66 The ICJ has not excluded this possibility in its judgment *Legal Consequences for States of the Continued Presence of South Africa in Namibia (South West Africa) Notwithstanding Security Council Resolution 276 (1970)*, Advisory Opinion, ICJ Rep. 1971, p. 45, but so far it has not accepted the authority to judge the validity of acts of the UNSC.

67 Della Cananea (2009) 519, 523.

However, also in the European multilevel system, judicial review was mute.[68] Both legal constraints and self-imposed judicial practices prevented the ECJ, the national courts of the EUMS and the ECtHR to step in and review the counter-terrorism acts of the UNSC. This generated a major problem of ineffectiveness in the protection of fundamental rights in the European multilevel system, since there was no remedy available at any level for the persons who wished to challenge the lawfulness of the UNSC measures adversely affecting them. Paragraph 1 following will consider the limitations of the jurisdiction of the ECJ in the CFSP codified by the EU Treaty and the jurisprudence of the CFI refusing competence to review an EC regulation implementing a UNSC anti-terrorism resolution. Paragraph 2 will take into account the structural limits of the jurisdiction of the national courts and of the ECtHR.

1. The ECJ

The EU Treaty excludes the jurisdiction of the ECJ over the acts adopted by the EU Council in the framework of CFSP: according to Article 46(1)(d) EU Treaty, the jurisdiction of the ECJ in the intergovernmental pillars is limited to what is specified by Article 35, which acknowledges a limited role for the ECJ only in the field of Justice and Home Affairs (JHA). A preliminary reference may be submitted (by the judiciaries of the EUMS that have accepted the jurisdiction of the ECJ)[69] on the validity and interpretations of decisions and framework decisions and on the interpretation of conventions; action for the annulment of decisions and framework decisions may then be brought by the EUMS or by the Commission.[70] Common positions instead are not contemplated among the acts that may be subject to review before the ECJ.[71]

The jurisdiction of the ECJ over the measures adopted in the EC pillar is formally recognized in the EC Treaty. The validity of EC acts may be challenged ex Article 230 – the action for annulment[72] – and ex Article 234 – the prelimi-

68 See: Cameron (2003) 159; Lavranos (2006) 471; Eeckhout (2007) 183; Adam (2009).

69 See *infra* note 140 and accompanying text.

70 According to Article 35(1) EU Treaty, the ECJ 'shall have jurisdiction, subject to the conditions laid down in this Article, to give preliminary rulings on the validity and interpretation of framework decisions and decisions, on the interpretation of conventions established under this title and on the validity and interpretation of the measures implementing them'. According to Article 35(6) then the ECJ 'shall have jurisdiction to review the legality of framework decisions and decisions in actions brought by a Member State or the Commission on grounds of lack of competence, infringement of an essential procedural requirement, infringement of this Treaty or of any rule of law relating to its application, or misuse of powers.' See also Spaventa (2008).

71 Peers (2007) 883, 886. The CFI in Case T-228/02 *Organisation des Modjahedines du peuple d'Iran (OMPI) v. Council of the EU* [2006] ECR II-4665 has confirmed the inadmissibility of an action of annulment against a common position.

72 According to Article 230(4) EC Treaty 'any natural or legal person may, under the same conditions, institute proceedings against a decision addressed to that person or against a decision which, although in the

nary reference procedure.[73] In the *Yusuf*[74] and *Kadi*[75] decisions of 2005, however, the CFI denied *proprio motu* the power to review the compatibility with human rights principles of an EC regulation implementing the counter-terrorism sanctions established by the UNSC in the EU legal space. The *Kadi* case originated from an action of annulment: the applicant, a Saudi national with substantial funds in the EU who had been black-listed by the UNSC Sanction Committee, alleged that the EC regulation[76] implementing the UNSC resolution[77] violated EU constitutional principles (in particular, the right of due process) and asked the CFI to quash the act insofar as it applied to him.

The CFI found it appropriate, in order to answer the question raised by the petitioner, 'to consider, in the first place, the relationship between the international legal order under the UN and the domestic or Community legal order.'[78] In the CFI's view, the Charter of the UN enjoyed supremacy 'over every other obligation of domestic law and international treaty law,'[79] including the EC Treaty and the same primacy extended to the resolutions adopted by the UNSC.[80] Furthermore, the EC should 'be considered to be bound by the obligations under the UN Charter in the same way as its Member States'[81] by virtue of the assumption of powers 'previously exercised by Member States in the area

---

form of a regulation or a decision addressed to another person, is of direct and individual concern to the former'. See Cartabia & Weiler (cf. *supra*: note 5) 55. For a critical assessment of the debate concerning the restrictive interpretation of the *locus standi* provision of Article 230(4) EC Treaty see Lewis (2007) 1469.

73 According to Article 234(1) EC Treaty the ECJ 'shall have jurisdiction to give preliminary rulings concerning (a) the interpretation of this Treaty; (b) the validity and interpretation of acts of the institutions of the Community' upon referral by a national court. See Adinolfi (1997).

74 Case T-306/01 *Ahmed A. Yusuf & Al Barakaat International Foundation v. EU Council and Commission* [2005] ECR II-3533.

75 Case T-351/01 *Yassin A. Kadi v. Council of the EU and Commission of the EC* [2005] ECR II-3649.

76 Council Regulation 881/2002 OJ 2002 L 139/9.

77 S/RES/1390 (2002).

78 *Kadi* at §178.

79 Id. at §181.

80 The judgment therefore confirms great respect for international law, and is consistent with a constitutional reading of the UN Charter. See Fassbender (1998) 529. With specific regard, however, to the due process concerns posed by the UNSC sanctioning process see also Fassbender (cf. *supra*: note 61) 437 and the text accompanying note 63 *supra*. As such, the internationalism of the CFI decision has been praised by some: see Stangos & Gryllos (2006) 466. Nonetheless a series of questions have been raised about the relationship between the legal orders of the UN, the Community and the EUMS: For an assessment of the debate in light of the subsequent ECJ judgment, distinguishing in particular between constitutionalist versus pluralist approaches to international law see in particular Halberstam & Stein (cf. *supra*: note 43) 43 ff and De Burca (2009) 37 ff as well as the literature cited *infra* note 191.

81 *Kadi* at §193 According to Nettesheim (cf. *supra*: note 56) 574, this argument is 'somewhat surprising.'

governed by the UN Charter.'[82] The CFI held that the UN Charter (and the acts adopted under it) prevailed even over EC constitutional rules.[83]

The CFI therefore took the view that 'a limitation of [its] jurisdiction [wa]s necessary'[84] here, since 'any review of the internal lawfulness of the contested regulation, especially having regard to the provisions or general principles of EC law relating to the protection of fundamental rights, would [...] imply that the court is to consider, indirectly, the lawfulness of'[85] a superior UNSC resolution. However, to avoid a full 'judicial abdication'[86] which would have produced a complete 'deficiency in the protection of fundamental rights'[87] the CFI found itself 'empowered to check, indirectly, the lawfulness of the resolution of the SC in question with regard to *jus cogens*, understood as a body of higher rules of public international law binding on all subjects of international law, including the bodies of the UN, and from which no derogation is possible.'[88]

Nonetheless, the review on the basis of *jus cogens* of the alleged violations of the fundamental rights of the petitioner turned out to be extremely limited.[89] The CFI excluded that it had the power to 'verify that there has been no error of assessment of the facts and evidence relied on by the SC in support of the measure it had taken.'[90] It instead affirmed, leaving a wide margin of appreciation to the UNSC, that 'the question whether an individual or organisation poses a threat to international peace and security, like the question of what measures must be adopted *vis à vis* the person concerned in order to frustrate the threats, entails a political assessment and value judgment which in principle falls within the exclusive competence of the authority to which the international community has entrusted primary responsibility for the maintenance of peace and security.'[91]

---

82 *Kadi* at §203 For a description of the theory of succession, according to which the EC has assumed all the responsibilities of the Member States in the fields now covered by Community law (a theory first developed with relation to the GATT: Joined Cases C-21/72 and C-24/72 *International Fruit Company* [1972] ECR 1219) and its defence in the present case see Tomuschat (2006) 537, 542-543.

83 This positions seems to contradict the normal understanding of the hierarchy of norms within the EC legal order: see Rosas (2008) 71, 78.

84 *Kadi* at §218.

85 Id. at §215.

86 Eeckhout (cf. *supra*: note 68) 205.

87 Nettesheim (cf. *supra*: note 56) 574.

88 *Kadi* at §227 For a critique of this reasoning see Conforti (2006) 333.

89 Lavranos (cf. *supra*: note 68) 475. *Contra* Tomuschat (cf. *supra*: note 82) 551, who claims that 'the judgment show that the CFI did not confine its assessment to *jus cogens* proper, but resorted to applying to their full extent the standards evolved in the practice of the EC judicial bodies.'

90 *Kadi* at §284.

91 Id. According to Adam (cf. *supra*: note 68) 10, the CFI has essentially adopted here 'the theory of the *actes de gouvernement* or political question.' The political question doctrine was originally crafted by the US Supreme Court in *Luther v. Borden* 48 U.S. 1 (1849) but is still today contested in legal scholarship. See, *e.g.*, Henkin (1976) 597; Franck (1992).

In conclusion, the CFI decided that none of the applicant's arguments alleging breach of fundamental due process right was well founded and it upheld the EC regulation, an instrument necessary 'as the world now stands'[92] to fight international terrorism. By limiting the scope of its judicial review,[93] however, the first decision of the CFI dealing with the legality of EU counter-terrorism measures 'raised several perplexities, since it ended sacrificing entirely the needs of the protection of fundamental rights,'[94] giving 'a *carte blache* to the member states'[95] to disregard the rule of law in implementing resolutions of the UNSC.[96] The EU constitutional principles were in fact 'outweigh[ed by] the essential public interest in the maintenance of international peace and security'[97] pursued by the political branches of the EU.

2. The National Courts and the ECtHR

The rulings of the CFI in *Yusuf* and *Kadi* had also a detrimental spill-over effect on judicial review at the national level.[98] In most EUMS, (administrative) courts are competent to review the compatibility of a specific national administrative decision (i.e. one freezing the assets of a blacklisted person) with the legislative act that enables it, in this case an EC regulation.[99] Following the well-established *Foto-Frost*[100] doctrine, however, national courts do not have the power to invalidate an EC measure on their own but must refer the matter to the ECJ via the preliminary reference procedure.[101] In the case of doubt as to the effective compatibility between an EC counter-terrorism act implementing a UNSC resolution and fundamental rights as general principles of EC law, national courts could activate the mechanism established by Article 234 EC Treaty.[102]

Once the matter would have reached the EU courts, however, the immunity-shield of the *Yusuf* doctrine would have again prevented the ECJ from reviewing the legality of a regulation implementing a UNSC resolution. Since the CFI in *Yusuf* refused to review the EC regulation challenged ex Article 230 EC Treaty

92 *Kadi* at §133.

93 Eckes (2008) 74, 82.

94 Cartabia (cf. *supra*: note 2) 49.

95 Tridimas & Gutierrez-Fons (cf. *supra*: note 45) 682.

96 Eeckhout (cf. *supra*: note 68) 205-206. See also Almqvist (cf. *supra*: note 45), 303. A defensive view of the ruling of the CFI is however taken by Brown (2006) 456, 468, who argues that the CFI 'has a responsibility not to hinder the effective implementation of peaceable measures adopted to combat terrorism. [Freezing of funds] broadly speaking, therefore, should receive judicial backing.'

97 *Kadi* at §289.

98 Lavranos (cf. *supra*: note 68), 486.

99 See Chiti (2004).

100 Case 314/85 *Foto-Frost*, [1987] ECR 4199.

101 Tesauro (2005) 299. See also Lenaerts (2006) 211.

102 Gautron (2006) 175.

– through a direct action for annulment by the interested parties – because the act was simply the implementation of a hierarchically superior norm of international law, perhaps the very same conclusion would also have been reached if the validity of that regulation had been challenged ex Article 234 EC Treaty – through a preliminary reference submitted by a national judge who had doubts about the legality of the regulation.[103]

Finally, no judicial resort against the contested counter-terrorism measures could be found by the interested persons before the ECtHR. To begin with, the ECtHR is not competent *rationae personae* to review the acts of the UNSC. This was recently affirmed in the *Behrami and Saramati* judgment.[104] Here, although the applicants, three Albanian nationals living in Kosovo, brought complaints against France, Germany and Norway for various violations of the ECHR that occurred in the course of and after the Kosovo War,[105] the ECtHR denied jurisdiction *ratione personae*.[106] According to the ECtHR, in fact, the defendants were operating under the aegis of the UN, which had authorized the military intervention with a SC resolution in the fulfilment of its 'unique'[107] responsibility of maintaining international peace and security.

'Since operations established by UNSC resolutions under Chapter VII of the UN Charter are fundamental to the mission of the UN to secure international peace and security',[108] in the ECtHR's view the ECHR could not 'be interpreted in a manner which would subject the acts and omissions of the Contracting Parties which are covered by UNSC resolutions and occurred prior to or in the course of such missions, to the scrutiny of the Court.'[109] The decision of the ECtHR, by indirectly attributing the conduct of war operations of several Contracting Parties to the UNSC and at the same time denying any jurisdiction over the former, came close to the 'non-justiciability argument'[110] utilized by the

---

[103] This hypothesis is developed *in abstracto* since it assumes that the ECJ would have followed the reasoning of the CFI in a preliminary reference challenging the validity of a EU act operating as a legal basis for a national administrative measure. As a matter of fact this hypothesis never came to being, since the ECJ was already able to review the CFI ruling in the *Kadi* case on appeal. See *infra* note 185 and accompanying text.

[104] Joined Cases *Behrami and Behrami v. France* and *Saramati v. France, Germany and Norway* ECHR [2007], Application No.71412/01 and 78166/01.

[105] For a comment on the judgments see Sari (2008) 151; Bordeau-Livenec, Buzzini & Villalpando (2008) 323.

[106] According to De Burca (cf. *supra*: note 80) 45 'the approach of the ECHR – paradoxically the court from which the strongest human-rights-protective approach might have been expected – seems disappointing as it abdicated any role in monitoring compliance with human rights.' See also Tridimas & Gutierrez-Fons (cf. *supra*: note 45) 685.

[107] *Behrami and Saramati* at §148.

[108] Id. at §149.

[109] Id.

[110] Barak (cf. *supra*: note 11) 177.

CFI in the *Kadi* case.[111] Its effect was to deprive individuals and entities of the power to challenge a UNSC resolution adversely affecting them in front of the ECtHR.

Since the *CFDT* decision,[112] moreover, the ECtHR has declared inadmissible all challenges *versus* the EC, as neither it nor the EU is (yet) party to the ECHR.[113] The ECtHR can review the compatibility with the ECHR of measures adopted by the Contracting parties after the exhaustion of all the available domestic remedies,[114] hence operating as a last instance court for Europe.[115] In *Matthews v. UK*[116] the ECtHR also acknowledged a power to review domestic acts of the EUMS amending primary EU law. The case was brought by a Gibraltese citizen who contested the compatibility of the UK act regulating election to the European Parliament with the right to democratic election recognized by the ECHR. The ECtHR restated that 'EC as such cannot be challenged before the Court because the EC is not a Contracting Party'[117] but it retained jurisdiction over the case.

The decision to review the application was, however, largely due to the fact that the contested UK act could 'not be challenged before the European Court of Justice for the very reason that it [was] not a 'normal' act of the Community, but [it was] a treaty within the Community legal order'[118] and that therefore the UK held responsibility *ratione materiae* for the consequences of that Treaty.[119] As will be explained in detail in the next sub-section, on the contrary, since the ECtHR's ruling in *M. & co. v. Germany*,[120] if the domestic act implements a EC/EU disposition, a presumption of legality will apply. The ECtHR will hence exercise an

111 See De Burca (*supra* note 80) whose paper is a detailed and thorough comparison between the ruling of the ECtHR and the judgment of both the CFI and the ECJ in *Kadi* and the different approaches taken by the various European judicial instances on the question of the relationship between international law (UN law) and European law (both EU law and ECHR law) and thus on the nature and scope of judicial review. As underlined by Tzanou (cf. *supra*: note 58) 145, though, 'the *Behrami and Saramati* decision is to be distinguished from *Kadi*. The Strasbourg court ruled on the issue of jurisdiction [...]. On the contrary in *Kadi* [...] the ECJ did not have to deal with the question of jurisdiction, as the measure before it were [indisputably] adopted by the Community itself even if they derived from UNSC resolutions.'

112 *Confédération Française Démocratique du Travail v. EEC (CFDT)* ECHR [1978]. Application No. 8030/77.

113 See Alkema (1979) 508. In Opinion 2/94 *In re Accession by the EC to the ECHR* [1996] ECR I-1759 the ECJ furthermore excluded that the EC could accede to the ECHR without a modification of the EC Treaty. From a practical point of view, however, the EC and the ECHR have come closer in the recent years, especially thanks to the jurisprudence of the ECJ and the ECtHR: see on this Gennusa (cf. *supra*: note 7) 91, Scheeck (cf. *supra*: note 7) 40, Douglas-Scott (cf. *supra*: note 2) 629.

114 See Petersmann, (2008) 1.

115 Tanzarella (2007) 143, 150.

116 *Matthews v. United Kingdom* ECHR [1999], Application No. 24833/94.

117 Id. at §32.

118 Id. at §33.

119 See King (2000) 86.

120 *M & co. V. Germany* ECHR [1990], Application No. 13258/87.

indirect review of the legality of an EC measure through a review of the legality of the national measure only in specific (quasi hypothetical) cases.[121]

C. Unsatisfactory Developments

The gap in the protection of fundamental rights generated by the original unavailability, for the individuals and entities adversely affected by the UN counter-terrorism resolutions, of effective judicial review in each layer of the European multilevel structure, prompted the European courts to react by elaborating several possible antidotes in their jurisprudence.[122] For all practical purposes, however, all these judge-made doctrines, although remarkable, fell short of a truly adequate response to the problem of ineffectiveness that had manifested in the European multilevel system of rights protection. In paragraph 1 I will take into account some innovative judgments of the ECJ both in the I and in the III pillar of the EU. In paragraph 2 I will go on to consider the *Solange* jurisprudence of the national courts and the ECtHR, underlining its possible impact in the case *de qua*.

The mechanisms of review developed by the ECJ to overcome its *Yusuf* and *Kadi* doctrine are new.[123] The *Solange* method, instead, is a well-known tool for coordinating overlapping jurisdiction originally elaborated by the constitutional courts of the EUMS and later also adopted by the ECtHR.[124] Nonetheless, both techniques, while important in themselves, may be regarded as unsatisfactory here. On the one hand, they proved insufficient for the purpose of enhancing the degree of protection ensured to those natural and legal persons whose funds had been frozen without due process. On the other hand, they risked jeopardizing the consistency of the European multilevel structure by calling into question consolidated principles such as the ECJ's monopoly of the power to declare the invalidity of the acts adopted by EU institutions.

1. The ECJ

To begin with, the ECJ adopted a teleological interpretation[125] of the provisions of the EU Treaty regulating its jurisdiction in the intergovernmental pillars in order to expand its review over common positions – a legal

---

[121] According to Harris, O'Boyle, & Warbrick (1995) 28, cited in Besselink (cf. *supra*: note 7) 655, the case *M & co. v. Germany* 'involves a disappointing surrender of competence by [...] Strasbourg.'

[122] Rosenfeld (2004) 633, 635 has underlined how courts in general learn from direct experience and may progressively calibrate the scope of their response by taking into account the effects of their previous decisions.

[123] Nettesheim (cf. *supra*: note 56) 579.

[124] See Lavranos (cf. *supra*: note 38) 217; Petersmann (cf. *supra*: note 114), 13 ff.

[125] For a discussion on the employment of teleological interpretation in the legal reasoning of the ECJ see: Bengoetxea, MacCormick & Moral Soriano (2001) 43; Poiares Maduro (2007) 1.

act currently employed both in CFSP and JHA.[126] In the *Segi* case,[127] the ECJ was confronted with an action brought by a Basque organization: a common position[128] had listed the entity as a terrorist organization and subjected it to enhanced control by the EUMS, who were authorized to give each other the widest possible assistance through police and judicial cooperation in criminal matters in preventing and combating terrorism. No freezing measures were adopted against the legal person with EC regulations. The petitioner, nonetheless, claimed damages because of its inclusion in the list without having been afforded any due process warrantee.

The ECJ rejected the appeal,[129] arguing that 'Article 35 EU Treaty confers no jurisdiction on the ECJ to entertain an action for damages whatsoever.'[130] However, excluding the claim that the petitioner was 'deprived of all judicial protection,'[131] the ECJ argued that a common position 'is not supposed to produce of itself legal effects in relation to third parties. This is why in the system established by Title VI of the EU Treaty, only framework decisions and decisions may be the subject of an action for annulment [or a preliminary reference] before the ECJ.'[132] If, therefore, the EU institutions adopted a common position that was intended to produce legal effects on third parties, it was necessary not 'to interpret Article 35 narrowly'[133] and 'it ha[d] to be possible to make subject to review by the ECJ a common position which, because of its content, ha[d] a scope going beyond that assigned by the EU Treaty to that kind of act.'[134]

The result of the evolutionary jurisprudence[135] of the ECJ in *Segi* was that 'a national court hearing a dispute which indirectly raise[d] the issue of the validity or interpretation of a common position [...] and which ha[d] serious doubts whether the common position [wa]s intended to produce legal effects in relation to third parties, would be able [...] to ask the ECJ to give a preliminary ruling.'[136]

---

[126] See Peers (cf. *supra*: note 71) 888 and the text accompanying note 71 *supra*.

[127] Case C-355/04 *Segi et al. v. EU Council* [2007] ECR I-1657 See also: Case C-354/04 *Gestoras Pro Aministia v. EU Council* [2007] ECR I-1579.

[128] Common Position 2001/931/CFSP OJ 2001 L 344/93.

[129] The CFI in Case T-338/02 *Segi et al. v. EU Council*, [2004] ECR II-1647 had rejected the action of the petitioner. See Nettesheim (*supra* note 56), 576. It is worth noticing that the petitioners, before starting proceedings in front of the EC courts, had already brought a case before the ECtHR. In its judgment *Segi et al. and Gestoras et al. v. the 15 Members of the EU* ECHR [2002], Application No. 6422/02 and No. 9916/02, the ECtHR however declared the application inadmissible for the reasons that the petitioners lacked the victim status required by Article 34 ECHR to begin an action before the ECtHR. See Callewaert (2007) 511, 516.

[130] *Segi* at §46.

[131] Id. at §51.

[132] Id. at §52.

[133] Id. at §53 See *supra* note 70.

[134] *Segi* at §54.

[135] See Sanfutos Cano (2008) 51.

[136] *Segi* at §54.

Nevertheless, while creating a new cause of action against common positions,[137] the *Segi* doctrine was unable to resolve the problem of ineffective human rights protection.[138] *In primis*, the broad language adopted by the CFI in *Yusuf* seemed to exclude that EU courts could review all EU acts which were simply an implementation of a UNSC resolution, including common positions challenged *ex* Article 35 EU Treaty.[139]

Furthermore, the jurisdiction of the ECJ in the intergovernmental pillars is not mandatory. In particular, Article 35 makes the submission of preliminary references by the national courts dependent upon the acceptance by each EUMS of the jurisdiction of the ECJ:[140] the EUMS must accept the jurisdiction of the ECJ and may decide whether all their tribunals or only their final supreme courts may make references to the ECJ. Since only some EUMS have accepted the jurisdiction of the ECJ, with a few of them limiting the referring power to their national jurisdiction of last instance,[141] a variable geometry prevails in this field. From this point of view, the possibility for persons affected by a counter-terrorism common position to obtain review by the ECJ was limited and essentially uncertain, because it depended on the contingent fact of being

[137] Note that the common position that was challenged by Segi (*supra* note 128) was adopted on the basis of the provisions of both the II and the III pillar. Since the EU Treaty confers no jurisdiction to the ECJ over purely II pillar measures it is however uncertain whether the reasoning of the ECJ in *Segi* could be expanded also to a common position adopted only on the basis of CFSP.

[138] Peers (cf. *supra*: note 71) 895.

[139] As noted above in the accompanying text of note 84 the CFI in *Yusuf* and *Kadi* refused to review a EC regulation because this simply implemented a hierarchically superior UNSC resolution. The supremacy of UN law extends also over a CFSP common position, so it seems likely that no review could have been undertaken on this act, even under a preliminary reference activated *ex* Article 35 EU Treaty.

[140] According, in fact, to Article 35(2) EU Treaty, 'by a declaration made at the time of signature of the Treaty of Amsterdam or at any time thereafter, any Member State shall be able to accept the jurisdiction of the ECJ to give preliminary rulings as specified in paragraph 1.' Article 35(3) then states that 'a Member State making a declaration pursuant to paragraph 2 shall specify that either: a) any court or tribunal of that State against whose decisions there is no judicial remedy under national law may request the ECJ to give a preliminary ruling on a question raised in a case pending before it and concerning the validity or interpretation of an act referred to in paragraph 1 if that court or tribunal considers that a decision on the question is necessary to enable it to give judgment; or b) any court or tribunal of that State may request the ECJ to give a preliminary ruling on a question raised in a case pending before it and concerning the validity or interpretation of an act referred to in paragraph 1 if that court or tribunal considers that a decision on the question is necessary to enable it to give judgment.' See also Arnull (2000) 227.

[141] As reported by Peers (cf. *supra*: note 71) 886 fourteen EUMS have accepted the jurisdiction of the ECJ but two of these have limited the possibility to make references for preliminary rulings only to the supreme courts of their legal system.

a national of one EUMS (allowing for preliminary references) rather than of another EUMS.[142]

Attempts were made by the CFI to remedy the *lacuna* in the protection of fundamental rights generated by the *Yusuf* and *Kadi* jurisprudence in the I pillar of the EU too.[143] In *Ayadi*[144] in particular, the CFI, while confirming the *ratio decidendi* of its previous judgments, recognized that persons affected by a freezing measure imposed by the UNSC have a right to be protected diplomatically by the competent EUMS in front of the UNSC auxiliary committee[145] and that 'it is open to the persons concerned to bring an action for judicial review based on the domestic law of the state of the petitioned government, indeed even relying directly on the contested regulation and relevant resolutions of the SC which that regulation puts into effect, against any wrongful refusal by the competent national authority to submit their cases'[146] to the UN organs charged with the delisting procedures. 'It is for the domestic legal system of each EUMS to determine the detailed procedural rules governing actions at law intended to safeguard [these] rights.'[147]

Notwithstanding the creation of a new right to action in the national legal orders deriving directly from EC law,[148] the *Ayadi* doctrine certainly missed the target of remedying to the lack of judicial review over EC regulations implementing UN resolutions.[149] Since diplomatic protection is granted on the basis of a political decision, it is not possible to consider it as affording an equivalent degree of protection to that ensured by access to a judicial authority.[150] As highlighted above, the mechanism of listing and delisting of suspected terrorist financers at the UN level is based on consensus among the members of the auxiliary committee and is essentially confidential. Individuals cannot petition the committee directly and do not participate personally in its deliberation.[151] Requiring the EUMS to take their duty of representing the persons falling under their jurisdiction seriously was certainly a step forward but it was not enough to

[142] The perverse effects of this 'variable geometry' of the ECJ's jurisdiction in the III pillar have been largely pointed out, *e.g.*, by Lenaerts & Jadoul (2002).

[143] Nettesheim (cf. *supra*: note 56) 574.

[144] Case T-253/02 *Chakif Ayadi v. EU Council* [2006] ECR II-2139. See also Case T-49/04 *Faraj Hassan v. EU Council and EC Commission* [2006] ECR II-52.

[145] Ciampi (cf. *supra*: note 43) 282.

[146] *Ayadi* at §150.

[147] Id. at §151.

[148] From this point of view, the *Ayadi* judgment expands the concept of domestic acts falling under the scope of Community law. On the ECJ's review of national measures on the basis of EU human rights principle see in general Tridimas (cf. *supra*: note 62) 319.

[149] Nettesheim (cf. *supra*: note 56) 575.

[150] The ICJ has indeed recognized in its judgment in the case *Barcelona Traction, Light and Power Co. Lmt. (Belgium v. Spain)*, ICJ Rep. 1970, p. 45, §79 that the State is 'the sole judge to decide whether its [diplomatic] protection will be granted, to what extent its granted and when it will cease.'

[151] Frowein (cf. *supra*: note 41) 790, Feinaugle (cf. *supra*: note 55) 1530; See also Bierstaker & Eckert (2006).

ensure to the interested parties a review of their status as fair and equitable as that attainable through judicial scrutiny (if this is a full review on the merits).[152]

2. The National Courts and the ECtHR

One possible answer to the problem of ineffectiveness could perhaps have taken place at the national level. It is well known that a number of constitutional courts in the EUMS have accepted the supremacy of EU law only with the reserve of some 'counter-checks'.[153] Most constitutional tribunals claim to retain a power to review EU law on the basis of the domestic constitutional principles of human rights protection but affirm that they will not resort to their safety jurisdiction as long as the EU system ensures a protection of fundamental rights equivalent to the national one.[154] The lack of judicial review at the supranational level over EU acts implementing a UNSC resolution might thus have prompted national constitutional courts to recur to the *Solange* jurisprudence and to declare void the EC act on their own.[155]

AG Mengozzi recognized this possibility in his opinion in the *Segi* case,[156] acknowledging that were the ECJ to uphold the decision of the CFI excluding any power to hear an action brought against a common position adopted in the III pillar, hence 'endors[ing] the recognition of such a gap in the protection of fundamental rights in the field of police and judicial cooperation in criminal matters, the national courts of various Member States would feel entitled, if actions were brought before them, to verify whether the acts adopted by the Council on the basis of Article 34 EU were compatible with the fundamental rights *guaranteed by their respective national legal systems, but not necessarily in an identical manner.*'[157] This option *de facto* did not materialize, but it is likely that its effect would not have been very satisfactory.

The potential reassertion of the primacy of fundamental rights would indeed have taken place at the very high cost of the consistency and stability of the EU system, which requires that invalidity of EU acts be declared by EU courts.[158]

---

[152] Aust (2008) 51, 64.

[153] See Cartabia (1995); Lavranos (cf. *supra*: note 38).

[154] The doctrine of 'supremacy with reserve' was first elaborated by the Italian and the German Constitutional Courts. See: C. Cost s. 183/1973 *Frontini*; BVerfG 37, 271 (1974) *Solange I*; C. Cost s. 170/1984 *Granital*; BVerfG 73, 339 (1986) *Solange II*; BVerfG 89, 155 (1993) *Maastricht Urteil*. But has successively been adopted by other supreme courts and constitutional tribunals Europe-wide. See, *e.g.* the decisions on the constitutionality of the European Arrest Warrant of the Polish Constitutional Court P 1/05 (2005) and of the Czech Constitutional Court Pl US 66/04 (2006). The literature on the issue is vast, see among many, Komarek (2007) 9; Baquero Cruz (2008) 389; Sadusrki (2008a) 1; Martinico & Pollicino (2008) 97.

[155] Lavranos (cf. *supra*: note 68) 489.

[156] See Nettesheim (cf. *supra*: note 56) 596 and the accompanying text of note 127 *supra*.

[157] *Segi* (Opinion of AG Mengozzi) at §90 (emphasis in the original).

[158] See Besselink (cf. *supra*: note 7) 649; De Witte (1999b) 177; Claes (2006) 666.

There are doubts, furthermore, whether national courts would have been sensitive to the fundamental rights claims of the individuals targeted by UNSC counter-terrorism sanctions.[159] From the few national cases that are available on the issue, it emerges indeed that the jurisprudence of national courts on targeted sanctions has been as weak and deferential as that of the CFI.[160] It suffices here to consider two examples. The French *Conseil d'Etat* (CdE) in its *Association Secours Mondial* decision[161] found itself competent to review an administrative act freezing the funds of an entity allegedly involved in the financing of terrorism.[162]

In exercising its review, however, the CdE employed as a standard the manifest error of appreciation scrutiny[163] and concluded that 'considérant [...] que [...] quelques jours après la parution au Journal officiel de la République française du décret attaqué, l'association requérante a été inscrite sur la liste élaborée et mise à jour périodiquement par le comité du Conseil de sécurité créé par la résolution 1267 du Conseil de sécurité des Nations-Unies et que par le règlement CE n° 1893/2002 du 23 octobre 2002, la Commission des Communautés européennes a également inscrit [l'association] sur la liste des personnes et entités pour lesquelles le Conseil de l'Union européenne a institué des mesures financières restrictives, il ne ressort pas des pièces du dossier que le ministre [...] a, dans ces circonstances, commis une erreur d'appréciation.'[164]

---

159 For a comparative overview of the role of the judiciaries during times of emergencies see Ackerman (2006); Barak (cf. *supra*: note 11) and, if you want, Fabbrini (cf. *supra*: note 47).

160 Ciampi (cf. *supra*: note 43) 430. An interesting example of the deference with which the judiciary has reviewed UN counter-terrorism sanction in a non-EUMS is the Swiss case. In *Youssef Nada v. SECO* 1A.45/2007 / daa judgment of 14 November 2007 the Swiss Supreme Court (SSCt) in fact adopted exactly the same stand of the CFI, denying the power to review a national measure implementing a UNSC resolution listing suspected terrorist and freezing their assets, but for its conformity with *jus cogens*. The same reasoning was later employed by the SSCt also in *A v. Département federal de l'économie* 2A.783/2008 /svc judgment of 23 January 2008. For an overview of the financial measures adopted by Switzerland to fight international terrorism see Zagaris (2003) 45, 94.

161 C.E. No. 262626, *Association Secours Mondial de France*, judgment 3 November 2004.

162 Adam, in this book.

163 According to Sadurski (2008b) 4 the 'manifest error of appreciation' represents a weak test for judicial review and 'only extremely irrational, arbitrary, unwise legal rules will fall victim of such test of reasonableness.' As a matter of fact, however, since the ruling in the case C.E. *Ministre de l'Equipment et du Logement c. Fédération des Défenses des Personnes Concernes par le Projet Ville Nouvelle Est de Lille*, judgment 28 May 1971, it is customary for the CdE to employ a stronger test to review the legality of administrative acts, which resembles proportionality analysis. See Braibant (1974) 297; Bobek (2008) 5. The decision to recur to the 'manifest error of appreciation' review highlights from this point of view the willingness of the CdE to adopt a deferential scrutiny of the governmental act. See Adam (cf. *supra*: note 162).

164 *Association Secours Mondial*, 7éme considérant.

In *Al-Jedda*,[165] the UK House of Lords (UKHL) also adopted a similar stand, affirming that an act authorized by a UNSC resolution would escape judicial review of its conformity with the human rights principles recognized by the ECHR.[166] Here, the case did not truly concern the legality of a UNSC counter-terrorism sanction: a British citizen was challenging his detention by the military in Iraq. His detention was authorized by a UNSC resolution, however.[167] The UKHL rejected the claim, ruling that the UN Charter (and the resolutions adopted by the UNSC) enjoyed supremacy even over the ECHR,[168] since this was 'necessary for imperative reasons of security.'[169] As this short overview highlights, both the supreme British and French courts came, in the end, very close to adopting the *act de gouvernement* theory, showing their incapacity to ensure an effective protection of the fundamental rights of persons affected by UNSC acts.

Similar claims hold true with regard to the ECtHR.[170] Even if the EC/EU is not party to the ECHR, the ECtHR has acknowledged a power to review the compatibility with the ECHR of acts of the EUMS which simply implement EC/EU dispositions at the national level.[171] The conditions for exercising this review have been recently restated in a comprehensive manner in the *Bosphorus* judgment.[172] Bosphorus, a Turkish air carrier, had leased an aircraft from the Yugoslavian national airline, just before the beginning of the Yugoslav civil war. While in Ireland, the aircraft was impounded by the Irish authorities on the basis of an EC regulation[173] implementing a UNSC resolution[174] imposing sanctions on Yugoslavia. After the exhaustion of the national remedies and a preliminary ruling of the ECJ on the interpretation of the relevant EC regulation,[175] Bosphorus started proceedings before the ECtHR lamenting a violation of the right to property.

165 *R (on the Application of Al-Jedda) v. Secretary of State* [2007] UKHL 58.

166 See Messineo (2009) 35.

167 S/RES/1546 (2004). See also S/RES/1637 (2005); S/RES/1723 (2006).

168 A majority of four Lord Justices of the UKHL concluded that the UN Charter and the obligations stemming from it ought prevail over the other international treaties, including the ECHR. Another Lord Justice, L.J. Rodger, following the reasoning of the ECtHR in *Behrami and Saramati*, even denied the jurisdiction *ratione personae* to decide the dispute arguing that the British military in Iraq was for all effects a *longa manus* of the UNSC. For a comment to the decision see Sari (2009) 181.

169 *Al-Jedda* (Bingham of Cornhill L.J. at §39).

170 Lavranos (cf. *supra*: note 68) 484; Douglas-Scott (2006a) 243, 253.

171 See *supra* note 120 and 121 and among the vast literature on the issue: Canor (cf. *supra*: note 37) 3; Scheeck (cf. *supra*: note 7) 40; Harpaz (cf. *supra*: note 7) 105.

172 *Bosphours Hava Yollari Turizm v. Ireland* ECHR (Grand Chamber) [2005], Application No. 45036/98

173 Council Regulation 990/93/EEC OJ 1993 L 102/14.

174 S/RES/820 (1993).

175 Case C-84/95 *Bosphorus v. Minister of Transports* [1996] ECR I-3953. For a criticism of the judgment see Canor (1998) 137.

The ECtHR found itself competent to review the decision of the Irish authorities even if they were simply giving effect to an EC regulation. The ECtHR acknowledged that Ireland was complying 'with its obligation flowing from EC law.'[176] On the other hand, it reasserted that 'a Contracting Party is responsible under Article 1 ECHR for all acts of omissions of its organs.'[177] After balancing the EUMS obligations to comply with EC law with their duty to ensure the effectiveness of the ECHR, however, the ECtHR affirmed that it would not undertake any review of a national measure implementing a EC/EU act as long as the EC/EU ensures a level of human rights protection, 'as regards both the substantive guarantees offered and the mechanism controlling their observance, in a manner which can be considered at least equivalent to'[178] that guaranteed by the ECHR.

According the *Solange* doctrine of the ECtHR,[179] in other words, review of EC measures through the national implementing acts is to be considered only as an *extrema ratio* to which it is possible to resort if the overall EC/EU system of human rights protection suddenly falls below the ECHR standard[180] and if 'in the circumstances of a particular case, it is considered that the protection of ECHR rights was [at the EU level] manifestly deficient.'[181] From this point of view, the *Bosphorus* judgment was not able to provide the answer to the problem of ineffectiveness generated by the lack of judicial review of UNSC sanctions at the EC level.[182] The response of the ECtHR to the potential violation of human rights by the EU institutions therefore seems as unsatisfactory as that of the other European courts.

D. The Rise of Judicial Review

An important step in the direction of resolving the problem of ineffectiveness in the protection of fundamental rights in the European multi-level system has been taken by the ECJ in the recent *Kadi & Al Barakaat* decision.[183] By submitting the EU counter-terrorism measures implementing UNSC

[176] *Bosphorus* at §148.

[177] Id. at §153.

[178] Id. at §155.

[179] See Jacqué (2005) 756; Gaja (2006).

[180] According to Peers (2006) 443, 452 'the concept of conditional review as developed by the [ECtHR] is fraught with ambiguities and uncertainties and runs the risk that human rights will not be sufficiently guaranteed in certain cases.'

[181] *Bosphorus* at §156.

[182] As acknowledged by Lavranos (cf. *supra*: note 68) 484-485, the effect of the *Bosphorus* judgment is indeed that 'private parties (like Bosphorus) who are affected by UN sanctions or rather European and domestic implementing measures are unable to obtain judicial review from the ECtHR in order to assess their conformity with the ECHR.' See also Ciampi (2006) 85.

[183] Joined Cases C-402/05 P and C-415/05 P *Yassin A. Kadi & Al Barakaat International Foundation v. EU Council and Commission* judgment [2008], nyr.

resolutions to a full and strict review, the ECJ has assured a more effective and consistent protection of the fundamental rights enshrined in the European constitutional order and has clearly restated that the rule of law shall survive, and remain in force, even in times of emergency.[184] In paragraph 1, this decision will be analyze in some detail; in paragraph 2, I will go on to address some of the innovations that might be introduced by the Lisbon Reform Treaty, which will contribute to ensuring a more effective protection of fundamental rights *vis à vis* UNSC counter-terrorism sanctions.

1. The ECJ

The *Kadi* decision of the CFI was later appealed and the ECJ was called on to decide about the legality of an EC regulation implementing a UNSC resolution listing persons suspected of being terrorists and freezing their assets without due process of law. In contrast to the CFI,[185] the Grand Chamber of the ECJ began its reasoning by emphasizing that 'the EC is based on the rule of law, inasmuch as neither its Member States nor its institutions can avoid conformity of their acts with the basic constitutional charter, the EC Treaty.'[186] According to the ECJ, it followed from 'those considerations that the obligations imposed by an international agreement cannot have the effect of prejudicing the constitutional principles of the EC Treaty, which include the principle that all EC acts must respect fundamental rights.'[187]

On this premise, the ECJ left aside the argument of the CFI concerning the relationship between the UN and EU legal orders,[188] and, while not denying the binding nature of the UNSC resolutions and their 'supremacy in [...] international law'[189] (stemming from the UN Charter), reaffirmed the *primauté* of primary EU constitutional law, 'in particular the general principles of which fundamental rights form part'[190] within the EU legal system. As a consequence, the ECJ excluded the possibility that an EC regulation implementing a UNSC resolution could be immune from judicial review. By adopting a confident constitutionalist approach[191] the ECJ argued instead that 'the review of the Court

184 Tridimas (2009) 103.

185 Halberstam & Stein (cf. *supra*: note 43) 43; De Burca (cf. *supra*: note 80) 43.

186 *Kadi* at §281 quoting Case 294/83 *Les Verts v. Parliament* [1986] ECR 1339.

187 *Kadi* at §285.

188 The ECJ deals with the international obligations binding on the EUMS and the EC respectively on the basis of Article 300(7) and Article 307 EC Treaty but reasserts the original hierarchy of norms in the EU legal system stating that the international law displace only 'acts of secondary EC law' (*Kadi* at §307). See Rosas (cf. *supra*: note 83).

189 *Kadi* at §288.

190 Id. at §308.

191 The position of the ECJ is defended by community lawyers such as Lavranos (2009) 157, 174 who argues that with the *Kadi* ruling 'the normally applicable hierarchy of norms within the Community legal order remains intact also *vis-à-vis* the UN Charter.' Also according to Tzanou (cf. *supra*: note 58) 142, 'there

of the validity of any Community measure in the light of fundamental rights must be considered to be the expression, in a community based on the rule of law, of a constitutional guarantee stemming from the EC Treaty as an autonomous legal system which is not to be prejudiced by an international agreement.'[192]

The ECJ clearly ruled that 'the EC judicature must, in accordance with the powers conferred on it by the EC Treaty, ensure the review, in principle the full review, of the lawfulness of all EC acts in the light of the fundamental rights forming an integral part of the general principles of EC law, including review of EC measures which, like the contested regulation, are designed to give effect to the resolutions adopted by the SC.'[193] And it engaged directly in a strict and attentive scrutiny of the contested regulation,[194] simply disclaiming the argument put forward by the defendant that 'when the SC has spoken, the Court must remain silent'.[195] The advice of AG Maduro seems to have been particularly relevant here, as the AG had argued in his opinion that 'in situations where the Community's fundamental value are in the balance, the Court may be required to reassess and possibly annul, measures adopted by the Community institutions, even when those measures reflect the wishes of the SC.'[196]

are two reasons that advocate in favour of the ECJ's self-oriented approach: first, [...] the serious deficit of the UN system as regard the observance of fundamental rights [...]. Secondly, the ECJ does not seek to establish itself as the guardian of the global legal order, since it does not review the UNSC resolution but the EC implementing measure'. For an international law critique, however, see De Burca, (cf. *supra*: note 80), 2 according to which 'the judgment is a significant departure from the conventional presentation and widespread understanding of the EU as an actor which maintains a distinctive commitments to international law and institutions.' According then to Gattini (2009) 213, 224 from this point of view the judgment of the ECJ 'gives rise to mixed feelings. On the one hand one can not but welcome the unbending commitment of the ECJ to the respect of human rights, but on the other hand the relatively high price, in terms of coherence and unity of the international legal system [...] is worrying'. For an assessment of the various approaches to the relationship between international and EU law – 'thin internationalism' and 'constitutional resistance' and the identification of a possible third way, 'a *Solange* type dialogue' – see Eeckhout (cf. *supra*: note 68) 205; Halberstam & Stein (cf. *supra*: note 43) 49 ff. For a survey of the various critical and favourable position of lawyers on the *Kadi* judgment see Poli & Tzanou, (2009).

192 *Kadi* at §316 There is much convergence among scholars as to the fact that the ECJ approach is preferable to that of the CFI as far as the protection of fundamental rights is concerned. See Tridimas (cf. *supra*: note 184) 126 who argues that 'on the issue of fundamental rights protection, the ECJ's commitment is to be applauded.'

193 *Kadi* at §326.

194 Cappuccio (2008) 903, 904.

195 *Kadi* (Opinion of Maduro AG) at §1 According to Tridimas & Gutierrez-Fons (cf. *supra*: note 45) 701 'a distinct feature of the ECJ's reasoning, which differentiates its approach from that of the CFI, is [precisely] that it conceded little ground to the source of the security concerns.' See also *supra* note 91.

196 *Kadi* (Opinion of Maduro AG) at §43.

On the merit of the fundamental rights claim raised by the appellant, the ECJ displayed 'distrust toward any invasion of due process'[197] and held that 'in the light of the actual circumstances surrounding the inclusion of the appellants' names in the list of persons and entities covered by the restrictive measures [...] the right of defence, in particular the right to be heard, and the right to effective judicial review were patently not respected.'[198] In addition, according to the ECJ, the freezing of assets deriving from inclusion on the list also 'constituted an unjustified restriction of [the] right to property.'[199] As a result, confirming that 'in the EU's flawed system of governance, democracy finds solace in judicial review,'[200] the ECJ declared the appeal to be well founded and annulled the contested EC regulation insofar as it concerned the applicants.[201]

In *Kadi*, the ECJ rejected the deferential stand of the CFI and followed the suggestions given by AG Maduro to take seriously the duty to preserve the rule of law as 'constitutional court of the municipal order that is the EC'.[202] The ECJ also reasserted the role of the judiciary in times of emergency by simply excluding that a 'regulation [could] escape all review by the EC judicature once it ha[d] been claimed that the act [...] concern[ed] national security and terrorism.'[203] As indeed the AG had again correctly pointed out, 'especially in matters of public security, the political process is liable to become overly responsive to immediate popular concern, leading the authorities to allay the anxiety of the many at the expenses of the rights of the few. This is precisely when courts ought to get involved',[204] with 'constitutional confidence.'[205] Through its decision, the ECJ re-established a judicial remedy at the EC level for the persons listed by UN resolutions in disregard of the due process guarantees.

2. The Lisbon Treaty

The judgment of the ECJ in *Kadi* fills the gap in the protection of fundamental rights in the European multilevel system by recognizing a remedy at the supranational level, and to some extent it anticipates the effects

---

197 Tridimas & Gutierrez-Fons (cf. *supra*: note 45) 698.

198 *Kadi* at §334

199 Id. at §370.

200 Tridimas (cf. *supra*: note 184) 103.

201 The ECJ, however, maintained on the basis of Article 231 EC Treaty the effects of the regulation for a period of no more than three months running from the date of delivery of the judgment in order to allow the EU Council to remedy the infringements found and to avoid 'seriously and irreversibly prejudicing the effectiveness of the restrictive measures.' (*Kadi* at § 373). See Tzanou (cf. *supra*: note 58) 152.

202 *Kadi* (Opinion of Maduro AG) at §37 According to Gattini (cf. *supra*: note 191), 234-235 'the ECJ in its own understanding is not an international supervisory body but a juridical body analogous to a domestic court.' See also D'Argent (2008) 265.

203 *Kadi* at §343. See also Della Cananea (cf. *supra*: note 67) 521.

204 *Kadi* (Opinion of Maduro AG) at §45.

205 Tridimas (cf. *supra*: note 184) 114.

that might be produced by the entry into force of the Lisbon Treaty. Even if the destiny of the reform treaty concluded by the EUMS in 2007 is still uncertain, it is worth analyzing its new provisions here.[206] While in fact, on the one hand, the EUMS had already shown their agreement on the need to introduce such novelties in the defunct Constitutional Treaty,[207] on the other, a discussion of the potentially positive impacts of these modifications may be useful *de jure condendo*. To begin with, if and when the Lisbon Treaty comes into force, it will reassert the importance of the protection of fundamental rights in the EU by granting *valeur juridique* to the EU CFR.[208]

The Lisbon Treaty, furthermore, will abolish the pillar structure of the EU by extending the *méthode communautaire* (including the full jurisdiction of the ECJ) also to the area of JHA.[209] While the CFSP will maintain several *ad hoc* rules,[210] according to the new Article 275 of the (renamed) Treaty on the Functioning of the EU, 'the ECJ shall have jurisdiction to [...] rule on proceedings, brought in accordance with the conditions laid down in the fourth paragraph of Article 230 of this Treaty, reviewing the legality of decisions providing for restrictive measures against natural or legal persons adopted by the Council on the basis of [the CFSP]'. Combined with the recent *Kadi* doctrine, this provision of the Lisbon Treaty will allow the ECJ to review a common position listing persons suspected of financing terrorism (as well as its implementing EC regulation) effectively.[211] The reasoning of the ECJ in *Segi* will hence acquire teeth, given that the text of the amended Treaty will exclude *de jure* a jurisdictional immunity for EU acts providing for restrictive measures and render the jurisdiction of the ECJ mandatory.[212]

Finally, the new Article 6(2) EU Treaty will mandate the formal accession of the EU (which will acquire legal personality and replace the EC[213]) to the ECHR.[214] To this end (after the entry into force of the Lisbon Treaty as well as of the 14th additional protocol to the ECHR, which expressly allows for the accession of the EU to the ECHR), a special agreement will have to be negotiated between the EU and the Council of Europe and then ratified by all the 47

206 See *supra* note 39. For a general overview of the Treaty and its impact on the functioning and the policies of the EU see Bilancia et al. (2009).

207 See De Witte (2007) 919.

208 On the impact of the Lisbon Reform Treaty on fundamental rights see Cartabia (2008) 81.

209 Ziller (2007) 70.

210 Id. 142.

211 Dougan (2008) 617, 674-675.

212 According to Dougan (cf. *supra*: note 211) 675 the decision of the ECJ in *Segi* was of 'little value in the case of [EUMS] which ha[d] refused to accept the [ECJ]'s jurisdiction to deliver preliminary rulings under the Third pillar. Under the revised Treaties, by contrast, the [ECJ] will have jurisdiction over all Union acts imposing restrictive measures on individuals.'

213 Ziller (cf. *supra*: note 209) 142.

214 Dougan (cf. *supra*: note 211) 671. On the accession of the EU to the ECHR, see among many Benoit-Rohmer (2000) 57; De Schutter (2002) 205.

Contracting Parties to the ECHR.[215] One of the major effects of accession will be that the acts of the EU institutions will be subject to judicial review before the ECtHR on their conformity with the ECHR.[216] The *Bosphorus* doctrine of indirect and limited reviewability will hence be replaced by a full human rights control of EU acts. Should the EU accede to the ECHR, a gap in the protection of fundamental rights such as the one generated by the *Yusuf* jurisprudence of the CFI would hence easily be filled by the review of the ECtHR.

E. 'A Judge in Berlin'

In conclusion, the substantive transformation that has recently taken place in the case law of the ECJ provides the right answer, especially if coupled with the formal transformations that would be produced by the entry into force of the Lisbon Reform Treaty, to the problem of ineffectiveness in the protection of human rights in the European multilevel system. Indeed, structural features of the multilayer structure – aggravated by the decisions of the CFI in *Yusuf* and *Kadi* to withhold scrutiny over domestic acts implementing UNSC resolutions – had made it impossible for the individuals and entities targeted by the UNSC counter-terrorism sanctions to have a court review the lawfulness of such measures.[217]

As chart 1 summarizes, judicial review of UN counter-terrorism measures was initially lacking in both the law in the books and in the law in action of all the layers of the European multilevel system of human rights protection. European courts therein attempted to introduce judge-made responses to overcome the gap in the protection of fundamental rights, but their efforts, although important in themselves, proved unsatisfactory. Finally, in the *Kadi* case, the ECJ took a decisive step in acknowledging the power to review the legality of EC acts implementing UNSC resolutions, anticipating the major reforms that (hopefully) are about to be introduced by the Lisbon Treaty.

»»		UN »»	CFSP »»	EC »»	EUMS »»	ECHR
	Legal acts under scrutiny	SC Resolution	Common Position	Regulation	Domestic act	-
time	Lack of judicial review	-	EU Treaty	*Yusuf*	*Foto-Frost*	*CFDT*
	Unsatisfactory developments	-	*Segi*	*Ayadi*	*Solange*	*Bosphorus*
»»	Rise of judicial review	-	Lisbon Treaty	*Kadi*	-	Accession Treaty

Chart 1: Judicial review of UN counter-terrorism sanctions: how effective is the protection of human rights in the European multilevel system?

It is commonplace in constitutional commentaries to recall that already in XVIII century Prussia a miller unlawfully expropriated of his assets by King

215 Ziller (cf. *supra*: note 209) 103.

216 See Kruger & Polakiewicz (2001) 1; Bribosia (2007) 995.

217 Eeckhout (2005) 20; Kunoy & Dawes (2009) 73.

Friedrich II was able to claim that the discretionary powers of his monarch were limited since there was a judge in Berlin to review the legality of that measure.[218] Three centuries later, the same principle still holds true: counter-terrorism measures adopted by the UN are not above the law: there is *encore* a judge somewhere in Europe willing and able to review their lawfulness.

IV Conclusion

The protection of fundamental rights in Europe is based on a multilevel system where national, supranational and international norms and institutions interlace to provide to the individual greater shield against the illegitimate exercise of public authority. Notwithstanding the existence of three different layers of human rights protection, however, there might be situations in which in the European legal space no rights or remedies are available at any layer of the system against severe infringements of fundamental rights. This situation, which I address as the problem of ineffectiveness, represents one of the major challenge to the European multilevel system of human rights protection and has to be carefully analyzed.

At the same time, several transformations in the law are affecting the scenario of human rights protection in Europe. In substantive terms, the continuous evolution in the jurisprudence of the highest European courts (i.e. the ECJ, the ECtHR and the national constitutional and supreme courts dialoguing together) reshapes the traits of the multilevel system in order to adapt European law to the new human rights challenges. Formal changes in the law are then elaborated through legislative and constitutional reform, especially in the context of EU Treaty amendments. These transformations have (at least potentially) the capacity to overcome some of the *lacunae* of the European multilevel system and resolve the problem of ineffectiveness.

As the case of judicial review of UN counter-terrorism measure in the European multilevel system indeed demonstrates, no review was originally available for the individuals and entities affected by the counter-terrorism sanctions of the UNSC who wished to contest the lawfulness of such measures. Some jurisprudential routes have therein been attempted to resolve the problem of ineffectiveness in the protection of fundamental rights, but most of them have proved to be unsatisfactory. In the end, however, the recent *Kadi* decision of the ECJ has furnished an adequate response to the problem *de qua*, partially anticipating the favourable formal innovations that would be introduced with the entry into force of the Lisbon Reform Treaty.

---

[218] The legendary history of the so called 'Miller of Sans Souci' is often considered as the emblematic case of the rise of the rule of law in Europe highlighting symbolically the passage from the *Ancient Régime* where the King and its officers were '*summa legibus soluta potestas*' (supreme power unbound by the law) to the liberal State where the exercise of power by public authorities is subjected to judicial review.

Bibliography

B. Ackerman, *Before the Next Attack: Preserving Civil Liberties in an Age of Terrorism* (New Haven, 2006).

S. Adam, *Les résolutions du Conseil de sécurité de l'Onu à l'épreuve des juridictions communautaires: Variations autour de la jusiticiabilité*, in Francis Snyders, *The Evolution of the European Court* (Bruxelles 2009 forthcoming).

S. Adam – in this book.

A. Adinolfi, *L'accertamento in via pregiudiziale della validità degli atti comunitari* (Milano, 1997).

D. Akande, 'The International Court of Justice and the Security Council: Is there Room for Judicial Control of Decisions of the Political Organs of the United Nations' [1997] 46 *International and Comparative Law Quarterly*, 341.

E. Alkema, 'The EC and the European Convention on Human Rights: Immunity and Impunity for the Community?' [1979] 16 *Common Market Law Review*, 508.

J. Almqvist, 'A Human Rights Critique of European Judicial Review: Counter-Terrorism Sanctions' [2008] 57 *International Comparative Law Quarterly*, 303.

P. Alston – J. Weiler, *An 'Ever Closer Union' in Need of a Human Rights Policy: The European Union and Human Rights*, in P. Alston, *The EU and Human Rights* (Oxford 1999).

A. Arnull, 'Les incidences du traité d'Amsterdam sur la Cour de Justice des CE' [2000] *Revue des Affaires Européennes*, 227.

H. Aust, 'Between Self-Assertion and Deference: European Courts and their Assessment of UN Security Council Resolutions' [2008] 8 *Anuario Mexicano de Derecho International*, 51.

J. Baquero Cruz, 'The Legacy of the Maastricht *Urteil* and the Pluralist Movement' [2008] 4 14 *European Law Journal*, 389.

A. Barak, *The Judge in a Democracy* (Princeton, 2006).

A. Barbera, *Le basi filosofiche del costituzionalismo* (Roma – Bari, 1997).

A. Barbera, 'Esiste una 'costituzione europea'?' [2000] 1 *Quaderni Costituzionali*, 59.

M. Barberis, *Filosofia del Diritto. Un'introduzione teorica* (Torino, 2005).

J. Bengoetxea, N. MacCormick – L. Moral Soriano, *Integration and Integrity in the Legal Reasoning of the European Court of Justice, in* G. De Burca & J. Weiler *The European Court of Justice* (Oxford, 2001).

F. Benoit-Rohmer, 'L'adhésion de l'Union à la Convention européenne des droits de l'homme' [2000] *Revue Universelle des Droits de l'Homme*, 57.

L. Besselink, 'Entrapped by the Maximum Standard: On Fundamental Rights, Pluralism and Subsidiarity in the European Union' [1998] 35 *Common Market Law Review*, 629.

L. Besselink, *A Composite European Constitution* (Groningen, 2007).

A. Bianchi, 'Assessing the Effectiveness of the UN Security Council's Antiterrorism Measures: The Quest for Legitimacy and Cohesion' [2006] 17 *European Journal of International Law*, 881.

T. Bierstaker – S. Eckert, *Strengthening Targeted Sanctions Through Fair and Clear Procedures. White Paper prepared by the Watson Institute, Targeted Sanctions Project* (Brown University, 2006).

P. Bilancia et al., *La nuova Europa dopo il Trattato di Lisbona* (Milano, 2009).

R. Bin, *Lo stato di diritto* (Bologna, 2004).

N. Bobbio, *L'età dei diritti* (Torino, 1992).

M. Bobek, 'Reasonableness in Administrative Law: A Comparative Reflection of Functional Equivalence' [2008] 2 Eric Stein Working Papers, 5.

P. Bordeau-Livenec, G. Buzzini & S. Villalpando, 'Case Note on *Behrami* and *Saramati*' [2008] 102 *American Journal of International Law*, 323.

G. Braibant, *Le principe de proportionnalité*, in *Melanges Waline* volume II (Paris, 1974).

S. Breyer, *Active Liberty* (New York, 2005).

E. Bribosia, *L'avenir de la protection des droits fondamentaux dans l'Union Européenne*, in G. Amato et al., *Genesis and Destiny of the European Constitution* (Bruxelles, 2007).

R.S. Brown, '*Kadi v. Council*: Executive Power and Judicial Supervision at the European Level' [2006] 4 *European Human Rights Law Review*, 456.

J. Callewaert, 'The European Court of Human Rights and the Area of Freedom, Security and Justice' [2007] 8 *ERA Forum*, 511.

I. Cameron, 'UN Targeted Sanctions, Legal Safeguards and the European Convention on Human Rights' [2003] *Nordic Journal of International Law*, 159.

I. Canor, "Can Two Walk Together Except They Be Agreed'? The Relationship Between International Law and European Law: The Incorporation of United Nations Sanctions Against Yugoslavia into European Community Law through the Perspective of the European Court of Justice' [1998] 35 *Common Market Law Review*, 137.

I. Canor, '*Primus Inter Pares.* Who is the Ultimate Guardian of Fundamental Rights in Europe?' [2000/1] 25 *European Law Review*, 3.

E. Cannizzaro, 'The Machiavellian Moment? The UN Security Council and the Rule of Law' [2006] 13 *International Organizations Law Review*, 195.

L. Cappuccio, 'E' illegittima la decisione delle istituzioni comunitarie che non rispetta il diritto di difesa?'[2007] 2 *Quaderni Costituzionali*, 416.

L. Cappuccio, 'Il controllo della Corte di Giustizia sugli atti comunitari tra tutela giurisdizionale dei diritti e lotta al terrorismo internazionale' [2008] 4 *Quaderni Costituzionali*, 903.

M. Cartabia, *Principi inviolabili e integrazione europea* (Milano, 1995).

M. Cartabia, *L'ora dei diritti fondamentali nell'Unione Europea*, in M. Cartabia, *I diritti in azione*, (Bologna, 2007).

M. Cartabia, *I diritti fondamentali e la cittadinanza dell'Unione*, F. Bassanini & G. Tiberi, *Le Nuove Istituzioni Europee: Commento al Trattato di Lisbona* (Bologna, 2008).

M. Cartabia, 'Europe and Rights: Taking Dialogue Seriously' [2009/1] 5 *European Constitutional Law Review*, 5.

M. Cartabia & J. Weiler, *L'Italia in Europa: profili istituzionali e costituzionali* (Bologna, 2000).

A. Cassese, 'Terrorism is Also Disrupting Some Crucial Legal Categories of International Law' [2001] 12 *European Journal of International Law*, 993.

A. Cassese, A. Clapham & J. Weiler, *1992 – What are our rights? Agenda for a Human Rights Action Plan*, in A. Cassese et al., *European union – The Human Rights Challenge: Volume II. Human Rights and the European Community: Methods of Protection* (Baden Baden 1991).

S. Cassese, *L'Unione europea come organizzazione pubblica composita*, in S. Cassese, *La crisi dello Stato* (Roma – Bari 2002).

S. Cassese, *Il diritto amministrativo e i suoi principi*, in S. Cassese, *Istituzioni di diritto amministrativo* (Milano, 2006a).

S. Cassese, 'A Global Due Process of Law' [2006b] NYU Hauser Papers Series.

S. Cassese, *I tribunali di Babele. I giudici alla ricerca di un nuovo ordine globale* (Roma 2009).

E. Cheli, *Il giudice delle leggi* (Bologna, 1996).

E. Cheli, *Lo stato costituzionale: radici e prospettive* (Napoli 2006).

M. Chiti, *Diritto amministrativo europeo* (Milano, 2004).

A. Ciampi, 'L'Union Européenne et le respect des droits de l'homme dans la mise en œuvre des sanctions devant la Cour Européenne des droits de l'homme' [2006] *Revue Générale de Droit International Public*, 85.

A. Ciampi, *Sanzioni del Consiglio di Sicurezza e diritti umani* (Milano, 2007).

M. Claes, *The National Court's Mandate in the European Constitution* (Oxford 2006).

L. Condorelli, 'Les attentats du 11 septembre et leur suites: où va le droit international?' [2001] *Revue Générale de Droit International Public*, 829.

B. Conforti, 'Decisioni del Consiglio di Sicurezza e diritti fondamentali in una bizzarra sentenza del Tribunale di Primo Grado' [2006] 11 *Diritto dell'Unione Europea*, 333.

P. Craig, *The Jurisdiction of the Community Courts Reconsidered*, in G. De Burca & J. Weiler, *The European Court of Justice* (Oxford 2001).

M. Cremona, 'The Union as a Global Actor: Roles, Models and Identity' [2004] 41 *Common Market Law Review*.

M. Cremona, *The Union's External Action: Constitutional Perspectives*, in G. Amato et al., *Genesis and Destiny of the European Constitution* (Bruxelles 2007) 1173.

P. D'Argent, 'L'arret *Kadi*: le droit communautaire comme droit interne' [2008] *Journal de droit européen*, 265.

A. D'Atena, *Tutela dei diritti fondamentali e costituzionalismo multilivello* (Milano, 2004).

G. De Burca, 'Human Rights, the Charter and Beyond' [2001] 10 Jean Monnet Working Paper.

G. De Burca, *The European Court of Justice and the Evolution of EU Law*, in T. Borzel & R. Cichowski, *The State of the European Union (Volume 6): Law, Politics and Society* (Oxford 2003).

G. De Burca, 'The European Court of Justice and the International Legal Order after *Kadi*' [2009] 1 Jean Monnet WP.

E. Defeis, 'Targeted Sanctions, Human Rights and the Court of First Instance of the European Community' [2007] 30 *Fordham International Law Journal*, 1449.

G. Della Cananea, *L'Unione Europea. Un ordinamento composito* (Roma – Bari 2003).

G. Della Cananea, 'Return to Due Process of Law: the European Union and the Fight against Terrorism' [2007] 6 32 *European Law Review*, 896.

G. Della Cananea, 'Global Security and Procedural Due Process of Law Between the United Nations and the European Union: *Kadi v. Council*' [2009] 15 *Columbia Journal of European Law*, 519.

C. Denis, *Le pouvoir normatif du Conseil de Sécurité des Nations Unies: Portée et limites* (Bruxelles, 2004).

O. De Schutter, *L'adhésion de l'Union à la Convention européenne des droits de l'homme comme élément du débat sur l'avenir de l'Union*, in E. Bribosia et al., *L'avenir du système juridictionnel de l'Union européenne* (Bruxelles, 2002).

G. De Vergottini, *Le transizioni costituzionali* (Bologna, 1998).

E. De Wet, *The Chapter VII Powers of the United Nations Security Council* (Oxford, 2004).

E. De Wet, *The role of Human Rights in Limiting the Enforcement Power of the UN Security Council: a Principled View*, in E. De Wet & A. Nollkaemper, *Review of the Security Council by Member States* (Antwerp, 2003).

B. de Witte, *Direct Effect, Supremacy and the Nature of the Legal Order*, in P. Craig & G. De Burca, *The Evolution of EU Law* (Oxford, 1999a).

B. De Witte, *The Past and Future Role of the European Court of Justice in the Protection of Human Rights*, in P. Alston, *The EU and Human Rights* (Oxford, 1999b).

B. De Witte, *Saving the Constitution? The Escape Routes and their Legal Feasibility*, in G. Amato, *Genesis and Destiny of the European Constitution* (Bruxelles, 2007).

M. Dougan, 'The Treaty of Lisbon 2007: Winning Minds not Hearts' [2008] 45 *Common Market Law Review*, 617.

S. Douglas-Scott, 'Case Note *Bosphorus v. Ireland*' [2006a] 43 *Common Market Law Review*, 243.

S. Douglas-Scott, 'A Tale of Two Courts: Luxembourg, Strasbourg and the Growing European Human Rights *Acquis*' [2006b] 43 *Common Market Law Review*, 629.

J. Dugard, *Judicial Review of Sanctions*, in V. Gowlland-Debbas et al., *United Nations Sanctions and International Law* (The Hague, 2005).

C. Eckes, 'Judicial Review of European Anti-Terrorism Measures – The *Yusuf* and *Kadi* Judgments of the CFI' [2008/1] 14 *European Law Journal*, 74.

P. Eeckhout, *External Relations of the European Union: Legal and Constitutional Foundations* (Oxford, 2004).

P. Eeckhout, *Does Europe's Constitution Stop at the Water's Edge?* (Groningen, 2005).

P. Eeckhout, 'Community Terrorism Listing, Fundamental Rights and UN Security Council Resolution: In Search of the Right Fit' [2007/2] 3 *European Constitutional Law Review*, 183.

F. Fabbrini, 'The Role of the Judiciary in Times of Emergency: Judicial Review of Counter Terrorism Measures in the United States Supreme Court and the European Court of Justice' [2009] *Yearbook of European Law* (forthcoming).

A. Facchi, *I diritti nell'Europa multiculturale* (Roma – Bari, 2006).

J. Farrall, *The United Nations Sanctions and the Rule of Law* (Cambridge, 2007).

B. Fassbender, 'The UN Charter as Constitution of the International Community' [1998] 36 *Columbia Journal of Transnational Law*, 529.

B. Fassbender, 'Targeted Sanctions Imposed by the UN Security Council and Due Process Rights' [2006] 13 *International Organizations Law Review*, 437.

C. Feinaugle, 'The UN Security Council Al-Qaida and Taliban Sanctions Committee: Emerging Principles of International Institutional Law for the Protection of the Individuals?' [2008/11] 9 *German Law Journal*, 1513.

P. Fitzgerald, 'Responding to Rogue Regimes: from Smart Bombs to Smart Sanctions. Managing 'Smart Sanctions' Against Terrorism Wisely' [2002/4] 36 *New England Law Review*, 957.

E. Flynn, 'The Security Council Counter Terrorism Committee and Human Rights' [2007] 7 *Human Rights Law Review*, 371.

T. Franck, *Political Questions, Judicial Answers* (Princeton, 1992).

J. Frowein, *The Anti-Terrorism Administration and the Rule of Law*, in P.M. Dupuy et al., *Festschrift Tomuschat* (Kehl – Strasbourg – Arlington, 2006).

J. Frowein – N. Krish, *Chapter VII: Action with Respect to Threats to Peace, Breaches of Peace and Acts of Aggression*, in B. Simma, *The Charter of the United Nations. A Commentary Volume I* (Oxford, 2002).

G. Gaja, *New Instruments and Institutions for Enhancing the Protection of Human Rights in Europe*, in P. Alston, *The EU and Human Rights* (Oxford, 1999).

G. Gaja, *The Review by the European Court of Human Rights of Member States' Acts Implementing European Union Law: 'Solange' Yet Again?,* in P.M. Dupuy et al. *Festschrift Tomuschat* (Kehl – Strasbourg – Arlington, 2006).

A. Garde, 'Is it really for the European Community to Implement Anti-Terrorism UN Security Council Resolutions?' [2006] *Cambridge Law Journal,* 284.

A. Gattini, 'Case Note *Kadi v. Council*' [2009] 46 *Common Market Law Review,* 213.

J.C. Gautron, *Droit européen* (Paris, 2006).

M.E. Gennusa, *La Cedu e l'Unione Europea,* in M. Cartabia *I diritti in azione* (Bologna, 2007).

E. Guild, 'The Uses and Abuses of Counter-Terrorism Policies in Europe: The Case of the 'Terrorist Lists'' [2008/1] 46 *Journal of Common Market Studies,* 173.

P. Haberle, *Verdad y Estado constitucional* (Ciudad de Mexico, 2006).

J. Habermas, *Lotta di riconoscimento nello stato democratico di diritto,* in J. Habermas & C. Taylor, *Multiculturalismo* (Milano, 2005).

D. Halberstam – E. Stein, 'The United Nations, the European Union and the King of Sweden: Economic Sanctions and Individual Rights in a Plural World Order' [2009] 46 *Common Market Law Review,* 13.

C. Harlow, *Access to Justice as a Human Right: the European Convention and the European Union,* in P. Alston, *The EU and Human Rights* (Oxford, 1999).

C. Harlow, 'Global Administrative Law: The Quest for Principles and Values' [2006/1] 17 *European Journal of International Law,* 206.

G. Harpaz, 'The European Court of Justice and its Relationship with the European Court of Human Rights: the Quest for Enhanced Reliance, Coherence and Legitimacy' [2009] 46 *Common Market Law Review,* 105.

D. Harris, M. O'Boyle, – C. Warbrick, *Law of the European Convention on Human Rights* (London, 1995).

H. L. Hart, *Positivism and Separation of Law and Morals,* in Herbert L. Hart, *Essays in Jurisprudence and Philosophy* (Oxford, 1983).

L. Henkin, 'Is There a 'Political Question' Doctrine?' [1976] 85 *Yale Law Journal,* 597.

M. Herdegen, *Review of the Security Council by National Courts: A Constitutional Perspective* in E. De Wet & A. Nollkaemper *Review of the Security Council by Member States* (Antwerp, 2003).

F. Jacobs, 'Judicial Dialogue and the Cross-Fertilization of Legal Systems: The European Court of Justice' [2003] 38 *Texas International Law Journal,* 547.

F. Jacobs, *The Sovereignty of Law* (Cambridge, 2007).

J.P. Jacqué, 'Droit communautaire et Convention européenne des droits de l'homme: L'arrêt *Bosphorus,* une jurisprudence '*Solange II*' de la Cour européenne des droits de l'homme?' [2005] 41 *Revue trimestrelle de droit européen,* 756.

P. Kapteyn, *The Role of the ECJ in Implementing Security Council Resolutions* in E. De Wet & A. Nollkaemper, *Review of the Security Council by Member States* (Antwerp, 2003).

T. King, 'Ensuring Human Rights Review of Intergovernmental Acts in Europe' [2000] 25 *European Law Review*, 86.

J. Komarek, 'European Constitutionalism and the European Arrest Warrant' [2007] 44 *Common Market Law Review*, 9.

P. Koutrakos, *Security and Defence Policy within the Context of EU External Relations: Issues of Coherence, Consistency and Effectiveness*, in M. Trybus et al., *European Security Law* (Oxford, 2007).

N. Krisch, 'The Open Architecture of European Human Rights Law' [2008/2] 71 *Modern Law Review*, 183.

H.C. Kruger – J. Polakiewicz, 'Proposal for a Coherent Human Rights Protection System in Europe: The European Convention on Human Rights and the EU Charter of Fundamental Rights' [2001] 22 *Human Rights Law Journal* 1.

P.J. Kuijper, *Implementation of Binding Security Council Resolutions by the EU/EC*, in E. De Wet & A. Nollkaemper, *Review of the Security Council by Member States* (Antwerp, 2003).

B. Kunoy – A. Dawes, 'Plate Tectonics in Luxembourg: the *Ménage à Trois* between EC Law, International Law and the ECHR Following the UN Sanctions Cases' [2009] 46 *Common Market Law Review*, 73.

N. Lavranos, 'Judicial Review of UN Sanctions by the CFI' [2006] 11 *European Foreign Affairs Review*, 471.

N. Lavranos, *Toward a* Solange-*Method between International Courts and Tribunals?*, in T. Broude & Y. Shany, *The Shifting Allocation of Authority in International Law: Considering Sovereignty Supremacy Subsidiarity* (Oxford, 2008).

N. Lavranos, 'Case Note: *Kadi v. Council*' [2009] *Legal Issues of Economic Integration*, 157.

K. Lenaerts, *The Unity of European Law and the Overload of the ECJ: The system of Preliminary Rulings Revisited* in I. Pernice et al, *The Future of the European Judicial System in a Comparative Perspective* (Baden-Baden, 2006).

K. Lenaerts & E. De Smijter, 'The Charter and the Role of the European Courts' [2001] 8 *Maastricht Journal of European and Comparative Law*, 90.

K. Lenaerts & L. Jadoul, *Quelle contribution de la Cour de Justice des Communautés européennes au développement de l'espace de liberté, de sécurité et de justice* in G. De Kerchove et al., *L'espace pénal européen: enjeux et perspective* (Bruxelles, 2002).

X. Lewis, 'Standing of Private Plaintiffs to Annul Generally Applicable European Community Measures' [2007] 30 *Fordham International Law Journal*, 1469.

J. Locke, *Second Treatise of Government* (1690): Edited by C. Macpherson (Indianapolis, 1980).

F. Maitland, *The Forms of Action at Common Law* (Cambridge, 1948).

G. Martinico & F. Fontanelli, 'Alla ricerca della coerenza: le tecniche del 'dialogo nascosto' tra i giudici nell'ordinamento costituzionale multilivello' [2008/2] *Rivista Trimestrale Diritto Pubblico*, 351.

G. Martinico – O. Pollicino, 'Between Constitutional Tolerance and Judicial Activism: the 'Specificity' of European Judicial Law' [2008/1] 10 *European Journal of Law Reform*, 97.

M. Matheson, *Council Unbound: The Growth of Un Decision Making on Conflict and Post-conflict Issues After the Cold War* (Washington DC, 2006).

Ugo Mattei, *Il modello di* Common Law (Torino, 1996).

F. Mayer, 'The European Constitution and the Courts: Adjudicating European Law in a Multilevel System' [2003] 9 *Jean Monnet WP*.

C. McCrudden, 'A Common Law of Human Rights? Transnational Judicial Conversation on Constitutional Rights' [2000/4] 20 *Oxford Journal of Legal Studies*, 499.

C.H. McIlwain, *Constitutionalism: Ancient and Modern* (Cornell, 1947).

F. Mégret & F. Hoffman, 'The UN as a Human Rights Violator? Some Reflections on the United Nations Changing Human Rights Responsibilities' [2003] 25 *Human Rights Quarterly*, 314.

F. Messineo, 'The House of Lords in *Al Jedda* and Public International Law: Attribution of Conduct to UN-Authorized Forces and the Power of the Security Council to Displace Human Rights' [2009] 56 *Netherlands International Law Review*, 35.

E. Miller, 'The Use of Targeted Sanctions in the Fight Against Terrorism: What About Human Rights?' [2003] 97 *American Society of International Law Proceedings*, 46.

A. Morrone, *Il custode della ragionevolezza* (Milano, 2001).

M. Nettesheim, 'UN Sanctions Against Individuals: a Challenge to the Architecture of the EU Governance' [2007] 44 *Common Market Law Review*, 567.

S. Peers, 'Limited Responsibility of European Union Member States for Action within the Scope of Community Law. Case Note to *Bosphorus Airways v. Ireland*' [2006] 2 *European Constitutional Law Review*, 443.

S. Peers, 'Salvation Outside the Church: Judicial Protection in the Third Pillar After the *Pupino* and *Segi* Judgments' [2007] 44 *Common Market Law Review*, 883.

I. Pernice, 'Multilevel Constitutionalism and the Treaty of Amsterdam' [1999] 36 *Common Market Law Review*, 703.

I. Pernice, 'Multilevel Constitutionalism in the European Union' [2002] 27 *European Law Review*, 511.

E.U. Petersmann, 'Human Rights and 'Constitutional Justice' Require Citizen-oriented Adjudication in International Economic Law' [2008/1] 20 *European Journal of International Law*, 1.

A. Pizzorusso, *Il patrimonio costituzionale europeo* (Bologna, 2002).
M. Poiares Maduro, 'The Importance of Being Called a Constitution: Constitutional Authority and the Authority on Constitutionalism' [2005] 3 *International Journal of Constitutional Law*, 332.
M. Poiares Maduro, 'Interpreting European Law: Judicial Adjudication in a Context of Constitutional Pluralism' [2007/1] 2 *European Journal of Legal Studies*.
S. Poli & M. Tzanou, *Survey on the Literature on* Kadi, in M. Cremona et al., *Challenging EU Counter-Terrorism Measures Through the Courts* (EUI Working Paper, 2009 forthcoming).
V. Ramraj et al., *Global Anti-terrorism Law and Policy* (Cambridge, 2005).
A. Reinish, 'Developing Human Rights and Humanitarian Law Accountability of the Security Council for the Imposition of Economic Sanctions' [2001] 95 *American Journal of International Law*, 851.
M. Reisman & D. Stevick, 'The Applicability of International Law Standards to United Nations Economic Sanctions Programs' [1998] 9 *European Journal of International Law*, 226.
E. Rosand, 'The Security Council's Efforts to Monitor the Implementation of Al Qaeda/Taliban Sanctions' [2004] 98 *American Journal of International Law*, 745.
A. Rosas, *The European Court of Justice and Public International Law*, in Jan Wouters et al., *The Europeanisation of International Law* (Cambridge, 2008).
M. Rosenfeld, 'Constitutional Adjudication in Europe and the United States: Paradoxes and Contrasts' [2004] 2 *International Journal of Constitutional Law*, 633.
W. Sadurski, ''*Solange*, Chapter 3': Constitutional Courts in Central Europe – Democracy – European Union' [2008a] 14 *European Law Journal*, 1.
W. Sadurski, ''Reasonableness' and Value Pluralism in Law and Politics', [2008b] 13 *EUI Working Paper*.
A. Saio, *Limiting Government: An Introduction to Constitutionalism* (Budapest, 1999).
E. Sanfutos Cano, *The third pillar and the European Court of Justice: a 'Praetorian Communitarisation' of Police and Judicial Cooperation in Criminal Matters?*, in Elspeth Guild et al., *Security v. Justice? Police and Judicial Cooperation in the EU* (London, 2008).
A. Sari, 'Jurisdiction and International Responsibility in Peace Support Operations: the *Behrami and Saramati* Cases' [2008/1] 8 *Human Rights Law Review*, 151.
A. Sari, 'The *Al-Jedda* Case Before the House of Lords' [2009] 13 *Journal of International Peacekeeping*, 181.
B. Saul, *Defining Terrorism in International Law* (Oxford, 2006).
M. Savino, 'La disciplina italiana della lotta al finanziamento del terrorismo' [2008/5] *Giornale di Diritto Amministrativo*, 497.

L. Scheeck, 'Solving Europe's Binary Human Rights Puzzle. The Interaction Between Supranational Courts as a Parameter of European Governance' [2005] *Questions de recherche de Science Po* 15.

M. Scheinin, *Is the ECJ Ruling in* Kadi *Incompatible with International Law?*, in M. Cremona et al., *Challenging EU Counter-Terrorism Measures Through the Courts* (EUI Working Paper, 2009 forthcoming).

F. Schimmelfenning, *Competition and Community: Constitutional Courts, Rhetorical Action and the Institutionalization of Human Rights in the European Union* in Berthold Rittberger et al., *The Constitutionalization of the European Union* (London, 2007).

M. Shapiro, *Courts: A Comparative and Political Analysis* (Chicago, 1981).

M. Shapiro, *The European Court of Justice*, in P. Craig – G. De Burca, *The Evolution of EU Law* (Oxford, 1999).

M. Shapiro, *Rights in the European Union: Convergent with the USA?*, in N. Jabko & C. Parson *The State of the European Union (Volume 7): With US or Against US? European Trends in American Perspective* (Oxford, 2005).

D. Shelton, *Remedies and the Charter of Fundamental Rights of the European Union*, in S. Peers & A. Wards, *The European Charter of Fundamental Rights: Politics, Law and Policy* (Oxford, 2004).

A.M. Slaughter, 'A Typology of Transjudicial Communication' [1994] 29 *University Richmond Law Review*, 99.

A.M. Slaughter, 'A Global Community of Courts' [2003] 44 *Harvard International Law Journal*, 191.

F. Snyder, 'The Effectiveness of European Community Law: Institutions, Processes, Tools and Techniques' [1993/1] 56 *Modern Law Review*, 19.

E. Spaventa, *Fundamental What? The Difficult Relationship Between Foreign Policy and Fundamental Rights*, in M. Cremona & B. De Witte, *EU Foreign Relations Law: Constitutional Fundamentals* (Oxford, 2008).

D. Spielmann, *Human Rights Case Law in the Strasbourg and Luxembourg Courts: Conflicts, Inconsistencies and Complementarities*, in Philip Alston, *The EU and Human Rights* (Oxford, 1999).

P. Stangos – G. Gryllos, 'Le droit communautaire à l'épreuve des réalités du droit international: lecons tirées de la jurisprudence communautaire récente relevant de la lutte contre le terrorisme international' [2006] *Cahiers de Droit Europeen*, 466.

J. Sterba, *Terrorism and International Justice* (Oxford, 2003).

E. Storskrubb & J. Ziller, *Access to Justice in European Comparative Law*, in F. Francioni, *Access to Justice as a Human Rights* (Oxford), 177.

P. Tanzarella, *Il margine di apprezzamento*, in Marta Cartabia, *I diritti in Azione* (Bologna, 2007).

G. Tesauro, *Diritto comunitario* (Padova, 2005).

C. Tomuschat, 'Case Note: *Kadi v. EU Council and Commission*' [2006] 43 *Common Market Law Review*, 537.

T. Tridimas, *The General Principles of EU Law* (Oxford 2006).

T. Tridimas, 'Terrorism and the ECJ: Empowerment and Democracy in the EC Legal Order' [2009/1] 34 *European Law Review*, 103.

T. Tridimas – J. Gutierrez-Fons, 'EU Law, International Law and Economic Sanctions against Terrorism: the Judiciary in Distress?' [2008] 32 *Fordham International Law Journal*, 660.

N. Trocker, ''*Civil Law*' e '*Common Law*' nella formazione del diritto processuale europeo' [2007] *Rivista Italiana di diritto pubblico comunitario*, 421.

M. Troper, 'Judicial Power and Democracy' [2007/1] 2 *European Journal of Legal Studies*.

M. Tzanou, 'Case Note *Kadi v. Council*' [2009/2] 10 *German Law Journal*, 123.

L. Van Den Herik, 'The Security Council's Targeted Sanctions Regime: in Need of Better Protection of the Individual' [2007] 20 *Leiden Journal of International Law*, 729.

A. Von Bogdandy, 'The European Union as a Human Rights Organization? Human Rights at the Core of the European Union' [2000] 37 *Common Market Law Review*, 1307.

A. Von Bogdandy, P. Dann & M. Goldmann, 'Developing the Publicness of Public International Law: Towards a Legal Framework for Global Governance Activities' [2008/11] 9 *German Law Journal*, 1375.

N. Walker, 'Multilevel Constitutionalism: Looking Beyond the German Debate' [2008] *London School of Economics Europe in Question Discussion Paper Series No. 8*.

C. Walter et al., *Terrorism as a Challenge for National and International Law* (Berlin – Heidelberg, 2004).

A. Ward, *Access to Justice*, in S. Peers & A. Wards, *The European Charter of Fundamental Rights: Politics, Law and Policy* (Oxford, 2004).

J. Weiler, *Methods of Protection of Fundamental Human Rights in the European Community: Towards a Second and Third Generation of Protection*, in A. Cassese et al. eds., *European Union – The Human Rights Challenge: Volume II. Human Rights and the European Community: Methods of Protection* (Baden Baden, 1991).

L. Wildhaber, 'A Constitutional Future for the European Court of Human Rights?' [2002] 23 *Human Rights Law Review*, 161.

L. Wildhaber, 'The European Court of Human Rights in Action' [2004] 21 *Ritsumeikan Law Review*, 83.

B. Zagaris, 'Merging of the Counter-Terrorism and Anti-Money Laundering Regimes' [2003] *Law and Policy in International Business* 34.

G. Zagrebelsky, *Il diritto mite* (Torino, 1992).

G. Zagrebelsky, *Diritti e Costituzione nell'Unione Europea* (Roma – Bari, 2003).

G. Zagrebelsky, *La legge e la sua giustizia* (Bologna, 2008).

J. Ziller, *Il nuovo Trattato europeo* (Bologna, 2007).

CHAPTER 6

Overcoming Dissonance to Reshape Coherence

The European Court of Justice, Terrorist Lists and the Rule of Law

Stanislas Adam*

This chapter highlights the ongoing dialogue entered into by Community Courts and political actors – either at UN, European or even domestic level – regarding the necessary balance between the efficiency of actions undertaken to combat terrorism through restrictive measures affecting individuals or entities and the respect for fundamental rights. The starting point is the judgment pronounced by the Grand Chamber of the European Court of Justice (hereafter, the ECJ) on 3 September 2008 in the *Kadi and Al Barakaat International Foundation* case (hereafter, the *Kadi* case/judgment).[1] The appellants in this case were included in UN lists of persons suspected of (aid to) terrorism. The dilemma the ECJ faced concerned the ability for Community Courts to review in full the legality of a Regulation whose normative content originates in a Resolution adopted by the UN Security Council (hereafter, the UNSC) or a committee placed under its auspices. Whereas the Court of First Instance (hereafter, the CFI) had drastically limited the scope for judicial review in this context, the ECJ on the contrary assumed the consequences of the autonomy of the Community legal order and annulled the disputed regulation. This was mainly rendered possible by firmly rejecting the idea that such review would amount to an indirect challenge of the legality of UN sanctions.

A correct understanding of the constitutional significance of this judgment first requires to look into the previous dichotomy in the case law of the CFI regarding the implementation of individual sanctions adopted at UN level (1) and into the initial attempts by the latter to soften the consequences of this discrepancy for the protection of fundamental rights in the Community legal order (2). As will be further demonstrated, the answer proposed by the ECJ in the *Kadi* judgment, that in essence follows the conclusions delivered by Advocate General (hereafter, A.G.) Poiares Maduro,[2] rests on a clear division of the Community and international legal orders. It is argued that this 'pluralistic approach'[3] enhanced a coherent protection of fundamental rights in the Community legal order, irrespective of whether the acts under scrutiny carry out UNSC measures or not (3). It is not the ambition of this chapter to enter into an in-depth analysis of the standards of fundamental rights applied by the ECJ in *Kadi*, nor to present all consequences of this judgment.[4] One rather tries

* PhD. Research Fellow, Flemish Fund for Scientific Research, Ghent University (*Jean Monnet Centre of Excellence*); Academic advisor at the University of Namur (*Projucit*). The author would like to thank Kirstyn Inglis, Nikolaos Lavranos and Peter Van Elsuwege for their valuable comments on earlier drafts. The usual disclaimer applies.

1 ECJ: Joined Cases C-402/05 P and 415/05 P *Kadi and Al Barakaat Foundation v. Commission and Council* [2008] nyr. M. Ali Yusuf was also a requesting party in Case C-415/05 but abandoned the proceedings he had started (see Order of the President of the ECJ of 13 November 2007).

2 See the conclusions delivered on 16 January 2008 in Case C-402/05 P and on 23 January in Case C-415/05 P.

3 de Burca (2009) 65.

4 See Lavranos (2009); Rijken (2009); Della Cananea (2009); Moiny (2009); D'Aspremont – Dopagne (2008); Griller (2008); Gattini (2009).

to underline the conceivable parallels between the reasoning followed by the ECJ in this case with other recent judgments pronounced in the context of the fight against terrorism or, more generally, concerning the relations between the Community and the international legal orders. Finally, it is argued that the *Kadi* judgment reinforces the legitimacy of the ECJ as a key interlocutor in the global debate on how to balance fundamental rights with efficiency when combating international terrorism through restrictive measures (4).

1 The Previous Discrepancy in Judicial Review

The practice of international sanctions has dramatically evolved since the middle of the Nineties, particularly following the terrorist attacks of 11 September 2001. A great majority of the measures adopted by the UNSC to maintain or restore international peace and security formerly focussed on States. However, attention was increasingly paid to the harmful consequences such measures entailed for citizens not responsible for the situation which motivated the sanctions. Consequently, an increasing number of sanctions have been directed against individuals since the late Eighties. Theoretically, *smart sanctions* directly target individuals, groups or organisations held responsible for infringements of international law in order to balance collective peace and security goals with individual rights.[5] While at first sight it appeared simple, this exercise revealed difficult in practice.[6]

At UN level, the fight against international terrorism through *smart sanctions* is essentially binomial. Resolution 1267 (1999)[7], which aims to combat the Taliban regime in Afghanistan and is therefore known as the *Taliban Resolution*, set up a special Committee (hereafter, the Taliban Committee). The latter is entrusted with the elaboration and update of a blacklist of individuals and entities presumably associated with Usama bin Laden, including those in the Al-Qaeda organisation. The list is based on information provided by the States and regional organisations. Resolution 1373 (2001),[8] on the other hand, rather aims to fight terrorism in general by requiring the UN Member States to freeze all assets of persons, groups or entities when they committed, or attempted to commit terrorist acts or participated in or facilitated the commission of terrorist acts. This Resolution set up a Counter-Terrorism Committee which, contrary to the Taliban Committee, is not competent to identify those persons, groups or entities. As a result, whereas the States cannot depart from the list instituted by the Taliban Committee, they are fully responsible for such identification in the

5 See on this evolution: Reinisch (2001).

6 See on the controversy surrounding the opportunity to replace trade and diplomatic sanctions by restrictive measures affecting individuals, Vermeulen – De Bondt(2008) 380 and 381.

7 Resolution 1267 (1999), 15 October 1999. See also Resolution 1333 (2000), 19 December 2000 and Resolution 1390 (2002), 16 January 2002.

8 UNSC Resolution 1373 (2001), 28 September 2001.

context of Resolution 1373 (2001). Implemented by different instruments in the EC/EU legal order, these Resolutions eventually led to a striking discrepancy in the case law of the CFI.

a. The Taliban Committee's list

The lists elaborated by the Taliban Committee were annexed to Common Position 1999/727/CFSP concerning restrictive measures against the Taliban[9] and were subsequently (and for the first time) carried into Community law by Regulation 337/2000 concerning a flight ban and a freeze of funds and other financial resources in respect of the Taliban of Afghanistan.[10] Since their adoption, these lists have been updated on a regular basis, especially on grounds of successive amendments of the annex to Regulation 881/2002.[11]

Kadi, Yusuf and *Al Barakaat International Foundation* challenged Regulation 881/2002 by arguing that the EC was not competent to adopt such restrictive measures against individuals. They relied on the fact that Articles 60 and 301 EC only evoke sanctions targeting third countries and not persons, groups or entities, unless when the latter can be identified with the regime to be sanctioned. Furthermore, they claimed that their fundamental rights had been violated, in particular their right to property, their right to be heard (*audi alteram partem*) and their right to an effective remedy. It should be borne in mind that, at that time, persons, groups or entities targeted by restrictive measures neither had the opportunity to be heard by the Taliban Committee on the appropriateness of such measures, nor did they enjoy any opportunity to directly challenge their inclusion in the list. Any re-examination was subject to State's petition, with the result that the persons, groups and entities concerned were entirely dependant on the diplomatic protection afforded by States to their nationals. Moreover, a de-listing was – and is still – only possible if decided by the Taliban Committee by consensus, each of its members enjoying a right of veto.

Before answering the arguments based on fundamental rights, the CFI dealt with a general objection to judicial review raised by the Council, the Commission and the United Kingdom. According to the latter, the obligations imposed on the Community and its Member States by the UN Charter prevail over every other obligation of international, Community or domestic law.[12] This is especially the case when action is undertaken by the UNSC on grounds of Chapter VII in order to combat threats to the peace, breaches of the peace and acts of aggression. Consequently, no judicial review of EC measures would be

9 15 November 1999, OJ 1999 L 294/1.

10 14 February 2000, OJ 2000 L 43/1.

11 Council Regulation (EC) N° 881/2002 imposing certain specific restrictive measures directed against certain persons and entities associated with Usama bin Laden, the Al-Qaida network and the Taliban, 27 May 2002, OJ 2002 L 139/9.

12 According to Art. 103 UN Charter, *'(i)n the event of a conflict between the obligations of the Members of the United Nations under the [...] Charter and their obligations under any other international agreement, their obligations under the [...] Charter shall prevail'.*

possible to the extent that their normative content (in this case, the identification of persons, groups or entities suspected of terrorism) originates in decisions adopted by the Taliban Committee, since the latter is entirely incorporated in and placed under control of the UNSC. Otherwise, an annulment of the disputed EC acts could make it difficult if not impossible for the Member States to comply with their obligations resulting from the UN Charter.

The CFI substantially upheld this objection, considering that UNSC Resolutions (as well as decisions adopted by the Taliban Committee) of the type of those at stake, from the standpoint of international law, *'clearly prevail over every other obligation of domestic law or of international treaty law including, for those (States) that are members of the Council of Europe, their obligations under the ECHR and, for those that are also members of the Community, their obligations under the EC Treaty'*.[13] This primacy would be inherent in the supremacy clause contained in Article 103 of the UN Charter and confirmed by Article 307 EC, providing that the EC Treaty does not affect the rights and obligations arising from international treaties concluded before its entry into force or, for acceding States, before the date of their accession.[14] Considering that five of the six founding Member States were a party to the UN Charter before that date, and that all acceding States were also members of the UN before becoming members of the EC/EU, the EC Treaty would in no way impair the obligations arising from the UNSC resolutions or the decisions of the Taliban Committee.[15]

The CFI moreover argued that, even though the EU is not a party to the United Nations, it is bound by the San Francisco Charter. This results from the EC Treaty itself as the latter empowers the Community with sanctioning competences that are potentially covered by UN measures.[16] As a consequence, in so far as under the EC Treaty the Community has assumed powers previously exercised by Member States in areas governed by the UN Charter, the provisions of that Charter have the effect of binding the Community. Applying the GATT line of reasoning,[17] the CFI acknowledged that treaties other than those concluded by the EC as such may be binding on latter's institutions, beyond the scope of Article 300 (7) EC.

Assuming what it deemed to be the normal consequence of both this primacy and the binding character of the UN Charter for the EC, the CFI drastically limited the scope of judicial review granted to *Kadi*, *Yusuf* and *Al Barakaat International Foundation*. In fact, much depends on the normative autonomy enjoyed by the Community institutions when implementing measures adopted at UN level. Considering that they are instituted and updated by a UN Commit-

---

13 CFI: Case T-306/01 *Yusuf and Al Barakaat International Foundation v. Council and Commission* [2005] ECR II-3533, para. 231; CFI: Case T-315/01 *Kadi v. Council and Commission* [2005] ECR II-3649, para. 181.

14 Art. 307 EC. See on this provision the chapter of Nikolaos Lavranos in this book.

15 Case T-306/01 above at fn 13, para. 240; Case T-315/01, above at fn 13, para. 190.

16 Case T-306/01 *idem* para. 250; Case T-315/01 *idem* para. 200.

17 ECJ, Joined Cases C-21 to 24/72 *International Fruit Company* [1972] ECR 1219, esp. at para. 18.

tee,[18] in principle the lists disputed in these cases escape judicial scrutiny by national or Community courts.[19] Strikingly enough, this line of reasoning nevertheless did not imply a full immunity for the disputed act. Acting as if it was a court of the UN legal order, the CFI accepted a judicial control confined to *ius cogens*, understood as a *'body of higher rules of public international law binding on all subjects of international law, including the bodies of the United Nations, and from which no derogation is possible'*.[20]

On the merits, the CFI dismissed the claims of the applicants regarding their fundamental rights, mentioning in particular the availability of humanitarian exemptions and derogations, the importance and the legitimacy of the aims pursued by the assets freezing measures, the temporary character of the sanctions, the periodical review mechanisms at UN level, the existence of a procedure for the re-examination of individual cases before the Taliban Committee and, finally, the complete system of judicial review available in Community law. As would be borne out further by the *OMPI*, *Sison* and *Al-Aqsa* judgments[21] and was even admitted by the CFI itself,[22] the 'universal' standard of fundamental rights here was much lower than the guarantees usually applicable within the Community legal order. In other terms, the Court's approach of the relations between acts of secondary Community law and Resolutions of the UN Security Council eventually led to curtailing the requirements regarding fundamental rights generally applicable before Community courts.

It is worth comparing the CFI's reasoning with that followed by the French *Conseil d'Etat* in annulment proceedings started by the *Association Secours Mondial de France* against measures adopted by the French Minister of economy, finance and industry implementing a list drafted by the Taliban Committee. This association challenged a decree subordinating any exchange operation, movement of capital or financial deal with this association, entailing an international dimension, to a preliminary authorisation.[23] Whereas explicitly confirming its judicial competence despite the circumstance that the disputed act gave effect to measures adopted at the level of the UN and the EC/EU, the review of legality proposed by the *Conseil d'Etat* was only marginal. The fact that the elements on grounds of which the association had been included in the list were classified for defence purposes, was deemed sufficient to justify the lack of motivation of the restrictive measures. Furthermore, the sole circumstance that this association had been included in the lists drafted by the Taliban Committee

---

[18] Case T-306/01 above at fn 13, para. 265; Case T-315/01 above at fn 13, para. 214.

[19] Case T-306/01 *idem* para. 270; Case T-315/01 *idem* para. 219.

[20] Case T-306/01 *idem* para. 277; Case T-315/01 *idem* para. 226. This would stem from the customary character of the rule enshrined in Article 5 of the Vienna Convention on the Law of the Treaties and from the fact that the UN Charter necessarily presupposes the existence of mandatory norms of international law.

[21] See below, 2.

[22] See for example CFI: Case T-306/01 above at fn 13, para. 289; CFI: Case T-315/01 above at fn 13, para. 238.

[23] C.E.: *Association Secours Mondial de France*, req. 262626, 3 Nov. 2004.

and subsequently implemented by the EU Council, excluded any error of assessment by the competent French Minister. Even if based on different theoretical grounds, the *Conseil d'Etat* being seemingly less reluctant than the CFI to identify a *political question* in this context,[24] the solutions reached by both courts were almost identical. By contrast, the Federal Tribunal of Switzerland explicitly endorsed the reasoning of the CFI on the primacy of UNSC resolutions in order to dismiss a request lodged against restrictive measures carried out by the bodies of the Federal Government.[25]

More generally, the reluctance of judges to even indirectly review the compatibility of resolutions adopted by the UNSC or by organs placed under its authority with superior principles of law, including human rights, is illustrated in recent judgments of the European Court of Human Rights (hereafter, the ECtHR)[26] and of the United Kingdom's House of Lords.[27]

---

24 To put it briefly, the *political questions* doctrine means that a court may not pronounce a judgment on the merits in a case that is too political in nature. The *political question* is a traditional element in the debate on judicial control in most Anglo-Saxon legal systems, especially the United States and the United Kingdom. See for a famous illustration of this doctrine, Supreme Court of the United States of America, *Baker v. Carr,* 369 US 186 (1962). This theory is often compared to the doctrine of the *actes de gouvernement* met in (mostly) civilian legal systems such as France, Belgium or Italy.

25 Federal Tribunal of Switzerland, *Youssef Mustapha Nada*, 14 November 2007, accessible at: www.bger.ch/fr/index/juridiction/jurisdiction-inherit-template/jurisdiction-recht/jurisdiction-recht-urteile2000.htm. M. Nada lodged an action before the European Court of Human Rights against Switzerland. The case was still pending when finishing this chapter.

26 See in particular ECtHR (Grand Chamber): *Behrami and Behrami v. France* (App. No 71412/01) and *Sarmati* v. *France, Germany and Norway* (App. No 78166/01), 2 May 2007 (Decision on the admissibility); ECtHR: *Kasumaj v. Greece* (App. No 6974/05), 5 July 2007 (Decision on the admissibility); ECtHR: *Gajic v. Germany* (App. No 31446/02), 28 August 2007 (Decision on the admissibility); ECtHR: *Beric and others v. Bosnia and Herzegovina* (App. Nos 36357/04, 36360/04, 38346/04, 41705/04, 45190/04, 45578/04, 45579/04, 45580/04, 91/05, 97/05, 100/05, 101/05, 1121/05, 1123/05, 1125/05, 1129/05, 1132/05, 1133/05, 1169/05, 1172/05, 1175/05, 1177/05, 1180/05, 1185/05, 20793/05 and 25496/05), 16 October 2007 (Decision on the admissibility). It should be noted that the claims lodged by these applicants were rejected on grounds of the lack of competence of the ECtHR *vis-à-vis* military operations or the administration of a territory upon operational control of an international organisation which is not a party to the ECHR, such as the UN or NATO. It is however difficult to deny that at least some of these decisions reveal that the attitude adopted by the ECtHR tends to warrant a smooth implementation of measures adopted at the international level to maintain or to restore peace and security. See in particular De Sena – Vitucci (2009). See on the *Behrami* Case the chapter of Antonella Angelini in this book.

27 See *Al Jedda, R v. Secretary of State for Defence* [2007] UKHL 58 (12 December 2007). Al Jedda, suspected of being a member of a terrorist group, challenged his detention by British troops in Irak without being charged with any offence. The House of Lords rejected his claim essentially on grounds of the obligations resting on the UN Member States on grounds of Art. 103 UN Charter.

b. The EU 'autonomous' list

This line of reasoning contrasts with the case law of the CFI in the context of Resolution 1373 (2001) and the measures implementing that Resolution in EU law[28] and in Community law.[29] Taking into account the room for manoeuvre left by this Resolution for the identification of targeted persons, groups and entities, the CFI opted here for a 'classical' review of legality and assessed the disputed Community measures in the light of fundamental rights as they are usually protected under EC law. The *Organisation des Modjahedines du peuple d'Iran* case (hereafter, the *OMPI* case)[30] concerned an organisation that had been proscribed in the United Kingdom according to the *Terrorism Act* 2000. As a result of Resolution 1373 (2001) and of the information provided for by the British authorities to the EU Council, all OMPI's assets had been frozen. Meanwhile, OMPI lost the two parallel actions it had lodged against the prohibition before the Proscribed Organisations Appeal Commission (hereafter, the POAC) and the High Court of England and Wales. OMPI therefore started proceedings against the EC/EU measures before the CFI. Significantly, when it went on to examine the pleas on the merits, the CFI emphasized that:

> '(i)n the present case, [...] Security Council Resolution 1373 (2001) [...] does not specify individually the persons, groups and entities who are to be the subjects of (restrictive) measures. Nor did the Security Council establish specific legal rules concerning the procedure for freezing funds, or the safeguards or judicial remedies ensuring that the persons or entities affected by such a procedure would have a genuine opportunity to challenge the measures adopted by the States in respect of them.' [31]

The restrictive measures did not come within the exercise of powers circumscribed at UN level and, accordingly, did not benefit from the primacy effect of UNSC resolutions or decisions of the Taliban Committee, highlighted in the *Kadi* and *Yusuf/Al Barakaat* judgments.[32] The CFI furthermore considered that EC implementing measures, adopted on grounds of Articles 60 and 301 EC, are not necessarily conditioned in their content and even in their existence by Common Positions. Despite the fact that Community Courts enjoy almost no competence regarding the latter, the CFI refused to apply here any 'paralysing

---

28 See especially Common Position 2001/931/CFSP on the application of specific measures to combat terrorism, OJ 2002 L 116/75.

29 See especially Regulation 2580/2001 on specific restrictive measures directed against certain persons and entities with a view to combating terrorism, OJ 2002 L 160/26. It should be borne in mind that this Regulation only concerns non-EU residents. Restrictive measures against EU residents and carrying out Common Position 2001/931/CFSP are adopted by the Member States.

30 CFI: Case T-228/02 *Organisation des Modjahedines du peuple d'Iran v. Council and Commission* [2006] ECR II-4665.

31 *Idem* paras 99 ff.

32 *Idem* para. 103 *juncto* 104.

effect' on judicial review, unlike in cases of normative similarity between the disputed act and a decision of the Taliban Committee. In light of the seriousness of the sanctions, the absence of any specific hearing and the vague motivation of the sanction, the CFI concluded that OMPI had not been able to prepare an adequate defence and had been deprived of any effective remedy.[33] The lack of a genuine statement of reasons deprived the CFI of any possibility to properly review the lawfulness of the disputed act.[34] As a result, OMPI's request for annulment was upheld. The CFI confirmed this standpoint in several subsequent cases.[35]

In the aftermath of the first *OMPI* and *Sison* and *Al Aqsa* judgments, the Council dramatically improved the procedure for listing individuals suspected of (aid to) terrorism.[36] Accordingly, the persons, groups and entities concerned may submit a request to the Council to obtain the statement of reasons for maintaining them on the list and may submit at any time to the Council a request that the decision to include or maintain them on the list should be reconsidered. On top of that, a 'Working Party 931' was set up with the specific mission of advising the Council on listing and de-listing requests, preparing regular review of the list and making administrative or legislative recommendations.[37]

Quite surprisingly, OMPI was not immediately removed from the EU autonomous list.[38] OMPI therefore challenged subsequent acts maintaining the assets freezing measures. In a first judgment of 23 October 2008, the CFI partly rejected the request made by OMPI against a decision maintaining the freezing of its funds and assets, which was based on the same evidence than the previously annulled act.[39] It held that the annulment of a measure for formal or procedural defects in no way prejudices the possibility to adopt a new measure on the basis of the same matters of law and fact as those serving as the basis for the annulled measure, *'provided that on this occasion (the competent authority)*

33 *Idem* paras. 164 to 166.

34 *Idem* paras. 172 and 173.

35 CFI: Case T-47/03 *Sison v. Council* [2007] ECR II-73; CFI: Case T-327/03 *Stichting Al-Aqsa v. Council* [2007] ECR II-79; CFI: Case T-229/02 *PKK and KNK (Osman Ocalan) v. Council* [2008] ECR II-45; CFI: Case T-253/04 *Kongra-Gel and others v. Council* [2008] ECR II-46.

36 Notice for the attention of the persons, groups and entities on the list provided for in Article 2(3) of Council Regulation (EC) No 2580/2001 on specific restrictive measures directed against certain persons and entities with a view to combating terrorism (see Annex to Council Decision 2007/445/EC of 28 June 2007), OJ 2007 C 144/1. See also OJ 2008 C 179/1 and OJ 2009 C 20/24.

37 Decision of the Council of 28 June 2007 establishing a Council Working Party on the implementation of Common Position 2001/931/CFSP on the application of specific measures to combat terrorism.

38 See in particular, for a last decision, Council Decision 2008/583/CE of 15 July 2008, OJ 2008 L 188/21, esp. Annex, points 1.26, 2.3 and 2.19. The resistance shown in particular by the British government to implement the ECJ's judgment in the case of OMPI has been strongly denounced. See Spitzer (2008).

39 CFI: Case T-256/07 *People's Mojahedin Organisation of Iran v. Council* [2008] nyr. OMPI lodged an appeal against this judgment before the ECJ. See ECJ: Case C-576/08 P *People's Mojahedin Organisation of Iran v. Council*, still pending.

observes the formal and procedural rules whose breach gave rise to the annulment and that the legitimate expectations of the persons concerned are duly protected'.[40] The CFI added that the rights of defence did not necessarily entail the right to be heard at a formal hearing, in so far as the targeted persons, groups or entities were able to make their case properly regarding the incriminating evidence and that the Council took sufficient consideration of the observations made on that occasion. By rejecting OMPI's claims, the CFI implicitly endorsed the improvements brought by the Council to the procedure leading to restrictive measures.

By contrast, the CFI declared void a subsequent decision maintaining OMPI on the lists notwithstanding the circumstance that an administrative authority of the United Kingdom (the POAC) had decided that there no longer exist any reason to justify the proscription of OMPI.[41] To put it briefly, the CFI observed that the Council was unable to explain the specific reasons that had led it to consider that the continued inclusion of OMPI in the list remained justified, in spite of the findings of fact made by the POAC.

This, however, was not the end to the OMPI judicial saga. The order proscribing OMPI in the United Kingdom was withdrawn in June 2008, following the dismissal of an appeal brought by the British Home Secretary against POAC's decision.[42] The Council nevertheless decided to maintain OMPI on the list. This decision followed a claim by France that it possessed new evidence that persons alleged to be members of this organization had taken part, in the past, to terrorist activities. In a judgment pronounced on 4 December 2008, the CFI upheld OMPI's requests against the new Council decision,[43] echoing the specific link made in previous judgments between EU restrictive measures and the risk assessment conducted by the competent national authority.[44]

This was partially because the new materials justifying the maintenance of OMPI on the list had not been communicated to this entity. The Council argued that it had adopted the disputed regulation in urgency, following the withdrawal of the national decision which formed the basis of the initial decision to freeze funds. Any interruption in the restrictive measures would have given the opportunity to OMPI to gain access to its funds and to render any subsequent sanction ineffective. The CFI rejected this argument and considered that the contested regulation disregarded the guidelines laid down in the aforementioned OMPI judgment.[45] Balancing the interests at stake, the CFI emphasized in particular that *'the Council's arguments totally fail to substantiate its claim that it was impossible for it to adopt the contested decision under a procedure that would have*

40 CFI: Case T-256/07 *idem* para. 75.

41 CFI: Case T-256/07 *idem* paras 167 to 187.

42 See below, fn 94.

43 CFI: Case T-284/08 *People's Mojahedin Organisation of Iran v. Council* [2008] nyr. France appealed this judgment before the ECJ. At the time of writing, the case was still pending. See ECJ: Case C-27/09 P *France v. People's Mojahedin Organization of Iran.*

44 See CFI: Case T-228/02 above at fn 30, para. 124; CFI: Case T-256/07 above at fn 39, para. 133.

45 See esp. CFI: Case T-228/02 above at fn 30, paras 120, 126 and 131.

respected the applicant's rights of the defence.'[46] In other words, it would have been possible to maintain the freezing order provisionally while communicating the new evidence justifying restrictive measures to OMPI. It was irrelevant in this respect that a statement of reasons had been sent by the Council to OMPI for enabling it to communicate its views. Such safeguards, laid down by the Council in the abovementioned Notice, only concern the right to an effective remedy *after* a final administrative decision has been adopted and not the right to a fair hearing *during* an administrative procedure. The CFI subsequently recalled that the list in question must be drawn up on the basis of precise information or material in the relevant file which indicates that a decision has been taken by a competent authority in respect of the persons, groups and entities concerned. According to the CFI:

> '[...] the procedure which may culminate in a measure to freeze funds under the relevant rules [...] takes place at two levels, one national, the other Community. In the first phase, a competent national authority, in principle judicial, must take in respect of the party concerned a decision meeting the definition in Article 1(4) of Common Position 2001/931. If it is a decision to instigate investigations or to prosecute, it must be based on serious and credible evidence or 'clues'. In the second phase, the Council, acting by unanimity, must decide to include the party concerned in the disputed list, on the basis of precise information or material in the relevant file which indicates that such a decision has been taken. Next, the Council must, at regular intervals, and at least once every six months, be satisfied that there are grounds for continuing to include the party concerned in the list at issue. Verification that there is a decision of a national authority meeting that definition is an essential precondition for the adoption, by the Council, of an initial decision to freeze funds, whereas verification of the consequences of that decision at the national level is imperative in the context of the adoption of a subsequent decision to freeze funds.'[47]

In a subsequent challenge of the funds-freezing measures, the Community Courts must, without substituting their own assessment of what is appropriate for that of the Council, not only establish whether the evidence relied on is factually accurate, reliable and consistent, but also ascertain whether that evidence contains all the relevant information to be taken into account in order to assess the situation. This information should moreover be capable of substantiating the conclusions drawn from it. Notwithstanding a specific request by the CFI, the Council was unable to communicate solid evidence of any new elements that could have justified the maintenance of the freezing of the assets of OMPI. Considering that this prevented the CFI from assessing whether the contested Regulation was well-founded in law, OMPI's plea concerning violation of the

---

[46] CFI: Case T-284/08 para. 39.

[47] *Idem*, para. 51. See also CFI: Case T-228/02 above at fn 30, para. 117.

right to an effective remedy was upheld. As a consequence, the Council finally removed OMPI from the EU autonomous list in January 2009.[48]

2 First Attempts towards Convergence: the *Ayadi*, *Hassan* and *Minin* Cases (CFI)

This two-pronged case law of the CFI resulted in a parallel discrepancy in the judicial protection afforded to persons, groups or entities essentially suffering from the same type of restrictive measures and, moreover, motivated by comparable objectives. This was especially striking since the ECJ had observed in the *Ocalan and Vanly* case that these restrictive measures have *'serious consequences'* for targeted persons and entities, including not only the prohibition of all financial transactions and financial services but also damages caused to their reputation and political activity.[49] For many observers, this situation was unacceptable in the light of the fundamental principles whereupon the Community is based.[50]

The CFI's sensitivity to this criticism appears in two subsequent judgments concerning restrictive measures affecting persons listed by the UN Taliban Committee, *Ayadi* and *Hassan*[51] and, later on, in the annulment proceedings started by Mr. *Minin*, albeit in a different legal and factual context.[52] The CFI eventually rejected the claims made by the applicants and dismissed their request seeking the annulment of Regulation 881/2002, essentially on the same grounds as in *Kadi* and *Yusuf/Al Barakaat*.[53] Interestingly however, these judgments laid down specific obligations on the EU Member States when they receive a request for removal from the list drafted by the Taliban Committee. Mr. Ayadi in particular had argued that he had twice requested the assistance of the

48 See Council Decision 2009/62/EC of 26 January 2009 implementing Article 2 (3) of Regulation (EC) No 2580/2001 on specific restrictive measures directed against certain persons and entities with a view to combating terrorism and repealing Decision 2008/583/EC, OJ 2009 L 23/25.

49 ECJ: Case C-229/05 P *PKK and KNK* v. *Council* [2007] ECR I-439, para. 110.

50 See S. Adam (2009); Almqvist (2008); Bianchi (2007); T. Biersteker, E. Eckert (2006) 58; Cremona (2006) 357-360; G Della Cananea (2007); Dewulf – Pacquée (2006); Eckes (2007); Eckes (2008); Eeckhout (2005); Eeckhout (2007); Etienne (2006); Heliskoski (2007); Jacqué (2006); Karayigit (2006); Lavranos (2006); Miron (2007); Nettesheim (2007); Simon (2005); Uyen Do (2005); Vlcek (2006); Van Ooik – Wessel (2006); Zašova (2008). See also the report of the Committee on international monetary law of the International Law Association, Rio de Janeiro Conference (2008) 27-30. See also Marty, 'United Nations Security Council and European Union blacklists', Report, Committee on Legal Affairs and Human Rights, Parliamentary Assembly of the Council of Europe, 16 November 2006, especially at paras 21, 41 to 45 and 91. For a less critical standpoint, see Brown (2006); Tomuschat (2006).

51 CFI: Case T-253/02 *Chafiq Ayadi* [2006] ECR II-2139; CFI: Case T-49/04 *Faraj Hassan* [2006] ECR II-52.

52 CFI: Case T-362/04 *Leonid Minin* [2007] II-2003.

53 CFI: Case T-253/02, above at fn 32, paras 116 and 117; CFI: Case T-49/04, above 32, paras 92 and 93.

Irish authorities in having him removed from the list but that, at the time of the hearing, no such procedure had been started before the Taliban Committee.[54]

The CFI argued that the de-listing procedure before the Taliban Committee, albeit not comparable with a genuine judicial review, took into account as far as possible the fundamental rights of the persons, groups or entities affected by restrictive measures. Admittedly, the latter did not have at that time a direct access to the Taliban Committee, nor did they have any guarantee to be heard in their claims. The CFI nevertheless considered that the Member States, in the light of the fundamental rights applicable in the Community legal order, must ensure that targeted persons, groups or entities are in a position to make their point before the competent national authorities when they present a request for their case to be reviewed. The margin of assessment that the authorities of those Member States enjoy in this respect must be exercised in such a way as to take due account of the difficulties that those persons may encounter in ensuring the effective protection of their rights at UN level, having regard to the specific context and nature of the measures affecting them and taking due account of the fact that they might not be aware of the specific reasons that justified their inclusion in the list.[55]

Considering that persons, groups or entities targeted by restrictive measures are not entitled to be heard before any UN organ, the CFI moreover required Member States to act promptly. They should ensure that any request for de-listing is presented without delay and fairly and impartially to the Committee, with a view to a re-examination, if that appears to be justified in the light of the relevant information supplied. By this approach, the CFI, although partially founding its reasoning on the UN legal order, drew direct consequences from Community law for the exercise by the Member States of diplomatic protection. Any wrongful refusal by the competent domestic authority to submit the case to the Taliban Committee should be subject to judicial review.[56] Arguably, the fact that a UN organ (in this case, the Taliban Committee) had identified the existence of an *obligation* for the Member States to exercise diplomatic protection played a major role in the CFI's reasoning, all the more since Community law is to be interpreted as far as possible in light of UNSC Resolutions.

Be this as it may, these attempts by the CFI to soften the consequences of the *Kadi* line of reasoning understandably did not satisfy Messrs. Ayadi and Hassan, who appealed these judgments before the ECJ.[57] These cases reflect a

---

54 *Idem* at para. 102.

55 Case T-253/02, paras 146 and 147. Case T-49/04, para. 116 and 117.

56 This was confirmed by the order given by the *Tribunal de première instance* of Brussels to a department of the Belgian government to request the Taliban Committee to remove the names of some individuals from the list. See Civ. Brussels (réf.), 11 February 2005, *Sayadi and Vinck*, R.G. 2004/2435/A, not published. This order however revealed ineffective in practice since these persons are still included in the list many years after that judgment.

57 ECJ: Case C-399/06 P *Hassan v. Council and Commission* still pending; ECJ: Case C-403/06 P *Ayadi v. Council* still pending. Even if there was not yet a judgment on these appeals at the time of writing, there

broader discussion at UN level on how to balance efficiency with transparency and human rights standards when adopting smart sanctions. As a consequence of increasing concern regarding the list established by the Taliban Committee, the UNSC created a *Focal Point for de-listing*.[58] Petitioners seeking to submit a request for de-listing can now do so either through the focal point or through addressing a request to their State of residence or citizenship. This evolution was allegedly pushed by the claims of Mr. Kadi, a national of Saudi Arabia, who had never been able to persuade this country to submit a request for his de-listing to the Taliban Committee.[59]

The procedure for listing and de-listing too improved in many respects, especially regarding the motivation of the decision to include a name in the list and the administrative burden resting on the requesting State. Exemptions were moreover refined.[60] A few months after A.G. Poiares Maduro had delivered his opinions in the *Kadi* and *Yusuf/Al Barakaat* cases, the Analytical Support and Sanctions Monitoring Team even suggested the creation of an independent panel to review the lists and to require the Taliban Committee to make public its statement of reasons justifying the inclusion or the maintenance of names on the lists.[61] The UNSC was nonetheless reluctant to abandon to an independent body what it deemed to be a substantial part of its responsibility to maintain international peace and security. Resolution 1822 (2008) therefore merely provides that each proposal by a Member State to include a name on the consolidated list must identify those parts of the statement of the case that may be released to the public.[62] The Committee has to make accessible on its website a narrative summary of reasons for listing the corresponding entry or entries on the consolidated list.[63] The States receiving notification of the restrictive measures are required to take, in accordance with their domestic laws and practices, all possible measures to notify or inform in a timely manner the newly listed individuals and entities of the measures imposed on them as well as of any information on reasons for listing available on the Committee's website.[64] Alongside an improvement of the de-listing procedure, the Committee received the task to conduct by 30 June 2010 a one-off review of all names that were

seems to be no reason why the ECJ will not follow the same reasoning as in the *Kadi and Al Barakaat International Foundation* case, analysed in following section, and therefore reform the CFI's judgments.

58 UNSC Resolution 1730 (2006), 19 December 2006.

59 Hudson (2007) 219.

60 UNSC Resolution 1735 (2006), 22 December 2006.

61 Report of the Analytical Support and Sanctions Monitoring Team pursuant to Resolution 1735 (2006) concerning Al-Qaida and the Taliban and associated individuals and entities, S/2008/324, 31 March 2008, esp. Section IV.

62 Art. 6 *d in fine* Guidelines.

63 Art. 6 *h* Guidelines. It is to be noted that some statements for reasons were not yet published at the time of writing (June 2009), especially those concerning individuals associated with the Taliban. Y. Moiny, above at fn 4, pp. 51 and 52.

64 Art. 6 *j* Guidelines.

inscribed on the consolidated list as at 30 June 2008, in order to ensure that it is as updated and accurate as possible and to confirm that the listing remains appropriate.[65]

3 The Judgment of the ECJ in *Kadi*: Reintroducing Coherence through Reshaping Core Constitutional Principles

As mentioned in the opening remarks, the judgment of the ECJ of 3 September 2008 put an end to appeal proceedings started by *Kadi* and *Al Barakaat Foundation* against judgments whereby the CFI had dismissed their action for annulment of a Regulation freezing their assets and financial resources. Not surprisingly, the most important issue raised by these proceedings was whether the ECJ could exercise a full review of legality even when this would indirectly amount to reviewing a UNSC Resolution (*a*). However, the audacity of the ECJ's answer to this question, that followed a key ruling of the High Court of England and Wales (*b*), should not overshadow the Court's comity towards political actors involved in the fight against terrorism through smart sanctions (*c*).

a. Beyond impunity: a full review of legality as a safeguard of fundamental rights

In the judgment pronounced on 3 September 2008, the Court first recalls that the Community is based on the rule of law and the respect for fundamental rights. As a consequence, neither its institutions nor the Member States can avoid review of the conformity of their acts with the EC Treaty.[66] The ECJ justifies this solution by the fact that, as such, an annulment of the disputed Regulation would leave unaffected the international obligations stemming from UNSC Resolution 1267 (1999) and the decisions adopted by the Taliban Committee. Admittedly, the Community must respect international law in the exercise of its powers.[67] More particularly, Community institutions should attach *'special importance'* to the primary responsibility attributed to the UNSC when acting on grounds of Chapter VII of the UN Charter in order to maintain international peace and security.[68] This had already been made clear in *Bosphorus*, where the ECJ acknowledged that measures implementing UNSC Resolutions, in light of the importance of the aim(s) they pursue, could entail negative consequences, even of a substantial nature, for some individuals.[69] The Lisbon Treaty fully

---

[65] Art. 9 Guidelines.

[66] ECJ: Joined Cases C-402/05 P and 415/05 P above at fn 1, paras 281 to 285.

[67] See ECJ: Case C-286/90 *Poulsen and Diva Navigation* [1992] ECR I-6019, para. 9; ECJ: Case C-162/96 *Racke* [1998] ECR I-3655, para. 45. See also CFI: Case T-115/94 *Opel Austria* [1997] ECR II-39, paras 90 to 95.

[68] ECJ: Joined Cases C-402/05 P and 415/05 P above at fn 1, para. 294.

[69] ECJ: Case C-84/95 *Bosphorus* [1996] ECR I-3953, para. 23.

confirms this by stressing the respect that the EU must have for the principles of the UN Charter.[70] Significantly however, the ECJ added in *Kadi* that neither the principles governing the international legal order nor the EC Treaty can be understood as authorising any derogation from the principles of liberty, democracy and respect for human rights and fundamental freedoms, which form the *'very foundations of the Community legal order'*.[71] Accordingly, the possibility to review in full the legality of any act of Community law must be considered to be the expression, in a Community based on the rule of law, of a constitutional guarantee stemming from the EC Treaty as an autonomous legal system which is not to be prejudiced by an international agreement.[72]

It is interesting to observe how subtle the ECJ has been in reaching this conclusion, without tackling the tricky issue of the relationship between EC law and the UN Charter. The Court simply observes that *'supposing'* the UN Charter would be binding on the Community and its Member States according to Article 300 (7) EC, this would in any case not mean that the Charter enjoys any supremacy over EC primary law.[73] Even though the EU is not a Member of the UN and notwithstanding the fact that a UNSC Resolution cannot easily be equated with an international agreement binding on the Community, the ECJ dispells any ambiguity by stressing that such a Resolution may in no way affect the autonomy of the Community legal order. Nor may it prejudice the Court's competence to protect it. This part of the judgment obviously echoes A.G. Poiares Maduro's standpoint that *'in the final analysis, the Community Courts determine the effect of international obligations within the Community legal order by reference to conditions set by Community law'*.[74] In this sense, the *Kadi* judgment is a perfect illustration, alongside for example the procedure for an opinion on an international agreement envisaged by the EC (Art. 300 (6) EC), of the constitutional function assumed by the ECJ in delineating the boundaries and controlling the interplay between the Community and international/domestic legal orders.

Consequently, the ECJ concluded that the fundamental rights of the appellants had been disregarded, in particular their right to be heard, their right to an effective remedy and, as a corollary, their right to property.[75] The disputed Regulation was therefore annulled. The *Kadi* judgment reflects in my opinion a correct understanding of the scope and limits of the Community Courts' competence and of the relations between the Community and the UN legal orders.

---

70 Art. 3, para. 5 *in fine* TEU and 21, paras 1 and 2c TEU. See also Declaration 13 annexed to the Lisbon Treaty, which recalls that *'the European Union and its Member States will remain bound by the provisions of the Charter of the United Nations and, in particular, by the primary responsibility of the Security Council and of its Members for the maintenance of international peace and security'* (OJ 2008 C 115/343).

71 ECJ: Joined Cases C-402/05 P and 415/05 P above at fn 1, paras 303 and 304.

72 *Idem* paras 316 and 326.

73 *Idem* paras 306 to 308.

74 See the conclusions delivered on 16 January 2008 in Case C-402/05 P and on 23 January 2008 in Case C-415/05 P, above at fn 1, para. 23.

75 ECJ: Joined Cases C-402/05 P and 415/05 P above at fn 1, paras 333 to 371.

Firstly, Article 27 of the Vienna Convention on the Law of the Treaties[76] and Article 103 of the UN Charter cannot result in an absolute supremacy of UNSC resolutions over EU primary law. The Community legal order is built upon the EC Treaty, which forms its constitutional charter and protects its autonomy, notably through the judicial mission assigned to the ECJ. This is especially true for basic principles of the Community legal order such as fundamental rights. For the same reason, Article 307 EC may not be interpreted as a *carte blanche* for interferences with the core principles whereupon the Community is founded.[77] Conversely, this rationale understandably invalidates a direct review by the Community Courts of the legality of UNSC Resolutions, even restricted to *ius cogens*. This is not so much because this concept is vague and controversial[78] but first and foremost because Community Courts would go beyond their role by *de facto* reviewing the legality of UNSC Resolutions, in the light of (supposed) peremptory norms of public international law.

Secondly, the *Kadi* judgment is a new vocal demonstration of the ECJ's constitutional maturity in the protection of the autonomy of the Community legal order. After all, just to mention one example, the logic in *Kadi* does not fundamentally differ from the protection of fundamental rights in German constitutional law offered by the *Bundesverfassungsgericht* in its ruling on the European Arrest Warrant (EAW).[79] Like the ECJ in *Kadi*, the German constitutional Court did not review directly the legality of the norm of 'international' law at stake (in this case, the EU Framework Decision on the EAW) but rather, reviewed measures implementing that norm at domestic level. Most importantly, while both admitting that international commitments have to be complied with, these Courts nevertheless give precedence to the constitutional foundations of the legal order from which they derive their legitimacy. In that sense, the ECJ's consistency in the protection of fundamental rights of persons, groups or entities targeted by restrictive sanctions, no matter their legal basis, reconciles the Community case law with the horizontality of human rights in the EC legal order.

Thirdly, the ECJ rightly points out that the improvements brought to the procedure for listing and de-listing before the Taliban Committee do not change its essentially diplomatic and intergovernmental nature, and for that reason do not justify any restriction in the judicial review of targeted sanctions by

---

76 Article 27 VCLT (1969) prevents a party from invoking provisions of internal law to justify a failure to comply with a treaty.

77 See on the articulation between Article 307 EC and the core principles of the EC legal order the chapter of Nikolaos Lavranos in this book.

78 It is generally considered that *ius cogens* does not include the right to a fair hearing, to obtain a statement of reasons and to an effective remedy. See Couzigou (2008).

79 BVerfG, 2 BvR 2236/04, 18 July 2005 (*Europäisches Haftbefehlsgesetz*). In this judgment, the German constitutional Court held the German Act implementing the EU Framework Decision on the EAW unconstitutional because it encroached upon the right of Germans not to be extradited in a disproportionate manner and because it lacked any possibility to judicially review a decision granting surrender.

Community Courts.[80] The Court's standpoint is all the more understandable since several studies and reports unequivocally criticise the lack of transparency of the sanctioning system under Resolution 1267 (1999).[81] At the same time, it fits better in a Community legal order based on the rule of law than the CFI's attempt to fill in the gap through diplomatic protection.

Although revolutionary in its consequences, the rationale behind *Kadi* perfectly reflects other cases where the ECJ balanced respect for international law with the necessary protection of the 'very foundations' of the Community legal order or the Community's interests. Whereas fully acknowledging the possibility for external sources of law to permeate the Community legal order, the ECJ demonstrates an incremental ability to protect the latter's integrity. This was already made clear in several opinions rendered by the ECJ on grounds of Article 300 (6) EC, especially those concerning the creation of the European Economic Area (EEA)[82] and the European Common Aviation Area (ECAA).[83] Consequently, and despite the different meaning long defended by some authors,[84] the ECJ confirmed the possibility to set aside international agreements concluded by the Community in breach of the EC Treaty.[85] The ECJ's propensity to protect Community interests is also reflected in the impossibility to plead before a Court of a Member State or before the ECJ that Community legislation is incompatible with some international agreements, even if they are binding on the EC.[86]

In order to be effective, the protection afforded by the ECJ must provide for a full review of legality of Community acts implementing international commitments in EC law. In that sense, the Court's dualistic approach in *Kadi* echoes the *Mox* judgment pronounced by the ECJ on 30 May 2006, albeit in a different context.[87] Neither the EC nor the Member States may, by way of concluding an

80 On these improvements, see below, 4.

81 See *e.g.* Fassbender (2006); T. Biersteker, E. Eckert (dir.) (2006); Report of the Informal Working Group of the Security Council on General Issues of Sanctions, S/2006/997, 18 December 2006, esp. at pp. 4 and 5; Fifth report of the Analytical Support and Sanctions Monitoring Team appointed pursuant to resolutions 1526 (2004) and 1617 (2005) concerning Al-Qaida and the Taliban and associated individuals and entities, S/2006/750, 31 July 2006.

82 ECJ: Opinion 1/91 *EEA I* [1991] ECR I-6079; ECJ: Opinion 1/92 *EEA II* [1992] ECR I-2821.

83 ECJ: Opinion 1/00 *ECAA* [2002] I-3493.

84 See esp. Joliet (1981) 59, 60,198.

85 ECJ: Case C-327/91 *France v. Commission* [1994] ECR I-3641.

86 See, on the GATT/WTO, ECJ: Joined Cases C-21 to 24/72 *International Fruit Company* [1972] ECR 1219; ECJ: Case C-149/96 *Portugal v. Conseil* [1999] ECR I-8395, para. 47; ECJ (ord.): Case C-307/99 *OGT Fruchthandelsgesellschaft* [2001] ECR I-3159 para. 24; ECJ: Joined Cases C-27/00 and 122/00 *Omega Air* [2002] ECR I-2569, para. 93; ECJ: Case C-377/02 *Léon Van Parys* [2005] ECR I-1465, para. 54. The Court recently extended this reasoning to the United Nations Convention on the Law of the Sea (UNCLOS). See ECJ: Case C-308/06 *Intertanko* [2008] ECR I-4057, paras 64 and 65.

87 ECJ: Case C-459/03 *Commission v. Ireland* [2006] ECR I-4635. See also Lavranos (2006) p. 349. In that case, the Commission sought a declaration by the ECJ that, by instituting dispute-settlement proceed-

international agreement or implementing a commitment under international law, affect the exclusive jurisdiction of the ECJ to rule on any dispute concerning the interpretation and application of Community law.[88] This does not only mean that legal sources external to the Community may not deprive the ECJ from the competences it enjoys according to the EC Treaty; it also means that they may not undermine the role of the ECJ as the ultimate guardian of Community law, as it results from the its judgments in *ERTA*[89] and *Les Verts*.[90]

b. The judicial interplay between the ECJ and the High Court of England and Wales

It is interesting to note that the High Court of England and Wales incidentally took part in the debate that led the ECJ to set aside the judgments of the CFI in the *Kadi* and *Yusuf/Al Barakaat* cases. Five individuals challenged freezing orders issued by the UK Government and implementing Resolutions 1267 (1999) and 1373 (2001). In a ruling adopted several months before the ECJ judgment in *Kadi*, the High Court expressed harsh criticism of the CFI's auto-limited judicial review.[91] Expressly sharing the standpoint of A.G. Poiares Maduro in his conclusions delivered in January 2008,[92] the High Court set aside the freezing orders on grounds *inter alia* that these orders overrode the listed persons' fundamental rights and disregarded the principle of legal certainty. Even if the ECJ's judgment of 3 September 2008 does not refer to this judgment, both procedures illustrate a comparable concern regarding the extent to which the legitimacy of the fight against terrorism may validate derogations to human rights and fundamental freedoms. Both procedures are illustrative of the (unspoken) judicial dialogue of Community and domestic courts in reshaping the rule of law in the context of smart sanctions.

The appeal lodged by Her Majesty's Treasury against the judgment of the High Court of Justice before the Court of Appeal of England and Wales (hereafter, the EWCA) is a new illustration of this interplay between Community and domestic judicatures. Whereas partly upholding the appeal, the EWCA confirmed the point made by the first judge that listed individuals are entitled to a 'merits based review', contrary to what the CFI had decided in the first *Kadi* judgment.[93]

---

ings against the United Kingdom under the United Nations Convention on the Law of the Sea concerning the MOX plant located at Sellafield, Ireland had failed to fulfil its obligations under Community law, especially Articles 10 EC and 292 EC.

88 Art. 220 EC *juncto* Art. 292 EC.

89 ECJ: Case 22/70 *Commission v. Council* [1971] ECR 263, para. 39.

90 ECJ: Case 294/83 *Parti écologiste Les Verts v. European Parliament* [1986] ECR 1339, para. 23.

91 *A, K, M, Q & G v. HM Treasury* [2008] EWHC Admin 869 (24 April 2008).

92 See in particular paras 30 to 40 of the judgment cited at footnote 98.

93 *'[...] the court has power to consider an application for judicial review by a person to whom the [freezing order] applies as a result of designation by the [Sanctions] Committee and, on such an application, to ask the court, so far as it can, to consider what the basis of the listing was.'* See *A, K, M, Q & G v. HM Treasury* [2008] EWCA Civ 1187 (30 October 2008) paras 120 and 121.

It is precisely on grounds of a review of this kind that the EWCA, albeit in a different context, concluded that the closed material adduced by the Home Secretary could not reasonably be understood as meaning that the *People's Mojahedin Organisation of Iran* intended in future to revert to terrorism and subsequently forced the United Kingdom to lift the proscription of this organisation.[94] As said above, this eventually forced the Council to withdraw that organisation from the EU autonomous blacklist, even though after new judicial proceedings before the CFI.[95]

c. The subtle way through scrutiny and comity

That being said, it is certainly worth underlining the ECJ's ability to balance the admittedly far-reaching consequences of its judgment in *Kadi*, revealing a certain 'comity' *vis-à-vis* the political actors responsible for smart sanctions.[96]

Firstly, the Court maintains the effects of the annulled Regulation for a brief period not exceeding three months, in order to allow the Council to re-examine the case of Kadi and Al Barakaat. An annulment with immediate effect undoubtedly would jeopardise new restrictive measures, whereas it could not be excluded that funds-freezing measures be justified against the appellants.[97] More than a technical adjustment, this temporary suspension of the effects of the annulment illustrates the Court's eagerness to reconcile as far as possible judicial review with international commitments binding upon the EC and its Member States.[98]

Secondly, the ECJ to some extent anticipates some of the problems the EU Council would face in the re-examination of the case of Kadi and Al Barakaat. Even if the judgment does not provide full guidance in this respect, the Court observes that *'overriding considerations to do with safety or the conduct of the international relations of the Community and of its Member States may militate against the communication of certain matters to the persons concerned and, therefore, against their being heard on those matters.'*[99] This is to avoid that persons or entities affected by restrictive sanctions claim the automatic communication of their

94 *Lord Alton of Liverpool and others v. Secretary of State for the Home Department* [2008] EWCA Civ 443 (7 May 2008). The Court of Appeal dismissed an application by the Home Secretary for permission to appeal against the decision of the POAC on 30 November 2007 to allow an appeal by Lord Alton of Liverpool and thirty-four other members of the two Houses of Parliament against the Home Secretary's refusal to allow their application pursuant to remove OMPI from the list of proscribed organisations.

95 See above, 1.

96 See also Della Cananea (2009) 524-525.

97 ECJ: Joined Cases C-402/05 P and 415/05 P above at fn 1, paras 373 to 376.

98 See, for a recent example in the context of the annulment of a Council decision concluding an international agreement, ECJ: Joined Cases C-317/04 and 318/04 *Parliament v. Council (PNR)* [2006] ECR I-4721, paras 71 to 74.

99 ECJ: Joined Cases C-402/05 P and 415/05 P above at fn 1, para. 342. This reiterates a statement already made by the CFI in the OMPI judgment of 12 December 2006 (CFI: Case T-228/02 above at fn 30, para. 133).

whole file, an obligation which could have placed the Council in an awkward position *vis-à-vis* the Taliban Committee.[100] Moreover, in order not to jeopardize the surprise effect, no hearing is required before the adoption of the freezing measures.[101]

Another manifestation of comity is to be found in the Court's implicit reference to the *Solange* theory when it concludes that a generalised immunity from jurisdiction, constituting a significant derogation from the scheme of judicial protection of fundamental rights laid down by the EC Treaty, appears unjustified *'for clearly that (UN) re-examination procedure does not offer the guarantees of judicial protection'*.[102] If the Court deems it necessary to proffer such a justification, it cannot be excluded that it could well also refrain from a judicial review *in concreto* 'as far as' the guarantees afforded at UN level would be equivalent to those applicable in the Community legal order. As will be illustrated in the next section, the negative presumption in the *Kadi* case provides an incentive for the UNSC and the Taliban Committee to reform the listing and de-listing procedures under Resolution 1267 (1999).

In order to comply with the judgment of the ECJ, the Commission communicated the narrative summaries of reasons provided by the Taliban Committee to Mr. Kadi and to Al Barakaat International Foundation. They were given the opportunity to comment on these grounds in order to be heard. Notwithstanding their observations, both Mr. Kadi and Al Barakaat International Foundation failed in their request to be de-listed. The Commission vaguely defended the maintenance of their names on the list by confirming their *'association with the Al-Qaida network'*.[103] New proceedings were brought by Mr. Kadi before the CFI, especially on grounds of the fact that the Council's decision, despite its far-reaching consequences, lacked any proper answer to the arguments put forward by him to plead the removal of his name from the list.[104] At the time of writing, other proceedings were still pending whereby individuals, groups and entities pursue the annulment of Community measures implementing Resolution 1267 (1999) on the same grounds as in the *Kadi* case.[105]

---

[100] Only the statement of reasons is made publicly available at UN level. It consists in a (relatively short) summary of the motivation justifying the inclusion or maintenance of a name on the list.

[101] ECJ: Joined Cases C-402/05 P and 415/05 P above at fn 1, para. 341.

[102] ECJ: Joined Cases C-402/05 P and 415/05 P above at fn 1, para. 322. See also on this implicit reference to the *Solange* theory, De Sena – Vitucci (2009) 223-225.

[103] Commission Regulation (EC) No 1190/2008 of 28 November 2008 amending for the 101st time Council Regulation (EC) No 881/2002 imposing certain specific restrictive measures directed against certain persons and entities associated with Usama bin Laden, the Al-Qaida network and the Taliban, OJ 2008 L 322/25.

[104] CFI: Case T-85/09 still pending.

[105] CFI: Case T-318/01 *Othman v. Council and Commission* still pending; CFI: Case T-135/06 *Al –Faqih v. Council* still pending; CFI: Case T-136/06 *Sanabel Relief Agency v. Council* still pending; CFI: Case T-137/06 *Abdrabbah v. Council* still pending; CFI: Case T-138/06 *Nasuf v. Council* still pending.

4 Reshaping the Rule of Law through Multi-Level 'Incentive Dialogue'

Admittedly, the case law of the Community Courts on smart sanctions so far has proactively influenced and determined the discussion and reasoning of politicians and judges regarding the fight against terrorism. The Community Courts' judgments on smart sanctions can therefore be regarded as the cornerstone of an 'incentive dialogue'. As underlined above, the Council, responding to the desiderata formulated by the CFI in the *OMPI*, *Sison* and *Al-Aqsa* judgments, significantly improved the procedure for an EU autonomous identification.[106] Nowadays, for each person, group or entity subject to restrictive measures under Council Regulation 2580/2001, the Council provides a statement of reasons that is sufficiently detailed to allow those listed to understand the reasons for their listing as well as to allow the Community Courts to exercise their power of review where a formal challenge is brought against that listing. The person, group or entity concerned may send a file to the Council with supporting documents asking for their listing to be reconsidered. The inclusion of a person or entity on the list is reviewed regularly and at least every six months. Each person, group or entity listed enjoys the opportunity to send observations to the Council. It remains to be seen whether the CFI will be satisfied with these improvements.[107] In two recent judgments both pronounced on 3 April 2008 (*Kongra-Gel*[108] and *Osman Ocalan*[109]), the CFI observed that in any case the sending of a statement of reasons according to the new procedure but after the submission of new annulment requests did not cover the unlawfulness of the disputed act.[110]

Most striking is the coherence brought in that dialogue by the *Kadi* judgment. The ECJ could only recognise – even if implicitly – that the restrictive measures adopted by the EC/EU on grounds of Resolution 1373 (2001) do not differ fundamentally from those adopted to carry out Resolution 1267 (1999), or more precisely the lists elaborated and updated by the Taliban Committee. Hence, both categories of measures entail analogous consequences for the persons, groups or entities whose names are mentioned in the lists. Arguably influenced by this similarity, the ECJ strongly rejected any attempt to diminish its role as a constitutional court in the field of fundamental rights. In that sense, the *Kadi* judgment sends a particularly unambiguous message to the EU

[106] See Factsheet, European Council, The EU list of persons, groups and entities subject to specific measures to combat terrorism, 15 July 2008, available at: www.consilium.europa.eu/uedocs/cmsUpload/080715_combat%20terrorism_EN.pdf.

[107] See *e.g.* CFI: Case T-49/07 *Sofiane Fahas* still pending; CFI: Case T-362/07 *Nouriddin El Fatmi* still pending; CFI, Case T-75/07, *Ahmed Hamdi*, still pending; CFI, Case T-323/07, *Mohamed El Morabit*, still pending.

[108] CFI: Case T-253/04 above at fn 35 nyr.

[109] CFI: Case T-229/02 above at fn 35.

[110] CFI: Case T-253/04, above at fn 35, para. 101; CFI: Case T-229/02 *idem* para. 68.

institutions, the Member States and the UN organs competent to fight terrorism through smart sanctions regarding the constraints implied by the autonomy of the Community legal order.

Significantly, the procedures for listing and de-listing before the Taliban Committee remain diplomatic and intergovernmental in nature since no independent review of a decision to include or to maintain a name on a list is available, and this despite the common proposal made in this sense by Denmark, Germany, Liechtenstein, the Netherlands, Sweden and Switzerland.[111] Moreover, de-listing still requires a consensus within the Taliban Committee. The State of citizenship or residence decides which information can be disclosed to the person or entity whose assets are frozen. These procedures clearly do not protect human rights and individual freedoms with the same intensity as in the Community legal order.

Interestingly, the UN Analytical Support and Sanctions Monitoring Team anticipated the possible consequences of the judgment of the ECJ in *Kadi* on the procedures applicable before the Taliban Committee.[112] According to the Team, it could not be excluded that, in the future, the ECJ will decide to examine evidence behind the reasons for listing provided by the Committee, or even conduct a complete review of the listing decisions. This could eventually raise problems since not all evidence motivating decisions of the Taliban Committee are publicly available. In these circumstances, the risk that the ECJ considers itself not to be in a position to fully review the legality of the restrictive measures cannot be underestimated. Acknowledging that the solution to such a dilemma depends on the circumstances, the Team nevertheless believes that *'the Committee may benefit from consideration of listings by the courts, assessing their judgments against the full body of evidence available'*.[113]

The case law of the ECJ simultaneously finds an echo in the recent Commission Proposal for a Council Regulation amending Regulation 881/2002[114] and following Resolution adopted by the Parliament the day after the judgment of the ECJ in *Kadi*.[115] The Commission promotes an upgrading and a clarification of the procedures applicable for the inclusion, maintenance or withdrawal of a name on the lists implementing decisions of the Taliban Committee. Fully in

[111] See the identical letters dated 23 June 2008 from the Permanent Representative of Switzerland to the United Nations addressed to the President of the general Assembly and the President of the Security Council, S/2008/428.

[112] Ninth report of the Analytical Support and Sanctions Monitoring Team, submitted pursuant to resolution 1822 (2008) concerning Al-Qaida and the Taliban and associated individuals and entities, S/2009/245, 11 May 2009.

[113] *Idem* para. 23.

[114] Commission's proposal for a Council regulation amending Regulation (EC) No 881/2002 imposing certain specific restrictive measures directed against certain persons and entities associated with Usama bin Laden, the Al-Qaida network and the Taliban, COM(2009) 187 final, 22 April 2009.

[115] Resolution of 4 September 2008 on the evaluation of EU sanctions as part of the EU's actions and policies in the area of human rights (2008/2031(INI)).

line with the coherence pursued by the ECJ in *Kadi*, the new procedure would be similar to the mechanism for the adoption of EU 'autonomous' sanctions. The proposal nevertheless preserves the surprise effect of the smart sanctions system since the Commission is to take a provisional decision to freeze the funds and economic resources of the individual or entity identified by the Taliban Committee. Against this background, the Commission is required to send the statement of reasons to this individual or entity without delay, in order to give him/her/it the opportunity to express his/her/its views. Before adopting a final decision, the Commission examines the arguments put forward by persons targeted by the UN and consults an advisory committee of experts of the Member States.[116] In parallel, the proposal also addresses the situation of those persons, groups and entities listed before the ECJ's judgment in order to respect their rights of defence, in particular their right to be heard. Accordingly, those persons, groups or entities concerned should be able to submit a request to the Commission in order to obtain the statement of reasons on grounds of which the Taliban Committee included them on the list and, eventually, to make observations.

If confirmed, the approximation of the two procedures will allegedly result in a more coherent system of EU restrictive measures, whether the latter implement UN lists or not, although it will not necessarily imply a full parallelism between both regimes since the political authority holding competence over (de)listing is different in each case.[117]

5 Conclusion

The above analysis underlines the critical role assumed by Community Courts in promoting the rule of law in the current multi-levelled dialogue surrounding the fight against terrorism. Based on the idea that collective security purposes primarily pursued by the UNSC cannot justify – beyond reasonable limits – derogations to the core principles upon which the Community legal order is based, the *Kadi* judgment is seminal in this respect. Almost one year later, one may conclude that the ECJ's approach does not fundamentally threaten the fundaments of the UNSC smart sanctioning regime. Rather, it is suggested here that the ECJ, by convincingly balancing the various interests at stake,[118] subtly disavowed the discrepancy resulting from the case law of the CFI and simultaneously denounced the lack of procedural guarantees before the Taliban Committee, without fundamentally jeopardising the efforts under-

[116] This is a mere codification of the practice followed by the Commission since the judgment of 3 September 2008. See the Report on the implementation of the revised Strategy on Terrorist Financing, 8864/1/09, 5 May 2009 6.

[117] The Commission is competent under Regulation No 881/2002 (UN lists) whereas the Council is competent under Regulation No 2580/2001 (EU autonomous lists).

[118] 'Editorial Comments' [2008] *C.M.L. Rev.* 1578.

taken by the international Community to devitalise the roots of terrorism.[119] The incentive effect of this case law clearly appears in the recent proposal made by the Commission for an improvement of the Regulation implementing decisions of the Taliban Committee. It remains to be seen whether this dialectical reshaping of the rule of law will be sufficiently echoed at the UN to bring about a reversal of the 'negative' – and implicit – *Solange* presumption by the ECJ in the *Kadi* judgment, a shift that undoubtedly could facilitate a smooth implementation of restrictive sanctions. Whatever the final result may be, the refusal by the ECJ to recognise any *supra*-constitutional status to UNSC resolutions in EU law encourages a global remodelling of the regime of smart sanctions with the aim of appropriately balancing individual rights and collective interests in the fight against international terrorism.

[119] For that reason, I do not share the view that the ECJ failed in that it did not enunciate more precisely the procedure to be followed for an initial inclusion in the EU list of persons, groups or entities targeted by the Taliban Committee or for their maintenance on that list. See Moiny (2009) 51, 52.

Bibliography

'Editorial Comments – The Court of Justice in the limelight – again ' [2008] *C.M.L. Rev.* 1571-1580.

S. Adam, 'Les résolutions du Conseil de sécurité de l'ONU à l'épreuve des juridictions communautaires. Variations autour de la justiciabilité' *in* F. Snyder (ed.), *L'avenir des juridictions communautaires: changement et continuité. The Future of European Courts: institutional change and continuity* (Brussels, Bruylant 2009) forthcoming.

J. Almqvist, 'A Human Rights Critique of European judicial Review: Counter-Terrorism Sanctions' [2008] *I.C.L.Q.* 303-331.

A. Bianchi, 'Assessing the Effectiveness of the UN Security Council's Anti-terrorism Measures: The Quest for Legitimacy and Cohesion' [2007] *E.J.I.L.* 881-919.

T. Biersteker, E. Eckert (dir.), *Strengthening Targeted Sanctions through Fair and Clear Procedures*, White Paper prepared by the Watson Institute, Targeted Sanctions Project, Brown University, 30 March 2006.

R. Brown, '*Kadi v. Council of the European Union and Commission of the European Communities*: Executive Power and Judicial Supervision at European Level' [2006] *E.H.R.L.R.* 456-469.

I. Couzigou, 'La lutte du Conseil de sécurité contre le terrorisme international et les droits de l'homme' [2008] *R.G.D.I.P.* 49-84.

M. Cremona, 'Community Report' *in* X.L. Xenopoulos (ed.) *External Relations of the EU and the Member States: Competence, Mixed Agreements, International Responsibility and Effects of International Law* (Nicosia, FIDE 2006 – National reports, 2006).

J. D'Aspremont, F. Dopagne, '*Kadi*: The ECJ's Reminder of the Elementary Divide between Legal Orders' [2008] *Int. Org. Law Rev.* 371-379.

G. de Burca, 'The European Court of Justice and the International Legal Order after Kadi', *NYU School of Law Jean Monnet Working Paper No 1/09* (www.jeanmonnetprogram.org/papers/09/090101.html accessed on 15 June 2009).

G. Della Cananea, 'Return to the due process of law: the European Union and the fight against terrorism' [2007] *E.L. Rev.* 896-907.

G. Della Cananea, 'Global Security and Procedural Due Process of Law between the United Nations and the European Union: Yassin Abdullah Kadi & Al Barakaat International Foundation *v.* Council' [2009] *Col. Journ. Eur. L.* 511-530.

P. De Sena – M.C. Vitucci, 'The European Courts and the Security Council: Between Dédoublement Fonctionnel and Balancing of Values' [2009] *E.J.I.L.* 202-209.

S. Dewulf – D. Pacquée, 'Protecting Human Rights in the War on Terror: Challenging the Sanctions Regime Originating from Resolution 1267 (1999)' [2006] *Netherlands Quarterly of Human Rights* 607-640.

C. Eckes, 'Comment on CFI: Case T-228/02 *People's Mojahedin Organisation of Iran* v. *Council and Commission*' [2007] *C.M.L. Rev.* 1117-1129.

C. Eckes, 'Judicial Review of European Anti-Terrorism Measures – The *Yusuf* and *Kadi* Judgments of the Court of First Instance' [2008] *E.L.J.* 74-92.

P. Eeckhout, *Does Europe's Constitution Stop at the Water's Edge? Law and Policy in the EU's External Relations*, Walter Van Gerven Lectures (Groningen, Europa Law Publishing, 2005).

P. Eeckhout, 'Community Terrorism Listings, Fundamental Rights, and UN Security Council Resolutions. In Search of the Right Fit' [2007] *E.C.L.R.* 183-206.

J. Etienne, 'Sur certains rapports entre le droit communautaire et le droit international public. Un bref commentaire de l'arrêt Yusuf et Al Barakaat du Tribunal de première instance des Communautés européennes' [2006] *C.D.P.K.* 373-376.

B. Fassbender, *Targeted Sanctions and Due Process. The responsibility of the UN Security Council to ensure that fair and clear procedures are made available to individuals and entities targeted with sanctions under Chapter VII of the UN Charter*, Study commissioned by the United Nations – Office of Legal Affairs, Humbolt-Universität zu Berlin, 20 March 2006.

J. Heliskoski, 'T- 253/02, Chafiq Ayadi *v.* Council and T-49/04, Faraj Hassan *v.* Council and Commission' [2007] *C.M.L. Rev.* 1143-1157.

A. Hudson, 'Not a Great Asset: The U.N. Security Council's Counter-Terrorism Regime: Violating Human Rights' [2007] *Berk.J.I.L.* 223-227.

J.-P. Jacqué, 'Le Tribunal de première instance face aux résolutions du Conseil de sécurité des Nations Unies. « Merci monsieur le Professeur »' [2006] *L'Europe des Libertés* 2-6.

R. Joliet, *Le droit institutionnel des Communautés européennes. Le contentieux* (Faculté de droit, d'économie et de sciences sociales de Liège, 1981).

M. Karayigit, 'The *Yusuf* and *Kadi* Judgments : The Scope of EC Competences in Respect of Restrictive Measures' [2006] *L.I.E.I.* 379-404.

N. Lavranos, 'Judicial Review of UN Sanctions by the Court of First Instance' [2006] *E.F.A.R.* 471-490.

A. Gattini, 'Comment on ECJ, Joined Cases C-402/05 P & 415/05 P, *Yassin Abdullah Kadi, Al Barakaat International Foundation v. Council and Commission*' [2009] *C.M.L. Rev.* 213-239.

S. Griller, 'International law, Human Rights and the European Community's Autonomous Legal Order: Notes on the European Court of Justice Decision in *Kadi*' [2008] *E.C.L.R.* 528-553.

N. Lavranos, 'Judicial Review of UN sanctions by the European Court of Justice' [2009] *N.J.I.L.* 343-359 (forthcoming).

D. Marty, 'United Nations Security Council and European Union blacklists', Report, Committee on Legal Affairs and Human Rights, Parliamentary Assembly of the Council of Europe, 16 November 2006.

A. Miron, 'La jurisprudence du Tribunal de première instance à propos de l'inscription sur les listes terroristes' [2007] *R.M.C.U.E.* 526-531.

Y. Moiny, 'Aperçu de la jurisprudence communautaire développée dans le cadre de la lutte contre le financement du terrorisme international' [2009/1] *R.D.U.E.* 31-54.

M. Nettesheim, 'U.N. Sanctions against Individuals – A Challenge to the Architecture of European Union Governance' [2007] *C.M.L. Rev.* 567-600.

C.R.J.J. Rijken, 'Het Hof als hoeder van de fundamentele rechten in de zaak Kadi en Al Barakaat' [2009/4] *N.T.E.R.* 140-146.

A. Reinisch, 'Developing Human Rights and Humanitarian Law Accountability of the Security Council for the Imposition of Economic Sanctions' [2001] *A.J.I.L.* 851-871.

D. Simon – F. Mariatte, 'Le Tribunal de première instance des Communautés: Professeur de droit international?' [2005] *Europe* 6-10.

J.P. Spitzer, 'Bending the law does democracy no good' [2008] *European Voice* 9.

C. Tomuschat, 'Comment on: CFI, Case T-306/01 *Ahmed Ali Yusuf and Al Barakaat Foundation v. Council and Commission* and Case T-315/01 *Yassin Abdullah Kadi v. Council and Commission*' [2006] *C.M.L. Rev.* 537-551.

T. Uyen Do, 'Droit institutionnel (arrêt Ahmed Ali Yusuf et Al Barakaat International Foundation c/ Conseil et Commission)' [2005] *R.D.U.E.* 637-640.

R.H. Van Ooik, R.A. Wessel, 'De Yusuf en Kadi-uitspraken in perspectief. Nieuwe verhoudingen in de interne en externe bevoegdheden van de Europese Unie' [2006] *S.E.W.* 230-241.

G. Vermeulen – W. De Bondt, 'European Report: Listing of Terrorists. Finding the Right Balance between Effective measures and Fundamental Human Rights Guarantees' [2008] *I.R.P.L.* 379-402.

W. Vlcek, 'Acts to Combat the Financing of Terrorism : Common Foreign and Security Policy at the European Court of Justice' [2006] *E.F.A.R.* 491-507.

S. Zašova, 'La lutte contre le terrorisme à l'épreuve de la jurisprudence du Tribunal de première instance des Communautés européennes' [2008] *R.T.D.H.* 481-505.

CHAPTER 7

Preliminary Reference and Constitutional Courts

Are You in the Mood for Dialogue?

Giuseppe Martinico*

Preliminary Remarks

There is a new intriguing frontier for judicial dialogue: the potential beginning of an era of cooperation between the European Court of Justice and some constitutional courts. Recently, the Belgian,[1] Austrian,[2] Lithuanian,[3] and-lastly-Italian[4] Constitutional Courts accepted to raise the preliminary reference to the ECJ.

Constitutional Courts are progressively accepting the cooperative mechanism set up by Article 234 of the European Community Treaty (hereafter ECT); the latest episode of this new trend is an historical decision by the Italian Constitutional Court (hereafter ICC). The aim of this work is to reflect on the latest trend of the relationship between Constitutional Courts (thereinafter CCs) and the European Court of Justice (thereinafter ECJ) within the first pillar.[5]

This article is divided into three parts:

1) in Part I, after briefly recalling the cases in which CCs other than the ICC raised preliminary references, the article will focus on the Italian case;
2) in Part II, after a summary of the main reasons which compelled the ICC to change its strategy, it will try to identify the macro-reasons which might favour a new cooperation between CCs and ECJ, namely the margin of appreciation doctrine-to which the ECJ refers in the latest years-and the emersion of an untouchable core of absolute rights (cfr. *Schmidberger*[6]) in the case-law of the ECJ.
3) In Part III, the article will refer to the problematic factors still existing between these courts. One should pay attention to these, before 'officially' affirming that a new era of cooperation between courts is beginning.

---

* STALS Senior Assistant Editor; Visiting Research Fellow, King's College, London, martinico@sssup.it.

1 *Cour d'Arbitrage*, 19 Febr.1997, no. 6/97, available at www.arbitrage.be/fr/common/home.html.

2 *VfGH*, 10 March 1999, B 2251/97, B 2594/97, available at www.vfgh.gv.at/cms/vfgh-site.

3 *Lietuvos Respublikos Konstitucinis Teismas*, decision of 8 May 2007, available at www.lrkt.lt/dokumentai/2007/d070508.htm.

4 *Corte Costituzionale*, sentenza no. 102/2008 and ordinanza no. 103/2008, available at www.cortecostituzionale.it. The preliminary reference was raised during *principaliter* proceedings.

5 The situation in the third pillar is in fact very different as the tensions existing between CCs and ECJ about the European Arrest Warrant saga demonstrate. For an overview on that see: Komarek (2005)and Pollicino (2008).

6 ECJ: Case C-112/00 *Schmidberger* [2003] ECR I-5659.

1 The Phenomenon in a Nutshell

Accepting the risk associated with simplification, one can identify three kinds of position with regard to the possibility for CCs to raise the preliminary reference to the ECJ:[7]

a) Some Courts have denied the possibility to raise the preliminary question to the ECJ. This is the case of German *Bundesverfassungsgericht* (BvG) and of the ICC with regard to *incidenter* proceedings. Courts can support this conclusion in several ways: some of them do not consider themselves as 'judges' pursuant to Article 234 ECT (for instance, the ICC did so until 2008). Although in *Solange I* the BvG accepted to be in principle bound by Article 234 ECT, it is interesting to notice that, in practice, the German constitutional judges never tackled the question, as Mayer points out.[8] Indeed, if in order to solve a question of EC law interpretation in the proceedings culminating in the 1993 *Maastricht* decision[9] the BvG decided to hear the testimony of the Director General of the Commission Legal Service, this was done precisely to avoid raising the preliminary reference to the ECJ. The position at hand is also that of the Spanish Constitutional Tribunal, according to which the possible contrast between EC and domestic law is a mere question of 'legality', not one of 'constitutionality'.[10]

b) Other Courts yet have initially denied such a possibility, but later changed their mind and entered a preliminary ruling proceeding. This is the case of the ICC with regard to ordinanza 103/2008.[11]

c) Finally, some Courts accepted to raise preliminary questions to the ECJ a long time ago. This is the case of the Belgian and Austrian Courts. The Austrian *Verfassungsgerichtshof*[12] first raised the reference in 1999, four years after Austria's accession. Yet, the most active CC in this sense is undoubtedly the Belgian *Cour Constitutionnelle*. This tribunal has set the 'record' of preliminary references so far: having a look at the 2008 Annual Report, one can remark that the number of references raised since 1952 is very high (12).[13] Moreover, the Belgian Court is the only one to have referred preliminary questions concerning both the interpretation and the validity of instruments of EC law.[14]

---

7 The most complete analysis of the relations between national judges and the ECJ is that carried out by Claes (2006). See also F.C. Mayer (2006) 281- 334.

8 Mayer (2006) 281-334, 287.

9 *BVerfGE* 89, 155, available at www.bundesverfassungsgericht.de/en/index.html.

10 See on that Vidal Prado (2004) 156-159.

11 *Corte Costituzionale*, ordinanza 103/2008, available at www.cortecostituzionale.it.

12 On the Austrian case see Jedliczka (2008) 301-305.

13 http://curia.europa.eu/jcms/jcms/J02_7000/annual-report.

14 *'Thus, the Constitutional Court of Belgium broke at least three records. Among national constitutional courts it is the court that has referred most questions to the ECJ (five,* at that time*); moreover it is the first to have made preliminary references on the validity of EC law (Money Laundering) as well as on the validity of EU law (Advocaten voor de Wereld)'*, Vandamme (2008) 127-148, 128.

The openness of the Belgian Constitutional Court has historical roots: initially born as an arbiter, the *Cour Constitutionnelle 'grew into a full-fledged constitutional court'*[15] just a few years after its creation. The Austrian *Verfassungsgerichtshof* was a pioneer, too.[16] Broadly speaking, as this article will argue below, these two courts paved the way for the Italian *revirement*. Dealing with the Italian case is necessary because the ICC, together with the BvG, has historically been the most famous competitor of the ECJ.

This history was enriched by an unexpected decision by the ICC: on April 15, 2008, for the first time in its history, the Court accepted to raise a preliminary question to the European Court of Justice.[17]

The decision the article is about to comment is relevant for several reasons, which can be summarized as follows:

- the ICC accepted the preliminary ruling mechanism under Article 234 ECT, and fully acknowledged the interpretative authority of the ECJ;
- the ICC confirmed its views on the distinction between the two ways in which the constitutionality of a domestic norm can be reviewed, i.e. direct (*principaliter*) proceedings and indirect *(incidenter)* proceedings. It further made it clear that this distinction influences the choice on whether to resort to EC law or not when solving a question of constitutionality;[18]
- in light of the above, this decision marks a veritable shift away from the doctrine of *procedural impermeability* between constitutional procedural law and EC law, which the ICC had devised since the earliest years of its case-law.

---

15 Vandamme (2008), 147.

16 'Generally it can be said that, if the Court has jurisdiction in a certain case under The Austrian Constitution – in other words, in a case where a question of constitutionality has to be answered – and has reason to believe that the Austrian provision in question conflicts with a European Law Provision, the Court will move for a preliminary ruling. However, the Court has come in some cases to the conclusion that it is obvious that an Austrian provision conflicts with a European Law Provision and is therefore not applicable and cannot be the subject-matter of a constitutional proceeding. On other occasions, an inferior court has failed to ask the ECJ for a preliminary ruling, even though it was bound to do so. In such cases, the constitutional right to a lawful judge has been violated; the case was reversed and remanded by the Constitutional Court without referring it to the ECJ', U. Jedliczka (2008), 304.

17 *Corte Costituzionale* ordinanza No. 103/2008, available at www.cortecostituzionale.it.

18 The *principaliter* proceedings is the ordinary definition for constitutional claims lodged directly before the Constitutional Court by the Central Government or the Regions. The *incidenter* proceedings, on the contrary, consists of a claim filed by an ordinary judge (known as judge *a quo*, a Latin expression meaning 'from which', since the question stems 'from' the judge) and is carried out while the underlying proceedings is pending (it is suspended). The former is a direct review of a piece of legislation which also entails an abstract nature, while the latter is a form of indirect review of legislation that bears a concrete nature (i.e., the outcome of the constitutionality review is decisive for the settlement of the dispute before the referring judge). This article refers to *incidenter* and *principaliter* proceedings by using descriptive definitions concerning the quality of the control involved, as the Latin expressions could be misleading for non-Italian readers: namely, I will use indirect/concrete (*incidenter*) and direct/abstract (*principaliter*), when referring to this distinction.

In dealing with the questions of constitutionality raised by the referring ordinary judge, the ICC adopted a two-step approach. The Court tackled and solved a first set of issues in judgment No. 102, while it postponed the decision upon a second set of issues, reluctant as it was to rule on those before a suggestion by the ECJ. A careful reading of the decision allows one to draw a distinction between the legal reasoning and the political motivations put forward by the udges. The present article will also describe the context in which this ruling is set, as well as its technical groundings and political consequences[19].

[19] The Italian Constitutional Court decided to raise the question during a trial opened by the application of the Italian Government and devoted to the so called 'Luxury Tax' ('Tassa sul lusso') established by the Sardinia district authority in 2006 and amended in 2007. In particular, under Article 4 of Law No 4 of the Sardinia Region of 2006, Sardinia imposed a tax on planes and boats (not including cruise ferries, boats used in sport competitions and boats spending the whole year in Sardinia's harbors); this tax levied from June 1st to September 30th, and payment thereof was due i) in case of each call made in regional airports for the purpose of transport of individuals, and ii) yearly, by the owner of any boat larger than 14 meters who intended to make call at any harbor or mooring point placed on the territory of the Region. The ICC referred the following questions:
'(a) Is Article 49 of the Treaty to be interpreted as precluding the application of a rule, such as that laid down in Article 4 of Law No 4 of the Region of Sardinia of 11 May 2006 (Miscellaneous provisions on revenue, reclassification of costs, social policy and development), as amended by Article 3(3) of Law No 2 of the Region of Sardinia of 29 May 2007 (Provisions for the preparation of the annual and long-term budget of the Region-2007 Finance Law), under which the regional tax on aircraft making stopovers for tourist purposes is levied only on undertakings, operating aircraft which they themselves use for the transport of persons in the course of 'general business aviation' activities, which have tax domicile outside the territory of the Region of Sardinia?
(b) Does Article 4 of Law No 4 of 2006 of the Region of Sardinia, as amended by Article 3(3) of Law No 2 of 2007 of the Region of Sardinia, by providing for the imposition of the regional tax on aircraft making stopovers for tourist purposes only on undertakings, operating aircraft which they themselves use for the transport of persons in the course of 'general business aviation' activities, which have tax domicile outside the territory of the Region of Sardinia, constitute, within the meaning of Article 87 of the Treaty, State aid to undertakings carrying on the same activities which have tax domicile in the Region of Sardinia?
(c) Is Article 49 of the Treaty to be interpreted as precluding the application of a rule, such as that laid down in Article 4 of Law No 4 of 2006 of the Region of Sardinia, as amended by Article 3(3) of Law No 2 of 2007 of the Region of Sardinia, under which the regional tax on recreational craft making stopovers for tourist purposes is levied only on undertakings, operating recreational craft, which have tax domicile outside the territory of the Region of Sardinia and whose commercial operations involve making such craft available to third parties?
(d) Does Article 4 of Law No 4 of 2006 of the Region of Sardinia, as amended by Article 3(3) of Law No 2 of 2007 of the Region of Sardinia, by providing for the imposition of the regional tax on recreational craft making stopovers only on undertakings, operating recreational craft, which have tax domicile outside the territory of the Region of Sardinia and whose commercial operations involve making such craft available to third parties constitute, within the meaning of Article 87 of the Treaty, State aid to undertakings carrying on the same activities which have tax domicile in the Region of Sardinia?'.

The present article will not deal with the facts out of which the question originated-all the more so because the case is still pending. Rather, it will seek to explain the reasons of such a *revirement* by the ICC.

1.1 The Italian Decision in Context

It is possible to appreciate the groundbreaking nature of such a decision simply by contrasting its findings with the previous case-law on the preliminary reference mechanism.

In the past years, case-law of the ICC has been characterized by a sort of procedural mutual exclusion between EC law and domestic constitutional law (that is, the non-usability of EC law within the framework of the domestic constitutional review). The ICC refused to use the preliminary reference on the basis of this exclusion: the ICC does not use EC law as a constitutional parameter; hence, it is not interested in asking for the exact meaning of an EC act, because it would not be relevant for the resolution of the case.

Moreover, the ICC recalled another technicality.

Since 1995,[20] the Constitutional Court has emphasized the nature of its functions and the peculiarity of its task, and consequently refused to raise the preliminary question to the ECJ; nevertheless, we could also maintain that the constitutional review of the national legislation shares some features with the normal jurisdictional function, I will try to provide some short remarks on this point.

First of all, scholars have stressed the Constitutional Courts' distinguishing features, that are rooted (i) in the broadness of the constitutional norms regulating the Court's activity, (ii) in the inapplicability of the set of general rules on interpretation (codified by Article 12 of the preliminary provisions to the Civil Code),[21] (iii) in the impossibility to apply those constitutional provisions conceived to regulate the judicial function (since in principle they are addressed to ordinary and administrative judges only), and (iv) in the uniqueness of constitutional proceedings.[22]

In order to describe the mandate of the ICC the scholars have conceived a fifth function/power (the function of 'constitutional control, the supreme guarantee of the Constitution[23]'), along with the classic tripartite division of powers (legislative, judicial and executive power), and in addition to the fourth function of 'political direction' ('*indirizzo politico*[24]'), owned by the constitutional subject who is capable of deciding and defining the State's fundamental policies (in a given historical period), and of adopting 'political acts' (that is, acts escaping any judicial review).

---

20 *Corte Costituzionale*, sentenza no. 536/1995, www.cortecostituzionale.it.

21 On the peculiarity of the constitutional interpretation see Crisafulli (1952) 11; Dogliani (1982) 90.

22 On this, see Zagrebelsky (1990) 105 ff.; Pizzorusso (1996) 133 ff.

23 Cartabia (2007).

24 Cheli (1968); Grottanelli De Santi (1988).

The Italian Constitutional Court's *revirement*, therefore, can be explained as consequence of several factors:

- the 2001 constitutional reform;
- the distinction between the *principaliter* (direct) proceedings and the *incidenter* (indirect) proceedings;
- the 'good' example given by the Belgian and Austrian Constitutional Courts;
- the previous case-law concerning the relationship between the European Court of Human Rights' (hereafter ECHR) and Article 117, par.1 of the Constitution;
- the lack of coherence concerning the ICC's nature (judicial or non-judicial) within the case-law of the Court itself, and
- the external pressure coming from cases like *Traghetti* and *Köbler*.

These six factors are explored here, with the aim of coming across the reasons that might have led the Italian Constitutional Court to review its jurisprudence.

A pre-emptive remark is needed, in fact, before entering the analysis of the factors mentioned above: as obvious, the refusal by the Italian Constitutional Court to raise the preliminary question to the ECJ cannot be explained only by technical elements, as it involves also political motivations. The Italian (and German) Constitutional Courts supported their refusal to consider themselves as judges in the meaning of Article 234 ECT with some typically political considerations, such as their poor consideration of the level of protection of fundamental rights provided by the EC, and with the purported non-democratic nature of the Community.[25]

However, there are also some important 'technical' (i.e. 'purely legal') factors, which can be very helpful to appreciate the Italian *Consulta*'s coherence, and this is the reason why a study of these judicial practices can be of much importance, even if we acknowledge the influence of the political choices drawn by the Court.

A. The 2001 Constitutional Reform

The Italian Constitution's new Article 117, paragraph 1 expressly codifies the limit that *supra*-national obligations represent for domestic law by providing that: '*Legislative power belongs to the State and the regions in accordance with the constitution and within the limits set by European Union law and international obligations*'.

Soon after the reform, the interpretation of this provision divided the scholars.[26] According to some of them, Article 117, paragraph 1 would simply codify the pre-existing situation: it would just grant a sort of *a posteriori* assent to the

[25] See, for example, *Solange I* cit: 'The Community still lacks a democratically legitimated parliament directly elected by general suffrage which possesses legislative powers and to which the Community organs empowered to legislate are fully responsible on a political level'.

[26] For an overview, see Chieppa (2007) 493-511, 499 ff.; Ruggeri, (2007).

European primacy[27] as it was developed by the ECJ and accepted across the Community.

Other scholars, instead, emphasized the importance of the constitutional *status* given to the European primacy, and asserted that Article 117 paved the way for the acceptance of the Italian monistic thesis.[28]

Such a codification would bring about the necessity of centralizing the task of controlling the relationship between EC law and national law[29] or – at least – a more active role of the ICC in this respect (along with common judges, who would maintain their role as main guardians of the primacy of EC law).[30]

The occasion of testing these theories was given in case no. 406/2005, where the ICC accepted a State claim against a regional law where Article 117, paragraph. 1 was the only parameter of constitutionality invoked, and in case no. 129/2006.[31]

In both cases, the Italian *Consulta* decided to appoint the Italian Constitution Article 117, paragraph 1 as the only parameter upon which to decide the question, and refrained from using the other constitutional standard of review invoked by the plaintiff.

In fact, the *Consulta* declared the regional laws challenged in this case unconstitutional for the first time, after many 'failed attempts'[32] (see cases no. 65, 150, 161, 304, 355, 393, 428, 434, 469 of 2005[33]).

Although these two decisions do not mention the intentional avoidance of preliminary ruling by the ICC, nevertheless they reflect a certain 'judicial activism', and support the view that the new explicit mention of EC law in Article 117, paragraph 1 changed the map of the relationship between the ICC and the EC system.

B. The distinction between direct proceedings and indirect proceedings

The above mentioned judgments were drawn in a direct proceeding, where the ICC acts as the 'true' judge of the controversy, as opposed to indirect proceedings ('*incidenter*' proceedings), where the 'true' judge of the question is the *a quo* national judge.

In direct proceedings EC norms are '*interposed norms* [norme interposte] *that can integrate the parameter for the control of consistency of the regional legislation with Article 117, par. 1, of the Constitution*' (see *sentenze* no. 129/2006; no. 406/2005; no. 166 and no. 7/2004) or, better, they '*make the parameter of Article*

27 Pinelli (2001) 194 ff.

28 Paterniti (2004) 2101 ss; Pajno (2003) 814-842.

29 S. Catalano(2006) 129 ff.

30 A. Celotto (2006) 121 ff.

31 *Corte Costituzionale*, sentenza no. 129/2006, www.cortecostituzionale.it.

32 In these terms Calvano (2005) 4417 ff.

33 See www.cortecostituzionale.it.

117, par. 1, actually efficient,[34] [and this can give rise to a] *declaration of constitutional illegitimacy of the regional norms judged incompatible with EC law.'*[35]

Moreover, since no form of appeal against its decisions is foreseen (Article 137 Cost), the Constitutional Court could not avoid raising the preliminary ruling without infringing the general interest to the uniform application of EC law.

According to the Italian Constitution, the legislation's constitutional review[36] can be triggered and pursued in two different ways: indirect proceedings and direct proceedings. In *incindeter* proceedings an *a quo* judge (either ordinary or administrative) can raise the question of constitutionality (i.e. of consistency between the Italian law and the Constitution) before the Constitutional Court during a trial. The Constitutional Court can regard the question as admissible only if it is 'relevant' (i.e. significant for the solution of the case) and non-manifestly groundless.

On the contrary, direct proceedings are regulated under by Article 127 of the Italian Constitution, that reads:

> '(1) Whenever the government regards a regional law as exceeding the powers of the region, it may raise the question of its constitutionality before the Constitutional Court within sixty days of the publication of the law.
> (2) Whenever a region regards a state law, another act of the state having the force of law, or a law of another region as infringing on its own sphere of powers, it may raise the question of its constitutionality before the constitutional court within sixty days of the publication of said law or act'.

According to the scheme provided therein, in case of a constitutional controversy arising between the Regions and the State, the Government can appeal directly against a regional law, and a Region can appeal directly against a national law, or a law enacted by another Region. In such cases, constitutional proceedings are conceived to resolve disputes between the State and the Regions concerning the limits of their respective powers.[37]

It is well known that direct proceedings represent another exception to the diffuse review of consistency between internal and Community law (i.e. the power that ordinary or administrative judges have to monitor the consistency between domestic and EC law); as argued above, the ICC had already agreed to rule on the issue of contrasts between national and EC law within this type of proceedings.

---

34 This passage is borrowed from sentenza No. 348/2007.

35 *Corte Costituzionale*, ordinanza no 103/2008.

36 The task of reviewing the legislation, in the traditional models of centralized constitutional justice, is usually attributed to a *ad hoc* Constitutional Court.

37 A huge difference between Regions and State exists: whilst the former can raise the constitutional question only when their sphere of competence is infringed by a State act, the State can raise the constitutional question on a regional norm grounded on any kind of constitutional 'defect'.

According to decisions no. 384/1994 and no. 94/1995,[38] indeed, a centralized decision could be envisaged when a question of consistency between national and EC law was raised before the ICC via direct proceedings (both by the Regions and by the State). In particular, in case no. 384/1994 the ICC acknowledged that, due to the particular dynamics of direct proceedings (where the role of the ordinary judge-who normally guarantees the respect of EC law-is irrelevant), its refusal to rule on such questions would have implied a dangerous gap in the protection of rights, and a breach of the legal certainty principle. Therefore, it can be said that, due to the unique features of direct proceedings, the residual possibility to involve the Constitutional Court is justified only because the ordinary judge, who is the natural guardian of EC law primacy at domestic level, is totally missing from the scene.

Scholars pointed out that, if the Constitutional Court were really coherent with this assumption, it should also provide for the centralization of the questions of consistency between national and EC laws in indirect proceedings.[39]

Probably, the key to understand the rationale underlying the choice made by the ICC rests in the absence of the *a quo* judge who normally non-applies the domestic norm in conflict with the EC law in direct proceedings.

The distinction between direct and indirect proceedings was initially drawn in case no. 129/2006, where the ICC declared that- as the Court had already had the chance to clarify (see cases no. 406/2005 and no. 166/2004)- EC directives work as interposed norms ('*norme interposte*'), and can then integrate the constitutional standard of review used in the constitutionality test over regional provisions, as regards their consistency with Article 117, paragraph 1 of the Constitution.

Italian scholars have already stressed how there is no particular reason for confining this view to direct proceedings alone.[40] The conflict between national norms and EC norms can be brought about in several ways besides in direct proceedings, as confirmed in an *ordinanza* raised to the ICC by the Italian Corte di Cassazione (see *Corte di Cassazione* III Criminal Section, order no. 1414/2006[41]). In that case the ICC's intervention was urged by the *Corte di Cassazione* because it was impossible to non-apply the Italian norms in conflict with interpretative ECJ rulings, since those interpretative rulings were based on an EC provision lacking direct applicability.[42]

---

38 Both available at www.cortecostituzionale.it.

39 Cartabia – Weiler (2000) 185.

40 Carbone (2007) 707-717, 711.

41 Recalled by Carbone, (2007) 711.

42 In its case-law (mainly in 113/1985 and 389/1989), the Italian Constitutional Court has recognized erga omnes effects to the ECJ's rulings because they share certain characteristics with the classic EC legal sources. In the Italian Constitutional Court's reasoning, these interpretive rulings present the normal effect of the classical EC legal sources when they contain the interpretation of EC legal provisions characterized by the following effects: direct applicability and direct effect. This way the Italian Court put ECJ interpretive rulings on an equal footing with classic EC acts (regulations, directives). Following this

The question was then referred back to the *Corte di Cassazione* because in the meanwhile the Italian regulation had been modified,[43] and this prevented the ICC from ruling on it (indeed, in cases of *ius superveniens* the requisite of relevance-see above-can obviously be missing). I am going to review this point at a later stage, when dealing with the Constitutional Court as *a quo* judge.

C. The 'good' example given by the Belgian and Austrian Constitutional Courts

As a matter of fact, it could be sound to claim that one of the most important reasons which led the *Consulta* to change its mind is the gradual acceptance of the constitutional dialogue by certain Constitutional Courts, through the use of Article 234 ECT. Apart from a couple of very well known cases,[44] it is interesting to notice that the case that probably persuaded these Constitutional Courts to accept the *formal* dialogue with the ECJ is the *Carlsen* case.[45] This is a bit of a paradox, because the 'main player' of that case was not a Constitutional Court, but the Danish Supreme Court (in Denmark, in fact, a real Constitutional Court does not exist).

In *Carlsen* the Danish Court specified the relationship existing between counter-limits and preliminary ruling as follows. According to the *Carlsen* doctrine, if there is a doubt about the consistency of an EC act with the Constitution, the Supreme (or Constitutional) Court can raise the question by asking the ECJ to clarify the exact meaning of the norm. Once it has received the ECJ's opinion, the the national (Constitutional or Supreme) court can decide: if it still has doubts regarding the constitutionality of the EC act, it can resort to the use of the 'counter-limits'.

This precedent obviously supports the view that Constitutional Courts do have the last say, even when they accept to raise the preliminary referral, and

reasoning, according to the Italian Constitutional Court, the ordinary judge's duty to non-apply internal law contrasting with the EC law must be extended to the case of contrast between national law and interpretive rulings of the ECJ. The reasoning of the Italian Constitutional Court builds upon the particular position of the ECJ in the EC legal system. The interpretive rulings of the ECJ would be second degree sources because they infer their legal power from the provisions they interpret. In fact, the Italian Court acknowledged the content and effects of the classic Community sources (direct effect and direct applicability) onto ECJ interpretive rulings only if the interpreted provisions have such effects. This is an indirect recognition of the strong role of the ECJ and it implies the extension of the national judge's obligation to non-apply national law contrasting with the interpretive rulings of the ECJ.

43 This is normally referred to in Italy with the Latin formula *jus superveniens*, used when an amendment of the applicable regulations results in changing the terms of a preexisting legal relationship, which was born (and regulated) under the previous set of norms.

44 *Cour d'Arbitrage*, 19th February 1997, No. 6/97, in http://www.arbitrage.be/fr/common/home.html; *VfGH*, 10 March 1999, B 2251/97, B 2594/97, in http://www.vfgh.gv.at/cms/vfgh-site. See also *Lietuvos Respublikos* Konstitucinis Teismas, Decision of 8 May 2007, available at www.lrkt.lt/dokumentai/2007/d070508.htm.

45 *Højesteret*, *Carlsen v. Rasmussen* [1999] 3 CMLR 854.

therefore encourages Constitutional tribunals to behave in the same way, without the fear of being outclassed by the ECJ.

D. The case-law on the relationship between the ECHR and Constitution Article 117, par.1

In Order no. 103/2008 the ICC recalled the recent twin cases no. 348 and 349/2007, where some national provisions[46] were declared unconstitutional for being in conflict with the international obligations stated in the European Convention of Human Rights, Protocol 1, Article 1.

These decisions are very innovative '*because not only has the Italian Constitutional Court clarified, by using Article 117, paragraph 1, the European Convention's actual efficacy in the domestic legal system, but it has also interpreted international obligations as an interposed standard of review, on the basis of which the constitutionality of domestic law must be assessed.*'[47]

There is no room here to analyze these two decisions in depth, but it is fundamental to point out the increasing openness of the constitutional jurisprudence towards external sources of law that is reflected in the text of the decisions. It is nevertheless curious to emphasize that in the above mentioned decisions the ICC entered a long reasoning in order to underline the difference between EC law and the law of the European Convention, based on the difference of their effects on domestic law, whereas in *order* no. 103/2008 the Court seems to refer to this precedent only with the view of supporting its findings on EC law. In other words, the ICC is more interested in using the similarities between EC and conventional (international) law, rather than in drawing the attention on those passages of the decisions no. 348 and 349/2007 where the Court itself had provided a careful distinction between them.

E. The lack of coherence of the Constitutional Court's case-law concerning its judicial – non judicial nature

As Prof. Groppi[48] pointed out, the fact that the Italian Constitutional Court did not consider itself as an *a quo* (referring) judge was hardly compatible with its own 'internal' case-law. According to a consolidated case-law, indeed, the ICC considers itself a potential *a quo* judge who can raise to itself (*sic*!) questions of consistency between ordinary statutory norms and constitutional provisions; this clear-cut judicial trend is consolidated in each area of its jurisdiction (see orders no. 22/1960, no. 225-297/1995, no. 183-197/1996, no. 42, 156, 288/2001, no. 2/1977). In each of these cases the ICC agreed to refer to itself (thus acting as an *a quo* judge) the question of constitutionality, but it argued that a difference still existed between itself and 'normal' judicial bodies (see *sentenze* no. 13/1960 and 536/1995).

46 Namely, the provisions ruling the quantification of compensation amounts due for public purposes expropriation and for unlawful expropriation.

47 See Biondi Dal Monte – Fontanelli, (2008), 889-932, 889.

48 Groppi (1997) 171 ff, 186-187.

It is common knowledge that the domestic notion of '*a quo* judge' is somehow different with the one pertaining to the EC order, but either of them is very broad, and allows for a wide interpretive margin.[49]

As for the ECJ's approach, it has been maintained that the Luxembourg Court follows a functional or '*fuzzy*[50]' logic, as its choices reveal a high degree of malleability and changeability. On this issue, the core elements of the ECJ's position-as expressed in its case-law-are summarized as follows: '*In order to determine whether a body making a reference is a court or tribunal for the purposes of Article 234 TEC, which is a question governed by Community law alone, the Court takes into account a number of factors, such as whether the body is established by law, whether it is permanent, whether its jurisdiction is compulsory, whether its procedure is* inter partes, *whether it applies rules of law and whether it is independent*'.[51]

According to these criteria it can be inferred that the ICC fits the 'tribunal or court' Community definition. Here, on the contrary, it is worth remembering how Italian scholarship had stated that indirect proceedings lack a perfect *inter partes* structure,[52] and that, for this reason, they differ from direct proceedings, and the ICC cannot be seen as playing the judge role in the indirect framework. Secondly, as the *Consulta* has repeatedly assessed, the ICC is not the actual judge deciding on the dispute of the trial before the *a quo* judge.

From this perspective, it is possible to appreciate the coherence of the Italian Constitutional Court, which raised the preliminary ruling in direct proceedings, arguing that in this context, in a dispute between a Region and the State, the judge is the Court itself (both formally and substantially).

F. The external pressure coming from cases like Traghetti and Köbler

In the cases *Traghetti del Mediterraneo*[53] and *Köbler*[54] the ECJ carried out something that was already anticipated in the *Francovich*[55] *and Brasserie*[56] decisions. Indeed, it had pointed out that:

> 'In international law a State whose liability for breach of an international commitment is in issue will be viewed as a single entity, irrespective of whether the

---

49 As Cartabia wrote 'The ECJ, for example, considered the Council of State capable of the preliminary ruling, ECJ judgement 16 October 1997, joined cases 69 to 79/96, while the selfsame court (Council of State) is not authorised to approach the Constitutional court with questions of constitutional review of legislation.' Cartabia, (2007).

50 D'Alessio – Pecchioli (1998), 699 ff.

51 See ECJ: Case C-96/04 *Standesamt Stadt Niebüll* [2006] ECR I-3561. See also Basile (2006) 696 ff.; Bassi, (2000) 155 ff.

52 Romboli, (1985).

53 ECJ: Case C-173/03 *Traghetti del Mediterraneo* [2006] ECR I-5177.

54 ECJ: Case C-224/01 *Köbler* [2003] ECR I-10239.

55 ECJ: *Francovich and Bonifaci v. Italy*, C-6/90 [1991] ECRI-5357.

56 Joined cases ECJ, Case C-46/93 and C-48/93, *Brasserie du pêcheur/Bundesrepublik Deutschland and The Queen v. Secretary of State for Transport, ex parte Factortame and others* [1996] ECR I-1029.

> breach which gave rise to the damage is attributable to the legislature, the judiciary or the executive. This must apply a fortiori in the Community legal order since all State authorities, including the legislature, are bound in performing their tasks to comply with the rules laid down by Community law directly governing the situation of individuals'.[57]

As the ECJ specified, a typical case of manifest infringement of community law is precisely *'the non compliance with the obligation to make a reference for preliminary ruling under the third paragraph of Article 234 EC.'*[58]

It was argued that these two judgments have to be read in the light of the ECJ's necessity to 'control' its relationship with national judges, after some questionable decisions were taken by the latter not to raise the preliminary question. As Cartabia pointed out: *'The fact remains, however, that the Court of Justice wants to punish the high courts that do not use, when necessary, the preliminary ruling ex Article 234 ECT.'*[59]

Besides, it is possible to link this judicial trend with other judgements issued by the ECJ, whereby the Court recognized that *'the liability of a member state under Article 169 arises whatever the agency of the state whose action or inaction is the cause of the failure to fulfil its obligations, even in the case of a constitutionally independent institution.'*[60]

Although Constitutional Courts are not expressly 'targeted' by these rulings, undoubtedly their own condition can be 'touched' by these judgments. It is therefore acceptable to suggest that the Constitutional Court could have given up a portion of its interpretative sovereignty also under the pressure coming from the judgements described above.

As Cartabia sharply concluded, somehow anticipating the latest events: 'The evolution of State liability as exemplified in the decisions *Köbler* and *Traghetti del Mediterraneo*, should solicit an overruling by the constitutional courts, preferably before facing the unpleasant hypothesis of requests for claims for damages on the part of individuals due to the constitutional courts' behaviour.'[61]

1.2 Final Remarks on this Point[62]

One should not overestimate the value of this *revirement* by enemy-CCs such as the ICC with regard to the ECJ: the Court was careful in preventing the revolutionary component of the decision from spreading and causing unexpected consequences. This means that the use of the preliminary

57 *Brasserie cit.*

58 *Köbler cit.*

59 Cartabia (2007).

60 ECJ: Case C-77/69 *Commission v. Belgium* [1970] ECR 243 ff; ECJ: Case C-8/70 *Commission v. Italy* [1970] ECR 966 ff; ECJ: C-100/77 *Commission v. Italy* [1978] ECR 887 ff.

61 Cartabia, (2007).

62 This paragraph reproduces the joint remarks contained in F. Fontanelli-G. Martinico (2010).

referral is undoubtedly limited to direct proceedings, and that this latter adjustment intervened to confirm the Court's traditional choice not to avail itself of Article 234 ECT. Whilst this minor overruling removed an unreasonable consequence of the Court's denial (the impossibility to obtain the ECJ's view in direct proceedings), the denial itself must stay, and it continues to raise a barrier between the ICC and the ECJ.

If, taken alone, this decision has no revolutionary impact, it is worth to consider it in a wider set of circumstances that could let one appreciate its peculiar value. In fact, this decision is not the only one dealing with the sensible matter of inter-judicial dialogue, although it is one out of few that actually treat it from a formal (*rectius*: procedural) perspective.

For instance, one can contrast this decision with the one issued in the *Berlusconi* case,[63] where the ICC decided to suspend a constitutionality proceeding it was handling, because a preliminary question was pending at the same time before the ECJ on the interpretation of an EC norm in relation to the same domestic provisions challenged before the ICC. The ICC preferred to prevent the possibility of issuing a decision in conflict with the ECJ, thus preferred to wait, and halted its proceeding. By doing this, the ICC re-created the effects of the preliminary referral to the ECJ (the suspension of the proceeding, the conformity with the ECJ's interpretation), still without using the procedure set forth in Article 234 ECT.

With order no. 103/2008, instead, the ICC decided to give up this unorthodox strategy. Finally aware of its 'judge' status, it could go for the institutional way and make use of Article 234 ECT. What is more, the ICC did not give up any of its competences, nor did it restrict its authority: by involving the ECJ, the ICC wishes to find authoritative/technical support to strengthen its own decision, but no transfer of jurisdiction to the ECJ actually occurred.

This new strategy (the preservation of its authoritativeness and of its apical position in the interpretive hierarchy, pursued involving the competitors, rather than excluding them) can be found also in the recent decisions no. 348 and 349/2007. There, the ICC acknowledged the obligation upon the ordinary judge to take into account the interpretation of the European Court of Human Rights, while applying the European Convention of Human Rights. In this case also, the ICC pledged allegiance to the interpretation of the European counterpart (the Strasbourg Court), but still kept for itself the possibility to assess the importance that this interpretation can bear in the domestic order (and to declare the unconstitutionality of the provisions of the Convention as interpreted by the Strasbourg Court).

This is why the commented decision embodies a significant change in the Court's case-law: after some informal attempts as the one described in the case of the 'double preliminarity' in *Berlusconi*, and after having instituted a formal relationship with another European Court (the Strasbourg Court), the ICC perceived that the dialogue with the ECJ had attained a degree of ripeness that

[63] *Corte Costituzionale*, ordinanza no. 165/2004, www.cortecostituzionale.it.

allowed for the opening of a formal channel such as the use of the preliminary referral.

In addition, the ICC will have to take the ECJ's ruling into account for the first time; the ECJ, in turn, will be called to demonstrate that it deserves the trust showed by the ICC, and it will probably behave in a careful and cooperative way. In sum, this order of reference opens a series of interesting procedural 'first times'. The contribution of this decision consists in having paved a (narrow) way for a new integration scheme between national and Community law, monitored by the ICC and ECJ-a scheme that now accompanies the traditional ordinary judge-ECJ relationship.

Nevertheless, taking into account the nature of the hidden dialogue,[64] which is characterized by a high level of 'discretion', it is too early to foresee what will happen. The interpretive struggle we have seen between courts was deeply influenced by the historical period it was set into; in the future, different conditions will most probably lead to different behaviour, in consistency with the dynamics of the comity principle. In other words, judicial cooperation must often be set into an egoistic framework, given that the reasons triggering comity could well be the same that, in other occasions, determine the rise of competition between courts[65]. In the next pages, the article will explain why one cannot really tell what will happen in the future with regard to this complicated *love/hate affair* between the ECJ and the CCs.

2 Looking for the Macro-Reasons for Such a New Trend

In this part, the article will focus on some factors which might have favoured the cooperation between CCs and the ECJ and contributed to the creation of a common ground between judicial actors.

In this respect, I have two arguments: first of all, the 'respect' shown by the ECJ towards the national constitutional structures of the Member States (and

64 By the formula 'hidden dialogue' I mean that unexplored side of the relationship between Constitutional Courts and the ECJ which feeds upon the somehow non-orthodox ways of judicial communication (that is, ways of judicial communication which are different from the preliminary ruling and which are not formalized according to the letter of the Treaties, i.e. art 234 ECT). Looking at the case-law of national constitutional courts', one can find some examples of such a phenomenon: the distinction between 'primacy' and 'supremacy ' (*Tribunal Constitucional*, Declaración 1/2004); admissibility of *recurso de amparo* against the refusal by domestic judges to raise the preliminary ruling (Tribunal Constitucional, sentencia 58/2004); the acknowledgment of *erga omnes* effects of ECJ's interpretive rulings (Corte Costituzionale, sentenza No. 113/1985 and 389/1989); dual preliminarity ('doppia pregiudizialità') see Corte Costituzionale, ordinanza No. 165/2004; Corte Costituzionale, ordinanza No. 536/1995); distinction between disapplication and non-application (Corte Costituzionale, sentenza No. 168/91). I used this formula in some papers of mine: Fontanelli- Martinico (2008); Martinico (2008); Martinico-Pollicino, (2008) 97-125.

65 Allard and Garapon (2005).

the consequent transformation of the primacy principle with the progressive emergence of a margin of appreciation doctrine in the ECJ's case-law); secondly, the latest developments of the ECJ's case-law in the field of fundamental rights.

2.1 Margin of Appreciation

Three years ago, Shany[66] wrote about a general margin of appreciation doctrine in international law to describe the process of progressive extension of this doctrine in tribunals other from the European Court of Human Rights.

Recently, some scholars in EU law[67] have taken this idea into further consideration in order to describe how the ECJ is attempting to *'locate the 'line' between EC review and legitimate Member State autonomy'*.[68]

As Weiler had already suggested, in fact, *'if fundamental rights are about the autonomy and self-determination of individual, fundamental boundaries are about the autonomy and self-determination of communities'*.[69]

When adopting this perspective, one can appreciate the ECJ's increasing attention to the peculiarities of the Member States in many sensitive areas.

Moreover, the ECJ has recently started to[70] quote the constitutional materials of the national judges or finding exceptions to obligations under EC law in national (rather than common) constitutional traditions:

> 'In that connection, it is not indispensable that restrictive measures laid down by the authorities of a Member State to protect the rights of the child, referred to in paragraphs 39 to 42 of this judgment, correspond to a conception shared by all Member States as regards the level of protection and the detailed rules relating to it (see, by analogy, Omega, paragraph 37). As that conception may vary from one Member State to another on the basis of, inter alia, moral or cultural views, Member States must be recognised as having a definite margin of discretion.'[71]

---

66 Shany (2006) 907-940. On this doctrine see also: Benvenisti (1998-1999), 843 ff; Hutchinson, (1999) 638 ff.; Lord Marclay of Clashfern (2000) 837; Prebensen (1998) 13 ff; de la Rasilla del Moral (2006) 611-624; Letzas (2006) 705-732.

67 For example, Shuibhne (2009) 230-256.

68 Shuibhne (2009), 243.

69 Weiler (1999) 102-129, 104.

70 This approach can be seen in many other cases: recently, for example, in *Gouvernement de la Communauté française et Gouvernement wallon*, where the ECJ attempted to prevent national constitutional law from standing in the way of the effectiveness of EC law, but, in the meantime, left manoeuvring room for those constitutional courts dealing with such issues. ECJ, Case C-212/06 *Gouvernement de la Communauté française et Gouvernement wallon*, not yet published. For a comment on this case see Van Elsuwege-Adam (2008) 655-711.

71 ECJ, Case C-244/06 *Dynamic Medien* [2008] ECR I-505.

These statements reveal the necessity to preserve national diversity as a fundamental value of integration, as expressed (also) in Article I-5 of the Constitutional Treaty (Article 4 of EUT after the Reform Treaty of Lisbon).[72]

According to Shany[73], the doctrine of margin of appreciation is based on two core elements:

a) Judicial deference. The courts should grant each other a certain degree of deference and respect each other's discretion.
b) Normative flexibility. International norms subject to this doctrine can be characterized as being open-ended or unsettled. Such norms provide the States with limited guidance and establish a broad zone of legality within which they are free to operate.

> 'Application of margin of appreciation doctrine depends on a variety of factors: a) the comparative advantage of local authorities-broader margins are afforded to local authorities with respect to questions they are better situated to assess (eg. Local moral sensitivities); b) the indeterminacy o the applicable standard- broader margins are granted over issues lacking a European consensus; and c) the nature of the contested interests- broader margins are granted when more important national interests are at stake and the alleged violation appears less fundamental'.[74]

This doctrine requires a certain attention to the legislative and factual situation of the national order involved in the case. It also implies the need for the ECJ to immerge itself in the constitutional structure of the national laws in order to make a preventive evaluation of its judgments.

This would require a case-by-case approach by the ECJ and a more frequent use of comparative law tools before the EC judge in order to evaluate the nature of the contested interests, the specificity of the domestic legal order at hand and the possible impact of its decision thereon.

We can find support for this approach in the latest judgements dealing with the issue of State liability in case of breach of the EC law. In *Konle*:[75]

---

72 The model for Article I-5 is undoubtedly Article 6 EUT ('current' version), which efficaciously describes the proximity between common constitutional traditions and national fundamental principles. In this article, in fact, these two kinds of legal sources are mentioned in two subsequent paragraphs. Here, suffice it to recall the reference that Article 6 ('current' version), par. 2 makes to the common constitutional traditions, and the reference to the 'national identities' of its Member States that is set in par. 3 of Article 6. I argue that, within a legal context, by the formula 'national identities' the European legislator referred to the constitutional identities of the Member States, that is to counter-limits, as defined by each national constitutional court. In this sense, one can say that Article I-5 of the Constitutional Treaty has simply codified such an interpretation expressly, by speaking about 'constitutional structure,' thus delivering the interpretation of counter-limits to the ECJ.

73 Shany (2007) 185.

74 Shany (2007) 187.

75 ECJ: C-302/97 *Konle* [1999] ECR I-3099.

> 'The answer to the fourth question must therefore be that, *in Member States with a federal structure*, reparation for damage caused to individuals by national measures taken in breach of Community law need not necessarily be provided by the federal State in order for the obligations of the Member State concerned under Community law to be fulfilled'.

At the same time, it is possible to read *Grant*[76] and *P v. S*[77] coherently by looking at the different impact of the ECJ's decisions on the factual background. In those cases, it was self-evident that the acknowledgement of rights of homosexual couples would have had much heavier financial repercussions on the Member States than those caused by the possible acknowledgement of transsexuals' rights. Consequently, such a decision would have been less understood by the States.

The ECJ plays its role of systemic actor well when it pays attention to the impact of its decision on the member states and to the current phase of European integration, such as it does in *Grant*:

> 'In the present state of the law within the Community, stable relationships between two persons of the same sex are not regarded as equivalent to marriages or stable relationships outside marriage between persons of opposite sex, and an employer is not therefore required by Community law to treat the situation of a person who has a stable relationship with a partner of the same sex as equivalent to that of a person who is married to or has a stable relationship outside marriage with a partner of the opposite sex. It is for the legislature alone to adopt, if appropriate, measures which may affect that position'.

These are only two examples of the attention given by the ECJ to the constitutional structures of the Member States; they reveal a strong hint to an attitude of judicial comity by the Court. Recently, the ECJ has demonstrated a tendency to allow for national constitutional traditions and structures which are not common to all Member States, but specific to one Member State (*Azores,*[78] *Omega*[79]). Such a behaviour may be related to the increasing use of comparative law by the ECJ:

> 'The methodology of comparative law to be employed by the Court has, therefore, to balance the respect of national legal traditions with the need to accommodate them to the specific needs of the EU legal order [...] in other words, it is not simply a question of determining what legal solution is common to the national legal orders. It is also, or mostly, a question of determining what legal solution fits

76 ECJ: C-249/96 *Grant v. South west trains Ltd* [1998] ECR I-621.

77 ECJ: C-13/94 *P/S and Cornwall County Council* [1996] ECR I-2143. See Pollicino (2004) 283-317

78 ECJ: Case C-88/03 *Portugal v. Commission* [2006] ECR I-7115, especially paras. 62-67.

79 ECJ: Case C-36/02 *Omega* [2004] ECR I-9609, paras. 34-35, 39-41. On *Omega* see Alemanno (2004709-751.

better with the EU legal order (in the light of its broader set of rules and principles and of its context of application). Comparative law becomes, in this way, one more instrument of what is the prevailing technique of interpretation at the Court: teleological interpretation'.[80]

As we will see, such a methodology might act as a boomerang and create many problems for the ECJ, should CCs feel that an external judged deprived them of their constitutional materials.

2.2 One Step Further: From Constitutionalization to the Idea of the Untouchable Core (i.e. the Absolute Rights in the Case Law of the ECJ)

After such judgements as *Kadi*,[81] scholars insisted on the definition of the ECJ as a constitutional court. Although it is questionable, this conclusion underlines the importance acquired by fundamental rights in the constitutional discourse of Europe. Without recalling the massive literature on the process of constitutionalization in the European Union in the past few years, I would like to stress a slightly different (but parallel) process. In this respect, having a look at the latest judgements of the ECJ one could pay attention to a further development in this process of constitutionalization: the progressive emergence of the category of absolute rights which may not be subjected to the balancing. The best example is given by the *Schmidberger* case:

> 'Thus, unlike other fundamental rights enshrined in that Convention, such as the right to life or the prohibition of torture and inhuman or degrading treatment or punishment, which admit of no restriction, neither the freedom of expression nor the freedom of assembly guaranteed by the ECHR appears to be absolute but must be viewed in relation to its social purpose. Consequently, the exercise of those rights may be restricted, provided that the restrictions in fact correspond to objectives of general interest and do not, taking account of the aim of the restrictions, constitute disproportionate and unacceptable interference, impairing the very substance of the rights guaranteed'.[82]

In *Schmidberger* the Court of Justice distinguished between two groups of fundamental rights: absolute rights, which admit of no restrictions, and other fundamental rights. Concerning the second category of rights, the Court of Justice admitted the necessity to evaluate the proportionality of their possible restrictions on a case-by-case basis. The Court went back to this selective,

80 Poiares Maduro (2007).

81 ECJ, Case C- 402/05 P *Kadi/Council and Commission*, not yet published

82 See, to that effect, ECJ, Case C-62/90 *Commission v. Germany* [1992] ECR I-2575, paragraph 23, and case ECJ C-404/92 *P X v. Commission* [1994] ECR I-4737, paragraph 18.

case-by-case approach to fundamental rights (conceived in *Schmidberger*) in the *Laval*[83] and *Viking*[84] cases.

In these judgements, the Court of Justice recognized the fundamental right to collective action as an integral part of EU Community law. The need to protect this right can justify restrictions on the fundamental freedom of establishment or on the freedom to provide services guaranteed under the EU Treaty, in order to protect workers and their conditions of employment. The Court of Justice added that this action is legal *'only if it pursues a legitimate aim such as the protection of workers'* and it has left the decision of legitimacy in this case up to national courts to decide, balancing the rationale of market integration with that of social policies.

The ECJ came back to the idea that an untouchable core of absolute rights exists in the *Kadi* case where the ECJ said:

> 'Fundamental rights form an integral part of the general principles of law whose observance the Court ensures. For that purpose, the Court draws inspiration from the constitutional traditions common to the Member States and from the guidelines supplied by international instruments for the protection of human rights on which the Member States have collaborated or to which they are signatories [...] It follows from all those considerations that the obligations imposed by an international agreement cannot have the effect of prejudicing the constitutional principles of the EC Treaty, which include the principle that all Community acts must respect fundamental rights, that respect constituting a condition of their lawfulness which it is for the Court to review in the framework of the complete system of legal remedies established by the Treaty.'

Beside this progressive attention to the fundamental rights issue, there is another relevant factor, which has been summarized by the double formula 'unionisation and conventionisation of fundamental rights':[85] the mutual influence of the two European legal systems (EC/EU law and ECHR) on one another.

On the one hand, in fact, ECtHR expressions entered the language of the ECJ thanks to two main tools: the general principles of Community law[86] and the Charter of fundamental rights of the EU.

Although the latter document is still not binding from a *stricto sensu* legal point of view, its proclamation favoured the emergence of a huge debate among scholars, especially among constitutional lawyers in continental Europe. Moreover, the ECJ has already begun to quote the Charter and refer to it[87] in spite of

---

83 ECJ, Case C-341/05 *Laval un Partneri Ltd/Svenska Byggnadsarbetareförbundet et a.* [2007] ECR I-11767.

84 ECJ, Case C-438/05 *The International Transport Workers' Federation and The Finnish Seamen's Union* [2007] ECR I-10779.

85 Callewaert (2008) 109-135.

86 On the interplay between ECHR and EC/EU Law see Groussot (2006) 63 ff.

87 Among the other cases, see ECJ: C-438/05 *The International Transport Workers' Federation and The Finnish Seamen's Union* [2007] ECR I-10779 and C-341/05, C-341/05 *Laval un Partneri Ltd /Svenska*

the Constitutional Treaty's (CT) failure to come into force and in the wait of the Reform Treaty (RT), which would make it legally binding (although the position of some Member States, such as the UK and Poland, is not clear because of the so called opt-out signed by these countries[88]).

More generally, the proclamation of the Charter of fundamental rights of the EU[89] brought new life to the debate about the drafting of a European Constitu-

---

Byggnadsarbetareförbundet. [2007] ECR I-11767.

88 Recently scholars have stressed the absurdity of the so called opting out by Poland and the UK with regard to the EU Charter of fundamental rights and the exclusion of the Charter itself from the text of the Reform Treaty. As we know, in fact, Article 6 EUT (Lisbon version) states that:
'The Union recognises the rights, freedoms and principles set out in the Charter of Fundamental Rights of the European Union of 7 December 2000, as adapted at Strasbourg, on 12 December 2007, which shall have the same legal value as the Treaties'. This article makes the Charter of fundamental rights part and parcel of EU primary law. In order to escape the risk of being subject to this document's provisions, the UK and Poland insisted on signing a specific protocol (n. 30), to the effect that:
'Article 1:
1. The charter does not extend the ability of the Court of Justice of the European Union, or any court or tribunal of Poland or of the United Kingdom, to find that the laws, regulations or administrative provisions, practices or action of Poland or of the United Kingdom are inconsistent with the fundamental rights, freedoms and principles that it reaffirms.
2. 'In particular, and for the avoidance of doubt, nothing in Title IV of the charter creates justiciable rights applicable to Poland or the United Kingdom except in so far as Poland or the United Kingdom has provided for such rights in its national law.'
'Article 2
To the extent that a provision of the charter refers to national laws and practices, it shall only apply to Poland or the United Kingdom to the extent that the rights or principles that it contains are recognised in the law or practices of Poland or of the United Kingdom'.
It was rightly observed that the goal of this protocol consisted in limiting the effect of the Charter without saying – as it would have been impossible to say under Article 6 EUT – that it is not binding for the UK and Poland. In fact, '*The opt-out is not an opt-out at all*' (Barnard 2008); one could find support for this hypothesis in the words of the House of Lords' Select Committee, according to which: 'The Protocol is not an opt-out from the Charter. The Charter will apply in the UK, even if its interpretation may be affected by the terms of the Protocol. The Preamble itself of the document does not use the qualification in terms of opt-out, its goal consists of the clarification of certain aspects of the application of the Charter' House of Lords EU Select Committee 'The Treaty of Lisbon: an impact assessment', http://www.publications.parliament.uk/pa/ld200708/ldselect/ldeucom/62/62.pdf. This protocol will not change much as long as the two Countries remain subject to those European acts that include reference to the EU Charter and the ECJ begins to quote and use the Charter of fundamental rights.

89 For a commentary see Feus (2000); Braibant (2001); UK House of Commons, Human Rights in the EU(2000); For a complete bibliography on the Nice Charter see http://www.arena.uio.no/cidel/cwatch/bibliography.html; Menéndez, (2001). For a very interesting introduction to the idea of a European constitutional law see: S. Douglas-Scott (2002) 3-44 and 515-530.

tion[90] and the possibility of a Bill of Rights at EU level,[91] since it testified the possibility to provide rights through a written instrument at supranational level, overcoming the ECJ's logic of *ius praetorium* in this field.

In its decision on case n. 540/03, the ECJ acknowledged a certain legally relevant role for the Charter. The Court reasoned:

> 'The Charter was solemnly proclaimed by the Parliament, the Council and the Commission in Nice on 7 December 2000. While the Charter is not a legally binding instrument, the Community legislature did, however, acknowledge its importance by stating, in the second recital in the preamble to the Directive, that the Directive observes the principles recognised not only by Article 8 of the ECHR but also in the Charter. Furthermore, the principal aim of the Charter, as is apparent from its preamble, is to reaffirm 'rights as they result, in particular, from the constitutional traditions and international obligations common to the Member States, the Treaty on European Union, the Community Treaties, the [ECHR], the Social Charters adopted by the Community and by the Council of Europe and the case-law of the Court [...] and of the European Court of Human Rights''.[92]

On the other hand, in the *Bosphorous*[93] case, the European Court of Human Rights, refused to review an EC regulation implementing a resolution of the UN Security Council, although the content of the EC act was restrictive of the property right.

The Strasbourg Court reached this conclusion under the conviction that the system of fundamental rights' safeguard guaranteed at the EC level and that provided by the ECHR are comparable.

In *Bosphorous*, the ECtHR used the same formula the German Constitutional Court adopted in *Solange* ('as long as') to introduce a sort of presumption of comparability, preventing a clash between jurisdictions.[94]

Such a presumption might be rebutted if, in the circumstances of a particular case, it was considered that the protection of Convention rights was manifestly deficient. Due to its ambiguity, this notion attracted fierce critique by the literature as well as by some components of the Court itself in their concurring opinions:

> 'In spite of its relatively undefined nature, the criterion 'manifestly deficient' appears to establish a relatively low threshold, which is in marked contrast to

[90] See the image by Pinelli (2002).

[91] Grimm (2003) 15 ff.; Mayer (2003) 175-196; Skouris (2004) 254 ff.

[92] ECJ: Case C-540/03 *Parliament v. Council* [2006] ECR I-5769.

[93] ECHR *Bosphorus Hava v. Ireland*, judgment of 30 June 2005.

[94] 'Paradoxically, the safeguard of core rights, far from being the reason for the application of the counter-limit doctrine, was used as harmonizing platform, and both tribunal sacrificed their own particular conception to pledge allegiance to the Court of Justice, or to support it' Fontanelli in Martinico-Fontanelli (2008).

> the supervision generally carried out under the European Convention on Human Rights. Since the Convention establishes a minimum level of protection (Article 53), any equivalence between it and the Community's protection can only ever be in terms of the means, not of the result'.

In the same decision, the ECtHR also paid attention to the Nice Charter, adding:

> 'Moreover, it seems all the more difficult to accept that Community law could be authorised, in the name of 'equivalent protection', to apply standards that are less stringent than those of the European Convention on Human Rights when we consider that the latter were formally drawn on in the Charter of Fundamental Rights of the European Union, itself an integral part of the Union's Treaty establishing a Constitution for Europe. Although these texts have not (yet) entered into force, Article II-112(3) of the Treaty contains a rule whose moral weight would already appear to be binding on any future legislative or judicial developments in European Union law: 'Insofar as this Charter contains rights which correspond to rights guaranteed by the Convention for the Protection of Human Rights and Fundamental Freedoms, the meaning and scope of those rights shall be the same as those laid down by the said Convention'.[95]

In *Bosphorus*, the ECtHR, despite the *prima facie* impression of judicial clash, preferred to act as a cooperative actor. In this sense one would be tempted to conclude for the birth of an instance of cooperative constitutionalism, as the outcome of a process of '*integration through rights*'.[96] Nevertheless, before reaching such an optimistic conclusion, I would like to enrich the picture by spotlighting some possible factors of tension between judicial actors.

3 Are We Watching a Happy Ending? The ECJ under Siege

Bearing this conclusion in mind, one could notice that there have recently been many factors of contrast between the ECJ and national Courts. As we saw, in the wake of the *Köbler* and *Traghetti del Mediterraneo* cases, there was a huge debate over the possibility for the ECJ to jeopardize the principle of national *res judicata* in order to ensure the uniformity of interpretation. The problem of the equilibrium between the need for interpretive uniformity and the respect for the principle of *res judicata* was tackled by the ECJ in the *Kühne & Heitz* case.[97] There (with regard to administrative decisions), the ECJ clearly expressed its preference for the overcoming of the national *res judicata*, where the applicable national law allows it. This reference to national autonomy (suggested by the *a quo* judge himself when raising the preliminary question)

95 Judges Rozakis, Tulkens, Traja, Botoucharova, Zagrebelsky and Garlicki.

96 Scheeck (2005) 837-885.

97 ECJ: Case C-453/00 *Kühne & Heitz* [2004] ECR I-837.

seems to mitigate the strong acceleration for the ECJ's interpretive uniformity. In *Kapferer*,[98] the ECJ answered a preliminary question raised by the *Landesgericht Innsbruck* (Austria) in the proceedings *Rosmarie Kapferer* versus *Schlank & Schick GmbH*. The *a quo* judge expressly proposed the possibility to extend the *Kühne & Heitz* principle to the case of *res judicata* in a judicial decision. The ECJ highlighted that:

> 'It should be added that the judgment in Kühne & Heitz, to which the national court refers in Question 1(a), is not such as to call into question the foregoing analysis. Even assuming that the principles laid down in that judgment could be transposed into a context which, like that of the main proceedings, relates to a final judicial decision, it should be recalled that that judgment makes the obligation of the body concerned to review a final decision, which would appear to have been adopted in breach of Community law subject, in accordance with Article 10 EC, to the condition, inter alia, that that body should be empowered under national law to reopen that decision (see paragraphs 26 and 28 of that judgment). In this case it is sufficient to note that it is apparent from the reference for a preliminary ruling that that condition has not been satisfied.'[99]

The *Kapferer* doctrine seemed to resolve the issue. Yet, a few months after that decision, the ECJ dealt with another interesting case: *Lucchini*.[100] In *Lucchini* the ECJ, following the Opinion of General Advocate Geelhoed, concluded that: '*Community law precludes the application of a provision of national law, such as Article 2909 of the Italian Civil Code, which seeks to lay down the principle of res judicata in so far as the application of that provision prevents the recovery of State aid granted in breach of Community law which has been found to be incompatible with the common market in a decision of the Commission which has become final.*' As I have elsewhere[101] argued, my impression is that one can explain the final conclusion reached in *Lucchini* by the fact that the contested decision was issued *ultra vires*. Indeed, as the ECJ itself recalled, that the challenged decision had been adopted on a subject of undisputed Community competence, given that national courts '*do not have jurisdiction to give a decision on whether State aid is compatible with the common market.*'[102] As Advocate General Geelhoed said, the principle of *res judicata* cannot permit the persistence of a judicial decision which amounts to a clear violation of the simplest separation of competences between the ECs

---

98 ECJ: Case C-234/04 *Kapferer* [2006] ECR I-2585.

99 ECJ: Case C-234/04 *Kapferer* [2006] ECR I-2585, par. 23.

100 ECJ: Case C-119/05 *Ministero dell'Industria, del Commercio e dell'Artigianato v. Lucchini SpA* [2007] ECR I-6199. About *Lucchini* see: Groussot- Minseen (2007) 385-417.

101 Martinico (2009).

102 ECJ: Case C-119/05 *Ministero dell'Industria, del Commercio e dell'Artigianato v. Lucchini SpA* [2007] ECR I-6199.

and the Member States.[103] *Lucchini* seemed to be an extra-ordinary judgement, unlikely to set a precedent on the point; broadly speaking, the judicial autonomy of the Member States did not seem to be put in doubt. However, a few months ago, in *Cartesio* the ECJ '*has opened the possibility for national Courts to make references and maintain them, even if they are quashed on appeal by a superior Court on points of EC Law*'[104] thus jeopardizing the '*national judicial autonomy*' of the States.[105]

Alongside this decision-which once more raised the question whether the aim of the ECJ is to build a sort of judicial hierarchy to be considered as alternative to the national one – one should pay attention to other contested decisions, which pawed the way to several critiques against the ECJ's work. suffice it to recall the heated debate raised after the *Mangold* decision.

As seen, the national and the supranational legal order are progressively converging in the field of fundamental rights. Moreover, the ECJ started acknowledging an important role to the national constitutional materials in its decision.

This 'partial' appropriation of the fundamental rights' discourse by the ECJ emerges in a long series of judgements, and it is most evident in cases such as *Omega*[106]and *Dynamic Medien*.[107] As some authors pointed out, having a look at

---

[103] 'In short, the key question is whether a final judgment which came about in the circumstances referred to above, which, as is evident from the previous point, may have serious implications for the division of powers between the Community and the Member States, as this results from the Treaty itself, and which would also make it impossible for the powers assigned to the Commission to be exercised, must be considered inviolable. To my mind, that is not the case', Opinion of the AG Geelhoed on the *Lucchini* case, delivered on 14 Sept. 2006.

[104] Sarmiento (2009). See the point: 'Where rules of national law apply which relate to the right of appeal against a decision making a reference for a preliminary ruling, and under those rules the main proceedings remain pending before the referring court in their entirety, the order for reference alone being the subject of a limited appeal, the second paragraph of Article 234 EC is to be interpreted as meaning that the jurisdiction conferred by that provision of the Treaty on any national court or tribunal to make a reference to the Court for a preliminary ruling cannot be called into question by the application of those rules, where they permit the appellate court to vary the order for reference, to set aside the reference and to order the referring court to resume the domestic law proceedings' ECJ: Case C-210/06 *Cartesio*, not yet published.

[105] 'Cartesio raises many questions about the degree of interference that the ECJ is willing to inflict on national judicial autonomy, but it is clear from its wording that national Courts that engage in a preliminary discourse with the Luxembourg Court are protected from most appellate intrusions of superior domestic Courts. When the ECJ states that a revocation or an amendment from the appellate jurisdiction is a matter that the inferior court 'alone is able to take a decision on', it is conferring on the said Court a power to disregard a judgement delivered by an appellate Court, on a case that will eventually return to that same jurisdiction when the judgements of the ECJ and the referring court are dictated', Sarmiento (2009)

[106] ECJ: Case C-36/02 *Omega* [2004] ECR I-9609.

[107] ECJ: Case C-244/06 *Dynamic Medien*, not yet published.

those cases one can perceive a certain concern over the 'octroyée *methodology of construing common constitutional traditions*'.[108]

Now, such a methodology has its own risks, as shown in the *Mangold* case, where the ECJ stated that:

> 'Directive 2000/78 does not itself lay down the principle of equal treatment in the field of employment and occupation. Indeed, in accordance with Article 1 thereof, the sole purpose of the directive is 'to lay down a general framework for combating discrimination on the grounds of religion or belief, disability, age or sexual orientation', the source of the actual principle underlying the prohibition of those forms of discrimination being found, as is clear from the third and fourth recitals in the preamble to the directive, in various international instruments and in the constitutional traditions common to the Member States [...] The principle of non-discrimination on grounds of age must thus be regarded as a general principle of Community law [...].'[109]

Some German scholars strongly contested the possibility to infer such a principle from the constitutional traditions common to the Member States. In an article published in English on *Euobserver,* Herzog and Gerken stressed:

> 'However, this 'general principle of community law' was a fabrication. In only two of the then 25 member states namely Finland and Portugal is there any reference to a ban on age discrimination, and in not one international treaty is there any mention at all of there being such a ban, contrary to the terse allegation of the ECJ. Consequently, it is not difficult to see why the ECJ dispensed with any degree of specification or any proof of its allegation. To put it bluntly, with this construction which the ECJ more or less pulled out of a hat, they were acting not as part of the judicial power but as the legislature'.[110]

In his critique of *Mangold,* Hatzopoulos[111] stressed how this reference to general principles weakens the legal reasoning of the ECJ and contested the resort thereto in other judgements like *Carpenter*[112] and *Karner.*[113]

Recently, another strong attack to the ECJ came from an Editorial of the *European Law Review.*[114] In a sort of short case-note on the *Commission/Italy*[115] decision, it was argued that the enlargement and the massive case load of the ECJ might jeopardize the coherence of its case-law:

108 Dani (2008).

109 ECJ: Case C-144/04 *Mangold* [2005] ECRI-9981.

110 Herzog-Gerken (2008).

111 Hatzopoulos (2007) 309-342, 337.

112 ECJ: Case C-60/00 *Carpenter* [2002] ECR I-6279.

113 ECJ: Case C-71/02, *Karner* [2004] ECR I-3025.

114 (2009) 173-174.

115 ECJ: Case C-110/05 *Commission v. Italy,* not yet published.

> 'The European Court of Justice is manifestly no longer 'tucked away in the fairyland Duchy of Luxembourg'. The new Palais, inaugurated on December 4, 2008, is a complex collection of buildings that, quite literally, consume the original Palais within a ring-like structure, alongside the original Court of First Instance and, most prominently, two high-rise towers (making unfortunate allusions to Tolkien difficult to suppress). The overall visual impact is one of enormous scale; but also, seeing the mismatched structures that differ from one another in almost every way – size, materials, scale – dysfunction. Within the Court of Justice, another striking image comes from the cavernous room in which the full court holds its réunion générale. In particular, to accommodate 27 judges, eight Advocates General and the Registrar, the long table in that room is, quite simply, vast. What that picture suggests is that the possibility for organic, unstructured discussion is impossible to reconcile with the present size of this judicial college'.

These are just a few instances showing how the picture is much more complicated than one could expect looking exclusively at the mentioned decisions of national constitutional courts. Before talking about a new era of stability and cooperation between courts, one should take account of the tensions between national and domestic legal orders: was it just a temporary truce?

4 Synopsis

This article aimed at describing the new trends in the relationship between the ECJ and Constitutional Courts. From a situation characterized by the reluctance by the latter to raise preliminary references to the former, we moved to a context where CCs do raise preliminary references. After trying to identify the main reasons for this strategy-change, the article explained why one ought to consider this situation as a temporary truce rather than the beginning of a stable cooperation.

References

J. Allard, A. Garapon, *Les juges dans la mondialisation*, Seuil, 2005.

D. Basile, 'La nozione di 'giurisdizione nazionale' nella giurisprudenza della Corte di giustizia. Aspetti problematici e profili comparativi' [2006] *Foro Amm. C.d.S.* 696 ff.

N. Bassi, 'Ancora sul rinvio pregiudiziale alla Corte di giustizia e sulla nozione di 'giudice nazionale': è il momento della Corte Costituzionale?' [2000] *Riv. It. Dir. Pubbl. Comunitario* 155 ff.

E. Benvenisti, 'Margin of appreciation, consensus, and universal standards' [1999] *New York University Journal of International Law and Politics* 843 ff.

F. Biondi Dal Monte, F. Fontanelli, 'The Decisions No. 348 and 349/2007 of the Italian Constitutional Court: The Efficacy of the European Convention in the Italian Legal System' [2008] *German Law Journal* 889 ff.

G. Braibant, *La Charte des droits fondamentaux de l'Union européenne. Témoignage et commentaires*, Seuil, 2001.

R. Calvano, 'La Corte costituzionale 'fa i conti' per la prima volta con il nuovo Articolo 117 comma 1 Cost.' [2005] *Giur. Cost.* 4417 ff.

J. Callewaert, ''Unionisation' and 'conventionisation' of fundamental rights in Europe: the interplay between union and convention law and its impact on the domestic legal systems of the member states', in J. Wouters, A. Nollkaemper, E. de Wet (eds.), *The Europeanisation of International Law. The Status of International Law in the EU and its Member States*, T.M.C. Asser Press, 2008, 109 ff.

S.M. Carbone, 'Corte Costituzionale, pregiudiziale comunitaria e uniforme applicazione del diritto comunitario' [2007] *Il Diritto dell'Unione Europea* 707 ff.

M. Cartabia, 'Taking Dialogue Seriously' The Renewed Need for a Judicial Dialogue at the Time of Constitutional Activism in the European Union' [2007] *Jean Monnet Working Paper* 12/07.

M. Cartabia – J.H.H. Weiler, *L'Italia in Europa, Il Mulino*, 2000.

S. Catalano, 'L'incidenza del nuovo articolo 117, comma 1, Cost. sui rapporti fra norme interne e norme comunitarie', in N. Zanon (ed.), *Le Corti dell'integrazione europea e la Corte costituzionale italiana*, ESI, 2006, 129 ff.

A. Celotto, 'Le fonti comunitarie', in G. Corso – V. Lopilato (eds), *Il diritto amministrativo dopo le riforme costituzionali – parte generale*, Giuffrè, 2006, 121 ff.

E. Cheli, *Atto politico e funzione di indirizzo politico*, Giuffrè, 1968.

R. Chieppa, 'Nuove prospettive per il controllo di compatibilità comunitaria da parte della Corte costituzionale' [2007] *Il Diritto dell'Unione Europea* 493 ff.

M. Claes, *The national courts' mandate in the European Constitution*, Hart Publishing, 2006.

V. Crisafulli, *La Costituzione e le sue disposizioni di principio*, Giuffrè, 1952.

M.T. D'Alessio, N. Pecchioli, 'Ricorso straordinario al presidente della repubblica e rinvio pregiudiziale: la logica «fuzzy» della Corte di giustizia' [1998] *Riv. It. Dir. Pubbl. Comunitario* 699 ff.

M. Dani, 'Tracking Judicial Dialogue-The Scope for Preliminary Rulings from the Italian Constitutional Court' [2008] *Jean Monnet Working Paper* 10/2008.

I. de la Rasilla del Moral ,'The Increasingly Marginal Appreciation of the Margin-of-Appreciation Doctrine' [2006] *German Law Journal* 611 ff.

M. Dogliani, *Interpretazioni della Costituzione*, F. Angeli, 1982.

S. Douglas-Scott, *Constitutional law of the European Union*, Longman, 2002.

Editorial, 'A court within a court: is it time to rebuild the court of justice' [2009] *European Law Review* 173 ff.

K. Feus (ed.), *The EU Charter of Fundamental Rights – text and commentaries*, Federal Trust, 2000.

D. Grimm, 'Il significato della stesura di un catalogo europeo dei diritti fondamentali nell'ottica della critica dell'ipotesi di una Costituzione europea', in G. Zagrebelsky (ed.) *Diritti e Costituzione nell'Unione Europea*, Laterza, 2003, 15 ff.

T. Groppi, 'La Corte costituzionale come giudice del rinvio ai sensi dell'art. 177 del Trattato CE', in P. Ciarlo, G. Pitruzzella, R. Tarchi (eds.), *Giudici e giurisdizione nella giurisprudenza della Corte costituzionale*, Giappichelli, 1997, 171 ff.

G. Grottanelli De Santi, 'Atto politico e atto di governo', *Enciclopedia Giuridica*, Vol. IV, Istituto della Enciclopedia Italiana, 1988.

X. Groussot, *General Principles of Community Law*, Europa Law Publishing, 2006.

X. Groussot, T. Minseen, '*Res Judicata* in the Court of Justice Case-Law: Balancing Legal Certainty with Legality?' [2007] *European Constitutional Law Review* 385 ff.

V. Hatzopoulos, 'Why the Open Method of Coordination is Bad for You: A Letter to the EU' [2007] *European Law Journal* 309 ff.

R. Herzog, L. Gerken, '[Comment] Stop the European Court of Justice', available at http://euobserver.com/9/26714.

M.R. Hutchinson, 'The Margin of Appreciation Doctrine in the European Court of Human Rights' [1999] *International and Comparative Law Quarterly* 638 ff.

U. Jedliczka 'The Austrian Constitutional Court and the European Court of Justice' [2008] *International Journal of Constitutional Law* 301 ff.

J. Komarek, 'European Constitutionalism and the European Arrest Warrant: in search of the limits of contrapunctual principles' [2005] *Jean Monnet Working paper* 10/05.

G. Letzas, 'Two Concepts of the Margin of Appreciation' [2006] *Oxford Journal of Legal Studies* 705 ff.

F. Mayer, 'La Charte européenne des droits fondamentaux et la Constitution européenne' [2003] *Revue trimestrielle de droit européen* 175 ff.

F.C. Mayer, 'The European Constitution and the Courts', in A. von Bogdandy, J. Bast (eds.), *Principles of European Constitutional Law*, Hart Publisher, 2006, 281 ff.

M. Poiares Maduro, 'Interpreting European Law: Judicial Adjudication in a context of constitutional pluralism' [2007] *European Journal of Legal studies*, available at http://www.ejls.eu/2/25UK.html.

Lord Marclay of Clashfern, 'The Margin of Appreciation and the Need for a Balance', in Protection des droits de l'homme: la perspective européenne, in P. Mahoney et al. (eds.), *Protection des droits de l'homme: la perspective européenne. Mélanges à la mémoire de Rolv Ryssdal*, Verlag, 2000, 837 ff.

G. Martinico, F. Fontanelli, 'The Hidden Dialogue: When Judicial Competitors Collaborate' [2008] *Global Jurist Advances*, available at http://www.bepress.com/gj/vol8/iss3/art7.

G. Martinico, 'A Matter of Coherence in the Multilevel Legal System: Are the 'Lions' Still 'Under the Throne'?' [2008] *Jean Monnet Working Paper* 16/08.

G. Martinico, O. Pollicino, 'Between constitutional tolerance and judicial activism: the 'specificity' of the European judicial law' [2008] *European Journal of Law Reform* 97 ff.

G. Martinico, 'Constructivism, Evolutionism and Pluralism: Europe's Constitutional Grammar' [2009] *King's Law Journal* 309 ff.

J.A. Menéndez, 'Chartering Europe: The Charter of Fundamental Rights of the European Union' [2001] *Arena Working Paper* 01/13.

A. Pajno, 'Il rispetto dei vincoli derivanti dall'ordinamento comunitario come limite alla potestà legislativa nel nuovo Titolo v. della Costituzione' [2003] *Le Istituzioni del federalismo* 814 ff.

F. Paterniti, 'La riforma dell'Articolo 117, comma 1, Cost. e le nuove prospettive nei rapporti tra ordinamento giuridico nazionale e Unione Europea' [2004] *Giur. Cost.* 2101 ff.

C. Pinelli, *Il momento della scrittura*, Il Mulino, 2002.

C. Pinelli, 'I limiti generali alla potestà legislativa statale e regionale e i rapporti con l'ordinamento comunitario' [2001] *Foro italiano* (V), 194 ff.

A. Pizzorusso, 'Uso e abuso del diritto processuale costituzionale', in M.Bessone (ed.), *Diritto giurisprudenziale*, Giappichelli, 1996, 133 ff.

O. Pollicino, 'New Emerging Judicial Dynamics of the Relationship Between National and the European Courts after the Enlargement of Europe' [2008] *Jean Monnet Working Paper* 14/08.

O. Pollicino, 'Legal Reasoning of the Court of Justice in the Context of the Principle of Equality Between Judicial Activism and Self-restraint' [2003] *German Law Journal* 283 ff.

S.C. Prebensen, 'The Margin of Appreciation and Articles 9, 10 and 11 of the Convention' [1998] *Human Rights Law Journal* 13 ff.

R. Romboli, *Il giudizio costituzionale incidentale come processo senza parti*, Giuffrè, 1985.

A. Ruggeri, 'Riforma del titolo V e giudizi di 'comunitarietà' delle leggi', available at http://www.associazionedeicostituzionalisti.it/dottrina/ordinamentieuropei/ruggeri.html.

D. Sarmiento, 'The Silent Lamb and the Deaf Wolves Constitutional pluralism, preliminary references and the role of silent judgments in EU Law', paper presented at the conference 'Constitutional Pluralism in the European Union and Beyond', held at St Anne's College, Oxford, 20-21 March 2009.

L. Scheeck, 'The relationship between the European Courts and integration through human rights' [2005] *Zeitschrift für ausländisches öffentliches Recht und Völkerrecht* 837 ff.

Y. Shany, 'Toward a General Margin of Appreciation Doctrine in International Law?' [2006] *European Journal of International Law* 907 ff.

Y. Shany, *Regulating jurisdictional relations between national & international courts*, Oxford University Press, 2007.

V. Skouris, 'La protezione dei diritti fondamentali nell'Unione europea nella prospettiva dell'adozione di una Costituzione europea', in L.S. Rossi (ed)., *Il progetto di Trattato-Costituzione, verso una nuova architettura dell'Unione europea*, Il Mulino, 2004, 254 ff.

N. Nic Shuibhne 'Margins of Appreciation: National Values, Fundamental Rights and EC Free Movement Law' [2009] *European Law Review* 230 ff.

T. Vandamme, 'Prochain Arrêt: La Belgique! Explaining Recent Preliminary References of the Belgian Constitutional Court' [2008] *European Constitutional Law Review* 127 ff.

P. Van Elsuwege, S. Adam, 'Situations purement internes, discriminations à rebours et collectivités autonomes après l'arrêt sur l'assurance soins flamande' [2008] *Cahiers de droit européen* 655 ff.

C. Vidal Prado, *El impacto del nuevo derecho europeo en los Tribunales Constitucionales*, Colex, 2004.

J.H.H. Weiler, 'Fundamental Rights and Fundamental Boundaries: On Standards and Values in the Protection of Human Rights', in J.H.H.Weiler, *The Constitution of Europe*, Cambridge University Press, 1999, 102 ff.

G. Zagrebelsky, 'Diritto processuale costituzionale?', in AA.VV., *Giudizio 'a quo' e promovimento del processo costituzionale*, Giuffrè, 1990, 105 ff.

CHAPTER 8

ECJ and Administrative Courts in EU Member States

Towards a Common Judicial Reasoning?

Fulvio Cortese*

1 Introduction

This paper briefly analyses selected judgements of administrative judges operating within the EU Member States.

It pays special attention to certain trends in case law within the legal systems that traditionally represent the core of the community integration process, namely France, Italy, Germany and Belgium.

To be precise, the scope of this analysis is to assess the *methods* applied by the courts in these legal systems to reiterate their State's belonging to the European Union on the one hand, and the effects of European administrative law on the principles and rules of national administrative law on the other.

Issues that are quite far from being original or unexplored fields of research. European legal theory and practice has long been trying to understand how national judges operate as direct players in implementing and interpreting community law.[1]

The majority of researchers are also well aware of the vital role national judges play in implementing community law, particularly if we look at the progressive consolidation of a continuous exchange between these judges and the European Court of Justice. In fact, we feel right in affirming that up to now this kind of exchange has been converting national judges into European judges and the effect has been that the European legal system can currently count on a close network of jurisdictions, often very different from one another, although from an operative point of view it is perfectly suited to ensuring an effective, uniform application of both European written law and European law resulting from the ECJ interpretation activity.[2]

Despite these significant achievements, the question nevertheless remains of which *methodological approach* would make judges in each single state feel part of a this integrated judicial system and, moreover, what is the *system-based assumption* underpinning each Court's reasoning.

2 A Possible Interpretation

We will try to formulate an initial, and maybe partly contrasting, interpretation of this specific issue.

Over and beyond the many occasions where national judges prove to be means of the contingent reiteration of the prevalence of community law and its principles, with a consequent *tangible implementation* of real and exclusive

* Researcher of Public Law (Faculty of Law – University of Trento, Italy).

1 See, for some examples, the recent study of Backes/Eliantonio (2009); Stone Sweet/T.L. Brunell, (1997); Tridimas/Tridimas (2002).

2 There is a wide literature on this subject. For an overview of the different approaches and interpretations as well as for further bibliographical references, see, from an Italian perspective, Ferrari (2006). In general, see the fundamental studies collected by Slaughter/Stone Sweet/Weiler (1998); Koopmans (2003).

community rules, it has to be verified whether it is possible for references to European law sources or to the ECJ's jurisprudence to represent a fundamental chance to development or rearrange the typical national debates on interpretation and, as a result, if they can be seen as an opportunity to *re-establish* some very important *traits and differences* in the legal system. In other words, we do not merely want to draw attention to the fact that national judges usually treat European law as they would foreign law, that is to say as a support for the logic or theoretical correctness behind a given decision when put under *comparative analysis*. This is a common situation, which has been a privileged field of implementation in many interesting, in-depth studies.[3]

This brief analysis mainly focuses on the fact that references made by national judges to European law and to its ECJ interpretation often play key roles in endorsing specific reasoning or interpretation that already exists in *national law*. This aspect is well worth our attention. In each case it can lead to the paradoxical assessment of the full suitability or the partial/total unsuitability of internal law concerning specific standards of protection, depending on the effective utility any one of these two results can provide to recognise whichever applicability the internal law considers as a necessary *constant* in its identity.[4]

In fact, it could arise that, in the same moment national judges feel European and realise the real need to leave room for the laws produced by the ECJ, the integration of judicial systems becomes a way to recover traditional theories and typically national recovery characteristics. Another question can now be made: is this a wholly negative issue or are we facing yet another important confirmation of the fact that the success of European integration is inherently based on a delicate process of constantly balancing uniformity and difference?

Before answering this question we have to deal directly with this theme, recalling cases and judgements that offer very significant signs of this problem, as previously said.

3 See Markesinis/Fedtke (2006).

4 For a first introduction to the concept of 'invariant' within the administrative law, see Giannini (2000) 3.

3 Relationships between Legal Systems: European Solutions and [...] National Reasoning

First of all, to test the reliability of this thesis it would be useful to consider the way in which administrative judges in national legal systems describe and justify the relationship between community law and internal law.

A recent, famous judgement by the French *Conseil d'Etat* offers an excellent example: specifically, it refers to the *arrêt Arcelor* (8th February 2007) concerning air-borne pollution[5]. The judgement was welcomed by national press as *'un noveau transfert de la souveraineté française au niveau europèen'*.[6]

In fact, in this case, despite the longstanding commitment to guaranteeing the *primauté* of community law over internal law,[7] for the first time the *Conseil d'Etat* openly acknowledged the *constitutional significance* of France as a member of the European Union. However, this was achieved by permitting administrative judges to perform, within their own independent control, a complex series of evaluations concerning the constitutionality of legislative acts or regulations resulting from the integral transposition of community directives.

In effect, in this specific case the *Conseil d'Etat* established that, with respect to the aforesaid legislative acts, the possibility of a direct judgement of constitutionality is connected to the preparatory need for determining the existence of a community principle (even resulting from the ECJ legal theory) that can ensure the same guarantees as the internal constitutional principle.

If this is the case, the judging body would be entitled to evaluate the existence of a contrast between the transposition law decrees and the community principle. For the case on hand, under this evaluation: a) *'in absence de difficultè seriouse'* in the possibility of finding a contrast, the judge should reject the constitutionality issue; b) *vice versa*, when in doubt, the judge should sustain the preparatory reference procedure under EC Article 234.

On the contrary, if a community legal principle 'equivalent' to the national principle is not found, the judge may reserve the right to independently ascertain the unconstitutionality of the source of the internal law.

---

5 The case is well known. To counteract the harmful consequences of the airborne pollution, the EU (25th April 2002) ratified the Kyoto Protocol: the EU Member States agreed to reduce their gas emissions in accordance with Protocol. Concerning these emissions, the EU Institutions (13th October 2003) adopted the Directive 2003/87/CE, to establish a quota system. The Directive was transposed in France too, without modifications (*ordonnance*, 15th April 2002; *decret*, 19th August 2004). The multinational firm *Arcelor*, leading manufacturer of steel in Europe, lodged an administrative appeal to the *Conseil d'Etat*, to obtain the annulment of the *decret*. In particular *Arcelor* alleged a breach of the national constitutional principle of equality, because the *decret* excluded the producers of plastic and aluminium from the number of the firms forced to reduce their emissions.

6 From *Le Monde*, 9th February 2007. For commentaries on this subject, see Chaltiel (2007) 335; Magnon (2007) 578; Pollicino (2007) 895; Mayer/Lenski/Wendel (2008) 63.

7 See Dicosola (2007) 615.

This interpretation is, at least, ambiguous and it is quite possible that French case law gives a similar interpretation, by which the *Conseil d'Etat* is thought to have further consolidated the principle of community law *primauté*. However, a much more significant point immediately comes to light in the situation where the French administrative judge actually concludes by underscoring a totally restrictive interpretation of the directions proposed by the *Conseil constitutionnel*, thereby choosing a *given interpretation* of the principles applied by the constitutional judge.[8]

This latter case, in 2004 (see judgement n. 496 dated 10th June) clearly explained that the principle of community law's prevalence must be balanced with the principle of a superior role of the Constitution, and therefore any verification of unconstitutionality of the internal transposition law decrees of community law is only possible if the laws clash with the '*identitè constitutionelle de la France*', in other words with any constitutional principles having no specific equivalent in the community legal system.

In the reasoning of the *Conseil d'Etat*, the reconstruction made by the constitutional judge is *interpreted* in a certain way, meaning that '*in the logical reasoning*' of the former '*there is an extra passage which makes all the difference*', namely '*the case by case verification of the suitability of the principle identified on a community level to guarantee an equivalent protection standard to the one provided by the principle applied on a constitutional level*'.[9]

However, a further element has to be highlighted: as we have seen, according to the *Conseil d'Etat* the verification of equivalence between the transposition law and the so-called 'equivalent' community principle can generally fall under the sole jurisdiction of national judges, since they can appeal to Article 234 EC only in cases of '*difficultè seriouse*'.

Although this theory can be given different interpretations – on the one hand, it leaves ample room to the national administrative judge; on the other hand it first reveals the *Conseil d'Etat's* historical will to admit the need for a regular recourse to the mechanism provided by Article 234 EC – there is no doubt that the methodological direction chosen by the administrative judge leads to the emergence, even in the specific case, of a characteristic technique of the French legal system, namely that of the 'clear act', purposely outlined in order to consent the control in legal theory a certain amount of discretionary power within the evaluation of its field of choice.[10]

It is quite possible that the *regulatory* use of this technique can produce effects that are *regularly* conflicting, both with those partially accepted by the ECJ in the renowned *Foto-Frost* case (judgement 22nd October 1987, C-314/85),[11]

8 For a reconstruction of French constitutional judges' directions, see Dutheillet De Lamothe (2006); Cassia (2007) 406; Costanzo (2007) 3763.

9 See Pollicino (2007).

10 *Ibid.*

11 ECJ: Case C-314/85 *Foto-Frost v. Hauptzollamt Lübeck-Ost* [1987] ECR I-4199. See Arnull (1988) 125; Goffin(1990) 216.

and with any cases that some Constitutional Courts (*e.g.* the German and Italian courts) have traditionally suggested within the self-attribution of the power of declaring the constitutionality of community law in defence of fundamental rights and/or freedoms ensured by internal law.[12]

This shows that even in the relationship between internal law and national law, there are still significant differences of approach and that, in balancing the needs of national sovereignty and the executive needs of community law, the national judge tends to perform a recovery actions, which commits him to a delicate and often 'implicit' case history activity aimed at assessing, even indirectly, the interpretative techniques that are typical of his tradition and directly connected to the historical acknowledgement of his institutional role within the legal system.

This approach is generally found in the German administrative legal theory and practice, which at times appears quite in unique in its exchange with the ECJ.

It may help to remember the renowned *Omega* case (judgment 14th October 2004, C-36/02),[13] which at times is quoted as one of the main cases where the Court is thought to have guaranteed a certain concept of 'human dignity', with particular reference to the concept given by the German constitutional law system. Actually, the case is not important for this situation, which is not really the most apt choice. In fact, the Court does not see a conflict with community law in the case law that allows an administrative authority to prohibit the opening of a specific business for reasons of public order, therefore for reasons that are considered by treaties as extraordinary grounds for limitation of the fundamental freedom of business in the European Community.

The fact that behind the reasoning on public order was an appeal to the constitutional public order, and with this the need to protect human dignity as a keystone of similar concepts, does not prevent us from noting that the community judge stopped at public order in a strict sense of the term, without setting down specific provisions on the coherence of the European legal system to a precise concept of dignity. For that matter the ECJ clearly states: '*It is not indispensable in that respect for the restrictive measure issued by the authorities of a Member State to correspond to a conception shared by all Member States as regards the precise way in which the fundamental right or legitimate interest in question is to be protected*'.

The *Omega* judgement is worthy of carefully analysis for the issues dealt with in this paper, since the reasoning of the German judges (who legitimated the decision to prohibited the opening of a laserdrome where 'war games' would be simulated) aims at protecting the concept of internal law (i.e. *constitutional* public order) on the concept of Community law (i.e. public order as a *limitation*

[12] See Pollicino (2007).

[13] ECJ: Case C-36/02 *Omega Spielhallen- und Automatenaufstellungs GmbH v. Oberbürgermeisterin der Bundesstadt Bonn* [2004] ECR I-9609. For a comment, see Alemanno (2004) 709; Frenz (2005) 48; Gennusa (2005) 174; Toggenburg (2005) 2.

to the freedom of opening a given business), as well as the recognition, within the definition of the same concept, of a power of discretion that the national case law traditionally recognises the city authorities (in this case, the burgomaster).

This so-called 'nationalisation' process of the institutions governed by community law is not a sporadic event: this can be confirmed by the highly restrictive trends used by German administrative judges in controlling the *Führerscheintourismus* issue.

This issue applies to individuals who have their driving licence withdrawn for any reason can obtain a new one in another European Member State, not under the national case law but under Statutory law. The community judge has often sentenced on this matter (and not by chance he awarded on cases remitted in the German legal system; see the *Kapper*[14] judgement, the *Halbritter* and *Kremer*[15] orders, as well as, finally, the *Wiedemann*[16] judgement), specifying that the Member States are not authorised to *indefinitely* refuse an individual who had his/her driving licence withdrawn within their territory the validity of any other kind of driving licence subsequently issued by another Member State where that person resided, even temporarily. This would not be admissible for the ECJ, even if the national law required a new driving test to ascertain that the reasons for the first withdrawal no longer exist. However, there would be the room to exercise the power of withdrawal based on *future behaviour* of the new driving licence holder's, even though still punishable by national law.

Before this situation, the German administrative judges have partly accepted the ECJ statements, although they have reserved the German authority further reasons for withdrawal, moreover justifying substantiation according to the actual community law. For instance, on this theme we should mention the interesting judgement by the *Verwaltungsgerichts Koblenz* of 30th April 2007,[17] which legitimated the failure to recognise the validity of a driving licence subsequently obtained in a Member State when the holder, on behaviour after the first withdrawal does not undergo a psycho-physical examination.

The court's reasoning is very interesting and partly can be understood: individuals who have been issued a new driving licence in another Member State in order to elude the internal law cannot be allowed to drive. Nonetheless, as far as this analysis is concerned, the court's justification of this reasoning is quite interesting: the so-called driving licence 'tourism' is prohibited as an unlawful behaviour ('*rechtsmissbräuchlich*'), and as such to be considered as prohibited by the community law as well.

A typical national category (i.e. the 'abuse of a right') in this particular case yet again becomes a way to make the principles formulated by the Court of

14 See ECJ: Case C-476/01 *Felix Kapper* [2004] ECR I-5205.

15 See ECJ: Case C-227/05 *Daniel Halbritter v. Freistaat Bayern* [2006] ECR I-49*, Summ.pub.; ECJ: Case C-340/05 *Stefan Kremer* [2006] ECR I-98*, Summ.pub.

16 See ECJ: Case C-329/06 *Arthur Wiedemann v. Land Baden-Württemberg* [2008] ECR I-4635.

17 This judgement can be easily found *on line* at the following address: www.ra-kotz.de/eu_fuehrerschein_entziehung_drogenkonsum.htm.

Justice more flexible. Another example, this time taken from the Italian judge's jurisprudence, can be used to show another orientation. In a famous judgement of 2003 (i.e. n.35 dated 10th January 2003[18]), the Council of State concluded a debate that had been especially opened in legal theory and that is still creating occasional yet significant notes of criticism: it is the definition of the system of Italian administrative acts conflicting with community laws which have direct effectiveness.[19] Some researchers were inclined to affirm that, on the grounds of the principle of the necessary prevalence of community law over internal law, the 'community' invalidity described has to give rise to a different legal theory to the general theory of annulment. Particularly, according to a certain reconstruction, an administrative act conflicting with the directly effective community law has to give rise to a case of invalidity, while another reconstruction, that the act should not be considered null and void but should be 'disapplied' (as happens for national law when it conflicts with community law).[20]

On the other hand, other researchers affirmed that the prevalence of a given 'right' cannot change the nature of the legitimacy parameter. From this standpoint, any infringement of the directly applicable community law falls under the 'infringement of the law', as in any other breach of the law within the internal legal system; the consequence of 'lawbreaking' is not its invalidity, but rather the annulment, which has to be required within a set period of time.[21]

In this judgement the Council of State sustained the second thesis, rejecting both the interpretation in favour of nullity and the one in favour of 'disapplication', and confirming the traditional uniqueness of the illegitimacy regime: '*The infringement of a rule that regulates the activity of the Administration, so as to exclude any discretionary choice in the exertion of the relevant power, actually involves the burden for the subject injured by the vitiated regulation to appeal against it within a compulsory term, in order to have its legitimacy assessed and to have it annulled, since there is no possibility for the administrative judge to decree its ineffectiveness, apart from contesting it before a court*'.

Apart from the specific reference made by the administrative judge to the ECJ legal theory and practice that would seem better suited to enable such an achievement – in other words, a reference to the trend by which the Member States' legal autonomy is guaranteed if individual situations protected by community law rely on effective procedures, equivalent to those of internal law and not more expensive – the fact that the Italian administrative judge confirms the integrity of his/her reasoning is significant: '[...]*also considering the compulsory respect for the general principles inherent to the national judicial system, the certainty of law and the stability of the effects of administrative orders not immediately appealed against*'.

---

18 See (2004) *Foro italiano*, III, 413.

19 An exhaustive examination of the different theories is given by Chiti (2004) 464.

20 The last thesis is supported by Chiti (2004).

21 This thesis is supported, among the others, by Greco (2008) 51.

There is a clear reference to the theory of administrative order's effectiveness, as it has evolved within the national administrative law and it is also evident that the reference is based on the classic principles of the Italian administrative judge's reasoning, that is to say the principle of the certainty and indefeasibility of law, before which the 'best' interpretation of the principles deriving from community law seems to be consistent with the structural identity of an administrative trial and its traditional features.

In order to recognise the significance of this approach, we have to note that, from a systematic standpoint, the Italian administrative judge does not even change his/her thought as a consequence of the ECJ *Santex* judgement (closely following the aforesaid judgement: 27th February 2003, judgement case C-327/00).[22] It concerned the same case in point on which the Council of State had already awarded, namely the case of the late impugnment of a call for tenders that included clauses in conflict with the directly effective community law.

It is known that in this specific case, despite reaffirming that legal theories on administrative invalidity, such as the Italian legal theory, are not contrary to community law, however, the ECJ specified that the rule of 'non application' of a non valid act (since it is in conflict with the directly effective community law) should be guaranteed in some special cases.

Particularly, according to the Court, the Community law concerning calls for tender '*must be interpreted as imposing on the competent national courts, where it is established that, by its conduct, a contracting authority has rendered impossible or excessively difficult the exercise of the rights conferred by the Community legal order on a national of the Union who has been harmed by a decision of that contracting authority, an obligation to allow as admissible pleas in law alleging that the notice of invitation to tender is incompatible with Community law, which are put forward in support of an application for review of that decision, by availing itself, where appropriate, of the possibility afforded by national law of disapplying national rules on limitation periods, under which, when the period prescribed for bringing proceedings for review of the notice of invitation to tender has expired, it is no longer possible to plead such incompatibility*'.

Nevertheless, according to the administrative judge, the possibility of 'bypassing' the periods of limitation for impugnment is hardly used: on the one hand, because on this issue the judge is often inclined to apply restrictive considerations similar to those normally given within the well-known institution of 'excusable error' in national law (a legal concept allowing, even if only in exceptional circumstances, not to regard as decisive mere the expiring of such period, and to admit claims concerning the deceptive behaviour of the administrative authority as well as the difficulty of interpretation); on the other hand, because, as far as the consideration of the ability to understand the need for an immediate impugnment of the call for tender is concerned, there is the strange trend to regard the 'acquiescence' of competitors through their mere participa-

[22] ECJ: Case C-327/00 *Santex SpA v. Unità Socio Sanitaria Locale n. 42 di Pavia* [2003] ECR I-1877. For a comment, see Ferrari (2003) 477.

tion in the procedure as decisive (in fact, their participation in the call for tender, without questioning the difficulty to understand the real value immediately prejudicial of the invitation to tender, is supposed to prove their original ability to evaluate its illegitimacy, and thus their original ability to act for its prompt impugnment: this way judged the Italian supreme administrative court of Milan, Lombardia, Sect. III, 18th July 2007, n.5429;[23] it helps to observe that the institution of acquiescence as well represents a well-known institution within the traditional legal theory of Italian administrative trial).

Again, like in the previous French case, the flexibility of national solutions before any principle formulated by the ECJ is necessarily connected to the recourse to reasoning categories or methods typical of the traditional case law of internal law, of which it becomes further cause for affirmation or even 'radicalization'. Once again, on this point, the Italian case is representative.

The same principles of the certainty of law and the stability of the effects of administrative orders have been appealed to, by the Council of State, in order to reaffirm the effectiveness of 'administrative preliminary reference procedure' that, is the rule under which, in order to assert before a court the administration's liability arising from the adoption of illegal and prejudicial acts, the citizen previously has to contest, within the periods of limitation, the prejudicial provision itself'.[24]

This is a trend as rooted within the administrative jurisdiction[25] as it is opposed by the civil jurisdiction, particularly by the Supreme Court of Cassation, which instead fervently supported the opposite thesis, on the grounds that the solution aimed at achieving the compensation for damages has to be considered autonomous and independent from the preliminary use of the remedy intended for the annulment of the order.[26]

With regard to this, it is convenient to highlight the administrative judge's tendency to appeal to the European community law and to the principles formulated by the ECJ to sustain his/her reasoning, and in particular the tendency to appeal to the community judge's declaration of conformity of national legal systems providing for annulment remedies, which have to be applied within a period of time (see the *Alcatel*[27] case), that is to say the judge's declaration of the judicial autonomy of Member States when the national legal practices comply with the principle of effectiveness and equivalence of judicial protection (see also the *Santex* case above).

---

23 See [2007], *Foro amministrativo – TAR*, 2280.

24 On this subject, see Cortese (2007).

25 Council of State, plenary meeting, 22nd October 2007, n.12. For a comment, see Gallo (2008) 339.

26 The Supreme Court of Cassation, United Sections, 23rd December 2008, n. 30254. For a comment, see Torchia (2009) 385; Greco (2009) 460. The Council of State confirmed the opposite solution: Council of State, Sec. VI, 21th April 2009, n.2436. For a comment, see Cortese (2009) 498.

27 ECJ: Case C-81/98 *Alcatel Austria AG and Others, Siemens AG Österreich and Sag-Schrack Anlagentechnik AG v. Bundesministerium für Wissenschaft und Verkehr* [1999] ECR I-7671.

It is obvious that, in this case, the reference to the preliminary Community law is a clear way of supporting the thesis by which the administrative order, even if not valid, produces effects that identify citizens' 'rights' and, therefore, limits the possibility for such rights to be compensated. It is also evident that this is only one of the possibilities given by 'community' reasoning, since the Supreme Court of Cassation actually sustains a negative interpretation, for instance remembering that, within the legal theory of the compensatory solution, provided for by Treaties with reference to community institutions (EC Article 288), the ECJ traditionally affirmed the rule of formal autonomy of such a remedy, and this as a result of a hermeneutic action aimed at identifying those principles that are shared by the Member States' legal systems.[28]

Thus, the Italian debate on the administration's liability system is interesting not only because, as in other examples analysed so far, the national judge is inclined to follow the community judge by looking at the methods, the institutions, the interpretative rules and traditions of internal law, but also because community law is often observed for its 'rhetorical' function: the principle of community law's prevalence is also referred to in order to acknowledge superiority to certain theories or practices, beyond the real assessment of the actual relevance of community law or the real need for it so as in order to guarantee a precise result.

4 Effectiveness of European Law: 'Simple' Cases and [...] 'Rhetorical' Decisions

This last aspect of the case discussed in this study emerges with particular strength when the national administrative judges attempt to settle certain controversies assumed by them due to their reference to community law and its specific efficiency.

Two interesting law cases emerge from this critical situation: the first case regards the Belgian administrative law, the second regards a certain Italian ruling.

The first case was decided by the Belgian Council of State and is referred to as the *Housieaux* case (after the party who orginated the controversy). It is significant because in the judgement leading to the Council of State even the ECJ pronounced on the limits and the legal procedures for public access to environmental information, as in directive 90/313/CE.[29]

The matter does not seem to pose particular problems. Mr. Pierre Housieaux simply asked to look up the text of an agreement drawn up between the *Société de développement régional de Bruxelles* (SDRB) and a temporary association of companies made up of the companies *Batipont Immobilier SA.* and *Immomills*

[28] On this subject, see Cortese (2009).

[29] Conseil d'Etat, Section d'administration, arret n° 161.407 du 19 juillet 2006, *Pierre Housieaux contre les Délégués du Conseil de la Région de Bruxelles-Capitale*. The text is available at: www.raadvst-consetat.be.

Louis de Waele Development. The agreement was aimed at fixing terms and conditions for the realization of some constructions to be built on an area previously expropriated for that purpose by the Région de Bruxelles-Capitale.

But the SDRB refused the request, saying that the regulatory discipline applicable to this kind of petition does not provide access, as it establishes that the government is to determine the organizational procedures for access to administrative documentation for any administration and proceeding. Mr. Housieaux lodged an administrative appeal to the Board of delegates of Région asking for a renewal of his request and once again asserting his right of access granted by the Community law before the SDRB.

The petition was granted by the Board through a disposition of partial access, which allowed the party to examine and receive only a copy of two separate attachments to the agreement; solely the attachments regarding the environment, which did not jeopardize any business interests of the contracting parties.

Mr. Housieaux lodged another petition and the Board replied that this petition was unacceptable, as it went against an act that was exclusively confirmatory in respect to the tacit decision of dismissal which in the meantime had been developed on the basis of SDRB's lack of action regarding the renewal of the petition of access.

The Council of State, before settling the controversy, asked ECJ to solve some issues of interpretation regarding the regulation within the abovementioned directive. The Court, in particular, affirmed an important principle and explained that even in presence of a national regulation which admits tacit decisions of dismissal, an explicit reasoning is always necessary; otherwise, the dismissal, even if it is tacit, is unlawful.[30]

The Council of State apparently applied this principle and rejected the inadmissibility plea exerted by the Council, though not on the basis that the tacit dismissal should be considered illegitimate, but rather on the basis that Mr. Housieaux appealed against a different explicit act containing a brief and assertive but formal reasoning.

This aspect is relevant because while the Council of State *seems* to apply the principles formulated by the Court, it actually demonstrates that it does not need them for the *aims* for which the community judge was asked to intervene (i.e. in order to understand wether the non contested tacit decision had the 'power' to make the next impugnment of the expressed act inadmissible). The judge, without taking into consideration the Court ruling, came to his verdict:

> 'Considérant que s'il est exact que le requérant n'a pas attaqué la décision implicite de refus résultant du silence pendant deux mois de la partie adverse, il n'en demeure pas moins que, par la suite, celle-ci a pris une décision expresse accueillant partiellement la demande du requérant et ce, nécessairement, à la suite d'un

[30] ECJ: Case C-186/04 *Pierre Housieaux v. Délégués du conseil de la Région de Bruxelles-Capitale* [2005] ECR I-3299.

> nouvel examen de sa demande; que le recours introduit contre cette décision expresse est recevable même si le requérant n'a pas attaqué la décision implicite, laquelle au demeurant était illégale à défaut d'être motivée; que l'exception ne peut être accueillie'.

Firstly, the Council of State, in practice, uses the principles formulated by the Court to infer implicitly and *in opposition*, as it is already provided for by the national law, that an act cannot be exclusively 'confirmatory' if it contains a reasoning that didn't previously appear (and that according to the European law should actually have appeared).

Secondly, the administrative judge uses the principle of the 'essential' character of the reasoning to reaffirm, *on a different level*, that the best interpretation of national laws on transparency of administration and access is the one having a 'formal' and 'substantive' reasoning: i.e. the expressed refusal of access is unlawful, as it is based on a completely generic and stereotyped justification.

In this controversy, in the narrower sense, the promotion of the interpretation issue before ECJ made by the Council of State assumes a 'rhetorical' value: the administrative judge, as was noted, does not need the Court's principles in order to decide on the matter; or more accurately, the judge needs them to affirm that the essential nature of the reasoning is so strong in the Community law that an elusive or apparent reasoning is equivalent to a lack of reasoning.

The possibility of having only 'rhetorical' references to the prevalence of the Community law and its effectiveness is a fact which became even clearer in a case settled in 2005 by a regional administrative Court in Italy.[31]

In this case the power of the 'rhetorical' reference is so strong that the administrative judge appears more 'European' than ECJ; giving statements which are as significant as they are mistaken. The effects of the 'rhetorical' use of European law can be harmful.

On this occasion as well, the actual events are easy to reconstruct. An Italian representative of the Military Staff of the European Union claimed to have not received his relocation allowance, according to the regulation established by the Council of European Union. In fact, the Ministry of Defence, despite his request, paid him his salary according to the national disposition only (Art. 1, letter c law 8 July 1961 n.642), which states that the relocation allowance and other compensations regarding a stay abroad should be deducted from the salary.

The *ratio* of the National rule is easy to understand: avoid any form of unjust enrichment in favour to the employee, who already benefits from additional compensation from his duties abroad. However, the Council's decision, asserted by the claimer, established that the salary of military personnel relocated abroad must be established by an 'exchange of letters' agreement between the community authority in charge and the Member State. The 'exchange of letters'

[31] Regional Administrative Court of Lazio, Sec. I-bis, 18 May 2005, n.4103. Ruling available at: *www.giustizia-amministrativa.it*.

agreement occurred, and the Italian State agreed to pay *also* the relocation allowance, as an additional compensation to the normal salary (which was expressly granted).

Faced with such controversy, the administrative Court of Lazio region did not decide to choose 'the easiest' solution – the one most feasible according to the national administrative law – in fact the administrative judge could have accepted the claim and invalidated the Ministry of Defence's refusal for excess of power, as it went unreasonably and unfairly against a previous decision made by the Ministry itself, one not univocally modifiable, as there had been a decision on the 'exchange of letters' agreement already mentioned.

On the contrary, the administrative judge chose the 'maximalist' solution: the refusal of the Ministry of Defence is unlawful, since the decisions made by the Council and the Commission (*in general*), when they meet the '*integrity*' requirement, produce binding effects within the Member States, not only upon the States involved, but also upon those different subjects who may be entitled to certain 'rights'. The result is notable as the administrative judge does not hesitate to affirm that even decisions can have 'horizontal' effects within the Member States and '*all the indications obtained from the fundamental judicial arrêt given by the Court of Justice from the well-known decision 6 October 1970 n.9/70 (Grad c/ Finanzamt Traustein case)*' can be applied to them.

Though this conclusion does not appear so unorthodox with regards to the decisions adopted within the EC, it must be remembered that in this case the 'decision' was adopted in a different area – the foreign policy of the Union – within a context and with a content which did not provide for a specific right in favour of a single subject: it was declined as a claim to obtain certain benefits according to what was set out in a subsequent 'exchange of letters' agreement, i.e. a short international agreement which is a typical and common regulatory form of a subject, where even within the European Union, inter-governmental features prevail and it is not possible to apply *sic et simpliciter* principles effective for acts adopted within the area of Community law.

The case is of interest, not so much for its reference to the Community law which can also assume a 'rhetorical' value (given the previously mentioned possibility of solving the case solely through the application of national law), but because such a reference, in this *event* separated from a specific need for dialogue with principles and rules concretely applicable to this case by the domestic administrative law, could lead to wrong solutions and spread interpretative misunderstandings on the efficacy of the European law.

5 Conclusions

At the end of this brief *excursus* regarding rulings more or less known concerning administrative judges of some Member States of the European Union, it is possible to derive useful principles for confirming the theory of interpretation previously discussed and its clarification. This also provides an answer to the questions regarding the positive or negative aspect of the above-mentioned cases.

A first proof of the theory elaborated at the beginning of this short essay derives from an observation: within the flexibility margins granted to the Member States by the Community law and the principles elaborated by ECJ, the national administrative judges do not hesitate to improve the value of the national law and its interpretative traditions.

However, from the cases studied, a trend emerges – one of defending national concepts only when they are 'not against' the Community law. That is a different trend of 'doing more', of updating or developing the national law by highlighting those characteristics more compatible with the Community law and more representative of the internal process for a *certain representation* of the domestic regulation.

In all the cases studied, though, the important role played by the administrative judge is evident. In some rulings (*e.g.* the *Arcelor* case) the judge's role reveals an institutional side-taking in order to perform the evolutionary processes of interpretation directly and independently, as required by the European integration.

In other rulings (usually held by German administrative judges; but the Belgian case belongs to this category as well), the domestic judge's knowledge seems to apply to specific and individually fixed areas only, but the approach used reveals a tendency to keep in line with the national administrative law and which takes advantage of those cases not yet expressly examined by ECJ.

In other rulings (and this is the case of the Italian ones) the issue of relation with the principles of the Community law is solved openly by means of a necessary convergence between the structural features of the domestic law system and the protection standards provided for at an international level, which are often misunderstood, re-interpreted or overrated.

It should also be considered that the so described administrative judge's attitude does not change according to how the legal system represents its willingness to the European case: basically, considering the cases previously analyzed, the debate on a possible predominance within the single legal system of monist or dualist concepts of the relation between member States and European Union proves in part useless because, as was shown, the administrative judge tends naturally to use the conceptual instruments according to his/her tradition of interpretation.

In fact, the projection system of National contents deriving from the Community is not affected by the previous acceptance of the theory that the States systems and the Union systems are united or separate: it confirms both positions.

The judges' reasoning, actually, cannot be considered common or homogeneous: it is inevitably affected by the 'starting point' of any judge, i.e. how their technical knowledge of the administrative law has developed during the time in their system. However, the *nationalizing* approach is common indeed, as all the judges analyzed reveal a tendency to be affected by their *forma mentis*.

This last characteristic allows for an evaluation of the overall positive character of the action performed by the administrative judges, because it shows the action's neutral character, i.e. its 'identity is not ideological' compared to the objectives of the European integration; and because it proves, *ex post*, that the European integration also allows these differences of interpretation and method. This permits the member States, when possible, to implement certain objectives through independent reassessments of their national regulation.

It is important to remember that the individuals responsible for these delicate balancing operations are the judges, i.e. those public bodies able to apply the community law empirically and as they are directly linked to the ECJ, may ask for help and verify the conformity and proportion of their solutions through dialogue, which is not necessarily one-way.[32] In fact, this is the very definition of *dialogue*.

32 For some suggestions in this specific direction see Sandulli (2008) 209.

References

A. Alemanno, *À la recherche d'un juste équilibre entre libertés fondamentales et droits fondamentaux dans le cadre du marché intérieur* (2004), *Revue du droit de l'Union européenne.*

A. Arnull, *National Courts and the Validity of Community Acts* (1988), *European Law Review.*

C. Backes, M. Eliantonio, *The Influence of the ECJ's Case Law on Indirect Effect in the Italian, German, Dutch and English Administrative Legal Systems and its Application by the National Administrative Courts,* Working Paper (June 29, 2009), http://ssrn.com/abstract=1427255.

P. Cassia, '*Le droit communautaire dans et sous la Constitution française*' [2007], *Revue trimestrielle de droit européen.*

F. Chaltiel, '*Le Conseil d'État reconnaît la spécificité constitutionnelle du droit communautaire. À propos de la décision Arcelor du 8 février 2007*' [2007] *Revue du marché commun et de l'Union européenne.*

M.P. Chiti, *Diritto amministrativo europeo,* Giuffrè (2004).

F. Cortese, '*Corte di Cassazione e Consiglio di Stato sul risarcimento del danno da provvedimento illegittimo: motivi ulteriori contro e per la c.d. «pregiudizialità amministrativa»*' (2009) *Diritto processuale amministrativo.*

F. Cortese, *La questione della pregiudizialità amministrativa. Il risarcimento del danno da provvedimento illegittimo tra diritto sostanziale e diritto processuale* (2007) Cedam.

P. Costanzo, *La giurisprudenza del Conseil Constitutionnel nel biennio 2005-2006* (2007), *Giurisprudenza costituzionale.*

M. Dicosola, '*La primauté in Francia tra giurisprudenza amministrativa, costituzionale e comunitaria*' (2007), *DPCE.*

V.O. Dutheillet De Lamothe, *Il Conseil Constitutionnel ed il processo di integrazione comunitaria* (2006), *www.associazionedeicostituzionalisti.it.*

G.F. Ferrari, *Corti nazionali e Corti europee* (2006) ESI.

E. Ferrari, '*La Corte di giustizia indica al giudice amministrativo una terza via tra perentorietà del termine di impugnazione e disapplicazione dei provvedimenti amministrativi*' (2003), *Foro italiano.*

W. Frenz, '*Menschenwürde und Dienstleistungsfreiheit*'(2005) *Neue Zeitschrift für Verwaltungsrecht.*

T. Koopmans, *Courts and Political Institutions: a Comparative View* (2003) Cambridge University Press.

C.E. Gallo, *L'adunanza plenaria conferma la pregiudizialità amministrativa* (2008), *Urbanistica e appalti.*

M.E. Gennusa, *La dignità umana vista dal Lussemburgo* (2005) *Quaderni costituzionali.*

L. Goffin, *De l'incompétence des juridictions nationales pour constater l'invalidité des actes d'institutions communautaires* (1990), *Cahiers de droit européen.*

G. Greco, *Argomenti di diritto amministrativo* (2008) Giuffrè.

G. Greco, '*La Cassazione conferma il risarcimento autonomo dell'interesse legittimo: progresso o regresso del sistema*' (2009) *Diritto processuale amministrativo.*

M.S. Giannini, *Istituzioni di diritto amministrativo* (2000) Giuffrè.

A.M. Slaughter, A. Stone Sweet, J.H.H. Weiler (eds.), *The European Courts & National Courts. Doctrine and Jurisprudence* (1998) Hart Publishing.

X. Magnon, '*La sanction de la primauté de la Constitution sur le droit communautaire par le Conseil d'Etat. Commentaire sous Conseil d'Etat, Assemblée, 8 février 2007, Société Arcelor Atlantique et Lorraine et autres*' [2007], *Revue française de droit administratif.*

B. Markesinis, J. Fedtke (eds.), *Judicial Recourse to Foreign Law: A New Source of Inspiration?* (2006) UCL Press.

F.C. Mayer, E. Lenski, M. Wendel, Der Vorrang des Europarechts in Frankreich – zugleich Anmerkung zur Entscheidung des französischen Conseil d´Etat vom 8. Februar 2007 (Arcelor u.a.) (2008) Europarecht.

O. Pollicino, '*Tanto rumore per (quasi) nulla? Sulla decisione Arcelor del Conseil d'Etat in tema di rapporti tra ordinamento interno e diritto comunitario*' [2007] *Il diritto dell'unione europea.*

A. Sandulli, *La Corte di giustizia europea e il dialogo competitivo tra le corti* (2008), in S. Battini, G. D'Auria, G. della Cananea, C. Franchini, A. Massera, B.G. Mattarella, G. Napolitano, A. Sandulli, L. Torchia, G. Vesperini, *Il diritto amministrativo oltre i confini. Omaggio degli allievi a Sabino Cassese* (2008) Giuffrè.

A. Stone Sweet, T.L. Brunell, *The European Court and the National Courts: A Statistical Analysis of Preliminary References, 1961-95*, Working Paper (n.14/1997), *http://www.jeanmonnetprogram.org/papers/97/97-14-.html.*

G.N. Toggenburg, *Grundrechte, Grundfreiheiten, Grund zum Nachfragen anlässlich der Rechtssache Omega* (2005), *European Law Reporter.*

L. Torchia, *La pregiudizialità amministrativa dieci anni dopo la sentenza 500/99: effettività della tutela e natura della giurisdizione* [2009] *Giornale di diritto amministrativo.*

G. Tridimas, P. T. Tridimas, *National Courts and the European Court of Justice: A Public Choice Analysis of the Preliminary Reference Procedure*, Working Paper (November 12, 2002), http://papers.ssrn.com/sol3/papers.cfm?abstract_id=320784.

CHAPTER 9

Behrami and *Saramati*: When Silence Matters

Antonella Angelini*

1 Introduction

As David Kennedy once lucidly said, international lawyers – further than sharing a view of their context and of themselves as professionals – tend to 'generate a set of common ideas about what the problems are to which their skills and tools are appropriate'.[1]

Even a cursory glance suffices to realize that, today, scholars deem as potential frets a staggering number of issues; be that due to the increased density of the international legal environment or induced by a renewal of recurrent fears.[2] If a review of such a variegate catalogue is likely to bear foremost in descriptive terms, more analytically intriguing might be reflecting on a trend which, far from being new in its dynamic, is both challenging in its content and remarkable in pace. What we refer to is the progressive convergence between two of the major drifts pervading the academic debate: on one side, the extension of the UN Security Council's scope of action, especially under Chapter VII of the UN Charter;[3] on the other, the legalisation – and tribunalisation, one should add – of certain realms at length barely touched by law in international intercourses.[4]

Whilst academics have thoroughly been speculating on the respective consequences of such tendencies, the troublesome aspects lying at their interface had remained shrouded in conjecture[5] until the decisions recently handed down by the main European regional courts in the *Kadi* and *Saramati* cases (hereafter, respectively *Kadi* and *Behrami*).[6] Ushering the said *problèmatique*, this triad of instances has casted a profound spell on the regard of the scholarly community and swiftly imparted a net direction, detectable in commentators' tendency to discuss the cases as a unit and to hint at systemic considerations. Thus, notions such as monism, dualism,[7] allegedly objective boundaries between legal orders[8]

* PhD Candidate at the Graduate Institute of International and Development Studies, Geneva.

1 See Kennedy (1999-2000) 346.

2 *Idid* 375-394. On the recurrent fear towards fragmentation and normative conflict, two umbrella concepts sheltering many others tendencies feared by scholars, see also Martineau (2009).

3 Among the many contributions to this topic, see de Wet (2004); more precisely on the expansion of the Matheson (2006); see also Gowlland- Debbas (2000).

4 See Shany (2009) 83.

5 See, for instance, Wellens (2005) 1159; see also Kolb – Porretto – Vité (2005) 423-430; see also Costello (2006) 125.

6 See Case T-315/01 *Kadi v. Council and Commission* [2005] ECR II-3649; Case T-306/01 *Yusuf and Al Barakaat International Foundation v. Council and Commission* [2005] ECR II-3533. See also Joined Cases C-402/05 & C-415/05 P *Kadi and Al Barakaat International Foundation v. Council and Commission* judgments of 3 September 2008. See also *Behrami and Behrami v. France, Saramati v. France, Germany and Norway*, App. Nos, 71412/01 & 78166/01, Grand Chamber, Decision on admissibility, 2 May 2007. Whilst in the course of the essay we will use the abbreviation of *Behrami* to refer to the two joined cases, in case of descriptive necessity or in order to discuss the legal issues respectively at stake, we will distinguish *Behrami* from *Saramati*.

7 See de Burca (2009).

8 See d'Aspremont – Dopagne (2008) 371.

and, conversely, *dédoublement fonctionnel* of organs amenable to a rather intricate bundle of orders within the global arena vividly revived.[9]

The texture of the discussion is, as it appears, particularly thick and the attempt to unravel all its knots could hardly suit the scope of the present contribution. Accordingly, our more modest purpose is to broach only a few points emerged through these pronouncements.

First, the substantive scope of analysis is limited to the *Behrami* case, dealt with by the European Court of Human Rights (hereafter, ECtHR). That, in turn, entails two major consequences. On the one hand, the factual circumstances at stake concern a specific kind of UN-authorised activity, namely the conduct of an organ belonging to a Member State of the European Convention and acting extraterritorially within the framework of a peace-keeping mission. On the other, the judicial actor involved is rooted in a context fairly different from that of the Community courts, masters of the *Kadi* decisions. Evident as it might seem, the latter observation reveals why the ECtHR could not so easily have grappled with the situation by relying on a constitutional discourse as strong as the one adopted by the European Court of Justice (hereafter, ECJ) in order to underpin its *de facto* dualist reasoning in the *Kadi* saga. Notwithstanding whether the delimitation of a legal order is a matter of objective assessment or of stipulative construction,[10] the constitutional tint of the ECtHR jurisprudence is by far paler than that of the ECJ and, at any rate, not enough pronounced to sustain a posture close to 'a declaration of independence from general international law'.[11] If the conundrums posed by the *Behrami* case tend to slip away from the 'home backyard' of a defined constitutional order, seizing the fact pattern in its wholeness requires to regard at any subject possibly involved therein.

There comes the second point informing our reflection. The matrix underneath *Behrami* – incidentally, common to *Kadi* as well – is imbued with a value-based component, reflected in the sensibility of the normative bodies at stake, namely the provisions on collective security enshrined in – and coming along with – the UN Charter and the human rights norms contained in the European Convention on Human Rights (thereafter, ECHR). There is, then, an almost intrinsic tendency to look at facts – and carve their judicial outcome – with reference to a broad, value-driven *desideratum*. In that respect, the endorsement of the internal human rights norms at the expenses of those on collective security is less straightforward as a solution than one may expect it to be in view of the vigorous rule-of-law oriented ethos animating the court.[12] If bluntly pursued, such an attitude would, in fact, be tantamount to neglecting the anything but marginal role played by the Security Council as the primary actor operating

9 See, De Sena and Vitucci, (2009) 209-213.

10 On the root of the notion of legal order see Kennedy (1999-2000) 348; Leben (2001) 19; Halpérin (2001) 48 and Abi-Saab (1987) 105-124.

11 See Milanović (2009) 73.

12 See Shany 88.

through this set of rules and determining to a large extent their features.[13] Far from coming in isolation, the normative component is thus deeply entrenched with an authoritative one; whence the twofold task pertaining to the ECtHR. First, articulating the relationship between the respective legal branches; second spelling out the relationship between itself as a regional court within the international legal order and the universal political organ *par excellence*.

In the light of these remarks, it is not much of a surprise if, expressly or not, the arguments expounded by the ECtHR, as well as the comments thereon made by scholars, turn on two concepts: fragmentation – with its corollary of normative conflict – and judicial review. Following this track, our reflection will attempt to grasp how both dimensions have framed the Court's reasoning and then eventually propose a few thoughts on a different approach to the matter. Normative conflict and judicial review hint to – or are quite automatically assimilated with – a 'black and white' posture: the choice between two rules/principles, putting aside the defeated one and the pronouncement confirming or quashing the legality of a given act performed by or attributable to a political organ. Our claim is that a regional court, such as the ECtHR, is neither compelled nor advised to feel straight-jacketed into such boundaries. An orientation towards normative-harmonization and an expressive mode of interaction are, respectively, two alternatives likely to yield, if cumulated, a more satisfying result than the legally faltering and policy disturbing one we are left with the current version of *Behrami*.

2 The Posture of the ECtHR in *Behrami*

Ever since its decision, *Behrami* has aroused such a rich flurry of criticism that perhaps it is in vain to search for an aspect yet to be touched. Commentators have progressively unfolded the numerous facets of the pronouncement, assessed its impact within the framework of the ECHR and its reflexes on general international law as well as on UN institutional law.[14] Rather than tracing out this chain of scholarly reflection, we will, as anticipated, concentrate on two axis informing the reasoning of the Court and eventually leading to its highly objectionable conclusions. The first concerns the relationship with the Security Council and its effects on both the Court's attitude and jurisdiction; the second turns on the normative relationship between the ECHR and the UN Charter. Before entering their discussion, let us briefly recall the

13 See Gowlland-Debbas (2007) 251-277.

14 With regard to the contributions solely dealing with *Behrami* see Farrior (2007) 743; Klein (2007) 43; Palchetti (2007) 681; Bodeau-Livinec, Buzzini, Villalpando (2008) 323; Sari (2008) 151; Lagrange (2008) 85; Larsen (2008) 509; Maneggia (2008) 191-210; Sarl (2008) 151; De Sena and Vitucci (2009); Krieger 159; Milanović and Papić (2009) 267. As to other contributions mentioning or discussing the case, see, *inter alia* Milanović (2009); de Burca, (2009); Breitegger (2009), 155.

factual circumstances which have given rise to the case and the overall approach adopted by the ECtHR.

2.1 A. Summary of the *Behrami* Decision

That the ECHR States' implication in the intricate Kosovo situation would have created further hurdles than those sweepingly disposed of through the *Banković* decision[15] is hardly surprising. Following the signing of the Military and Technical Agreement between Serbia and the NATO whereby the former agreed to withdraw its forces from Kosovo, the UN Security Council resolution 1244 of 10 June 1999 inaugurated a new phase by establishing an international presence comprising a civil administration – entrusted to the United Mission in Kosovo (UNMIK) – and a NATO-led military force (KFOR).[16] The participation of several Member States in both entities triggered the recourse to the Court in the two instances at stake.

In *Behrami*, the claim arose from the explosion of an undetonated cluster bomb killing one young boy and seriously injuring the latter's brother. The plaintiffs – the boy's father and his surviving son – claimed a violation of Article 2 (right to life) of the ECHR, ensuing from the omission to clear the mine field. They argued that France, the KFOR leading nation in the region where the accident occurred, was responsible for that task.[17]

The *Saramati* case, for its part, concerned Articles 5 (right to liberty and security) and 13 (right to an effective remedy) of the ECHR. Their breach allegedly stemmed from Mr. Saramati's extra-judicial detention on preventative grounds in furtherance of a KFOR Commander's order. The applicant addressed his complaint to those States – France and Norway – whose nationals had decided and repeatedly confirmed the said measure.[18]

Though the submissions of the parties[19] primarily hinged on whether the applicants fell within the respondent States' jurisdiction according to the meaning of Article 1 of the Convention,[20] the Court decided to approach the

---

15 See *Banković v. Belgium*, App. No 52207/99, Grand Chamber, Decision on admissibility, 12 December 2001, hereinafter *Banković*. We also recall the *Marković* Case, disposed by the Court relying on the *Banković* precedent; see *Marković and Others v. Italy*, App. No 1398/03, Grand Chamber, Judgment, 14 December 2006. On the latter see Shah, 'Seeking Remedies for Violations of International Humanitarian Law: *Marković v. Italy*', 7 *HRLR* (2007) 412.

16 See S/RES/1244 (1999), 10 June 1999. On the specific mandates of the civil and military presences see, respectively, paras. 10-11 and paras. 7 and 9 of the resolution. On this part see also *Behrami*, paras. 1-17.

17 See *Behrami*, paras. 5-7 and 73-81.

18 See *Behrami*, paras. 8-17 and 73-81. The applicant had initially included Germany among the respondent, but in the course of the proceedings asked the Court – and received the permission – to withdrawn such allegation for lack of proof, see paras. 64 and 65.

19 It is worth stressing that seven more states and the UN as well had submitted observations in quality of interveners.

20 See *Behrami*, par. 67.

matter from a different angle, namely from that of the Court's *ratione personae* competence. As it has been aptly remarked by two commentators,[21] this shift of perspective was the 'first and most important' step of a threefold move. After swiftly resolving that UNIMIK was the entity vested with the mandate to de-mine,[22] the Court proceeded, in fact, by asking whether the 'impugned action of KFOR (detention in *Saramati*) and inaction of UNMIK (failure to de-mine in *Behrami*) could be attributed to the UN' and finally addressed the issue of its competence '*ratione personae* to review any such action or omission found to be attributable to the UN'.[23] Answering affirmatively to the first question yields the solution of the case: given the patent lack of personal jurisdiction towards the UN, the joined cases could only be incompatible with the provisions of the Convention and, therefore, be quashed.[24]

One cannot help perceiving a sort of mismatch between the mechanic of this logic pattern and the decision as a whole. The articulation of the Court's reasoning does not, *prima facie*, suffer of flaws severe enough to prompt the sharp criticisms raised in many quarters. Among these voices, the most recurrent drawback traced in *Behrami* concerns the gap in the protection and guarantee of the Conventional set of rights and correlated remedies.[25] More subtly, it has been noticed that – far from being confined to the operative side – the latter trend is likely to impact on the deeper fabric of general international law, primarily by instilling a message of unaccountability utterly at odds with the rationale of international responsibility.[26] Common to these fears, lies a sort of feeling that the attitude shown in *Behrami* might thoroughly be reiterated by the Court in similar cases. And yet, the virtual automaticity thereby supposed does not stem – at least not necessarily – from the path guiding the ECtHR in its decision. The essence of the problem, in fact, lies elsewhere. On the one hand, it resides in the way the Court interpreted and used the rules on the international responsibility of International Organisations (IOs);[27] on the other it derives from the considerations purported in paragraph 149 – and similarly reiterated later–[28] whereby the Court held that:

> 'since operations established by the UNSC Resolutions under Chapter VII of the UN Charter are fundamental to the mission of the UN to secure international peace and security and since they rely for their effectiveness on the support from

[21] See Milanović and Papić (2009) 270-274.

[22] See *Behrami*, paras. 123-127.

[23] See *Behrami*, para. 121.

[24] See *Behrami*, paras. 144-152.

[25] Whereas almost all the cited Authors discuss or at least hint to this aspect, for the analysis more focused on this point see the essay by Fabbrini in this volume; Sari, *supra*, note 14.

[26] See Milanović and Papić (2009) 268, 281-289.

[27] On this point, see particularly Palchetti, *supra*, note 14, 686-694; Sari, *supra*, 14, 162-166; Milanović and Papić, *supra* note 14, 274-281, Larsen, *supra* note 14; Maneggia, *supra* note 14.

[28] See particularly, *Behrami*, para. 151.

> member states, the Convention cannot be interpreted in a manner which would subjects the acts and omissions which occur prior to or in the course of such missions, to the scrutiny of the Court.'[29]

One might feel a little puzzled in realizing that, when it comes to a Chapter VII missions, most discussions on attributions become almost dubious, given that any act – attributable or not to the UN – is anyway protected from any interference of the Court. Certainly, that sheds light on scholars' anxieties for a lock stock and barrel repetition of *Behrami*. However, the Court's goal in carving this approach remains unclear. Inquiring on that aspect entails an attempt to reveal the 'hidden rings' of the reasoning chain followed by the Court. In this respect, it seems quite unlikely that either the discourse on attribution of acts to IOs or the Court's position in paragraph 149 might simply be a redundancy. Likely, the two axis are not primarily aimed at reinforcing one another, but rather at furthering different goals sought by the Court. We believe, that the ECtHR's interpretation of the rules in IOs' responsibility and the overtly policy-grounded position expressed on Chapter VII missions were instrumental to a double avoidance: first, on Article 1 of the ECHR – more precisely on the extraterritorial scope of the obligations posed by the instrument – second, on Article 103 of the UN Charter as a rule injecting a quasi-hierarchical dimension within the international legal system.[30] More profoundly, the latter remarks flesh out the features assumed in *Behrami* by those knots that regional courts have to disentangle if confronted with issues of collective security. On the one hand, the matter of delimiting the contours of its field and mode of action as a judicial organ, thereby spelling out the relationship with the Security Council; on the other articulating the bundle of rules flowing, in turn, from the Charter, general international law and the conventional regime.

2.2 When Silence Matters; What the Court Avoids in *Behrami*

A hidden move on jurisdiction and attribution

A trend of cases decided on similar grounds of admissibility as *Behrami* confirm that the latter was foreseen by the Court as a standard it would use in the future.[31] It is fair to say that the Court has once more been able to turn a potentially bogging-down situation into a golden opportunity to revise its set of

---

29 See *Behrami*, para. 149.

30 On this latter point, see also the observations of Milanović and Papić, *supra*, note 14, 289-293.

31 See See *Kasumaj v. Greece*, App. Nos 6974/05, First Section, Decision on admissibility, 5 July 2007; *Galić v. Germany* App. No. 31446/02, First Section, Decision on admissibility, 28 August 2007; *Berić and Others v. Bosnia and Herzegovina*, App. Nos 36357/04, 36360/04, 38346/04, 41705/04, 45190/04, 45578/04, 45579/04, 45580/04, 91/05, 97/05, 100/05, 101/05, 1121/05, 1123/05, 1125/05, 1129/05, 1132/05, 1133/05, 1169/05, 1172/05, 1175/05, 1177/05, 1180/05, 1185/05, 20793/05, and 25496/05, Forth Section, Decision on admissibility, 16 October 2007; *Dragan Kalinić and Milograd Bilbiija v. Bosnia and Herzegovina*, App. Nos 45541/04 and 16587/07, Forth Section, Decision on Admissibility, 13 May 2008.

jurisdictional tools and mainly try to limit the scope of the jurisdictional provision of the Convention. *Banković*, which is the Court's most notable attempt to curtail the extra-territorial application of the Convention, immediately comes to mind. Indeed, as pointed out by one early commentator of *Behrami*, 'it is striking that the Court has preferred to evaluate the admissibility of the instances relying on attribution [...] as it could simply have acknowledged that the alleged violations had not occurred within the 'legal space' of the Convention'.[32] *Banković* represented a Pyrrhic victory for the Court[33] and sufficiently explains the shift endorsed in *Behrami* however, assessing the strategic or tactic character of the latter move requires further investigation. It seems thatthe Court, not wishing to fall in another *cul de sac*, sought a jurisdictional tool to grasp with complex extra-territorial issues. *Behrami* illustrates that: by embracing a more subtle technique for phrasing jurisdictional matters and relying – at least nominally – on the rules on IOs' responsibility, the Court crafted a brand-new approach to delimit the scope of ECHR States' obligations and, thereby, of its own jurisdiction.

The Court's first step was to redirect the focus from Article 1 of the ECHR – as framed by the parties – to its own *ratione personae* jurisdiction:

> [T]he question raised by the present cases is, less whether the respondent States exercised extra-territorial jurisdiction in Kosovo but far more centrally, whether this Court is competent to examine under the Convention those States contribution to the civil and security presences which did exercise the relevant control of Kosovo.
>
> Accordingly, the first issue to be examined by this Court is the compatibility *ratione personae* of the applicants' complaints with the provisions of the Convention.[34]

The adjustment thereby purported is not of minor relevance.

Marco Milanović and Tatjana Papić noticed that 'the notion of 'jurisdiction' found in the ECHR and in many other human rights treaties refers to the jurisdiction of a *State*, not to the jurisdiction of a *court* [...] and it is a trigger for the application of the treaty obligations to arise in the first place'.[35] Although different, the two concepts are closely related to each other. On the one hand, if a human rights instrument does not apply i.e., if the State does not have obligations under that instrument, then the relevant court – or monitoring body – does not have *ratione materiae* jurisdiction in that specific instance. This also applies if an allegedly wrongful act is not attributable to the defendant State, then the judicial or quasi-judicial organ at stake lacks *ratione personae*

[32] See, Palchetti, *supra*, note 14, 685. (translated from Italian by the present Author).

[33] On the plethora of comments raised by *Banković* see, among others, Greenwood, 'Jurisdiction, NATO and the Kosovo Conflict', in Capps (2003) 145-171; Lawson (2004) 55-136; Wilde (2005) 115.

[34] See, *Behrami*, paras. 71-72.

[35] See Milanović and Papić, *supra*, note 14, 272; see also Milanović (2008) 411.

jurisdiction to review the argued conduct. Spelt with reference to the present case, the latter remarks unveil the first choice made by the ECtHR: avoiding to directly determine the *existence* of ECHR obligations for the respondent States. Approaching the facts of *Behrami* from the standpoint of attribution the Court was not a mistake; however, it somehow blurred the logical relationship between the two dimensions we have spotted.[36]

The notion of jurisdiction in human rights treaties is primarily a 'question of fact, of effective overall control that a State has over a territory or of authority or control that it has over a particular person'.[37] Without venturing into a thorough inquiry, it is fair to say that the the Court's case-law – though less tersely – hinges on similar basis.[38] Spelt with reference to the circumstances at stake, the latter approach would require consider the *single* impugned acts and ascertain whether the respondent States were exercising authority or control over the relevant portion of the territory (*Behrami*) or over the plaintiff (*Saramati*). Additionally, given that whatever the circumstances, a State operates through its own organs or agents, assessing the issue of control entails a concurrent determination of the attribution. The two facets of the analysis stand, in fact, on the same logical level and are equally determining. In *Behrami,* the body of rules normally relevant for attribution – those relative to State responsibility – matters little because the contingents deployed in Kosovo are undoubtedly organs of the defendant States.[39] But within the framework drawn by SC Resolution 1244, determining the entity – the contributing State or the UN – to which the

36 A certain drift of the debate on the ECtHR judgement bears witness of that, notably in some scholars' discussion on the logical order and mutual relationship between the issues of jurisdiction and attribution. One of the first commentators of the decision had in fact maintained that 'the Court was mistaken in *Behrami* to venture in the issue of attribution, since the question of State jurisdiction is a preliminary matter which logically must be dealt with before attribution' see, Sari, *supra*, note 14, 159. The latter stance had later been criticised by two other commentators, who had in turn hold that 'State jurisdiction is not strictly speaking a preliminary issue, certainly not any more so than is attribution', see Milanović and Papić, *supra*, note 14, 273.

37 *Ibid.*, 272. On the notion of jurisdiction in human rights treaties see also Meron (1995) 78; De Schutter (2006); Wilde (2007) 503, especially at 508, 513-514; 183. Whereas, more specifically on Article 1 of the ECHR see De Sena (2002); Cohen-Jonatan (2002) 1069-1082.

38 Further than *Banković*, see *Drozd and Janousek v. France and Spain*, App. Nos.12747/87, ECtHR (plenary session), Judgment of 26 June 1992; *Loizidou v. Turkey*, 15318/89, ECHR, Judgment, 18 December 1996; *Cyprus v. Turkey*, App. No. 25781/94, Grand Chamber, Judgment, 10 May 2001; *Issa and Others v. Turkey*, App. No. 31821/96, Second Section, Judgment, 16 November 2004; *Ilaşcu and Others v. Moldova and Russia*, App. No. 48787/99, Grand Chamber, Judgment, 8 July 2004; *Öcalan v. Turkey*, App. No. 46221/99, Grand Chamber, Judgment, 12 May 2005; *Hussein v. Albania and Others*, App. No. 23276/04, Forth Section, Decision on admissibility, 14 March 2006.

39 At Art. 4, Draft Articles on Responsibility of States for Internationally Wrongful Acts, see ILC Report on its 53rd session (23 April–1 June and 2 July–10 August 2001) *General Assembly Official Records*, Fifty-sixth Session, Supplement No. 10. (A/56/10) at 40.

conducts at stake are to be attributed is decisive. Hence, we will examine IOs' responsibility rules.

In case of state organs placed at the disposal of the UN for the purposes of peace operations,[40] Article 5 of the Draft Articles on the Responsibility of International Organizations[41] is the pertinent evaluation criterion. After précising that for the purpose of attribution of acts to IOs, control plays a different role than with reference to State responsibility,[42] the commentary of the provision foresees control as follows: '[...] when an organ or agent is placed at the disposal of an international organization, the decisive question in relation to attribution of a given conduct appears to be who has effective control over the conduct in question'.[43] Hence, two main consequences follow: first, in deciding whether a contingent acted in its national or international capacity, the analysis purports on the specific act at stake; second, the question to be answered comes down to deciding in whose name an organ was acting at the moment when the act occurred.

In summary, it appears that the process of evaluation the Court might have been expected to follow is a two-tiered one, comprising an assessment of the jurisdictional link existing between the claimants and the respondents States – i.e., whether any organ of the latter was exercising authority or control over the former – and the determination of the entity with effective control on the acting organ. However, the Court proceeded in a rather different way.

While approaching the case as one of *ratione personae* jurisdiction, the Court added an element into its framing of the matter when it stated that 'the civil and security presences [...] did exercise the relevant control of Kosovo'. Indeed, while hinting at control, the latter stance keeps the contours of the matter undefined with regard to ECHR States, by means of a general reference to the UN missions on the terrain. Essentially, the overall reference to control, if not incorrect at a starting point, cannot stand on its own in the circumstances at stake. The assessment of a jurisdictional link – and concurrently of attribution – neces-

---

40 The term is taken from the 'Brahimi Report' and refers to 'operations of conflict prevention and peacemaking; peacekeeping; and peace-building', see Report of the Panel on UN Peace Operations (Brahimi Report) UN Doc. A/55/305-S/2000/809, 21 August 2001; see also Bourtos-Ghali, (1992).

41 For the provisionally adopted text of the Draft Articles on Responsibility of International Organizations see ILC Report on its 60th Session (5 May to 6 June and 7 July to 8 August 2008) *General Assembly Official Records*, Sixty-second Session, Supplement No. 10 (A/63/10), ch. VII, 249-299.

42 See para. 4, which reads as follows: 'With regard to States, the existence of control has been mainly discussed in relation to the question whether conduct of persons or of groups of persons, especially irregular armed forces, is attributable to a State. In the context of the placement of an organ or agent at the disposal of an international organization, control plays a different role. It does not concern the issue whether a certain conduct is attributable at all to a State or an international organization, but rather to which entity – the contributing State or organization or the receiving organization – conduct is attributable.', see ILC Report 56th session (3 May-4 June and 5 July-6 August 2004) *General Assembly Official Records*, Fifty-ninth session, Supplement No. 10 (A/59/10), ch. V. 94-142, at 111-113.

43 *Ibidem*, 113.

sitate, as stressed above, an analysis tailored to the specific allegedly unlawful conduct. A similar attitude then also pervades the interpretation given to the rules on IOs' responsibility. Many commentators have highlighted the flaws in this part of the decision.[44] One word suffices to convey the most noticeable trait of the Court's overall approach: formalism. Indeed, the reference to Resolution 1244 in order to ascertain *who* – of KFOR or UNIMIK – detained the mandate to de-mine and detain, as well as the attempt to ascertain the link between the Security Council and KFOR on the basis of the notion of delegation of powers under Chapter VII of the Charter were both purely formalistic.

The repartition of competence contained in the resolution is, at best, of little guidance for the purpose of deciding on attribution. Indeed, the framework sketched therein is certainly far from reflecting the administrative and institutional matrix existing in Kosovo.[45] Such a reliance, although understandable in view of the said complexity, remains *per se* insufficient. Moreover, in light of the following discussion on the delegation of powers by the SC, one is induced to conclude that, rather than attempting to disentangle the Kosovo byzantine situation, the Court was apparently casting its spell in interpreting the rules on attribution.

Indeed, in paragraphs 128-141 of the decision, we undeniably notice the distance between the posture of the Court and the relevant factual background; which reflects the deductive reasoning carried out in tracing the actions of the TCNs' contingents back to the SC. There are two pivotal steps: first, articulating the link between the SC and KFOR (paras. 132-136) and second, rejecting the arguments advanced by the parties with regard to the level of TCNs' involvement allegedly detaching troops from their international NATO mandate (paras. 137-141). Interestingly, the Court adopted two different modalities to define the notion of control. With regards to the NATO-TCNs relationship, it upheld a *factual* criterion based on the ultimate retention of operational command; whereas – just a few lines before – it had grounded the attribution of KFOR's acts to the SC on the *legality* of the delegation of powers supposedly disposed by Resolution 1244.[46] The effort in forging a construction as convincing as possible is remarkable as well as the ability in juggling with the scholarly sources cited to bolster the discussion on the SC's Chapter VII powers.[47] The result, however,

44 See particularly, Palchetti, *supra*, note 14 particularly at 686-694; Milanović and Papić, *supra* note 14, particularly at 274-289; Larsen, *supra* note 14; Maneggia, *supra* note 14.

45 On the latter aspect, see Picone (2005) 50-51, see also refereces in footnotes 131-133 therein.

46 On this lack of coherence see also Maneggia, *supra*, note 14,. 200. As to the notion of delegation, incidentally never used by the SC in the dispositive of its resolution, the Court had previously made a distinction between authorization and delegation, see para. 43 ' [...] use of the term 'delegation' in the present decision refers to the empowering by the UNSC of another entity to exercise its functions as opposed to 'authorizing' an entity to carry out functions which it could not itself perform.', see *Behrami*, para. 43.

47 In the latter respect, it is quite remarkable to notice not only the extensive reference made to scholarly contributions but also the distortive way of using the latter. Indeed, among the Authors cited in square

is far from meeting the intended goal. In fact, an important conceptual loophole, deprives the reasoning of consistency: the fact that a SC resolution might provide for a legal delegation of powers i.e., respecting the institutional criteria determining its legality has nothing to do with attribution, neither in the light of previous UN practice, nor within the scope of Article 5 of the Draft Articles on the responsibility of IOs. The implied *non sequitur* is evident when conjunctly reading paragraphs 133 and 136 of the decision:

> 'The Court considers that the key question is whether the UNSC retained ultimate authority and control so that operational command only was delegated. This delegation model is now an established substitute for the Article 43 agreements never concluded'.
>
> [...]
>
> 'This *delegation model demonstrates* that, contrary to the applicants' argument at paragraph 77 above, direct operational command from the UNSC is not a requirement of Chapter VII collective security missions.' (emphasis added)

First, the standard endorsed in the first part of the above extract is doubtful. Notwithstanding that the expression is squarely taken from the work of one scholar,[48] it is arguable whether the maintenance of the 'ultimate authority and control' might be compatible with a complete divestment of control over the conduct of operations or, at any rate, whether the reporting system might provide a sufficient toll to exercise 'overall control and authority'.[49] The whole inquiry on any sort of 'delegation model' is irrelevant altogether, given that the parties had put forward operational command as a potential indicator of effective control for the purpose of attribution, and not as a matter of Charter legality. Consequently, these two aspects are conflated in the argumentation of the Court, which – already faltering as a reconstruction of the Charter framework for peace missions – is far from passing the muster when it comes to demonstrating why the 'ultimate authority and control' test is a pertinent attribution criterion.[50] Unsurprisingly, the risk that such a dangerous move may creep into the practice of other courts or, even worse, be endorsed by States has prompted the reaction of the 'generalists', beginning with the ILC Special Reporter on the responsibility of IOs, Giorgio Gaja. He has commented 'without denying the

brackets at para. 132 only the contribution of Prof. Sarooshi had, in fact, drawn the link between the notion of delegation of powers by the SC with that of attribution. The other Authors mentioned had rather dealt with the practice of delegation and legality thereof, without raising the matter of attribution. On this point, see also Milanović and Papić, *supra*, note 14, 285-286.

48 See Sarooshi, *The United Nations and the development of collective security. The delegation by The UN Security Counci of its Chapter VII powers* (1999) 268-284.

49 See *Behrami*, para.134.

50 On this point, see particularly Larsen and Maneggia, *supra*, note 14. It should be noticed that in a later case decided on the same basis of *Behrami*, namely *Berić*, the Court had recourse to the expression of 'effective overall control' instead of 'ultimate authority and control', see *Berić*, para. 27.

importance of this jurisprudence that it would be difficult to accept, simply on the strength of the judgment in *Behrami* and *Saramati*, the criterion applied in those cases as a potential universal rule. Also as a matter of policy, the approach taken by the European Court of Human Rights is unconvincing. It would lead to attributing to the United Nations conduct which the organization has not specifically authorized and of which it might have little knowledge or no knowledge at all.'[51]

It seems that both the elusive mention of control and the thorough discourse on attribution have been crafted with the purpose of avoiding an analysis of the alleged violations taken in isolation. Furthermore, such an approach demonstrates the Court's attempt to skip the confrontation with its previous jurisprudence on the meaning of the jurisdictional clause of the Convention and, especially with the related thorny question of effective control. The reasons behind a similar choice of judicial policy might be manifold – definitely including the wish to limit *à la Banković* ripples effects on jurisdictional matters– and hard to seize from an external standpoint. Contrarily, its major effect is quite patent: considerably curtailing the coverage of the Convention. The all-encompassing approach taken in *Behrami* resembles – if not conceptually, at least in its functioning – to the notion labelled in *Banković* as the 'legal space of the Convention'. In other terms, it operates as a jurisdictional tool to dispose of complex situations, whose context may give rise to a bundle of claims the Court is not willing to deal with. Similarly, certain commentators have maintained that *Behrami* 'sends a clear message to States saying they are free to do whatever they wish to do and escape any human rights scrutiny as long as they protect themselves by obtaining the imprimatur of an international organization'.[52] To clarify, it is wrong to expect the Court to uphold its *Behrami* doctrine on attribution – and thereby refrain from exercising its jurisdiction – in any situation implicating an IO. Proof of this resides in the arguments relative to distinguishing the circumstances of *Behrami* from those of its previous pronouncement in *Bosphorus*,[53] particularly in paragraph 151 whereby the Court held that:

> 'in the present cases, the impugned acts and omissions of KFOR and UNMIK cannot be attributed to the respondent States and, *moreover, did not take place on the territory of those States or by virtue of a decision of their authorities.* [...] There exists, in any event, a fundamental distinction between the nature of the international organization and of the international cooperation with which the Court was there concerned and those in the present cases. As the Court has found above, UNMIK was a subsidiary organ of the UN created q under Chapter VII and KFOR was exercising powers lawfully delegated under Chapter VII of the Charter by the

51 See Gaja, *Seventh Report on responsibility of international organizations*, ILC 61st session (4 May-5 June and 6 July-7 August 2009) A/CN. 4/610 at 12.

52 See Milanović and Papić, *supra*, note 14, 268.

53 See *Bosphorus Hava Yollari Turizm Ve Ticaret Anonim Sirketi v. Ireland*, App. No. 45036/98, Grand Chamber, Judgment, 30 June 2005.

> UNSC. *As such, their actions were directly attributable to the UN, an organization of universal jurisdiction fulfilling its imperative collective security objective.* (emphasis added).[54]

Therefore, we should see the Court's move not exactly as granting a 'blank check' to ECHR States acting under the aegis of any IO, but rather as defining an approach easily adjustable to extra-territorial contexts as well as to situations – whether or not within the 'legal space of the Convention' – implying multiple layers of governance. Cases so far decided *à la Behrami* bear evidence of that, the gamut of claims having aroused from the UNMIK-KFOR presence in Kosovo but also from some acts performed by the High Representative in Bosnia and Herzegovina.[55]

Along with such versatility, the posture endorsed in *Behrami* strikes for being replete with overt policy considerations to one main addressee: the Security Council, depositary of the 'imperative collective security objective' pursued by the UN. Here comes the second turning point of our reflection. The avoidance of Article 1 ECHR sought to forge an alternative jurisdictional tool to resolve *en bloc* situations charged with issues of collective security. The reasons underpinning – almost compelling – a similar choice of self-restraint clearly stand out by reading the previously cited paragraphs 149 and 151. Indeed, the reference to the need to not interfere with the ECHR States' participation in peace operations and the mentioning of the imperative collective security objective fostered by the UN are moves which, arguably, leave little room for any sort of activism.

In conclusion, the Court decided to refrain from scrutinizing the acts of the ECHR States acting within the framework of the UN system of collective security and has therefore attempted to define a doctrine capable of meeting this need. Yet, the very fact that the latter arguments are endorsed and reiterated so prominently, spurs further speculation. In other words, their phrasing in terms of the primacy of *certain Charter values* raises the question of their correspondent on the *normative* side. At this point, Article 103 of the Charter, the so called 'supremacy-clause' of the Charter immediately springs to mind.[56] Therefore,

---

54 See *Behrami*, para. 151.

55 For the list of cases so far decided relying on the *Behrami* precedent see *supra*, note 31. Most of them concern the situation in Kosovo within the framework of SC Resolution 1244. Those related to tin Bosnia and Herzegovina are – at the moment of writing – only two, namely the *Berić* and *Kalinć* cases. As to the legal background of the case and the role of the High Representative – a figure instituted by the so-called 'Peace Agreement' (Annex 10 thereto) and lately endorsed by the SC through its resolution 1031 of 15 December 1995 – see *Berić*, paras. 10-19.

56 Article 103 of the UN Charter reads as follows: 'In the event of a conflict between the obligations of the Members of the United Nations under the present Charter and their obligations under any other international agreement, their obligations under the present Charter shall prevail.' The latter provision has progressively attracted a growing number of scholarly reflections, on some of its aspects see Liivoja (2008), see also Kolb (2004). In more general terms, see Bernhardt (2002) 1297.

what is the relationship articulated by the ECtHR between the two normative bodies of the UN Charter and the ECHR? Additionally, how does the overtly disclaimed value-oriented dimension enter such a dimension?

Supremacy of values, conflict of norms: a thorn ECtHR

The interplay between the normative and the value-based dimensions permeates the reasoning of the Court to such an extent that their contours are not that easy to seize. One may compare it to the illusion created by a ventriloquist: understanding who is speaking for whom – the person or his puppet – can sometimes be quite a tricky exercise. On the one hand, in fact, the numerous stances reiterating the primacy of the goals of collective security pursued by the UN would have stood completely in the air without a reference – at least nominal – to Article 103 of the UN Charter. On the other, the legal implications deriving from the cited article are neither spelt out in their scope, nor articulated with reference to the legal obligations enshrined in the ECHR. The Court is, in this respect, completely silent. Although a complete neglect of the provision – incidentally, extensively quoted by the respondent and the intervening States–[57] could have hardly been possible, the Court still remained reluctant to pick up and address the main issue adumbrated by Article 103, namely normative conflict. Most importantly, normative conflict is, indeed, the big elephant in the courtroom. As subtly noted by two commentators, the ECtHR was certainly not willing to spell out once and for all the *hierarchical* relationship supposedly existing between the obligations imposed by the Charter and those enshrined in its own constitutive instrument.[58] Hence, the need to fall back on policy arguments which is an argumentative device arguably much easier to mould and eventually refine according to future needs. In other words, the daunting perspective of seeing the ECHR displaced by a bunch of norms external to the 'constitutional instrument of the European public order'[59] led the Court to blur the problem of conflict by purporting a value-based, rather than normative, primacy.

The successful attempt to merge the two mentioned dimensions is not only reflected in the relevant part of the decision – the pivotal paragraphs, quite tellingly, following one another[60] – but is also confirmed by a certain trend of doctrinal contributions.

The recourse to Article 103 has been widely deemed as the trigger of the solution purported by the Court. Seeing the final outcome of *Behrami* as the transposition of the Court's view on Article 103, commentators have at length criticized the far-reaching scope allegedly accorded to that provision.[61] Consequently, extending 'the primacy of any act and omissions of contracting States covered by SC Resolution 1244, irrespective of whether they are

57 See *Behrami*, paras. 97, 102, 106, 113.

58 See Milanović and Papić, *supra*, note 14, 293.

59 See *Behrami*, para. 145.

60 See *Behrami*, paras. 147 -149.

61 See particularly Palchetti, *supra*, note 14, 696-704; De Sena and Vitucci, *supra*, note 14, 204-205.

imposed [...] whether they are only *authorized* or even whether they are only voluntary'(emphasis in the original) has been seen as tantamount to stretch the intended purpose of Article 103 up to tearing it into pieces.[62] Undoubtedly, that would squarely have been the case if the Court had taken a similar stance. As a matter of fact, it did not. Instead, it reached a similar result through the considerations of primacy of the alleged main objective of the Charter which are collective security and peace maintenance.

Thus, the ensuing question is twofold. First, what does such a posture say about the Court's perception of its own relationship with the SC as the main universal political organ? Second, did the ECtHR – as a regional judicial organ vested with the task of protecting human rights – have any alternative choice?

A swift conclusion on either the policy stances or the use of Article 103 may, as shown, be oblivious of some deeper – at time contrasting – drifts lying at their root. Whether the Court tried or not to constrain itself for the future when eluding the riddle of normative conflict, the result we are confronted with today does not leave much room for nuances. The strength of the endorsement of values pursued by the Court goes far beyond a mere posture of self-restraint. Accordingly, some authors have even ventured as far as to saying that the *Behrami* ruling might be seen through the lenses of Georges Scelle's theory of *dédoublement fonctionnel.*[63] They believe that, through its decision the ECtHR has *de facto* aimed at furthering certain values emanating from the UN legal order, at the expenses of those enshrined in their own order. The lack of a solid normative construction and the blunt statement made by the Court may probably yield sufficient evidence to share such a position, at least in its main tenants.[64] Yet, we cannot help thinking that the endorsement made by the ECtHR was imbued with a further component. Mindful of the remarks made on the *internal* effects of the *Behrami* doctrine on attribution and jurisdictional matters, it is quite tempting to conclude that the primacy attributed to the UN objective of collective security gives a sort of 'final imprimatur' to the reject of claims systematically made by the Court. As mentioned above, if one looks at the effects entailed by the sweeping stance of paragraph 149 and then turns to the whole discussion on attribution, the feeling is that the former hollows out the latter, even if it were only to be for the actions performed by ECHR States in connection with a Chapter VII operations. As a matter of fact, whatever the shortcomings and strains suffered by the discourse on attribution, the Court found a way to protect the result it sought. By putting forward an almost overriding argument, it underpinned its wish to discard a whole bunch of situations having the features we have spotted above. However, an inquiry on motives may, eventually risk to see too much in certain stances or passages of the reasoning

62 See De Sena and Vitucci, *supra*, note 14, 205.

63 *Ibid.*, 209-213.

64 The starting point of the two Authors is, in fact, different from ours as far as the Court's use of Article 103 is concerned. They, in fact, start from the premise of insufficiency of the supremacy clause as spurring a fall back on the value-based dimension; *Ibid.*, 204.

developed by a Court. Therefore, rather than further delving into the folds of *Behrami*, we would like to address an ultimate question arising from the actual discussion. What was, in the end, the compelling need to *perceive* the relationship between the UN Charter legal system and the one defined by the ECHR as one *of conflict*? Plus, why should the relationship between itself – as a judicial organ – and a political one be described according to the dichotomy of either an unwarranted interference or unfettered liberty of action? Providing a thorough answer to both questions certainly represents a broad task but simply suggesting a few hints in this respect will definitely be useful.

Although it explicitly mentioned Article 31. 3 c) of the Vienna Convention on the Law of Treaties (VCLT),[65] the Court with regard to the UN legal order, restrained itself to considering Articles 25 and 103 of the UN Charter.[66] Such a narrow reading calls for several critical considerations. Overall, one may notice that in its previous case-law, the Court had not shied away from using the cited provision in order to open up the conventional legal order to a considerable number of external norms.[67] Thus, there were no obstacles preventing the inclusion of those Charter provisions referring to human rights; eventually the Court might even have had regard to the many important human rights treaties concluded in the framework of the UN. Incidentally, a similar conclusion would be warranted also by a more careful reading of Article 103, which makes reference to 'the obligations under the present Charter' thereby putting on the same level – and according the same primacy – to the *whole bundle* of Charter obligations, rather than those stemming from a given resolution. In other terms, a contextual reading of the Charter was not only an available but was also a legally sounder option at the disposal of the Court.[68] Indeed, that might have put in perspective the compelling need to avoid any normative conflict, precisely because such a conflict would, to a large extent, have faded away.

If a path of normative harmonization to reconcile the Charter provision and those of the ECHR was then possible, that does not completely unravel the core

65 See Vienna Convention on the Law of Treaties, opened for signature May 23, 1969, 1155 U.N.T.S., 331, 8 I.L.M. 679 (entered into force on January 27, 1980). The Court introduces Article 31.3 c) by holding that 'It also recalls that the principles underlying the Convention cannot be interpreted and applied in a vacuum. It must also take into account relevant rules of international law when examining questions concerning its jurisdiction and, consequently, determine State responsibility in conformity and harmony with the governing principles of international law of which it forms part, although it must remain mindful of the Convention's special character as a human rights treaty' see, *Behrami*, para. 122.

66 See *Behrami*, para. 147.

67 We refer to the following cases: *Al-Adsani v. the United Kingdom*, App. No. 35763/97, Grand Chamber, Judgment, 21 November 2001; *Fogarty v. the United Kingdom*, App. No. 37112/97, Grand Chamber, Judgment, 21 November, 2001; *McElhinney v. Ireland*, App. No. 31253/96, Grand Chamber, Judgment, 21 November, 2001; *Banković*, see *supra*, note 15. For a discussion on the use of the said article see particularly McLachlan (2005) 304-306. As to a critical appraisal of the Court case-law on the triad of cases on immunity, see particularly Orakhelashvili (2003) 529.

68 In a similar vein, see also De Sena and Vitucci, *supra*, note 14, 213.

issue in *Behrami*. Indeed, as mentioned above, the problem hinged on a value-based dimension. At the forefront, one feels puzzled by the Court's assertion that the 'imperative objective' of the UN is one of collective security. Leaving aside the fact that, literally, collective security is *one of* the aims of the UN rather than the *one and only*, one should not be oblivious of the fact that 'collective security' is a goal which has progressively acquired a number of facets, certainly, not excluding altogether human rights.[69] Plus, the fear of interfering with the effectiveness of the operations engaged in by ECHR States looses much of its strength once the relationship between the two branches of obligations incumbent on States as Members of the UN and concurrently of the ECHR is crated in a more harmonic way. What probably remains is the wish to avoid engaging in any kind of relationship with the Security Council in its quality of universal political organ. Whether the latter reticence stems from a genuine concern of putting unwarranted laces to the SC's efforts in maintaining peace and security or, from a quite opportunistic desire to discard many delicate situations, we leave the issue up to the reader's own assessment. Nevertheless, it is worth noticing that both hypothesis stand on the quite debatable assumption that the interaction between a political and a judicial organ primordially turns on either an interference or a quasi-indifference. Without lifting the lid of a debate as rich as the one on this matter, our perception can aptly be illustrated through some observations made by José Alvarez during the post-*Lockerbie* debate on the relationship between the ICJ and the Security Council. Once revealed that the main positions of that moment – namely, those of the 'legalist' and of the 'realist' – had engendered the fake perception that judicial review had to be seen ' as a choice between hegemonic (or systemic) needs and the 'rule of law'',[70] he argued that 'the Court and the Council faced a continuum of options and interpretative modes [...] judicial review [being] an evolutionary process, emerging from a dialogue among all international actors'.[71]

The ECtHR, though potentially partaking in this dialogic pattern, has not seized the occasion provided by *Behrami* to cast its own spell on the matter. In the end, this probably represents the most strident silence of the ECtHR in *Behrami*.

3 Concluding Observations

In an intriguing essay, Vaughan Lowe maintained that the establishment of the Permanent Court of International Justice – and the ensuing shift from arbitral to judicial dispute settlement – had also entailed a shift in perception as far as the normative completeness – or lack thereof – of the international legal system was concerned.[72]

---

69 See Gowlland-Debbas, *supra*, note 13, particularly at 259-266.

70 See Alvarez (1996) 39.

71 *Ibid.*, 39.

72 See Lowe (2000) 207-236.

The flurry of claims brought before the major European judicial bodies may, today, mark a drift of a similar importance. They might, in fact, trigger an effort to articulate the relationship between two pivotal moves informing the international legal system, namely the hierarchical judicialisation of several of its normative branches and the centralization of certain functions of collective interest, often merging political and legal aspects. To a certain extent, the fact that such a process has been spurred by the action of certain individuals does not have to be underestimated. Just a few years ago, one might have hardly expected a similar upsetting drift to have this as its *primum movens.* If anything, the latter novelty has at least revealed how deep the value-based dimension has crept into the international legal system; that, in return, leaves the door open for improvements.

From a more general perspective, one may spot a further aspect of interest in these cases taken as a whole. They have, in fact, brought to light a need which has silently been pervading the 'community' of international scholars since a while: 'facing – and grappling with – the growing complexity not only of the legal system(s), but also of their own perception of the latter'.

In conclusion, the recent cases and the reflection thereon can be seen as a piece of a broader trend, whereby international lawyers are trying to re-define their 'common view' of both problems and the appropriate solutions thereto. In the light of this latter observation, the timidity or the opportunism of the ECtHR in *Behrami* – and its manifold shortcomings – can, at least intellectually, be seen in a less frustrating way. However, we cannot stop lingering over its bitter taste.

References

G. Abi-Saab, 'Le système du droit international ou le droit interantional en tant qu'ordre juridique', *Cours général de droit international public.* Collected Courses of the Hague Academy of International Law 207 (The Hague: Martinus Nijhoff Publishers, 1987).

J. Alvarez, 'Judging the Security Council' [1996] 90 *American Journal of International Law.*

R. Bernhardt, *'Article 103'*, in B. *Simma* et al. (eds.), *The Charter of the United Nations: A Commentary* (New York: Oxford University Press, 2002).

P. Bodeau-Livinec, G. P. Buzzini, and S. Villalpando, '*Agim Behrami & Bekir Behrami v. France; Ruzhdi Saramati v. France, Germany & Norway*. Joined App. Nos 71412', [2008] 102 *American Journal of International Law.*

B. Bourtos-Ghali, 'An Agenda for Peace', Report of the Secretary General, UN Doc. A/47/277-S/24111, 17 June 199.

A. Breitegger, 'Sacrificing the effectiveness of the European Convention on human rights on the altar of the effective functioning of peace support Operations: A Critique of *Behrami & Saramati* and *Al Jedda'* [2008] 11 *International Community Law* Review.

E. Capps, P. Evans and S. Konstadinidis (eds.), *Asserting Jurisdiction: International and European Legal Perspectives* (Oxford: Hart Publishing, 2003).

J.D. Cohen-Jonatan, 'La territorialisation de la juridiction de la Cour européenne des droits de l'homme', [2002] *Revue trimestrielle des droits de l'homme.*

C. Costello, 'The *Bosphorus* ruling of the European Court of Human Rights: fundamental rights and blurred boundaries in Europe', [2006] 6 *Human Rights Law Review.*

J. d'Aspremont and F. Dopagne, '*Kadi*: the ECJ's reminder of the elementary divide between legal orders', [2008] 5 *International Organizations Law Review.*

G. de Burca, 'The European Court of Justice and the international legal order after *Kadi*', Jean Monnet Working Paper 01/09, available at www.jeanmonnetprogram.org.

O. De Schutter, 'Globalization and Jurisdiction: Lessons from the European Convention on Human Rights' [2006] 6 *Baltic Yearbook of International Law.*

P. De Sena, *La nozione di giurisdizione statale nei trattati sui diritti dell'uomo* (Torino: Giappichelli, 2002).

P. De Sena and M. C. Vitucci, 'The European Court and Security Council: between *dédoublement fonctionnel* and balancing of values', [2009] 20 *European Journal of International Law.*

E. de Wet, *The Chapter VII powers of the United Nations Security Council* (Oxford: Hart Publishing, 2004).

S. Farrior, 'Introductory Note to *Behrami and Behrami v. France and Saramati v. France, Germany & Norway*, European Court of Human Rights (31 May 2007)', [2007] 46 *International Legal Materials*.

V. Gowlland-Debbas, 'The functions of the United Nations Security Council in the international legal system', in M. Byers (ed.) *The role of law in international politics* (Oxford: oxford University Press, 2000).

V. Gowlland-Debbas, 'Collective security revised in light of the flurry over UN reform: an international law perspective', in V. Chetail (ed.) *Conflicts, sécurité et cooperation/Conflict, security and cooperation. Liber amicorum Victor-Yves Ghebali* (Brussels : Bruylant, 2007).

J.L. Halpérin 'L'apparition et la porté de la notion d'ordre juridique dans la doctrine internationaliste du XIXe siècle', [2001] 33 *Droits*.

D. Kennedy, 'When renewal repeats. Thinking against the box', [1999-2000] 32 *New York University Journal of International Law and Politics*.

P. Klein, 'Responsabilité pour les faits commis dans le cadre d'opérations de paix et étendue du pouvoir de contrôle de la Cour Européenne des droits de l'homme: quelques considérations critiques sur l'arrêt *Behrami* et *Saramati*' [2007] 53 *Annuaire Français de Droit International*.

R. Kolb, 'Does Article 103 of the Charter of the United Nations apply only to decisions or also to authorizations adopted by the Security Council?',]2004] 64 *Zeitschrift für ausländisches öffentliches Recht und Völkerrecht*.

R. Kolb, G. Porretto and S. Vité, *L'application du droit international humanitaire et des droits de l'homme aux organisations internationals. Forces de paix et administrations civiles transitoires* (Brussels: Bruylant, 2005).

H. Krieger, 'A Credibility Gap: the *Behrami* and *Saramati* decision of the European Court of Human Rights' 13 [2009] *Journal of International Peacekeeping*.

F. Lagrange, 'Responsabilité des Etats pour actes accomplis en application du chapitre VII de la Charte des Nations Unies ' [2008] 112 *Revue Générale de Droit International Public*.

K. Larsen, 'Attribution of Conduct in Peace Operations: the 'Ultimate Authority and Control ' test ' [2008] 19 *European Journal of International Law*.

C. Leben 'De quelques doctrine de l'ordre juridique', [2001] 33 *Droits*.

R. Lawson, 'Life after *Bankovic´*: on the extraterritorial application of the European Convention on Human Rights', in F. Coomans & M.T. Kamminga (eds.) *Extraterritorial application of human rights treaties* (Oxford: Intersentia, 2004).

R. Liivoja, ' The scope of the supremacy clause of the United Nations Charter'[2008] 57 *International and Comparative Law Quarterly*.

V. Lowe, 'The politics of law-making: are the method and character of norm creation changing?' in M. Byers (ed.), *The role of law in international politics. Essays in international relations and international law* (Oxford: Oxford University Press, 2000).

A. Maneggia ' 'Controllo efftettivo' e imputabilità della condotta nella decisione *Behrami/Saramati* della Corte europea dei diritti dell'uomo', in C. Focarelli *Le nuove frontiere del diritto internazionale* (Perugia: Morlacchi Editore 2008).

A.C. Martineau, 'The rhetoric of fragmentation: fear and faith in international law', [2009] 22 *Leiden Journal of International Law.*

M.J. Matheson, *Council unbound: the growth of the UN decision making on conflict and post-conflict issues after the Cold War* (Washington: USIP Press, 2006).

C. McLachlan, 'The principle of systemic integration and Article 31.3 c) of the Vienna Convention', [2005] 54 *International and Comparative Law Quarterly.*

T. Meron, '*Extraterritoriality of Human Rights Treaties*', [1995] 89 *American Journal of International Law.*

M. Milanović and T. Papić, 'As bad as it gets: the European Court of Human Rights' *Behrami* and *Saramati* decision and general international law', [2009] 58 *International and Comparative Law Quarterly.*

M. Milanović, 'Norn conflict in international law: whither human rights?', [2009] 20 *Duke Journal of Comparative and International Law.*

A. Orakhelashvili, 'Restrictive Interpretation of Human Rights Treaties in the Recent Jurisprudence of the European Court of Human Rights' [2003] 14 *European Journal of International Law.*

P. Palchetti, 'Azioni di forza istituite o autorizzate dalle Nazioni Unite davanti alla Corte Europea dei Diritti dell'Uomo: i casi *Behrami* e *Saramati*', [2007] 3 *Rivista di Diritto Internazionale.*

P. Picone, 'Le autorizzazioni all'uso della forza tra sistema delle Nazioni Unite e diritto internazionale generale' [2005] 88 *Rivista di Diritto Internazionale.*

A. Sarl, 'Jurisdiction and International Responsibility in Peace Support Operations: The *Behrami* and *Saramati* Cases', [2008] 8 *Human Rights Law Review.*

D. Sarooshi, *The United Nations and the development of collective security. The delegation by The UN Security Counci of its Chapter VII powers* (Oxford: Oxford University Press, 1999).

Y. Shany, 'No longer a weak department of power? Reflections on the emergence of a new international judiciary', [2009] 20 *European Journal of International Law.*

K. Wellens, 'Fragmentation of international law and establishing an accountability regime for international organisations: the role of the judiciary in closing the Gap', [2005] 25 *Michigan Journal of International Law.*

R. Wilde, 'The "Legal Space" or "Espace Juridique" of the European Convention on Human Rights: is it relevant to extraterritorial state action?', [2005] 2 *European Human Rights Law Review.*

R. Wilde, 'Triggering State Obligations Extraterritorially: The Spatial Test in Certain Human Rights Treaties' [2007] 40 *Israel Law Review.*

CHAPTER 10

The Relationship between the ICC and Other International Tribunals

An Analysis of the Lubanga Confirmation of Charges

Rosa Raffaelli*

1 Introduction

This Chapter will take into examination some of the problems related to the proliferation of international criminal tribunals, and the conflicts that can arise between them and the International Court of Justice. In particular, I will analyse the first decision of the International Criminal Court (ICC, Pre-Trial Chamber, Case *Prosecutor v. Thomas Lubanga Dyilo*, Decision on the confirmation of charges, 29 January 2007), and the way in which the Pre-Trial Chamber (PTC) based itself on the assessment of facts made by the ICJ in the *Democratic Republic of the Congo v. Uganda* case in order to adjudicate on the nature of the armed conflict in the Democratic Republic of the Congo.[1] I will also take into consideration other cases in which international criminal tribunals made reference to the jurisprudence of the ICJ and *vice versa*, in order to determine whether the decision under examination follows the same lines.

At first sight, it might seem that the coexistence of a plurality of international criminal courts and of the ICJ cannot give rise to any type of conflict. Indeed, while the ICJ only has jurisdiction over States, as it is called to ascertain their international responsibility, international criminal courts can only rule over individuals and their criminal responsibility under international law; moreover, while the ICJ hears cases brought before it by States, international criminal courts are seized by their Prosecutors.[2] Thus, it is clear that conflicts – in a formal sense – between these two types of Tribunals cannot arise: as has been noted,[3] a strict notion of 'conflict of jurisdiction' requires two conditions – same parties of the conflict and same issue (meaning same factual and legal grounds) – which can never be satisfied in cases brought before the two different types of Tribunals. However, it would be overly simplistic to state that, merely because their jurisdictions regard different subjects and different objects, there can be no overlap: indeed, both types of Tribunals are tasked with the interpretation of international law and its application to internationally relevant facts; thus, they might have to decide on the scope of application of the same rule of law, or on the existence and legal qualification of the same facts. For instance, the commission of an international crime might give rise both to criminal responsibility of the individual who committed it, and to State responsibility: thus, both the ICJ and an international criminal tribunal might have to adjudicate on the same facts in order to establish different types of responsibility.[4] In this case, the principles that have been developed to avoid conflicts of jurisdiction between different courts, such as the principle of litispendence and the *res judicata* rule would not apply, as the differences in the jurisdiction *ratione personae* and *materiae* of

---

* PhD candidate in Criminal Law, Sant'Anna School of Advanced Studies, Pisa.

1 ICJ, *Case concerning armed activities on the territory of the Congo*, Judgment, 19 December 2005.

2 See Hafner (2002).

3 See Shany (2003) 24 ff.

4 See Hafner (2002) 595 ff.; Fujita (2002) 576.

the two tribunals would not allow for it.[5] Thus, when both types of Tribunals have to adjudicate on partially identical issues, there is no formal route to avoid clashes or tensions; an informal solution might be for one Tribunal to cite the jurisprudence of the other in order to support its own judgment, but there exists no rule binding an international tribunal to cite, follow or take legal notice of the jurisprudence of another.

2 Conflicts with Regard to Rules of International Law: The *Nicaragua* and *Tadic* Cases

We can identify two possible types of conflicts between international criminal courts and the ICJ: tensions can arise either when both types of Courts have to apply the same rule of international law, whose existence and content are disputed, or when both courts have to adjudicate on the same facts. Most attention seems to have been paid to the first type of conflict: indeed, it is not unusual that international tribunals, deciding on the responsibility of different subjects, have to apply the same rules. Even in national legal systems, where rules are generally more precisely defined, conflicts often arise with regard to the interpretation that has to be given to a specific provision: most legal systems are therefore organized hierarchically, with a Supreme Court tasked with interpreting the law, while lower Courts might either be bound to follow its interpretation (according to the principle of *stare decisis*) or tend to do so due to the persuasive force of the interpretation given by the Supreme Court.

In the international legal system, the lack of any hierarchy between Courts and the customary nature of most rules of law leaves a broad space for conflicting interpretations: thus, one Tribunal might state that a customary rule of law exists, while another denies it, or they might disagree on its interpretation and scope of application. While conflicts of this type might be inevitable in a system which has no hierarchical organization or structure, and where therefore no judicial body has a duty to follow the decisions of another, this does not mean that such conflicts are desirable. As has been stated, while each international tribunal is autonomous in applying the law, in its law-finding activity it should take into account judgments of other tribunals on the same subject; in particular, when an international criminal tribunal is called to apply customary international law, the need for consistency implies that it should also pay respect to the views of the ICJ on what is international customary law.[6]

A well known example of conflict related to the interpretation of a rule of customary law is surely the one concerning the rules regarding State's responsibility for the conduct of one individual or group, which is not a *de jure* organ of that State but somehow depends on or is controlled by it. In the well known

---

5 See Shany (2003) 22.

6 Shahabuddeen (2002) 647; Buergenthal (2001) 267 ff.

Nicaragua case,[7] the ICJ was, *inter alia*, confronted with the problem of how to attribute the actions of individuals or groups who are not *de jure* organs of a State to that State; in particular, it had to determine whether the USA could be deemed responsible for violations of international humanitarian law committed by the *contras*, an armed group acting on the territory of Nicaragua with the support of the US. The Court, after judging that the *contras* were not completely dependent on the USA's aid and support, stated that the test to be used in order to establish whether the US could be held responsible for the rebels' actions was a test of 'effective control': thus, in order for the USA to bear responsibility for specific actions committed by the *contras*, it would have to be proved that 'that State had effective control of the military or paramilitary operations in the course of which the alleged violations were committed' (para. 115).

Around ten years later, in the first case brought before the ICTY, the Trial Chamber of this Tribunal found that, in order to establish whether the conflict in the former Yugoslavia was of an international character, it had to determine whether some of the armed forces involved were acting on behalf of a State: in this case, the conflict would have been internationalized, and therefore Article 2 of the Statute of the Tribunal would have been applicable. Thus, the Court had to identify the test to be used in order to attribute actions committed by an armed group to a State: in this case, however, the test was not applied in order to establish State's responsibility, but merely in order to characterize the nature of the Yugoslav conflict. The Trial Chamber,[8] applying the *Nicaragua* test of effective control, stated that the armed forces of the *Republika Srpska* could not be considered as *de facto* organs of the Government of the Federal Republic of Yugoslavia, and that the conflict could therefore not be considered as an international one; however, the Presiding Judge, Judge Gabrielle Kirk McDonald, issued a Dissenting Opinion stating that the Trial Chamber had mistakenly interpreted and applied the Nicaragua test, and that the armed conflict could be considered as an international one (see the dissenting opinion to the Judgment). Subsequently, the Prosecutor appealed against the conclusion of the Chamber, claiming that the conflict was international. The Appeals Chamber[9] therefore had to re-examine the issue of the applicability of the test of 'effective control' in order to qualify the armed conflict; the Chamber deemed it necessary to take into examination the ICJ's judgment in the Nicaragua case, contesting the validity of the test as enounced in that decision and coming to the conclusion that the test applied in the *Nicaragua* case did not correspond to customary international law, and thus that it was not valid. It is very interesting to briefly recall how the Appeals Chamber proceeded: the Court did not contest the appropriateness of using a test, originally drafted with regard to State's responsibility, in order to establish whether an armed conflict could be considered as international, but

7 ICJ, *Case concerning military and paramilitary activities in and against Nicaragua – Nicaragua v. United States of America*, Judgment of 27 June 1986.

8 ICTY, Trial Chamber, Case IT-94-1-T *Prosecutor v. Dusko Tadić*, Judgment of 7 May 1997.

9 ICTY, Appeals Chamber, Case IT-94-1-T *Prosecutor v. Dusko Tadić*, Judgment of 15 July 1999.

it contested the existence of a rule of international customary law corresponding to the one enounced by the ICJ. This procedure could not but lead to a clash between the two judgments; indeed, the ICTY did nothing to minimize the conflict, and in its analysis of the ICJ's jurisprudence it stated that the *Nicaragua* test did not seem to be persuasive as it was not consonant with the logic of the law of State responsibility and was at variance with judicial and State practice (paras. 99 ff., in particular 115 ff.). The Appeals Chamber thus concluded that the test to be used to assess the responsibility of a State for the actions of groups depending on its aid and assistance should be one of 'overall control'; applying this test, it concluded that the Yugoslav Army exercised the requisite measure of control over the Bosnian Serb Army, and therefore that the armed conflict could be characterized as international.

It is interesting to note that the Appeals Chamber of the ICTY cited the ICJ's jurisprudence on the existence and scope of application of a rule of customary international law merely in order to claim that this rule had been misinterpreted, and thus that the real content of the provision was different from that claimed by the ICJ. It is clear that, in order to adjudicate on the existence and content of a rule of law, especially if customary, international tribunals cannot but take into account the relevant jurisprudence of other courts, as they might already have analysed State practice in order to determine the existence and scope of application of the provision. However, the *Tadić* judgment has been criticized for the use it made of the *Nicaragua* case: indeed, the Appeals Chamber made reference to the ICJ's jurisprudence, which had already been cited in front of the Trial Chamber, exclusively in order to state that the rule of law enounced by the ICJ did not exist, and therefore that the provision to be followed was different.[10]

This case is an emblematic example of a conflict relating to the existence and scope of application of a rule of law: indeed, the fact that the ICTY made reference to the ICJ's jurisprudence did not serve to the purpose of ensuring uniformity in the interpretation or application of the law, as the Chamber contested the basis and the validity of the ICJ's findings. The outcome of this procedure was that two different international courts, each being the Court of last instance in their separate ambits of jurisdiction, came to different conclusions on the scope of application and on the interpretation of a specific rule of international law: although this cannot be considered as a conflict of jurisdiction, as the two Courts have competence over different subjects and different objects, the outcome did, indeed, bear negative effects on the unity of international law.[11]

---

10 See Milanovic (2006) 553.

11 See Rosenne (2004) 102.

3 Reiteration of the Conflict: The *Genocide* Case

The tension between the interpretations adopted by the two Courts has not been solved, but rather reiterated, by the recent ICJ's judgment in the case relating to the application of the Genocide Convention.[12] The Genocide case is particularly interesting as the ICJ was called to adjudicate on State's responsibility for facts that had already been proved before the ICTY, although for the different purpose of establishing individual criminal responsibility; thus, in this case tensions could arise with regard to the facts that had to be proven, to their legal qualification, and to the existence and scope of application of rules of international law. The Genocide case has already been analysed by a number of Authors, and there is no need to re-examine it in detail.[13] However, I will briefly point to some of the most interesting elements of the judgment.

To start with, the ICJ heavily relied on the fact-finding activity of the ICTY, thus showing more than mere deference for this Tribunal's findings. Indeed, in its evaluation of the evidence presented by the parties, the ICJ stated that it would accept as 'highly persuasive' relevant findings of fact made by the Tribunal at trial, unless upset on appeal (para. 223): the Court made reference to its previous jurisprudence on the evaluation of evidence, and in particular to its statements on this issue in the *Democratic Republic of the Congo v. Uganda* case (para. 61), to assess the value to be given to the ICTY's findings. In particular, it stated that the ICTY's conclusions deserved high consideration, as the fact-finding process of this Tribunal can be considered as 'evidence obtained by examination of persons directly involved', tested by cross-examination, the credibility of which has not been challenged subsequently, and to which therefore the ICJ should assign the greatest value. Thus, by giving high consideration to the credibility of the ICTY's statements on facts brought as evidence by the parties, the ICJ prevented the insurgence of conflicts in the assessment of the same facts: in this case, the ICJ had been asked to adjudicate on facts which also fell within the jurisdiction of the ICTY, and on which the latter had already rendered its judgments, and therefore there was a high risk that the two tribunals could have made conflicting statements on the facts of the case.

The ICJ has also shown great deference for the interpretation given by the international criminal tribunals of rules of international criminal law, whose application falls within their specific jurisdiction; thus, for instance, the ICJ cited the ICTY's jurisprudence on ethnic cleansing (para. 190) and the scope of protected groups in cases of genocide (paras. 195 ff.). Indeed, as the notion of genocide and the constituent elements of this crime have been interpreted by highly specialized international tribunals, such as the ICTY and the ICTR, the ICJ, which has a general jurisdiction to interpret international law, can only be praised for citing and following their jurisprudence, as this clearly suits a

[12] ICJ, *Application of the Convention on the Prevention and Punishment of the Crime of Genocide – Bosnia and Herzegovina v. Serbia and Montenegro*, Judgment, 26 February 2007, hereinafter Genocide case.

[13] Cassese (2007); Halink (2008); Milanovic (2006); Cannizzaro (2007).

need for coherence in the interpretation of international law and serves to avoid conflicts. The deference shown to the ICTY's jurisprudence went to the point that, when the ICJ had to adjudicate on State's responsibility and on the rules governing the attribution of actions of an individual or a group to a State of which the person or group is not an organ, it took into consideration the judgment of the Appeals Chamber of the ICTY in the *Tadić* case, and expressed reasoned grounds not to follow the test of 'overall control' developed in it. The ICJ was very careful in its analysis of the *Tadić* case, and did not contest the validity of the 'overall control' test enounced in the judgment; indeed, the Court tried to minimize the conflict between its jurisprudence and the ICTY's on the interpretation of the rules on State's responsibility. The International Court of Justice moved from the observation that the ICTY had not been called upon to rule on questions of State responsibility, as its jurisdiction only regards the international criminal responsibility of individuals: thus, when the Appeals Chamber, in the *Tadić* case, addressed the issue of the rules governing State responsibility, this was not indispensable for the exercise of its jurisdiction. The ICJ therefore stated: 'the Court attaches the utmost importance to the factual and legal findings made by the ICTY in ruling on the criminal liability of the accused before it and, in the present case, the Court takes fullest account of the ICTY's trial and appellate judgments dealing with the events underlying the dispute. The situation is not the same for positions adopted by the ICTY on issues of general international law which do not lie within the specific purview of its jurisdiction and, moreover, the resolution of which is not always necessary for deciding the criminal cases before it' (para. 403). Thus, the ICJ seemingly assigned authority only to the decisions taken by the ICTY for which this court was the 'competent' tribunal, while it decided not to follow the ICTY's interpretation of international customary law when this interpretation concerned a provision that the ICTY was not competent to apply. Moreover, according to Cannizzaro, in the *Genocide* case the ICJ was obliged to follow the ICTY's factual findings, as these were binding for the parties of that case: the Author claims that, as judicial decisions are rules of law applying to specific situations, the judgments of the ICTY are rules of law compelling not only the individuals tried in front of this tribunal, but also the States that are bound by the UN Resolution establishing the ICTY (Security Council Resolution 827/1993) and by the Statute of this Tribunal. According to this 'normative approach' to the role and significance of the ICTY's judgments, the ICJ is required to show deference to their findings; however, the judgments of the ICTY do not represent a *definitive* judicial decision on the matter (in accordance with the principle of *res judicata*), but they must be taken into account by the ICJ as they represent valid international law for those States that are bound by the UN Resolution, and thus also for the States parties of the *Genocide* case.[14] However, according to the same theory, this assertion is only valid with regard to the relevance of decisions taken by the ICTY in cases brought before the ICJ by States bound to respect the

[14] Cannizzaro (2007) 8 ff.

ICTY's judgments, while it would not apply in the reverse situation: if the decisions of the ICTY can be considered as applicable law in disputes between States in front of the ICJ, this does not imply that a decision of the ICJ could bind the ICTY, or any other international criminal tribunal.[15] Indeed, international criminal trials are developed in the interest of the international community as a whole, in application of higher standards of proof than the ones applicable in front of the ICJ and following specific rules on the admissibility of evidence: no international criminal tribunal can therefore be bound by a decision taken by another court, not even the ICJ. This last comment leads us to the specific object of this note: the ICC's decision on the confirmation of charges in the case *Prosecutor v. Thomas Lubanga Dyilo*, and the reference it made to the ICJ's jurisprudence.

4 Overlaps in Factual Assessments: the Qualification of the Armed Conflict in Ituri, DRC

As is well known, the International Criminal Court, established in July 2002 as the first permanent international criminal tribunal, rendered its first ever decision on the confirmation of charges in January 2007. The procedure in front of the ICC, which is a mixture between the inquisitorial and the accusatorial systems, requires that the charges brought against the accused are confirmed by a Pre-Trial Chamber, whose task is to determine whether there is 'sufficient evidence to establish substantial grounds to believe that the person committed the crime charged' (Article 61(7) of the Rome Statute). The confirmation hearing allows the Court to ensure that prosecution is not frivolous or abusive, thus protecting the accused from the risk of being subjected to a criminal trial for committing international crimes when there are actually no grounds to believe him guilty.[16] The decision on the confirmation of charges, however, is not a final decision, but it merely represents the last stage of the Pre-Trial phase. The first accused brought before the Pre-Trial Chamber of the ICC was Thomas Lubanga Dyilo, the founder and president of the *Union des Patriotes Congolais* (UPC) and the former commander in chief of the *Forces patriotiques pour la libération du Congo* (FPLC), who was charged of conscripting and enlisting children under the age of 15 into the FPLC and using them to participate actively in the hostilities, in the context of a non-international armed conflict. The defendant was surrendered by the DRC to the ICC in March 2006; the confirmation of charges hearing took place in November 2006.

The ICC's jurisdiction on the Democratic Republic of the Congo stems from a self-referral by this State: the President of the DRC referred to the Prosecutor the situation of crimes within the jurisdiction of the Court committed in the territory of the DRC and asked him to investigate on this situation; the Pros-

[15] Cannizzaro (2007) 15.

[16] See Schabas (2004) 140; Marchesiello (2002) 1235.

ecutor, after an evaluation of the situation in the Congo, decided to initiate the investigations, and up until now has brought charges against four defendants, all of whom are accused of committing international crimes in the region of Ituri (North-Eastern DRC). The DRC, however, has also filed applications against Uganda, Rwanda and Burundi before the International Court of Justice, alleging that these States have perpetrated acts of armed aggression against the Republic itself on its territory, thus violating the UN Charter. While the cases against Burundi and Rwanda have not been decided and have been removed from the list, the case against Uganda led the ICJ to adopt its judgment on 19 December 2005: the Court declared, i.a., that Uganda was the occupying power in Ituri until 2 June 2003, when the Ugandan army (UPDF) withdrew from the territory of the DRC, and that Uganda was responsible for a number of violations of international humanitarian and human rights law committed by its army on the territory of the DRC.

It should already be clear where the tension between the findings of the ICC and those of the ICJ could lie: indeed, the latter has ascertained that Uganda was the occupying power in Ituri until June 2003, while the Prosecutor of the ICC, in indicting Lubanga of war crimes committed between September 2002 and August 2003 in Ituri, claimed that these crimes had been committed in the context of an armed conflict not of an international character. The Pre-Trial Chamber of the ICC, in confirming the charges against Thomas Lubanga, decided to make reference to the jurisprudence of the ICJ, giving it such a high importance as to amend the charges against the suspect; thus, the Chamber avoided the risk of the ICC giving a divergent assessment of facts than the ICJ. However, while the case under examination clearly is one of partial overlap between the competence of two international tribunals, each one of them having been called to adjudicate on the same factual issues for different purposes, it seems that the PTC went beyond its powers in taking notice of the ICJ's judgment and using it to amend the charges. Moreover, although coherence between international tribunals, both on legal and factual issues, is surely desirable, it seems that different factual assessments do not have the same negative consequences on the unity and coherence of the international legal system as conflicting interpretations of the law: I will therefore try to question the appropriateness of using the ICJ's factual assessments at a criminal trial as a means of avoiding conflicts.

Firstly, it might be useful to briefly recall the way in which the PTC proceeded in order to determine that the conflict in Ituri was to be qualified as an international armed conflict. The Chamber moved from the consideration that, although the Prosecutor, in the document containing the charges, had stated that the crimes had been committed in the context of a non-international armed conflict, the characterisation of the conflict had been disputed: both the Defence and Legal Representative of one of the victims had made reference to the involvement of foreign elements in the conflict in Ituri, and in particular to the role of Uganda, Rwanda and (in the case of the Defence) the MONUC (para.

200). The Chamber subsequently proceeded to examine the notion of international armed conflict, in order to assess whether the conflict in Ituri should have been qualified as such.

Article 21 of the Rome Statute allows the Court to take into account, as applicable law, in the first place, the Statute, Elements of Crimes and Rules of Procedure and Evidence of the ICC; in the second place, where appropriate, applicable treaties and the principles and rules of international law, including the established principles of the international law of armed conflict. Failing the first and second sources of law, the Court can also apply general principles of law derived from national laws of legal systems of the world including, as appropriate, the national laws of States that would normally exercise jurisdiction over the crime.[17] The Chamber therefore took into account firstly its internal sources (which it considered of little use, as the only provision on the qualification of an armed conflict is footnote 34 of the Elements of Crimes, according to which the term international armed conflict includes military occupation) and subsequently the principles of international law. With regard to the latter, the PTC took into consideration not only common Article 2 of the Geneva Conventions (and their commentary), but also the jurisprudence of the ICTY, and in particular of its Appeals Chamber in the case *Prosecutor v. Dusko Tadić*. It is interesting to see that the PTC, while acting in accordance with Article 21(1)(b), and thus applying 'the established principles of the international law of armed conflict', took into account the interpretation of these principles given by another international criminal tribunal, thus reaffirming the validity of cross-references in the judgments of international tribunals when interpreting rules of international law that have already been applied by other tribunals.

The Pre-Trial Chamber then moved to examine the facts and the evidence of an involvement of Uganda in the territory of the DRC; its conclusion that Uganda was present in Ituri as an occupying power until June 2003 seems however to be based more on the ICJ's judgment than on the evidence presented for the purpose of the confirmation of charges (which, in any case, was not presented in order to prove the international characterization of the armed conflict, as it was originally not included in the charges). Indeed, of the 8 paragraphs that the Court devotes to an analysis of the facts, only two make reference to evidence related specifically to the *Lubanga* case, and – although the relevant portion is heavily redacted in the public version of the decision – it seems that most evidence was very general and vague; for instance, none of the cited statements seems to have made specific reference to the date of Uganda's withdrawal from the DRC. In the remaining six paragraphs, the PTC quoted the ICJ's judgment, and the evidence on which the ICJ had relied, to confirm its statement on the presence of Uganda as an occupying force in Ituri.

This way of proceeding seems to be quite problematic: indeed, while there is nothing wrong in one Court citing the jurisprudence of another tribunal to support its statements and its interpretation of the law, using the judgment of

[17] See Pellet (2002) 1015 ff.

one Court as the main basis for a factual finding by another Tribunal is highly disputable, and the more so if we consider that the ICC, as an international criminal tribunal, is governed by rules of evidence and applies standards of proof that are not the same as the ones applicable in front of the ICJ. In the present case, the PTC seemingly decided to make a different evaluation of the facts than the one alleged by the Prosecutor, basing its decision mainly, if not entirely, on the ICJ's Judgment. Of course, this last assertion is disputable, as we do not know how much evidence of the presence of Uganda in Ituri the PTC had in front of itself; however, the evidence that the PTC cites mostly comes from the ICJ's Judgment. To confirm this impression, we can take into account para. 221 of the Decision on the confirmation of charges: in this portion, the PTC concedes that some of the evidence admitted for the purpose of the confirmation hearing bears on the role of Rwanda in the conflict in Ituri, and in particular on Rwanda's backing the UPC; however, although this evidence is described as 'substantial', and summarized in paras. 222 to 225, the PTC concludes that the paucity of the evidence before it does not allow it to find that there are substantial grounds to believe that Rwanda intervened, directly or indirectly, in Ituri. It is of course impossible to know what would have happened, had the ICJ also adjudicated on the case *DRC v. Rwanda*; however, reading the confirmation decision one is left with the feeling that the PTC might have had, in front of itself, as much evidence on the role of Rwanda as on that of Uganda, and thus, that the decision to only consider Uganda's occupation derives primarily from the fact that it could base this decision on a judgment coming from the ICJ.[18] As the ICJ had already considered proven the responsibility of Uganda for occupying the territory of Ituri, as well as for the violations of human rights and humanitarian law committed in that area by the UPDF, the Pre-Trial Chamber seemingly took judicial notice of the ICJ's decision, treating the facts underlying Uganda's occupation in a manner that is not very different from the one resulting from the application of the principle of *res judicata*. Although this was clearly done in order to avoid characterizing the same factual situation, at the international level, both as an occupation and a non occupation, and thus to avoid a conflict on the qualification of the same facts, and although the role of Uganda in the conflict in the DRC is a historically well proven fact, there are a number of grounds that allow criticism of the PTC's decision.

5 Did the PTC Have the Power to Amend the Charges?

The first problematic aspect of the decision under consideration is the interpretation that the PTC gave of Article 61 of the Rome Statute, which concerns the powers of the Pre Trial Chamber after the confirmation hearing. It might be useful to recall the wording of Article 61(7), which states that the Chamber may:

[18] See de Beco (2008) 325.

a) confirm those charges in relation to which it has determined that there is sufficient evidence, and commit the person to a Trial Chamber for trial on the charges as confirmed;
b) decline to confirm those charges in relation to which it has determined that there is insufficient evidence;
c) adjourn the hearing and request the Prosecutor to consider:
(i) providing further evidence or conducting further investigation with respect to a particular charge; or
(ii) amending a charge because the evidence submitted appears to establish a different crime within the jurisdiction of the Court.

What emerges from this provision is that the PTC has no discretional power to amend the charges: according to the wording of Article 61, even if the evidence appears to establish a different crime within the jurisdiction of the Court, the Chamber can only adjourn the hearing and request the Prosecutor to consider amending the charges. In the case against Lubanga, however, the PTC interpreted this provision in quite an imaginative way,[19] and therefore determined that it had the power to amend the charges in that specific case. The Chamber argued that the purpose of the provision is to prevent the PTC from committing a person for trial for crimes which would be materially different from those set out in the Document Containing the Charges and for which the Defence would not have had the opportunity to submit observations at the confirmation hearing (para. 203 of the Decision). Consequently, it stated that, in that specific case, it was not necessary to adjourn the hearing and request the Prosecutor to amend the charges because the relevant articles of the Rome Statute, which criminalize conscripting, enlisting and using actively in hostilities children under the age of 15 in an international or a non-international armed conflict (articles 8(2)(b)(xxvi) and 8(2)(e)(vii) of the Statute), 'criminalise the same conduct' (para. 204).

However, by confirming charges that were different from the ones alleged by the Prosecutor, the Chamber seems to have acted *ultra vires*: as the Prosecutor himself claimed, when requesting the PTC to grant the Office leave to appeal the Decision, 'the Pre-Trial Chamber, by proceeding in this manner, has altered the characterization of the charge. This has been done despite the clear language of the Statute, which only allows the Chamber to adjourn the proceedings and request the Prosecution to consider amending a charge, if the Chamber is of the view that the evidence submitted appears to establish a different crime. As a result, the Prosecution is forced to proceed with a crime that it had already determined, after careful examination of the evidence in its possession, should not be charged, and to devote time and resources to supplement that evidence, if possible, in order to adequately substantiate that crime at trial'.[20] It seems worth to recall that the request for leave to appeal was rejected by the PTC, which

[19] Bekou (2008) 343.

[20] ICC, Office of the Prosecutor, Case *Prosecutor v. Thomas Lubanga Dyilo*, Application for Leave to Appeal Pre-Trial Chamber I's 29 January 2007 'Décision sur la confirmation des charges', para. 2.

made reference to the fact that the legal characterisation of the conflict as of an international nature had already been mentioned in the *Decision on the arrest warrant against Thomas Lubanga Dyilo* (issued on 10 February 2006), and that pursuant to regulation 55 of the Regulations of the Court, the Trial Chamber has the power to 'change the legal characterisation of facts to accord with the crimes under articles 6, 7 or 8, or to accord with the form of participation of the accused'.[21]

It seems that the PTC both went beyond its powers, adjudicating on an issue which the Rome Statute leaves to the Prosecutor's autonomy, and gave a very reductive interpretation of the term 'crime'. Indeed, while the crime, in its material elements, may well be the same if committed in an international or in a national armed conflict, there are huge differences if one takes into consideration a broader notion of crime: for instance, in this case the accused had not been charged with committing war crimes in the context of an international armed conflict, and thus could not defend himself, at the confirmation hearing, by claiming that the conflict was not international. Moreover, between the material elements of the two crimes specifically charged there is a difference, which the PTC analysed and tried to minimize, but which calls into question the interpretation and scope of application of the two provisions: indeed, while the conduct, in the case of a non international armed conflict, is described as 'conscripting or enlisting children under the age of fifteen years into armed forces or groups or using them to participate actively in hostilities', in an international conflict the crime is that of 'conscripting or enlisting children under the age of fifteen years into the national armed forces or using them to participate actively in hostilities.' There is a clear difference between the letter of the two provisions; however, the PTC declared this difference to be irrelevant, and gave an interpretation of the term 'national armed forces' which, although partly persuasive, tends to minimize the divergence and to imply that, even if the Rome Statute uses different words, the meaning of the terms cannot but be the same (see the decision, paras. 268 to 285). Now, irrespective of the reasons for such a difference (purportedly not casual, as according to some Authors it is due to the pressure coming from Arab States, afraid that otherwise the participation of children into the *intifadah* would have been prohibited,[22] it is clear that the difference exists, and therefore the crimes cannot be considered to be the same, as the PTC claimed. Thus, the Chamber actually confirmed charges against the suspect which were different from the ones originally formulated by the Prosecutor, both forcing the latter to find evidence that would, at Trial, prove beyond any reasonable doubt that the conflict in Ituri was international and that the UPC/FPLC was a 'national armed force', and depriving the suspect of his right to challenge these two elements at the pre-trial phase.[23]

21 ICC, Pre Trial Chamber I, Decision on the Prosecution and Defence applications for leave to appeal the Decision on the confirmation of charges, 24 May 2007.

22 See Cottier (1999) 473; von Hebel and Robinson (1999) 118.

23 Ochoa (2008) 53.

6 Is a Different Factual Assessment by Different International Tribunals to be Avoided at All Costs?

Another very interesting issue relates to the general problem of the different characteristics of factual and legal conflicts between international tribunals, and in particular between international criminal tribunals and other types of Courts: in particular, the question is whether, in the case under examination, a conflict between the qualification of the facts given by the ICJ and the ICC would have been as problematic as if the ICC had given an interpretation of rules of customary international law divergent from that of the ICJ.

When two international tribunals declare the existence of incompatible rules of law, this can jeopardize the unity, coherence and thus authority of the international legal system as a whole: for instance, as seen above, if the ICJ applies one criterion to assess State's responsibility, while the ICTY declares the existence of another, this clearly gives rise to a tension between the two courts. Indeed, as the same legal system cannot contain two rules of law which are incompatible with each other on the very same issue, either the ICJ or the ICTY erred in its law-finding function, applying a rule of law that does not correspond to that existing at the international level. However, while these types of conflicts lead to uncertainties on the existing rules of international customary law, the same does not hold true for conflicts on facts and on their legal qualification. Indeed, even in national legal systems different types of Courts can, and often do, qualify differently the same facts: this is not considered to be symptomatic of an incoherence in the system, as different courts have to apply different standards of proof and can use, to form their judgment, different types of evidence. Thus, while conflicting statements on the exact content of a rule of law always give rise to a conflict, as the law cannot regulate differently the same situation depending on the type of Tribunal that applies it, contradictory statements regarding the facts and their qualification are often unavoidable, and justified by the circumstances. For instance, in the case of the decision on the confirmation of charges against Thomas Lubanga, had the Chamber confirmed the charges, not even considering that the nature of the armed conflict in the DRC was disputed, such a decision would not have implied a violation of the ICJ's judgment, even if reiterated by the Trial Chamber in its final judgment: indeed, the ICC, as a criminal tribunal, has to apply a different (much higher) standard of proof, and to decide only taking into account the evidence brought before it by the parties according to its own rules of procedure and evidence.

The questionability of the PTC's decision to amend the charges with regard to the nature of the armed conflict, taking into account the ICJ's decision on this issue, also emerges from an analysis of the latter judgment, and of the evidence that the Court used in order to adjudicate on Uganda's responsibility. In the *DRC v. Uganda* case, the ICJ had to deal with a great number of highly factual issues, as the outcome of the case depended more on an assessment of the facts than on their legal qualification: indeed, the questions at stake were mainly factual (whether Uganda was in the DRC, for how long, and what did its troops do). It has been noted[24] that the ICJ, in this case, based its decision mainly on some MONUC reports and on the report of the Porter Commission; in the final judgment, the ICJ made a general statement on the way in which it would evaluate the evidence before it, stating that it would treat with caution evidentiary materials specially prepared for the case and also materials emanating from a single source, and would prefer contemporaneous evidence from persons with direct knowledge, giving particular attention to reliable evidence acknowledging facts or conduct unfavourable to the State represented by the person making them. Moreover, it added that it would also give weight to evidence that had not been challenged by impartial persons for the correctness of what it contains, and noted that evidence 'obtained by examination of persons directly involved, and who were subsequently cross-examined by judges skilled in examination and experienced in assessing large amounts of factual information, some of it of a technical nature, merits special attention' (para. 61). In the evaluation of the evidence, the Court did, indeed, apply these standards; thus, it rejected as unreliable some of the evidence produced by the DRC in order to substantiate its claims, finding the items of evidence 'uncorroborated, based on second-hand reports, or not in fact saying what they are alleged to say by the DRC, or even in some cases partisan' (para. 159). Notwithstanding these exclusions, the ICJ based its decision mainly on secondary, documentary evidence; in particular, with regard to the portion of the judgment concerning Uganda's occupation, the ICJ based its decision primarily on one fact, not disputed between the parties, that was proven mainly through documentary evidence. Indeed, the Court, having stated that 'it is not disputed between the Parties that General Kazini, commander of the Ugandan forces in the DRC, created the new 'province of Kibali-Ituri' in June 1999 and appointed Ms Adèle Lotsove as its Governor', proceeded to state that this conduct was clear evidence of the fact that Uganda established and exercised authority in Ituri as an occupying power. Thus, this portion of the ICJ's judgment is based mainly on one fact, which is clearly considered to be proven even because it is not disputed between the parties: however, an agreed fact between Uganda and the DRC, while relevant for the decision of the International Court of Justice, cannot form the basis of a decision on the criminal responsibility of an accused before the ICC.

Another problematic aspect, with which the Pre-Trial Chamber was not directly confronted but that will emerge again at Trial, concerns the different standards of proof applicable in front of the two tribunals. Indeed, while the standard of proof that the ICJ applies is not determined in its Statute and Rules, and therefore the ICJ has to set its own standards for each decision it takes, depending of course on the seriousness of the allegations (see the judgment in the Genocide case, para. 210), the ICC has to apply a fixed standard of proof in each of the phases of its procedure: thus, while the PTC only has to determine whether there is sufficient evidence to establish substantial grounds to believe

[24] Halink (2008).

that the person suspected committed the alleged crimes (Article 61 of the Rome Statute), at Trial the standard is that of 'beyond any reasonable doubt', which is typical of criminal trials (Article 66(3) of the Statute). Thus, the evidence that the ICJ considers as sufficient to prove a fact might be insufficient to prove the same fact before the Trial or the Appeals Chambers of the ICC. From this viewpoint, the fact that two distinct international tribunals reach a different factual conclusion on the same issue does not give rise to any conflict; indeed, the unity and coherence of the international legal system is not jeopardized by the coexistence of two judgments, taken according to different standards of proof, reaching opposite conclusions on the facts. Indeed, even national legal systems, which are organized in order to attain coherence and to avoid any type of conflict, often allow different types of courts to take diverging decisions on the same fact: an accused might well be acquitted of the criminal charges against him but sentenced to pay compensation for the damages caused by the same conduct. While part of the general public might find this to be inexplicable, as it is understood to mean that the same person both did and did not commit a fact, lawyers tend to agree that there is no tension between the two decisions: the evidence against a person might well satisfy a civil court, while insufficient to prove guilt beyond any reasonable doubt.

Although we can agree that divergences at the international level should be minimized, and that too much difference in the assessment of the same facts, or in the law that is applicable to them, may not be easily understood by the general public, thus weakening the image of international law,[25] there is a huge difference, from a legal point of view, between different assessments of the facts and of the law, especially when the facts are assessed differently by two tribunals that have to take into consideration different types of evidence and to assess its value according to different standards of proof. A divergence on the existence and scope of application of the same rule of law always reduces the unity of international law, as one legal system cannot include contradictory rules of law that apply to the same issue. On the other hand, a different assessment of the facts might, in some cases, be unavoidable, due to the higher standard of proof that applies before international criminal tribunals: although it is clear that divergences should be, to the extent possible, minimized, there are cases where they cannot be, and thus where a different assessment of the same facts is just unavoidable. In such cases, trying to acquire coherence at all costs between tribunals that have different jurisdictions might only be possible by violating basic principles of law, such as those regarding the standards of evidence to be applied in front of criminal tribunals and the role of the parties at Trial.

[25] Van den Wyngaert (2006) 68.

7 Conclusions

The solution that the Pre Trial Chamber of the ICC adopted, which is seemingly, at least partly, due to its willingness to avoid conflicting assessments of the same facts before different international tribunals, gives rise to some perplexities. Surely, the choice to take into account the ICJ's judgment cannot but be praised: the PTC recognized that another international court had already adjudicated on matters that could bear consequences on the nature of the armed conflict, and acted so as to minimize the risk of conflicts on the evaluation of the same facts. Moreover, the PTC, by citing both the jurisprudence of the ICJ and ICTY, proved its willingness to follow their reasoning and their interpretation of international rules, thus avoiding the insurgence of unnecessary conflicts. However, it seems that the best way to proceed would have been, according to Article 61(7), to ask the Prosecutor to reconsider the charges, allowing him to use his discretionary powers in assessing the evidence in his possession: this would have minimized the risk of a divergent assessment of the same facts, as the Prosecutor would have been bound to reconsider the evidence in his possession, without giving the impression of one Court treating the factual assessments of the other as *res judicata*.

A different assessment of the same facts might be, in the present or in any future case, unavoidable, due to the differences in the jurisdiction and rules of evidence of the two international tribunals. While deference should be paid, at the international level, to the decisions of the ICJ, other international tribunals, in particular those having jurisdiction over international crimes, are not bound to follow them, and their evaluation of the facts, and for good reasons: thus, if the practice of cross-reference can only be praised, as it ensures uniformity in the interpretation and application of the law, the need for coherence should not be extended too much, crossing the line between a (desirable) consistency in the application of the law and evaluation of the facts and the unnecessary creation, at the international level, of a principle of *res judicata* whose content would be even broader than in national systems.

References

O. Bekou, 'Prosecutor v. Thomas Lubanga Dyilo, Decision on the confirmation of charges' [2008] 8 *Human rights law review* 343.

T. Buergenthal, 'Proliferation of international courts and tribunals: is it good or bad?' [2001] *Leiden Journal of International Law* 267.

E. Cannizzaro, 'Interconnecting international jurisdictions: a contribution from the Genocide Decision of the ICJ' [2007] 1 *European Journal of Legal Studies*, available at http://www.ejls.eu/1/5UK.pdf.

A. Cassese, 'The Nicaragua and Tadić tests revisited in light of the ICJ Judgment on Genocide in Bosnia', [2007] 18 *European Journal of International Law* 649.

M. Cottier, *Article 8 (2)(b)(xxvi)*, in O Triffterer, *A commentary to the Rome Statute of the International Criminal Court* (Baden Baden 1999) 466 ff.

G. de Beco, 'The Confirmation of Charges before the International Criminal Court: evaluation and first application' [2007] 7 *International Criminal Law Review* 469.

G. De Beco, 'War crimes in international versus non-international armed conflicts: 'new wine in old wineskins'?' [2008] 8 *International Criminal Law Review* 319.

Pierre-Marie Dupuy, 'The danger of fragmentation or unification of the International legal system and the International Court of Justice' [1999] 31 *New York University Journal of International Law and Politics* 791.

H. Fujita, 'Chevauchements juridictionnels et tribunaux internationaux' *Liber amicorum Judge Shigeru Oda* [2002] Kluwer Law International 575.

G. Hafner, 'Der IGH und der Internationale Strafgerichtshof', in *Liber amicorum Judge Shigeru Oda* [2002] Kluwer Law International 587-619.

S. Halink, 'All things considered: how the International Court of Justice delegated its fact-assessment to the United Nations in the Armed Activities case' [2008] 40 *New York University Journal of International Law and Politics* 13.

M. Marchesiello, 'Proceedings before the Pre-Trial Chambers', in A. Cassese, P. Gaeta, D. Jones (ed.), *The Rome Statute of the International Criminal Court: A Commentary*, (Oxford 2002) 1231.

M. Milanovic, 'State Responsibility for Genocide' [2006] 17 *European Journal of International Law* 553.

M. Milanovic, 'State Responsibility for Genocide: a follow up', [2007] 18 *European Journal of International Law* 669.

J.C. Ochoa S, 'The ICC's Pre-Trial Chamber I Confirmation of charges decision in the case of Prosecutor v. Thomas Lubanga Dyilo: between application and development of international criminal la' [2008]16 *European Journal of Crime, Criminal Law and Criminal Justice* 39.

A. Pellet, 'Applicable law', in A Cassese, P Gaeta, D Jones (eds), *The Rome Statute of the International Criminal Court: A Commentary*, (Oxford 2002) 1051.

C.P.R. Romano, 'The proliferation of international judicial bodies: the pieces of the puzzle' 31 *New York University Journal of International Law and Politics* 709.

Shabtai Rosenne, *The perplexities of modern international law* (Leiden 2004) Nijhoff publisher.

W.A. Schabas, *An introduction to the International Criminal Court* (2004) Cambridge University Press.

M. Shahabuddeen, 'Consistency in holdings by International Tribunals' *Liber amicorum Judge Shigeru Oda* [2002] Kluwer Law International 647.

Y. Shany, *The competing jurisdictions of international courts and tribunals*, Oxford University Press, 2003.

G. Stessen, C. Van den Wyngaert, 'The international non bis in idem principle: resolving some of the unanswered questions' [1999] 48 *International and Comparative Law Quarterly* 779.

C. van den Wyngaert, 'International criminal courts as fact (and truth) finders in post-conflict societies: can disparities with ordinary international courts be avoided' [2006]100 *American society of International Law proceedings* 63.

H. von Hebel and D. Robinson, 'Crimes within the jurisdiction of the Court' in R.S. Lee (ed), *The international criminal Court: the making of the Rome Statute*, (1999) Kluwer Law International 79.

CHAPTER II

Trade Remedies Disputes – Reciprocal Relationship between WTO and NAFTA Tribunals

Jorge A. Huerta-Goldman*

Outline of the Chapter

This article is about the reciprocal relationship between two independent tribunals – the WTO and the 1904 NAFTA Panel – reviewing antidumping or countervailing duty Orders. Subject to certain jurisdictional requirements, both tribunals may review even the same trade remedy Order imposed within the NAFTA region. After a brief overview of trade remedy cases, I present the main elements of both tribunals. Later, I describe the cases where both tribunals reviewed the same Order. I argue that 1904 NAFTA legal remedies are narrower than those of WTO but 1904 Panellists are more open to stretch the provisions of these legal remedies in issuing their findings. Also, 1904 Panellists often follow the reasoning and findings of the WTO Panel/AB when reviewing the same determination. Sometimes, they even import WTO law into their ruling even though 1904 Panels rule based on national law.

Introduction

A WTO Panel/Appellate Body (AB) may review an antidumping (AD) or countervailing (CVD) Order at the same time as a NAFTA 1904 Panel.[1] The Order has to be imposed by a NAFTA Party and affect exports from another NAFTA Party. The WTO tribunals give standing to WTO Members, whereas the NAFTA 1904 Panel not only gives standing to the NAFTA Parties – all of them WTO Members – but also to private parties.

At first sight, this duplication of tribunals might appear to create issues of double *fora*. I have argued that this is not the case.[2] The NAFTA 1904 Panel replaces domestic tribunals reviewing the AD/CVD Order in the NAFTA Party imposing it. The WTO Panel/AB has ruled out arguments on *estoppel* when domestic courts review the same AD/CVD Orders. Furthermore, the parties are not the same when a private party triggers the 1904 Panel; and the substantive law is not the same: one is based on WTO Law and the other on domestic law.[3]

---

* The author is currently working for the Mexican Ministry of Economy and may be contacted at jahg@mexico-wto.org or jorge.huerta@unine.ch. The opinions expressed in this work are entirely those of the author and he alone is responsible for the accuracy of the information. I would like to thank Peter Bennett, Pablo Klein-Bernard and Marisa Goldstein for their comments and guidance in writing this article. I would also like to thank and recognize Luis Fraile Nogal for his excellent research assistance.

1 In addition to the procedures under Chapter 19 of NAFTA, which include 1904 Panels, NAFTA has two more main dispute settlement procedures. Chapter 20 contains the general dispute settlement mechanisms of the NAFTA (Country vs Country procedures), and Chapter 11 contains investment disputes and substantive commitments (private party vs Country procedures). These two chapters are outside the scope of this article.

2 See Huerta-Goldman (2009).

3 Under Mexican law, international treaties are part of domestic law. The WTO covered agreements are, accordingly, part of Mexican law.

After a brief description of trade remedy Orders, I describe the main elements of the WTO dispute settlement and the 1904 NAFTA Panels (Section 1). The reciprocal relationship between these two tribunals in specific cases is presented in section 2. The subsequent section presents my observations (Section 3), followed by the conclusions.

1 Background

1.1 The AD/CVD Investigations in a Nutshell

Assume *US Pens* sells pens in the US territory for US$ 1.50 (normal value) and exports the same pens to Mexico for US$ 1 (export price), as presented in Table 1. For determining the margin of dumping, the comparison of both prices has to be made at the same level of trade, normally at the ex-factory level (Art 2.4 of the ADA), through deductions and adjustments to the raw data from the transactions. Also, the dumped imports have to affect competing producers in Mexico (*Plumas MEX*) producing pens that are like products (Art. 2.6 of the ADA).

Table 1. Hypothetical example of Dumping

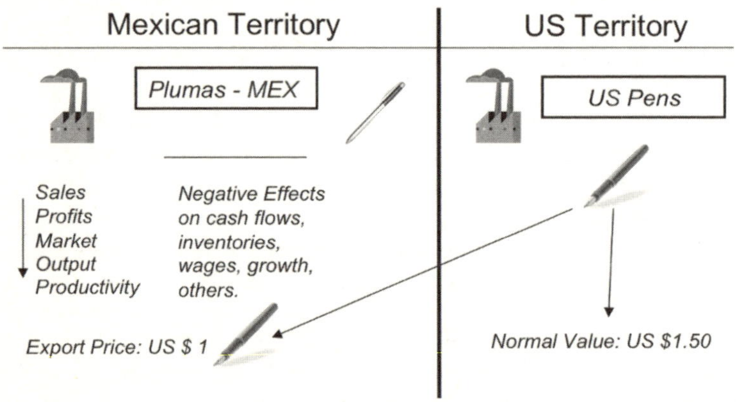

Dumping exists, under Art. 2.1 of the ADA, if '[...] the export price of the product exported from one country to another is less than the comparable price, in the ordinary course of trade, for the like product when destined for consumption in the exporting country.'

Injury, under Art. 3 of the ADA, means 'material injury', 'threat of material injury' or 'material retardation of the establishment of an industry.' Two elements are to be objectively assessed in an injury determination: a) the volume of the dumped imports and their effects on prices in the importer WTO

Member; and b) the impact of these imports on domestic producers of such products.

The determination on causation between dumping and injury must be based on all relevant evidence, and may not attribute the injurious effects of factors other than the dumped imports (Art. 3.5 of ADA).

When applicable, and in compliance with the ADA requirements, the importing Member may apply an AD duty to the dumped imports. In our hypothetical example, Mexico would be entitled to impose an AD duty of 50% on pens coming from US Pens.[4]

There are some procedural requirements for each stage of the AD Order: standing and initiation (Art. 5 of the ADA), thresholds on the provisional AD determination (Art. 7 of the ADA), thresholds on the final AD determination (Art. 9 of the ADA), price undertaking with the exporter to eliminate injury (Art. 8 of the ADA), publicity (Art. 12 of the ADA), duration and subsequent reviews (Art. 11 of the ADA) among others.

Summarizing, from a procedural perspective an AD/CVD Order may have different determinations as it develops. The AD investigation starts with a public notice of initiation, followed by a public notice of imposition, or if not, of a provisional measure and, if applicable, a public notice of the final determination.[5] Yearly reviews may apply and a sunset-review must be undertaken after each period of five years. These reviews require the assessment of the likelihood of the continuation or recurrence of injury, and likelihood of dumping, if the Order were to be revoked. Other special procedures may take place if, for example, there is a new shipper. Each of these procedural stages has different thresholds with respect to the substantive requirements on initiation, dumping, injury and causation. The dispute settlement procedures of the WTO and the NAFTA 1904 Panel offer the possibility of reviewing most of the determinations of these procedural stages, as explained below.

CVD Orders are applied in a very similar way to AD duties. But the element of dumping is replaced by a subsidy provided by the exporting WTO Member (Art. 10 *et seq.* of ASCM).[6] Note that a subsidy may be challenged by two means: the imposition of CVDs by the importing Member in order to protect its territory from the injurious effects of the subsidy; and a direct challenge to the subsidy (prohibited subsidies or serious prejudice) through a WTO case in order to eliminate the whole subsidy or its effects (Art. 3 to 7 of the ASCM). The

4 The mathematical equation for determining the margin of dumping is as follows: D=NV-EP/EP, where NV is normal value and EP export price. So, in our hypothetical example the equation would be as follows: 1.50–1/1=0.5*100=50%.

5 The US AD/CVD orders offer an additional complication when trying to understand their development. The US has a dual system where the investigating authority is split: the International Trade Commission investigates the injury and the Department of Commerce the dumping/subsidy. So, for instance, a final AD order would have a determination from each agency.

6 Agreement on Subsidies and Countervailing Duties.

former protects the market of the importer Member whereas the later attacks the WTO legality of the subsidy.

1.2 WTO Dispute Settlement Procedures

A WTO Member can file a complaint against another WTO Member. This is a dispute in the sense of Art. 1 of the DSU. The DSU process contains various stages,[7] as shown in Table 2. Each stage comprises a variety of steps. For instance, the Panel stage begins with the request for a Panel, followed by its establishment.[8]

Table 2. Procedural Stages of the DSU with their Questions to be Solved

Procedure	*Question to be solved*
Consultations[1]	Can the Parties negotiate a solution by themselves?
Panel procedure[2]	Are the facts in violation of WTO law?[3]
Appellate Body procedure[4]	Are the legal interpretations and issues of law correctly applied and assessed by the Panel?[5]
Reasonable period of time or RPT (by negotiation or arbitration)[6]	What is the time the defendant has to comply with the Panel/AB recommendations?
Panel/AB under Art. 21.5 of the DSU[7]	Is the measure taken to comply with the Panel/AB report: a) existent, and/or b) consistent with the Covered Agreements?
Arbitration under Art. 22.6 of the DSU[8]	What is the impact caused by the illegal measure?[9] Or what is the level of countermeasures?[10]

1) See Art. 4 of the DSU. 2) See Art. 6 to 16 and 19 of the DSU. 3) Two basic and simple questions must be answered in order to tackle the main issue: what are the facts? And what are the WTO obligations? 4) See Art. 17 to 19 of the DSU. 5) See Art. 17.6 of the DSU. 6) See Art. 21.3 of the DSU. 7) See Art. 21.5 of the DSU. In practice, the provisions for consultations, Panel and AB procedure may apply *mutatis mutandis*. 8) Art. 22.6 and 22.7 contain most of the procedural guidance for this arbitration. But most of the paragraphs under Art. 22 of the DSU can be relevant for the substance of the arbitration. 9) The arbitrator may have to answer the following specific issues: a) is the level of suspension equivalent to the level of nullification or impairment? b) is the suspension allowed by the Covered Agreements? and c) have the principles of Art. 22.3 of the DSU been followed? 10) See Art. 4.11 and 7.9 of the SCM Agreement.

The DSU does not contain any specific Article dealing with the jurisdiction of Panels, unlike Article 36 of the Statute of the International Court of Justice. Nonetheless, different DSU provisions deal tacitly with the jurisdiction of

---

7 Since they are not necessarily used in the whole DSU process (they are not part of the sequence of procedures), we do not include two procedures in this chart: good offices, conciliation and mediation (Art. 5 of the DSU) and arbitration as an alternative dispute settlement mechanism (Art. 25 of the DSU).

8 For further reading on the work of the DSU, see the comprehensive and detailed work by Palmeter and Mavroidis (2004). Further research on the DSU process has been developed by the following authors: Huerta-Goldman (2009); Bhala (2008); Mavroidis (2007); Jackson, Davey and Sykes (2001) and Jackson (2000).

Panels/AB/arbitrators.[9] These provisions provide the WTO with the capacity for compulsory jurisdiction depending on the subject matter (*ratione materiae*), and the Parties to the dispute (*ratione personae*) (Palmeter and Mavroidis 2004, page 17 *et seq.*).

The WTO requires compliance with the Panel report – temporary compensation or retaliation are transitional options. A dispute can, of course, always be settled through a mutually agreed solution (MAS). Compliance, and to some extent MAS, are usually referred to as 'property rules' – which capture the idea that the Parties to a contract must *always* perform the contract. Compensation and retaliation are 'liability rules' – which provide the Parties to the contract with the possibility of compensating *in lieu* of performing the contract.[10] The WTO DSU takes an unambiguous stance in favour of 'property rules' (compliance). For instance, if a 'liability rule' such as compensation has been agreed, but the illegality persists, the author of the illegal measure may face new complaints by other WTO Members.

Table 3. Legal Remedies in the WTO Broken up into Property/Liability Rules, Procedural Stages and the Member Implementing the Legal Remedy

	MAS	*Compliance*	*Compensation*	*Retaliation*
Property rules vs liability rules	Property rules and/or liability rules[1]	Property rules	Liability rules	Liability rules
WTO Procedural Stage	Any procedural stage	The end of the RPT	The end of the RPT[2]	*De jure*: the end of the RPT *De facto*: after a possible 21.5 Panel/AB
Member Implementing the Legal Remedy	Complainant and defendant	Defendant	Complainant and defendant	Complainant

1) A MAS may include steps to comply, terms of compensation or even characteristics of retaliatory measures. 2) *De jure*, negotiations on compensation start at the end of the RPT. However, the so-called 'sequencing agreement' contains a *de facto* lacuna on when the negotiations have to take place. Since, according to this agreement, Art. 21.5 of the DSU takes effect before any retaliatory measures are authorised, the negotiations on compensation are omitted.

9 See for instance the following provisions of the DSU: Art. 1 (coverage and application), Art. 2 (establishment of a Dispute Settlement Body), Art. 3.1 (member's adherence to the principles applied by the GATT), Art. 6 (establishment of Panels), Art. 7 (terms of reference), Art. 17.6 (issues of law on appeals), Art. 17.13 (authorizing the AB to uphold, modify or reverse the legal findings of the Panel).

10 See Mavroidis (2007 § 4.9) for a classification of WTO legal remedies into property rules and liability rules. Schwartz and Sykes (2002) advocate legal remedies that provide 'efficient breach' of WTO law – *i.e.*, the defendant would give to the victorious complainant something of equal value in exchange for what he was obliged to give by WTO law had the contract been fulfilled.

1.3 Panels under Art. 1904 of NAFTA (Chapter 19 of NAFTA)

An Art. 1904 Panel,[11] usually triggered by a private party,[12] revises final AD/CVDs imposed by one of the three NAFTA Parties. It is a substitute for domestic legal procedures challenging those final AD/CVDs. A 1904 Panel may remand or affirm the final determination subject to review. There may be several remands with respect to the same final determination and several 1904 Panels reviewing different final determinations within the same AD/CVD Order.

The following hypothetical example serves to explain the situation of an AD Order that has been challenged through a 1904 Panel.

Assume that the investigating authority of a NAFTA Party has an AD Order in place and issues different final AD determinations: final determination, first administrative review, second administrative review, third administrative review, fourth administrative review and a sunset review.

Table 4 shows a case where a given exporter, for instance, challenged three final decisions (within the same AD Order) through the 1904 Panel: the definitive AD determination, the first administrative review and the third administrative review.

The Panel dealing with the final AD determination remanded the determination to the investigating authority for correction. The investigating authority then sent back its re-determination to the Panel, which sent it back again (remanded) for further amendments. Finally, the investigating authority sent its second re-determination back and the 1904 Panel affirmed it. The same situation occurred in our example, with respect to the third administrative review where we have three Procedures under a 1904 Panel. Still in our example, the Panel affirmed the investigating authority's determination on the first administrative review. Hence, there were no further Panels with respect to the final determination of the first review.

---

11 Chapter 19 of NAFTA contains three other dispute settlement procedures: the Extraordinary Challenge Committee's procedure covering review of possible behaviour by the Panel – *i.e.*, misconduct, conflict of interest, due process, jurisdiction; the review of AD/CVD statutory amendments; and involvement of the Special Committee safeguarding the functioning of the system whose role is to avoid obstruction in the establishment of Panels and to monitor the implementation of its decisions.

12 A NAFTA Party on its own initiative may request an Art. 1904 Panel. It seeks the initiation of an Art. 1904 Panel on request of a person who would otherwise be entitled under the law of the importing NAFTA Party to commence domestic procedures for judicial review of that final determination.

Table 4. Timeline of 1904 Panels under NAFTA

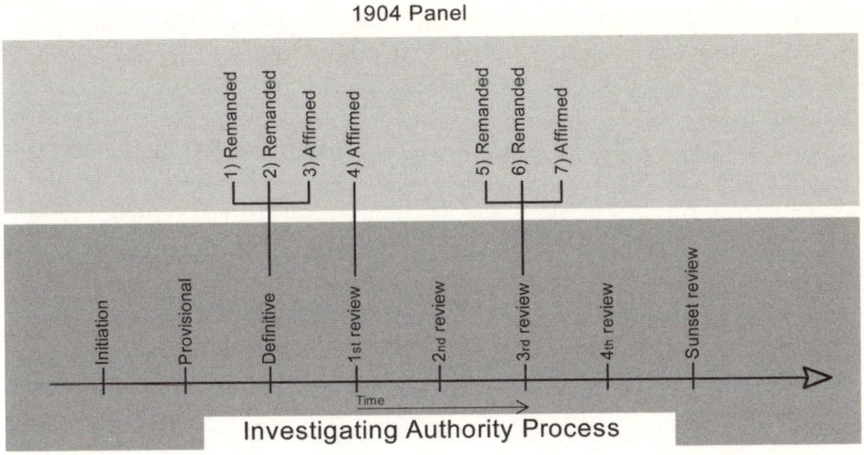

The main legal remedies in a 1904 Panel – to uphold or to remand the final determination – are 'property rules.' But if a NAFTA Party considers that a 1904 Panel has been undermined it can trigger the Special Committee. This procedure may lead to the suspension of NAFTA benefits or the suspension of Art. 1904 Procedures – 'liability rules.'

Table 5. The Legal Remedies of Art. 1904 Panels and the Special Committee

	Upheld	Remand (time)	Through the Special Committee: a) Suspension of Art. 1904 Panels b) Suspension of NAFTA benefits
Property rules vs liability rules	Property rules	Property rules	Liability rules

2 The Reciprocal Relationship between NAFTA and WTO Tribunals

There is no direct communication between a WTO Panel/AB and a NAFTA 1904 Panel as a procedural option. But nothing prohibits one tribunal from observing the findings and reasoning of the other, especially when both review the same determination within a given AD/CVD Order. I classified the cases into those where the finding by one of the tribunals was observed or followed by the other (Section 2.1) and those cases where the situation did not allow for that to happen, even though the two procedures were in place – for instance, when one of them did not produce a report (Section 2.2.).

2.1 Cases where one Tribunal Followed the Findings of the Other

2.1.1 Mexico's AD Order on Corn Syrup HFCS

The 1904 Panel on *HFCS (MEX-USA-98-1904-01)* closely observed the injury findings[13] and the procedures under WTO case *Mexico – HFCS (DS132)* as presented in Table 6.

Table 6. HFCS – Injury Findings

WTO	*1904 Panel*
Ordinary Panel (24 February 2000) inconsistency with Art. 3 of ADA (threat of material injury): - by considering only a part of the domestic industry's production, and - the potential effect of the restraint agreement. It recommended that the measure be brought into conformity.	1st remand (3 August 2001)[1] - prompt termination / refund; or - new justification of threat of injury - it noted the WTO ruling on threat of material injury.
21.5 Panel/AB (21 November 2001) inconsistency with Art. 3 of ADA (upheld by the AB): - impact of dumped imports and - the potential effect of the restraint agreement. It recommended that the measure be brought into conformity.	2nd remand (15 April 2002): - no later than 30 days to take action that the duties had been illegally imposed and collected - the imposition and collection of the duties violated international provisions and applicable laws; and - linked its findings to the WTO Panel/AB findings and concluded that the record does not support a conclusion of threat of injury. Basically, it ordered termination of the Order

1) The 21.5 Panel circulated its report on 22 June 2001, which is before the issuance of the first remand of the 1904 Panel.

The HFCS AD Order was withdrawn by Mexico on 21 May 2002 in compliance with the findings of the 1904 Panel. The complainants in the 1904 Panel linked the WTO dispute with the case at issue; and more importantly, the Art. 1904 Panel reacted accordingly.

13 There were other findings, but not fundamental to the interaction between the two tribunals.

2.1.2 US AD Order on OCTG

The WTO case in *US – OCTG from Mexico (DS282)* and *USA-MEX-2001-1904-03 (1904 of NAFTA)* concerned more or less the same subject matter. The WTO Panel/AB found that the likelihood-of-dumping determination in the First Sunset Review was inconsistent with WTO Law. The report was adopted by the DSB on 28 November 2005. The 1904 Panel reviewing the Sunset Review, on the other hand, issued five reports remanding the file back to the investigating authority on the likelihood determination of dumping (February 2005, February 2006, July 2006, January 2007, and June 2007). In its last report, the 1904 Panel ordered the investigating authority to issue a determination '[...] to the effect that the evidence [...] does not support a finding of likelihood of [...] dumping,' as it assumed that the US authorities were not able to issue a reasonable affirmative likelihood determination. Even though both Panels found on the lack of likelihood of dumping, the 1904 Panel did not use the same categorical language as the 1904 Panel in *HFCS 1904* with respect to the WTO report mentioned above.[14] There was no contradiction on the findings, from the WTO and the 1904 tribunals, with respect to the sunset review.

On 22 June 2007, the US revoked the OCTG AD Order pursuant to the Second Sunset review. The investigating authority found that the revocation of the Order would not be likely to lead to a continuation or recurrence of material injury. Even though the 1904 Panel ordered, within the limitations of its legal remedies available, the revocation of the Order on grounds of deficiencies in the first sunset review on the dumping determination, the US eliminated the Order for injury deficiencies in the second sunset review. It seems that the US decided to disregard the WTO and the 1904 Panel rulings on the antidumping determination with respect to the first sunset review.

2.1.3 US AD Order on Cement

The US *AD Order on Cement* produced two Multilateral Panels and the sixteen 1904 Panels on Cement.

The WTO Panel in *US – Cement from Mexico (DS281)* did not issue a report as the parties notified a MAS distributed on 21 May 2007 (WT/DS281/8), which provided for a gradual elimination of the AD duties and the settlement of NAFTA Chapter 19 cases and the WTO case.[15]

The only multilateral ruling with respect to this *AD Order on Cement* is the GATT report reviewing the initiation of the *AD Order on Cement from Mexico.*[16]

---

14 The findings of the WTO Panel/AB, which determined that there was no WTO violation, and the 1904 Panel findings affirming some claims are not taken into account.

15 For the text of the MAS relating to the *US AD order on Cement*, see http://ia.ita.doc.gov/cement-agreement/cement-final-agreement.pdf (Consulted in July 2009).

16 As noted above, the initiation of an AD order is a prerequisite for yearly reviews, sunset reviews and subsequent procedures within the same AD order.

The *US – Cement (GATT)*[17] case was initiated by Mexico against the imposition by the US on 30 August 1990 of an *AD duty order on imports of cement from Mexico*. Mexico's request for consultations was presented on 24 October 1990[18] claiming the violation of several provisions of the AD Code.[19] The products protected by the US were industrial Goods (cement). The GATT Panel ruled in favour of Mexico and:

- found the US initiation of the investigation on cement from Mexico inconsistent with Art. 5.1 of the Agreement on Implementation of Article VI of the General Agreement on Tariffs and Trade (Tokyo AD Code). The initiation was not on behalf of producers of all or almost all of the production in the regional market.[20] Other claims from Mexico were unresolved by the Panel.

With respect to NAFTA claims, the *AD order on Cement from Mexico* was challenged 16 times under NAFTA Chapter 19, contesting different final determinations within the same order. Some of them were remanded several times. Ten challenges against final determinations within the AD order on Cement did not produce a Panel report.[21] Three 1904 Panels eventually confirmed the final

[17] GATT Panel Report, *United States – Anti-Dumping Duties on Gray Portland Cement and Cement Clinker from Mexico*, ADP/82, 7 September 1992, unadopted.

[18] See Panel report, *United States – Anti-Dumping Duties on Gray Portland Cement and Cement Clinker from Mexico*, ADP/82, 7 September 1992, unadopted, para. 1.

[19] Mexico's claims were on Arts. 1, 3, 4, 5, and 6 of the Agreement on Implementation of Article VI of the General Agreement (Tokyo AD Code – the predecessor to the current ADA). See the Report of the GATT Panel, *United States – Anti-Dumping Duties on Gray Portland Cement and Cement Clinker from Mexico, ADP/82, 7 September 1992, unadopted*, para. 3.3.1 to 3.4.88.

[20] See the report of the Panel, *United States – Anti-Dumping Duties on Gray Portland Cement and Cement Clinker from Mexico, ADP/82, 7 September 1992, unadopted*, para. 5.34, 6.1 and 6.2.

[21] They are as follows:

i) Cement from Mexico; DOC final Results of the 8th AD duty administrative review (USA-MEX-2000-1904-03);

ii) Cement from Mexico; DOC final Results of the Full Sunset Review of the AD Duty Order (USA-MEX-2000-1904-05);

iii) Cement from Mexico; DOC final results of the 9th AD duty administrative review (USA-MEX-2001-1904-04);

iv) Cement from Mexico; USITC final results of the five year review of the AD duty order and USITC Dismissal of a Request to Institute a Section 751(b) Investigation (USA-MEX-2002-1904-01);

v) Cement from Mexico; DOC final results of the 10th AD duty administrative review (USA-MEX-2002-1904-05);

vi) Cement from Mexico; DOC final Results of the 11th AD duty administrative review (USA-MEX-2003-1904-01);

vii) Cement from Mexico; DOC final Results of the 12th AD duty administrative review (USA-MEX-2003-1904-03);

viii) Cement from Mexico; DOC final Results of the 13th AD duty administrative review (USA-MEX-2004-1904-03);

determination or the re-determination on remand subject to its review.[22] The remaining three 1904 Panels are mentioned below.[23]

There is no direct dialogue between the multilateral tribunals and the NAFTA 1904 Panels reviewing this AD order. There is no parallel ruling with respect to the same determination within the *AD order on Cement.* As mentioned above, the only multilateral ruling reviewed the initiation of the order – *i.e.*, the GATT Case – and neither the WTO tribunal nor the 1904 Panels dealt with the initiation of the order. Also, even though some of the determinations (yearly or sunset) of the *AD order on Cement* were challenged through a NAFTA 1904 Panel and the WTO, the WTO Panel did not issue a report. Accordingly, the 1904 Panel tribunals did not have any guidance from the WTO Panel/AB with respect to the same determinations within the same *AD order on Cement.*

Still, an issue with respect to reciprocal relationship is whether the GATT Panel had any influence on the three NAFTA 1904 Panel cases that were not ultimately affirmed and remained with unresolved remanded issues. Two of these cases had unresolved issues that were not related to the GATT Panel ruling on *cement,* that is the petition was not presented on behalf of 'all or almost all of the production in the regional market':

- The 1904 Panel dealing with the *sixth administrative review (USA-MEX-98-1904-02)* had unresolved remanded issues, which were not related to the ruling of the GATT Panel.[24]
- The 1904 Panel dealing with the seventh administrative review (USA-MEX-99-1904-03) had an unresolved remanded issue, which was not related to the ruling of the GATT Panel.[25]

---

ix) Cement from Mexico; DOC final Results of the 14th AD duty administrative review (USA-MEX-2006-1904-03); and

x) Cement from Mexico; DOC final Results of the AD duty administrative review (USA-MEX-2007-1904-02).

22 The 1904 Panels are:

• The 1904 Panel dealing with the *third administrative review (USA-95-1904-02)* found that the US final determination (60 Fed. Reg. 26,865 (19 May 1995)) had been based upon substantial evidence on the record and was in accordance with law.

• The 1904 Panel dealing with the *fourth administrative review (USA-97-1904-02)* issued its report affirming the Department of Commerce's determination.

• The 1904 Panel dealing with the *fifth administrative review (USA-97-1904-01)* issued its report affirming the re-determination on remand issued by the investigating authority.

23 These cases did not finish with a Panel report affirming the re-determination by the investigating authority. There is no clear information on whether they are active or terminated. The only clear reference would be that there is a MAS with respect to the AD order on Cement from Mexico as notified at the WTO.

24 The unresolved remanded issues relate to the determination that certain home market sales were outside the ordinary course of trade, and the calculation of differences in merchandise.

25 It remanded the decision to apply adverse facts available to a company that fully cooperated in calculating 'Cementos de Chihuahua's' importer-specific rate. The Panel made the pointed comment that it

However, the 1904 Panel dealing with the *five-year review (USA-MEX-2000-1904-10)* issued a finding that in some ways is similar to that of the GATT Panel. The 1904 Panel remanded, among others things, the issue on the conclusion by the US investigating authority that all, or almost all, of the production in the Southern Tier region was likely to suffer material injury if the order were revoked.[26] I found an indirect similarity between the two findings. As mentioned before, the GATT Panel in the *Cement* case found violation on the issue of 'all or almost all' in the request for initiation. The 1904 Panel, on the other hand, remanded the issue of the 'all or almost all' of the production for determination of the likelihood of injury. The GATT Panel ruled on the initiation and the 1904 Panel on the five-year Sunset Review with respect to the likelihood of injury.

2.1.4 US AD/CVD Orders on Softwood Lumber

On 12 September 2006, Canada and the US signed the 'Softwood lumber Agreement,' which, among others things, terminated the Softwood Lumber Orders retroactively. Accordingly, the DOC revoked the CVD Order effectively as from 22 May 2002, without the possibility of reinstatement.[27] This agreement terminated several disputes under NAFTA 1904 and the WTO related to the *Softwood lumber Orders.*

Five 1904 Panels did not produce a report.[28] Two more 1904 Panels finished their work with a motion to dismiss related to the 'Softwood lumber Agreement.'[29] On the other hand, the US and Canada notified the agreement to the

found particularly disturbing DOC's decision deliberately to disobey its instructions.

[26] Other remanded issues that were unresolved are the standard of 'probable' or 'more likely than not;' the further explanation of the likely volume of subject imports, their likely price effects and the likely impact on the domestic industry if the order were revoked; and the full evaluation of the Southdown acquisition.

[27] *Notice of Rescission of Countervailing Duty Reviews and Revocation of Countervailing Duty Order: Certain Softwood Lumber Products From Canada; 71 FR 61714, 61715 (DOC, 19 October 2006).*

[28] They are:

i) CVD (Section 129) on Softwood Lumber (USA-CDA-2005-1904-02) from 18 January 2005;

ii) Section 129 Softwood Lumber (USA-CDA-2005-1904-03) from 21 January 2005;

iii) Section 129 Softwood Lumber (USA-CDA-2005-1904-04);

iv) AD on Softwood Lumber (USA-CDA-2006-1904-01) from 11 January 2006; and

v) CVD on Softwood Lumber (USA-CDA-2006-1904-02) from 11 January 2006.

[29] The 1904 Panel on *Softwood Lumber (USA-CDA-2006-1904-05)* from 3 April 2006 and the 1904 Panel in *Countervailing order and Rescission for Softwood Lumber (USA-CDA-2005-1904-01)* from 18 January 2005 were terminated through a Motion to Dismiss.

WTO as a MAS. With this notification, they terminated all the WTO disputes related to the *Softwood lumber Orders,*[30] one of which was at consultations stage.[31]

Two other WTO procedures, also terminated though the MAS, relate to the provisional determinations of the *Orders on Softwood Lumber* and did not have an equivalent 1904 Panel Procedure.[32] In *US – Preliminary Determinations with respect to Certain Softwood Lumber from Canada (DS236)*, the WTO Panel found violations of WTO Law. In *US – Provisional Anti-Dumping Measure on Imports of Certain Softwood Lumber from Canada (DS247)* there was no report.

One of these two cases influenced the reasoning of the 1904 Panel in *Countervailing Duty order for Softwood Lumber (USA-CDA-2002-1904-03)*. In its first remand from 13 August 2003, it followed the reasoning of the WTO Panel in *US – Preliminary Determinations with respect to Certain Softwood Lumber from Canada (DS236)*. The 1904 Panel noted that the WTO ruling is not binding upon it, but it clearly stated that it concurred with the WTO Panel on its finding that certain Canadian programmes provided financial contributions to the exporters. The 1904 Panel compared the language of the WTO SCM Agreement and the US corresponding laws on CVD and found no significant differences. Hence, the 1904 Panel affirmed the investigating authorities' finding on financial contribution.[33]

In sum, the WTO Panel/AB and a 1904 Panel simultaneously reviewed only three determinations within the *Softwood lumber Orders*: the injury, the AD and the CVD determinations, as presented below.

---

30 The disputes suspended were:

i) US – Preliminary Determinations with respect to Certain Softwood Lumber from Canada (DS236);

ii) US – Provisional Anti-Dumping Measure on Imports of Certain Softwood Lumber from Canada (DS247);

iii) US – Final Countervailing Duty Determination with respect to Certain Softwood Lumber from Canada (DS257);

iv) US – Final Dumping Determination on Softwood Lumber from Canada (DS264);

v) US – Investigation of the International Trade Commission on Softwood Lumber from Canada (DS277); and

vi) US – Reviews of Countervailing Duty on Softwood Lumber from Canada (DS311).

31 See *US – Reviews of CVD on Softwood Lumber from Canada (DS311).*

32 As noted above, the 1904 Panel reviews final, and not provisional, determinations. The only situation where a 1904 Panel may have jurisdiction over a provisional determination is when the investigating authority terminates the AD/CVD order without the imposition of a duty. In these situations, the petitioners may trigger the 1904 Panel procedure against a provisional determination that becomes *de facto* a final determination terminating the order.

33 See *Countervailing Duty order for Softwood Lumber (USA-CDA-2002-1904-03)* from 2 April 2002, first remand from 13 August 2003, section VI. FINANCIAL CONTRIBUTION.

2.1.4.1 The Dumping Determination on Softwood Lumber

The WTO Panel report, as amended by the AB, in *US – Final Dumping Determination On Softwood Lumber From Canada (DS264)*[34] revised the AD determination in the *Softwood Lumber order.*[35] The Panel mainly found that the US violated Art 2.4.2 of the ADA in determining the existence of margins of dumping on the basis of a methodology incorporating the practice of 'zeroing'.[36] The AB upheld this finding. I omit the other finding of no inconsistency and the claims where the WTO Panel applied judicial economy. Later, the 21.5 procedures deal with the 129(b) new determination by the US, which was still using zeroing for the dumping calculation, and was held to be WTO inconsistent.

On the other hand, the 1904 Panel on *Antidumping Order for Softwood Lumber (USA-CDA-2002-1904-02)*, reviewing the same determination, issued its first report on 17 July 2003. It remanded the determination on thirteen specific instructions on technical issues with respect to the calculation of the margin of dumping. The same 1904 Panel issued its second report on 5 March 2004 reviewing the first re-determination by the investigating authority. It remanded the first re-determination to the DOC with three specific instructions.

But the third report, ordering a remand, from the same 1904 Panel (9 June 2005) presents a novelty with respect to the US legal perspective on WTO law. It ordered the DOC not to use the methodology of 'Zeroing' to recalculate the AD margins for all the remaining respondents, as it had previously ordered the elimination of the AD margin for one of the exporters. Based on the WTO ruling mentioned above, the 1904 Panel indicated that zeroing in this investigation was inconsistent with a US international obligation and, by application of the Charming Betsy doctrine, was unreasonable and not in accordance with the law. It sustained its finding with the fact that the *WTO Softwood lumber* dispute involved not only the same AD Order but also the US as defendant. This strongly contradicts the US longstanding position that zeroing is allowed in its internal legal system.

But data on this 1904 Panel does not offer information on what happened with this remand. On 5 January 2007, the same 1904 Panel concluded this 1904 Panel procedures with the motion to dismiss, which had been requested as a consequence of the 'Softwood lumber Agreement' that terminated the Orders.

---

34 See the Report of the Panel (WT/DS264/R) from 13 April 2004 and the Report of the AB (WT/DS264/AB/R) from 11 August 2004.

35 See *Certain Softwood Lumber Products from Canada (Notice of Amended Final Determination of Sales at Less Than Fair Value and Antidumping Duty Order)*, 67 Fed. Reg. 36, 068 (22 May 2002), corrected, 30 May 2002, 67 Fed. Reg. 37,775 (30 May 2002).

36 One Member of the Panel issued a dissenting opinion. It argued that the US '[...]interpretation of Articles 2.4.2 and 2.4 as not prohibiting zeroing is a permissible one[...]' This member of the Panel concluded, in the dissenting opinion, that the US did not violate 2.4 of the ADA in zeroing with respect to a fair comparison.

2.1.4.2 The Injury Determination on Softwood Lumber

The WTO Panel report in *US – Investigation of the International Trade Commission on Softwood Lumber from Canada (DS277)*,[37] revised the injury determination in the *Softwood Lumber order*.[38] There was no appeal and the WTO Panel found that:

- The ITC determination violates Art. 3.7 of the ADA and Art. 15.7 of the SCM Agreement in that the finding of a likely imminent substantial increase in imports is not objective and unbiased in light of the totality of the factors considered. The other aspects of the ITC determination do not violate the covered agreements cited.
- The ITC determination violates Art. 3.5 of the ADA and Art. 15.5 of the SCM Agreement with respect to the causal analysis, which is, itself, in violation of Art. 3.7 of the ADA and Art. 15.7 of the SCM Agreement. The Panel did not address the allegations with respect to other aspects of the ITC determination in light of the provisions cited by the complainant.

Findings on non-inconsistency and claims not addressed are omitted.

According to Canada's request for a 21.5 Panel (WT/DS277/8), the new measure taken by the US to comply with the original WTO Panel report did not implement the ruling of the Panel. Canada considered that the new measures,[39] allegedly taken by the US to comply with the DSB's recommendations and rulings, violate Art. 3.5 and 3.7 of the ADA and Art. 15.5 and 15.7 of the SCM Agreement.

On the other hand, the 1904 Panel on *Injury Order for Softwood Lumber (USA-CDA-2002-1904-07)* from 22 May 2000 reviewed the final determination by the ITC on injury. In its first report, dated 5 September 2003, the 1904 Panel remanded three main issues to the investigating authority: threat of material injury determination, like products with respect to square-end bed frame components and flangestock, and cross-cumulation.[40] This Panel issued its

---

37 See the Report of the Panel (WT/DS277/R) from 22 March 2004.

38 Softwood Lumber from Canada, Inv. Nos. 701-TA-414 and 731-TA-928 (Final), USITC Pub. 3509 (May 2002, 67 Fed. Reg. 36,022 (ITC 22 May 2002) ('Final Determination').

39 The measures identified by Canada are:

- *Section 129 Consistency Determination, Softwood Lumber from Canada, (24 Nov. 2004), Inv. Nos. 701-TA-414 and 731-TA-928*, and
- *Notice of Amendment to AD and CVD Orders on Certain Softwood Lumber Products from Canada (20 December 2004), 69 Fed. Reg. 75,917 (DOC, 20 December 2004) and the 22 May 2002 orders, as purportedly amended by this notice.*

40 The remanded issues in more details are as follows:

- The Commission's threat of material injury determination. The Commission should consider, in its analysis, all of the information and data (the 1904 Panel included several directions with respect to this remanded issue).
- The Commission's holdings that square-end bed frame components and flangestock are part of the

second report on 19 April 2004 and remanded the re-determination on *threat of injury*.[41] Finally, the 1904 Panel issued its third report on 31 August 2004 remanding the second re-determination for a determination consistent with the decision of the 1904 Panel that the evidence on the record does not support a finding of *threat of material injury*. No further information was found on this remand.[42]

There is a similarity in the findings of these two panels. The WTO Panel from 22 March 2004 found violation on the likely imminent substantial increase in imports. The 1904 Panel, in its second report from 19 April 2004 found that the re-determination was not supported by substantial evidence on the likelihood of substantially increased imports of the subject merchandise into the US.

2.1.4.4 The CVD Determination on Softwood Lumber

The WTO Panel report, as amended by the AB, in *US – Final Countervailing Duty Determination with respect to Certain Softwood Lumber from Canada (DS257)*[43] revised the CVD determination in the *Softwood Lumber order*.[44]

- The WTO Panel found DOC's determination that provision of stumpage constituted a financial contribution in the form of the provision of a good or service *was not inconsistent* with Article 1.1 (a) (1) (iii) SCM Agreement, and rejected Canada's other claim (Upheld by the AB).

---

single domestic like product for the continuum of species that comprise softwood lumber.
• The Commission's decision to cross-cumulate in the context of a threat of material injury determination and instruct the Commission to reconsider its interpretation of the statute with respect to cross-cumulation.

41 The 1904 Panel concluded that the following DOC findings were not supported by substantial evidence:
i. the Canadian producers' excess production and projected increases in capacity, capacity utilization and production, indicating the likelihood of substantially increased imports of the subject merchandise into the US;
ii. the domestic industry is threatened with material injury by reason of a significant rate of increase of the volume or market penetration of imports of the subject merchandise, indicating the likelihood of substantially increased imports into the US;
iii. the domestic industry is threatened with material injury by reason of the fact that imports of the subject merchandise are entering at prices that are likely to have a significant depressing or suppressing effect on domestic prices, and are likely to increase demand for further imports; and
iv. the domestic industry has curbed its overproduction of softwood lumber.

42 Apparently, the US Court of International Trade resolved the issue, as one of the parties to the 1904 Panel requested its assistance.

43 See the Report of the Panel (WT/DS257/R) from 29 August 2003 and the Report of the AB (WT/DS257/AB/R) from 19 January 2004.

44 See *Notice of Final Affirmative Countervailing Duty Determination and Final Negative Critical Circumstances Determination: Certain Softwood Lumber Products from Canada, 67 Fed. Reg. 15545 (April 2, 2002) ('Final Determination')*.

- The WTO Panel found DOC's determination of the existence and amount of benefit to the producers of the subject merchandise *was inconsistent* with Articles 14, 14(d), 10 and 32.1 of the SCM Agreement.
  – The AB reversed this finding with respect to the interpretation of Article 14(d) of the *SCM Agreement*, and found, instead, that an investigating authority may use a benchmark other than private prices in the country of provision, with some conditions.[45]
  – Hence, the AB reversed the consequential finding that the US acted inconsistently with Articles 10, 14, 14(d) and 32.1 of the *SCM Agreement* with respect to DOC's determination of the existence and amount of benefit in the underlying CVD investigation.
  – However, the AB found that there was not sufficient factual basis to complete the analysis and apply the legal test mentioned above.
  – Therefore, the AB did not make any finding on whether DOC's determination of the existence and amount of benefit in the underlying countervailing duty investigation is consistent or inconsistent with Articles 14 and 14(d) of the *SCM Agreement*, or on whether the imposition of countervailing duties based on that determination is consistent or inconsistent with Articles 10 and 32. 1 of the *SCM Agreement.*
- The WTO Panel found DOC's failure to conduct a pass-through analysis in respect of upstream transactions for log and lumber inputs between unrelated entities *was inconsistent* with Article 10 and 32.1 of the SCM Agreement and Article VI:3 of GATT 1994.[46]
  – The AB Upheld the finding on the pass-through in respect to *logs*, but;
  – the AB reversed the finding on the pass-through in respect to *lumber.*
- The WTO Panel found DOC's determination that the provincial stumpage programmes are specific *was not inconsistent* with Art. 2.1(c) SCM Agreement, and rejected Canada's other claim.

I have omitted the claims where the WTO Panel applied judicial economy and those not addressed by the Panel.

The 21.5 Panel/AB dispute relates to the measures applied by the US in implementing the original Panel/AB report (WT/DS257/15). On 20 December 2004, the DOC published the final results of the first administrative review.[47]

---

45 The two conditions are as follows:
• that private prices of the goods in question in the country of provision are distorted, because of the predominant role of the government in the market as a provider of the same or similar goods; and
• the alternative benchmark relates or refers to, or is connected with, prevailing market conditions in the country of provision (including price, quality, availability, marketability, transportation and other conditions of purchase or sale).

46 It applied judicial economy on Art. 19.1 and 19.4 of the SCM Agreement.

47 *Notice of Final Results of Countervailing Duty Administrative Review and Rescission of Certain Company-Specific Reviews: Certain Softwood Lumber Products from Canada*, 69 Fed. Reg. 75,917 (DOC 20 Decem-

Even though Canada also mentioned the original final CVD determination, its main objective in this 21.5 procedure was to review the first administrative review,[48] which is a new determination.

On the other hand, the 1904 Panel in *Countervailing Duty order for Softwood Lumber (USA-CDA-2002-1904-03)* from 2 April 2002 issued its first report on 13 August 2003. In essence, it ruled that the final determination properly found the elements necessary to support the conclusion that the Canadian Provincial governments provided a countervailable subsidy to timber harvesters, but that the DOC had not properly determined the benefit flowing from the subsidy. The case was remanded to the DOC to, *inter alia*, re-determine the benefit.

Several times, the 1904 Panel remanded the re-determinations back to the DOC. It issued its second report on 7 June 2004, remanding the first re-determination. After agreeing with some requests for remands from the DOC, it remanded the file back for the recalculation of the benchmarks for different regions, among other adjustments and recalculations. On 1 December 2004, it remanded the second re-determination on twelve highly detailed technical corrections with respect to the information from different regions, the specific benchmarks and other issues with respect to logs. The 1904 Panel issued its fourth report on 23 May 2005. It remanded the third re-determination on recalculations for Québec and Ontario with respect to the profits and benchmarks, among others things. Later, it issued its fifth report on 5 October 2005, remanding the fourth re-determination to determine the amount of log seller profit and to adjust the profit figures for some provinces. Finally, the 1904 issued its sixth report on 17 March 2006, where it upheld the fifth re-determination. The 1904 Panel decided that some issues were not properly before it, as they had not been previously remanded. These included log seller profit, log export restraints and revocation of the order.

There are some parallels between the two procedures – the WTO and 1904 Panel of NAFTA. First, both tribunals found that there was no violation of WTO or US law, on the financial contribution. Hence, both tribunals focused on the illegalities as to the existence or amount of the benefit. But, the WTO AB reversed the legal test used by the WTO Panel on this issue. As the factual basis was not sufficient, it could not complete the analysis and apply the correct legal test. Accordingly, the AB made no findings on the claims related to this issue.

Also, there appears to be one contradiction between the two tribunals. On the one hand, the WTO Panel found violation, upheld by the AB, on the failure to conduct a pass-through analysis in respect of upstream transactions or log inputs between unrelated entities. On the other hand, the 1904 Panel in its

ber 2004); and *Issues and Decision Memorandum: Final Results of Administrative Review: Certain Softwood Lumber Products from Canada*, December 13, 2004.

48 *Notice of Final Results of Countervailing Duty Administrative Review and Rescission of Certain Company-Specific Reviews: Certain Softwood Lumber Products from Canada*, 69 Fed. Reg. 75,917 (DOC 20 December 2004) and *Issues and Decision Memorandum: Final Results of Administrative Review: Certain Softwood Lumber Products from Canada from 13 December 2004.*

first report affirmed the determination of the DOC not to undertake a pass-through analysis of certain transactions, since the record lacked evidence of the extent of arms-length transactions in sales by independent loggers to sawmills in Saskatchewan and Manitoba. Further analysis on this contradiction may be required, for instance, on the similarity of the evidence presented to each tribunal.

2.2 Parallel Procedures with no Finding by one Tribunal

2.2.1 Mexico's AD order on Bovine

The NAFTA 1904 Panel (*MEX-USA-2000-1904-02*) and the WTO case (*Mexico – Beef and Rice (DS295)*) were initiated to review the same measure.[49] The 1904 Panel issued two reports. But the measure at issue was not put before the WTO tribunals, as the US did not pursue its review at Panel Stage. Even though it included this measure in is request for consultations, it was not included in its Panel request. So, the US decided not to have the WTO review of this AD order imposed by Mexico.[50]

2.2.2 US AD Order on Tomatoes

The WTO case in *US – Tomatoes (49)* remained at consultations stage. Mexico requested consultations with the US on 1 July 1996. The measure at issue was the *AD investigation on US imports of fresh or chilled tomatoes of any kind from Mexico.* Mexico claimed violation of the principle of non-discriminatory treatment in international trade, Art. VI and X of GATT´94, and Art. 2, 3, 5, 6 and 7.1 of the ADA. The WTO records offer nothing more than the request for consultations by Mexico.

The US and Mexican exporters reached a MAS, in the form of price undertaking, which was not notified to the WTO. The following information is relevant:

- the US Department of Commerce published the suspension of the AD investigation through a price undertaking (61 FR 56617) on 1 November 1996;
- the Mexican exporter of tomatoes signed a price undertaking with the US

[49] *The Final Determination of 27 April 2000, published in the Official Gazette of the Federation of Mexico on 28 April 2000, of the AD Investigation on imports of Bovine Beef and Eatable Offal, goods classified under tariff fractions 0201.10.01, 0202.10.01, 0201.20.99, 0202.20.99, 0201.30.01, 0202.30.01, 0206.21.01, 0206.22.01, and 0206.29.99, of the Tariff of the General Import Tax Law, originating from the US, independent of the country of origin.*

[50] A 1904 Panel established in 2002 dealt with an AD order on Bovine (MEX-USA-2002-1904-01). But as there is no report from the Panel, it is not possible to know whether it covered the same AD order as the WTO case on Mexico – Beef and Rice (DS295).

investigating authority;[51]
- there are no further DS documents after the request for consultations; and
- the price undertaking was extended in January 2008.[52]

Two NAFTA 1904 Panel cases were initiated on Canadian exports of tomatoes and the limitation placed on them by an *AD Order of tomatoes* imposed by the US (USA-CDA-2002-1904-04 from 27 March 2002 and USA-CDA-2002-1904-06 from 1 May 2002). But as the 1904 Panels were terminated without a report, there is no way of knowing whether these cases related to the *AD order on tomatoes* affecting Mexico's exports.

2.2.3 US AD Order on Stainless Steel and Strip

Three 1904 Panels may be related to the WTO cases on Stainless Steel from Mexico (DS235 and DS433).[53] But there is not enough NAFTA information to know whether they are related to the same AD order imposed by the US. These three NAFTA cases relating to the *AD order, or orders, on Stainless Steel Sheet and Strip* are active but there was no report available a the time of writing: *USA-MEX-2007-1904-01* from 22 January 2007; *USA-MEX-2008-1904-01* from 12 March 2008; and *USA-MEX-2009-1904-02* from 11 March 2009.

2.2.4 US AD Order on Live Cattle

One 1904 Panel may be related to the WTO case *US – Countervailing Duty Investigation on Live Cattle from Canada (DS167)*. Canada requested consultations on 19 March 1999,[54] but did not go further to the Panel stage. Mexico sought third party status in the consultations (WT/DS167/2). The 1904 Panel that may be related to this WTO case is *US CVD on Live Cattle (USA-CDA-1999-1904-06)* from 22 December 1999, which was terminated without report or any further information.[55]

---

[51] See http://ia.ita.doc.gov/tomato/1996-agreement/1996-agreement.html (Consulted in July 2009).

[52] See 'US and Mexico agree on a new suspension agreement for tomato AD case.' Published by INSIDE U.S. TRADE (www.InsideTrade.com) on 1 February 2008, Vol. 26, No. 5.

[53] *US – Anti-Dumping Determinations regarding Stainless Steel from Mexico (DS325) and US – Final Anti-dumping Measures on Stainless Steel from Mexico (DS433).*

[54] It alleged violations of the ASCM on the initiation of the CVD investigation and the Agreement on Agriculture with respect to the Peace Clause, Art. 13, on due restraint. See WTO document (WT/DS167/1).

[55] Another 1904 Panel, which may be related, was terminated without further information: *Live Cattle (IN) USA-CDA-1999-1904-07 from 14 March 2000.*

2.2.5 US AD/CVD Order on Wheat

Canada sought consultations (WT/DS310/1), followed by a request for the establishment of a WTO Panel (WT/DS310/2) in *US – Determination of the International Trade Commission on Hard Red Spring Wheat from Canada (DS310)*. There is no further information on this case, after the request for a Panel on 10 June 2004. Canada alleged the violation of both the ADA and the ASCM with respect to initiation, causality and the effect of dumping and injury with respect to AD/CVD Orders.[56]

One 1904 Panel certainly relates to the Canadian WTO complaint: *Injury order for 'Wheat' USA-CDA-2003-1904-06* from 24 November 2003.[57] On June 7, 2005, the Panel, with one partially dissenting opinion, affirmed in part and remanded in part the agency's determination. On December 12, 2005, Panel unanimously affirmed the agency's determination on remand.

A second 1904 Panel was terminated without a report[58] and a third 1904 Panel reviewed a different measure.

3 Observations

NAFTA 1904 legal remedies are narrower than those of WTO, though only to a small degree. Starting with the property rules, a 1904 Panel report remanding the file back to the investigating authority would contain details on how to correct the determination, whereas a WTO Member would have ample room for manoeuvre on means to comply with the Panel/AB report. Suspension of concessions (liability rule) has been used as a remedy in the WTO, but the suspension of the 1904 Panel system might not constitute a credible threat.

The NAFTA 1904 Panel procedure requires the defendant to amend its determination so that it complies with domestic law, whereas the WTO obliges

56 The measures identified by Canada relate to AD and CVD:
- the US ITC investigation on Hard Red Spring Wheat from Canada (Investigations Nos. 701-TA-430B and 731-TA-1019B (Final));
- the ITC's final determination that an industry in the US is materially injured by reason of imports from Canada of hard red spring wheat that have been found by the DOC to be subsidized by Canada and sold in the US at less than fair value (68 Federal Register (FR) 60707 (23 October 2003));
- the DOC's CVD duty order (68 FR 60642 (23 October 2003)) and AD order (68 FR 60641 (23 October 2003)) with respect to hard red spring wheat from Canada; and
- the final definitive ADD and CVD applied as a result.

57 It reviewed the final affirmative injury determination of the US ITC involving imports of hard red spring wheat from Canada. See *Hard Red Spring Wheat from Canada, Inv. Nos. 701-TA-430B and 731-TA-1019B (Final), USITC Pub. 3639 (Oct. 2003), (68 Fed. Reg. 60,707, 60,708(23 October 23))*.

58 In *Antidumping order on Wheat (USA-CDA-2003-1904-04)* from 3 October 2003, the Panel review was terminated by the sole requester without the issuance of a report.

the defendant to bring the measure into conformity, which may take the form of a new determination. For instance, a 1904 Panel would require the amendment of an illegal final determination, whereas a WTO Panel/AB may allow an illegal final determination to be remedied through the first administrative review.

NAFTA 1904 Panels stretch the provisions of the main legal remedies beyond simply remanding or upholding (the 1904 Panel in *HFCS* ordered the elimination of the AD Order). On the other hand, WTO Panels and the AB take a more conservative approach and limit themselves to recommending that the defendant bring the measure into conformity. WTO tribunals seldom use their right to suggest ways of implementation. Perhaps the reaction from WTO Members to the suggestion in *Guatemala – Cement from Mexico (DS60)* was a strong disincentive against including suggestions in subsequent reports.

1904 Panels very often reach findings similar to WTO tribunals when reviewing the same determination. 1904 Panels reviewing AD/CVD imposed by Mexico may follow WTO rulings very directly (*Mexico AD on HFCS*). But, without specifically saying so, 1904 Panels reviewing US AD/CVD orders produce findings similar to the corresponding WTO tribunal (*US AD on OCTG*). When the same determination imposed by the US has been found to be WTO inconsistent, a 1904 Panel may order its amendment even if the US Congress has not passed such obligations into US Law – the practice of Zeroing (*US AD Orders on Softwood lumber*) is an example. This would allow parties interested in an AD/CVD order to achieve direct implementation of WTO law and rulings in the US system (direct effect).

Complainants in both *fora*, may recycle claims presented in the other *forum*. A WTO Member may present claims to a WTO Panel that were made by the exporters in a 1904 Panel or *vice versa*. It is natural that private lawyers representing exporters in an AD/CVD investigation would advise WTO Members in a parallel dispute reviewing the same AD/CVD Order.

The remand procedure in a 1904 Panel may be very long and this may reduce the efficiency of the system.

Several potential cases for parallel litigation exist. But many of the reviews have not produced a report either in the WTO or in the 1904 Panel procedure.

4 Conclusions

WTO dispute settlement and 1904 Panels are tools for reviewing AD/CVD orders within the NAFTA region. They seem to be closely related, even though they have marked differences relating to issues such as standing and substantive law. It is difficult to litigate against trade remedy cases, but the parallel utilization of these procedures seems to be of use to the complainant. Two MAS were found in such scenarios (*Cement and Softwood lumber*). But, from the procedural point of view, parallel litigation in these two *fora* is highly complicated.

Bibliography

Appleton, Barry; *Navigating NAFTA: A Concise User's Guide to the North American Free Trade Agreement*; Carswell (1994).

Bhala, Raj; *International Trade Law: Interdisciplinary Theory and Practice*, Third Edition; LexisNexis (2008).

Clyde-Hufbauer, Gary – Goodrich, Ben; *Lessons from NAFTA – Free Trade Agreements, US Strategies and Priorities*; Institute for International Economics (2004).

Czako, Judith – Human, Johann – Miranda Jorge; *A Handbook on Anti-Dumping Investigations*; Cambridge University Press (2003).

Gantz, David; 'Dispute Settlement under the NAFTA and the WTO: Choice of Forum Opportunities and Risks for the NAFTA Parties'; 14 *Am. U. Intl L. Rev.* 1025 (1999).

Huerta-Goldman, Jorge A.; *Mexico in the WTO and NAFTA: Litigating International Trade Disputes*; Kluwer Law International (2009).

Jackson, John H.; *The Jurisprudence of GATT and the WTO*; Cambridge University Press (2000).

Jackson, John H. – Davey, William J. – Sykes, Alan O.; *Cases, Materials and Texts on Legal Problems of International Economic Relations*; West Group (2001).

Mavroidis, Petros C; *Trade in Goods, The GATT and Other Agreements Regulating Trade in Goods*; Oxford University Press (2007).

Mavroidis, Petros C.; Messerlin; Patrick A. and Wauters, Jasper M.; *The Law and Economics of Contingent Protection in the WTO*; Elgar International Economic Law (2008).

Palmeter, David and Mavroidis, Petros C.; *Dispute Settlement in the World Trade Organization*; Cambridge University Press (2004).

Pauwelyn, Joost; 'Adding Sweeteners to Softwood Lumber: the WTO-NAFTA 'Spaghetti Bowl' is Cooking'; *Journal of International Economic Law* 9(1), 197-206 (2006).

Perezcano-Diaz, Hugo; El Arbitraje a Nivel Internacional y Dentro del Marco del TLC – El Arbitraje en las Relaciones de Consumo; *Procuraduría Federal del Consumidor* (1997).

Schwartz, Warren F. and Sykes, Alan O.; The Economic Structure of Renegotiation and Dispute Resolution in the World Trade Organization; *The Journal of Legal Studies*, vol. 31 (January 2002).

Vermulst, Edwin – Graafsma, Folkert; *WTO Disputes: Anti-Dumping, Subsidies and Safeguards*; Cameron May (2002).

CHAPTER 12

The Dialogue between Judges & Experts in the EU and WTO

Alberto Alemanno*

1 Introduction

While the entry of science into the courtroom is not an entirely new phenomenon, the integration of scientific knowledge into the international courts legal environment is a more recent one. Today not only the outcomes of criminal, paternity and civil liability cases may turn on scientific evidence, but also those of major international trade disputes may depend on the scientific element.

The legal review of science-based measures represents not only one of the most difficult, but also one of the most unexplored aspects of the controversial relationship between law and science.

As the US Supreme Court stated in *Daubert*, while the goal of science is epistemic – to achieve 'cosmic understanding', the goal of the judicial process is the 'particularised resolution of legal disputes'.[1] Indeed, the role of a judge facing questionable scientific issue has little to do with questions of cosmic truth, it rather deals with the most immediate issue of determining the admissibility and reliability of the scientific data provided by the parties. However, the accomplishment of these tasks may involve criteria and notions that may derive, somehow, from science itself.

Against this backdrop, this study examines the role of expertise in the European judicial architecture and in the WTO Dispute Settlement System.[2] As both the WTO and the EC require the presence of scientific justification to determine the legitimacy of many national (and supranational) health regulations to avoid disguised forms of protectionists,[3] international adjudicators are increasingly called upon reviewing the scientific soundness (whether a scientific justification exists) of these measures while assessing their legality.

But how a judge, by definition a non scientist, may conduct an assessment on whether a measure is scientifically supported? Which is the level of intensity of the scrutiny that this judge may exert over the risk regulation being reviewed?

These questions are currently sources of endlessly controversy in the international legal arena[4] and at the centre of some international trade disputes.[5]

---

* Associate Professor of Law, HEC Paris.

1 *Daubert v. Merrell Dow Pharmaceuticals, Inc.*, 509 U.S. 579 (1993).

2 If the liberalization of trade has occurred at bilateral, regional and multilaterals levels, the two most successful experiences are the European Union (EU), formerly the European Economic Community established in 1957 by the Treaty of Rome (ECT), and the World Trade Organisation (WTO), created in 1995 upon the 1947 General Agreement on Tariff and Trade's framework (GATT). For a comparative legal analysis of these trade liberalization efforts see Ortino (2004).

3 The broad area of public health measures is unique for the moment in its explicit invocation of scientific and quasi-scientific notions, such as the elements identifying their correctness.

4 See Ehlermann (2002) at 612-13, who, while leaving the organ, has noted that 'during the last months, the question of standard of review has thus become one of the most controversial aspects of the Appellate Body's jurisprudence'.

5 *European Communities – Certain Measures Affecting Poultry Meat and Poultry Meat Products from the United States*, WT/DS 389/4; *Australia – Measures Affecting the Importation of Apples from New Zealand*, WT/DS 367.

Their answers are relevant to the extent they determine not only the immediate outcome of some legal disputes, but also how much regulatory autonomy WTO and EU Members enjoy in regulating to protect the health of their people. The final question is obviously more sensitive within the WTO framework than within the EC, where not only EC courts have more adjudicatory power, but also Member States have transferred regulatory competences to the EC.

The next section provides an overview of the scientific justification disciplines existing within the EU and the WTO and illustrates their rationales. After analyzing the role played by expertise in the judicial review of science-based measures in both legal systems, the following sections formulate some proposals aimed at reorienting the role of the WTO and EU judicial bodies in order to make them less involved with science when reviewing science-based measures.

2 The Scientific Evidence Requirement

Science in the trade liberalization process has become a decisive factor to distinguish between legitimate and illegitimate domestic policies in the trade policy arena. Indeed, under both the WTO and the EC, the presence of scientific justification is required to determine the legitimacy of many national regulations aimed at safeguarding public health and safety. If both the WTO and the EC recognize to their members the basic right to establish their own appropriate level of public health protection, the exercise of this domestic regulatory power is constrained by the imposition to apply trade disciplines that are not only non-discriminatory but also scientifically-based. A showing of scientific justification immunizes (*iuris tantum*) health regulations against a trade-challenge. Instead, failure to satisfy this requirement, unless a regulatory measure is based on an international standard or on an agreed discipline, implies inconsistency with the trade agreement, triggering the obligation to remove the contested measure.

Thus, science has been invested with the role of mediating tensions between national regulatory concerns and the demands of the international community. Science, as universal knowledge grounded in physical experience, is perceived as the only rational and testable methodology able to depoliticize international trade disputes. The hope in science as the decisive factor lies on the belief that science, as an objective standard, brings constraints on the regulatory process by spotting all protectionist regulations and saving only those genuinely motivated on public health grounds.

However, the difficulty stemming from this use of science as neutral arbiter in trade liberalization is to make science speak the language of the law, that is integrating scientific data into both the regulatory and the adjudicatory process. Depending on the role played by science, several 'law and science' models have developed throughout the liberalization trend that has emerged in recent years.

Among the different models for managing law and science interactions, it is worth considering the models that have emerged from the European Community and from the WTO by examining their disciplines of health regulation. This broad area of regulation is unique for the moment in its explicit reference to scientific factor as the identifying marker for a presumption of regulatory correctness.[6]

The described emphasis on the integrity of the scientific justification required within the regulatory process in both the GATT/WTO and EC disciplines for health regulations implies that their respective adjudicatory bodies may be called upon to evaluate the validity of the scientific analysis underlying national measures to protect public health.

At the time of the negotiation of the SPS Agreement, rather than relying solely on discrimination to identify illegitimate health regulations, Member States decided to choose a neutral-value criterion such as scientific evidence. Similarly, the EC courts, followed by the EC legislator, quite soon began to refer to science as the main organising criterion allowing distinction to be drawn between legitimate and illegitimate health measures. The logic of the scientific requirement is easy to understand. If a regulation aimed at protecting public health is not supported by scientific evidence proving the danger to be avoided by means of that regulation, then the suspicion may legitimately arise that the regulation disguises protectionist intent. At the same time, however, the introduction of a scientific discipline may also cause difficulties for regulators who genuinely have legitimate non-protectionist intentions.

In the light of the above, the challenge is, when interpreting the scientific discipline, to reconcile its primary goal of spotting sham health regulations with Member States' recognised right to pursue the level of protection they deem appropriate for their society.

In so doing, it is crucial to bear in mind that, while the goal of the judicial process is the 'particularised resolution of legal disputes' the goal of science is epistemic, i.e. to achieve 'cosmic understanding'.[7] Hence, unlike law, science by its nature tends to be highly tentative and, accordingly, somewhat inconclusive. As a result, persuasive evidence of certain types of risk, especially those surrounded by scientific uncertainty, may be difficult to generate. As a result, 'in the face of such scientific uncertainty, scientific evidence requirements may stand in the way of honest regulatory efforts to manage risk'.[8]

Yet, since both the WTO and the EC require the presence of detailed scientific justification to determine the legitimacy of national (and supranational) regulations to avoid disguised forms of protectionism,[9] their courts are increas-

6 However, it is likely that in the near future scientific requirements for regulatory validity may be introduced into new areas.

7 *Daubert v. Merrell Dow Pharmaceuticals, Inc.*, 509 U.S. 579 (1993).

8 Sykes, *Domestic Regulation, Sovereignty and Scientific Evidence Requirements: A Pessimistic View*, at 258.

9 The broad area of public health measures is unique for the moment in its explicit invocation of scientific and quasi-scientific notions, such as the elements identifying their correctness.

ingly called upon to review the scientific soundness (whether a scientific justification exists) of these measures, when assessing their legality.

But how may a judge, generally a non scientist, assess whether a given measure has a sound scientific basis? What degree of scrutiny does a judge exercise, lawfully and practically, over the food regulations he is called upon to review? These are but some of the questions addressed in this chapter.

3 How to Improve the Role of the Judge in the Review of Science-Based Measures?

The WTO and EC risk regulation disciplines and, accordingly, the standards of judicial review of science-based measures, as interpreted and applied by their respective courts, show the struggle faced by WTO and EC judges when they are called upon to interact with science in their activity of *dicere legem*.

Though developed in a domestic law context, the most authoritative formulation of this struggle belongs to the US Supreme Court Chief Justice Rehnquist. In his dissenting opinion in the *Daubert* case, he noted that

> 'the various briefs filed in this case are markedly different from typical briefs [...] they deal with definitions of scientific knowledge, scientific method, scientific validity, and peer review – in short, matters far afield from the expertise of judges [...]'.[10]

It is indeed true that, in international legal *fora*, most legal opinions and judgments do not ordinarily rest on this kind of intellectual foundation, but rather are based on other sources of knowledge which are closer to the educational background of the judges. However, given the specificity of certain subject matters, it may happen that most of the scientific sources cited in a legal decision could not be easily read and understood by the majority of the judges composing the court.

Not only the intrusive standard of review adopted by WTO panels, but also that followed by EC courts (a sort of 'reasonable deference standard') when reviewing science-based national measures may seem to implicitly require some scientific expertise from these judges. This seems particularly true, in the EC context, after the adoption of the *Pfizer*[11] and *Vitamins* line of cases.[12]

---

10 *Daubert v. Merrell Dow Pharmaceuticals, Inc.*, 509 U.S. 579 (1993), paras 598-599.

11 ECJ: Case T-13/99 *Pfizer Animal Health v. Council*, 2002 ECR II-3305, at 143-144. For a brief review of the judgment, Alemanno (2002), 842-845 and Walker (2003) 221-225; for a critical assessment of the judgment, see also Ladeur (2003) 1465 and the reaction to this article by Wolf (2004) 1175-1180.

12 ECJ: Case 192/01 *Commission v. Denmark* [2003] ECR 9693; ECJ: Case C-24/00 *Commission v. France* [2004] ECR I-1277; ECJ: Case C-270/02 *Commission v. Italy* [2004] ECR I-1559; ECJ: Case C-41/02 *Commission v. Netherlands* [2004] ECR I-11375. See on these judgments, Alemanno (2003).

Even if the EC courts and the WTO judicial bodies are not being directly asked to establish whether a certain risk exists or, more generally, to settle a scientific debate, they tend to evaluate the competing scientific claims made by the parties in order to determine whether the contested measures conform to the scientific discipline in force within their legal system.

However, one would not reasonably expect any AB Member or panellist or any European court judge called upon to decide a science-based case to have any specific scientific knowledge in the scientific field in question. The members of these courts are typically staffed by individuals without scientific expertise and, moreover, operate under time constraints. Indeed, these judicial bodies lack the resources to carry out a more informed and independent evaluation of the risk assessment outcomes submitted by the parties. In that light, it is of no surprise that both EC and WTO courts, being poorly equipped to evaluate scientific evidence, struggle in accomplishing this task. Nevertheless, notwithstanding the lack of scientific knowledge and appropriate resources, under the applicable standards of review, both European and WTO courts tend to carry out their own examination of the quality of the scientific data advanced by the parties.

These factors raise the question as to how the judiciary, notably the WTO and EC courts, may deal with scientific evidence.

3.1 The Role of Experts in Judicial Review: The External Expert Consultation in the WTO

To somehow mitigate such difficulties the WTO panels, unlike the EC judiciary, tend to rely on external advisors.[13] According to the Dispute Settlement Understanding, a panel may consult 'experts', either individually, or by convening an 'expert review group', to obtain their opinion on scientific and technical matters in dispute settlement.[14] Similar provisions already existed

---

[13] Such consultations have taken place in most of the health and environmental disputes that have been settled by the WTO DSB. See Pauwelyn (2006) 235.

[14] Article 13 DSU (*Right to Seek Information*) reads as follow: '1. Each panel shall have the right to seek information and technical advice from any individual or body which it deems appropriate. However, before a panel seeks such information or advice from any individual or body within the jurisdiction of a Member it shall inform the authorities of that Member. A Member should respond promptly and fully to any request by a panel for such information as the panel considers necessary and appropriate. Confidential information which is provided shall not be revealed without formal authorization from the individual, body, or authorities of the Member providing the information. 2. Panels may seek information from any relevant source and may consult experts to obtain their opinion on certain aspects of the matter. With respect to a factual issue concerning a scientific or other technical matter raised by a party to a dispute, a panel *may* request an advisory report in writing from an expert review group. Rules for the establishment of such a group and its procedures are set forth in Appendix 4'. It seems that while panels may ask experts their views on the matter, they cannot dispose any new risk assessment. On the scope of WTO external expertise, see *infra* 4.1.2.

under the GATT system.[15] Both the SPS and TBT Agreements contain some additional provisions relating to the expert assistance procedure and encourage the panels to rely on this opportunity for external help.[16]

Generally, the selection process of experts and the operation of an expert consultation procedure take places according to the steps indicated below.[17] However, it must be noted from the outset that any WTO Agreements provide for detailed rules and procedures for the appointment and the operation of experts acting on an individual basis, but that they only do so for expert review groups.[18]

---

15 Christoforou remarks that the 1966 Conciliation-Procedures under Article XXIII (in Decisions and Conclusions of the Contracting Parties, 5 April 1966, GATT B.I.S.D, 14th Suppl., 1966, at 18) contained virtually the same provisions as those of Article 13.1 and the first sentence of paragraph 2 of the same article. See Christoforou (2000) 254.

16 Article 11.2 SPS provides that a panel should seek advice from experts chosen by the panel in consultation with the parties. To this end, the panel may, when it deems appropriate, establish an advisory technical experts group, or consult the relevant international organizations, at the request of either party to the dispute or on its own initiative. Article 14.2 TBT states that, at the request of a party to a dispute or at its own initiative, the panel may establish a technical assistance expert group.

17 The detailed description of the general expert consultation procedure which follows builds upon the previous cases in which the panels have selected and consulted scientific experts. For an analysis of these modalities see Pauwelyn (2002) 328.339-340; Motaal (2005) 499 and Christoforou (2000) 258-259.

18 Appendix 4 of the DSU, entitled Expert Review Groups, states: 'The following rules and procedures shall apply to expert review groups established in accordance with the provisions of paragraph 2 of Article 13. 1. Expert review groups are under the panel's authority. Their terms of reference and detailed working procedures shall be decided by the panel, and they shall report to the panel. 2. Participation in expert review groups shall be restricted to persons of professional standing and experience in the field in question. 3. Citizens of parties to the dispute shall not serve on an expert review group without the joint agreement of the parties to the dispute, except in exceptional circumstances when the panel considers that the need for specialized scientific expertise cannot be fulfilled otherwise. Government officials of parties to the dispute shall not serve on an expert review group. Members of expert review groups shall serve in their individual capacities and not as government representatives, nor as representatives of any organization. Governments or organizations shall therefore not give them instructions with regard to matters before an expert review group. 4. Expert review groups may consult and seek information and technical advice from any source they deem appropriate. Before an expert review group seeks such information or advice from a source within the jurisdiction of a Member, it shall inform the government of that Member. Any Member shall respond promptly and fully to any request by an expert review group for such information as the expert review group considers necessary and appropriate. 5. The parties to a dispute shall have access to all relevant information provided to an expert review group, unless it is of a confidential nature. Confidential information provided to the expert review group shall not be released without formal authorization from the government, organization or person providing the information. Where such information is requested from the expert review group but release of such information by the expert review group is not authorized, a non-confidential summary of the

The Panel requests relevant international bodies (such as the WHO, IOE or the IPPC) and the parties to indicate the names of suitably qualified scientific experts and asks for their CVs. After having circulated all CVs to the parties for comments, the panel then appoints the best experts, generally ranking them with numbers between 3 and 5. In general, panels do not select experts that are nationals of the parties to the dispute, unless they are expressly authorized by the parties to do so.[19]

Before the appointment of the experts, the panel prepares specific questions to be addressed to them. To the extent possible, these questions are also provided to the parties. The parties then have the possibility not only of expressing their objections to any particular expert[20] but also to comment on the proposed questions before these are sent to the experts. At this stage, the panel appoints the experts by informing the parties of its selection.

The experts are required to provide answers in writing to the questions and their answers are provided to the parties. Moreover, should the panel feel it necessary, or on a party's request, a meeting with experts may take place in which the panel, parties and experts gather just before the second substantive meeting with the parties.

Finally, the panels' practice in expert consultation shows that panels may have recourse to scientific experts even if none of the parties to the dispute requests it or if a party objects to it.[21]

In all the health cases in which expert consultations have taken place to date – *EC-Hormones,*[22] *US-Shrimp/Turtle,*[23] *Australia-Salmon,*[24] *Japan-Agricultural products, EC-Asbestos, Japan-Apples* and, finally *EC-Biotech* – the panels have consulted more than one expert, but always on an individual basis. In other words, to date not a single panel has set up an expert review group. The last

information will be provided by the government, organization or person supplying the information. 6. The expert review group shall submit a draft report to the parties to the dispute with a view to obtaining their comments, and taking them into account, as appropriate, in the final report, which shall also be issued to the parties to the dispute when it is submitted to the panel. The final report of the expert review group shall be advisory only'.

19 This exclusion rule is expressly provided by Appendix 4 of the DSU establishing rules and procedures applicable to expert review groups.

20 The parties may raise 'compelling objections' by, for instance, pointing to the fact that the experts were employees of either party to the dispute or that they were involved in the procedures at issue. See *EC-Biotech* panel report, at 7.21.

21 Thus, for instance, neither in the *Salmon* case nor in the *Agricultural products* the parties to the dispute have requested expert advice.

22 The same set of experts has been appointed for two panels.

23 *United States-Import prohibition of certain shrimp and shrimp products*, DS58/R, DS58/AB/R, DS58/AB/RW, DS58/RW.

24 Here, the implementation panel has appointed a different set of experts than that used in the original panel.

example is given by *United States – Continued Suspension of Obligations in the EC – Hormones Dispute*, where the Panel decided not to establish an expert review group as had been suggested by the European Communities, but to consult experts on an individual basis.[25]

The issue as to whether the panels, in a dispute involving scientific or technical matters, are limited to seeking advice from an expert review group or whether they may consult experts on an individual basis is controversial. Unfortunately, neither the relevant DSU and SPS provisions nor the panels/AB case law contribute to resolving the matter.

As will be shown below, though it might appear to be a mere procedural question, the choice of appointing an expert review group or individual scientists is pivotal in determining the level of scientific involvement requested from the WTO judicial bodies.

A. Individual Experts vs. Expert Review Group

Each time a party expressly asked for the appointment of an expert review group (typically the EC), the panel appointed individual experts instead.[26] The Appellate Body has endorsed this preference by interpreting Article 13 DSU as referring to expert review groups as a mere option (a panel *may* request). This constant practice raises several procedural and substantive questions which deserve closer scrutiny.

Although rendered controversial by the wording of the WTO texts, this preference for the appointment of individual experts tends to be justified on practical grounds.[27] The main argument presented in favour of such an option is that expert individual consultation is not only less time-consuming than group review (not having to generate a common written report) but it would also ensure more flexibility in the consultation process. In an expert individual consultation – the argument goes – a panel, by asking specific questions of each expert and by adding questions during the process, would obtain the individual opinion of each expert rather than a common and monolithical consensus position. This would help the panel in better assessing the scientific evidence brought by the parties. However, contrary to conventional wisdom, the provision

[25] Panel Report, US – Continued Suspension of Obligations in the EC – Hormones Dispute, WT/DS320/R, 21 March 2008, para. 7.71; Panel Report, Canada – Continued Suspension of Obligations in the EC – Hormones Dispute, WT/DS321/R, 21 March 2008, para. 7.69. The European Communities initially indicated that the Panel did not have to consult experts (Panel Report, US – Continued Suspension, para. 7.56; Panel Report, Canada – Continued Suspension, para. 7.54).

[26] This has happened notwithstanding the expressed request of the complaining party to appoint an expert review group in the *Shrimps-Turtles* case and notwithstanding the complainant and defendant common request in the *Hormones* case. See for a criticism of this position, Christoforou (2000) 630-1. See, more recently, Panel Report, *US – Continued Suspension*, para. 7.71; Panel Report, *Canada – Continued Suspension*, para. 7.69.

[27] For a complete description of the practical arguments generally invoked to justify the panels' preference for individual expert consultation, see Pauwelyn (2002) 328.

of expertise by individual experts within the judicial review context is not necessarily more efficient than the setting up of an expert review group.

While reliance on individual experts may appear to render the expertise consultation process more expeditious and flexible than the expert advisory group scheme, past cases have clearly shown how these expectations cannot realistically be met. In fact, the provision of various opinions by individual experts inevitably produces the effect of providing the judge with further scientific material to consider and evaluate. This has been expressly recognized by the panel in *Japan – Agricultural Products*, which stated that

> 'we are called to examine and to weigh all the evidence [...] including the opinions we received from the experts advising the panel'.[28]

In particular, being opinions elaborated on an individual basis and according to different methodologies, they lead the panel to engage in a complex quasi-scientific analysis aimed at verifying whether there is a common ground among these opinions. This evaluation becomes even more complex when individual experts hold divergent views.

While the main objective of the expert consultation procedure should be to prevent the panellists from getting involved in scientific issues by providing them with an assessment of the plausibility of the scientific evidence advanced by the parties to the dispute, the individual consultation practice described is likely to achieve the exact opposite result. Indeed, by introducing into the review process additional (often conflicting) scientific materials to be assessed together with the competing scientific claims brought by the parties, reliance on individual experts renders, paradoxically, the task of the judges even more (scientifically) cumbersome. How can judges be expected to be epistemically capable of assessing the possibly conflicting individual scientific opinions expressed by the experts?

In the light of the above, it is argued here that the appointment of an expert review group, though apparently more time-consuming, may potentially simplify the scientific task that judges are increasingly called upon to accomplish. Being entrusted with the duty of coming up with a written report, the expert group would be forced to either find common grounds on the different specific scientific issues at stake or, at least, to genuinely represent the whole spectrum of scientific opinions (i.e. majority and minority) existing in the current scientific state-of-the-art research on that controversial issue. In fact, adherents to different schools of thought should be represented among the experts. By borrowing the AB's language, the expert review group may set out, according to this model

[28] Panel Report in *Japan – Agricultural Products*, para 7.408.

> 'both the prevailing view representing the mainstream opinion, as well as the opinions of scientists taking a divergent view'.[29]

Furthermore, besides these arguments of merit, there also exist some textual reasons for privileging reliance on expert review groups over that of individual experts. As has been observed, although the wording of the relevant WTO texts does not help in identifying the appropriate form of expert consultation in a scientific-based controversy, it is undisputed (and perhaps meaningful) that they do provide for detailed rules and procedures solely for an expert review group.[30] This has meant that the panels' current practice of appointing individual experts has taken place not only contrary to the customary rules of interpretation of international treaties, as codified by the relevant 1969 Vienna Convention,[31] but also in a sort of legal vacuum in which panels had to determine by themselves the rules to follow in the following matters: appointment of the experts, decision of the terms of reference, nationality of the experts, etc.

Thus, for instance, it should be observed that the current trend of WTO panels to request the assistance of competent international bodies (such as the WHO, IOE or the IPPC) in selecting the experts does not find any textual support in the WTO Agreements. Although the panels have limited their requests for assistance in the selection of experts to those international organizations mentioned in the SPS Agreement (in the quality of standard-setting bodies), this does not necessarily mean that the experts should come exclusively from those organizations. In particular, this practice looks controversial to the extent that the appointed experts are likely to come from the same organizations which have set the international standards the WTO Members may have tried to depart from. Against this backdrop, it is unavoidable that these experts will tend to defend the existing international standards elaborated by their organization, if not by themselves.[32]

The most forceful and most articulated *j'accuse* expressed against the current expert consultation practice has been formulated by Christoforou who foresees that

---

29 *Hormones*, AB Report, para 194.

30 It is by relying on this systematic argument that the EU has contested the current expert consultation practice based on individual experts in the *Asbestos* case, *supra* note.

31 According to Article 31 of the 1969 Vienna Convention on the Law of Treaties the interpretation must give meaning and effect to all the 'terms of a treaty'. See Christoforou (2000) 264 (footnote 115).

32 As an example of this phenomenon, one may refer to the *Hormones* case where 3 experts out of the 5 appointed by the panel were scientists regularly participating in the Codex Alimentarius committees and one of them was even the *rapporteur* in the risk assessment on the hormones at issue in the dispute. This example is provided by Christoforou (2000) 256 (footnote 98).

> 'the developing practice of panels seeking advice only from experts individually, if applied systematically, would render the provisions of the DSU and the SPS and TBT Agreements on expert review groups useless and obsolete'.[33]

It is in the light of the above arguments that scientific advice from an expert review group should be preferred over individual expertise. It is not only more efficient, objective and clear, but is also the sole procedure capable of attaining the main purpose of external expertise: to avoid the judges having to face troubling scientific issues by providing a report reflecting the current scientific debate on a specific issue (i.e. mainstream and minority scientific opinions). Besides this, major reliance on expert review groups would be more respectful towards the WTO Agreements' *littera legis* and more in line with the current practice in relation to the use of science.

B. The Scope of the Expert Consultation: What Role for Scientific Experts?

It is appropriate to leave aside the expertise consultation procedural issues and to move to the nature and scope of this procedure.

The expert consultation finds its rationale in the assumption that panel Members, by consulting scientists specialized in the areas related to the dispute, may be better placed to understand and critically assess the scientific evidence advanced by the parties. In fact, as stated by the panel in the *Salmon* case, the

> 'expert opinions are opinions on the evidence submitted by the parties'.[34]

Accordingly,

> 'a panel is entitled to seek information and advice from experts and from any other relevant source it chooses [...] to help it to understand and evaluate the evidence submitted and the arguments made by the parties, but not to make the case for a complaining party'.[35]

However, panels have shown some confusion about the appropriate role for scientific expertise. Although it might seem that the expert advice should not cover more than the evidence submitted by the parties, panels tend to directly ask experts the very same disputed scientific question that the panel itself has

---

33 *Ibid.*, p. 264.

34 See also panel report on *Australia – Salmon*, paras 8.41, 8.126 and 8.172. In full conformity to this approach, in the *Agricultural Products* case, Dr. Ducon simply stated: '[t]he arguments put forward by Japan for requiring varietals trials are not based on scientific data. They are supported by a few experimental data in which varietals difference exists, in terms of LD50, among a lot of other data in which it does not'. See Panel Report, *Agricultural Products*, para 8.36.

35 *Japan-Agricultural Products*, AB Report, para 129.

to answer.[36] This clearly happened in the *Agricultural products* case, where the experts advising the panel were asked whether

> 'in their expert opinion, there is an objective or rational relationship between, on the one hand, the varietal testing requirement imposed by Japan and, on the other hand, any evidence submitted by the parties'.[37]

This trend towards a 'delegation' of responsibility in deciding the outcome of a dispute has caused uneasiness with an expert appointed in the *Hormones* dispute. On the occasion of the joint meeting with experts, Dr Ritter vocally denounced the fact that the provision of an answer to the question of whether residual hormones in beef would produce a biological effect on consumers would 'really pre-empt the outcome of the dispute'.[38]

Although it might clearly seem to be abusive, this practice may find some support in the open-textured formulation of Article 13 DSU, which recognizes the almost unfettered right of the panel to seek information and technical advice from any individual or body which it deems appropriate and to seek information from any relevant source. Therefore, to avoid the abovementioned risk of 'delegation', it might be necessary to somehow constrain the scope of the expertise consultation. In order to achieve that result, the main purpose of the expert consultation must be borne in mind, which is to avoid panels getting involved in scientific issues by them providing an assessment of the plausibility of the scientific arguments brought by the parties. In other words, if we want to reduce the role of the panel in addressing and deciding scientific issues without delegating the decision on the final outcome of the dispute there is a need to frame from the outset the scope of the external consultation.

Ideally, experts' review should therefore be limited to a determination of whether that scientific opinion represents a sufficiently sound application of scientific principles to justify its conclusions.

This analysis will help the judges in determining whether the measure conforms to the risk assessment requirements imposed by the SPS Agreement, thus freeing them from any scientific involvement.

Further confusion would seem to exist concerning the tasks with which experts might be entrusted. Thus, for instance, in the *Hormones* case, the panel asked the appointed experts to address questions that touched upon the cost effectiveness of different regulatory alternatives.[39] But, how can laboratory natural scientists give answers to questions dealing with regulatory politics and economics?

---

36 See Mc Ginnis/Movsesian (2000) 594; Stewart/Karpel (2000) 593.

37 *Japan-Agricultural Products*, Panel Report, para 8.35.

38 *EC-Hormones*, Panel Report, Annex: Joint Meeting with Experts, para 64.

39 *Ibidem*, at paras 24, 172, 236, 268, 828, 838-848.

After the famous Appellate Body's statement according to which the risk that is to be evaluated in a risk assessment under Article 5.1 is 'not only risk ascertainable in a science laboratory, but *also risk in human societies as they actually exist*',[40] one may legitimately wonder whether the relevant expertise within the WTO system should be limited to natural scientists.[41] Should the focus of risk analysis remain on 'the real world in which people live and die', it might be reasonable to imagine that panels will also consult experts coming from other fields, capable, for example, of assessing the effectiveness and the consequences stemming from a particular regulatory decision.

Thus, for instance, in the EC Commission's practice of collection and use of expertise it is considered 'appropriate to mobilise experts beyond the scientific community'.[42] These experts may include lawyers, ethicists, or those with practical knowledge gained from day-to-day involvement in an activity.

C. The Legal Status and Authority of the Experts' Opinions

A further drawback of the current expert consultation practice must be found in the panels' tendency towards attributing undue authority to the opinion of any one expert. In the *Hormones* case, for instance, the panel dismissed one of the EC arguments by relying solely on the opinion of one of the experts.[43] While the EC argued that an alternative to carbadox existed with the same therapeutic action, the panel dismissed this argument by relying on the sole advice of one expert who argued that oxytetracycline was a readily available alternative.[44]

This 'pick and choose' approach from individual experts' opinions does seem to bring the panels back to the original problem of having judges playing with science. It shows how panellists may resort to scientific advice for the sole reason of imbuing a determined outcome with apparent 'scientific legitimacy'.

Although expert advice is not legally binding,[45] the panel must show deference to it to the extent that it comes from a source that has epistemically more authority.

Finally, the readiness of WTO panels to call on experts contrasts with the reluctance of the EC courts to rely on external advice. EC courts prefer to review the contested measures by relying solely on their (by definition, non-scientific) evaluation of the scientific evidence brought to the dispute by the parties. As will

---

40 *EC-Hormones*, AB Report, para. 187.

41 See, on this point, Howse/Mavroidis (2000) 320 (who argue that '[...] expertise concerning the effectiveness and consequences – social and economic, or even cultural – of particular forms of risk management and regulatory intervention may be appropriate').

42 EC Commission, Communication on the Collection and Use of Expertise by the Commission: Principles and Guidelines COM (2002) 713 final, at 16.

43 This example is provided by Walker 311 (footnote 282).

44 *Hormones*, Panel Report, para 8.234.

45 This is expressly established by Appendix 4 of the DSU, paragraph 6, which states that 'the final report of the expert review group shall be advisory only'.

be illustrated below, although in principle both EC courts would have the expertise option open through their internal rules, they tend not to use it.

D. Conclusions on the WTO Expert Consultation System

While recourse to expert advice undoubtedly increases the ability of WTO panels to understand and assess the scientific evidence brought by the parties, there seem to be some flaws in the current practice of external consultation as developed by WTO panels.

In primis, the current practice of appointing solely individual experts may be perceived as ineffective and not entirely in conformity with the letter of the WTO treaty. Past cases have shown how recourse to individual experts inevitably entrusts panel Members with an extra scientific role. Instead of avoiding judges having to face the troubling scientific issues raised by the dispute, the current (individual) expert consultation practice entrusts them with an even more demanding scientific task: to assess the merits of the expert opinions formulated on the plausibility of the scientific evidence brought by the parties and to verify whether there exists common ground among the diverging opinions of individual experts, thus legitimizing an even more complex involvement in scientific matters. Furthermore, the panels, when 'picking and choosing' among the various individual experts' opinions, may be tempted to accord undue authority to the opinion of any one of these experts and this notwithstanding their own lack of scientific knowledge.

As to the scope of the requested expertise, there is a growing risk that panels will ultimately delegate the responsibility of deciding on a dispute to the chosen individual experts it traditionally relies upon. This outcome is quite unfortunate to the extent that these experts, not belonging to a WTO institution, do not enjoy the legitimacy necessary to accomplish this task.[46] More sensitively, there is no real control on their scientific activity within the current WTO framework.

Last but not least, following the Appellate Body's famous statement according to which the risk that is to be evaluated in a risk assessment under Article 5.1 is 'not only risk ascertainable in a science laboratory, but *also risk in human societies as they actually exist*',[47] one may legitimately wonder whether the relevant expertise within the WTO system should be limited to natural scientists. Should the focus of risk analysis remain on 'the real world in which people live and die', it might be reasonable to imagine that panels will also consult experts coming from other fields, capable, for example, of assessing the effectiveness and the consequences stemming from a particular regulatory decision.[48] This position would seem to find some textual support within the same SPS Agree-

---

46 However, it may be noted that neither the WTO judicial bodies nor the experts are politically accountable.

47 *EC-Hormones*, AB Report, at 187.

48 For example, in the *Hormones* case, some risk management issues such as cost effectiveness, relative efficacy of regulatory responses and compliance have been discussed during the meeting with the experts. See Annex to the Panel Report: Joint Meeting with Experts, paras 24, 172, 268, 828, 838-847.

ment, where Article 5.6 conditions the application of the least trade-restrictive test to the 'technical and economic feasibility'. Technical and economic feasibility are therefore factors that may play a role in assessing an SPS regulatory measure. Although these factors have not received particular attention within the WTO case law so far, they are believed to be supportive of the introduction of multidisciplinary expertise within the WTO dispute settlement system.

Some signs of an opening towards non-exclusively scientific oriented expertise may be found in the Article 21.5 implementation panel in *Japan-Apples*.[49] Here, the panel, when revisiting the previous finding of the experts in the original panel, according to which 'it would be appropriate not to export apples from (severely) blighted orchards',[50] asked its experts to further elaborate on the matter. In answering that request, Dr Geider said 'There may be no strict scientific basis to say that this is something that you should not do. On the other hand there are practical reasons. I think this is what we say is good practice so it's good orchard practice not doing that'.[51] From his side, Dr Hale stated that 'it would not be economic to even harvest [fruits from severely blighted orchards], never mind export them'.[52] Against this backdrop, the panel concluded that, to the extent that these concerns relate to 'good agricultural and commercial practice', they do not override the scientific conclusion that mature symptomless apples pose only a negligible risk of transmitting fire blight, even if harvested from several blighted orchards.[53]

It is submitted that multidisciplinary and multi-sectoral expert review groups may not only encourage a cross-fertilization of ideas but also stimulate debate and lead to 'better' opinions.

Despite the abovementioned limits of the current expert consultation practice, the increasing use of expert advice within the WTO is a positive development that must be applauded.[54] Expert advice not only ensures quality, transparency and legitimacy to WTO decisions but, if adequately fine-tuned, it might potentially reduce the level of scientific involvement currently required by the standard of legal review of science-based measures. In particular, to make the expert consultation a useful tool to somehow lighten the panels' involve-

49 *Japan-Apples* Article 21.5 Panel Report WT/DS245/RW.

50 Panel Report on *Japan-Apples*, para. 8.226.

51 Dr. Geider, Transcript, Annex 3, para. 187.

52 Dr. Hale, Transcript, Annex 3, para. 188.

53 *Japan-Apples* Article 21.5 Panel Report, para 8.88.

54 Similarly, also the International Court of Justice's experience with the use of experts may be seen as a positive development (Article 50 of the Statute of the Court states that: 'The Court may, at any time, entrust any individual, body, bureau, commission, or other organization that it may select, with the task of carrying out an enquiry or giving an expert opinion.' Article 51 of the Statute continues by stating that: 'During the hearing any relevant questions are to be put to the witnesses and experts under the conditions laid down by the Court in the Rules of Procedure referred to in Article 30.'). See, notably, for an excellent survey of expert evidence in the first fifty years of the International Court of Justice, White 2005.

ment with scientific matters, it is necessary to favour reliance on expert advisory groups (instead of on individual experts) and to determine the exact scope of the consultation expertise.

4 Towards an EC Expert Consultation System?

Although in need of some adjustments, the WTO expert consultation system may potentially inspire the development of a similar mechanism within the EC judicial system. As the *Pfizer/Alpharma* judgments have recently clearly shown, the EC courts might also need to rely on external expertise to assess the scientific plausibility of the scientific claims of both Member States and EC institutions. There are good reasons to believe that reliance on this external help tool might facilitate the role that EC courts are increasingly called upon to play with science when reviewing science-based measures.

Although under the current Statute[55] and their respective Rules of procedure,[56] both the CFI and ECJ 'may at any time entrust any individual, body, authority, committee or other organizations it chooses with the task of giving expert opinion', they have so far been quite reluctant to rely on external advice.[57] This seems to be especially true for scientific matters. While the courts, notably the CFI, have ordered expert reports to *inter alia* assess the quality of a translator's work,[58] an official's mental state,[59] to examine the rates for and conditions of transport of mineral fuels,[60] price rises and the market in dyestuffs[61] and the economic consequences of certain gas tariffs,[62] in order to verify the conclusions drawn in the contested act, the evidence relied on and the characteristics of the market,[63] they have rarely done so in scientific matters. Occasionally, the parties have themselves submitted an expert's report or, at the hearing, an expert has addressed the Court on behalf of one of the parties.[64]

The decision to obtain an expert's report is made by the Court in the form of an order after the parties have been given an opportunity to be heard. The same order appoints the experts, defines the scope of the expertise and sets a time limit for the drafting of the report.

55 EC Statute, Article 25.

56 ECJ Rules, Article 49 and CFI Rules, Article 70.

57 For an excellent review of the European Courts's practice on consultation of experts, see Sibony/Barbier de la Serre 2008.

58 ECJ: Case 10/55 *Mirossevich v. High Authority* [1954-56] ECR 333.

59 ECJ: Case 12/68 *X v. Audit Board* [1969] ECR 109

60 ECJ: Case 24 and 34/58 *Chambre syndicale de la Sidérurugie de l'Est v. High Authority* [1960] ECR 281.

61 ECJ: Case 48/69 *ICI Ltd v. Commission* [1972] ECR 619.

62 ECJ: Case C-169/84 *Société CdF Chimie Azote et Fertilisants SA* [1990] ECR 3083.

63 ECJ: Cases C-89, 104, 114, 117, 125 to 129/85 *Ahlstrom v. Commission* [1993] ECR 1307.

64 ECJ: Case 204/80 *Procureur de la République v. Vedel* [1982] ECR 465.

Despite this rather simple framework for having expertise at its disposal, EC courts have traditionally been unwilling to use it.

Therefore, before sketching out a possible expertise system within the EC judicial system, it might be crucial to look at the reasons that have so far discouraged the EC courts from relying on this possibility. An explanation for the European courts' reticence in asking external advice may be found within the EC institutional framework itself. As EC courts, especially when reviewing a Community measure, may be called upon to review scientific studies coming from the EC scientific committees, they might feel that submitting one of these studies to a third party review would amount to putting into question both the scientific and institutional legitimacy of these committees, which ultimately belong to the same system of governance. However, this argument, which boils down to the idea according to which the CFI/ECJ is an institution among other institutions, does not seem to be entirely persuasive if examined from a US perspective. In fact, US Federal Courts do not hesitate to review the risk assessments undertaken by federal regulatory agencies. It is therefore controversial whether this legitimacy argument may justify by itself the EC courts' deferential attitude vis-à-vis the scientific reports prepared by the European scientific committees.

A more credible argument aimed at explaining this deferential approach to science marked by a Europe label refers to judicial tradition. Having hardly ever relied on scientific expertise, judges (notably the judge *rapporteur* in the EC judiciary jargon) might be somehow discouraged in proposing to other Court members to have recourse to expertise under the courts' rules of procedure. Finally, if tradition continues to play a crucial role in explaining the courts' wariness, fears of ultimately delegating the task of solving a dispute may also exist.

In attempting to develop a credible and effective expert consultation system for EC courts when dealing with scientific matters, it is important to take due account of the institutional scientific framework upon which the Community relies when adopting legislation.

In fact, unlike the WTO judicial bodies, the European courts, when called upon to judicially review a science-based measure, are likely to already dispose of a scientific study supporting that measure or, at least, dealing with its scientific foundations. While this is certainly the case when the courts are called upon to examine the legality of an EC measure, it might not be the case when the contested regulation has been adopted by a Member State. In the latter case, the national measure is supported instead by a national scientific opinion coming from its own authorities.

Against this backdrop, one may wonder who might be consulted by the EC courts to examine the scientific adequacy of the evidence brought by the parties to the dispute. Should they ask the EC scientific committee members, perhaps those sitting within EFSA, to review the evidence they have themselves developed? Or should they rely on some third-party scientists? And *quid* in case of science-based national measures? Should the Court submit the national scientific evidence to the scrutiny of the EC scientific committees?

It is extremely difficult to answer that question as there is no hierarchy between research bodies and their scientific advice.[65] It is therefore difficult to see how, in the event of conflicting scientific studies, it could be justified to follow one set of scientific opinions rather than another.

In the light of the above, an expertise consultation system might be imagined in which the courts may rely respectively on national experts to examine the European studies advanced by the EC institutions and on the EC scientific committees to review the national scientific opinions brought by the parties to the dispute. A similar consultation procedure may be more than adequate to assist the EC judges in verifying the existence of a minimum scientific level in the studies put forward by the parties. Furthermore, through its cross-consultation mechanism between Member States and EC experts, this procedure could effectively avoid a situation where the same scientist who has developed the scientific opinion supporting the contested measure may be called upon to review *ex post* the same study. Last but not least, this system would be in line with the European idea according to which scientific studies could not be ranked depending on their national or European origin. In fact, as shown somewhere else, EFSA's scientific opinions do not have precedence over diverging national opinions.[66]

5 The Role of Peer Review in Judicial Control

A valid alternative method to external expertise might be represented by reliance on peer review.[67] This is a formal science-based process that is traditionally used after a scientific work is nearly complete, and utilises independent experts who were not involved in the development of the scientific study.

Although it is used primarily by publishers, to select and to screen submitted manuscripts,[68] and by funding bodies, to decide the awarding of monies for research, peer review process is also utilised for risk assessment products. In these circumstances, it involves an in-depth assessment of the assumptions, calculations, alternate interpretations, methodology and conclusions. In particular, by taking the form of a deliberation, it involves an exchange of judgments about the appropriateness of methods and the strength of the author's infer-

65 On the lack of a principle of supremacy of European scientific advice over national one, see Alemanno (2007).

66 See Alemanno, (2007). See also Regulation 178/2002.

67 For an introduction to peer-review, see, *e.g.*, Office of Management and Budget, Final Information Quality Bulletin for Peer Review, 15 December, 2004.

68 As a result, publications and awards that have not undergone peer review are likely to be regarded with suspicion by scholars and professionals in many fields.

ences.[69] Peer review panels tend to seek to reach consensus or common agreement regarding the adequacy of the product review. The final goal pursued by peer review is endorsement of the work product's conclusions.

In the United States, the Office of Management and Budget (OMB) has established since 2004 that 'important scientific information shall be peer reviewed by qualified specialists before it is disseminated by the federal government'.[70] Within this context, the purpose followed by peer review is 'to enhance the quality and credibility of the government's scientific information'.[71] The introduction of the peer review mechanism in the federal legislative mechanism is part of the Information Quality Act,[72] under which Congress has directed OMB to issue guidelines 'to provide policy and procedural guidance to Federal agencies for ensuring and maximising the quality, objectivity, utility and integrity of information' disseminated by Federal agencies.

The practice of peer review of risk assessment products is not entirely unknown in the Community or in the WTO. Thus, for instance, within the framework of the European directive on the placing of plant protection products on the market, EFSA has launched the peer review process of the assessments made by Member States aimed at creating a 'positive lists' of pesticides.[73] This

69 See the Final Information Quality Bulletin for Peer Review by the Office of Management and Budget (OMB), December 2004, at 2.

70 *Ibid.*, p. 1.

71 *Ibid.*

72 The Information Quality Act was developed as a supplement to the Paperwork Reduction Act, 44 U.S.C. §3501 *et seq.*, which requires OMB, *inter alia*, to 'develop and oversee the implementation of policies, principles, standards and guidelines to [...] apply to Federal agency dissemination of public information'. Besides this Act, Executive Order 12866 (58 Fed. Reg. 51,735 (October 4, 1993)), establishes that the Office of Information and Regulatory Affairs (OIRA) is 'the repository of expertise concerning regulatory issues' and it directs OMB to provide guidance to the agencies on regulatory planning. The same Order also requires that 'each agency shall base its decisions on the best reasonably obtainable scientific, technical, economic, or other information' (§ 1(b)(7)).

73 Council Directive 91/414/EEC of 15 July 1991 concerning the placing of plant protection products on the market (OJ L 230, p. 1-32) was required to be implemented by Member States from 26 July 1993. The main elements of the Directive are as follows: a) to harmonize the overall arrangements for the authorization of plant protection products within the European Union (EU). This to be achieved firstly by harmonizing the process for considering the acceptability of active substances at a European Community level to environment and health and, secondly, even though individual product authorization remains the responsibility of individual Member States, by establishing harmonized risk assessment criteria for Member States to use when considering the safety of those products. b) The Directive provides for the establishment of a positive list (Annex I) of active substances which have been shown to be without unacceptable risk to people or the environment. c) Member States are only permitted to authorize marketing and use of plant protection products where the active substances are listed in Annex I, except where transitional arrangements apply. d) The Directive provides for a series of transitional arrangements and derogations until 25 July 2003 to allow for the progressive re-evaluation of those active substances already on the market in the EU on 25 July 1993. e) The Directive also makes

process is managed by EFSA's Pesticide Risk Assessment Peer Review Unit (PRAPeR).

Within the WTO, the Appellate Body has even shown some propensity towards the idea of relying on peer-review in order to assess the quality of scientific expertise. In fact, in *Hormones*, the AB has recognised that Member States may also rely on minority opinions in order to satisfy the risk assessment requirement, but provided they come from 'qualified and respected sources'.[74]

The scope mandated in a peer review is generally called 'charge' and aims at providing instructions regarding the objective of the analysis and the specific advice sought. These tend to be determined in advance of the selection of the reviewers.

It is suggested that not only decision-makers but also courts may rely on peer review, by either asking some experts to peer review some of the scientific evidence advanced by the parties or by simply showing deference to that evidence whenever this has been subject to peer review.

One of the main advantages stemming from judges' reliance on peer review is that via this tool they might determine the exact scope of experts' review, by, for instance, asking them to distinguish scientific facts from professional (science policies) judgments.

This might turn out to be especially useful in both the EC and WTO legal contexts, where neither risk analysis frameworks recognise that uncertainty is inherent in science and that in many cases scientific studies do not produce conclusive evidence.

In the light of the above, it is submitted that peer review mechanisms might either be used by courts or simply inspire the WTO and EC external expert consultation system, by providing guidance on how to define the scope of the expert advice.

Whatever the case may be, both EC and WTO courts should show deference to the scientific evidence which has been advanced by the parties to the dispute and which has been previously peer reviewed. In particular, it is suggested that proof of a prior peer review must give rise to a presumption of conformity of that evidence with the relevant scientific evidence. However, prior peer review is not by itself sufficient ground for triggering such a presumption. There is clearly a need for some evidence proving the adequacy of prior peer review. Thus, for instance, publication in an important scientific journal may mean that adequate peer review has been performed.

---

provision for a system of mutual recognition, such that following the listing of an active substance on Annex I of the Directive, Member States are obliged to grant authorizations (on request) on the basis of those granted in other Member States; insofar as it can be shown that the agricultural, plant health and environmental conditions are comparable in the two Member States.

74 *EC-Hormones*, AB Report, para 194.

An example of such a deferential approach to peer reviewed scientific evidence may be seen in *Methanex*,[75] a recent case decided by NAFTA under the provisions in the North American Free Trade Agreement's (NAFTA) Chapter 11 on investment and the UNCITRAL arbitration rules.[76] At the heart of this case there is an investment dispute between Canada-based Methanex Corporation and the United States. Methanex is a major producer of methanol,[77] a gasoline additive which has been banned by California in 2002 on environmental and human health grounds. Methanex, after having submitted a claim before NAFTA, argued, *inter alia*, that the ban was not a genuine environmental measure but a disguised restriction of trade.[78] In replying to this argument the NAFTA Tribunal, 'having considered all the expert evidence adduced', accepted the scientific evidence underpinning the contested measure 'as reflecting a serious, objective and scientific approach to a complex problem in California'.[79] In particular, the Tribunal came to this conclusion by taking account of the fact that this scientific evidence 'was subject at the time to public hearings, testimony and peer-review'. In light of the above, it concluded that

> 'its emergence as a serious scientific work from such an *open and informed debate* is the best evidence that it was not the product of a political shame engineered by California'.[80]

It is believed that there is a great deal to be learned from this use of peer-review within judicial review of science-based measures and, as will be illustrated below, there is even more to be learned from the application of such a procedure-based standard of review in both the EC and WTO.

---

75 *Methanex Corp. v. the United States of America*, Final Award of the Tribunal on Jurisdiction and Merits, in the matter of an international arbitration under chapter 11 of the north American free trade agreement and the uncitral arbitration rules. S. Sagarika (2006) 110-114.

76 The text of the NAFTA Agreement is available at http://www.nafta-sec-alena.org/.

77 This substance is a key component in MTBE (methyl tertiary butyl ether), which is used to increase oxygen content and act as an octane enhancer in unleaded gasoline.

78 In particular, the plaintiff argued that the California ban was tantamount to an expropriation of the company's investment; a violation of NAFTA's Article 1110, and was enacted in breach of the national treatment (Article 1102) and minimum international standards of treatment (Article 1105) provisions. By relying on these arguments, Methanex seeked financial compensation from the United States in the amount of over $900 million U.S.

79 Part III, Chapter A, 51, para 101 of the Final Award.

80 *Ibidem*.

6 Some Proposals to Help the Judge When Reviewing Science

While the scientific process is engaged with scientific research and publication of formulation, corroboration, and advancement of scientific principles and theories, the legal process does not establish nor attempt to develop scientific theories, principles or 'truth' for the purposes of science, but only for the purposes of adjudication.

Accordingly, EC courts and WTO judicial bodies are not being directly asked to establish whether a certain risk exists or, more generally, to settle a scientific debate, they are, rather, increasingly required to evaluate the competing scientific claims made by the parties in order to determine whether the contested measures conform to the scientific discipline in force within their legal system. While this tendency is particularly significant with the WTO, EC courts would also seem to be increasingly playing a quasi-scientific role, by engaging in scientific controversies in order to adjudicate between diverging scientific claims.

As these courts began referring to 'the quality and quantity' of the scientific evidence (WTO) and the requirement for a 'detailed assessment' (EC) they have invested themselves with a non-legal task which, as shown above, they cannot realistically carry out. Indeed, on the courts' benches do not sit scientists, but lawyers.

This interpretation of their respective scientific disciplines inevitably opens up the Pandora's box of scientific discussion to these judicial bodies, thereby somehow legitimizing their involvement in controversial scientific matters.

The problem raised by this approach is that judges, being non-scientists, are not epistemically capable of discerning between good science and bad science. And this is exactly what EC and WTO courts (must) aim at doing when reviewing science-based measures. They want to make sure that the contested measure is adequately backed up not simply by a claim of science, but by a proper and adequate scientific study.

In fact, under the current interpretation adopted by the respective courts, both the EC and WTO scientific disciplines, by requiring the authorities to base their measure on science, not only establish a procedural requirement (necessity of scientific evidence or risk assessment), but also introduce a substantive test ('detailed risk assessment'; 'quality and quantity of scientific evidence') which finally boils down into a *minimum scientific threshold*. Indeed, the Panel in the *Apples* case has clearly stated that the evidence to be considered under Article 2.2 SPS should be

> '[...] evidence gathered *through scientific methods*, excluding by the same token information not acquired through a scientific method'.[81]

---

[81] *Japan – Apples*, Panel Report, para 8.92.

Similarly, the ECJ in the *Vitamins* line of cases has held that public authorities must justify their health regulations on 'a detailed assessment of the risk' alleged.[82]

By borrowing the language used by the Supreme Court in *Daubert*, it would seem that both the WTO and the EC courts have interpreted their scientific disciplines as requiring that the submitted evidence must be 'grounded in the methods and procedures of science'.[83]

However, to be 'good science' the scientific evidence supporting a measure does not merely have to be a scientifically-dressed study, but has to meet some minimum criteria assuring its scientific character.

It is by engaging in this exercise that judges, though not adequately equipped for the inevitable scientific evaluations required, attempt to adjudicate between diverging scientific claims, by 'picking and choosing' among different scientific opinions advanced by the parties. This happens because judges must, somehow, draw lines between scientific evidence that is 'detailed enough' or 'sufficient enough' and scientific evidence that is not 'detailed enough' or 'sufficient enough'. The result is that some scientific studies pass the legal test and are considered adequate in backing up a certain measure and others do not. Thus, the minimum scientific threshold reveals itself as a 'pass or fail' test.

Since it is *how* the conclusions have been reached, not *what* the conclusions are that make good science today, both WTO and EC courts have interpreted their respective scientific discipline as requiring the evidence submitted by the parties to satisfy some *minimum scientific requirements*. This trend seems to challenge the traditional uncritical view that the law has embraced vis-à-vis science's claims of universal truth.[84]

While this approach to the review of science-based measures may seem reasonable to the extent that it simply allows the judge to verify *how* the scientific study supporting a contested measure has been conducted and *what* its conclusions are, this task cannot be done by the judge alone and it also presupposes the development of some general guidelines establishing which *minimum criteria* a scientific study must satisfy to be considered 'scientific'.

6.1 How Can a Judge Assess Whether a Scientific Study is 'Scientifically Adequate'?

In answering this question it is crucial to take due account of the limited role that courts and tribunals may play in reviewing scientific information, notably in assessing the 'quality' of the scientific studies quoted by the parties to a dispute. In fact, judges can neither develop by themselves the criteria determining whether a study is 'scientific enough' nor judge whether these criteria are met by a scientific opinion brought by the parties to the dispute.

---

82 ECJ: Case 192/01 *Commission v. Denmark* [2003] ECR 9693, at 47.

83 *Daubert v. Merrell Dow Pharmaceuticals, Inc.*, 509 U.S. 579 (1993).

84 Atik (1996-97) 740.

Therefore, since a court may not realistically assess whether the scientific evidence advanced by one party meets the *minimum scientific requirements* required to consider it 'good science', reliance on external advice, in the form of external experts or peer-review mechanisms, is increasingly needed.

As seen above, the WTO expert consultation system may reveal itself to be a useful experience upon which to build in order to develop an external scientific support for international courts called upon to review science-based measures.[85] In fact, this system of external help has been generally successful in facilitating the scientific tasks judges are increasingly called upon to perform when reviewing science-based measures. Although presenting some drawbacks, such as, for example, the continual preference of panels for the appointment of individual experts rather than expert review groups, the WTO dispute settlement body practice with external expert consultation has been positive. In the light of the above, it has been submitted that, though in need of some adjustments, the WTO external consultation system could also be extended and become current practice within the EC judicial architecture.

Thus, it could be envisaged that, not only the WTO judicial bodies but also the EC courts, when reviewing either a Member State or an EC science-based measure, might rely on some external scientific advice in order to assess whether the scientific evidence brought by the parties is 'adequately scientific'. This use of experts would help the judge in ascertaining whether a minimum scientific threshold claimed by the contested measure has been met, thereby preventing the judge from engaging in scientific tasks.

Alternatively, courts, as seen above, may also rely on peer review as an effective tool aimed at establishing whether the scientific study underpinning a contested measure is adequately grounded on science. They may do so by either asking some experts to peer review the scientific evidence advanced by the parties or by merely showing deference to that evidence whenever this has previously been subject to peer review. Of course, in the latter case, peer review should, in turn, satisfy certain minimum scientific soundness requirements, which may boil down to, for instance, a publication in an internationally renowned publication.

As illustrated above, an excellent example of this use of peer-review within judicial review of science-based measures is represented by the abovementioned *Methanex* case.

6.2 What is a Minimum Scientific Threshold?

As to the issue of determining what is the minimum scientific threshold that both WTO and EC courts seem to hint at when reviewing science-based measures, it is neither for the judge nor for the external experts to develop

[85] The use of experts by other international organizations is not the object of this chapter. For an excellent survey of expert evidence in the first fifty years of the International Court of Justice, see White (2005).

minimum standards of scientific adequacy to be met by scientific evidence advanced by the parties to a dispute.

There is currently a strong trend, internationally, to formalize procedures for dealing with risk analysis issues and to promote commonalities of approaches throughout the different sectors where risk assessment may be developed.[86] Thus, for instance, at EC level, some efforts have been deployed to develop a harmonized approach to risk assessment procedures among the Scientific Committees advising the European Commission in the area of human, animal and plant health and on the environment.[87] At international level, this trend towards formalizing procedures for risk assessment is even more significant and is traditionally led by some of the international standardization bodies mentioned within the SPS Agreement. In recent years, these standards organizations have contributed more to the trade system by setting out scientific approaches to regulation than by promulgating standards that are identical across countries.[88] Thus, as illustrated above, the *Codex Alimentarius Commission* is engaged, since 1995, in developing Working Principles for Risk Analysis aimed at determining the main steps and procedures that scientific assessors must follow when engaging in risk analysis applied to food safety issues.[89] Similarly, the UN Food and Agricultural Organization (FAO) has developed new guidelines that will help countries assessing the risks of living modified organisms (LMOs) to determine whether some should be considered to be weeds or other organisms that damage plants.[90]

---

86 This trend is also visible at national level. See, for example, in the US, the Envtl. Protection Agency, Proposed Guidelines for Carcinogenic Risk Assessment, 61 Fed. Reg. and, especially, the more general Office of Management and Budget (OMB) Proposed Bulletin on Risk Assessment, which aims at providing clear minimum standards for the scientific quality and presentation of federal risk assessments.

87 To this end, it has been established a Working Party on 'Harmonization of Risk Assessment Procedures' to address specifically the general principles of risk assessment and its application to broad consumer health issues, with a particular reference to measures that would enhance compatibility of approaches between the Scientific Advisory Committees. See the Updated Opinion of the Scientific Steering Committee on Harmonization of Risk Assessment Procedures, adopted on 10-11 April 2003. A full Second Report on the Harmonization of Risk Assessment Procedures was expected by the end of the following year but it has not yet seen the light of the day.

88 Atik (1996-97) 740, 46.

89 The Codex Alimentarius Commission has been discussing policies for risk analysis since its 20th Session (1995), when it adopted an Action Plan for Codex-wide Development and Application of Risk Analysis Principles and Guidelines. The Joint FAO/WHO Committee on General Principles, meeting in Paris in April 2005, is elaborating further guidance specific to the food safety field, see Proposed Draft Working Principles on Risk Analysis for Food Safety.

90 These guidelines are available at http://www.fao.org/newsroom/en/news/2004/43684/. Similarly, FAO has established Guidelines for Pest Risk Analysis. These guidelines have been discussed in the *Japan-Agricultural Products* case. See, *e.g.* Panel Report, paras 2.25-2.33.

The objective of these international efforts is to provide guidance to their respective Member States so that food safety and health related aspects of their decisions and recommendations are based on risk analysis.

From a conceptual point of view, it might be useful to underscore that the harmonization activity brought forward by these bodies does not aim at setting up technical standards, but merely at developing a common approach to the risk analysis in a specific field.[91] These common approaches to risk analysis have been dubbed as 'meta-standards'.[92]

It is argued that this task, which may be called 'light harmonization' or 'soft convergence' in risk analysis, carries the potential of not only guiding scientists in conducting risk assessment but also facilitating the task of the experts called to determine the scientific adequacy of the opinions and studies adduced by the parties. In other words, these guidelines may help the experts in evaluating not the validity of scientific studies, but instead their methodologies. Should these scientific studies satisfy the general guidelines on risk analysis developed on that particular scientific area, experts and, accordingly, panels should show deference to them.

This approach does not seem to be totally unknown to the WTO/SPS system. As seen above, under Article 5.1 SPS, if a national requirement is not based on a specific international standard, the WTO Member adopting that requirement must justify its measure by a risk assessment that takes into account 'the risk assessment techniques' developed by Codex, the International Office of Epizootics (OIE) and the International Plant Protection Convention (IPPC). It is submitted that the insertion of this provision within the SPS Agreement legitimises the possibility for the interpreter to rely upon 'light harmonisation' tools in order to find guidance on how to apply risk analysis requirements.

This seems to be further confirmed by the *EC-Biotech* panel report, where the Panel, after consulting the Parties, has requested several international organisations (Codex, FAO, the IPPC Secretariat, WHO, OIE, the CBD Secretariat and UNEP)

> '[...] to identify materials (reference works, glossaries, official documents of the relevant international organisations, *including conventions, standards and guidelines*, etc.) that might aid [the panel] in determining the ordinary meaning of certain terms used in the definitions provided in Annex A to the SPS Agreement'.

---

91 See also the efforts deployed by WHO in harmonization of risk analysis within its area of competence. WHO, jointly with FAO, are developing guidelines documents for undertaking each of the four components of a risk assessment namely hazard identification, hazard characterization, exposure assessment and risk characterization. To date guidelines for hazard characterization of pathogens in food and water have been finalized, and the draft guidelines for exposure assessment of pathogen in food have been prepared and are currently under review. FAO and WHO are now planning the development of practical guidelines for risk characterization of microbiological hazards in foods. See http://www.who.int/foodsafety/micro/en/.

92 Jostling, *supra* note 5, at 46.

> In light of the above, '[t]he materials' the panel has obtained in this way 'have been taken into account [...], as appropriate'.[93]

As has been argued above, such an interpretation by an AB proves that Article 5.1, by referring to the 'risk assessment techniques developed' by the international standard-setting organisations, may prove to be a useful legal basis for the WTO judicial bodies to rely upon in order to find some guidance when reviewing complex science-based measures.

7 Conclusions

Given the increasingly intrusive scrutiny applied by EC and WTO courts to science-based measures, which has led their judges to become enmeshed in scientific debates, this chapter, by adopting a critical stance on the current trend, has attempted to reorient the role of the judge when reviewing science-based regulations. After having illustrated the struggle faced by both EC and WTO judicial bodies when reviewing strictly science-based measures, it has been found that their growing scientific involvement has to be redirected towards the effort to assess whether the scientific evidence advanced by the parties to the dispute constitutes 'good science'. This effort seems to be more justified within the WTO context than in the EC, since WTO judicial bodies, by not disposing of a complete risk analysis framework upon which to rely when reviewing a food safety measure, tend to be more demanding vis-à-vis the scientific basis of a contested measure.

Since it is *how* the conclusions have been reached, not *what* the conclusions are that make 'good science' today, both WTO and EC courts have interpreted their respective scientific discipline as requiring that the evidence submitted by the parties satisfies some scientific quality requirements. This interpretation of their respective scientific disciplines inevitably opened up the Pandora's box of scientific discussion to these judicial bodies, thus somehow legitimizing their involvement in controversial scientific matters. However, judges, being non-scientists, are not epistemically capable of discerning between 'good science' and 'bad science'.

In particular, it has been argued that this task cannot be done by the judge alone and that it presupposes the development of some general guidelines establishing which *minimum criteria* a scientific study must satisfy in order to be considered 'scientific enough'.

To solve the first problem it has been suggested to improve (within the WTO) and to develop (within the EC) the external experts' consultation practice, as this might facilitate the current attempt by judicial bodies to verify whether the scientific evidence advanced by the parties to the dispute is 'scientifically adequate'. This method, however, might become superfluous should the scientific study which has been advanced by the parties be subject to peer-review.

---

93 *EC-Biotech* panel report, at 7.96.

As to the second related problem of facilitating the task of the expert in accomplishing her task, it might be advisable to rely on those guidelines, currently elaborated by several international standardization organisations and by the same EC scientific committees, aimed at promoting commonalities of approaches in risk analysis for different sectors. This solution not only finds a solid textual basis within the WTO but has also been endorsed by the *EC-Biotech* panel report.

In the light of the above, it is advisable that courts, notably when reviewing the scientific basis of a contested measure, rely, first, on peer review as a tool aimed at verifying – loosely speaking – the scientific plausibility of a contested measure and, second, when necessary, on external experts in order to attain the same goal.

Reliance on these external expertise tools will ensure that courts won't get involved in the scientific merits of the evidence, thereby allowing an objective and scientifically-restrained review. In particular, by engaging into an effective dialogue with external experts, the courts might obtain not only a critical assessment of the scientific evidence submitted to them, but also a useful translation of these studies into a non-scientific jargon.

It is believed that this dialectic interdisciplinary dialogue, by reducing the level of scientific involvement of courts and by giving an operational meaning to what 'minimum science' is, might prove successful in finding a more appropriate role for the international judge in risk analysis.

Bibliography

A. Alemanno, 'Protection des consommateurs: Arrêts Alpharma/Pfizer', 4 *Revue du droit de l'Union Europénne*, (2002).

A. Alemanno, 'Les affaires vitamines, *Commission/Danemark et al.* ', *Revue du Droit de l'Union Européenne*, issue 3, (2003).

A. Alemanno, *Trade in Food, Regulatory and Judicial Approaches to Food Safety*, Cameron May (2007).

J. Atik, 'Science and International Regulatory Convergence', 17 *Northwestern J. Int'l L. & B.* 736 (1996-97).

Claus-Dieter Ehlermann, 'Six Years on the Bench of the 'World Trade Court': Some Personal Experiences as Member of the Appellate Body of the World Trade Organization', in 36 *J. World Trade* (2002).

T. Christoforou, *Settlement of Science-Based Trade Disputes in the WTO: A Critical Review of the Developing Case Law in the Face of Scientific Uncertainty*, 8 *N.Y.U. Environmental Law Journal* 622 (2000).

C.-D. Ehlermann, 'Six Years on the Bench of the 'World Trade Court': Some Personal Experiences as Member of the Appellate Body of the World Trade Organization', in 36 *J. World Trade* 605 (2002) .

R. Howse/P.C. Mavroidis, *Europe's Evolving Regulatory Strategy for GMOs – The Issue of Consistency with WTO Law: of Kine and Brine*, 24 *Fordham Int.' L.J.* (2000)

K.H. Ladeur, 'The Introduction of the Precautionary Principle into EU law: A Phyrric Victory for Environmental and Public Health Law? Decision-making Under Conditions of Complexity in Multi-Level Political Systems', 40 *Common Market Law Review*, 1455-79 (2003).

F. Ortino, *Basic Legal Instruments for the Liberalization of Trade*, Oxford and Portland Oregon (2004).

J.O. Mc Ginnis/M.L. Movsesian, 'The World Trade Constitution', 114 *Harvard Law Review* 511, (2000).

D.A. Motaal, 'Is the World Trade Organization Anti-Precaution?', *Journal of World Trade*, 39(3) (2005).

J. Pauwelyn, 'Expert Advice in WTO Dispute Settlement', in G. Bermann and P.C. Mavroidis, *Trade and Human Health and Safety* (2006) Cambridge University Press.

J. Pauwelyn, 'The use of Experts in WTO Dispute Settlement' [2002]51 *ICQL*.

S. Sagarika, 'Methanex Corporation and the USA: The Final NAFTA Tribunal Ruling' *Review of European Community & International Environmental Law* 15 (1) (2006).

A. Sibony and E. Barbier de la Serre, *Common Market Law Review*, (2008).

A. Sykes, *Domestic Regulation, Sovereignty and Scientific Evidence Requirements: A Pessimistic View*, 3 *Chicago J. Int.' L.* 353 (2002)

T.P. Stewart/A.A. Karpel, 'Review of the Dispute Settlement Understanding: Operation of Panels' 31 *Law & Pol'y Intl Bus* (2000).

Walker, *Keeping the WTO from Becoming the 'World Trans-Science organization': Scientific Uncertainty, Science Policy, and Factfinding in the Growth Hormones Dispute.*, 31 *Cornell International Law Journal* 251 (1988)

V.R. Walker, 'The Myth of Science as a 'Neutral Arbiter' for triggering Precautions' 26 *Boston College International and Comparative Law Review* (2003).

G. White, 'The Use of Experts by the International Court', in V. Lowe and M. Fitzmaurice eds., *Fifty years of the International Court of Justice, Essays in Honour of Sir Robert Jennings* Cambridge University Press (2005).

S. Wolf, 'Risk Regulation, Higher Rationality, and The Death of Judicial Self-Restraint: A Comment on Ladeur' 41 *Common Market Law Review*, 1175-1180 (2004).

Final Information Quality Bulletin for Peer Review by the Office of Management and Budget (OMB), December 2004.

U.S. vs. EC Biotech Products Case – WTO Dispute Backgrounder, The Institute for Agriculture and Trade Policy, September 2005.

CHAPTER 13

Whose Margin Is It?

State Discretion and Judges' Appreciation in the Necessity Quicksand

Filippo Fontanelli*

1 Introduction

This work rests heavily on some studies that have been carried out on the notion of 'margin of appreciation', a concept that was originally minted and employed by the European Court of Human Rights (ECtHR), and which then served as a model for other international judiciary actors vested with the power of reviewing the conduct of State authorities.

This formula and the concept underlying it formed the subject of various definitions and critiques. Nevertheless enough to say, in general terms, that it accounts for the freedom that Members to the Council of Europe enjoy in treating certain values that could enter into conflict with the rights protected by the European Convention of Human Rights (ECHR).[1] The Strasbourg Court has made use of this doctrine in two different sets of occasions: notably, consideration of national appreciation can lead the ECtHR not to review a measure under the ECHR either because there is a violation, but it amounts to a necessary and proportional limitation of the ECHR (in light of the necessity to strike the balance between conventional rights and national interests) or because there is no violation at all (the measure regulates matters under the sole State sovereignty).[2]

The margin of appreciation entails obvious implications for the general interplay among legal orders: it is designed to create a deferential link between the *supra*-national judiciary body and the normative set of the Member State,[3] but also between the former and the national colleagues.[4]

Deference towards national authoritative acts (whatever they might be: legislative measures, administrative decisions, judgments) is an effective instrument to manage diversity, and therefore several *supra*-national courts have applied it, although using different definitions (see, for instance, the doctrine of constitutional tolerance of the European Court of Justice).[5] In a recent study,[6] Shany observed that 'margin-of-appreciation like' approaches have gradually spread across the practice of courts whose mandate includes the review of State action,

---

* LL.M. 2010 candidate, Global Hauser scholar, NYU School of Law, New York. Ph.D. 2011 candidate, Scuola Superiore di Studi Universitari e Perfezionamento, Pisa. Comments are welcome at f.fontanelli@sssup.it.

1 See Council of Europe, Convention for the Protection of Human Rights and Fundamental Freedoms, Nov. 4, 1950, 213 U.N.T.S. 222, Artt. 8-11, 18. It is important to stress that this concept 'denot[es] the discretion of states to strike the proper balance *in the first instance.*' (emphasis added), that is before any adjudication phase. See Stone Sweet (2008) 148.

2 Letsas (2006).

3 See the wording of the ECHR in the Judgment of December 19, 1989, ECHR, Series A, No. 169, p. 53, *Mellacher and others.*

4 Yourow (1996); Arai-Takahashi (2002).

5 Weiler (2002).

6 Shany (2006).

and welcomed its diffusion, in spite of the criticism that this doctrine has attracted, mostly because of its essentially political nature.

The use of similar techniques is clearly more crucial when a *supra*-national legal order does not enjoy a status of absolute prevalence over the national ones, in terms of competence, supremacy of the higher laws, direct applicability, power to review findings of national authorities: the lack of any of these aspects could give rise to situations where the *supra*-national authority needs to step back *vis-à-vis* national policies, whatever they be.[7]

Besides, the rationale of these techniques is strictly related to the general purpose of the *supra*-national organization concerned: organizations whose purpose is the creation of common rules for, or the regulatory harmonization of, member States with respect to certain matters (for instance, the common market for the European Community or Third Pillar issues for the European Union) are naturally inclined to fight regulatory diversity and fragmentation, and to allow for State discretion only subject to certain conditions. On the other hand, objective-based organizations tend to acknowledge a wider freedom to their Members as regards the choice of domestic policies: the focus is rather on the attainment of the agreed objectives, and regulatory diversity is a commonly accepted standard ('*laissez-régler*').[8] This is the case of the organizations promoting negative integration among their members,[9] such as the Council of Europe (whose normative production is limited to the principles established by the Convention) and the WTO, among whose objectives can be listed the gradual elimination of pre-existing protectionist national regulation and the systematic eradication of new one.

Indeed, the de-regulating process *par excellence* is certainly the one built upon the WTO system, at least in its original layout.[10] It is therefore not surprising that the quasi-judicial bodies acting within the Dispute Settlement Mechanism (DSM) devote particular attention to the margin of maneuver left to national authorities both in pursuing extra-WTO policies and to adjudicate WTO-regulated issues at the national level, such as anti-dumping cases.

The negative integration framework set forth by the Covered Agreements (other than the TRIPS)[11] could not but codify deference towards national diversity in catch-all provisions like Art. XX of the GATT.[12] A symptomatic instance of this trend is the exception under Art. XX (d), providing for a safe haven to national regulations that are not linked to a particular protected value

7 For a complete appraisal of trade-off devices used to settle 'trade and [...]' issues, see Trachtman (1998) 35-36.

8 Trachtman (1998) 37-39.

9 For an accurate account of the concept of negative integration and its application in economic communities, see Ortino (2004) 18 and bibliography referred to therein, in particular F. Scharpf.

10 Mavroidis (2008).

11 Trachtman (2007) 648.

12 For an explanation of the concepts of negative and positive integration, see Tinbergen (1955) 77-79, referred to in Shaffer (2008) 48.

and appear to be *prima facie* WTO-inconsistent, but are designed to comply with WTO-consistent rules.[13] More specifically, Art. 17(6) (ii) of the Antidumping Agreement provides for a presumption of conformity of State authorities' conduct with the Agreement, unless such consistent interpretation is simply not permissible.[14] Both provisions, although clear in their *Chevron*-like wording, were often interpreted quite strictly, and could not prevent DSM bodies from squashing national practices brought before them.[15]

This chapter aims at testing the status of deferential practice in the field of WTO, by scrutinizing a sample case-law of the panels and the Appellate Body (AB) that specifically questions the right of Members States to pass measures *necessary* to promote certain values. Since we intend to focus on the necessity principle (with the purpose of expanding the study conducted by Sykes, see below), we will not enlarge our research to other landmark cases that dealt with the issue of national discretion more broadly, nor will we analyse the SPS cases, to which the very question necessity often applies as well.[16]

Such analysis shall account for the diversity-friendly approach of the WTO system *vis-a-vis* national regulations and policies. However, even if the somewhat codified 'margin of appreciation' clauses should serve as a limit for judicial discretion (at least in principle) in that they would grant Members' conduct with a presumption of WTO-consistency, we shall demonstrate how the strict interpretation of the necessity requirement *de facto* partially impaired the diversity-friendly rationale of Art. XX GATT, and left the judges with the power to implement a case-by-case appreciation.

In other words, if any margin of discretion originally belonged to the States, it could have shifted from State authorities to the WTO judges. Indeed, these latter are the ones enjoying the power to decide (that is, to appreciate) when State action amounts to legitimate implementation of national policies or rather to WTO-inconsistent conduct.

Whereas such outcome could not be surprising, it should be noted that, quite differently from what occurs in other *supra*-national systems, the WTO is based on a general purpose of pursuing integration through an objective-based deregulation rather than through harmonization of State laws. In such scenario,

---

13 Zleptnig (2002).

14 Croley, Jackson (1996).

15 Tarullo (2002); Huerta (2009).

16 Among them, see *US – Restrictions on Import of Tuna*, ('Tuna-Dolphin II'), DS29/R, (1994); *US – Restrictions on Imports of Cotton and Man-made Fibre Underwear* ('Underwear'), WT/DS24/R (1997); *EC – Measures Concerning Meat and Meat Products (Hormones)*, WT/DS26/AB/R (1998); *EC – Regime for the Importation, Sale and Distribution of Bananas – Recourse to Arbitration by the European Communities under Article 22.6 of the DSU*, WT/DS27/ARB/ECU (2000); *Argentina – Safeguard Measures on Imports of Footwear*, WT/DS121/AB/R (2000); *EC – Measures Affecting Asbestos and Asbestos-Containing Products*, WT/DS135/AB/R (2001); *US – Tax Treatment for 'Foreign Sales Corporations' – Recourse to Arbitration by the United States under Article 22.6 of the DSU and Article 4.11 of the SCM Agreement*, WT/DS108/ARB (2002).

therefore, the margin of appreciation towards State action entails a very fundamental relevance: States have committed themselves to WTO obligations but retained the willingness and the right to pass national regulations without being second-guessed by a superior judge. In other words, in the international trade law order this appreciation would not be a courtesy of the judges, but the natural counter-weight of the terms of the general agreement between the parties (WTO shall not limit State action, *as far as* it does not encroach upon WTO obligations).

We should keep in mind that – as it often occurs when negative integration is pursued – unilateral policies are not harmful to the WTO framework, at least until the non-discrimination rule applies.[17] If the norms providing for such legislative and executive freedom are ineffective and if the judicial trend appears to be discretionary and hardly foreseeable, we could reasonably allege that deregulation is not a general principle of the system, or at least that it is not the main one anymore, and that a sort of positive integration may be taking place.

2 The Necessity Test and the Least-Restrictive Means Doctrine

Obviously, the treatment of WTO-inconsistent state practices in DSM litigation cannot be the subject matter of a short study: every single case litigated before panels or the AB (and many others that are settled before litigation) involves the review of state measures claimed inconsistent with WTO law. Therefore, we will rather narrow down our analysis to those reports in which the application of Art. XX GATT is invoked and discussed: the mechanism of the general exception represents perhaps the best venue where 'appreciation' occurs, that is where purposeful violation of WTO agreements is reviewed by the panels and the AB.[18]

A seminal study from Prof. Sykes (dating of 2003) demonstrated that WTO judicial bodies alternate 'deferential' and 'interferential' behaviors with respect to national policies. This study also showed how deference often occurs when certain particular values are attached to the measures at stake (notably, public health), whilst decreases in other cases.[19] The privileged point of view to embark on in this analysis is the construction by the WTO judiciary bodies of Art. XX

---

17 Mavroidis (2008) 7: 'Policies are being unilaterally defined and, to the extent that there is an international spillover, it will be internalized through nondiscrimination. [...] Trade will not harmonize societal preferences. Trade is not the overarching value in the WTO contract. Trade comes after respect of regulatory diversity.' This is the core of the Korean claim in the *Korea – Beef* case (see *infra*), as synthesized at 240 of the panel's report: 'Regulatory diversity, Korea continued, to the extent that it is applied in a non-discriminatory manner, is not put into question in the WTO system.' See Trachtman (2007) 632.

18 Stone Sweet (2008) 153.

19 Syke's article also argues that the construction of the 'necessity' requisite triggers a cost-benefit analysis. Even though we will incidentally mention similar theories, we do not intend to ascertain the implications of this argument in this work.

GATT, in particular of the term 'necessary' used in the exceptions under Art. XX (a), (b) and (d).[20]

Art. XX GATT empowers Member States to pass GATT-inconsistent measures, provided that they belong to one of the categories listed, each related to a different societal value, and that they are applied in a non-discriminatory way. In particular, exceptions designed to promote public morals, human (and animal and plant) health, and compliance with GATT-consistent national norms make reference to the requisite of necessity.

The principle of necessity is a well-known tool in public international law, designed to shelter states from the overly rigid application of rules that could result in unfair outcomes.[21] In the three above-mentioned clauses, the necessity test aims at securing that only least trade-restrictive measures are duly adopted by States, thus substantiating the idea that the State actually finds itself in a 'state of necessity' with respect to its trade obligations: whenever another measure entailing a lighter impact on WTO obligations is reasonably available and could have been adopted to attain the same objective, the measure under consideration cannot be justified under Art. XX (a), (b) or (d).[22]

For the purpose of this brief analysis, we will take into consideration only the necessity test under Art. XX GATT (plus Art. XIV (a) GATS, see below), therefore we won't dwell into other necessity-related provisions of the Covered Agreements, in particular those of the SPS.[23]

---

20 These provisions refer to measures: '(a) necessary to protect public morals; (b) necessary to protect human, animal or plant life or health; [...] (d) necessary to secure compliance with laws or regulations which are not inconsistent with the provisions of this Agreement, including those relating to customs enforcement, the enforcement of monopolies operated under paragraph 4 of Article II and Article XVII, the protection of patents, trade-marks and copyrights, and the prevention of deceptive practices.' See Garcia (2006) 11, taking up one of Schoenbaum's remarks regarding the necessity test: 'it is the most important test within WTO jurisprudence for determining the balance to be struck between trade and non-trade values in cases involving GATT law.'

21 In a way, the principle of necessity favors the shift from rules to principles, as Montini (1997; 2001) sharply puts it.

22 See the next section for a description of the seminal cases where this least trade-restrictive test was first established.

23 For a comprehensive list of WTO provisions referring to necessity, see Delimatsis (2008) 370: 'Necessity in obligation provisions is to be found in Articles VI(4), and (5), and XII(2)(d) GATS; 2(2), (3), and (5) TBT; 2(2) and 5(6) SPS; and 8(1) TRIPs. Paragraph (2) of the draft accountancy disciplines also falls into this category. Provisions that comprise necessity as part of an exception include: Article XIV GATS and paragraph (5)(e) of the Annex on Telecommunications; Articles XI(2)(b) and (c), and XX GATT; Articles 3(2) and 27(2) TRIPs; and Article 23(2) GPA. The provisions entailing an exception could be further refined into provisions that are part of an exception to the provisions where they belong (*e.g.*, Article XI(2)(b) GATT or paragraph (5)(e) of the GATS Annex on Telecommunications), and provisions that constitute a general exception (*e.g.*, Article XX GATT or XIV GATS).' See, generally, Neumann, Tuerk (2003).

The necessity test is also a fundamental element of the ECtHR margin of appreciation doctrine as described above. Whereas it can be the only criterion under which a measure is reviewed (type A: if the measure is necessary to protect certain values, States can pass it), it can also be coupled with the proportionality test (type B: States are granted a limited scope of action, thus if the limitation of the protected right is not disproportionate to the benefit the measure can ensure, it is legitimate).

It goes without saying that type A is merely an automatic test, whilst type B is a quantitative one, and implies the power to assess whether a certain threshold was attained or not in the case at stake. We endeavor to examine the case-law related to Art. XX (a), (b) and (d) in order to understand if the WTO necessity resembles more to type A or B. This would allow us to define the extent of the margin Member States enjoy under WTO-law, and to understand the deferential techniques used by the panels and the AB towards governmental policies.

We will then be able to say whether the record of the necessity test case-law can help Member States shape their prospective measures in order to ensure WTO-compliance *ex ante*, that is, whether the review of the necessity prerequisite has attained a significant degree of predictability and technicality. This question is fundamental because it is argued that, on the contrary, the use of the margin of appreciation doctrine by the ECtHR often amounts to an oracular exercise, in which the reason why a judgment finds a measure legitimate (or not) seems to be the judgment itself.[24]

We chose to put the cases in a merely chronological order and to discuss the incremental evolution of the necessity test. Despite an obsessive referral to relevant precedents, indeed, the jurisprudence is often changing and yet not fully established, thus we have got reason to believe that some further adjustments may occur in the future, as the *China – Audiovisual* panel report showed.

3 Previous Case Law

3.1 GATT Precedents and Analogies with Art. XXI GATT

The application of the three exceptions at stake was invoked and treated by the judicial bodies only in few cases (in the WTO era).Therefore it is easy to briefly review all of them and account for the position of the AB

[24] See for instance Letsas (2006) 712, according to whom in the judgments of the Strasbourg Court references made to the margin of appreciation are the *result* of the Court's review, rather than a tool to facilitate it. The author also argues that this concept is of little use since the Court, when supporting its findings with some argumentative evidence, tends to resort to other instruments: '[w]e have no prior theory of what falls within the states' margin of appreciation, which we can use to find out what state acts (or omissions) amount to a violation. Rather, we use other tools, such as 'balancing' or the proportionality principle in order to find out the limits of the Convention rights.'

(and the panels) with respect to the principle of necessity. However, a laconic appraisal of the few fundamental GATT (pre-WTO) cases will be of help.[25]

In particular, it is worth here quoting the panel report of *United States – Section 337*:

> '[A] contracting party cannot justify a measure inconsistent with another GATT provision as 'necessary' [...] if an alternative measure which it could reasonably be expected to employ and which is not inconsistent with other GATT provisions is available to it [...] [I]n cases where a measure consistent with other GAT provisions is not reasonably available, a contracting party is bound to use, among the measures reasonably available to it, that which entails the least degree of inconsistency with other GATT provisions.'[26]

This test was later applied in the *Thailand – Cigarettes* case to disqualify Thailand's measure aimed at blocking the import of foreign cigarettes,[27] and in the *Tuna I* case, in which the Panel condemned the US for applying dolphin-mortality thresholds with respect to Mexico-sold tuna stocks.[28]

Since the first WTO case, the AB acknowledged the importance of the concept of necessity referred to in Art. XX (a), (b) and (d), as opposed to the other general exceptions.[29] The necessity condition, therefore, was designed to avoid

---

25 For a more detailed analysis of the GATT jurisprudence, see Sykes (2003) 412-415.

26 *United States – Section 337 of the Tariff Act of 1930*, 36th Supp GATT BISD 345, 392-93 (1990), at par. 5.26. Stone Sweet (2008) 156, explains that this test was advocated by the EC, which had in mind the EC and ECtHR-related doctrines of proportionality. The US had proposed a stricter test based on rational analysis of the measure.

27 *Thailand-Restrictions on Importation of and Internal Taxes on Cigarettes*, 37th Supp GATT BISD 200,223 (1991), at 74-75 (inconsistencies with GATT obligations arising from a national measure were deemed to be legitimate only as far as they were 'unavoidable').

28 See *United States – Restrictions on Imports of Tuna (Mex. v. U.S.)* GATT Panel Report 3 Sept. 1991 as reported in 2 IELR, 48-114, in which the panel uses the same wording of the Cigarettes report. US had subjected import of tuna to the respect of certain thresholds of dolphin-mortality. However, the way these thresholds were calculated made them often too strict in the practice, and since the US had not carried out any attempt to negotiate a cooperation strategy with the exporting countries the Panel found that the application of the thresholds was not necessary, because it was more trade-restrictive than another reasonably available alternative. We will simply mention that after this report, the US endeavored to collaborate with other countries to create the American Tropical Tuna Commission, and reached an agreement in 1992 establishing a conservation program to gradually reduce dolphin mortality.

29 See AB's report in WT/DS2, WT/DS4 – *United States – Standards for Reformulated and Conventional Gasoline*: 'In enumerating the various categories of governmental acts, laws or regulations which WTO Members may carry out or promulgate in pursuit of differing legitimate state policies or interests outside the realm of trade liberalization, Article XX uses different terms in respect of different categories: 'necessary' – in paragraphs (a), (b) and (d); 'essential' – in paragraph (j); 'relating to' – in paragraphs (c), (e) and (g); 'for the protection of' – in paragraph (f); 'in pursuance of' – in paragraph (h); and 'involving' – in paragraph (i). It does not seem reasonable to suppose that the WTO Members intended

instrumental behavior from Member States, and to prevent them from invoking Art. XX with respect to measures only vaguely related to the public interests listed therein, but actually concealing a protectionist intent.

Besides, the AB clarified how the test applies exclusively to the measures adopted and cannot involve the review of the value pursued or the national policy promoted.[30] Like Mavroidis lucidly puts it: '*a WTO adjudicating body [...] can extend its judicial review only with respect to the means used to achieve the ends: ends are not justiciable, means are.*'[31] We insist on this apparent neutrality of the reviewing bodies in respect of the national interest underlying the challenged measure: this approach plays a major role in the overall structure of the necessity test, and in shaping its difference from the 'margin of appreciation' test used by the Strasbourg court.

We deem it useful to mention in passing the debate surrounding another exception provided in the GATT, namely the security exception of Art. XXI GATT,[32] entitling each Member State to pass WTO-inconsistent measures subject to the condition it considers them 'necessary' for the protection of its security interests. Although there is no jurisprudence of a competent WTO body[33] on this Article, there is consensus on the fact that each Member State has the exclusive power to assess the scope and the nature of its own security interests, and this choice cannot be reviewed by the WTO bodies. In fact, since the interest invoked and the threshold of protection thereof are not questionable, the security defense could be challenged only as to the compliance with

---

to require, in respect of each and every category, the same kind or degree of connection or relationship between the measure under appraisal and the state interest or policy sought to be promoted or realized'.

30 See *US – Gasoline* cit., par. 7.1: 'It was not its task to examine generally the desirability or necessity of the environmental objectives of the Clean Air Act or the Gasoline Rule. Its examination was confined to those aspects of the Gasoline Rule that had been raised by the complainants under specific provisions of the General Agreement. Under the General Agreement, WTO Members were free to set their own environmental objectives, but they were bound to implement these objectives through measures consistent with its provisions, notably those on the relative treatment of domestic and imported products.'

31 Mavroidis (2005) 191.

32 Reading: 'Nothing in this Agreement shall be construed (*a*) [...]...]; or (*b*) to prevent any contracting party from taking any action which it considers necessary for the protection of its essential security interests (i) relating to fissionable materials or the materials from which they are derived; (ii) relating to the traffic in arms, ammunition and implements of war and to such traffic in other goods and materials as is carried on directly or indirectly for the purpose of supplying a military establishment; (iii) taken in time of war or other emergency in international relations; or (*c*) [...] .' This provision does not seem exhaustive as to the exact extent of a potential judicial review of DSM bodies, and this is why some authors refer to its opaqueness and broadness. See Weiler (2001) 197, Cann Jr. (2001) 422 and Browne (1997) 410.

33 For a useful review of the cases in which the Art. XXI exception was invoked or threatened prior to adjudication before a panel (including the EU-US controversy on the Helms-Burton Act), see Lindsay (2003) 1308.

the 'necessity' requirement, which has to be blatantly disregarded to trigger a review.[34]

When a sensitive issue such as national security is at stake it is somehow easier to conceive this pronounced judicial deference in respect of the interest the challenged measure is alleged to pursue; nonetheless, it is useful to keep this scheme in mind to address the necessity test under Art. XX GATT, because we will see that the trend is similar: public interests invoked are rarely challenged, and the national policy (the means) for which the measure is adopted is reviewed only in limited terms.[35]

3.2 WTO Case Law; Early Cases

DS-2 Gasoline

There is no need here to resume the facts of this landmark case. We will simply take note of the panel's fundamental lines with respect to the XX(b) exception and the 'necessity' condition thereof.[36] In particular, the panel on the one hand found fault with the defendant not being able to discharge the burden of the proof (that no less restrictive means were reasonably available), and on the other hand, actively explored potential alternatives to the measures adopted, and argued at length that, indeed, there were other less WTO-inconsistent measures that could have been adopted.[37]

The XX(d) exception was also invoked by the US, but the panel's review did not get to the analysis of the necessity aspect and rejected it. For the record, the US invoked the Art. XX(g) exception as well (relating to the protection of limited

---

34 See Emmerson (2008) 145-146, arguing that only the adequacy of the measure (and not the scope of the invoked essential security interest) can be subject to judicial review.

35 As to the distinction between the public interest and the national policy, see Diebold (2008) 47.

36 Namely, the panel introduced the three-tiered test to review Art. XX(b) exceptions, at 6.20, where the defendant is required to establish: '(1) that the policy in respect of the measures for which the provision was invoked fell within the range of policies designed to protect human, animal or plant life or health; (2) that the inconsistent measures for which the exception was being invoked were necessary to fulfill the policy objective; and (3) that the measures were applied in conformity with the requirements of the introductory clause of Article XX.' In fact, the US also raised the Art. XX(d) defense, and the panel spelled out at 6.30 an identical test to be used when reviewing this exception. The challenged measure was found to be covered by neither of the exceptions, but whereas the test stopped at the intermediate 'necessity' stage as regards the XX(b) defense, the XX(d) test failed at the first step. Neither of these findings was appealed by the US.

37 See panel's report, at 6.22-29. In particular, see 6.27: 'slightly stricter overall requirements applied to both domestic and imported gasoline could offset any possibility of an adverse environmental effect from these causes, and allow the United States to achieve its desired level of clean air without discriminating against imported gasoline. Such requirements could be implemented by the United States at any time.'

natural resources), but the AB found that the measure at stake was applied in a discriminatory way, thus violating the *chapeau* of Art. XX.[38]

DS-31 Periodicals

In this case,[39] Canada argued that the challenged measure (an import prohibition for foreign periodicals containing a certain amount of *ad hoc* advertisement directed at the Canadian market) was justified under Art. XX(d).[40] The necessity test was discussed by the parties, but the panel applied judicial economy and did not explore the issue, since it found that the measure did not 'secure compliance' with the national regulation referred to by the defendant.[41] This part of the report was not appealed, thus the AB did not pronounce on the necessity test.[42]

This case, as well as the Gasoline one commented above, are nevertheless important for our analysis, because they show how the exception of Art. XX(d) carries within a larger potential for judicial review than the XX(a) and (b) ones. Indeed, the protected interest (compliance with a national laws) is not an abstract value like 'public morals' or 'human health', and a reviewing body can reasonably assess whether the trade-restrictive measure is factually instrumental (and necessary) to the enforcement of the national norm invoked.[43] This test does not imply any review of the aim of the national laws itself or of the policy

[38] This case is therefore instructive as to the functioning of the three-tiered test, since each of the three objections raised by the US failed at a different stage of the review: the panel found that (i) the measure did not fall under Art. XX(d) in light of its purpose, that (ii) it fell under Art. XX(b), but did not meet the necessity condition; and the AB found that (iii) the measure fell under Art. XX(g), it was 'primarily aimed at' the conservation of natural resources, but it was applied in a discriminatory way, and therefore was WTO-inconsistent.

[39] WT/DS31 – *Canada – Certain Measures Concerning Periodicals.*

[40] See panel's report, at 3.5: 'The general objective of these measures is to help the Canadian periodical industry raise advertising revenues. Tariff Code 9958 ensures the achievement of this goal, with Section 19 of the Income Tax Act.'

[41] See panel's report at 5.8-11, referring to the *EEC – Parts and Components* GATT precedent: "to secure compliance with laws and regulations' in Article XX(d) of GATT 1994 [means] [...] 'to enforce obligations under laws and obligations', not 'to ensure the attainment of the objectives of the laws and regulations'.'

[42] Likewise, in the *Mexico – Soft Drinks* case, the panel and the AB did not examine whether the challenged measures were 'necessary' under Art. XX(d) GATT, since these latter did not 'secure compliance with [relevant national] laws and regulations', and therefore fell outside the scope of the exception. Quite curiously, instead, the panel of the *EC – Tariff Preferences* case, even after having found that the challenged measure did not fall under the health-related general exception, since it was 'not one designed for the purpose of protecting human life or health' (see report at 7.210), went on – on an *arguendo* basis – and endeavoured to demonstrate that it did not meet the necessity test and the chapeau requirements neither.

[43] We agree with the distinction proposed by Panama in the WT/DS-366 *Colombia – Indicative Prices and Restrictions on Ports of Entry* case, see panel's report at 7.495: whereas the Art. XX(b) exception is purpose-oriented, the Art. XX(d) exception is 'functional.' This would also entail a difference between

these latter are designed to promote: the panel and the AB can restrict their review to a merely logic and procedural activity, without touching politically sensitive issues.

Contrarily, when it comes to measures allegedly covered by the Art. XX(b) exception, the necessity test must be performed solely as regards to the 'abstract' value (health promotion), irrespectively of whether the measures are necessary to enforce any wider national regulation scheme.[44] It goes without saying that in such cases it is easier for the defendant to argue that the measure brings some contribution to the (even prospective) attainment of the public interest pursued. For these reasons, despite that the panel had clarified since the 1990 *Thailand – Cigarettes* report that the same construction of the word 'necessity' must apply in both provisions, the task of the adjudicatory body in either case is not quite the same.

DS-58 Shrimps

The Shrimp saga[45] does not need to be summarized here because the necessity issue is tackled neither by the panel[46] nor by the AB.[47] It is, nevertheless, discussed at length by the parties. It is interesting to note how the US criticizes the over-interpretation of the necessity test adopted in the *US-337* and *US-Gasoline* jurisprudence, claiming that the sophisticated test based on the search for least restrictive measures cannot be inferred by the normal meaning of the Art. XX(b) provision in light of the standards of the Vienna Convention on the Law of Treaties. Furthermore, such over-construction was allegedly not necessary, since it was arguably intended to avoid discrimination and disguised protectionism, a rationale already enshrined in the *chapeau* of Art. XX.

This claim of duplication is perhaps revealing in our research: it is at least *prima facie* reasonable, and leads us to think what the real rationale is beneath

the contribution to the attainment of the health interest (which could be perspective, or likely) and the enforcement of the national laws and policies (which ought to be actual).

44 See the panel's report, at 6.22: 'it was not the necessity of the policy goal that was to be examined, but whether or not it was necessary [to adopt the challenged measures]. It was the task of the Panel to address whether these inconsistent measures were necessary to achieve the policy goal under Article XX(b). It was therefore not the task of the Panel to examine the necessity of the environmental objectives of the Gasoline Rule, or of parts of the Rule that the Panel did not specifically find to be inconsistent with the General Agreement.'

45 Case WT/DS58 – *United States – Import Prohibition of Certain Shrimp and Shrimp Products.*

46 See panel's report at 7.29 and 7.3. The panel reversed the first two steps of the Art. XX test, as described above, and started by verifying the compliance with the introductory lines of Art. XX. Since a violation was found at this stage, the panel did not check whether the measure actually fell within Art. XX(b), nor whether the necessity condition was met. The AB reversed this part of the report, redressing the due order of the Art. XX test as described in the Gasoline report. See AB's report, at 122.

47 Even though the AB reversed the appraisal of Art. XX GATT performed by the panel, it started by conceding that the measure fell under Art. XX(g), then squashing it for not being compatible with the *chapeau*. The Art. XX(b) defense, therefore, was not discussed.

the need for a significant link between the challenged measure and each of the interests listed in the exceptions from (a) to (j), and notably beneath the necessity condition that we are studying. Given that the avoidance of disguised discriminatory and protectionist practices is already enhanced by the *chapeau* of Art. XX GATT,[48] and that the WTO deals with trade liberalization, what else do we need to justify a measure, irrespective of its purpose?

In fact, the enumeration of the protected interests is clearly an attempt to restrict the available exceptions only to values that the Contracting Parties deemed worthy of a special care, due to their apparent relation with state sovereignty. Although this would be tantamount to saying that the WTO-order is not value-neutral, we should recall how the quasi-judiciary bodies of the DSM can question neither the goodness of the invoked value nor the level of protection claimed by the defending Member.

In other words, the parties enjoy a considerable power to self-judge their own needs, to decide the preferred level of protection for their selected values[49] and to choose the relevant policies to ensure such protection. Accordingly, they are free to pass whatever measure they deem necessary. Such a wide margin of autonomous action makes it virtually impossible to question a measure only on the basis of the first step of the test, by challenging its pertinence to one of the enumerated categories (with the exception of Art. XX(d) measures, as seen above). Unless they consist of mundane effort to pass hidden protectionist measures, national policies enjoy the benefit of the doubt as to their good-faith origin.[50]

DS-155 Argentina

In this under-cited panel report[51] the application of Art. XX(d) was invoked by Argentina to justify a set of administrative and tax measures that, in the claimant's view, amounted to a ban on exports and an obstacle to imports of bovine hide. It is interesting to note the defendant's position, challenging the by then established least-restrictive means test, and complaining about the lack of discretion it grants States:

---

48 See the AB's report in *US – Gasoline*, at p. 22: ' [...] the purpose and object of the introductory clauses of Article XX is generally the prevention of 'abuse of the exceptions [...] '. In other words, the measures falling within the particular exceptions must be applied reasonably.'

49 See the AB's report in *Asbestos* (see below), at 168.

50 This does not mean that the burden of the proof is on the claimant, because Art. XX exceptions can be used as objections in a dispute, and require the defendant to provide evidence in favor of their application (see AB report *United States – Shirts and Blouses* on 23 May 1997, WT/DS33/AB/R, at p. 14). However, we want to stress that at least the *prima facie* stage of this evidentiary task is much facilitated by the self-assessment power States enjoy.

51 Case WT/DS155 – *Argentina – Measures Affecting the Export of Bovine Hides and the Import of Finished Leather.*

> Where does subparagraph (d) prescribe that the government of a State must analyze an array of options, and choose the least restrictive? What is the yardstick for defining what is less restrictive? Accepting this approach would mean supplanting the sovereignty of governments by a panel's evaluation. [...] A certain degree of discretion must therefore be allowed to the Member invoking the exception in determining which measure is necessary for securing observance of laws and regulations that are not inconsistent with the general agreement.[52]

This position is contested by the European Communities, both on the basis of relevant precedents and on a biased reading of the literal meaning of the word 'necessity'.[53] The panel acknowledges these different views, and dodges the thankless thank of taking a position on the point: since evidence submitted by the defendant meet the stricter standards advocated by the EC there is no need to ascertain whether Argentina's complaint about the overly invasive least-restrictive means doctrine was founded.[54] The measures were deemed to be 'necessary' because defendant's arguments were effective in creating a presumption to that end, even though the following review under the *chapeau* of Art. XX GATT led the panel to squash them.

DS-161 and 169 Korea – Beef

The late-2000 AB report on the *Korea – Beef* case[55] represents a landmark document for the appraisal of the necessity requirement in respect of GATT general exceptions, and especially the Art. XX(d) one.[56] The claimants held that Korea's measures requiring that imported beef be sold only in specialized imported beef stores, as well as Korean laws and regulations restricting the resale and distribution of imported beef, resulted in a violation of Art. III.4 GATT.

Korea objected, *inter alia*, that such measures[57] were necessary to comply with its Unfair Competition Act (a domestic regulation providing for consumers' protection), for the purpose of preventing retailers from deceiving consumers by selling exported beef as domestic beef. In order to prove compliance with the necessity requirement, Korea stated essentially that the preventive nature of

52 See panel's report, at 8.251-252.

53 See id., at 8.255, where the EC quotes the Webster Dictionary, and claims that 'necessary' means 'unavoidable,' 'that cannot be dispensed with,' 'essential.' Contrast this reading with the AB's report in *Korea – Beef* (cit. below) at 160.

54 See id., at 11.304-306. This is certainly due to judicial economy considerations, but also perhaps to the virtual impossibility to take into account the *Korea – Beef* AB report (see *supra*, in particular at 161), that was circulated only a week before the circulation of this report.

55 Case WT/DS161, WT/DS169 – *Korea – Measures Affecting Imports of Fresh, Chilled and Frozen Beef.*

56 See Sykes (2003) 407 ff, for an accurate comment on the case and of the AB's position as to the necessity requisite.

57 In particular, the obligation to set up a 'dual retail system' whereby retailers had to store imported and domestic beef in different sections of their premises.

the measure entailed higher effectiveness in policing fraudulent practices than possible *ex post* alternatives, and that Korean administrative authorities run on a limited budget and lacked the resources for setting up a non-stop police control of all beef retailers' premises.

We quote again a passage accounting for the defendant's position, as it seems to go to the core subject of our research, and unveils how awkward is the task of reconciling the diversity-friendly nature of the WTO system with an invasive construction of the necessity test:

> Korea noted that so far GATT/WTO case law has not explored the link between regulatory diversity, on the one hand, and the necessity requirement, on the other. Korea submitted that there is a correlation between the two in the sense that were a regulatory objective to be sought in a very strict manner, the choice of instruments would consequently be influenced. Since the level of protection sought cannot be put into question, the choice of instrument will have to be appreciated in the same context.[58]

The panel found the measures to be non-necessary, in light of two (related) facts: (i) Korea had not adopted similar regulations with respect to other tradable goods, and to beef sold in restaurants (amounting to some 45% of the total), and (ii) reasonably available GATT consistent alternatives existed.[59]

The AB (unlike the *Argentina – Hides and Leather* panel) starts by taking upon itself the task of clarifying the meaning of the term necessity, and finally concedes that not only 'indispensable' measures could fit the Art. XX(d) exception, but also measures whose link with the national regulation is slightly less direct, provided that they are not just 'making a contribution' thereto.[60] To help the adjudicator in handling such an indistinct test, the AB argues that it is helpful to 'take into account the relative importance of the common interests or values that the law or regulation to be enforced is intended to protect. The more vital or important those common interests or values are, the easier it would be to

[58] See panel's report, at 242. The right of every Member State to choose freely the level of protection of its interest is arguably derived from the jurisprudence on health-related measures concerning the application of the Sanitary and Phytosanitary agreement (SPS), see Orellana (2009) 144 and Atik (2009) 614.

[59] See for instance panel's report at 672: 'For instance, a generally applied record-keeping requirement backed with sanctions would constitute a WTO consistent alternative to the WTO inconsistent dual retail system. If foreign beef shops can keep book-records, it is difficult to see why the same could not be requested from domestic shops.'

[60] The famous passage referring to the 'range of degrees of necessity' is in the AB's report, at 161. At 164 the AB summarizes the test in a way that casts a diversity-unfriendly light thereon, since less than indispensible measures are said to be legitimate only on exceptional grounds (they can be '*nevertheless*' necessary, even though they are not indispensible), see Regan (2007) 358. See the similar holding of the ECtHR in the *Handyside* case, where the judges: 'observed that 'the adjective 'necessary,' [...] is not synonymous with 'indispensable' [and] neither has it the flexibility of such expressions as [...] 'admissible,' [...] 'useful,' 'reasonable,' or 'desirable.'

accept as 'necessary' a measure designed as an enforcement instrument.'[61] This principle, coupled with a newly re-worded least-restrictive means one (that actually reminds of proportionality),[62] contributes to establishing a less schematic and more unpredictable 'process of weighing and balancing a series of factors'[63] that obviously implies a decisive degree of discretion from the reviewing body.

These lines are fundamental for our analysis, since the AB introduces for the first time the possibility to review *the merits* of national policies, rather than just the logical and instrumental link between national measures and the public interest pursued. In addition, this analysis on the merits is spelled out with respect to an Art. XX(d) defense, which had been applied until then in a rather 'functionalist' way[64]: attaching the newly formulated balancing test to this exception was an unexpected move, that finds little or no justification in the legal texts.[65]

This step would entitle us to draw a comparison with the ECtHR's margin of appreciation doctrine: the value-neutral character of the DSM review did not seem to be an absolute feature anymore, and balancing values was an available tool for WTO bodies entrusted with the adjudication of Art. XX GATT general exceptions, according to proportionality benchmarks.[66] In fact, in the *Korea – Beef* case the AB did not need to carry out such sensitive analysis, since it upheld the findings of the panel as to the non-necessity of the dual-retail system.[67] As discussed below, in fact, this analysis was hardly ever attempted.

---

61 See AB's report at 162.

62 Paragraph 163 spells out a 'proportionality' requirement for the purpose of the overall test: the more effective and less restrictive the measure is, the more likely it is for the WTO body to apply Art. XX GATT.

63 See id., at 164.

64 See above, in the paragraph discussing the *Periodicals* case.

65 See Regan (2007) 355-356: 'there is nothing in the text of Article XX(d) to suggest that different regulatory purposes are accorded different values by Article XX(d). *A fortiori*, there is nothing to suggest that it is appropriate for the Appellate Body to rank Members' regulatory purposes according to the Appellate Body's intuitions about their value.'

66 We will show that, although admissible in theory, the consistency between the two tiers of this test (least-restrictive and balancing; logical and axiological) was not guaranteed by the AB in the subsequent case-law, it is therefore sound to state that in the least-restrictive test, as designed in *Korea*, there is no logical space left for cost–benefit weighing with respect to the underlying goal, see Regan (2007) 352. On the abstract possibility to use proportionality in order to manage the interplay between trade obligations and national interests, see Van Aaken (2009) 503, referring to the conception of applicable trade norms as principles (as opposed to rules) and to the work of Robert Alexy.

67 In fact, the AB correctly stresses the legitimacy of the reasoning by which the panel had noted the absence of similar measures in other market sectors. Korea had alleged that this fact could not imply that the stricter measures adopted for the beef sector were not necessary, as this finding would amount to an interference in Korea's right to set the level of protection at its sole discretion, and to set different levels of protection in different market sectors. The AB stated that this comparative analysis had in fact the different purpose of highlighting that efficient alternative measures were available, as the one Korea

DS-135 Asbestos

The facts are well-known: France had enacted a ban on the sale of products containing asbestos fibers, and argued before the panel (appointed upon Canada's request) that this measure was legitimate under the health-related general exception (Art. XX(b) GATT). The proclaimed level of health protection was 'zero-risk', and the EC stated that only a total prohibition of asbestos sale could reach this objective. In Canada's view, other alternatives (such as a controlled use of asbestos-containing materials) would be less-restrictive and would ensure a virtual cancellation of the risk, thus representing a preferable alternative to the ban.

However, the panel acknowledged the EC's right to set an absolute level of health protection based on a 'zero risk' policy, and stated that no other reasonable alternative for that purpose was available except the total ban.[68] The AB rebutted Canada's grounds for appeal and made reference to its *Korea – Beef* precedent, notably to the 'weighing and balancing process' and the 'importance' criterion;[69] noting that the preservation of human life and health is 'vital and important in the highest degree.' In fact, the ban was found to be legitimate irrespective of the balancing test, since it was indispensible to attain the level of protection sought, and only 'dispensable' measures have to pass the weighing step.[70]

3.3 WTO Case Law; Recent Cases

DS-285 Gambling and DS-302 Cigarettes

These cases[71] were adjudicated almost at the same time, and their reports were circulated only a few weeks away from each other, besides being similar in their content.

used to enforce in the non-beef sectors of the market. See AB's report, at 175-178. McGrady (2009) 159, notes that the panel and the AB characterized Korea's goal in different ways, somewhat contrary to the principle that each State has the power to define it autonomously, and that the loose formulation of the goal adopted by the AB made it easier to find equally efficient alternatives.

68 See panel's report at 8.217: 'controlled use does not constitute a reasonable alternative to the banning of chrysotile asbestos that might be chosen by a decision-maker responsible for developing public health measures, bearing in mind the objectives pursued by France [absolute halt to risk-spreading].'

69 See AB's report at 172: 'we observed, in that case, that '[t]he more vital or important [the] common interests or values' pursued, the easier it would be to accept as 'necessary' measures designed to achieve those ends.'

70 In this respect, see Regan (2007), and Howse, Tuerk (2001) 324.

71 Cases WT/DS285 – *United States – Measures Affecting the Cross-Border Supply of Gambling and Betting Services*; WT/DS302 – *Dominican Republic – Measures Affecting the Importation and Internal Sale of Cigarettes.*

The *Gambling* dispute[72] was referred to the panel by Antigua and Barbados, contesting that the US had adopted certain prohibition measures with respect to trans-border gambling services that amounted to unfair discrimination of foreign suppliers. The US, *inter alia*, argued that these measures were necessary to avoid a serious harm to national public morals and public order[73] and that, by enhancing their enforcements, these measures made an essential contribution to the compliance with other national laws restricting gambling, including criminal laws against organized crime.[74] The panel accepted to dwell on the multiple-criteria review put forward by the AB in the *Korea – Beef* case, but finally denied that the general exceptions applied because the necessity requirements were not met. Notably, since the US had not engaged in multilateral negotiation upon Antigua's request, the panel stated that it had not duly explored *every* possible alternative, and that therefore the adopted measures were not indispensable. The AB reversed this finding on the necessity, and found that the application of the ban was discriminatory under the introductory clause of Art. XIV GATS (the equivalent of Art. XX GATT's *chapeau*).

In the same period, Honduras challenged for being discriminatory and unjustified the special rules, procedures and administrative practices applied by the Dominican Republic to determine the value of imported cigarettes for the purpose of applying the domestic Selective Consumption Tax, and claimed that they violated WTO obligations. The Dominican Republic objected that the measures at stake were legitimate under Art. XX(d) GATT, because they were necessary to enforce the obligations under the national Tax Code, and were useful in preventing cigarette smuggling.[75] In this case, the panel accepted the defendant's assertion regarding the high importance of the public interest pursued and the minimal impact of the measures on the imports, both aimed at averting a potential 'balancing' unfavorable test (the measures had no significant trade-impact, and promoted a fundamental public value such as compliance with tax law). Accordingly, the panelists focused on the 'traditional' necessity test, conceived as a least-restrictive means analysis, and stated that the measures were unnecessary.[76] The AB upheld this position in its report, and rebutted the

---

72 Although this very famous case was about trade in trans-national gambling services, and therefore required the application of the GATS agreement rather than the GATT, it is well-known that the system of general exceptions of the GATS is virtually identical to the GATT one, at least as regards to the provisions at stake in this dispute, that is the public morals exception (Art. XX(a) GATT, Art. XIV(a) GATS) and the internal compliance one (Art. XX(d) GATT, Art. XIV(c) GATS). Accordingly, the findings of the panel and the AB relating to the 'necessity' requirement are helpful for our survey. See Molfa (2005).

73 See *Gambling* panel's report at 3.279: 'Remote supply of gambling raises significant concerns relating to the maintenance of public order and the protection of public morals.'

74 See id. at 3.273-277.

75 See *Cigarettes* panel's report at 4.88.

76 See id., at 7.228: 'Dominican Republic has not proved why, for example, providing secure tax stamps to foreign exporters [...] would not be equivalent to the current tax stamp requirement in terms of allowing

appellant's claim according to which the panel had not taken into due account all the relevant factors in its review.

The *Gambling* panel's report and the *Cigarettes* AB's report clarify where the 'balancing task' stands in the logical fabric of the overall necessity test: first, it must be ascertained that there is a causal link between the measure and the enforcement of national interests, then the balancing process can step in. Eventually, it must be ascertained that no reasonably available less-restrictive alternatives exist, before passing on to questioning its compliance with the *chapeau* clause of Art. XIV GATS or XX GATT.

Before these reports first circulated, the balancing process had been merely proclaimed (but not carried out) in the *Korea – Beef* case,[77] and was used merely *ad adiuvandum* in the *Asbestos* case (in which the case was decided solely upon a matter of indispensability). Therefore, these *Gambling* and *Cigarettes* cases are the first occasions where the role of such test should come clear: the panels and the AB take into account the three relevant aspects of the measure: (i) importance of the public interest, (ii) impact on trade, (iii) effectiveness with respect to the value pursued.[78]

At a closer look, one could argue that elements (ii) and (iii) were already included in the least-restrictive test: the search for an alternative measure that is equally efficient and less trade-restrictive is based on a comparison, thus it is implicit that the comparing subject knows such information, they are the fundamental points of reference for its task.[79] As to element (i), we deem it highly unlikely that a panel or the AB would state that the national interest invoked by

---

it to secure the same high level of enforcement with regard to tax collection and the prevention of cigarette smuggling.'

77 See Regan (2007) 348.

78 See AB's *Cigarettes* report at 71-72. See also the panel's report of the *Gambling* case at 6.477. In the *Cigarettes* case, after the AB confirmed the low level of effectiveness of the challenged measures, it went on and easily dismissed them as unnecessary: it was not difficult to find GATT-consistent alternative measures that could guarantee the same (low) level of contribution to the attainment of the public interest declared. The structure of this test recalls the proportionality test formulated by Robert Alexy and referred to by Van Aaken (2009) 504: 'The proportionality principle is comprised of three sub-principles: the principle of suitability [whether the measure is suitable to achieve the goal], the principle of necessity [non availability of less intrusive alternatives], and the principle of proportionality in a narrow sense [ratio between the seriousness of the intrusion and importance of the right].'

79 The same opinion is shared and brilliantly summarized by Regan (2007) 357: 'In fact, the only consideration in the Appellate Body's list that is relevant to a cost–benefit balancing test and not to a less-restrictive alternative test is the value of the regulatory purpose, which as we have already seen is a seriously suspect consideration.' Similarly, Stone Sweet (2008) 158: 'As it has developed, the WTO version of necessity analysis often absorbs the balancing in the strict sense phase, importing elements of Alexy's 'law of balancing' into its jurisprudence.' Stone Sweet also sharply notes that C.D. Ehlermann chaired the AB in this case, suggesting that this fact accounts for the similarities between the *Korea* test and the doctrine of proportionality in the EC (interestingly, the same could hold true for the seminal GATT *US – 337* case, since P. Pescatore was one of the panelists).

the defending party is of low or no importance: in such assessment self-judging is understandably the standard practice, as mentioned above.[80]

Both cases could also be decided by skipping the wearing phase of the 'weighing and balancing' process. US measures were squashed not due to a ruinous aggregate evaluation of their impact, efficiency and importance, but only because their application did not meet the clean-hands requirements of the *chapeau*. Dominican Republic's measures were unnecessary because they were so ineffective that many other GATT-consistent alternatives could be foreseen.[81]

In sum, the balancing process does not seem to add much to the original least-restrictive means test, and it does not really result in a balancing between values or rights, as it is in the margin of appreciation doctrine (and in every national constitutional experience).[82] Contrarily, the scope of the least-restrictive test seemed to expand gradually.[83]

---

80 See for instance the *Gambling* panel's report at 6.492, acknowledging that the interests and values protected by the challenged measures serve very important societal interests that can be characterized as 'vital and important in the highest degree' (see also id. at 6.558). Likewise, the *Cigarettes* panel's report reads, at 7.215: 'The Panel finds no reason to question the Dominican Republic's assertions in the sense that the collection of tax revenue [...] is a most important interest for any country and particularly for a developing country such as the Dominican Republic.' See also *Brazil – Tyres* panel's report at 7.112. Even with respect to China's mundane effort to invoke Art. XX(d) in the *China – Autombile case* (see *infra*) the panel could not help acknowledging the importance of the proclaimed interest (tax collection). See panel's report at 7.360. See also *US – Shrimp (Thailand)* AB's report at 313, and *Colombia – Entry Ports*, panel's report at 7.566 (fighting under-invoicing and money laundering). In this respect, see Regan (2007) 363, and McGrady (2009) 162.

81 Neither did the *Asbestos* case be of much help in clarifying the 'balancing' test, see Regan (2007) 350: 'none of the later opinions [mentioned] actually involves standard cost–benefit balancing, and none depends on a weighing of the underlying benefit.' See also Foster (2008) 437.

82 See Stone Sweet (2008) 138, according to which the proportionality test is a global constitutional standard, therefore each tribunal that applies it, including international ones, operates 'in a constitutional mode, inherently, irrespective of how one understands the 'constitutional' nature of the regime more broadly.'

83 In the *Asbestos* case the AB had refused to take into account the fact that the EC enforced less rigid measures with respect to other dangerous substances; in *Korea – Beef* it looked at the less restrictive policies adopted by Korea in other sectors in the market, but allegedly only for the purpose of finding reasonable alternatives to the dual-retail system. In the *Gambling* case, instead, the panel goes further and seems to review the US conduct in parallel sectors of the services market (namely, non-remote gambling services) in order to question the overly high level of protection of public morals pursued, see at 6.493: '[we ought to] determine whether particular aspects associated with the remote supply of gambling and betting services will justify a prohibition, particularly in light of the tolerant attitude displayed in some parts of the United States to the non-remote supply of such services.' The panel determined that on-line gambling entails some specific risks that could require a different regulation from the one governing non-remote gambling services (see id. at 6.521).

DS-332 Brazil – Retreaded tyres

In 2005, the EC summoned a panel complaining that Brazil had violated its GATT obligations by enacting an import ban on retreaded tyres, and also by lifting this ban only with respect to tyres originating from other MERCOSUR countries.[84] Brazil defended the ban on the basis of Art. XX(b) GATT (import of retreaded tyres allegedly generates unnecessary tyre waste, and consequently carries within the health and environmental risks that flow from tyre waste accumulation and disposal)[85] and the MERCOSUR exception on the basis of Art. XX(d) GATT (it was necessary to enforce MERCOSUR obligations set forth by international and national laws).[86]

In particular, Brazil contended that since health-related risks deriving from tyre waste cannot be eliminated, only non-generation of waste tyres, requiring an import ban on shorter-lifespan tyres, could achieve the chosen level of protection. It adopted a position recalling the EC's one in the *Asbestos* case (see above), and cited explicitly the *Asbestos* AB's report as regards the unquestionable importance of health policies and the discretion accorded to Member States in determining the environmental and health policies.[87]

The three relevant factors were considered and balanced by the panel: human life and health are very important (good), the ban is extremely trade-restrictive (bad) but likely to represent a certain contribution towards the overall policy of tyre waste reduction (average). At the appellate level, the AB confirmed the scope of the margin of discretion enjoyed by the panel in assessing the third factor, that entitles the panel to appreciate the nature of the contribution made by the measure in 'qualitative' (*lege*: rough) terms.[88] The panel then agreed to examine the least-restrictive means test, and essentially discarded all alternative measures proposed by the EC, as being unfeasible.[89]

84 Case WT/DS332 – *Brazil – Measures Affecting Imports of Retreaded Tyres.*

85 At 4.11 of the panel's report, Brazil mentions, *inter alia*, the risks related to cancer, dengue (and other mosquito-borne diseases), reproductive problems and environmental contamination.

86 See panel's report at 4.426: 'Brazil argues that it enacted the MERCOSUR exemption with no other purpose than to 'secure compliance' with Brazil's municipal law that made the MERCOSUR commitments and the rulings of the MERCOSUR dispute settlement body binding on Brazil.'

87 See panel's report at 4.16.

88 See AB's report at 147, stating that the panel was under no 'obligation to quantify the contribution of the Import Ban to the reduction in the number of waste tyres and to determine the number of waste tyres that would be reduced as a result of the Import Ban. In our view, the Panel's choice of a qualitative analysis was within the bounds of the latitude it enjoys in choosing a methodology for the analysis of the contribution.'

89 At the *chapeau* step, though, the panel noted that the parallel import of used tyres was likely to impair the beneficial effect of the ban on retreaded tyres, and found that the ban was applied in a discriminatory way, constituted a disguised protectionist measure, and could not be justified under Art. XX(b). See panel's report at 7.356. The AB adjusted this finding and found that the discriminatory application went beyond the consequences from the parallel import of used tyres. For an extensive discussion on the

In this case the 'weighing process' proved once again a burdensome and irrelevant step of the review, as argued by the EC.[90] It was already arguable from the precedents commented above that no veritable balancing was at stake: when striking the balance among various elements, the absolute and overwhelming weight of one of them should affect the outcome of the overall process and outweigh the importance of the other ones, in a fashion that vaguely recalls the famous Learned Hand formula.[91] It was already clear that this was not the case (utmost importance of the public interest is a constant that did not affect the result in the *Cigarettes* case, likewise, the ruinous effect on trade of the remote-gambling ban was not, *per se*, sufficient to prevent the AB from finding it 'necessary', and pass on to the *chapeau* test). The EC had warned Brazil that *Asbestos*-deference could not be easily obtained merely by stressing the importance of the health objective and proclaiming a high standard of protection, and the AB promptly dubbed this warning.[92]

DS-339, 340, 342 China – Automobile Parts

In this *monstre* litigation,[93] the Art. XX(d) exception played a secondary role, its application was denied by the panel and the defendant did not appeal this part of the finding.[94] It is worth noting that China relied on arguments similar to the Korean ones in *Korea – Beef*: restrictive measures were passed with the

---

role 'complementary measures' (as opposed to alternative ones) may have in the necessity analysis, see McGrady (2008).

90 See AB's report at 176. The EC contended that the weighing process was performed in a superficial way, and that no actual balancing had occurred, also because the 'contribution' factor had been assessed in terms too vague, and could not play a role in the weighing process.

91 See Trachtman (1998) 47. According to the AB (see AB's report at 182), this process 'is a holistic operation that involves putting all the variables of the equation together and evaluating them in relation to each other after having examined them individually, in order to reach an overall judgement.' The Hand formula is the Law and Economics device used to schematize efficient negligence rules, named after judge Billings *Learned Hand* (1872 –1961), see Kerkmeester, Visscher (2003) 8: 'Hand used the algebraic function $B<p^*L$, where B denotes the burden of precautions, p the probability of losses and L the magnitude of the losses if an accident occurs.' In the WTO framework, a national measure could be subject to a similar test in order to pass the scrutiny of the panel, according to the *Korea* balancing test: namely, the impact of the trade restriction should be lesser than the contribution to the goal times the importance of the goal. This cost-benefit analysis, however, was merely proclaimed and rarely applied, see Trachtman (2007) 647. For an enlightening analysis of the necessity test under cost-benefit terms that takes into account the Learned Hand test and other similar formulas, see Collins (2009) 27-32.

92 See panel's report at 4.43, and AB's report at 147: 'we disagree with Brazil's suggestion that, because it aims to reduce risk exposure to the maximum extent possible, an import ban that brings a marginal or insignificant contribution can nevertheless be considered necessary.' We recall in passing that the outcome of *Asbestos*, despite the discussion of the weighing process, depended essentially on the indispensible nature of the measure.

93 Cases WT/DS339, WT/DS340, WT/DS342 – *China – Measures Affecting Imports of Automobile Parts.*

94 See China's contentions in this respect in the panel's report at 4.187.

view of enforcing its domestic tariff schedule and prevent fraudulent behaviours ('tariff circumvention').[95] Nevertheless, unlike Korea (that at least established that fraudulent wrongdoing were contrary to the Unfair Competition Act) China failed in demonstrating that these circumvention techniques were in violation of its own laws, hence the dismissal of the Art. XX(d) defense.[96]

In this case, and in others that followed,[97] it looks like that the Art. XX(d) defense had turned into a standard boilerplate clause, that defendants always try to invoke regardless of whether it is founded; this trend is also due perhaps to the fragmentation of the adjudication of general exceptions into several micro-tests created by the jurisprudence. Whereas the purpose of this over-technicalisation was to discourage abusive recourse to the exceptions founded on a vague referral to general principles, the effect was in fact the opposite: every defendant gives it a try, and endeavours to fill the box of each sub-test, perhaps hoping that passing the 'easy' tests (the subsumption under Art. XX, the weighing and balancing process, the consistency of the 'laws and regulations' with the WTO) would give it enough momentum to pass the 'hard' ones (the least-restrictive means test, the *chapeau* test).[98]

One of the latest cases we can comment on is the *Colombia – Entry Ports*, in which Colombia tried to defend some border measures invoking Art. XX(d), namely compliance with national regulations aimed at the prevention of under-pricing techniques and smuggling. The panel, however, found that Colombia did not meet its burden relating to the actual contribution that the measures challenged ought to secure to the enforcement of the laws and regulations, and statistical data showing that smuggling did not decrease suggested that the measures adopted did not secure the enforcement of designated policies.[99] One of the three factors of the 'balancing' test being irremediably flawed, the panel could not but reject the Art. XX(d) defence, and declare the measures non-necessary.[100]

95 The same pattern was then followed by Colombia in the *Colombia – Entry Ports* litigation, see panel's report at 7.483.

96 See id. at 7.346. The panel, like in the *EC – Tariff Preferences*, tackled the necessity test only in *arguendo* terms, and found that it was not satisfied.

97 See the AB's report in the *US – Shrimp (Thailand)* case at 317-318.

98 There is another risk, according to Regan (2007) 350, that is the risk that the AB could finally be deceived by its own dicta about balancing, and actually starts looking into sovereignty interests to review them.

99 See panel's report at 7.586.

100 See id. at 7.619. Again, although phrased with reference to the balancing test, this outcome could have been the result of the least-restrictive test as well: given the low level of effectiveness, many alternatives are available to the defendant (like in *Korea – Beef*).

DS-363 China – Audiovisual

The most recent case is the *China – Audiovisual* one,[101] in which China defended some of its trade restrictions regarding various products from the US[102] (and distribution services related thereto) alleging, among other things, that these measures fell within the application of the public morals general exception (Art. XX(a) GATT).[103] According to the panel's analysis public morals is a high-importance value, and China legitimately set a high level of protection with respect thereto.[104]

Different measures were under scrutiny concerning the requisites national enterprises must meet to import: these measures are likely to be effective, and they do not restrict imports *a priori*, therefore they are legitimate.[105] Other measures,[106] to the contrary, need to pass a stricter test, since they are found not to be reasonably contributing to the attainment of the overall policy, and they raise protectionism concerns. However, in light of the low trade-restrictiveness they imply (and of the importance of the value they pursue) some of them pass the necessity test, whereas others that affect the importing rate more significantly (or qualitatively, setting *a priori* prohibitions) are rejected by the Panel.[107] This might be perhaps one of the rare cases where the balancing is actually carried out, and this could also be due to the wide range of diverse measures that were at stake: comparing them could somehow yield the same results of a proper least-restrictive analysis.

For those measures that had passed the necessity test, the Panel turns to the examination of alternatives proposed by the claimant. The main alternative consisted in entrusting the Government (rather than the importing companies) with the task of performing the content review upon imported products: this possibility is analyzed by the Panel, that rapidly states its feasibleness:

> It emerges [...] that implementing the US proposal would make a contribution that is at least equivalent to that of the relevant [China measures]. At the same time,

[101] Case WT/DS363 – *China – Measures Affecting Trading Rights and Distribution Services for Certain Publications and Audiovisual Entertainment Products.*

[102] Audiovisual products sound recordings, periodicals and newspapers, electronic publications, theatrical productions.

[103] See panel's report at 7.712. Notably, China held that it had the power to regulate the import of similar goods through a content review mechanism, with the view of protecting public morals from external threats.

[104] Id. at 7.817-818.

[105] Id. at 7.828. At first glance, these measures are comparable in nature to those required in the *Korea – Beef* case, which were found to be non-necessary.

[106] Measures that provide for numerical limitations and controlled geographical distribution of importing companies, or set forth a different procedure for the review of newspaper and periodicals, and for products of the audiovisual sector, or require the state-ownership of importing companies, or exclude foreign-invested companies.

[107] Id. at 7.836, 7.863, 7.868.

> the US proposal would have a significantly less restrictive impact on importers – in fact, it would have no such impact – without there being any indication that it would necessarily have a more restrictive impact on imports of relevant products than the [measures] at issue.[108]

A further potential cost-benefit objection is defused: shifting the control burden to the central Government does not *per se* impose additional costs on China's administration, since China already supports the entire cost of the review (the rules currently in force allow only State-owned companies to perform it).

If the method followed by the Panel is upheld at the appellate level, we could interpret this report as a normalization of the previously fuzzed multi-phased necessity test: the 'balancing' part boils down to an evaluation of the aspects on which the least-restrictive test is based (with the assessment of the state policy which bears an almost anecdotal character). The balancing test filters measures that would have failed the least-restrictive analysis upfront, being ineffective *and* much restrictive. No actual balancing is ever performed, but the procedure of the test is at least pretty clear in its articulation.

4 Tentative Conclusions: Who Gets the Margin in the WTO?

As mentioned in the introduction, a paradox seems to occur whenever, under the application of 'margin-of-appreciation like' doctrines, discretion abstractly accorded to States ends up being exercised by judges reviewing their conduct.[109] A first explication is perhaps that in these cases, the subsidiary role of the international trade law framework and the indispensable action of the WTO adjudicatory bodies create an irreconcilable tension that from time to time results in the sacrifice of State autonomy.[110]

One of the overarching principles governing the interplay between *supra*-national and national orders is the principle of subsidiarity, by which the intervention of the higher authority is legitimate only when it is necessary, that is when the higher subject is capable of producing a better result than the lower as regards to a particular objective. When this is not the case, the lower authority retains the general competence to act, and is supposed to be better placed with respect to issues that relate to its conduct and its interests. This paradigm fits the negative integration agenda of the WTO[111]: States are free to determine their policies, unless these affect the free-trade objectives that were agreed at the

108 Id. at 7.898.

109 See McGrady (2009) 163.

110 On the dynamics between intrusion and subsidiarity, see Shany (2006) 908. See id., 912 (especially fn 25) for a description of the link between the principle of subsidiarity and the margin of appreciation.

111 Shaffer (2008) 37. Trujillo (2008) frames this subsidiarity relationship in terms of 'reciprocal deference', 208.

international level, in which case international rules (and adjudicators thereof) intervene.[112]

Claiming that adjudication (and possible interference with State action) is foreseen only in case of necessity, however, could be misleading, if we think of the WTO Covered Agreements as an incomplete contract, an enlightening simile often referred to by scholars.[113] In this perspective, State obligations can be exactly determined *only* through the indispensable activity of the arbiter charged with the interpretation (and application) of the agreements. The utmost and systemic necessity of this action rules out subsidiarity aspirations.

This mixed situation can represent the optimal balance, or 'the right mix between deference and supervision, in light of the comparable advantages of the two sets of actors.'[114] However, it could also amount to a confused doctrine,[115] where contradictory elements are put together in the attempt of following different purposes, and a telling example could be the comparison of paragraphs 161 and 162 of the *Korea – Beef* case: locating 'necessity' significantly below 'indispensability' is a deferential move by the AB that is clearly inspired by margin-of-appreciation considerations, but at the same time its power to review the importance of the national goal is a very intrusive one, which intends to be instrumental to the appropriate application of Art. XX, by providing the adjudicator with the tools to unmask protectionist measures.[116]

States are not aware of the exact margin of discretion they are accorded to keep their measures legal. This doubt is surely related to the ambiguous wording of the applicable legal texts, that may as well be intentional, but the subsequent rulings of the adjudicator did not clarify the boundaries of the regulatory powers that still belong to Member States.[117]

---

112 Ehlermann, Lockhart (2004) 493. This is well expressed in Regan (2007) 350, stating that if the AB started to question the opportunity of a national interest '[t]hat would be at odds with the whole spirit of the WTO agreements.'

113 Among the others, Mavroidis (2008) 3, Trachtman (1998) 46 (referring to the work of G.K. Hadfield).

114 Shany (2006) 919.

115 McGrady (2009) 162, talks about 'an unfortunate midpoint between a proportionality test and a necessity test that is truly deferential to the regulatory goals of WTO Members.'

116 See id. In the paragraphs above we have given account of the unfeasibility of this mixed doctrine, that caused neither of these paragraphs to be strictly applied by the panels and the AB.

117 See Trachtman (2007) 645, discussing the methods used to allocate regulatory powers through property-based mechanisms: 'Muddy or Solomonic Entitlements. Where the cost of formal transfer is very high, it may be better to provide unclear and incomplete ('muddy') formal property rights, in order to reduce deadweight losses and encourage reallocative transactions through informal means or through adjudication. The question of whether, for example, states have the authority to block imports of goods due to the way they are produced is not clearly answered in WTO law, thereby inducing states to reveal information in order to bargain.'

5 Reallocation of Regulatory Authority and the Role of Principles

It has been argued that the necessity and the least-restrictive tests work as a device of positive integration since they can imply mutual recognition (namely, the recognition of the national measure as an effective least-restrictive measure). Further, the reallocation of discretion that we have described could just be the reflection of a parallel underlying process, that is, the (strategic) reallocation of regulatory authority from States to the WTO.[118]

This vision is striking as it accounts precisely for the impression this study is called to test: a margin-of-appreciation looking device such as the necessity test departs from its presumptive purpose and ends up delivering the discretion to the judges:

> The WTO's negative integration 'trade-off devices,' including national treatment, least-trade restrictive alternative testing and balancing testing, may be understood simply as mandates to judges to exercise discretion in the allocation of jurisdictional authority. [...] they leave much discretion to judges, they may plausibly be understood to orient and constrain judges towards, if not to, an approximation of efficiency. They do so under circumstances where it is difficult to imagine an alternative approach, other than one of positive integration. Positive integration has its own costs.[119]

Yet, it is more doubtful whether the WTO necessity test that we have studied has something in common with the margin of appreciation as applied by the ECtHR. We have argued that the balancing process is not a real proportionality device,[120] but ends up working as a preparatory exercise for the least-restrictive alternative test. In principle, the proportionality benchmark would require the relative sacrifice of right A, when in order to attain the protection thereof, right B must undergo a disproportionately unfavourable treatment, even if this is the only alternative available.

Proportionality works as a corrective of the margin of appreciation in the case law of the Strasbourg Court,[121] preventing States from promoting their public interests by totally disregarding their conventional obligations. This is not the case in the WTO system: absolute departure from trade obligations is acceptable under the notion of 'indispensability' (as we have seen in some of the cases hinging upon the adoption of 'total bans').

Furthermore, the doctrine also entails a *de minimis* character: the ECtHR will not question State choices that do not significantly affect the rights of the

---

[118] Trachtman (2007) 641, 646. For a first formulation and a wider discussion of this view, see Trachtman (1998) 82, and (2005b).

[119] Trachtman (2007) 647.

[120] Trachtman (1998) 75.

[121] Riza Çoban (2004) 204-205.

Convention, and will not endeavour to find alternative measures.[122] In the WTO, as we have seen, the least-restrictive test can only be avoided when the measure is proven to be indispensible for the attainment of the public interest sought.[123]

As we conjectured in the introduction, the difference lies in the very nature of the supranational organizations at stake: exceptions to the European Convention are treated as such, and undergo a case-by-case opportunity assessment, while the general exceptions of Art. XX GATT and XIV GATS represent the codification of Member States' background sovereign power to regulate. The test is not there to approve legitimate unilateral measures, but to unmask the illegitimate protectionism. Given the right of WTO Member States to autonomously set the level of protection sought, what is left is essentially a scrutiny of the Panel or the AB on the good faith[124] of a measure, whereas the ECtHR is rather interested in its effects.[125]

The *stricto sensu* proportionality test is never performed nor envisaged, and in any case the AB would have hard time trying to perform such exercise without an *ad hoc* legitimacy.[126] In this sense, *laissez-régler* seems to be the general guideline, indeed, but when a national measure fails to pass the indispensability test (type A test, see above in Section I), the least-restrictive means analysis is open (type B test), and it is hard to foresee its outcome, since panels and AB often base their rulings on common sense and impressionistic and qualitative assessments.[127]

This is probably where the (reciprocal?) margin of appreciation should intervene: if the unpredictable result of this kind of review is a physiological feature that cannot be prevented, at least some sort of actual margin of appreciation (based on the presumption of the legality of State conduct, along with some

---

[122] 'Tant que le législateur ne dépasse pas les limites de sa marge d'appréciation, la Cour n'a pas à dire s'il a choisi la meilleure façon de traiter le problème ou s'il aurait dû exercer son pouvoir différemment (arrêt du 19 décembre 1989, CEDH, série A n° 169, p. 53).'

[123] *Contra*, see Neumann, Tuerk (2003) 214.

[124] For an enlightening insight of the panels and AB's practice as regards general principles of law (including, for the purposes of this work, good faith and *in dubio mitius*) see Mavroidis (2008b) 443.

[125] Another distinction can easily be inferred from these arguments. States losing a dispute before the ECtHR can certainly be dissatisfied with the ruling and have to give up their policies, irrespective of any evidence of good faith. Contrarily (at least in principle), good faith WTO Members will have their interest protected in any case, since either they will win or – if they lose – they will be suggested reasonable alternative measures to replace the illegitimate measure.

[126] See Neumann, Tuerk (2003) 233, and bibliography referred to therein. For a definition of the narrow proportionality test, see Trachtman (1998) 35, and bibliography referred to therein. This test is used by the ECtHR (see *supra* at fn 66 and 78) and by the ECJ, even though this latter rarely actually applies it, see Delimatsis (2008) 389, Neumann, Tuerk (2003) 202 ff. The narrow proportionality test is not applied by the WTO bodies, see Trachtman (1998) 58.

[127] Sykes (2003) 415-416. In particular, the 'qualitative' shift of the *Brazil – Tyres* AB's report appears to strengthen the idea that adjudicatory basis can rely on non-scientific arguments to support their views.

degree of tolerance thereof[128]) could soften the impact of the review, even at the risk of letting some very well disguised protectionist measures pass.[129]

In passing, we note that some elements still deserve a better definition, such as the 'reasonable availability' of alternative measures[130] and the role of cost-benefit analysis, and also that the least-restrictive means test alone can fail to strike the right balance, since it is designed not to balance at all, when a *real* proportionality corrective is not set forth as well.[131]

The over-proceduralisation of the necessity test, far from guaranteeing non-discretionary efficiency or a greater deal of legal certainty, would perhaps benefit from an explicit assessment of the reasonableness of reviewed State action and of its good faith (would the State have *reasonably* adopted the same measure if it had no protectionist intent whatsoever?). Reasonableness, again, is rather a standard than a rule, but could be helpful in governing the reciprocal discretion:

> 'Le raisonnable apparaît ainsi à la fois comme l'instrument de préservation de la marge d'appréciation des Etats et comme l'instrument de contrôle par le juge de l'exercice du pouvoir discrétionnaire de l'Etat.'[132]

In sum, we acknowledged that despite a laborious case law and the influence of various deferential doctrines originated in other systems of law, the WTO necessity stays as a peculiar device of minimization of potential harms to trade. State interest comes first, unconditionally, and then trade interests come on stage and require compliance, to the (residual) highest extent possible. Yet, they are never on stage at the same time, as in a narrow proportionality scheme, or in the reasonable application of the margin of appreciation. WTO commits to pay respect to diverse national values exactly the same way insurance companies commit to pay for damages caused by the insured. They both will do so, eventually, but only if they have not managed to demonstrate that a fraud occurred, or

128 See Howse, Teitel (2009) 32, discussing Hormones II and stressing how '*responsible, representative governments*' are acknowledged deference by the AB.

129 Shany (2005) 913. *Contra*, Shaffer (2008) 60.

130 Does this concept imply a detailed assessment on the administrative costs the State could bear to implement them, or only the simple discarding of excessively burdening options, such as in *Brazil – Tyres*? Should these costs form part of a cost-benefit analysis, and if so, what should they be compared with: the lesser restriction of trade benefits? Would developing countries be credited with a particular presumption of good faith, and exempted from least-restrictive and more costly suggestions?

131 According to Trachtman (1998) 72, it can be overbroad and under-inclusive at the same time: '[n]ecessity testing engages in truncated maximization, or truncated comparative cost-benefit analysis, by keeping the regulatory benefit relatively constant and working on the trade detriment side. It thus evaluates a much more limited range of options, ignoring other groups of options that may be superior.'

132 Separate Opinon of judge J.-P. Cot in *Volga (Russian Federation v. Australia)*, ITLOS case no. 11, judgment of December 23, 2002, at 18. Our translation: 'Reasonableness appears to be both the tool which protects States' margin of appreciation and which judges apply to control States' use of their discretionary power.'

that a lesser sacrifice would be possible, keeping the same level of compliance with the commitment.

A limited opening to principles such as proportionality or reasonableness, along with a progressive establishment of the case law would be welcomed, also to divert the practice from the scenario evoked in a recent US Supreme Court case: 'Judges and defendants alike were left at large, wandering in deserts of uncharted discretion.'[133]

[133] *ExxonShippingCo. v. Baker*, 2008, 128 S.Ct.2605, citing Frankel (1973) 'Criminal Sentences: Law without order.'

Bibliography

D. Akande, S. Williams, 'International Adjudication on National Security Issues: What Role for the WTO?' [2003] *VA. J. INT'L L.*, 365-404.

Y. Arai-Takahashi, *The Margin of Appreciation and the Principle of Proportionality*, Intersentia, 2002.

E. Benvenisti, 'Margin of Appreciation, Consensus, and Universal Standards', [1999] *Int'l L. Pol.* 843-854.

R.E. Browne, 'Revisiting 'National Security' in an Interdependent World: The GATT Article XXI Defense After Helms-Burton' [1997] *GEO. L. J.* 405-432.

W.A. Cann, Jr., 'Creating Standards and Accountability for the Use of the WTO Security Exception: Reducing the Role of Power-Based Relations and Establishing A New Balance Between Sovereignty and Multilateralism' [2001] *YALE J. INT'L L.* 413-485.

D. Collins, 'Health Protection at the World Trade Organization – The J-Value as a Universal Standard for Reasonableness of Regulatory Precautions' [2009, forthcoming] *Journal of World Trade.*

S.P. Croley, J.H. Jackson, 'WTO Dispute Procedures, Standard of Review, and Deference to National Governments' [1996] *American Journal of International Law* 193-215.

P. Delimatsis, 'Determining The Necessity Of Domestic Regulations In Services – The Best Is Yet To Come' [2008] *Eur. J. Int'l L.* 365-408.

P. Delimatsis, T. Cottier, 'Article XIV bis GATS: Security Exceptions' [2008] Max Planck Commentaries On World Trade Law, WTO – Trade In Services, Rüdiger Wolfrum, Peter-Tobias Stoll, Clemens Feinäugle, eds., Vol. 6, 329-348, Martinus Nijhoff Publishers, 2008.

I. de la Rasilla del Moral, 'The Increasingly Marginal Appreciation of the Margin-of-Appreciation Doctrine' [2006] *G. L. J.* 611-624.

A. Desmedt, 'Proportionality in WTO Law' [2004] in M. C.E.J. Bronckers, G. N. Horlick (eds.) *WTO Jurisprudence and Policy: Practitioners' Perspectives*, Cameron May, 783-829.

N. F. Diebold, 'The Morals and Order Exceptions in WTO Law: Balancing the Toothless Tiger and the Undermining Mole' [2008] *Journal of International Economic Law* 43-74.

C.D. Ehlermann, N. Lockhart, 'Standard of review in WTO law' [2004] *Journal of International Economic Law* 491-521.

C.E. Foster, 'Public Opinion and the Interpretation of the World Trade Organisation's Agreement on Sanitary and Phytosanitary Measures', [2008] *Journal of International Economic Law* 427-458.

F.J. Garcia, 'The Salmon case: evolution for balancing mechanisms for non trade values in WTO' [2006] in P.C. Mavroidis e G.A. Bermann (eds.), *Trade and human health and safety*, Cambridge University Press, 2006.

C.Y. Howard, *The Margin of Appreciation Doctrine in the Dynamics of European Human Rights Jurisprudence*, Martinus Nijhoff, 1996.

R. Howse, 'Democracy, science, and free trade: risk regulation on trial at the World Trade Organization' [2000] *Mich. L. Rev.* 2329-2357.

R. Howse, E. Tuerk, 'The WTO Impact on Internal Regulations – A Case Study of the Canada – EC Asbestos Dispute', in G. De Burca, J. Scott (eds.) *The EU and the WTO: Legal and Constitutional Aspects*, Hart Publ., 2002.

J. Huerta, 'Trade Remedies Disputes – Dialogue between WTO and NAFTA Tribunals' [2009], F.Fontanelli-G.Martinico-P.Carrozza (eds), Shaping rule of law through dialogue: international and supranational experiences, Europa Law Publishing, Groningen, forthcoming.

H. Kerkmeester, L. Visscher, 'Learned Hand in Europe: a Study in the Comparative Law and Economics of Negligence' [2003] *German Working Papers in Law and Economics* Volume 2003 Paper 6.

G. Letsas, 'Two Concepts of the Margin of Appreciation' [2006] *Oxford Journal of Legal Studies* 705-732.

J. Meltzer, 'State sovereignty and the legitimacy of the WTO' [2005] *University of Pennsylvania Journal of International Economic Law* 693-733.

P.C. Mavroidis, 'Market Access in the GATT', STALS Research Paper n. 7/2008, available at http://www.stals.sssup.it/site/files/stals_Mavroidis.pdf.

P.C. Mavroidis, 'No Outsourcing of Law? WTO Law as Practiced by WTO Courts' [2008b] *Am.J.I.L.*, 421-474.

B. McGrady, 'Necessity Exceptions In Wto Law: Retreaded Tyres, Regulatory Purpose And Cumulative Regulatory Measures' [2008] *J. Int'l Econ. L.* 153-173.

C.M. McInerney, 'From Shrimps And Dolphins To Retreaded Tyres: An Overview Of The World Trade Organization Disputes, Discussing Exceptions To Trading Rules' [2009] *N.Y. Int'l L. Rev.* 153-200.

M. Molfa, 'US Legislation on Cross-Border Gambling Violates the GATS: Has a New Era for Internet Gambling Commenced? I Would Not Bet on It!' [2005] *Intl. T. L. R.* 205-213.

M. Montini, 'The Necessity Principle as an instrument to balance trade and the protection of the environment', in F. Francioni (ed.) *Environment, Human Rights and International Trade*, Oxford, 135-155.

M. Montini, 'The Nature and Function of the Necessity and Proportionality Principles in the Trade and Environment Context' [1997] *RECIEL* 121-130.

J. Neumann, E. Tuerk, 'Necessity Revisited: Proportionality in World Trade Organization Law After Korea – Beef, EC – Asbestos and EC – Sardines' [2003] *J World Trade* 199-233.

F. Ortino, *Basic Legal Instruments for the Liberalisation of Trade: a Comparative Analysis of EC and WTO Law*, Hart Publishing, 2004.

F. Ortino, 'Treaty Interpretation and the WTO Appellate Body Report in *US – Gambling*: A Critique' [2006] *Journal of International Economic Law* 117-148.

D. Osiro, 'GATT/WTO Necessity Analysis: Evolutionary Interpretation and its Impact on the Autonomy of Domestic Regulation' [2002] *Legal Issues of Economic Integration* 123-141.

H. Petzold, 'The Convention and the Principle of Subsidiarity', in R. St. J Macdonald and others (eds.) *The European System for the Protection of Human Rights*, Martinus Nijhoff Publishers, 1993, 41-62.

D. Regan, 'The meaning of 'necessary' in GATT Article XX and GATS Article XIV: the myth of cost–benefit balancing' [2007] *World Trade Review* 347-369.

M.A. Reiterer 'Article XXI GATT – Does the National Security Exception Permit 'Anything Under the Sun'?' [1997] *Austrian Review of International and European Law* 191-212.

A. Riza Çoban, *Protection of property rights within the European Convention on Human Rights*, Ashgate, 2004.

G. Shaffer, 'A Structural Theory Of WTO Dispute Settlement: Why Institutional Choice Lies At The Center Of The Gmo Case' [2008] *N.Y.U. J. Int'l L. & Pol.* 1-101.

Y. Shany, 'Towards a General Margin of Appreciation Doctrine in International Law?' [2006] *European Journal of International Law* 907-940.

A. Sykes, 'The Least Restrictive Means' [2003] *U. Chi. L. Rev.* 403-419.

A. Stone Sweet, J. Mathews, 'Proportionality Balancing and Global Constitutionalism' [2008] *Colum. J. Transnat'l L.* 73-165.

D.K. Tarullo, 'The hidden costs of international dispute settlement: WTO review of domestic anti-dumping decisions' [2002] *Georgetown Journal of International Law* 109-181.

R. Teitel, R. Howse, 'Cross-judging: tribunalization in a fragmented but interconnected global order' [2009] *New York University Public Law and Legal Theory Working Papers*. Paper 112.

J. Tinbergen, *International Economic Integration*, Elsevier Publ'g Co., 1965.

J.P. Trachtman, 'Trade and... Problems, Cost-Benefit Analysis and Subsidiarity' [1998] *European Journal of International Law* 32-85.

J.P. Trachtman, G. Marceau, 'TBT, SPS, and GATT: A Map of the WTO Law of Domestic Regulation' [2002] *Journal of World Trade* 811-881.

J.P. Trachtman, 'Lessons for the GATS from Existing WTO Rules on Domestic Regulation, in Domestic Regulation & Service Trade Liberalization' [2003] in A. Mattoo, P. Sauvé (eds.) *Domestic regulation and service trade liberalization*, Oxford, 2003, 205-219.

J.P. Trachtman, 'United States: Measures Affecting the Cross-Border Supply of Betting and Gambling Services' [2005] *American Journal of International Law* 861-867.

J.P. Trachtman, 'Transcending 'Trade and [...]' – an Institutional Perspective' [2005b] *Am. J. Int'l L.* 77-93.

J.P. Trachtman, 'Regulatory Jurisdiction and the WTO' [2007] *Journal of International Economic Law* 631-651.

E. Trujillo, 'Mission Possible: Reciprocal Deference Between Domestic Regulatory Structures and the WTO' [2007] *Cornell International Law Journal* 201-264.

A. Van Aaken, 'Defragmentation Of Public International Law Through Interpretation: A Methodological Proposal' [2009] *Ind. J. Global Legal Stud.* 483-512.

J.H.H. Weiler, *The Constitution of Europe*, Cambridge University Press, 1999.

J.H.H. Weiler, 'Federalism and Constitutionalism: Europe's *Sonderwerg*' [2002] in R. Howse, K. Nicolaïdis, *The Federal Vision*, Oxford University Press, 2002, 54-70.

H.C. Yourow, *The Margin of Appreciation Doctrine in the Dynamics of European Human Rights Jurisprudence*, Martinus Nijhoff Publishers, 2006.

S. Zleptnig, 'The Standard of Review in WTO Law: An Analysis of Law, Legitimacy and the Distribution of Legal and Political Authority' [2002] *European Integration online Papers* No. 2002-017.

CHAPTER 14

Global Threads: Weaving the Rule of Law and the Balance of Legal Software

Gianluigi Palombella*

1 Hardware to Software

Among the diverse reactions raised through the debate on 'fragmentation', the issue at stake in the International Law Commission 2006 Report,[1] there certainly were worries that the international environment could neither be depicted nor grasped anymore from *one* overarching *view*. Admittedly, the views from one single regulatory regime (think of NAFTA, or WTO, the WB or the IMF, UNCLOS and the like) in spite of its global reach, are after all 'self observing', looking at the world as an 'internal' space, depending on the regime's own functionalities. The general proliferation of normative legal fabrics jeopardises the reassuring belief that differentiation develops under *one and all encompassing frame* of law. Indeed, it does endanger the dogma of the *system* unity of law.[2]

All the more so, if some less institutionalised processes of global governance are taken into account that are following straightforwardly 'alternative' paths, cutting themselves free of traditional legal ties, basing on private autonomous pragmatism, or 'self made' normativities (if not legalities).[3]

In our more traditional mindset, we need to come to terms with the loss of such cultural, or logical, presupposition, according to which making sense of law is tantamount to making sense of it as a 'system'. And most attempts to 'constitutionalise' the global law, or alternatively, to recognise the thin threads that draw some trans-system connections, do simply try and compensate for this uninvited system's obsolescence.

Yet, questions like those concerning transnational rule of law and justice, the plurality of regulatory regimes, the segmentation of international law, communication among legal orders were barely unknown[4] and not reflected upon in the lessons of the most illuminating and influential legal theorists of the last

* Professor of Legal Philosophy at the University of Parma (Italy); fellow of the New York University Straus Institute for the Advanced Study of Law and Justice.

1 'Conclusions of the work of the Study Group on the Fragmentation of International Law: Difficulties arising from the Diversification and Expansion of International Law', Adopted by the International Law Commission at its Fifty-eighth session, in 2006, and submitted to the General Assembly as a part of the Commission's report covering the work of that session (A/61/10, para. 251). Available at http://untreaty.un.org/ilc/reports/2006/2006report.htm.

2 In his introduction to the 2006 International Law Commission Report on Fragmentation, Martti Koskenniemi signaled that the problems lurking in cases like the Mox Plant-nuclear facility at Sellafield, UK (involving three different institutional procedures, the Arbitral Tribunal at UN Convention on the Law of the Sea, the procedure under the Convention on Protection of the Marine Environment of the North-East Asiatic Atlantic, and under the European Community and Euratom Treaties within the European Court of Justice) are both substantive and procedural: they involve questions as to competence of diverse institutions and the hierarchical relations among them: an issue that the commission decided to leave aside (See *ibid.*, M. Koskenniemi, *Introduction*, § 13, p. 11).

3 In the huge bibliography, see at least Teubner (1997); Berger (1999); Teubner (2002).

4 A similar point is made by Twining (2006) 119-122.

century, like Kelsen, or Hart. European thought and practice as well had been imbued with the material and conceptual dominance of the State and, what is more, with the *strictly related unity* of law: whether reducing the law to the State or *vice versa*, the concept of law is essentially connected with the 'hardware' notion of 'a system'. Truly, the argument went, 'the compulsory nature of the rules in force, whatever their remote origin may be, appears henceforth as the effect of th[at] centralizing will [...] a true and proper subject [...] the State'.[5] It follows that juridical relations however created by individuals' transactions or groups' agreements are still dependent of the State's will, one granting for itself that 'exclusiveness rendered necessary in order to assure the unity of the system'.[6]

Although much of this narrative is now flawed, and some dogmas have been attenuated or definitely abandoned, still the connection with the *hard structure* of a 'system' shows some resistance in association with law. Properly so, however. It means the shift from a 'set' of rules to an organised rational 'order', and both in Kelsenian and Hartian representation it marks at least the passage from primitive to mature law. It allows for identity and stability, for more or less functional relations among norms, for the unending effort of border drawing, for implementing a selective notion of 'validity' as 'belonging'. The idea of such a structured and stable 'system'[7] often hinges also upon a genetic configuration of law, endowed with its own grammar, language, and 'anatomic' morphology.

To put it differently, law has been mainly conceived of as endowed with its *hardware*, one that insures its basic existence, pointing to predefined typology of rules, their formal hierarchical bonds, and the like. Of course, the *hardware* is, as much as computers are (at least for us 'normal' users), a pre-given capability and a constitutive support, and yet it is simply silent and empty, without its enabling *software*. The latter allows us to make sense of the thing, giving meaning and value, transforming some structural or technological potential into a working machinery, imbued with life.[8] Law resembles as well the idea of such a *software*,[9] generated by real world practice, and developed around principles and rules, regulations, legislation, custom, contracts, treaties, judicial decisions, and so forth.

When we face the multiple normative entities inhabiting the global sphere, we are, so to speak, bewildered with such a legal *software*, that thrives on the whole in lacking pre-given and all harmonising devices. Despite being very often produced by institutionalised authorities, it has fragmented our territorial law in the vertical supranational and in the horizontal transnational modes: it

---

5 Del Vecchio (1937) 8.

6 *Ibid.* 9.

7 The best work on this issue is due to Raz (1980).

8 This metaphor is suggested by the Yale law professor Jack Balkin, who elaborated through it upon his concepts of culture and ideology in his book, Balkin (1996). I am responsible for adapting the suggestion to law.

9 Needless to say, I am not referring here to the so called soft-law, but to law *sans phrase.*

generates a *pluralism*[10] *of self contained orders*, whose 'separability' is itself all but neatly construed: with the unintended effect that their field-scopes[11] actually *overlap* in controlling practices and cases.[12]

When at issue is global law, we therefore realise that *software* is increasing, differentiating and perfecting itself around the kernel of many distinctive rationalities, enabling to perform, in diverse 'windows', highly complex regulations, assessments and dispute resolution, from commerce to environment, from the law of the sea to internet domains, from labour to telecommunications, energy to human rights, to the law of war.

In coping with this coupled phenomena, that is, system fading and regulatory proliferation, we are thus witnessing *software* self expansion at the expense of some *hardware* capability. This prompts legal reasoning to realise once more that it is *the former to determine the latter*: we cannot proceed from the available hardware (system structure) to the permissible software (law & rules) as it was in XIX and XX century legal positivism. We have to run after the available software instead, come to terms with it, and then try to conceive, maybe, of some suited, ever changing, hardware.

One of the compensating strategies has been focussing on the judicial side: judicial work could advance, so to speak, some additional *software*, one of a distinctive kind though: shaped 'through cases' but providing for gap bridging criteria and connective texture, not directly found in the 'primary' rules that it is for judges to apply or enforce. Even Courts indirect 'communicative' strategies might either reflect or produce interfacial rules, purport to develop some shared working idioms helping coexistence and connections in the absence of the 'grand box'. One of the threads, one fundamental on the legal plane, is the rule of law. And whereas the 'system' might be out of sight, the rule of law might increase its relevance and role, up to becoming the closest thing to a post-'Babel'[13] legal understanding.

2 Contestability

The 'rule of law' is less part of argumentative tools of legal reasoning than a concluding label generally held to encompass, support and justify its overall result. One might recall the solemn appeal to 'the rule of law that prevails in this jurisdiction' as the ultimate rationale that the US Supreme

---

10 In the literature about pluralism and trans-nationalism, see Kennedy (2007).

11 It is this overlapping that is held to define legal pluralism, in the path breaking work of Engle Merry (1988).

12 This generates of course the well known phenomena of regimes collision, uncertainty, forum shopping and so forth. See *infra*.

13 The metaphor has become a *topos* and is recalled as a rather favourable opportunity both in Higgins, (2006) and in S. Cassese (2009).

Court invokes, in the whole, as a matter of legal justification.[14] The ECJ adopted the rule of law up to a stronger and system-building significance: by granting that every act be submitted to the principle of judicial reviewability by the ECJ,[15] it is the bedrock for the European Community to be a 'community of law', and it equally implies ensuring that 'in the interpretation and application of the Treaty the law is observed'.[16]

Even so, the rule of law actually lends itself to controversial results. This holds true in State legal orders as much as in the international and in the global sphere.[17] Instances are plentiful. In the EU well-confined supranational order, the European Court of Justice, that works since decades under the supremacy and direct effect principles,[18] is recently reaffirming its original attitude toward 'integration-through-law' by essentially resorting to its 'rule of law' supremacy: but the latter ultimately risks boiling down to a kind of 'law of rules'.[19] For this point to be clarified and expanded, some examples can be helpful.

In the *Volkswagen*[20] decision, the ECJ ruled that the 1960 Volkswagen statute violated the right to establishment, through free flow of capital, as laid down in Article 56 (1) EC.[21] To be sure, the decision was in line with previous judgements overturning national state regulations[22] and with policy inaugurated (1999-2004) by the Internal Market Commissioner Frits Bolkestein: however, invalidating the Volkswagen law is tantamount to overturning the idiosyncratic continental Europe Social-Market Capitalism model (the 'Rheinish'). The *internal* significance of the latter lies in workers' co-determination, state involvement,

---

14 See, *e.g.*, *Hamdan v. Rumsfeld*, 548 U.S. 557 (2006), at p. 635.

15 Case 294/83 *Partie Ecologiste 'Les Verts' v. European Parliament* [1986] ECR 1339.

16 *Opinion 2/94* (Accession by the Community to the European Convention for the Protection of Human Rights and Fundamental Freedoms) [1996] ECR I-1763.

17 I should refer here to the analysis I made elsewhere of the potential and weakness of the rule of law 'beyond the State': see Palombella (2009). Elaboration on the rule of law double edge goes through decisions like the European Court of First Instance Case T-306/01 *Yusuf and Al Barakaat Int'l Foundation v. Council and Commission*; Case T-315/01 *Kadi v. Council and Commission* both of 21 September 2005; US Supreme Court *Hamdan v. Rumsfeld* (2006) (see *supra* n. 14), the European Court of Justice Joined Cases C-402/05 P, *Yassin Abdullah Kadi and Al Barakaat International Foundation v. Council & Commission* [2005] ECR II-3649, Judgment of 3 September 2008.

18 ECJ, Case 26/62 (*Van Gend & Loos*) [1962] ECR 1.; and Case 6/64 (*Costa v. ENEL*) [1964] ECR 585.

19 In the rather textual and certainty-minded sense of Scalia (1989).

20 ECJ, decision of 23 October 2007, *Commission v. Federal Republic of Germany* (Case C-112/2005).

21 According to the Court, the statute prevented private investors from taking up shares in the company and effectively participating in its administration and control, mainly by giving the Federal government and the *Land* of Lower Saxony a veto against majority acquisition, through a special powers, privileged share (of 20%). Cf. *supra* at note 20, ECJ, *'Volkswagen'*, Grand Chamber Judgment, par. 22, paragraphs 38-56 and *passim*.

22 See Zumbansen – Saam (2007) 1028: 'a continuation and further accentuation of a line of argument that the Court has been unfolding over past few years with regard to the Member State provisions in conflict with the EC' guarantee of free movement of capital'.

social protection, while this deeply rooted and socially structured pattern might end up affording *external* resistance to market integration or global liberalization.

The controversial point is of course about fair interpretation of treaties,[23] but all in all, it concerns the 'rule of law' and its use: whether sheer 'dura lex' is fairly (and in the typical monist intra-european style) resorted to in pursuing some – admittedly, 'functional' – straightforward European policy, dictating a uniform overall economic model,[24] that 'political' institutions are unable to agree upon. Of course, this should be reflected upon regardless of our belief (or disbelief) in an 'undistorted market competition' (or of one's policy preferences) and with reference to the technical import and *use* of a legal notion such as the 'rule of law'.[25]

On a slightly different plane, some even more telling decisions draw a rule of law interrogation mark, directly pointing, this time, to one of the most cherished rule of law ingredients, *proportionality*.[26] The latter can be held to convey 'global' judicial dialogue just because it has obtained a recognized status among rule of law essentials, spreading through legal orders worldwide, from Europe to US, and so forth. It is literally what one might call a 'global constitutional standard'. Diverse scholars connect its requirement to a possible constitutionalisation of global functional regimes, like the WTO.[27] Thus, it should be taken seriously as a kind of universal pillar for all judicial bodies to understand each other. It is believed to be a *rule of law* 'golden rule'[28](Beattie) or one feasible basis for a tentative constructivism, building some rule of law constants between different actors confronted in the global setting.[29]

The ECJ had showed in its 2003 decision, *Schmidberger v. Austria*[30] (in times preceding the EU constitutional failure), its inclination to a wider self understanding then the court of an 'economic union': by granting (proportionality) equal ranking to the freedoms of assembly and expression as to the free movement of goods, it was furthering its prospective role as a potential 'constitutional court'. Some years later, the trend seems inverted. In *Viking*[31] the ECJ addressed,

---

23 See generally Spattini (2008) 303-64.

24 Cf. Spattini (2008), and Zumbansen – Saam (2007).

25 For the traditional meaning of the rule of law in the European Communities system see Fernandez Esteban (1999).

26 Classical reference for an analysis of proportionality in its logical steps and functionality is Alexy (2003) 131-40. See also Habermas (1996) 256-9.

27 Review of such tendencies, and distinction between the WTO as a 'constitution' v. the 'constitutionalisation' of WTO, in Cass (2005).

28 Beatty (2005). See also of the same author, the chapter *Law's Golden Rule*, in Palombella – Walker (2009) 99-116.

29 Stone Sweet – Mathews (2008) 73-165. However, see as well, recently, Tsakyrakis (2009).

30 Case C-112/00 *Schmidberger, Internationale Transporte und Planzüge*, judgment of 12 June 2003.

31 Case C-438/05 *Viking* 2007: A Finnish passenger shipping company, on the way of registering its ship Rossella under an Estonian flag, to be crewed by Estonian seafarers on lower wages, was faced by the

among the rest, the question whether the Unions' right to strike can be forfeited for the sake of Article 43 EC right of a Finnish company (Viking) trans-state free establishment. By submitting the right to strike to the reasonable requirement of proportionality (strictly meant) and necessity,[32] the ECJ actually stated that its use was unjustified, under the circumstances: thus, it turns out that it cannot be resorted too unless it is proved to be the *extrema ratio* and passes a test striking the balance with the company's and the general interest.

The ECJ reasoning sounds at least ambiguous: although virtually nothing in the abstract can be expected to escape proportionality in the given circumstances, it is all a matter of *when (or how)* to balance, and *whose* balance (and no less, *what* is to be balanced). The ECJ (rule of law and proportionality based) argument is about to make the 'right to strike' to collapse: it has been said that in some continental legal orders, like the Italian, this would hardly meet collective action's constitutional intention, and collides heavily with the intangible[33] Unions autonomy (within legal pre-fixed limits agreed upon in advance) in interpreting the collective good and the value of conflict within it.[34]

On a theoretical plane, it has been observed that although proportionality cannot 'dictate' the only one correct answer, it 'mitigates certain legitimacy problems' and it 'requires courts to acknowledge and defend, honestly and openly, the policy choices that they make when they make constitutional choices. Proportionality is not a magic wand that judges wave to make all of the political dilemmas of rights review disappear. Indeed, waving it will expose rights adjudication for what it is: constitutionally-based lawmaking'.[35] Let alone its 'realist' belief about judges as 'law makers' under constitutional limits, this considered statement does fail to see that the challenge, in the 'global' mode, looks very different: the point is not about the shortcoming of 'waving proportionality', while a constitutional system being constant, but precisely the opposite: i.e. that such a normative production develops (even) regardless of a constitutional basis, and even where it can hardly avail itself of some premised frame, as in the global realm.

Thus, I would rather maintain that if one can imagine the rule of law as something more than a 'law of rules' or 'formal' judicial protection, it is proportionality that comes into the scene as first; nonetheless, one would miss the point by relying on it as the 'ultimate' rule of law provider.

---

international transportation workers (ITF) Union's threat to strike, in defence from unemployment of the former Finnish workers likely to be replaced.

32 Case C-438/05, *Viking* 2007:§81-83.

33 This holds true, of course, in a legal frame where external *limits are fixed* (not balanced) relating to the protection of market survival potentiality of the companies or, in the public sector, to the intangible guarantee of a measure of functioning in essential public services (like health, transportation etc.).

34 For similar comments, see Zoppoli (2008) 157; and Rusciano (2009) 64.

35 Stone – Mathew (2008) 78.

3 Persistence

As regards the rule of law, controversiality is definitely unsurprising. The 'deconstructivist' strength of criticisms addressing the rule of law as much as human rights or democracy does traditionally stress their indeterminacy,[36] their openness as well as their dark side.[37] The deep reason for this to be so, is mainly in the conceptual status of the rule of law as an ideal.

If one looks at the European Union primary law and its western trinity of values, the rule of law comes to the fore with democracy and human rights, and it would be hard to deny the contested nature of each of them. Nonetheless, let us look below the surface: 'essentially contested' concepts[38] are still playing a channelling role. Despite the slipping ground provided, they function by gathering convergence over a space of normativity, thinking and deliberation. and still the very fact of choosing such words-concepts, as a forum of debate and principled pillars of our legal orders, retains its working function. Take human rights, and the unending warning about their side effects, like the sheer justificatory use of state interventionism; similar concerns apply should we consider the model of the 'rule of law'. Legal theorists know that its *importance* certainly derives from belonging in many 'comprehensive' conceptions of the legal system,[39] or dependence upon 'situated' and 'thick' cultural premises.[40] Nevertheless, the rule of law numbers as well among the 'essential', 'constitutive' elements over which current diverse views of legal orders end up 'overlapping': thus, its model says something, perhaps about legal and political justice, which quite disparate moral and ethical beliefs are asked to confront. As much as human rights discussion is forced to resist the allure of self reference and parochialism by resting on their inherent language of 'universalisability', the 'rule of law' calls upon national communities to focus on some logic of *law* as such, at the level of fundamental features, i.e. on that plane of self understanding, where communicative codes are clarified in advance, and can be exposed to some external check, confrontation and learning. All the more so, because the rule of law lies in the middle ground (at least in scholarship and judicial records) between on the one hand, (a) the necessary requirements for the law to be functioning as the most efficient method of guiding behaviours (being stable and constant, public, retrospective, possible to comply with, and the like),[41] and on the other hand, (b) the further, and more demanding, ideal that in comparative

36 Gordon (1984).

37 For example, see Sajo (2006). And in it, also Palombella (2006).

38 Waldron (2002).

39 I take the word 'comprehensive' here in the sense (evoking different views of the 'good') made clear by Rawls (1993) 154.

40 This time, say, in the sense of Walzer (1994).

41 The requirements list will give us something like an 'anatomy' of the rule of law (as such insufficient), as Krygier (2009) 47-52. However, in my view, the anatomic conception is represented at its best by Raz (1979) 214-18 and Fuller (1969). Fuller elaborates on: Generality, clarity, promulgation, stability,

constitutional history one can trace back to the Middle Ages, Dicey and current developments,[42] as encompassing some specific institutional tasks (regardless of external or heterogeneous domains like, say, political democracy), that relate to legality, as a matter of liberty, balance and non-domination (in the juridical sense of non-monopolisation of legal sources).[43]

Thus, its tendency is explained to be versatile vis-à-vis plural, diversified incarnations, and at the same time, to be an issue on the 'universal' arena. So it is that we dare to overstep the line of purely deconstructive theories, and elaborate on the 'virtuous' ambivalence of the rule of law underlying meaning.

Although I will not embark here on the definitional endeavour I have pursued elsewhere, I submit that the persistence of the rule of law is relying on some core meaning, making sense, instead of just an unqualified legality, of a set of wider and more appealing normativity: one that conveys our aspiration to put legality beyond the reach of instrumental use and the whim of the ruling powers, be they sovereigns, Kings or Parliaments, democratic powers or autocracies, unassailable supranational entities (like say, the Sanction Committees of the UN Security Council) or international conventional agreements, as well as specialised or functional global regimes (say, the WTO, or the ICANN, or the UNCLOS). In the global sphere, where legal orders face the danger of clash, reliance on the rule of law has to be reframed. It is not only a matter of granting some habeas corpus, due process, judicial review to individuals under the purview of State administrations (or equivalent entities), although it is much about that.[44]

One cannot deny that it comes to the fore firstly as a power of naming, or of classification: Whether *Asbestos and Asbesto Products*[45] are better classified under the chapters of human rights or health, or safety[46] will depend on a fight for law, competence, and jurisdiction, and will turn out to produce different outcomes. Is this classification power capable of falling under our concern for the 'rule of law'? Be aware that from the angle of the 'rule of law', though, the question does appear as a problem of legal countervailing or balancing devices, methods, not directly as a matter of social or economic power.

---

consistency between rules and behaviours, non-retroactivity, non-contradictory rules, nor requiring the impossible.

42 Among the references at least Dicey (1915) 195-6, 268-73; Haskins (1995) 535-6. and McIlwain (1940); for the modern period, Reid (2004).

43 I have dealt with this at length elsewhere, in Palombella (2010).

44 The vast literature on the CFI and ECJ cases, *Kadi* and *Al Baarakat* (see *supra* note 17 and *infra*) did flourish also on this issue.

45 See *European Community – Measures concerning Asbestos and Asbestos Products* 2001, p. 61 para 168, and the comment in Koskenniemi (2005).

46 For instance see Howse – Türk (2001); see also Bermann – Mavroidis (2006).

When, as in the famous *Swordfish* case,[47] a supranational entity (the EU) and a national State (Chile), defend their claims, they happen to find their own case as one potentially relevant, or 'belonging', in more than one regulatory regime (or system), each endowed with fundamental 'political' objectives, functional imperatives, scientific expertise, principles, rules, and finally, Tribunals: to this extent, the International Convention on the Law of the Sea, and the World Trade Organisation emerge as they are, separate in the space, each with an attracting and unifying force, and both can announce the rule of law *according to their own realm.*

What is of interest to us, is that their *parallel validity* has to face a crucial challenge, as a matter of Euclidean geometry, when from the point of view of the parties involved (Chile, or the EU, in *Swordfish,* or say, Mexico and US, between NAFTA and WTO in *Soft Drinks)*[48] the (parallels) *non intersection property* fails the evidence. Indeed, it is just through parties activity and their 'judicial' choices, that an otherwise inexistent crossroad materialises, and functional normative settlements as well as their rationalities, construed as mutually unrelated, risk to come to an embarrassing date.

Where the rule of law emerges, then, is precisely at this normative crossroad, much less imaginary than theories of legal systems can think. There is no superior rule, no *Grundnorm,* and should it exist, in the Kelsenian mode, it would hardly attach to such an environment: the latter is not the traditional international legality, where states' orders are meant to defer – and territorial sovereignties to surrender – to the international rule, and to assume its wider order to be the source of their normative validity. International order in the strict sense is itself just one among the many concurring in this wider 'space'. Indeed, we would hardly understand all regulatory governance from the viewpoint of the law between states.

When normative regimes and full-fledged legal orders of any typology whatsoever are about to come at some crossroad, where neither *Kompetenz Kompetenz* is available, nor a European Union *sui generis* model of an 'autonomous' multilevel community of law is in place, the problem of *authority* resurfaces, and it is here that the rule of law has to be projected. As it happens in the view of undesired 'third kind encounters',[49] diverse strategies (circumstances – relative)

47 The case: at WTO: Chile- WTO Doc. WT/DS193; at the ITLOS, *Chile v. Eur. Com.* (Mar. 15, 2001) (available at www.un.org/Depts/los/ITLOS/Order1_2001Eng_pdf) (suspended). For a presentation of the case, recently S. Cassese (2009) 31-35. Cf. also Treves (2008) 42; Orellana (2001); Orellana (2002) 55.

48 Cf. Panel Report, *Mexico–Tax Measures on Soft Drinks and Other Beverages,* WT/DS308/R (Oct. 7, 2005).

49 I take the liberty of appropriating the metaphor, invoked to all different respect elsewhere by Camroux – Lechervy (1996).

like comity,[50] mutual recognition, equivalent protection, subsidiarity, and more, hopefully begin to flourish.[51]

The point to be stressed, however, is that in the fragmented pluralism of legal orders we can find judges and courts as builders of a thin fabric of general principles, partly descending from the structural rules of judging, partly elaborated on dialogue, communication, and all in need to establish a common practice whose fortune will depend on their actual success in giving some stable principled lines and parameters of conflict resolutions, at least on the procedural side.[52] However, we should also refrain from asserting that the rule of law boils down to an a priori formal primacy that should be granted hierarchically to one 'higher' legal order's imperatives, as content independent. Moreover, it is to be rejected the parochial idea that the rule of law is something concerning 'one jurisdiction at time' and that its meaning is therefore jurisdiction-relative. Far from narrowing itself to these two last alternatives, it is instead depending on the trans-orders weaving of potential *meta-rules*, a third chance then, possibly promising a critical measure to which global law, as much as municipal and international law, should have been subscribing as a matter of coherence.[53]

Persistence of the rule of law will be then due to an *externalization* function, displayed by multiple sources, while engaging in real world events and confrontation. Again, the issue of the rule of law shall not resemble the sheer respect for laws that are in force in one's jurisdiction; its layer is where legal cultures, traditions, expertise, languages, can overlap. In such an environment, where poor reliance on a system of law (and even poorer on 'one' community values) is allowed, protection of pluralism might turn to be still the best practice.

---

50 As the President of the Arbitral Tribunal constituted for the UNCLOS in 2003 said, in dismissing the case filed by Ireland against UK concerning the Sellafield nuclear enrichment plant in Britain, after the European Court of Justice was assumed to be competent to decide: 'The Tribunal considers that a situation in which there might be two conflicting decisions on the same issues would not be helpful to the resolution of this international dispute. Nor would such a situation be in accord with the dictates of mutual respect and comity that should exist between judicial institutions deciding on rights and obligations as between States, and entrusted with the function of assisting States in the peaceful settlement of disputes that arise between them' (para 11). The text is available as President's Statement of June 13 2003 at http://www.pca-cpa.org/showpage.asp?pag_id=1148.

51 In his overview, S. Cassese recalls primacy (in European law, and in the different version of the primacy of the 'global' over the European order), the Spanish Constitutional Tribunal (largely isolated) distinction between primacy and supremacy, state constitutional doctrine of counter-limits; the doctrine of the so called 'norme interposte'; the principle of equivalent protection; the functional tasks' division; and eventually, subsidiarity. S. Cassese (2009).

52 Elaboration on such question has been hugely growing since (a) Slaughter (2005) to S. Cassese (2009). I will only add here Chester Brown, *A Common Law of International Adjudication*. Oxford, OUP, 2007.

53 I have argued along these lines elsewhere, in Palombella (2009).

4 Duality: the Balance of Legal Software as a Matter of the Rule of Law

As follows from the foregoing, the controversial nature of the rule of law is coupled with its persistence, and persisting normative value. What does mark the rule of law in the transforming scene of the 'global' legality is in some ways its dependence of a usable grammar that has come to transgress the borders, although bringing with itself its failures, ideology and contestability.

Cassese has rightly pointed out the habits and logic of judging as a constant resource that helps constructing some common communicative trend among peers in the global scene.[54] Kingsbury has maintained that a 'public' nature attaches to the entities that are producing law and regulation throughout the globe, and such a 'public' nature implies definable general qualities, affecting their mode of action: as he writes, this conception would 'encompass legal governance forms adopted in inter-societal relations (*e.g.* cross-border governance institutions of co-religionists), in transnational relations among elements of states (*e.g.* networks of government regulators, such as the Basle Committee of central bankers), and in the jurisgenerative work of bodies that do not depend on states' [...] I propose treating them as public entities. These entities, along with the states that are the archetypical public entities, are the actors in an inter-public order'.[55] The quality of 'publicness' would then entail a few conceptual consequences concerning the standard of their behaviour, namely, the principles of legality, rationality, proportionality, rule of law, human rights protection.[56]

In my view, one of the premises for the rule of law to be a stable reference depends on its added value pointing to the *non instrumental* role that the rule of law itself ought to play.

Although everything can be meant as usable to whatever pursuit, and this holds true, say, for rationality or the principle of legality for example, human rights and the rule of law appear to embody an inherent claim to be treated always as an 'end' and 'never merely as a means'.[57] In the case of the rule of law this embraces the creation of institutional arrangements (and/or legal principles of administrative or judicial behaviour), providing that positive law be capable of some resistance to instrumental use, thereby affording subjects with a *duality* of law: that is, each actor, endowed with normative capacity, should also find himself facing 'another' law[58] that from his viewpoint is not under his purview, however 'dominant' his position, as a ruler, or legislator, and its equivalents, might be. The pattern should be meant to hold even for judicial organs, since

---

54 See Cassese (2005).

55 Kingsbury (2009) 169.

56 *Ibid.*, pp. 178-9.

57 The Kantian formulation is: 'Act in such a way that you treat humanity, whether in your own person or in the person of any other, always at the same time as an end and never merely as a means to an end'. Kant (1785) 36.

58 I am referring to positive law to be actually practiced. I am not invoking sheer morality.

they appear multiple, *per se* 'ultimate', authorities, and yet responsible for the definition of general principles underpinning the viability of legal intercourses in the interconnected fields of the global sphere: from this angle, building up sharable criteria of mutual respect and communication *is itself a rule of law requirement,* and the premise for the rule of law to flourish in a setting where an ultimate authority and the ready-made legal 'system' are vague or missing.

This general precondition has a bearing on the connection of the rule of law with the idea of the 'right', of fairness in intersubjective relations, and inter-institutional 'respect'. It is not a sheer matter of comity, though[59]. One could find appealing and appropriate to further elaborate along the general lines of the idea that the 'principles of right, and so of justice, put limits on which satisfactions have value; they impose restrictions on what are reasonable conceptions of one's good'. Principles of justice 'specify the boundaries that men's systems of ends must respect [...] Interests requiring the violation of justice have no value.'[60] Although I cannot address here this background reference further,[61] it helps orienting toward the relevance of the idea of the 'right': the latter is to be meant as normatively implied by the rule of law as an *ideal,* and in this context it reflects a kind of Kantian requirement allowing for coexistence under circumstances of liberty, unmasking a power based conception of the 'good', and preventing parochial values from being imposed universally by the means of a dominant and unrivalled law.

In this same sense, a global rule of law could not be squared with only one dominating conception of the 'good', i.e. of unrestricted functional imperatives and policy goals, whether imposed by WTO regulations, or some imperial notion of democracy, and the like. Moreover, the existence of legal regimes counterbalancing with ecological concerns the free commerce oriented regulations in WTO, can imitate this logic[62] (one can say the same thing in the reverse order, though).

A significant case should be mentioned, concerning the principle developed in recent years, the 'responsibility to protect', firstly by the International Commission on Intervention and State Sovereignty.[63] It was then highlighted with emphasis by the UN Secretary General and re-elaborated by the 'High Level

59 Although comity has its standing as an ancient principle in international law, one should also bear in mind the comments on it by Koskenniemi (2005) 2, referring to 'dictates of mutual respect and comity', ironically as matters of 'Victorian politeness'. As he writes: 'This is a gentlemen's affair. Whatever environmental or economic interests may be involved, we must deal with this as civilised men'.

60 Rawls (1971) 31.

61 I have dealt with justice connection to the rule of law in Palombella (2009).

62 However, one should also attribute relevance to the *internal* limitations: see the WTO Appellate Body jurisprudence based on GATT, Art. XX, concerning trade law 'permissible exceptions' to be referred to a number of issues form morals to health to conservation of exhaustible natural resources, etc.: see Article XX, General Agreement on Tariffs and Trade (GATT) Oct. 30, 1947, 61 Stat. A-11, 55 U.N.T.S. 194.

63 Available online at http://www.iciss.ca/report-en.asp.

Panel on Threats, Challenges and Change' created by the UN, in a report with a meaningful title: *A More Secure World: Our Shared Responsibility*.[64] The Report has been interpreted as challenging the intrinsic value of the State per se.[65] The principle is capable of providing a criterion of prevalence when genocides, ethnic cleaning, crimes against humanity, and possibly natural disasters are at stake.

In principle, it says more than the *limits* that apply to sovereignty: the 'responsibility to protect' says that ultimately no sovereignty is justified unless it fulfils its promise and *raison d'etre*. Sovereignty, thus, is not the westphalian ultimate value, sovereignty is *conditional*.[66]

In different words, and in the 'rule of law' language that I suggest, one can focus on the premise that international sphere allows some other law to counterbalance the law of the state as a matter of sovereignty, by challenging not merely its scope and limits, but its very *self definitional power*, i.e. the entitlement to decide by itself what its final legitimate *rationale* must be. This holds true when other interests are allowed to get a 'voice', when 'others', subjects, individuals, peoples, are taken as inherently and independently worthy of legal protection. 'Another' (tentative and *in fieri)* law has been pitted against State sovereignty: one referring to 'peoples' and individuals instead of states, and deriving its validity well outside the State's legality.

In a further representation, it bears the notion of *balance* between the law of the sovereign and the *independent* rights of the individuals that is, since its origin, inscribed in the English conception of the rule of law.

The latter is thus all but a neutral category. Sovereignty under the rule of law means that its 'gubernaculum' power is as legitimate and legal as is an independent law that enshrines the rights of the (English) subjects and the countervailing entitlements of other public institutions.

---

[64] U.N. Doc. A/59/565 (Dec. 1, 2004), at http:// www.un.org/secureworld, where the report *A More Secure World: Our shared Responsibility*, is available online. Since security does not only relate to the 'political' border of States but also directly to human beings. according to the *High Level Panel*, the fact of assuming the status of 'signatory States' of the UN Charter redefines the meaning of their sovereignty (something that the International Commission on Intervention and State Sovereignty began to affirm in 2001 in 'The Responsibility to Protect').

[65] (b) Slaughter (2005).

[66] One can see for example what Feinstein (2005) 39, 10-11: 'In the face of the genocides of the 1990s and later the Security Council rupture over Iraq, the older ideas about sovereignty began to yield to newer ideas, in which a state's sovereign rights are a function of its behavior. The High- Level Panel speaks to these issues very eloquently, even if some of its members may disown these points. The first principle of conditional sovereignty is the idea that sovereignty entails rights as well as responsibilities. A government's first sovereign responsibility is to its people, to protect them from grave harm, atrocities, and crimes against humanity. If a state fails to live up to this primary responsibility, through acts of omission or commission, it cannot expect to enjoy the full benefits of sovereignty. The corollary principle is that when a state fails to live up to this fundamental responsibility, other states have a duty to take action to spotlight, prevent, or stop the oppression. By action I mean everything from diplomacy to economic pressure and, if necessary, the prompt use of force'.

Our task is to transfer such dynamics in the global sphere of legality *without a State and without an unequivocal legal system.* The responsibility to protect, as much as other principles and judicially held standards, contributes of itself to the establishment of legal threads that can represent the rule of law, as a legal service to coexistence. This applies (in the terms of 'the right' allure) to a global realm where the conceptions of the 'good' bear too different and strong contents to be the unifying cement of a universal community. However, the role of the rule of law is not to build up a 'community of the good', nor a global polity.

Certainly, the rule of law is also capable of being slowly tailored by the formation of judicial networks, the rise of bridges between regimes and legal orders, and even the adaptation to foreign law traditions: all involve a process of recognition that cannot be pursued on a pure authority-basis.[67] For example, the communicative endeavour, and the mainstreaming of the rule of law, interweave fairly when rules of engagement do not end up with some top-down supremacy principle, that would hardly work as a default rule in much of the trans-orders intercourses as increasing today.

The rule of law exerts its role by playing precisely the reverse function than an authority supporting legal tool. It does constrain whatever authority on the basis of generally agreed upon criteria of action that should appear to the relevant actors out of their (legally authorised) disposal. As a further instance one can recall the idea of imperative rules in international law: it is now recognised that a new layer[68] has taken shape, a *super partes*,[69] or a community law have developed, that cannot be simply overturned by conventional law.

The challenge of the rule of law indeed should be clear at this point. It is not only that some authority be acting within the limits of law and procedural requirements of law itself (in the standard tests). It is certainly this, but by no means just this.

One can return on the subject by observing the unassailable view of the World Bank, according to which: 'While defined in various ways, the rule of law prevails where (i) the government itself is bound by the law, (ii) every person in society is treated equally under the law, (iii) the human dignity of each individual is recognized and protected by law, and (iv) justice is accessible to all'.[70] This is the necessary general pattern of requirements. Separation of powers, judicial independence, equality before the law, protection of human dignity, access to justice.

However, what makes them real is their being embedded into a law that cannot be overwritten, and that on a substantive ground is capable of facing the tension against contingent legal policies ('gubernaculum', prevailing ideas of the

---

67 For the role of authority and 'content dependent assessments', cf. Palombella (2009).

68 Weiler (2004).

69 A. Cassese (2005) 217.

70 World Bank, *Legal and Judicial Reform: Observations, Experiences, and Approach of the Legal Vice Presidency* (Washington, D.C.: World Bank, July 2002), 1.

'good', functional regimes' imperatives, legislative majorities). Moreover, most of the times, it would be impossible to check[71] requirements like 'access to justice' or respect for 'dignity', outside the context of the balance between procedural or formal conditions and substantive laws. Since the rule of law is meant to be something different from a sheer law of rules, it might entail a more contextual and substantial recognition.

If we export the rule of law discourse onto the global sphere, framed through these lines, the tension between different, not erasable, sides of law resurfaces.

It is of some evidence, that the rule of law becomes significant only when there is some positive law that can be opposed, say, to Article 103 UN,[72] should the SC Sanctions Committee determine anti terrorist security goals to be almost absolute: it can be some interpretation of the *jus cogens*[73] extension to the right of judicial review, or the right to property in the human rights system; or it can be the European Treaties fundamental principles as capable of opposing the legality of contrary internal regulations.[74]

In the multifaceted global governance this is still to be proved, elaborated upon, and the construction of some confront – and – commensurability between legal arrangements generated out of diverse regimes (say the ECHR and EU market freedoms, IMF and HR, ISO standards and WTO, etc.) is slowly in search of a consistent definition.

The challenge is here to abandon a stereotyped version of the rule of law, construed around the state, and nevertheless bearing in mind the balance rationale, the English common law or the constitutional state dual (higher law based) scheme: a stable recurrence, that has made legislative law countered by a countervailing independent law, whether insured through the fabric of the common law or the aggravated authority of a constitution. The duality scheme, however implemented in diverse contextual incarnations, bears persistence, allows change and flexibility, and is meant to contrast against the mere instrumentalisation of law.

Exporting the rule of law[75] in foreign and underdeveloped countries, a matter that relates highly to the World Bank activities, or to the EU 'conditionality' strategies, is in need as well of not-purely parametrical rigidities, and more sensitive adjustment: pre fixed requirements have to be measured against the general distinctive rationale that the rule of law bears (a rationale that would otherwise simply be confused either with some generic legality, rationality, or with human

---

71 Illuminating analyses, with empirical research, are published in Amichai Magen – Morlino (2008).

72 'In the event of a conflict between the obligations of the Members of the United Nations under the present Charter and their obligations under any other international agreement, their obligations under the present Charter shall prevail'.

73 Note that in *Kadì* and *Al Baarakat* (see *supra* note 17) the European Court of First Instance did firstly consider the SC resolutions under the prevailing force of Jus Cogens, and secondly, excluded there was any evidence as to the Jus Cogens nature of rights to property or to defense.

74 This happened through the reasoning of the European Court of Justice in *Kadi* 2008 (see *supra* note 17).

75 Kleinfeld – Nikolaidis (2009) 139-170.

rights, solidarity, and so forth). And in the potential conflict between parochial or apologetic jurisdiction-based conceptions of the rule of law, the latter can only be addressed by confirming its background essential precondition: *in pending the global legal 'system', the rule of law amounts ultimately to a matter of equilibrium between concurring authorities, institutions, and, as explained in the above, especially* sides *of legal production (or application and interpretation)*. The requirements, common rules and principles, that are to be chosen as essential rule of law conditions in diverse spatial and historical settings, should replicate this logic, all things considered.

The stage is settled then, for multilateral and balanced rule of law guidelines, although the performed plays may still turn to be diverse.

References

R. Alexy, 'Constitutional Rights, Balancing and Rationality' [2003] *Ratio Juris* 131-40.

J. Balkin, *Cultural Sotfware* (Yale Un. Press, 1996).

D.M. Beatty, *The Ultimate Rule of Law* (Oxford, OUP, 2005).

D.M. Beatty, *Law's Golden Rule,* in G. Palombella, N. Walker (eds.), *Relocating the Rule of Law,* (Oxford, Hart Pub., 2009), 99-115.

K.P. Berger, *The Creeping Codification of the Lex Mercatoria,* (Leiden, Kluwer Law International, 1999).

G.A. Bermann, P.C. Mavroidis (eds.), *Trade and Human Health and Safety* (Cambridge University Press, Cambridge, 2006).

C. Brown, *A Common Law of International Adjudication* (Oxford, OUP, 2007).

D. Camroux, C. Lechervy, 'Close encounter of a third kind? The inaugural Asia-Europe meeting of March 1996' [1996] *The Pacific Review* 442-453.

D. Cass, *The Constitutionalisation of the World Trade Organisation* (Oxford, OUP, 2005).

A. Cassese, *International Law* (Oxford, OUP, 2005).

S. Cassese, 'Administrative Law without the State? The Challenge of Global Regulation' [2005] *New York University Journal of Int'l Law and Politics* 663-694.

S. Cassese, *I Tribunali di Babele* (Roma, Donzelli, 2009).

G. del Vecchio, '*On the Statuality of Law*' [1937] *Journal of Comparative Legislation and International Law* 1-20.

A.V. Dicey, *Introduction to the Study of the Law of the Constitution* (London, ECS Wade, 1915).

S. Engle Merry, '*Legal Pluralism*' [1988] *Law and Society Review* 869-896.

L. Feinstein, 'Symposium, Commentary by Experts' [2005] *Northwestern University Journal of Int'l Human Rights* 39-50.

M.L. Fernandez Esteban, *The Rule of Law in the European Constitution* (London and Cambridge, Kluwer Intern., 1999).

L. Fuller, *The Morality of Law* (New Haven, Yale University Press, 1969).

R. Gordon, 'Critical Legal Histories' [1984] *Stanford Law Review* 57-125.

J. Habermas, transl. by W. Rehg, *Between Facts and Norms* (Boston, The MIT Press, 1996).

G.L. Haskins, 'Executive Justice and the Rule of Law: Some Reflections on Thirteenth century England' [1995] *Speculum* 529-538.

R.Howse, E.Türk, *The WTO Impact on Internal Regulations: A Case Study of the* Canada-EC Asbestos *Dispute,* in G. De Burca, J.Scott (eds.), *The EU and the WTO: legal and constitutional issues* (Oxford, Hart, 2001), 283-328.

R. Higgins, 'A Babel of Judicial Voices? Ruminations from the Bench' [2006] *International & Comparative Law Quarterly* 791-804.

I. Kant, *Grounding for the Metaphysics of Morals* [1785], trans. by J. W. Ellington (Indianapolis, Hackett Publish. Co., 1993).

D. Kennedy, 'One, Two, Three, Many Legal Orders: Legal Pluralism and the Cosmopolitan Dream' [2007] *New York University Review of Law and Social Change* 641-659.

B. Kingsbury, *International Law as Inter-Public Law,* in H.R. Richardson, M.S. Williams (eds.), *NOMOS XLIX: Moral Universalism and Pluralism* (New York, NYU Press, 2009), 167-187.

R. Kleinfeld, K. Nikolaidis, *Can a Post-Colonial Power Export the Rule of Law? Elements of a General Framework,* in G. Palombella, N. Walker (eds.), *Relocating the Rule of Law* (Oxford, Hart Pub., 2009), 139-170.

M. Koskenniemi, *Global Legal Pluralism: Multiple Regimes and Multiple Modes of Thought,* paper presented at Harvard, 5 March 2005, p. 7 (available at http://www.helsinki.fi/eci/Publications/MKPluralism-Harvard-05d%5B1%5D.pdf.).

M. Krygier, *The Rule of Law: Legality, Teleology, Sociology,* in G. Palombella, N. Walker (eds.), *Relocating the Rule of Law* (Oxford, Hart Pub., 2009), 45-70.

A. Magen, L. Morlino (eds.), *International Actors, Democratization and the Rule of Law. Anchoring Democracy?* (London, Routledge, 2008).

C. McIlwain, *Constitutionalism: Ancient and Modern* (Ithaca, CA: Cornell University Press, 1940).

M. Orellana, *The EU and Chile Suspend the Swordfish Case Proceedings at the WTO and the International Tribunal of the Law of the Sea* (ASIL INSIGHTS, 2001), available at http://www.asil.org/insights/insigh60.htm.

M. Orellana, 'The Swordfish Dispute between the EU and Chile at the ITLOS and the WTO' [2002] *NORDIC Journal of International Law* 55-81.

G. Palombella, *The Abuse of Rights and the Rule of Law,* in A. Sajo (ed.), *The Dark Side of Fundamental Rights* (Utrecht, Eleven Intern. Publisher, 2006), 5-28.

G. Palombella, 'The Rule of law beyond the State: Failures, Promises and Theory' [2009] *International Journal of Constitutional Law* 442-467.

G. Palombella, 'The Rule of Law as an Institutional Ideal' [2010] *Comparative Sociology*, forthcoming.

J. Rawls, *Theory of Justice* (Cambridge, Harvard University Press, 1971).

J. Raz, *The Rule of Law and its Virtue* in J. Raz, *The Authority of Law: Essays on Law. and Morality* (Oxford, Clarendon Press, 1979).

J. Rawls, *Political Liberalism* (New York, 1993).

J. Raz, *The Concept of a Legal System* (Oxford, Clarendon Press, 1980, repr. 2003).

P. Reid, *Rule of Law. The Jurisprudence of Liberty in the Seventeenth and Eighteenth Century* (DeKalb, Northern Illinois University Press, 2004).

M. Rusciano, 'Diritto di sciopero e diritto costituzionale' [2009] *Rivista italiana di diritto del lavoro* 49-70.

A. Sajo (ed.), *The Dark Side of Fundamental Rights* (Utrecht, Eleven Intern. Publisher, 2006).

A. Scalia, 'The Rule of Law as a Law of Rules' [1989] *University of Chicago Law Review* 1175-1188.

(a) A.M. Slaughter, *A New World Order* (Princeton, Princeton University Press, 2005).

(b) A. M. Slaughter, 'Security solidarity, and Sovereignty: The Grand Themes of UN Reform' [2005] *American Journal of International Law* 619-631.

G.C. Spattini, ''Vere' e 'false' 'golden shares' nella giurisprudenza comunitaria e la 'deriva sostanzialista' della Corte di Giustizia ovvero il 'formalismo' del principio della 'natura della cosa', il case Volkwagen, e altro' [2008] *Rivista italiana di diritto pubblico comunitario* 303-364.

A. Stone Sweet, J. Mathews, 'Proportionality Balancing and Global Constitutionalism' [2008/47] *Columbia Journal of Transnational Law* 73-165.

G. Teubner, *Global Bukowina: Legal Pluralism in the World Society* in G. Teubner (ed.), *Global Law Without a State* (Dartmouth, Aldershot, 1997), 3-28.

G. Teubner, *Hybrid Laws: Constitutionalizing Private Governance Networks*, in R. Kagan, M. Krygier, K. Winston (eds.), *Legality and Community* (Lanham, Rowman and Littlefield, 2002), 311-331.

T. Treves, 'Fragmentation of International Law: the Judicial Perspective' [2008] *Comunicazioni e Studi* 821-875.

S. Tsakyrakis, 'Proportionality: An assault on human rights?' [2009] *International Journal of Constitutional Law* 468-493.

W. Twining, 'Schauer on Hart' [2006] *Harvard Law Review Forum* 119-122.

J.H.H. Weiler, 'The Geology of International Law. Governance, Democracy and Legitimacy' [2004] *Zeitschrift für ausländisches öffentliches Recht und Völkerrecht* 547-562.

J. Waldron, 'Is the Rule of Law an Essentially Contested Concept (in Florida)?' [2002] *Law and Philosophy* 21-137.

M. Walzer, *Thick and Thin. Moral Argument at Home and Abroad* (Notre Dame In., 1994).

A. Zoppoli, 'Viking e Laval: la singolare andatura della Corte di Giustizia (ovvero l'autonomia collettiva negata' [2008] *Diritti, lavori, mercati* 151-162.

P. Zumbansen, D. Saam 'The ECJ, Volkswagen and European Corporate Law: Reshaping the European Varieties of Capitalism' [2007] *German Law Journal* 1028-1051.